Introducing Communication Theory

FOURTH EDITION

Introducing Communication Theory

ANALYSIS AND APPLICATION

Richard West
Emerson College

Lynn H. Turner
Marquette University

McGraw-Hill
Higher Education

Boston   Burr Ridge, IL   Dubuque, IA   New York   San Francisco   St. Louis
Bangkok   Bogotá   Caracas   Kuala Lumpur   Lisbon   London   Madrid   Mexico City
Milan   Montreal   New Delhi   Santiago   Seoul   Singapore   Sydney   Taipei   Toronto

**McGraw-Hill
Higher Education**

Published by McGraw-Hill, an imprint of The McGraw-Hill Companies, Inc., 1221 Avenue of the Americas, New York, NY 10020. Copyright © 2010, 2007, 2004, 2000. All rights reserved. No part of this publication may be reproduced or distributed in any form or by any means, or stored in a database or retrieval system, without the prior written consent of The McGraw-Hill Companies, Inc., including, but not limited to, in any network or other electronic storage or transmission, or broadcast for distance learning.

This book is printed on acid-free paper.

4 5 6 7 8 9 0 QFR/QFR 1 5 4 3 2

ISBN: 978-0-07-338507-5
MHID: 0-07-338507-7

Editor in Chief: *Michael Ryan*
Publisher: *Frank Mortimer*
Executive Editor: *Katie Stevens*
Marketing Manager: *Leslie Oberhuber*
Developmental Editor: *Kate Scheinman*
Production Editor: *Holly Paulsen*
Manuscript Editor: *Rachel Hockett*
Design Manager: *Ashley Bedell*
Text Designer: *Elise Lansdon*
Illustrators: *Joan Carol, John and Judy Waller, Robin Mouat, Ayelet Arbel, Macmillan*
Media Project Manager: *Ron Nelms*
Production Supervisor: *Louis Swaim*
Composition: *10/12 Sabon by Macmillan Publishing Solutions*
Printing: *45# New Era Matte, Worldcolor*

Library of Congress Cataloging-in-Publication Data has been applied for.

The Internet addresses listed in the text were accurate at the time of publication. The inclusion of a Web site does not indicate an endorsement by the authors or McGraw-Hill, and McGraw-Hill does not guarantee the accuracy of the information presented at these sites.

www.mhhe.com

Brief Contents

Contents

Chapter 3   **Thinking About Theory and Research**   **44**

Chapter 4   **As We Begin . . .**   **67**

PART TWO   *Understanding the Dialogue*   73

PART THREE   *On the Horizon . . .*   517

Chapter 30   Moving in New Directions   519

Preface

It is with great enthusiasm that we provide the fourth edition of *Introducing Communication Theory: Analysis and Application*. The success of the three previous editions shows that communication theory courses are thriving and teachers and students of communication understand the importance of theoretical thinking. This text explores the practical, engaging, and relevant ways in which theory operates in our lives. It is written for students who have little or no background in communication theory. We originally wrote the book because we felt that students needed to know how theorizing helps us understand ourselves, our experiences, our environment, and our culture. We also wrote this book because we believe that students should have a text that relates theory directly to their lives. In this text we make a concerted effort to achieve the following objectives:

- Familiarizing students with the principles and central ideas of important theories they are likely to encounter in the communication discipline
- Demystifying the concept of theory and helping students see the application of theory in their everyday activities
- Helping students become more systematic and thoughtful critical thinkers
- Providing students with an overview and brief history of how the communication discipline is developing
- Introducing students to the research process and the place of theory within this process

The fourth edition of this book maintains its original focus of introducing communication theory to students in an accessible, appealing, and memorable way. We believe that students understand material best when it is explained in a clear, direct way through a number of realistic and applicable examples. Our hope is that students will take away a basic knowledge of, and appreciation for, communication theory from reading our text. Together, we have nearly fifty years combined of teaching communication theory. During this time, we have learned a great deal. *Introducing Communication Theory: Analysis and Application* utilizes and applies all that we as teachers have learned from our students. We continue to be indebted to both students and colleagues whose suggestions and comments have greatly influenced this fourth edition.

The theories in communication studies have roots in both communication and in other fields of study. This exciting interdisciplinary orientation is reflected in the selection of the various theories presented in the text. We not only include the unique contributions of communication theorists, but also theories with origins in other fields, including psychology, sociology, biology, and philosophy. Communication theorists have embraced the integration of ideas and principles forged by their colleagues across many disciplines. Yet the application, influence, and inherent value of communication are all sustained by the theorists in this text. In other words, although you will read theories that cut across various fields of study, their relevance to *communication* remains. We do not presume to speak for the theorists; our goal is to frame their words and illustrate their theories with practical examples and applications so that their explication of communication behaviors becomes accessible for students.

The Challenges of Teaching and Learning Communication Theory

The instructor in a communication theory course may face several challenges that are not shared by other courses. Because many students think of theory as distant, abstract, and obscure, teachers must overcome these potentially negative connotations. Negative feelings toward the subject can be magnified in classrooms where students represent a variety of ages and socioeconomic, ethnic, cultural, and linguistic backgrounds. *Introducing Communication Theory* addresses this challenge by offering a readable and practical guide that integrates content with examples, capturing the essence and elegance of theory in a straightforward manner. In addition, the book takes an incremental approach to learning about theory, resulting in a thoughtful and appropriate learning pace.

A second challenge associated with teaching and learning communication theory relates to preconceived notions of research: Students may view scholarship as difficult or remote. This book demonstrates to students that they already possess many of the characteristics of researchers, such as curiosity and ambition. Students will be pleasantly surprised to know that they operate according to many personal theories every day. Once students begin to revise their misconceptions about research and theory, they are in a position to understand the principles, concepts, and theories contained in this book.

A third challenge of teaching and learning communication theory is capturing the complexity of a theory in an approachable way without oversimplifying the theoretical process. To address this problem, instructors often present a skeletal version of a theory and then fill in the missing pieces with personal materials. By providing a variety of engaging examples and applications reflecting a wide range of classroom demographics, *Introducing Communication Theory* facilitates such an approach.

Special Features and Learning Aids

To accomplish our goals and address the challenges of teaching communication theory, we have incorporated a number of special features and learning aids into the fourth edition:

- *Part One, Setting the Stage.* The first four chapters of the book continue to provide students a solid foundation for studying the theories that follow. This groundwork is essential in order to understand how theorists conceptualize and test their theories. Chapters 1 and 2 define communication and provide a framework for examining the theories. We present several traditions and contexts in which theory is customarily categorized and considered. Chapter 3 provides an overview of the intersection of theory and research. We see Chapter 4 as a bridge to the theories that follow. In this chapter, we present students with a template of various evaluative components that we apply in each of the subsequent theory chapters.

- *Updated coverage of all 25 theories.* Separate chapters on each of twenty-five theories provide accessible, thorough coverage for students and offer flexibility to instructors. Because of the feedback we received from the previous edition, we retained the original theories from the third edition, but **each** chapter has been updated. This updating results in a more thoughtful, current, and applicable presentation of each theory.

- *Section openers.* The theory chapters in Part Two, Understanding the Dialogue, are organized into six sections. We have written section openers to introduce these groups of chapters. The overviews provide students with an explanation for our choices, placing the theories in context and allowing students to see the connections between and among theories.

- *Chapter opening vignettes.* Each chapter begins with an extended vignette, which is then integrated throughout the chapter, providing examples to illustrate the theoretical concepts and claims. These stories help students understand how communication theory plays out in the everyday lives of ordinary people. Students have commented that these opening stories help drive home the important points of the theory. In addition, the real-life tone of each vignette entices students to understand the practicality of a particular theory.

- *A structured approach to each theory.* Every theory chapter has a consistent format that begins with a vignette, followed by an introduction, a summary of theoretical assumptions, a description of core concepts, and a critique (using the criteria established in Part One). This consistency provides continuity for students, ensures a balanced presentation of the theories, and helps ease the retrieval of information for future learning experiences.

- **NEW** *Visual template for theory evaluation.* The critique section in every theory chapter has been extensively revised for this edition. Each theory is critiqued using the criteria for theory evaluation presented in Chapter 4. In addition, the theory's context, scholarly tradition, and approach to knowing are articulated. Each of these areas are elucidated in Part One of the text.

> "The first four chapters of the book continue to provide students a solid foundation for studying the theories that follow. This groundwork is essential in order to understand how theorists conceptualize and test their theories."

> "Every theory chapter has a consistent format that begins with a vignette, followed by an introduction, a summary of theoretical assumptions, a description of core concepts, and a critique (using the criteria established in Part One). This consistency provides continuity for students, ensures a balanced presentation of the theories, and helps ease the retrieval of information for future learning experiences."

- *Theory at a Glance boxes.* In order for students to have an immediate and concise understanding of a particular theory, we incorporate this feature at the beginning of each theory chapter. Students will have these brief explanations and short summaries before reading the chapter, thereby allowing them to have a general sense of what they are about to encounter.

- *Tables and figures.* To increase conceptual organization and enhance the visual presentation of content, we have added several **NEW** tables and figures throughout the text. Many chapters have new visual aids for students to consider, helping them to understand the material. These visuals provide a clearer sense of the conceptual organization of the theories, and they support those students who best retain information visually.

- **NEW** *End-of-book glossary.* Students have expressed interest in having a compiled list of definitions at the end of the text. This Glossary provides an easily accessible definition of all terms contained in the book.

- **NEW** *Significant revisions of several theories.* Coordinated Management of Meaning, Structuration Theory, Organizational Information Theory, Media Ecology Theory, and Cultural Studies have all undergone major revision.

- **NEW** *Incorporation of over 150 new references.* The explosion in communication research is reflected in the integration of dozens of new studies, essays, and books that help students understand the theory or theoretical issue.

- **NEW** *Integration of Robert Craig's "Seven Traditions of Communication Theory."* Craig's category system is discussed as one way to frame the discussion of communication theory.

- *Theory Into Practice (T∗I∗P) boxes.* These boxes, featured in every chapter, present student comments on a particular concept or theoretical issue. These student voices, extracted from journals in classes we have taught, illustrate the practicality of the topic under discussion and also show how theoretical issues relate to students' lives.

- *Research Notes boxes.* These boxes present annotated abstracts of research articles and essays that are relevant to the chapter and, like T∗I∗P boxes, appear in every theory chapter. Research Notes boxes demonstrate how theories or theoretical principles are utilized in research studies; they also serve to familiarize students with the content and conventions of original research.

- *Updated research and examples.* Each chapter has undergone a revision to reflect the most current thinking and research. Furthermore, examples reflect and include a variety of different situations and experiences, such as disagreements in a publishing company, health benefits at a small jewelry store, dating problems, a public speech about drunk driving, the struggles of a single father, public perceptions of spanking, and the problems encountered by celebrities such as Martha Stewart. In providing up-to-date scholarship and incorporating diverse examples, we wish to show students the depth and breadth of communication theory in society.

- *Running glossary.* Throughout each chapter, a running glossary gives students immediate access to unfamiliar terms and their meanings.

- *Theory Application in Groups (TAG) boxes.* Working with others can help students better appreciate the material. We developed this feature to encourage collaborative learning and to foster critical thinking across different learning styles. In Chapter 15, Structuration Theory, for instance, we ask small groups to think about ethical lapses in judgment from organizational leaders and how principles can inform their thinking about this issue.

- *Discussion Starters* conclude each chapter. These thought-provoking questions prompt students to critically examine the chapter and focus on critical issues.

Supplemental Resources

For the Student

The Online Learning Center at www.mhhe.com/west4e provides interactive resources to address the needs of a variety of teaching and learning styles. For every chapter, students and instructors can access chapter objectives, quizzes, and summary.

We believe that many theories cut across multiple contexts. Therefore, we ask students to look at how two theories from different contexts relate to each other. We also consider how some theories may deal with similar contexts but approach them in very different ways. The Theory Connection feature at the Online Learning Center asks students to think about these contrasts. For instance, we ask students to consider the role of silence in both Groupthink and Muted Group Theory.

For the Instructor

For instructors only, the Online Learning Center offers an online Instructor's Manual with general guidelines for teaching the basic theory course, sample syllabi for quarter and semester courses, chapter onlines, and classroom activities.

Also available at the Online Learning Center are PowerPoint lecture slides, which provide instructors with a comprehensive presentation to organize their lectures. In addition, a computerized test bank with multiple-choice and short-answer questions for every chapter is available.

Organization

Part One, Setting the Stage, provides a conceptual foundation for the discrete theory chapters in Part Two. Chapter 1 begins by introducing the discipline and describing the process of communication. Chapter 2 provides the prevailing traditions and contexts that frame the communication field. In this chapter, we focus on Robert Craig's guide to the ways in which communication theory can be considered. The chapter then turns to primary contexts of communication, which frame the study of communication in most academic settings across the country. Chapter 3 explores the intersection of theory and research. In this chapter, we provide students an understanding of the nature of theory and the characteristics of theory. The research process is also briefly discussed, as are perspectives that guide communication research. Our goal in this chapter is to show that research and theory are interrelated and that the two should be considered in tandem as students read the individual chapters. Chapter 4 provides a list of evaluative criteria for judging theories as well as for guiding students toward assessment of each subsequent theory chapter.

With this foundation established in Part One, Part Two, Understanding the Dialogue, introduces students to twenty-five different theories, each in a discrete, concise chapter. Many of these theories cut across communication contexts. For example, Relational Dialectics Theory can be understood and applied in an organizational context as well as in an interpersonal context. However, to facilitate understanding, we have grouped theories into six sections according to primary focus: The Self and Messages, Relationship Development, Groups and Organizations, The Public, The Media, and Culture and Diversity.

It was not easy for us to decide which theories to include because there are so many from which to choose. In making our selections, we were guided by four broad criteria: (1) whether the theory is significant in the field, (2) whether it reflects the interdisciplinary nature of the field, (3) whether it is important in the context of current thinking in the field, and (4) whether it contributes to a balance of pioneering and contemporary theories in the book. In addition, we were sensitive to the need to include theories developed by a diverse group of scholars.

Finally, in Part Three, On The Horizon . . ., Chapter 30 describes the constant evolution of theory and theory building based on new societal trends. To show students that the communication major provides practical knowledge leading to employment, we conclude with a focus on career paths that make use of communication theory. We also make suggestions for becoming more adept in a communication career.

Acknowledgments

Any book owes its existence to efforts made by others in addition to the listed authors, and some people who have helped with this book may not even realize the debt we acknowledge here. We would like to thank all those who have helped us as we worked our way through this large project. First, our work rests on the shoulders of the theorists whose creations we profile in this book. We are grateful for their creative thinking, which allows us to understand and predict the complexities of the communication process. Second, our insights represent the discussions that we have had with our communication theory students and colleagues over the years. Several parts of this book are based upon student input at both of our institutions. Students have contributed to this book in both direct and indirect ways. Our families, too, contributed in ways both large and small in helping us complete this project. For providing us with patience, support, and food, we cannot thank them enough.

As is customary in each book he writes, Rich would like to acknowledge his mother for her continual focus on what matters in life: family, fun, and spirituality. He remains grateful for her continued positive influence. Rich would also like to thank his partner, Chris, who knows precisely when to make things less intense and more relaxing. Finally, Rich would like to thank his colleagues and administration at Emerson College in Boston. Their continued support and ongoing student-centeredness are exemplary. Changing schools mid-career was much more palatable because of the encouragement and engagement at Emerson.

Lynn would like to thank her family: her husband, Ted; her daughter's family, the Spitznagles—Sabrina, Billy, Sophie, and Will; her stepdaughter's family, the Kissels—Leila, Russ, Zoe, Dylan; and her stepson's family, the Feldshers—Ted, Sally, Ely, and Lucas for invaluable lessons in communication theory and practice. Further, she is indebted to her parents and her brother and his family, as well as all of her extended family members who helped in ways great and small as this project continued over time. Friends and colleagues, especially Pat Sullivan, Helen Sterk, Bob Shuter, and Patrice Buzzanell, provided great support and have taught her many valuable lessons about scholarship and communication theory. She also owes a significant debt to her research assistant, Diana Turner, for tracking down those elusive sources and for a great deal of helpful copyediting.

We wish to thank Emerson College and Marquette University. They continue to offer supportive climates that allowed us to finish this project in a timely manner. We are grateful for the secretarial help, the research assistance, and the general tenor of encouragement fostered by the administration, faculty, and staff.

We also thank those people who worked hard to put this book into production. We need to first thank Katie Stevens, Executive Editor, at McGraw-Hill. She served as an excellent resource as we worked through ideas for this edition. In addition to Katie, several other people gave their time, talent, and expertise to make this a book of which we are proud. They include our developmental editor, Kate Scheinman, a stellar editor whose support has been invaluable; marketing manager Leslie Oberhuber; media project manager Ron Nelms; production editor Holly Paulsen; and design manager Ashley Bedell. We thank each of these individuals for their contributions to the fourth edition of the text. Their determination in making this an outstanding product is deeply appreciated.

Finally, we thank the manuscript reviewers who gave their time and expertise to keep us on track in our interpretation of the ideas of others. We are grateful for their careful reading and insightful suggestions, which expanded and clarified our thinking in many ways. The errors in this book are our own, but the strengths were established through their help. Our text is a much more useful product because of the comments and suggestions of the following reviewers who have shaped this book over the years:

Fourth Edition

Rebecca Dumlao,
East Carolina University

Edward T. Funkhouser,
North Carolina State University

Scott Guest,
Bowling Green State University

Anna Laura Jansma,
University of California, Santa Barbara

Anne M. Nicotera,
University of Maryland

Mark Zeigler
Florida State University

Third Edition

Randall S. Chase,
Salt Lake Community College

Chrys Egan,
Salisbury University

Kathleen Galvin,
Northwestern University

Reed Markham,
Salt Lake Community College

Rita L. Rahoi-Gilchrest,
Winona State University

Second Edition

Sue Barnes,
Fordham University

Jack Baseheart,
University of Kentucky

Jamie Byrne,
Millersville University

Thomas Feeley,
State University of New York, Geneseo

Amy Hubbard,
University of Hawaii at Manoa

Matthew McAllister,
Virginia Tech

Janet Skupien,
University of Pittsburgh

Jon Smith,
Southern Utah University

Katy Wiss,
Western Connecticut State University

Kevin Wright,
University of Memphis

First Edition

John R. Baldwin,
Illinois State University

Holly H. Bognar,
Cleveland State University

Sheryl Bowen,
Villanova University

Cam Brammer,
Marshall University

Jeffrey D. Brand,
North Dakota State University

Randy K. Dillon,
Southwest Missouri State University

Kent Drummond,
University of Wyoming

James Gilchrist,
Western Michigan University

Laura Jansma,
University of California–Santa Barbara

Madeline M. Keaveney,
California State University–Chico

Joann Keyton,
University of Kansas

Debra Mazloff,
University of St. Thomas

Elizabeth M. Perse,
University of Delaware

Linda M. Pledger,
University of Arkansas

Mary Ann Renz,
Central Michigan University

Patricia Rockwell,
University of Southwestern Louisiana

Deborah Smith-Howell,
University of Nebraska

Denise Solomon,
University of Wisconsin

Tami Spry,
St. Cloud State University

Rebecca W. Tardy,
University of Louisville

Ralph Thompson,
Cornell University

About the Authors

Richard West is Professor and Chairperson of Communication Studies at Emerson College in Boston. Prior to coming to Emerson, Rich was a professor at the University of Southern Maine. Rich received his B.A. and M.A. from Illinois State University and his Ph.D. from Ohio University. Rich has been teaching since 1984, and his teaching and research interests range from family diversity to teacher–student communication. He began teaching communication theory as a graduate student and has taught the class in lecture format to more than 200 students. Rich is the past President of the Eastern Communication Association (ECA), the oldest professional communication organization in the country. He serves on the Executive Committee of the National Communication Association, where he is also the Director of the Educational Policies Board. He is a past recipient of the Outstanding Alumni Award in Communication at Illinois State University and Ohio University. Rich is the co-author (with Lynn Turner) of *Gender and Communication, Perspectives on Family Communication,* and *Understanding Interpersonal Communication.* He has been recognized as an ECA Research Fellow and is a member of the editorial boards for six communication journals.

Lynn H. Turner is Professor in Communication Studies at Marquette University in Milwaukee, Wisconsin. Lynn received her B.A. from the University of Illinois and her M.A. from the University of Iowa, and she received her Ph.D. from Northwestern University. She has taught communication theory and research methods to undergraduates and graduates in the Diederich College of Communication at Marquette since 1985. Prior to coming to Marquette, Lynn taught at Iowa State University and in two high schools in Iowa. Her research interests include interpersonal communication, family communication, and gendered communication. She is the recipient of several awards, including Marquette's College of Communication Research Excellence Award and the Book of the Year award from the Organization for the Study of Communication, Language, and Gender for her book with Patricia Sullivan, *From the Margins to the Center: Contemporary Women and Political Communication.* Lynn is a past president of the Central States Communication Association and was recently elected 2nd Vice President of the National Communication Association.

PART One

Setting the Stage
Communication, Theory, and Research

Y OU MIGHT NOT HAVE THOUGHT ABOUT THIS, BUT each day the decisions we make, the media we consume, and the relationships we experience can be enriched and explained by communication theory. Communication theory helps us to understand other people and their communities, the media, and our associations with families, friends, roommates, co-workers, and companions. Perhaps most important, communication theory makes it easier to understand ourselves.

We begin our discussion of communication theory by asking you to consider the experiences of Morgan and Alex. After randomly being assigned as roommates, the two met on "move-in day" at Scott Hall. They were both pretty nervous. They had checked out one another on Facebook, e-mailed each other, and talked on the phone a few times, so they knew-quite a bit about each other. Once they met, they started talking. They went out for coffee the first few weeks of school, getting to know each other better. They spent a lot of time telling stories about their families and friends, and talking about what they look for in a partner. They both loved television, especially the "reality shows," because they loved to see how other people dealt with their lives in times of stress. After several weeks, Morgan and Alex became closer. They were going to have to balance their desire to hang out with each other with their need to be alone. And it was going to be give-and-take because their schedules were completely opposite. Eventually, the two became great friends.

To illustrate the various ways in which communication theory functions in the lives of Morgan and Alex, let's identify important aspects of their story and see how theory provides some understanding of Morgan's and Alex's behaviors. First, these roommates supported the research of Uncertainty Reduction Theory (Chapter 9) through their need to reduce their uncertainty about each other. They also probably self-disclosed some personal information to each other, underscoring a central feature of Social Penetration Theory (Chapter 10). Next, they discovered that they both watch television and use it to see how others live their lives, highlighting the essence of Uses and Gratifications Theory (Chapter 23). Balancing the need to be together with the need to remain private encompasses Relational Dialectics Theory (Chapter 12). Morgan and Alex also told personal stories to each other; storytelling is at the heart of The Narrative Paradigm (Chapter 20). In sum, at least five communication theories could help explain the experiences of the two roommates.

The first four chapters provide an important foundation for discussing each communication theory that follows. These chapters give you a general introduction to communication and to theory. First, to provide you some insights into the communication field, in Chapter 1 we present our definition of communication, the prevailing models of communication, and other important issues including ethics and communication. Chapter 2 is dedicated to a discussion of the various traditions and contexts of communication, two important frameworks to consider as you read the remainder of the book. We prepare you directly for understanding the intersection of theory and research in Chapter 3. As you will learn, when scholars develop a theory, it is a result of a great deal of research. Finally, in Chapter 4 we provide an important referent point for you as you review each theory in the text. This chapter provides important criteria for evaluating a theory and also includes a model for you to examine. This "bridge chapter" is differentiated from the rest of the text so you can quickly refer to its contents as you are introduced to various theories.

CHAPTER 1

Thinking About Communication: Definitions, Models, and Ethics

The Bollens

Jimmy and Angie Bollen have been married for almost thirty years, and they are the parents of three children who have been out of the house for years. But a recent layoff at the company where their son Eddy worked has forced the 24-year-old to return home until he can get another job.

At first, Eddy's parents were glad that he was home. His father was proud of the fact that his son wasn't embarrassed about returning home, and his mom was happy to have him help her with some of the mundane chores at home. In fact, Eddy showed both Jimmy and Angie how to instant message their friends and also put together a family website. His parents were especially happy about having a family member who was "tech-savvy" hanging around the house.

But the good times surrounding Eddy's return soon ended. Eddy brought his laptop to the table each morning, marring the Bollens' once-serene breakfasts. Jimmy and Angie's walks at night were complicated because their son often wanted to join them. At night, when they went to bed, the parents heard Eddy talking on his cell phone, sometimes until 1:00 A.M. When Eddy's parents thought about communicating their frustration and disappointment, they quickly recalled the difficulty of their son's situation. They didn't want to upset him any further. The Bollens tried to figure out a way to communicate to their son that although they love him, they wished that he would get a job and leave the house. They simply wanted some peace, privacy, and freedom, and their son was getting in the way. It wasn't a feeling either one of them liked, but it was their reality.

They considered a number of different approaches. In order to get the conversation going, they even thought about giving Eddy a few website links related to local apartment rentals. Recently, the couple's frustration with the situation took a turn for the worse. Returning from one of their long walks, they discovered Eddy on the couch, hung over from a party held earlier at his friend's house. When Jimmy and Angie confronted him about his demeanor, Eddy shouted, "Don't start lecturing me now. Is it any wonder that none of your other kids call you? It's because you don't know when to stop! Look, I got a headache and I don't want to hear it from you guys!" Jimmy snapped, "Get out of my house. Now!" Eddy left the home, slamming the front door behind him. Angie stared out of the window, wondering whether they would ever hear from their son again.

In the most fundamental way, communication depends on our ability to understand one another. Although our communication can be ambiguous ("I never thought I'd get this gift from you"), one primary and essential goal in communicating is understanding. Our daily activities are wrapped in conversations with others. Yet, as we see with the Bollen family, even those in close relationships can have difficulty expressing their thoughts.

Being able to communicate effectively is highly valued in the United States. Corporations have recognized the importance of communication. The National Safety Management Society (www.nsms.us/pages/opermishaps.html) reports that industrial safety is contingent on the ability of employees and management to communicate clearly and to avoid jargon when possible. Health care, too, is focusing more on the value of communication. In doctor–patient relationships, for instance, research shows that communication is essential for the recovery of patients and impacts the extent to which doctors offer medical advice to their patients (Blanquicett, Amsbary, Mills, & Powell, 2007; Jucks & Bromme, 2007). In the classroom, researchers (e.g., Goodboy & Myers, 2008) have concluded that affirming feedback positively affects student learning. And, with respect to social networking sites such as Facebook, individuals in romantic relationships report using communication (technology) as a way to check up on the status of their relationship—from commitment to fidelity (Stern & Taylor, 2007). Make no mistake about it: Abundant evidence underscores the fact that communication is an essential, pervasive, and consequential behavior in our society.

As a student of communication, you are uniquely positioned to determine your potential for effective communication. To do so, however, you must have a basic understanding of the communication process and of how communication theory, in particular, functions in your life. We need to be able to talk effectively to a number of very different types of people during an average day: teachers, ministers, salespeople, family members, friends, automobile mechanics, and health-care providers. Communication opportunities fill our lives each day. However, we need to understand the whys and hows of our conversations with others. For instance, why do two people in a relationship feel a simultaneous need for togetherness and independence? Why do some women feel ignored or devalued in conversations with men? Why does language often influence the thoughts of others? How do media influence people's behavior? These and many other questions are at the root of why communication theory is so important in our society and so critical to understand.

Defining Communication

Our first task is to create a common understanding for the term *communication*. Defining *communication* can be challenging. Katherine Miller (2005) underscores this dilemma, stating that "conceptualizations of communication have been abundant and have changed substantially over the years" (p. 3). Sarah Trenholm (1991) notes that although the study of communication has been around for centuries, it does not mean communication is well understood. In fact, Trenholm provocatively illustrates the dilemma when defining the term. She states "Communication has become a sort of 'portmanteau' term. Like a piece of luggage, it is overstuffed with all manner of odd ideas and

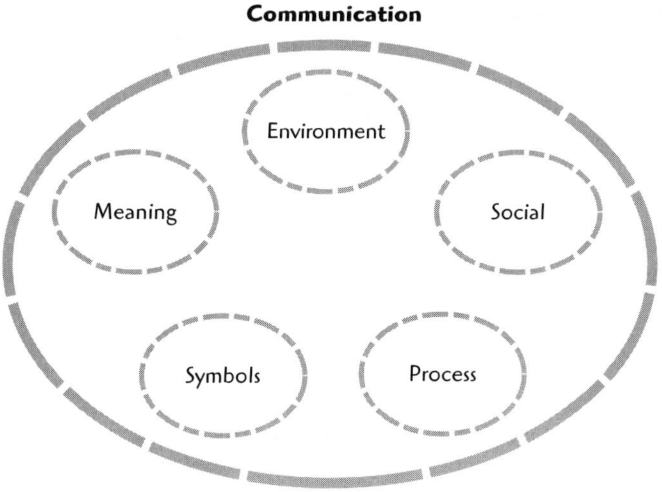

Communication

Figure 1.1
Key Terms in
Defining
Communication

meanings. The fact that some of these do fit, resulting in a conceptual suitcase much too heavy for anyone to carry, is often overlooked" (p. 4).

We should note that there are many ways to interpret and define *communication*—a result of the complexity and richness of the communication discipline. Imagine, for instance, taking this course from two different professors. Each would have his or her way of presenting the material, and each classroom of students would approach communication theory in a unique manner. The result would be two exciting and distinctive approaches to studying the same topic.

This uniqueness holds true with defining *communication*. Scholars tend to see human phenomena from their own perspectives, something we delve into further in the next chapter. In some ways, researchers establish boundaries when they try to explain phenomena to others. Communication scholars may approach the interpretation of communication differently because of differences in scholarly values. With these caveats in mind, we offer the following definition of *communication* to get us pointed in the same direction. **Communication** is a social process in which individuals employ symbols to establish and interpret meaning in their environment. We necessarily draw in elements of mediated communication as well in our discussion, given the importance that communication technology plays in contemporary society. With that in mind, let's define five key terms in our perspective: *social, process, symbols, meaning,* and *environment* (Figure 1.1).

First, we believe that communication is a social process. When interpreting communication as **social,** we mean to suggest that it involves people and interactions, whether face-to-face or online. This necessarily includes two people, who act as senders and receivers. Both play an integral role in the communication process. When communication is social, it involves people who come to an interaction with various intentions, motivations, and abilities. To suggest that communication is a **process** means that it is ongoing and unending. Communication is also dynamic, complex, and continually changing. With this view of

communication
A social process in which individuals employ symbols to establish and interpret meaning in their environment

social
the notion that people and interactions are part of the communication process

process
ongoing, dynamic, and unending occurrence

communication, we emphasize the dynamics of making meaning. Therefore, communication has no definable beginning and ending. For example, although Jimmy and Angie Bollen may tell their son that he must leave the house, their discussions with him and about him will continue well after he leaves. In fact, the conversation they have with Eddy today will most likely affect their communication with him tomorrow. Similarly, our past communications with people have been stored in their minds and have affected their conversations with us.

The process nature of communication also means that much can happen from the beginning of a conversation to the end. People may end up at a very different place once a discussion begins. This is exemplified by the frequent conflicts that roommates, spouses, and siblings experience. Although a conversation may begin with absolute and inflexible language, the conflict may be resolved with compromise. All of this can occur in a matter of minutes.

Individual and cultural changes affect communication. Conversations between siblings, for example, seem to have shifted from the 1950s to today. Years ago, siblings rarely discussed the impending death of a parent. Today, it's not uncommon to listen to children talking about nursing home care, home health care, and even funeral arrangements. The 1950s was a time of postwar euphoria; couples were reunited after World War II and the baby boom began. Today, with an ongoing U.S. troop presence in Iraq, Afghanistan, and elsewhere around the world, Americans rarely experience the euphoria they once had. The tensions and uncertainties are too vivid. As you can see, perceptions and feelings can change and may remain in flux for quite some time.

Some of you may be thinking that because the communication process is dynamic and unique it is virtually impossible to study. However, C. Arthur VanLear (1996) argues that because the communication process is so dynamic, researchers and theorists can look for patterns over time. He concludes that "if we recognize a pattern across a large number of cases, it permits us to 'generalize' to other unobserved cases" (p. 36). Or, as communication pioneers Paul Watzlawick, Janet Beavin, and Don Jackson (1967) suggest, the interconnectedness of communication events is critical and pervasive. Thus, it *is* possible to study the dynamic communication process.

To help you visualize this process, imagine a continuum where the points are unrepeatable and irreversible. Frank Dance (1967) depicts the communication process by using a spiral, or helix (Figure 1.2). He believes that

Figure 1.2
Communication Process as a Helix
Source: Reprinted by permission of Frank E. X. Dance.

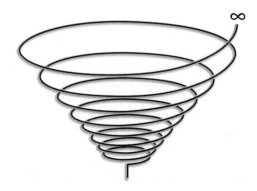

communication experiences are cumulative and are influenced by the past. He notes that present experiences inevitably influence a person's future, and so he emphasizes a nonlinear view of the process. Communication, therefore, can be considered a process that changes over time and among interactants.

A third term associated with our definition of communication is *symbols*. A **symbol** is an arbitrary label or representation of phenomena. Words are symbols for concepts and things—for example, the word *love* represents the idea of love; the word *chair* represents a thing we sit on. Labels may be ambiguous, may be both verbal and nonverbal, and may occur in face-to-face and mediated communication. Symbols are usually agreed on within a group but may not be understood outside of the group. In this way, their use is often arbitrary. For instance, most college students understand the phrase "this course has no prereqs"; those outside of college may not understand its meaning. Further, there are both **concrete symbols** (the symbol represents an object) and **abstract symbols** (the symbol stands for a thought or idea).

Robin Toner (2008, May 4) of the *New York Times* underscored the importance of symbols during presidential elections. She states that in 1988, presidential candidate Michael Dukakis vetoed legislation that would have required students to recite the Pledge of Allegiance. This veto was later used by George H.W. Bush to question the patriotism of Dukakis. In much the same way, as a 2008 presidential candidate, Barack Obama's earlier decision to campaign without wearing a lapel pin depicting the American flag drew questions about his patriotism. Despite Obama's assertion, that the "pins had become a substitute for true patriotism" (Rutenberg & Zeleny, 2008), he eventually wore the flag lapel pin. Clearly, symbolic meaning can be significant.

In addition to process and symbols, meaning is central to our definition of communication. **Meaning** is what people extract from a message. In communication episodes, messages can have more than one meaning and even multiple layers of meaning. Without sharing some meanings, we would all have a difficult time speaking the same language or interpreting the same event. Judith Martin and Tom Nakayama (2008) point out that meaning has cultural consequences:

> [W]hen President George W. Bush was about to go to war in Iraq, he referred to this war as a 'crusade.' The use of this term evoked strong negative reactions in the Islamic world, due to the history of the Crusades nearly 1,000 years ago . . . While President Bush may not have knowingly wanted to frame the Iraq invasion as a religious war against Muslims, the history of the Crusades may make others feel that it is (p. 70).

Clearly, not all meaning is shared, and people do not always know what others mean. In these situations, we must be able to explain, repeat, and clarify. For example, if the Bollens want to tell Eddy to move out, they will probably need to go beyond telling him that they just need their "space." Eddy may perceive "needing space" as simply staying out of the house two nights a week. Furthermore, his parents will have to figure out what communication "approach" is best. They might believe that being direct may be best to get their son out of the house. Or they might fear that such clear communication is not the most

symbol
arbitrary label given to a phenomenon

concrete symbol
symbol representing an object

abstract symbol
symbol representing an idea or thought

meaning
what people extract from a message

effective strategy to change Eddy's behavior. Regardless of how Jimmy and Angie Bollen communicate their wishes, without sharing the same meaning, the family will have a challenging time getting their messages across to one another.

The final key term in our definition of communication is *environment*. **Environment** is the situation or context in which communication occurs. The environment includes a number of elements, including time, place, historical period, relationship, and a speaker's and listener's cultural backgrounds. You can understand the influence of environments by thinking about your beliefs and values pertaining to socially significant topics such as same-sex marriage, physician-assisted suicide, and immigration into the United States. If you have had personal experience with any of these topics, it's likely your views are affected by your perceptions. Or, consider the time in history as another influential factor. Less than fifteen years ago, the idea that gay men and lesbians could marry was unthinkable. With the 2004 law in Massachusetts, the rights of gay and lesbian Americans to marry were affirmed in that state. Clearly, the environment and all of its components influence communication and behavior.

The environment can also be mediated. By that, we mean that communication can take place with technological assistance. It's highly likely that all of you have communicated in some sort of mediated environment; namely, through e-mail, chat rooms, or social networking sites. These mediated environments influence the communication between two people in that people in electronic relationships are not able to observe each other's eye behavior, listen to vocal characteristics, or watch body movement. This mediated environment has received a great deal of attention over the years as communication theory continues to develop (Aakhus, 2007).

environment
situation or context in which communication occurs

T*I*P

Theory Into Practice

Genie

The discussion in class about environment made a lot of sense to me. I can't begin to tell you how many different types of physical environments I'm in every day. I work in a nonprofit, so I'm always in and out of the office. Our office is on the third floor of a five-story building. It's quite small but we have a lot of fun. Sometimes, though, I have to go to a corporate office where everything is new and looks very expensive. A lot of the workers, though, seem up-tight! Then, I have to visit some people's homes and I can say that there is so much difference in the way people have arranged their home environments. And I haven't even begun to talk about how I use e-mail and the different mediated environments. It's unbelievable!

The Intentionality Debate: Did You Mean That?

Before we close our discussion on defining *communication,* let's talk briefly about an academic debate that took place about sixty years ago, and which the field continues to discuss today. The debate centered on this question: Is all behavior communication? For example, suppose that Eric and his landlady, Martha, are talking about renewing his lease for the upcoming year. Martha claims she has to raise the rent due to higher heating costs. As the two speak, Eric notices that Martha doesn't look him in the eye as she explains the $100 increase. He begins to wonder whether Martha is telling the truth, thinking that her shifting eyes and constant throat clearing must signify something deceptive. Can Martha's shifting eyes and throat clearing be considered communication? Are these behaviors within the boundaries of our definition of *communication*? Or is Eric's perception simply Eric's perception? What if Martha never intended to communicate anything other than that she needs the money to offset the cost of heating the apartment?

Some communication researchers have strongly favored the view that only intentional behaviors are communicative. For instance, Gerald Miller and Mark Steinberg (1975) interpret the communication process this way:

> We have chosen to restrict our discussion of communication to intentional symbolic transactions: those in which at least one of the parties transmits a message to another with the intent of modifying the other's behavior . . . . By our definition, intent to communicate and intent to influence are synonymous. If there is no intent, there is no message. (p. 15)

Despite this perspective, researchers have debated whether messages that are sent unintentionally—or mistaken meanings that people make ("I didn't mean *that*—you misunderstood me")—fit the definition of *communication*. Those who say that these sorts of messages are not communication (Miller and Steinberg) argue that only intentionally sent and accurately received messages can be called communication. However, other researchers believe that this approach narrows the definition too much.

This tension in interpreting what constitutes a communication event was a primary discussion point of researchers many years ago. In the early 1950s, a group of scholars from Stanford University in Palo Alto, California, collaborated on a new approach to human communication. These researchers represented a variety of disciplines, including psychiatry, anthropology, and communication. Among the many findings emanating from a series of scholarly papers was the assumption that "you cannot not communicate" (Watzlawick, et al., 1967). This thinking reflects the notion that all things can be considered communication. According to the **Palo Alto team,** when two people are together, they constantly communicate because they cannot escape behavior. Even silence and avoidance of eye contact are communicative. So, using our earlier example of Eric and Martha, Eric's perception of distrust would be legitimized under the Palo Alto rubric: One can say nothing and still say something. The Palo Alto group believed that anything we do, including ignoring or refusing to speak to another, is communication. This greatly broadens the definition of *communication*, making it virtually synonymous with *behavior*.

Although this line of thinking has enjoyed much popular support, it is potentially problematic for those of us interested in communication theory. In

Palo Alto team
a group of scholars who believed that a person "cannot not communicate"

fact, Michael Motley (1990) reasons that "not all behavior is communication, only interactive behavior is; so in noninteractive situations one can indeed 'not communicate,' but in interactive situations one indeed cannot not communicate" (p. 619). In other words, Motley believes that one *can* not communicate. To be fair, one of the original proponents of the "you cannot not communicate" argument later recanted her original thinking by concluding that "all behavior is not communicative, although it may be informative" (Beavin-Bavelas, 1990, p. 599).

If everything can be thought of as communication—our verbal and nonverbal unintended expressions—then studying communication in a systematic manner is not only challenging, but also nearly impossible. As we discussed earlier in this chapter, setting boundaries on behavior in conversations or relationships is necessary in theory building. By defining everything as communication, we inevitably undermine the field we wish to study. Defining communication requires both that we draw boundaries and that we still acknowledge some overlap. Definitions can be somewhat subjective, and you will soon discover as you review and understand communication theory that once you've defined *communication,* your understanding of communication and theory will necessarily guide your thinking. This happens with communication researchers and theorists as well. Each approaches his or her research with a personal way of looking at the communication process, and these views influence who and what is studied, and when and how the study is executed. We encourage you to consider the theories in this book and the theorists' views of communication before you make up your mind.

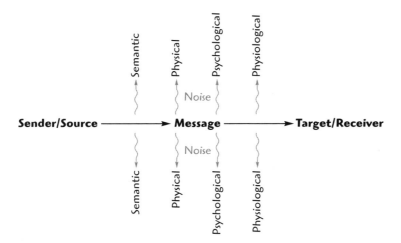

Figure 1.3
Linear Model of Communication
Source: Adapted from Shannon & Weaver, 1949.

Models of Understanding: Communication as Action, Interaction, and Transaction

Communication theorists create **models,** or simplified representations of complex interrelationships among elements in the communication process, which allow us to visually understand a sometimes complex process. Although there are many communication models, we discuss the three most prominent ones here. In discussing these models and their underlying approaches, we wish to demonstrate the manner in which communication has been conceptualized over the years.

Communication as Action: The Linear Model

In 1949, Claude Shannon, a Bell Laboratories scientist and professor at the Massachusetts Institute of Technology, and Warren Weaver, a consultant on projects at the Sloan Foundation, described communication as a linear process. They were concerned with radio and telephone technology and wanted to develop a model that could explain how information passed through various channels. The result was the conceptualization of the **linear model of communication.**

This approach to human communication comprises several key elements, as Figure 1.3 demonstrates. A **source,** or transmitter of a message, sends a **message** to a **receiver,** the recipient of the message. The receiver is the person who makes sense out of the message. All of this communication takes place in a **channel,** which is the pathway to communication. Channels frequently correspond to the visual, tactile, olfactory, and auditory senses. Thus, you use the visual channel when you see your roommate, and you use the tactile channel when you hug your parent.

models
simplified representations of the communication process

linear model of communication
one-way view of communication that assumes a message is sent by a source to a receiver through a channel

source
originator of a message

message
words, sounds, actions, or gestures in an interaction

receiver
recipient of a message

channel
pathway to communication

noise
distortion in channel not intended by the source

semantic noise
linguistic influences on reception of message

physical (external) noise
bodily influences on reception of message

psychological noise
cognitive influences on reception of message

physiological noise
biological influences on reception of message

Communication also involves **noise,** which is anything not intended by the informational source. There are four types of noise. First, **semantic noise** pertains to the slang, jargon, or specialized language used by individuals or groups. For instance, when Jennifer received a medical report from her ophthalmologist, the physician's words included phrases such as "ocular neuritis," "dilated funduscopic examination," and "papillary conjunctival changes." This is an example of semantic noise because outside of the medical community, these words have limited (or no) meaning. **Physical,** or **external, noise** exists outside of the receiver. **Psychological noise** refers to a communicator's prejudices, biases, and predispositions toward another or the message. To exemplify these two types, imagine listening to participants at a political rally. You may experience psychological noise listening to the views of a politician whom you do not support, and you may also experience physical noise from the people nearby who may be protesting the politician's presence. Finally, **physiological noise** refers to the biological influences on the communication process. Physiological noise, then, exists if you or a speaker is ill, fatigued, or hungry.

Although this view of the communication process was highly respected many years ago, the approach is very limited for several reasons. First, the model presumes that there is only one message in the communication process. Yet we all can point to a number of circumstances in which we send several messages at once. Second, as we have previously noted, communication does not have a definable beginning and ending. Shannon and Weaver's model presumes this mechanistic orientation. Furthermore, to suggest that communication is simply one person speaking to another oversimplifies the complex communication process. Listeners are not so passive, as we can all confirm when we are in heated arguments with others. Clearly, communication is more than a one-way effort and has no definable middle or end (Anderson & Ross, 2002).

Communication as Interaction: The Interactional Model

The linear model suggests that a person is only a sender or a receiver. That is a narrow view of the participants in the communication process. Wilbur Schramm (1954), therefore, proposed that we also examine the relationship between a sender and a receiver. He conceptualized the **interactional model of communication,** which emphasizes the two-way communication process between communicators (Figure 1.4). In other words, communication goes in two directions: from sender to receiver and from receiver to sender. This circular process suggests that communication is ongoing. The interactional view illustrates that a person can perform the role of either sender or receiver during an interaction, but not both roles simultaneously.

One element essential to the interactional model of communication is **feedback,** or the response to a message. Feedback may be verbal or nonverbal, intentional or unintentional. Feedback helps communicators to know whether or not their message is being received and the extent to which meaning is achieved. In the interactional model, feedback takes place after a message is received, not during the message itself.

interactional model of communication
view of communication as the sharing of meaning with feedback that links source and receiver

feedback
communication given to the source by the receiver to indicate understanding (meaning)

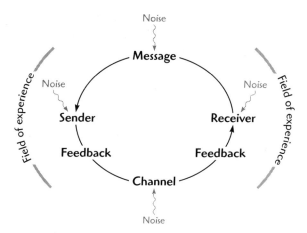

Figure 1.4
Interactional Model of Communication

To illustrate the critical nature of feedback and the interactional model of communication, consider our opening example of the Bollen family. When Eddy's parents find him on the couch drunk, they proceed to tell Eddy how they feel about his behavior. Their outcry prompts Eddy to argue with his parents, who in turn, tell him to leave their house immediately. This interactional sequence shows that there is an alternating nature in the communication between Eddy and his parents. They see his behavior and provide their feedback on it, Eddy listens to their message and responds, then his father sends the final message telling his son to leave. We can take this even further by noting the door slam as one additional feedback behavior in the interaction.

A final feature of the interactional model is a person's **field of experience,** or how a person's culture, experiences, and heredity influence his or her ability to communicate with another. Each person brings a unique field of experience to each communication episode, and these experiences frequently influence the communication between people. For instance, when two people come together and begin dating, the two inevitably bring their fields of experience into the relationship. One person in this couple may have been raised in a large family with several siblings, while the other may be an only child. These experiences (and others) will necessarily influence how the two come together and will most likely affect how they maintain their relationship.

Like the linear view, the interactional model has been criticized. The interactional model suggests that one person acts as sender while the other acts as receiver in a communication encounter. As you have experienced, however, people communicate as both senders and receivers in a single encounter. But the prevailing criticism of the interactional model pertains to the issue of feedback. The interactional view assumes two people speaking and listening, but not at the same time. But what occurs when a person sends a nonverbal message during an interaction? Smiling, frowning, or simply moving away from the conversation during an interaction between two people happens all the time. For example, in an interaction between a mother and her daughter, the mother may be reprimanding her child while simultaneously "reading" the

field of experience
overlap of sender's and receiver's culture, experiences, and heredity in communication

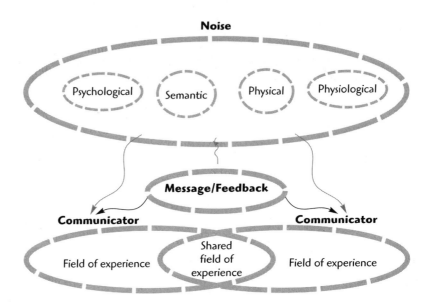

Figure 1.5
Transactional
Model of
Communication

child's nonverbal behavior. Is the girl laughing? Is she upset? Is she even listening to her mother? Each of these behaviors will inevitably prompt the mother to modify her message. These criticisms and contradictions inspired development of a third model of communication.

Communication as Transaction: The Transactional Model

**transactional
model of
communication**
view of communi-
cation as the
simultaneous sending
and receiving of
messages

The **transactional model of communication** (Barnlund, 1970; Frymier, 2005; Wilmot, 1987) underscores the simultaneous sending and receiving of messages in a communication episode, as Figure 1.5 shows. To say that communication is transactional means that the process is cooperative; the sender and the receiver are mutually responsible for the effect and the effectiveness of communication. In the linear model of communication, meaning is sent from one person to another. In the interactional model, meaning is achieved through the feedback of a sender and a receiver. In the transactional model, people build shared meaning. Furthermore, what people say during a transaction is greatly influenced by their past experience. So, for instance, at a college fair, it is likely that a college student will have a great deal to say to a high school senior because of the college student's experiences in class and around campus. A college senior will, no doubt, have a different view of college than, say, a college sophomore, due in large part to his or her past college experiences.

Transactional communication requires us to recognize the influence of one message on another. One message builds on the previous message; therefore, there is an interdependency between and among the components of communication. A change in one causes a change in others. Furthermore, the transactional model presumes that as we simultaneously send and receive messages, we attend to both verbal and nonverbal elements of a message. In a sense, communicators negotiate meaning. For instance, if a friend asks you about your family background, you may use some private language that your friend doesn't understand. Your friend may make a face while you are presenting your message, indicating some sort of confusion with what you've said. As a result, you will most likely back up and define your terms and then continue with the conversation. This example highlights the degree to which two people are actively involved in a communication encounter. The nonverbal communication is just as important as the verbal message in such a transactional process.

Earlier we noted that the field of experience functions in the interactional model. In the transactional model, the fields of experience exist, but overlap occurs. That is, rather than person A and person B having separate fields of experience, eventually the two fields merge (see Figure 1.5). This was an important addition to the understanding of the communication process because it demonstrates an active process of understanding. That is, for communication to take place, individuals must build shared meaning. For instance, in our earlier example of two people with different childhoods, the interactional model suggests that they would come together with an understanding of their backgrounds. The transactional model, however, requires each of them to understand and incorporate the other's field of experience into his or her life. For example, it's not enough for Julianna to know that Paul has a prior prison record; the transactional view holds that she must figure out a way to put his past into perspective. Will it affect their current relationship? How? If not, how will Julianna discuss it with Paul? The transactional model takes the meaning-making process one step further than the interactional model. It assumes reciprocity, or shared meaning.

You now have a basic understanding of how we define communication, and we have outlined the basic elements and a few communication models. Recall this interpretation as you read the book and examine the various theories. It is likely that you will interpret communication differently from one theory to another. Remember that theorists set boundaries in their discussions about human behavior, and, consequently, they often define *communication* according to their own view. One of our goals in this book is to enable you to articulate the role that communication plays in a number of different theories.

Thus far, we have examined the communication process and unpacked the complexity associated with it. We have identified the primary models of communication, trying to demonstrate the evolution and maturation of the communication field. We now explore a component that is a necessary and vital part of every communication episode: ethics.

Ethics and Communication

In the movie *The Insider*, which was based on a true story, the lead character's name is Jeffrey Wigand, a former tobacco scientist who violated a contractual agreement and exposed a cigarette maker's efforts to include addictive ingredients in all cigarettes. The movie shows Wigand as a man of good conscience with the intention of telling the public about the company and its immoral undertakings. Wigand clearly believed that saving lives was the right and only thing to do, and he made his actions fit his beliefs: He acted on his ethics.

ethics
perceived rightness or wrongness of an action or behavior

In this section, we examine **ethics,** or the perceived rightness or wrongness of action or behavior. Ethics is a type of moral decision making (Arnett, Harden-Fritz, & Bell, 2008), and determining what is right or wrong is influenced by society's rules and laws. For example, although some may believe Wigand's efforts were laudable, others may note that Wigand apparently knew what was going on when he signed a contract prohibiting him from disclosing company secrets. Furthermore, the murkiness of ethics is evidenced when one considers that Wigand made a lot of money before disclosing what was occurring.

The United States is built on standards of moral conduct, and these standards are central to a number of institutions and relationships (Alboher, 2008). Because ethical standards tend to shift according to historical period, the environment, the conversation, and the people involved (Englehardt, 2001), ethics can be difficult to understand. Let's briefly discuss ethical issues as they pertain to cultural institutions; a more comprehensive explanation of ethics can be found elsewhere (see Johanneson, Valde, & Whedbee, 2008). We begin by asking why we should understand ethics, next explain ethics as it relates to society, and finally, explain the intersection of ethics and communication theory. As you think about this information, keep in mind that ethical decision making is culturally based. That is, what we consider to be ethical and appropriate in one society is not necessarily a shared value in another society. For instance, though many in the United States can identify with the plight of the Bollen family, you should know that in many cultures, having a son return to his family-of-origin is revered and would not pose the problems that the Bollens are experiencing.

Why study ethics? The response to this question could easily be another question: Why not study it? Ethics permeates all walks of life and cuts across gender, race, class, sexual identity, and spiritual/religious affiliation. In other words, we cannot escape ethical principles in our lives. Ethics is part of virtually every decision we make. Moral development is part of human development, and as we grow older, our moral code undergoes changes well into adulthood. Ethics is what prompts a society toward higher levels of integrity and truth. Elaine Englehardt (2001) observes that "we don't get to 'invent' our own system of ethics" (p. 2), which means that we generally follow a given cultural code of morality. And Ken Andersen (2003) argues that without an understanding and an expression of ethical values, society will be disadvantaged: "Violating the norms of ethical communication is, I believe, a major factor in the malaise that has led many people to withdraw from the civic culture whether of their profession, their associations, their political arena" (p. 14).

From a communication perspective, ethical issues surface whenever messages potentially influence others. Consider, for instance, the ethics associated with telling your professor that you couldn't turn in a paper on time because a member of your family is ill, when such an illness doesn't exist. Think about the ethics involved if you take an idea of a co-worker and present it to your boss as if it were your own. Consider the ethical consequences of going out on

Table 1.1 Examples of Ethical Decision Making in the United States

INSTITUTION	EXAMPLES OF ETHICAL ISSUES
Business and industry	Should CEOs be given pay raises in companies that are not profitable?
Religion	Are same-sex marriages moral?
Entertainment	Does viewing violence in movies prompt violence in society? Should Hollywood develop a morality code?
Higher education	Should students be allowed credit for "life experiences" such as jobs? Should student fees go to political groups on campus?
Medicine	Can pharmaceutical companies be held responsible for sample medicines? Should medical professionals be given license to end the life of a patient?
Politics	Should political candidates make promises to citizens?
Technology	Should Internet sites be held accountable for their content? Who should monitor websites targeting children?

several dates with someone and choosing not to disclose a past felony for assault, or of posing as someone other than yourself in online communications. Television, too, carries ethical implications. For example, can television promote racial tolerance and harmony and simultaneously present portrayals of cultural groups in stereotypic and offensive ways? We continue our discussion of ethics by identifying some of the institutions whose ethical standards have been the subject of much conversation. Business and industry, religion, entertainment, education, medicine, politics, and technology are just a few of the many fields that have been prone to ethical lapses and have been challenged in communicating messages of integrity (Table 1.1).

Business and Industry

Perhaps no cultural institution has been under more ethical suspicions of late than "corporate America." Unethical behavior in corporations has reached proportions never before seen. Companies have tried to hide costs, use creative accounting practices, commit accounting fraud, and a plethora of other ethical breaches. The examples are plentiful: The former head of the World Bank engineers a job promotion and salary increase for his longtime companion; WorldCom declares bankruptcy after the discovery of an $11 billion accounting "error"; Enron inflates earnings reports and hides billions in debt, while increasing salaries of its executives; the founder of Adelphia Communications and his two sons commit bank and securities fraud, leading to the company's demise; and Boeing's chief financial officer inappropriately recruits a retired government official with whom he previously negotiated contracts. Sadly, each of these situations occurred within a six-year period (2001–2007). The list of business scandals has been especially prominent. But with the advent of Corporate Ethics Statements, improved transparent accounting practices, and increased accountability to stockholders, businesses are starting to improve their ethical standing. Of course, much, much more needs to be done to eliminate lingering levels of distrust, especially after the 2008 federal bailout of financial institutions in the United States.

Religion

Both Eastern and Western civilizations have stressed ethics in their moral traditions. For instance, according to Taoism, no one exists in isolation, and, therefore, empathy and insight will lead to truth. For the Buddhist, being moral requires that one use words that elicit peace and avoid gossip, self-promotion, anger, argument, and lying. From a Western perspective, many ethical issues derive from early Greek civilization. Aristotle first articulated the principle of the Golden Mean. He believed that a person's moral virtue stands between two vices, with the middle, or the mean, being the foundation for a rational society. For instance, when the Bollens are deciding what to say to their son Eddy about overstaying his welcome, their Golden Mean might look like this:

EXTREME	GOLDEN MEAN	EXTREME
lying	truthful communication	reveal everything

The Judeo-Christian religions are centered as well on questions of ethics. In fact, there is an online publication devoted solely to Religion and Ethics (www.pbs.org/wnet/religionandethics/current/headlines.html). Christianity is founded on the principle of good example—that is, live according to God's laws and set an example for others. However, some believe that such moral standards are not uniquely religious. For those not affiliated with organized religion, the secular values of fairness and justice and working toward better relationships are important as well. Affiliating with a religion may also pose some ethical difficulty if a person does not subscribe to a number of its philosophies or orientations. For instance, people who believe that gay men and lesbians should be able to marry may be challenged because most religions reject the legitimacy of such ceremonies.

Despite efforts to retain ethicality, religious institutions have had a number of ethical challenges over the years. Ministers frequenting prostitutes, pedophilic priests, drug abuse by church leaders, and sexual immorality among parishioners and pastors are just a few of the dozens of religious scandals that have caused outrage. Fortunately, many religious bodies are now developing clear ethical statements on appropriate behavior and clarifying the consequences of ethical violations.

Entertainment

The entertainment industry has also been intimately involved in dialogues about ethics and communication. Often, a circular argument surfaces with respect to Hollywood: Does Hollywood reflect society or does Hollywood shape society? Many viewpoints are raised in these arguments, but three seem to dominate. One belief is that Hollywood has a responsibility to show the moral side of an immoral society; movies should help people escape a difficult reality, not relive it. A second opinion is that Hollywood should create more nonviolent and nonsexual films so that all family members can watch a movie. Unfortunately, critics note, films like *Hostel, The Wicker Man, 300,* and *Gangs of New York* tend to exacerbate violent attitudes in young people. A third school of thought is that Hollywood is in show *business,* and therefore making money is what moviemaking is all about. Regardless of whether you agree with any of these orientations, the entertainment industry will continue to reflect *and* influence changing moral climates in the United States. Some might say that Hollywood leading the charge in any conversation on ethics is, in itself, a question of ethics.

Higher Education

A third cultural institution that has been charged with questionable ethics is higher education. Colleges and universities across the United States teach introductory courses in ethics, and these are required courses in many schools.

Despite this interest, many schools have lost their own moral compass. For instance, colleges and universities face an ethical choice about reporting crime statistics on their campus. Despite the fact that they are required to report campus crime via the "Jeanne Clery Act" (named after a Lehigh University student who was murdered in 1986), some campuses fear the bad publicity. As a result, crime is "contextualized" ("Our campus is in a large city; there's a lot of crime everywhere" or "Our campus is in a rural setting; we may have a few problems but we're still relatively safe"). Another ethical decision arises when schools are required to identify the enrollment patterns for legislative and financial support. Frequently, schools report statistical increases in enrollment over a number of years when in reality the school system has simply adopted a new way of counting heads. Although they are called institutions of "higher" learning, some campuses have reached new "lows" in ethical decision making.

Medicine

A fourth institution concerned with ethics and communication is the medical community. Specifically, with advances in science changing the cultural landscape, bioethical issues are topics of conversation around the dinner table. Physician-assisted suicide is one example of medicine at the center of ethical controversy. To some, the decision to prolong life should be a private one, made by the patient and his or her doctor. To others, society should have a say in such a decision.

Medical decisions can become publicly debated far from the hospital bed-side. In 2004, for instance, the state of Florida and Governor Jeb Bush tried to prevent the spouse of a terminally ill woman (Terry Schiavo) from shutting down the ventilator system that kept her alive. Eventually, the U.S. Supreme Court refused to intervene in a lower court's ruling (allowing the spouse to terminate his wife's life). Although one can imagine the personal pain Mr. Schiavo felt about such a decision, the story played out in public, with a debate on euthanasia at the center of the outcry. Late-term abortions, human cloning, drug-enhanced athletes, medicinal marijuana, and physician-assisted suicide are all topics that demonstrate the interrelationship among ethics, politics, and medicine. This topic has resonated sufficiently in our society that there is now a publication devoted to the topic of ethics and medicine (www.ethicsandmedicine.com).

Politics

Discussing the belief that politics is ethically challenged is like telling an *American Idol* contestant that there will be teenagers watching the program: It's obvious! Ethics and politics are often viewed as incompatible. We are living in cynical times and opinion polls consistently show that the public's view of political leaders rates lower than their view of paying taxes. The scandals associated with politics relate to lobbyists, campaign financing, infidelity, deception, conflicts of interest, cover-ups, bribery, conspiracy, tax evasion . . . Watergate, Filegate, Travelgate, Troopergate . . . the list goes on and on.

The ethical problems associated with politics may never go away, despite efforts to establish ethics commissions and oversight advisory boards in state and national governments. Though many of us wish to be optimistic in thinking that we are cultivating a new generation of political leaders who are ethical beings, there are those who are not as hopeful. Still, with nonprofit organizations such as Public Interest Research Group (PIRG) and the Government Accountability Project—groups that expose ethical shortcomings in our government and its leaders—and with aptly named laws such as the Honest Leadership and Open Government Act of 2007, there may be cause for increased confidence in the future.

Technology

Technology is at the center of many ethical debates today. Armed with a copy of the First Amendment, proponents of free speech say the Internet, for example, should not be censored. Free speech advocates stress that what is considered inappropriate can vary tremendously from one person to another, and consequently, censorship is arbitrary. Consider, for instance, the U.S. Supreme Court decision protecting "virtual" child pornography on the Internet. Noting that the Child Pornography Protection Act was overly broad, the justices felt that banning computer-generated images of young people was unjustified. In addition, social networking sites (MySpace, myYearbook, and classmates.com) are fast becoming prone to ethical problems. How much information is too much? Teenagers letting others know where they live, blogs that divulge too much information about a family's financial situation, and would-be employers looking over the shoulders of users are just a few of the many ethical challenges characterizing the online world.

As we become more and more reliant on technology in the United States, particularly on the Internet, ethical issues will continue to arise. Lying about one's identity online, downloading copyrighted material, inviting young people into violent and hate-filled websites, and watching executions on the Internet are all examples of potential technological ethics dilemmas.

Some Final Thoughts

The relationship between communication and ethics is intricate and complex. Public discourse requires responsibility. We presume that political leaders will tell the truth and that spiritual leaders will guide us by their example. Yet we know that not all elected officials are honest and that not all religious leaders set a spiritual standard. Organizations are especially prone to ethical dilemmas. For instance, whistle-blowing, or revealing ethically suspicious behavior in a company, can have lasting implications. Although some may view whistle-blowing as a courageous and morally sound act, others may view it as a violation of trust. This difference in perception usually rests on whether a whistle-blower is perceived as a disgruntled employee who may have been passed over for a promotion or as someone who is genuinely concerned about a company's ethical practices. Unethical practices do little to garner trust in people. As J. Michael Sproule (1980) concludes, "When people are misled they distrust the sources that have deceived them. If the majority of a society's information sources behave without concern for honest communication, then all communication is weakened" (p. 282).

There is an ethical dimension to listening as well. As listeners (or readers) we have a responsibility to give a fair hearing to the ideas of others. This responsibility extends to such ideas as the communication theories presented in this book. Rob Anderson and Veronica Ross (2002) point out six important ethical strategies to consider when reading communication theory:

1. Remain open to being persuaded by the statements of others.
2. Remain willing to try out new ideas that may be seen by others as mistakes, and invite others to experiment also.
3. Accept that multiple perspectives on reality are held as valid by different people, especially in different cultural contexts.
4. Attempt to test any tentatively held knowledge.
5. Live with ambiguity, but become less tolerant of contradiction.
6. Evaluate knowledge claims against personal experience and the everyday concrete pragmatics of what works. (p. 15)

In addition to these suggestions, we add one more: If a theory is a bit difficult to understand at first, don't gloss over it. Delve into the explanation once more to gain a clearer picture of the theorists' intentions. You may feel inexperienced or unprepared to challenge these theories. Yet we offer the theories for review, application, and comment and want you to ask questions about them. Although we would like to think that all theorists are open and receptive to multiple ways of knowing, the reality remains that theory construction is bound by culture, personality, time, circumstance, and the availability of resources. As students of communication theory, you must be willing to ask some difficult questions and probe some confusing areas.

The Value of Understanding Communication Theory

Finally, although we've alluded to this throughout the chapter, we'd like to emphasize the importance of communication theory to all of our lives. We realize that many of you may not be immediately aware of the value of this topic. Therefore, we want to give you a glimpse into the significance of communication theory. As you read and understand each chapter, you will likely develop your own personal understanding of the importance of communication theory. We encourage you to be open as you explore this exciting area.

Understanding Communication Theory Cultivates Critical Thinking Skills

One important value you glean from studying communication theory relates to your critical thinking skills. Without doubt, as you read and reflect on the theories in this book, you will be required to think critically about several issues. Learning how to apply the theory to your own life, recognizing the research potential of the theory, and understanding how a particular theory evolved will be among your responsibilities in this course. In addition, understanding communication can aid in your skill set. The information in Chapter 18 (The *Rhetoric*), for instance, will be instrumental when you are required to deliver a public speech. Chapter 14 (Groupthink) contains content that will aid your undertanding of working in decision-making groups. These skills notwithstanding, as Craig and Muller (2007) notes, many theories have a Western cultural bias, so we need to be cautious in a universal application of the theory.

These activities require that you cultivate your critical thinking skills—skills that will help you on the job, in relationships, and as you are introduced to media.

Understanding Communication Theory Helps You to Recognize the Breadth and Depth of Research

In addition to fostering critical thinking skills, being a student of communication theory will help you appreciate the richness of research across various fields of study. Regardless of what your current academic major is, the theories contained in this book are based on the thinking, writing, and research of intellectually curious men and women who have drawn on the scholarship of numerous disciplines. For instance, as you read about the Relational Dialectics Theory (Chapter 12), you will note that many of its principles originate in philosophy. Groupthink (Chapter 14) originated in foreign policy decision making processes. Face-Negotiation Theory (Chapter 26) was influenced by research in sociology. As you pursue a particular degree, keep in mind that much of what you are learning is a result of theoretical thinking.

Understanding Communication Theory Helps to Make Sense of Personal Life Experiences

Understanding communication theory also helps you make sense of your life experiences. It's nearly impossible to find a theory in this book that does not in some way relate to your life or to the lives of people around you. Communication theory aids you in understanding people, media, and events and helps you answer important questions. Have you ever been confused about why some men speak differently from some women? Chances are that reading Muted Group Theory (Chapter 28) will help you understand why that may be the case. Do the media promote a violent society? The theory of Cultivation Analysis (Chapter 22) will likely help you answer that question. What role does technology play in society? Media Ecology Theory (Chapter 25) responds to that question. And what happens when someone stands too close while talking to you? Expectancy Violations Theory (Chapter 8) explores and explains this type of behavior. Some of you may have entered this course thinking that communication theory has limited value in your life. You will see that much of your life and your experiences in life will be better understood because of communication theory.

Communication Theory Fosters Self-Awareness

Thus far, we observed that learning about communication theory helps your critical thinking skills, informs you about the value of research across different fields of study, and aids you in understanding the world around you. One final reason to study theories of communication pertains to an area that is likely to be most important in your life—you. Learning about who you are, how you function in society, the influence you are able to have on others, the extent to which you are influenced by the media, how you behave in various circumstances, and what motivates your decisions are just a handful of the possible areas that are either explicitly or implicitly discussed in the theories you will be introduced to in this book. Social Penetration Theory (Chapter 10) will help you consider the value of self-disclosing in your relationships. Chapter 5 (Symbolic Interaction Theory) will assist you in thinking about the meaning of the various symbols surrounding you. Yet these are not "self-help" communication theories; they do not provide easy answers to difficult questions. What you will encounter are theories that will help you as you try to understand yourself and your surroundings.

You are about to embark on an educational journey that may be new to you. We hope you persevere in unraveling the complexity of communication theory. The journey may be different, challenging, and tiring at times, but it will always be applicable to your life.

Conclusion

In this chapter, we introduced you to the communication process. We presented our definition of *communication* and reviewed the intentionality debate as a point of controversy in the communication field. In addition, we identified three prevailing models of communication: the linear model, the interactional model, and the transactional model. We discussed ethics and its relationship to communication theory. Finally, we provided several reasons why it is important for you to study communication theory.

You now have an understanding of the communication process and some sense of how complex it can be. As you read the many theories in this book, you will be able to view communication from a variety of perspectives. You will also gain valuable information that will help you understand human behavior and give you a new way to think about our society. We continue this examination in Chapter 2 when we present the traditions in communication study and important contexts in which communication takes place.

Discussion Starters

1. What led to the blowup between Eddy Bollen and his parents? Do you believe that Eddy and his parents were trying to handle his situation in an ethical way? Why or why not?

2. Do you believe that all slips of the tongue, conversational faux pas, and unintentional nonverbal behaviors should be considered communication? Why or why not? What examples can you provide to justify your thoughts?

3. Explain why the linear model of communication was so appealing years ago. Explain the appeal of the transactional model using current societal events.

4. Discuss the value of looking at communication theory from a variety of different disciplinary angles.

5. What are some recent ethical dilemmas related to communication? How was each dilemma resolved, if it was?

6. Comment on why so many definitions of communication exist.

7. Think of how you looked at communication before enrolling in this course. How has your perception changed after reading this chapter? How has your impression been verified by the content of this chapter?

Online Learning Center   (www. mhhe.com/west4e)

Visit the Online Learning Center at www.mhhe.com/west4e for chapter-specific resources, such as story-into-theory and multiple-choice quizzes, as well as theory summaries and theory connection questions.

CHAPTER 2

Thinking About the Field: Traditions and Contexts

Jenny and Lee Yamato

As the 18-year-old daughter of a single parent, Lee Yamato knows that life can be difficult. She is the only child of Jenny Yamato, a Japanese American woman whose husband died from a heart attack several years ago. Jenny raised her daughter in Lacon, a small rural town in the South. It was stressful being a single mom, and Jenny was sometimes the target of overt racist jokes. As a waitress, Jenny knew that college would be the way to a better life for her daughter. She saved every extra penny and worked at the children's library for several months to bring in extra income. Jenny knew that Lee would get financial aid in college, but she also wanted to be able to help her only child with college finances.

As Lee finished her senior year in high school, she knew that before too long she would be leaving to attend a public university. Unfortunately, the closest college was over 200 miles from Lacon. Lee had mixed feelings about her move. She was very excited to get away from the small-town gossip, but she also knew that leaving Lacon meant that her mom would have to live by herself. Being alone could be devastating to her mom, Lee thought. Still, Lee recognized that her education was her first priority and that in order to get into veterinary school, she would have to stay focused. Thinking about her mom would only make the transition more difficult and could sour her first year as a college student.

Jenny, too, felt ambivalent about Lee leaving. When Jenny's husband died, she didn't think that she could raise a 13-year-old by herself. In fact, given that single moms were not viewed with a lot of respect, Jenny felt even more overpowered. However, her own tenacity and determination had paid off, and she was extremely proud that her child was going away to college. Like her daughter, though, Jenny felt sad about Lee's departure. She felt as if her best friend was leaving her, and she couldn't imagine her life without her daughter. She knew that they would talk on the phone, but it couldn't replace the hugs, the laughter, and the memories.

On the day that Lee was to leave, Jenny gave her a box with chocolate chip cookies, some peanut butter cups (Lee's favorite), a photo album of Lee and Jenny during their camping trip to Arizona, and a shoe box. Inside the shoe box were old letters that Jenny and her husband had written to each other during their courtship. Jenny wanted Lee to have the letters to remind her that her dad's spirit lives on in her. When Lee looked at the first letter, she put it down, hugged her mom, and cried. She then got into her car and slowly drove away, leaving her house and her only true friend behind.

Chapter 1 provided a foundation for conceptualizing what communication is and understanding the complexity of the communication process. In this chapter, we further unravel the meaning of communication by articulating two primary ways of looking at the field of communication.

The communication discipline is vast, and its depth is reflected in the lives of people across the United States, people like Lee and Jenny Yamato. Their relationship is obviously a close one, marked now by a common and often emotional point in a family's development: college. As the two begin to adapt to a new type of relationship characterized by distance, their communication will also take on new levels of importance. As Bethani Dobkin and Roger Pace (2006) state, "communication has the potential to shape identities, relationships, environments, and cultures" (p. 6). The Yamato family will likely communicate with an appreciation for the full impact that communication can have on their lives. Let's begin our discussion of the communication field by looking at seven traditions in communication. We will then examine various settings in which communication occurs. These two approaches guide this chapter. The first approach ("The Seven Traditions") is theoretical in nature; the second framework ("The Seven Contexts") is more practical in its approach. We describe each in the following pages.

Theory Into Practice

Trish

To be honest, I wasn't sure how to explain my communication major to my mom and dad when I went home for Thanksgiving. They had no idea why I wanted to major in it! After I talked to them about what communication is (and what it isn't!), I think they were pretty happy that I found a major that made sense to me. I know I'm more employable by understanding communication, but I also just love knowing how broad a field it is. I think I convinced some of my dormmates to switch their major!

Seven Traditions in the Communication Field

Robert Craig (Craig, 1999; Craig & Muller, 2007) outlines communication theory in one of the more thoughtful, intellectually valuable ways. Craig believed that communication theory is a vast and often unwieldy area of study and, to this end, provided categories to aid over understanding of it. Craig and Muller note that trying to make sense of communication theory is often complicated because of different intellectual styles in the field. A classification system for understanding communication theory, then, helps us to break down the challenges associated with understanding theory.

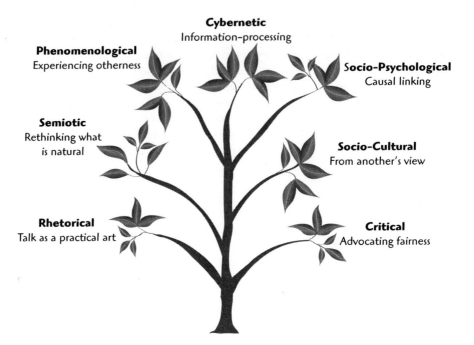

Cybernetic
Information-processing

Phenomenological
Experiencing otherness

Socio-Psychological
Causal linking

Semiotic
Rethinking what
is natural

Socio-Cultural
From another's view

Rhetorical
Talk as a practical art

Critical
Advocating fairness

Figure 2.1
Traditions in
Communication
Theory

Craig terms the following framework as "traditions" to highlight the belief that theoretical development doesn't just occur naturally. Indeed, theorizing in communication is a deliberative, engaging, and innovative experience that happens over time. As Craig and Muller (2007) point out, "theorists invent new ideas to solve problems they perceive in existing ideas in a particular tradition" (p. xiii). And, although traditions suggest adhering to a historical preference, Craig and Muller are quick to point out that traditions change frequently and, like communication, are dynamic. Further, they caution that many theories are not easily categorized: "Even a theory that rebels against its tradition and rejects major parts of it can still belong to the tradition in significant ways" (p. xiv). So let's examine the seven traditions of communication theory as advanced by Craig (1999). To honor the integrity of each tradition yet avoid irrelevant detail for this section of the chapter, we will provide you an overview of each tradition. If you'd like additional details, you are encouraged to consult Craig's research. See Figure 2.1 for an overview of the traditions.

The Rhetorical Tradition

At the heart of the rhetorical tradition is what Craig notes as the "practical art" (p. 73) of talk. This tradition suggests that we are interested in public address and public speaking and their functions in a society. Rhetorical theory is especially valued in many Western societies because it helps us understand the influence of speech and how we can cultivate our public speaking effectiveness. This tradition also includes the ability to reflect on different viewpoints before arriving at a personal view. It is the usefulness of the rhetorical tradition that remains attractive to researchers, theorists, and practitioners.

The rhetorical tradition necessarily involves elements pertaining to language and the audience. It also includes a discussion pertaining to audience appeals; how do audience members respond to emotions, for example? To what extent does the power of language move people to emotional and decisive action? How are we influenced or swayed by the appeals by mass media? What role does personal example play in having others accept our point of view? What effect does speaking to a large group of people have on the perceptions or actions of that group? Or, to what extent does the rhetorical tradition challenge the common belief that "telling the plain truth is something other than the strategic adaptation of a message to an audience" (Craig, 2007, p. 73)? Answering such questions is not easy and yet needs to be considered as we reflect on the value and historical importance of looking at communication theory using a rhetorical lens.

The Semiotic Tradition

Simply put, **semiotics** is the study of signs. Signs are part of a social life and *signs* stand for something else. Children laughing and running around is a *sign* of play. A ring on the ring finger of the left hand is a *sign* of a married individual. An adult crying in a funeral home is a *sign* of sadness. Most common among these signs are "words" or what we generally consider as language usage. According to the semiotic tradition, meaning is achieved when we share a common language. As noted in Chapter 1, people arrive at a communication exchange with various fields of experience and values placed on these experiences. Pioneer linguist I. A. Richards (1936) observed that words are arbitrary and have no intrinsic meaning. Consequently, achieving commonality in meaning is more difficult than first imagined—particularly if one is using language that is not recognized nor valued by another.

semiotics
the study of signs

Semiotics suggests that what we think of as "natural" or "obvious" in public discourse needs to considered in context. That is, our values and belief structures are often a result of what has been passed down from one generation to another (a tradition). What was considered to be a "given" years ago may simply not be that way today. Semiotics challenges the notion that words have appropriate meanings; indeed, words change as the people using those words change. Consider, for example, the use of the words "war" and "peace" in the 1940s (World War II), the 1960s/70s (Vietnam War), the 1990s (Gulf War), and today (Iraq War). There are also likely to be multiple meanings of these two words if, for example, someone lost a family member in one of these wars and if another person protests war on a regular basis. Consider the phrase "single parent." In the 1950s, it did not resonate deeply in society. However, as time evolved, the divorce rate soared and marriage was not a "default" choice; being a single mom (like Jenny Yamato) or single dad is now commonplace.

The Phenomenological Tradition

Let's explore the term *phenomenology*, a concept derived from the field of philosophy. **Phenomenology** is a personal interpretation of everyday life and

phenomenology
a personal interpretation of everyday life and activities

activities. Often, phenomenology is intuitive and involves looking at things and events through a personal lens.

Craig (2007) believes that the phenomenological tradition is marked by communication that he contends is an "experience of otherness" (p. 79). What this means is that a person tries to attain authenticity by eliminating biases in a conversation. Many phenomenologists believe that an individual's system of beliefs should not influence the dialogue taking place. As you're probably figuring out, this is quite challenging, or, as Craig points out, is a "practical impossibility" (p. 80). Consider, for example, the challenge many people have communicating with other people who have different points of view or are from different backgrounds. Craig notes that many phenomenological ideas are especially applicable to issues pertaining to diversity, identity, class, sexuality, and religion.

The Cybernetic Tradition

Communication as information science was first introduced by Shannon and Weaver, two scholars associated with the linear model we discussed in Chapter 1. Recall that this model's fundamental shortcoming pertained to the fact that human communication is not as simplistic as linearity suggests. Nonetheless, what Shannon and Weaver did advance was the belief that communication involves noise. Cybernetics in particular looks at problems such as noise in the communication process. But it goes further. Cybernetics tries to unravel the complexities of message meaning by underscoring the unpredictability of the feedback we receive.

By advocating a cybernetic approach, communication theorists are embracing an expansive view of communication. As Craig (2007) states: "[I]t is important for us as communicators to transcend our individual perspectives, to look at the communication process from a broader, systemic viewpoint, and not to hold individuals responsible for systemic outcomes that no individual can control" (p. 82). In other words, the cybernetic tradition asks us to understand that communication is not only information processing, but also that individuals enter into communication settings with different abilities in that information processing.

The Socio-Psychological Tradition

Those who adhere to the socio-psychological tradition uphold a cause–effect model. That is, communication theory is examined from a view that holds that someone's behavior is influenced by something else—something social psychologists call a "variable" (we return to the issue of quantitative research in Chapter 3). Craig (2007) believes that underlying this tradition is the assumption that our own communication patterns and the patterns of others vary from one person to another. It is up to the social psychologist to unravel the relationship among these patterns.

An early advocate of the socio-psychological tradition was Carl Hovland. Hovland, a Yale psychologist, examined attitude change and investigated the extent to which long- and short-term recall influences an individual's attitudes and beliefs. In the 1950s—long before personal computers came into existence—Hovland also was the first to experiment with computer simulations and the learning process. His work and the work of other social psychologists underscored the importance of experimental research and trying to understand causal links. It is this scientific evidence for human behavior that continues to pervade much communication theorizing from this tradition.

The Socio-Cultural Tradition

The essence of the socio-cultural tradition can be summed up this way: "Our everyday interactions with others depend heavily on preexisting, shared cultural patterns and social structures" (Craig, 2007, p. 84). The core of the socio-cultural tradition suggests that individuals are parts of larger groups who have unique rules and patterns of interaction. To theorize from this tradition means to acknowledge and become sensitive to the many kinds of people who occupy this planet. Theorists should not instinctively nor strategically "group" people without concern for individual identity.

Socio-cultural theorists advocate that we abandon the binary "you/me" or "us/them" approach to understanding people. Instead, appealing to the *co-creation* of social order/reality is a worthier goal for consideration. As people communicate, they produce, maintain, repair, and transform (Carey, 1989). Dialogue and interaction must be characterized by an understanding of what Craig (2007) calls "voice," (p. 84) an individual point of view that inevitably finds its way into everyday conversation.

The Critical Tradition

Individuals who are concerned with injustice, oppression, power, and linguistic dominance are those who would likely identify themselves as critical theorists. Critiquing the social order and imposing structures or individuals on that order are at the heart of critical theory. Among the critical theorists most known for protesting social order is philosopher and political economist/revolutionary, Karl Marx. Marx believed that power in society has been hijacked by institutions that have no real concern for the working class. In his book, *The Communist Manifesto*, Marx and his colleague Friedrich Engels (1848) contended that the history of a society is best understood by looking at the class struggles in that society. We explore more of Marx's influence in Chapter 21.

Critical theorists find that openly questioning the assumptions that guide a society is legitimate. In doing so, communicators expose the beliefs and values that guide their decision making and actions. As is suggested in our opening story of Jenny and Lee Yamato, Jenny felt that as a single mom, she could never achieve the level of respect afforded to other family types. Critical theorists would attempt to unravel how a society defines freedom, equality, and reason, three qualities identified by Craig (2007), in order to understand Jenny's experiences. Who or what are the principle forces on social order? How does one achieve the freedom to express one's will? These and a host of other questions are at the core of the critical tradition.

Putting It All Together

This discussion provides you one way of looking at the texture of the communication field. Communication theory, as you will discover, is not created in a vacuum. Scholars enter into the theory-building process with particular positions, some of which influence the direction of the theories they construct and refine.

With this backdrop, we now wish to explore a more practical framework from which to view communication theory. We turn our attention to the various contexts, or environments, of communication from which research and theory develop.

Seven Contexts in the Communication Field

In order to make the communication field and the communication process more understandable and manageable we now look at the various contexts of communication. What is a context? Contexts are environments in which communication takes place. Contexts provide a backdrop against which researchers and theorists can analyze phenomena. Contexts also provide clarity. Our discussion of context focuses on **situational contexts**. To suggest that a context is situationally based means that the communication process is limited by a number of factors—namely, the number of people, the degree of space between interactants, the extent of feedback, and the available channels.

Earlier we noted that the communication field is very diverse and offers various research opportunities. This can be a bit cumbersome, and at times even communication scholars lament the wide array of options. Still, there seems to be some universal agreement on the fundamental contexts of communication. In fact, most communication departments are built around some or all of the following seven communication contexts: intrapersonal, interpersonal, small group, organizational, public/rhetorical, mass/media, and cultural (Figure 2.2). Keep in mind, however, that communication departments in colleges and universities across the United States divide themselves uniquely. Some, for instance, include mass communication in a department of communication whereas others may have a separate department of mass communication. Some schools have a department of interpersonal communication and include every context therein. This diversity underscores that the discipline is permeable, that boundary lines among the contexts are not absolute.

Intrapersonal Communication

As you review theories in this book, keep in mind that a theory may focus on how individuals perceive their own behavior. At the root of this thinking is intrapersonal communication. Intrapersonal communication theorists frequently study the role that cognition plays in human behavior. Intrapersonal communication is communication with oneself. It is an internal dialogue and may take place even in the presence of another individual. Intrapersonal communication is what goes on inside your head even when you are with someone.

contexts
environments in which communication takes place

situational contexts
environments that are limited by such factors as the number of people present, the feedback, the space between communicators, among others

intrapersonal communication
communication with oneself

CONTEXT		SOME RESEARCH AND THEORETICAL CONCERNS
INTRAPERSONAL Communication with oneself		Impression formation and decision making; symbols and meaning; observations and attributions; ego involvement and persuasion
INTERPERSONAL Face-to-face communication		Relationship maintenance strategies; relational intimacy; relationship control; interpersonal attraction
SMALL GROUP Communication with a group of people		Gender and group leadership; group vulnerability; groups and stories; group decision making; task difficulty
ORGANIZATIONAL Communication within and among large and extended environments		Organizational hierarchy and power; culture and organizational life; employee morale; opinions and worker satisfaction
PUBLIC/RHETORICAL Communication to a large group of listeners (audience)		Communication apprehension; delivery effectiveness; speech and text criticism; ethical speechmaking; popular culture analysis
MASS/MEDIA Communication to a very large audience through mediated forms	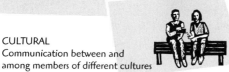	Use of media; affiliation and television programming; television and values; media and need fulfillment; effects of social networking sites
CULTURAL Communication between and among members of different cultures		Culture and rule-setting; culture and anxiety; hegemony; ethnocentrism

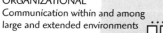

**Figure 2.2
Contexts of
Communication**

Intrapersonal communication is usually more repetitive than other communication; we engage in it many times each day. This context is also unique from other contexts in that it includes those times when you imagine, perceive, daydream, and solve problems in your head. Intrapersonal communication is much more than talking to oneself. It also includes the many attributions you may make about another person's behavior. For instance, an employer may want to know why an employee arrives late to work and looks disheveled each day. The supervisor may believe that the worker's tardiness and demeanor are a result of some domestic problems. In reality, the employee may have another job in order to pay for his or her child's college tuition. We all have internal dialogues, and these internalized voices can vary tremendously from one person to another.

Intrapersonal communication is distinguished from other contexts in that it allows communicators to make attributions about themselves. People have the ability to assess themselves. From body image to work competencies, people are always making self-attributions. You may have thought seriously about your own strengths and shortcomings in a number of situations. For example, do you find that you are an excellent parent but not so excellent as a statistics student? Are there times when you feel that you are a trusted friend, but not so trusted in your own family?

Although some people may believe that talking to oneself is a bit peculiar, Virginia Satir (1988) believes that these internal dialogues may help individuals bolster their self-esteem—the degree of positive orientation people have about themselves. Often, intrapersonal communication is difficult; it requires individuals to accept their accomplishments and confront their fears and anxieties. Looking in a mirror can be both enlightening and frightening. Of course, mirrors can also be distorting. Jenny Yamato, for example, may think that her world is over once her daughter leaves for college. The reality for the vast majority of parents, however, is that they survive the "loss." As a single parent, Jenny may think that she is incapable of moving on without Lee. Once Lee leaves, however, Jenny may find that she is more empowered living alone.

The research in intrapersonal communication centers a great deal on the cognitions, symbols, and intentions that individuals have. To this end, researchers in this area have examined attitudes toward specific behaviors and events, including dating (Guerrero & Bachman, 2008), father–daughter relationships (Punyanunt-Carter, 2007), dreaming (Ijams & Miller, 2000), imagination (Engen, 2002), self-embarrassment (Sharkey, Park, & Kim, 2004), and motivation of business executives (Millhous, 2004).

Our discussion of intrapersonal communication has focused on the role of the self in the communication process. Recall from Chapter 1 that as individuals communicate with themselves, the process may be either intentional or unintentional. Intrapersonal communication is at the heart of a person's communication activities. Without recognizing oneself, it is difficult to recognize another.

Interpersonal Communication

From its beginnings, interpersonal communication referred to face-to-face communication between people. Contemporary views of interpersonal communication incorporate a technological lens (e.g., dating websites, etc.). Several theories that you will read about in this book have their origins in the interpersonal context. This context is rich with research and theory and is perhaps the most expansive of all of the contexts. Investigating how relationships begin, the maintenance of relationships, and the dissolution of relationships characterizes much of the interpersonal context.

One reason researchers and theorists study relationships is that relationships are so complex and diverse. For instance, you may find yourself in dozens of relationship types right now, including physician–patient, teacher–student, parent–child, supervisor–employee, and so forth. Interacting within each of these relationships affords communicators a chance to maximize the number of channels (visual, auditory, tactile, olfactory) used during an interaction. In

self-esteem
the degree of positive orientation people have about themselves

interpersonal communication
face-to-face communication between people

this context, these channels function simultaneously for both interactants: A child may scream for his mom, for instance, and as she is able to calm him with her caress, she touches the child, looks in his eyes, and listens to his whimpering subside.

The interpersonal context itself comprises many related subcontexts. Interpersonal researchers have studied the family (Metts & Lamb, 2006), friendships (Patterson, 2007), long-term marriages (Hughes & Dickson, 2006), physician–patient relationships (Richmond, Smith, Heisel, & McCroskey, 2001), and relationships in the workplace (Bruning, Castle, & Schrepfer, 2004). In addition, researchers are interested in a host of issues and themes (for example, risk, power, teasing, gossip, liking, attraction, emotions, and so forth) associated with these relationships.

Researchers have also examined the link between interpersonal communication and mass media, organizations, and the classroom (Frymier & Houser, 2002). Finally, relationships that have not been studied enough, including gay and lesbian relationships, cohabiting relationships, and computer network relationships, are gaining researchers' attention (boyd & Ellison, 2007; Galvin, 2004; Peplau & Beals, 2004). As you can see, researchers have framed some very diverse and exciting work within the interpersonal communication context, and studying relationships and what takes place within them has broad appeal.

Small Group Communication

A third context of communication is the small group. Small groups are composed of a number of people who work together to achieve some common purpose. Small group research focuses on task groups as opposed to the friendship and family groups found in the interpersonal context. Communication theory centering on small groups frequently concerns the dynamic nature of small groups, including group roles, boundaries, and trust.

Researchers disagree about how many people make up a small group. Some scholars argue that the optimal number for a small group is five to seven members, whereas others put no limit on the maximum number of members. Nearly all agree, however, that there must be at least three people for a small group to exist (Schultz, 1996; Poole, 2007). For our purposes, then, small group communication is defined as communication among at least three individuals.

The number in a group, is not as important as the implications of that number. The more people, the greater the opportunity for more personal relationships to develop. This may influence whether small groups stay focused on their goals and whether group members are satisfied with their experiences (Shaw, 1981). A classic study (Kephart, 1950) revealed that as the size of the group increases, the number of relationships increases substantially. With a three-person group, then, the number of potential relationships is 6; with a seven-person group, there are 966 possible relationships! When there are too many group members, there is a tendency for cliques to form (Mamali & Paun, 1982). However, large numbers of group members may result in additional resources not present in smaller groups.

small group communication communication among at least three individuals

cohesiveness
the degree of
togetherness between
and among
communicators

People are influenced by the presence of others. For example, some small groups are very cohesive, which means having a high degree of togetherness and a common bond. This cohesiveness may influence whether the group functions effectively and efficiently. In addition, the small group context affords individuals a chance to gain multiple perspectives on an issue. That is, in the intrapersonal context, an individual views events from his or her own perspective; in the interpersonal context there are more perspectives. In the small group context, many more people have the potential to contribute to the group's goals. In problem-solving groups, or task groups in particular, many perspectives may be advantageous. This exchange of multiple perspectives results in **synergy**, and explains why small groups may be more effective than an individual at achieving goals.

synergy
the intersection of
multiple perspectives
in a small group

networks
communication
patterns through
which information
flows

roles
positions of group
members and their
relationship to the
group

Networking and role behavior are two important components of small group behavior. **Networks** are communication patterns through which information flows, and networks in small groups answer the following question: Who speaks to whom and in what order? The patterns of interaction in small groups may vary significantly. For instance, in some groups the leader may be included in all deliberations, whereas in other groups members may speak to one another without the leader. The small group context is made up of individuals who take on various **roles,** or the positions of group members and their relationship to the group. These roles may be very diverse, including task leader, passive observer, active listener, recorder, and so forth.

Before we close our discussion of small groups, we should point out that as with the interpersonal communication context, research on small groups spans a variety of areas. Small group communication scholars have studied power in small groups (Boulding, 1990), juries (Gastil, Leighter, Deess, & Black, 2008), gossip in public school classrooms (Jaworski & Coupland, 2005), conflict (Gross, Guerrero, & Alberts, 2004), creativity (Sabatine, 1989), and cultural diversity (Brooks & Ward, 2007). Much theory and research today continues to underscore the fact that groups exist to meet certain needs (Adams & Galanes, 2009).

Working in small groups seems to be a fact of life in society. At times, it may seem as if we cannot go anywhere without some sort of small group forming. From peer groups to task groups to support groups, the small group experience is a ubiquitous one. Very few students can receive their degree without working in small groups. From study groups to presentations, you may feel as if you are immersed in small group activities. Company supervisors relish team approaches to problem solving. Some families have weekly or monthly family meetings, at which the group discusses such issues as vacations, sibling rivalry, and curfew.

The United States will continue to rely on small groups, even as we increase our reliance on technology. Although we have reached a point at which nearly 71 percent of all U.S. adults are Internet users (www.pewinternet.org/pdfs/PIP_Broadband%202007.pdf), we're confident that person-to-person contact will never go out of style. Computers may crash and break down, but people will continue to function and communicate in small groups.

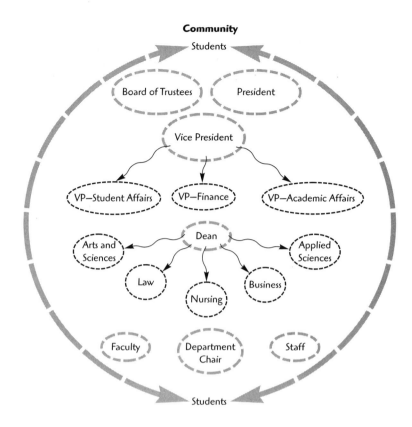

Community

Students

Board of Trustees
President

Vice President

VP—Student Affairs
VP—Finance
VP—Academic Affairs

Dean

Arts and Sciences
Applied Sciences

Law
Nursing
Business

Faculty
Department Chair
Staff

Students

Figure 2.3
Example of Hierarchy in Higher Education

Organizational Communication

It is important to distinguish between small group communication and organizational communication. Organizational communication pertains to communication within and among large, extended environments. This communication is extremely diverse in that organizational communication necessarily entails interpersonal encounters (supervisor–subordinate conversations), public speaking opportunities (presentations by company executives), small group situations (a task group preparing a report), and mediated experiences (internal memos, e-mail, and teleconferencing). Organizations, then, are groups of groups. Theories of organizational communication are generally concerned with the functionality of the organization, including its climate, rules, and personnel.

What distinguishes this context from others is that a clearly defined hierarchy exists in most organizations. Hierarchy is an organizing principle whereby things or persons are ranked one above the other. For an example of the hierarchy in many colleges and universities, see Figure 2.3. Does your school follow the same hierarchy? Michael Papa, Tom Daniels, and Barry Spiker (2008) point out that most Western organizations are traditionally hierarchical in that there are clear ideas about "division of labor, unity of command, and unity of direction" (p. 45). Organizations are unique in that much of the communication taking place is highly structured, and role playing is

organizational communication
communication within and among large, extended environments

hierarchy
an organizing principle whereby things or people are ranked one above the other

often specialized and predictable. Employees and employers alike are clear in their chain of command. Unlike in the interpersonal context, several modes of communication can substitute for face-to-face interaction: memos, e-mail, and teleconferencing.

The uniqueness of organizational communication is also represented by the research and theory conceptualized in this context. Many of the present-day organizational communication theories had their origins in a series of studies conducted in the mid-1920s to early 1930s. These studies, known as the **Hawthorne experiments,** were significant influences on modern theory in that they inaugurated the human relations approach to organizations. Researchers at the Western Electric Hawthorne Plant in suburban Chicago were interested in determining the effect of lighting levels on employee productivity. Interestingly, results of this research indicated that not only did the environmental conditions influence employee output but so did the interpersonal relationships with other employees and supervisors. One conclusion arising from these studies was that organizations should be viewed as social entities; to speed up production, employers must consider workers' attitudes and feelings. These studies were among the first to put a human face on the impersonal corporate world (Roethlisberger & Dickson, 1939).

Although the human relations approach has enjoyed a great deal of theoretical and research attention, today there are a number of additional organizational orientations, including cultural systems and scientific management. Further, organizational communication theory and research today address various eclectic issues, including the *Challenger* disaster (Gouran, Hirokawa, & Martz, 1986), uncertainty on the job (Waldeck, Seibold, & Flanagin, 2004), whistle-blowing (Gabriel, 2008), rumor (Jian, 2007), job training (Waldron & Lavitt, 2000), sexual harassment (Keyton, Ferguson, & Rhodes, 2001), and workplace aggression (Domagalski & Steelman, 2007). In addition, as with other contexts, the influence of ethnic and racial culture has also been examined (Nkomo & Cox, 1996) within organizations.

What is important to glean from this discussion is that, like other contexts, the organizational context has a rich tradition. The Hawthorne studies of human behavior on the job have led today's researchers and theorists to expand their perspectives of organizations and organizational life.

Public/Rhetorical Communication

The fifth context is known as the **public communication** context, or the dissemination of information from one person to a large group. This is not a new context; speech presentations have existed since the beginning of time and continue today. Colin Powell, Oprah Winfrey, Bill Gates, and Bono are just a few of the contemporary public figures who are in high demand as public speakers.

In public speaking, speakers usually have three primary goals in mind: to inform, to entertain, or to persuade. This latter goal—persuasion—is at the core of rhetorical communication. Many of the principles of persuasion—including audience analysis, speaker credibility, and verbal and nonverbal delivery of a message—are necessarily part of the persuasive process. As you

---

Hawthorne experiments
a set of investigations that ushered in a human relations approach to organizations

public communication
the dissemination of information from one person to many others (audience)

reflect on your own public speaking experiences, you may be surprised to learn that in actuality you have been following rhetorical strategies rooted in early Greek and Roman days. How people have constructed their persuasive speeches has been the focus of study for more than 2,500 years.

Effective public speakers owe their success to early rhetorical principles, a topic that we discussed earlier. For our purposes here, we define rhetoric as a speaker's available means of persuading his or her audience. This definition was advanced many years ago by Aristotle. Rhetoric has been described as an art that brings together speakers and audience (Hart, 1997). The study of rhetoric is expansive and can include the study of texts of speeches, presidential inaugural addresses, and rhetorical analyses of cultural themes and issues. Samples of rhetorical scholarship include analyses of the Catholic Church (Lamoureux, 1994), George W. Bush's war speeches (Zagacki, 2007), talk show host Rush Limbaugh (Appel, 2003), and abolitionist Frederick Douglass (Selby, 2000). We discuss rhetoric in more detail in Chapter 18.

rhetoric
a speaker's available means of persuasion

Theory Into Practice

Bradley

T*I*P

They say that people can manage communication apprehension. I have to admit I didn't believe that . . . at first. Then, I had to give a speech in front of my lecture class (there were around 100 students in there). I was running for student senate and the professor asked if I wanted to say a few words. I was so nervous! My hands were sweaty and I almost fell over my own feet when I walked up to the front of the class. As I talked for a few seconds, though, I slowed down and saw a lot of friendly faces out in the audience. I was so relieved when it was all over, but I did manage my anxiety quite a bit.

One area in the public/rhetorical context that has received significant scholarly attention is communication apprehension (CA), or the general sense of fear of speaking before an audience. Research by James McCroskey and Virginia Richmond has been quite valuable as the communication field tries to unpack the challenges of speech anxiety. You will recall that boundaries between and among the contexts are often blurred, and CA research is one example of that blurring. Although communication apprehension is a public speaking concern, CA focuses on intrapersonal issues. Furthermore, CA has been studied with a number of different populations, including student athletes (Stockstill & Roach, 2007), at-risk children (Ayres, Ayres, & Hopf, 1995), employees (Bartoo & Sias, 2004), and those in romantic relationships (Theiss & Solomon, 2006), as well as across cultures (Hsu, 2004). In addition, researchers have advanced ways to reduce communication apprehension. Clearly, the public communication/ rhetorical context addresses the confluence of theory, research, and skills.

communication apprehension
a general sense of fear of speaking before an audience

Mass/Media Communication

mass media
channels or delivery modes for mass messages

mass communication
communication to a large audience via various channels (radio, Internet, television, etc.)

new media
computer-related technology

The sixth context is the mass communication or mediated context, which targets large audiences. First, we need to define a few terms. **Mass media** refers to the channels, or delivery modes, for mass messages. Mass media include newspapers, videos, CD-ROMs, computers, TV, radio, and so forth. **Mass communication** refers to communication to a large audience via one of these channels of communication. Although mass communication frequently refers to "traditional" venues (e.g., newspapers), we expand our discussion to include **new media,** which encompasses computer-related technology. This communication technology includes the Internet, including emailing, blogging, and instant messaging; the influence of social networking sites (Facebook and MySpace) on communication; cell phone usage; and digital television. For our purposes, we identify mass communication as communication to a large audience via multiple channels of communication. The mass communication context, therefore, includes both the channel and the audience.

Like each of the preceding contexts, the mass communication context is distinctive. It allows both senders and receivers to exercise control. Sources such as a newspaper editor or a television broadcaster make decisions about what information should be sent, and receivers have control over what they decide to read, listen to, watch, or review. Suppose, for instance, that you are an advertiser who has slotted an expensive television commercial featuring Tiger Woods. You've paid Woods handsomely, and yet, to determine whether his endorsement has made a difference in sales, you have to wait for the numbers to come in. You have control over the choice of the endorser, but the audience also has control over what they watch and what they buy.

Some, like theorist Stuart Hall (see Chapter 21), suggest that mass media inherently serve the interests of the elite, especially big business and multinational corporations, who, Hall suggests, fund much of the research in mass communication. Many studies, however, are not underwritten by corporate sponsorship. They reflect the growing diversity of mass communication researchers and theorists. A myriad of topics using a mass media framework have been studied, including the portrayal of sex on prime-time television (Eyal & Finnerty, 2007), online support communities (Wright, 2000), heroes in the movie *The Matrix* (Stroud, 2001), television makeover programs (Kubic & Chory, 2007), email flaming (Turnage, 2007), grandparent personal websites (Harwood, 2000), and an analysis of quiz shows such as *Who Wants to Be a Millionaire?* (Hetsroni, 2001). As you can see, a wide array of research studies characterize the mass communication context.

As we write this, some of our comments may already be out of date. Mass communication is rapidly changing, and what was promised as a marvelous advance today is often considered outdated tomorrow. Because of the pervasiveness and availability of mass media in our society, media theorists will have to deal with the impact of media on the communication process itself. Some researchers (for instance, Turkle, 2005) suggest that computers help (re)define the way we conceive of ourselves. This redefinition may have an inevitable impact on the communication process. Furthermore, although a large number of homes and businesses subscribe to new technologies, a gap will always exist between those who have the resources and those who do not. Consequently, future mass communication theorists may have to rethink the universality of their theories.

Cultural Communication

The final communication context we wish to examine is cultural communication. To begin, we should define what we mean by *culture*. There are many definitions of *culture*. For our purposes, **culture can be viewed as a "community of meaning and a shared body of local knowledge"** (Gonzalez, Houston, & Chen, 2004, p. 5). **Cultural communication,** therefore, **refers to communication between and among individuals whose cultural backgrounds vary.** These individuals do not necessarily have to be from different countries. In a diverse country such as the United States, we can experience cultural communication variation within one state, one community, and even one block. It is not uncommon in many parts of this society, for instance, to see two people from different cultural backgrounds speaking to each other. Urban centers, in particular, can be exciting cultural arenas where communication takes place between members of different co-cultures. **Co-cultures are groups of individuals who are part of the same larger culture but who—through unity and individual identification around such attributes as race, ethnicity, sexual identity, religion, and so forth—create opportunities of their own.** The word *co-culture* is now widely accepted in the academic community as a replacement for *subculture,* a term suggesting that one culture has dominance over another culture.

Cultural communication is a relatively young academic context, with its beginnings traced back only to the 1950s (Leeds-Hurwitz, 1990). However, much exciting work has been done since then. The growth of this area of study can be attributed to the growth across organizational cultures, with more U.S. companies doing business abroad. In addition, technological availability, population shifts, and genuine efforts to understand other cultures contribute to the growing interest and frequent conversations pertaining to this context. Some of these dialogues are still difficult, nearly fifty years after the signing of the Civil Rights Act. Some cultural events have helped jumpstart 21st century cultural conversations (Senator Barack Obama becoming president), but these conversations are still fraught with challenges.

The intercultural context differentiates itself from other contexts in a few ways. First, as you may have determined, this context is the only context that specifically addresses culture. Although some contexts, such as the organizational context, comprise research on racial and ethnic cultures, this work is often ancillary, with culture being examined for its effects on the organization, for example. In the intercultural context, however, researchers and theorists purposely explore the interactions and events between and among people of different cultures. Second, study in the intercultural communication context means that researchers inherently accept the fact that human behavior is culturally based. In other words, culture structures how we perceive and how we act.

culture
a community of meaning and a shared body of knowledge

cultural communication
communication between and among individuals whose cultural backgrounds vary

co-cultures
groups of individuals who are part of the same larger culture, but who can be classified around various identites (race, sex, age, etc.)

To give you an indication of the type of research and thinking taking place in the cultural communication context, consider the following research titles: "*De Que Colores:* A Critical Examination of Multicultural Children's Books"(Willis-Rivera & Meeker, 2002), "Native American Culture and Communication Through Humor" (Shutiva, 2004), "Discursive Negotiation of Family Identity: A Study of U.S. Families with Adopted Children from China" (Suter, 2008), "When Mississippi Chinese Talk" (Gong, 2004), and "The Color Problem in Sillyville: Negotiating White Identity in One Popular 'Kid-Vid'" (Gonzalez & Gonzalez, 2002).

Although this research derives from a number of different cultural perspectives, you should be aware that much of what we know and how we relate is a result of a Western model of thinking—that is, many of us interpret events and behaviors through a European (American) lens (Asante, 1987). Gonzalez, Houston, and Chen (2004) state that when studying culture and communication, it's important to "invite *experience*" (p. 3) into the research arena. A great deal of intercultural communication theory and research embraces such an effort. This context is filled with opportunities to study areas that have not received a lot of attention in the past. Investigating culture and cultural groups holds continued promise as the United States grows more diverse.

Collating the Contexts

In discussing these seven contexts, we have provided you with a basic category system for dividing the broad field of communication. These seven categories help us discuss the communication process more clearly and specifically. Yet the template is not perfect, and as you have probably noted in our discussion, there is often overlap among the categories. For instance, when people belong to a cancer support group online, their communication has elements of at least four contexts: intrapersonal, interpersonal, small group, and mass communication. Thus, we caution you against viewing these categories as completely exclusive and distinctive from one another.

Conclusion

This chapter has provided a framework to use as you try to understand the communication field. We began by exploring the seven established traditions of communication theory that are inclusive of the theories you're about to read in this book. These traditions include Rhetorical, Semiotic, Phenomenological, Cybernetic, Socio-Psychological, Socio-Cultural, and Critical. We next examined the primary contexts of communication: Intrapersonal, Interpersonal, Small Group, Organizational, Public/Rhetorical, Mass/Media, and Cultural. As various theories are introduced to you, you will see that many of them fall neatly in these divisions. Other theories will cut across traditions and contexts.

You should now be able to discern the uniqueness of the communication discipline. As you read the next few chapters on theory building, you will begin to link the communication process with the theoretical process. These preliminary chapters offer important foundations to draw on as you encounter the theories presented later in the book.

Discussion Starters

1. Lee and Jenny Yamato's experiences fall across several of the contexts we identified in this chapter. Which of the contexts are in play in their story?

2. Which of the seven traditions in the communication field most appeals to you? Why?

3. Which context of communication most appeals to you? Why?

4. If you had to add another context of communication based on your experiences, what context would it be? How would you interpret the context for others? What examples illustrate the context?

5. How would you illustrate—with a picture—the overlap between and among the various communication traditions.

6. Explain how politics can influence each of the communication contexts.

7. Suppose you were asked to differentiate between a tradition and a context? What would guide your thinking in your response?

Online Learning Center (www. mhhe.com/west4e)

Visit the Online Learning Center at www.mhhe.com/west4e for chapter-specific resources, such as story-into-theory and multiple-choice quizzes, as well as theory summaries and theory connection questions.

CHAPTER 3

Thinking About Theory and Research

Rolanda Nash

Rolanda Nash had to hurry to class from work. She always seemed to be running late these days. She had a lot on her mind since she had decided to divorce Anton and move from Sheridan, Wyoming, to Chicago. She was pretty sure Anton was going to leave her alone now and just cooperate with the divorce. After her relationship with him, she felt she would never trust another man again. Meanwhile, she had to complete six credits to graduate and keep the new job she had secured in Chicago. In addition to doing her schoolwork, Rolanda was working thirty hours a week for one of her professors, Dr. Stevens. Dr. Stevens was testing a theory about communication behaviors, and so far it had been a fun job for Rolanda. The theory Dr. Stevens was interested in was called Communication Accommodation Theory. Dr. Stevens had told Rolanda that communication accommodation focused on how and when people made their own communication sound like their conversational partner's (a process of accommodation). According to the theory, when someone wants to get another's approval, there is a higher chance for them to mirror this person's talk. Dr. Stevens wanted to observe communication accommodation in an organizational setting. The professor had sent Rolanda into two different organizations with a tape recorder. Rolanda's task was to tape naturally occurring conversations between subordinates and managers. Stevens called it water cooler conversations, but so far Rolanda had not seen a single water cooler!

Rolanda thought it was very challenging to capture natural conversations. Although Stevens had obtained permission for her to record conversations in the organizations, some people recognized Rolanda and were self-conscious about talking around her. In addition, neither of the two organizations employed many African Americans. Rolanda felt she stuck out as she walked through the hallways. But she was used to that. In most of her university classes she was the only African American woman. At first it really bothered her, but she was used to it by now. She was hoping Chicago would be a better experience.

Now, if she could only get enough conversations to satisfy Dr. Stevens, she could go home to tackle her English assignment. Stevens hadn't really told her how many conversations she needed. Rolanda was hoping ten would be enough. That's all she had gotten in five days of taping. Dr. Stevens had mentioned last week that when Rolanda was finished taping, she would probably be sending her back to the organizations to do some follow-up interviews with the people she had taped. Rolanda wondered how that would work out. She hoped she could get what Dr. Stevens wanted.

Rolanda is involved in theorizing and researching about complex communication interactions both in her work and in her personal life. Although not everyone does research for a living, often people wonder to themselves, or ask one another, Why do we act the way we do? Why do we argue about some things and not others? Why are we successful in communicating sometimes and not at other times? How can we be better communicators? Scholars believe that we can provide answers to these kinds of questions with theory, because as Robert Craig and Heidi Muller (2007) observe, "theorizing is a formalized extension of everyday sense-making and problem solving" (p. ix). Furthermore, when we make observations and compare them to theory, we're doing research to help us in our efforts to make sense of situations and solve problems. Theory and research are inextricably linked. Paul Reynolds (2007) points out that some researchers begin with theory (theory-then-research) whereas others begin with research (research-then-theory), but all researchers need to think about both.

In this book we are discussing theory and research as professionals use them in their work; yet all of us in daily life think like researchers, using implicit theories to help us understand those questions we mentioned previously. Fritz Heider (1958) referred to everyday interactors engaging in theoretical thinking as "naïve psychologists." Whenever we pose an answer to one of our questions (for example, if we suggest that maybe we are really fighting over power and control and not what color to paint the living room), we are engaging in theoretical thinking.

In many ways, this text points out the similarities and differences between thinking as a "naïve" theorist and thinking as a professional theorist. First, as we have just mentioned, they are similar because both puzzle over questions encountered through observations and both seek answers for these questions. Both also set up certain criteria that define what an acceptable answer might be. For instance, when Ely, a student, wonders why his roommate talks so much more than what is comfortable for him, he might decide on the following criteria for an answer: The answer has to apply to all communication contexts (phone, face-to-face, and so forth); and the answer has to make sense (Ely wouldn't accept for an answer that his roommate comes from another planet where talk is more highly valued than here on Earth). When Ely and social scientists find answers that satisfy their criteria, they generalize from them and may apply them to other situations that are similar. If Ely concludes that his roommate is insecure and talks to cover up his insecurity, he may determine that others he meets who talk more than he does are also insecure.

In all those processes, everyday communicators follow the basic outline advanced by social science. However, there are very clear differences apparent in this description as well. First, social scientists systematically test theories whereas nonscientists test selectively. For instance, Ely will accept evidence that agrees with his theory about the relationship of insecurity and talking and tend to ignore evidence that contradicts it. Researchers are more rigorous in their testing and more willing to amend theories, incorporating information arising from inconsistencies in the original formulation of the theory. In the text, many of the theories we present have undergone extensive revisions as

T∗I∗P

Theory Into Practice

Martina

When we first started talking about the "naïve theorist" idea, I thought it was kind of weird. I was pretty sure I wasn't a theorist, naïve or not! Then I started keeping track of how I was thinking like a theorist in my everyday life. It was amazing how many times I did make a theory and then tried to test it. It seemed like it happened a lot at work. When I was being considered for a promotion, I watched carefully to see what the "higher ups" in my office did and how they reacted to my work. I developed a "theory" that the men in positions of power needed to think of me as their daughter but the women wanted me to perform as an equal. So, when I presented my work to the men, I was more deferential and asked them for advice. I never did that with the women. I decided my theory was correct when I got the promotion!

testing has posed challenges to the original theoretical principles or a need for expansion of them.

Now that you know that theory and research operate in some ways like the way we think already, we're ready to move on to an in-depth examination of our basic terms. In this chapter, we prepare you for reading about the twenty-five theories to follow by providing the following: (1) a definition of theory that maps the term onto intellectual traditions and explains how scholars' assumptions affect the process of theorizing, and (2) a brief description of the research process.

Defining Theory: What's in a Name?

theory
an abstract system of concepts and their relationships that help us to understand a phenomenon

Generally speaking, a **theory** is an abstract system of concepts with indications of the relationships among these concepts that help us to understand a phenomenon. Stephen Littlejohn and Karen Foss (2008) suggest this abstract system is derived through systematic observation. Jonathan H. Turner (1986) defined *theory* as "a process of developing ideas that can allow us to explain how and why events occur" (p. 5). This definition focuses on the nature of theoretical thinking without specifying exactly what the outcome of this thinking might be. William Doherty and his colleagues (1993) have elaborated on Turner's definition by stating that theories are both process and product: "Theorizing is the process of systematically formulating and organizing ideas to understand a particular phenomenon. A theory is the set of interconnected ideas that emerge from this process" (p. 20). In this definition, the authors attempt to be inclusive. They do not use Turner's word *explain* because the goals of theory can be more numerous than simply explanation, a point we explore later in this chapter.

In this brief discussion, you have probably noticed that different theorists approach the definition of *theory* somewhat differently. The search for a

DILBERT © Scott Adams/Distributed by United Feature Syndicate Inc.

universally accepted definition of *theory* is a difficult, if not impossible, task. When defining the term *theory,* as D. C. Phillips (1992) observes, "there is no divinely ordained *correct* usage, but we can strive to use the word consistently and to mark distinctions that we feel are important" (p. 121).

In part, the difficulty in defining *theory* is due to the many ways in which a theory can be classified or categorized. Here we refine our definition by examining the following features and attributes of theories: level of generality, components, and goals.

Level of Generality

One way to understand differences among theories pertains to their level of generality. Level of generality refers to how widely the theory can be applied. Theories can be grand (universal), mid-range (moderately general), or narrow (very specific). **Grand theories** purport to explain all of communication behavior in a manner that is universally true. Outside the discipline of communication, Marxism, an approach we mentioned in Chapter 2, is an example of a grand theory. A grand theory would have the ability to unify all the knowledge we have about communication into one integrated theoretical framework. This may or may not be a worthy goal (Craig, 1999), but most would agree that no grand theory of communication exists. There are too many instances where communication differs from group to group or when communication behavior is modified by changes in context or time to create a grand theory.

A **mid-range theory** explains the behavior of a specific group of people rather than all people, as a grand theory would do. A mid-range theory might try to explain the behavior of all people within a specified time or context.

grand theories
theories that attempt to explain all of a phenomenon such as communication

mid-range theory
a theory that attempts to explain a specified aspect of a phenomenon such as communication

Many theories of communication fall into the mid-range category. Mid-range theories explain a focused aspect of communication behavior, such as how people behave in initial encounters with strangers (see, for example, Chapter 9 describing Uncertainty Reduction Theory), how people agree on decisions in groups (see, for example, Chapter 14 describing Groupthink), or how people from different cultures engage in conflict (see, for example, Chapter 26 describing Face-Negotiation Theory). These theories are bounded by considerations such as time (the initial encounter between strangers explained by Uncertainty Reduction Theory), context (communication in small groups explained by Groupthink), or type of communication behavior (conflict behavior explained by Face-Negotiation Theory). In the case of Face-Negotiation Theory, the boundaries also include the context of cultural communication.

narrow theory
a theory that attempts to explain a very limited aspect of a phenomenon such as communication

Finally, a **narrow theory** "concerns only certain people in certain situations—for example, the communication rules pertinent to standing in an elevator" (Stacks, Hill, & Hickson, 1991, p. 284). Often theories are criticized for claiming to be grander than they really are. For instance, some critics of Standpoint Theory (Chapter 29) argue that it makes claims about all women, but these assertions have to be modified by other identifiers such as class and race.

Theories differ in their level of generality due to their difference in focus or what they try to explain. Some theories focus on the entire communication process (e.g., Symbolic Interaction Theory), whereas others focus more specifically on a given aspect of the process, such as the message or the sender (e.g., Rhetorical Theory). Still others attend to communication as a means for relationship development (e.g., Social Penetration Theory). Knowing a variety of ways to classify theories helps us see how very dissimilar works (such as Uncertainty Reduction, Uses and Gratifications, and Muted Group) can all be defined as theory.

Components

To understand *theory*, we also need to understand the components of theories. Theories are composed of several key parts, the two most important of which are called concepts and relationships. **Concepts are words or terms that label the most important elements in a theory.** Concepts in some of the theories we will discuss include *cohesiveness* (Groupthink), *dissonance* (Cognitive Dissonance Theory), *self* (Symbolic Interaction Theory), and *scene* (Dramatism). As you can see, sometimes theories are named using one of their key concepts, although this is not always the case.

concepts
labels for the most important elements in a theory

A concept often has a specific definition that is unique to its use in a theory, which differs from how we would define the word in everyday conversation. For example, the concept "cultivation" used in Cultivation Analysis (see Chapter 22) refers specifically to the way media, especially television, create a picture of social reality in the minds of media consumers. This use of the term differs somewhat from using it to mean hoeing your garden or developing an interest, skill, or friendship. In the theory, cultivation has a unique and relatively narrow definition. It is always the task of the theorist to provide a clear definition of the concepts used in the theory.

Concepts may be nominal or real. **Nominal concepts** are those that are not observable, such as democracy or love. **Real concepts** are observable, such as personal rituals or spatial distance. As we'll discuss later in the chapter, when researchers use theory in their studies, they must turn both nominal and real constructs into something concrete so that they can be observed. It is much easier to do this for real concepts than for nominal ones.

Relationships specify the ways in which the concepts in the theory are combined. For example, in Chapter 1 we presented three different models of the process of communication. In each model, the concepts are very similar. What is different is the relationship specified among them. In the first model, the relationship is a linear one where one concept relates to the second, which then relates to the next, and so forth. In the second model, the posited relationship is interactive, or two-way. The third model illustrates mutual influence (transaction), where all the concepts are seen as affecting one another simultaneously.

Goals

We can also clarify the definition of theory by understanding its purposes. In a broad, inclusive sense, the goals of theory can include explanation, understanding, prediction, and social change; we are able to *explain* something (why Anton behaved so badly in his relationship with Rolanda, for example) because of the concepts and their relationships specified in a theory. We are able to *understand* something (Rolanda's distrust of men) because of theoretical thinking. In addition, we are able to *predict* something (how Rolanda will respond to other men she meets) based on the patterns suggested by a theory. Finally, we are able to effect *social change* or empowerment (altering the institution of marriage so that it more completely empowers both partners, for example) through theoretical inquiry.

Although some theories try to reach all these goals, most feature one goal over the others. Rhetorical theories, some media theories, and many interpersonal theories seek primarily to provide explanation or understanding. Others—for example, traditional persuasion and organizational theories—focus on prediction. Still others—for instance, some feminist and other critical theories—have as their central goal to change the structures of society. As you learned in Chapter 2, for critical theorists, this means effecting social change, not simply improving individual lives. For instance, a theory about conflict management may help people understand how to engage in conflict more productively, thus enriching their lives. Yet it may do nothing to change the underlying structures that promoted the conflict in the first place.

Now we have a working definition for theory: an abstract system of concepts with indications of the relationships among these concepts that helps us to explain, understand, predict, or change a phenomenon (i.e., some aspect of communication). In addition, we can see that theories can be broadly generalized or more narrowly applied. Most theories have the ability to generalize moderately, called mid-range. From this discussion of the definition of theory, it should be clear that experience and theory are related, although experience is concrete and theory is abstract. We'll now address this relationship.

nominal concepts
concepts that are not directly observable

real concepts
concepts that are directly observable

relationships
the ways in which the concepts of a theory relate to one another

Relationship Between Theory and Experience

In 1952, Carl Hempel compared a scientific theory to a complex spatial network, saying that a theory's "terms are represented by the knots, while the threads connecting the latter correspond, in part, to the definitions and, in part, to the fundamental and derivative hypotheses included in the theory" (p. 36). Hempel then noted that this theory/network

> floats, as it were, above the plane of observation and is anchored to it by rules of interpretation. These might be viewed as strings which are not part of the network but link certain points of the latter with specific places in the plane of observation. . . . From certain observational data, we may ascend, via an interpretive string, to some point in the theoretical network, then proceed, via definitions and hypotheses, to other points, from which another interpretive string permits a descent to the plane of observation. (p. 36)

Hempel suggests that although a theory is abstract, it enables us to understand concrete experiences and observations, and that a theory itself is capable of being modified by observations. In addition, his statement asserts that our concrete experiences and observations are interpreted by us through the lens offered by the theory we are using.

Janet Yerby (1995), commenting on the notion that theories act as a lens, allowing us to see some things while ignoring others, refers to theories as "the stories we have developed to explain our view of reality" (p. 362). The strings of interpretation that Hempel mentions can be seen as the elements in the story we have chosen as satisfactory explanations for communication behaviors. In taking this approach, we have to be aware, as Yerby suggests, that theories, like stories, change and evolve over time as new information modifies and refines them.

This line of thinking prompts us to ask what motivates a scholar to choose one theory (or lens) over another in their work. The answer to this question comes in an examination of the varying approaches to knowing that scholars bring to their work before they even begin to do any research.

Approaches to Knowing: How Do You See (and talk about) the World?

Many scholars (Baxter & Babbie, 2004; Baxter & Braithwaite, 2008; White & Klein, 2008) have discussed how researchers think and talk about the world and their work. Most of these scholars have identified three general approaches: positivistic or empirical, interpretive, and critical. We will discuss each of these in turn, but remember that we're presenting each approach in its extreme form, and many researchers would not identify themselves as subscribing to the extremes. Most people find some way to adapt one of these approaches to fit the particular way they see the world.

The Positivistic, or Empirical, Approach

The **positivistic, or empirical, approach** assumes that objective truths can be uncovered and that the process of inquiry that discovers these truths can be, at least in part, value-neutral. This tradition advocates the methods of the natural sciences, with the goal of constructing general laws governing human interactions. An empirical researcher strives to be objective and works for **control,** or direction over the important concepts in the theory. In other words, when the researcher moves to the plane of observation, he or she carefully structures the situation so that only one element varies. This enables the researcher to make relatively definitive statements about that element.

As Leslie Baxter and Dawn Braithwaite (2008) observe, the researcher's task in the empirical approach is "to deduce testable hypotheses from a theory" (p. 7). In other words, the positivistic approach moves along the theory-then-research model to which Reynolds (2007) referred.

positivistic/ empirical approach
an approach assuming the existence of objective reality and value-neutral research

control
direction over the important concepts in a theory

The Interpretive Approach

The **interpretive approach** views truth as subjective and co-created by the participants, with the researcher clearly one of the participants. There is less emphasis on objectivity in this approach than in the empirical approach because complete objectivity is seen as impossible. However, this does not mean that research in this approach has to rely totally on what participants say with no outside judgment by the researcher. Martyn Hammersley (1992), for example, advocates a "subtle realism" that suggests that researchers "monitor [their] assumptions and the inferences [they] make on the basis of them" (p. 53). In this subtle realism, Hammersley suggests that research can find a way to be reasonably objective. The interpretive researcher believes that values are relevant in the study of communication and that researchers need to be aware of their own values and to state them clearly for readers, because values will naturally permeate the research. These researchers are not concerned with control and the ability to generalize across many people as much as they are interested in rich descriptions about the people they study. For interpretive researchers, theory is best induced from the observations and experiences the researcher shares with the respondents. This means that the interpretive approach is likely to follow Reynolds' (2007) research-then-theory model.

interpretive approach
an approach viewing truth as subjective and stressing the participation of the researcher in the research process

The Critical Approach

In the **critical approach,** an understanding of knowledge relates to power. As Art Bochner (1985) notes, this approach "assumes that science cannot exist without ideology" (p. 46). Critical researchers believe that those in power shape knowledge in ways that work to perpetuate the status quo. Thus, powerful people work at keeping themselves in power, which requires silencing minority voices questioning the distribution of power and the power holders' version of truth. Patricia Hill Collins (1991) speaks from this approach when she says that "the tension between the suppression of Black women's ideas and our intellectual activism in the face of that suppression, comprises the politics of Black feminist

critical approach
an approach stressing the researcher's responsibility to change the inequities in the status quo

Table 3.1 Three Approaches to Knowing

	EMPIRICAL	INTERPRETIVE	CRITICAL
Goal	Explanation of world	Probe the relativism of world	Change the world
Engagement of researcher	Separate	Involved	Involved
Application of theory	To generalize about many like cases	To illuminate the individual case	To critique a specific set of cases

thought" (pp. 5–6). Black feminists are not the only researchers who are comfortably rooted in the critical approach Marxists and feminists of all types, among others, also work from this intellectual tradition. For critical researchers, it is generally important to change the status quo to resolve power imbalances and to give voice to those who have been silenced by the power structure.

Some critical theorists, notably Stuart Hall (1981), whose work we feature in Chapter 21, have commented that power imbalances may not always be the result of intentional strategies on the part of the powerful. Rather, ideology, or "those images, concepts, and premises which provide the frameworks through which we represent, interpret, understand and 'make sense' of some aspect of social existence" (Hall, 1981, p. 31), is often "produced and reproduced" accidentally. For example, this may come about when certain images of masculinity work to sell a product. When advertisers observe this success, they continue creating ads with these images. In this fashion, the images of masculinity become entrenched in society. Thus, although the powerful are interested and invested in staying in power, they may not be fully aware of what they do to silence minority voices (Table 3.1).

Approaches to Knowing: What Questions Do You Ask About the World?

Implicit in the three approaches to knowing are answers to questions about the nature of reality (researchers call this **ontology**), questions about how we know things (researchers call these questions **epistemology**), and questions about what is worth knowing (or what researchers call **axiology**). It's important to recognize that each of the three approaches to knowing (empirical, interpretive, and critical) answers questions about ontology, epistemology, and axiology differently. We'll briefly address each of these terms and suggest how the three approaches to knowing treat them differently.

Ontology is the study of being and nonbeing, or in other words, the study of reality. The word *ontology* comes from the Greek language and means the science of being or the general principles of being. The What Is Ontology? website (www.formalontology.it/section_4.htm) provides the following definition for ontology: "a science or study of being: specifically, a branch of metaphysics

ontology
a branch of knowledge focused on the nature of reality

epistemology
a branch of knowledge focused on how we know things

axiology
a branch of knowledge focused on what is worth knowing

relating to the nature and relations of being; a particular system according to which problems of the nature of being are investigated; first philosophy." This definition focuses on the idea that ontology gives us a certain vision of the world and on what constitutes its important features. It is called the first philosophy because it is not possible to philosophize until the nature of reality is determined. Often questions of ontology cluster around how much free will people have. Researchers who subscribe to an empirical approach believe that general laws govern human interactions. Thus they also believe that people don't have a lot of free choice in what they do—people are predictable because they follow the laws of human behavior which, to a large extent, determine their actions. A researcher's job is to *uncover* what is already out there in reality. This differs from researchers with an interpretive bent, who would allow that people do have free choice, and see a researcher's job as to co-create reality with research participants. Finally, critical researchers see choice and constraint in the power structures they wish to change.

The questions surrounding epistemology focus on how we go about knowing; what counts as knowledge is intimately related to ontology. How researchers see the world, truth, and human nature necessarily influences how they believe they should try to learn about these things. The approach (positivistic, interpretive, or critical) Dr. Stevens took in our opening example would affect her way of collecting information, an epistemologic choice. For instance, if Dr. Stevens researched as a positivist, she would institute many more controls than we described in our opening case study. Furthermore, the number of observations would not be left to chance or to Rolanda's schedule. Dr. Stevens would have calculated the number of conversations she needed to support statistics testing relationships among status and communication accommodation. If Dr. Stevens operated in the interpretive tradition, she would not be content with her own analysis of the conversations. She might invite the participants to read the transcripts of their conversations so that they could tell her whether they were trying to accommodate to their partners. Stevens would probably be interested in the participants' explanations for why they changed (or did not change) their speech patterns as they conversed with superiors or subordinates in the workplace. Using a critical approach, Dr. Stevens might bring some of the following questions to her research: How is the relationship between workers of differing statuses communicatively constructed? Does convergence happen unequally based on status? Are there status differences other than occupation that impact communication accommodation? How can we change the prevailing power structures to improve the inequities we observe in the workplace?

The final set of questions focuses on the place of values in theory and research. The empirical position on axiology is that science must be value-free. However, most researchers do not take this extreme position and accept that some subjectivity, in the form of values, informs the research process (Bostrom, 2003). The question that is still debated concerns not *whether* values should permeate theory and research but *how* they should.

Here we briefly present three positions on this debate that correspond to the three ways of knowing: avoiding values as much as possible in research (empirical), recognizing how values influence the entire research process (interpretative), and advocating that values should be closely intertwined with scholarly work (critical). The first stance argues that the research process consists of many stages and that values should inform some of these stages but not others. For example, the part of the research enterprise that focuses on theory choice must be informed by the values of the researcher. Scholars choose to view a research problem through the lens that they believe most accurately describes the world. Thus, some researchers choose theoretical frameworks that are consistent with an ontology of free choice, whereas others choose frameworks that are more "lawlike" and deterministic. Yet, when they test these theories (the verification stage), they must eliminate "extra-scientific values from scientific activity" (Popper, 1976, p. 97). As you can see, this stance proposes a very limited role for values.

The second position argues that it is not possible to eliminate values from any part of theorizing and research. In fact, some values are so embedded in researchers' culture that researchers are unconscious that they even hold them. Sandra Bem (1993), for instance, observes that much of the research on differences between women and men was influenced by biases existing at the time. Many feminist scholars argue that social science itself suffers from a male bias (Harding, 1987). Some African American scholars make the same observations about the European American biases that exist in much social scientific research (Allen, 2007; Houston, 1992). Thomas Nakayama and Robert Krizek (1995) point out that communication researchers often take White for granted as the default race. Thus, the values and assumptions held by those with a European American perspective are never highlighted, questioned, or acknowledged; they simply inform a scholar's process. Yoshitaka Miike (2007) takes this one step further to advocate theories that would be Asiacentric (meaning rooted in Asian thinking).

The final position argues that not only are values unavoidable, but they are a desirable aspect of the research process. Earlier in this chapter we referred to the goals of theory as including social change. Those who embrace this goal are called critical theorists. Critical theorists advocate seeing theory and research as political acts that call on scholars to change the status quo. Thus, scholars must contribute to changing conditions rather than simply reporting conditions (Table 3.2).

Table 3.2 Answers Supplied by the Three Approaches to Knowing

	EMPIRICAL	INTERPRETIVE	CRITICAL
Ontology	No free choice	Free choice	Choice restrained by power
Epistemology	Theory first. Control study	Research first. Co-create study	Critique power. Seek change
Axiology	Reduce role of values	Acknowledge values	Celebrate values

Approaches to Knowing: How Do You Go About Theory Building?

When researchers seek to create theory, they are guided by all of the issues we've just discussed: their general approach to knowing things (empirical, interpretive, or critical) and the answers to questions about truth or reality, gathering information, and values (ontology, epistemology, and axiology). In addition, they have some guidelines about how to create theory (Craig, 1999). We will review three traditional guidelines: covering law, rules, and systems. The covering law approach and the rules approach represent two extremes, whereas the systems approach provides an intermediate position between the extremes. We must caution that few scholars take the extreme positions sketched out here. Rather, these positions form benchmarks from which researchers anchor their own stances on questions of communication.

The **covering law approach** seeks to explain an event in the real world by referring to a general law. Researchers applying a covering law approach believe that communication behavior is governed by forces that are predictable and generalizable. The **rules approach,** at the other end of the ontological continuum, holds that communication behavior is rule governed, not lawlike. The rules approach differs from the covering law approach in that researchers holding the rules approach admit the possibility that people are free to change their minds, to behave irrationally, to have idiosyncratic meanings for behaviors, and to change the rules. Ultimately, their differences focus on the concept of choice. The covering law model explains human choices by seeking a prior condition (usually a **cause**) that determines the choice that is made (usually an **effect**). From the rules model, rule following results from a choice made by the follower but does not necessarily involve antecedent conditions or any aspect of the cause–effect logic of the covering law approach.

A third view, the **systems approach,** subscribes somewhat to the beliefs of the rules approach while also suggesting that people's free will may be constrained by the system in which they operate. Further, this approach acknowledges the impossibility of achieving what the covering law approach requires: laws about human communication that are invariant and general. The systems approach proposes assumptions that are more easily met than those of the covering law approach (Monge, 1973). We now examine each of the three approaches in more detail and provide an overview in Table 3.3.

Covering Law Approach

This term was first introduced by William Dray (1957), a historian who defined *covering law* as that "explanation is achieved, and only achieved, by *subsuming what is to be explained under a general law*" (p. 1 [emphasis in original]). Some covering law explanations refer to universal laws that state all *x* is *y*. These laws are not restricted by time or space. However, as new information comes to light, even laws have to be modified. Covering law explanations do not always have to be cause–effect. They may also specify relationships of coexistence. We have a causal relationship when we say that self-disclosures by

---

covering law approach
a guideline for creating theory suggesting that theories conform to a general law that is universal and invariant

rules approach
a guideline for creating theory that builds human choice into explanations

cause
an antecedent condition that determines an effect

effect
a condition that inevitably follows a causative condition

systems approach
a guideline for creating theory that acknowledges human choice and the constraints of the systems involved

Table 3.3 Guidelines to Communication Theory Construction

APPROACH	DESCRIPTION/EXAMPLE
Covering law	Covering law theorists hold that there are fixed relationships between two or more events or objects. Example: Whenever Linda speaks, Bob interrupts her; this is a lawlike statement that expresses a relationship between Linda and Bob. These statements are commonly referred to as if-then statements.
Rules	Rules theorists contend that much of human behavior is a result of free choice. People pick the social rules that govern their interactions. Example: In an interaction between co-workers, much of their conversation will be guided by rules of politeness, turn taking, and so on.
Systems	Systems theorists hold that human behavior is part of a system. Example: Think of a family as a system of family relationships rather than individual members. This illuminates the complexity of communication patterns within the family.

one person cause self-disclosures from a relational partner. A claim of coexistence merely asserts that two things go together—that is, when one person self-discloses, the other does, too—but it does not claim that the first self-disclosure causes the second. It's possible that social norms of reciprocity cause the second self-disclosure or that both disclosures are caused by the environment (an intimate, dimly lit bar or consuming more alcohol than usual).

Critical attributes of covering law explanations are that they provide an explicit statement of a boundary condition and that they allow **hypotheses,** testable predictions of relationships, of varying levels of specificity, to be generated within this boundary condition. Furthermore, because the system is deductive, complete confirmation of theories is never possible. There will always be unexamined instances of the hypothesis.

The type of covering law that we have just described is considered outdated by most social scientists (Bostrom, 2004). Most researchers today recognize that this type of universal law is unrealistic. Instead, researchers might strive for "probabilistic laws," or statements we can predict with a certain degree of probability. For example, as Berger (1977) asserts, "We can predict with a certain probability that if males and females with certain eye colors have large numbers of children, a certain proportion of those children will have a certain eye color. However, we are *not* in a position to predict what the eye color of a *particular* child will be" (p. 10).

Overall, a covering law approach instructs researchers to search for lawlike generalizations and regularities in human communication. These lawlike generalizations may be culturally bound or may have some other complex relationship with culture. Covering law offers a theory-generating option that aims for complete explanation of a phenomenon. The law, in effect, governs the relationships among phenomena.

hypotheses
testable predictions of relationships between concepts that follow the general predictions made by a theory

Table 3.4 Rules Governing Initial Peer Encounters

In the first fifteen minutes of an encounter:	In the second fifteen minutes:
Politeness should be observed.	Politeness should be observed.
Demographics should be exchanged.	Likes and dislikes can be discussed.
Partners should speak in rough equivalence to each other.	One partner can speak more than another, but avoid dominance.
Interruptions and talk-overs should be minimal.	More interruptions can be tolerated, but avoid dominance.

Rules Approach

This approach assumes that people are typically engaged in intentional, goal-directed behavior and are capable of acting rather than simply being acted upon. We can be restricted by previous choices we have made, by the choices of others, and by cultural and social conditions, but we are conscious and active choice makers. Further, human behavior can be classified into two categories: activities that are stimulus–response behaviors (termed **movements**) and activities that are intentional choice responses (termed **actions**) (Cushman & Pearce, 1977). Rules theorists contend that studying actions is most relevant to theorists.

Rules theorists look inside communities or cultures to get a sense of how people regulate their interaction with others (Shimanoff, 1980). Rules do not require people to act in a certain way; rather, rules refer to the standards or criteria that people use when acting in a particular setting (Cushman & Cahn, 1985). For example, when two people meet, they normally do not begin at an intimate level of exchange. Rather, there is an agreed-upon starting point, and they will delve further into intimacy if the two see the relationship as having a future. The process of meeting another is guided by rules, although these rules are rarely verbally identified by either person. Don Cushman and Barnett Pearce (1977) believed that if the relationship evolves, the rules guiding inter-actions change. Rules, then, are important benchmarks for the direction of an interaction. Table 3.4 illustrates how rules guide initial encounters of many peers in the United States.

Several researchers (Lull, 1982; Wolf, Meyer, & White, 1982) have used a rules-based theoretical framework to study family television viewing behaviors. James Lull (1982) identified three types of rules that govern family television watching. First are **habitual rules,** which are nonnegotiable and are usually instituted by the authority figures in the family. When Roger and Marie tell their children that there can be no television until all homework is checked over by one of them and declared finished for the night, they are establishing a habitual rule.

Parametric rules are also established by family authority figures, but they are more negotiable than habitual rules. For example, the Marsh family may have a rule that members can engage in extended talk only during commercial breaks when they are viewing television. Yet, if something exciting has happened to one member, they may negotiate to talk about it during the program itself.

Finally, Lull identified **tactical rules,** or rules that are understood as a means for achieving a personal or interpersonal goal, but are unstated. For example,

movements
activities based on stimulus–response

actions
activities based on intentional choice responses

habitual rules
nonnegotiable rules that are usually created by an authority figure

parametric rules
rules that are set by an authority figure but are subject to some negotiation

tactical rules
unstated rules used to achieve a personal or interpersonal goal

if Rob and Jeremy are watching television together and Rob likes Jeremy, he may tune in to Jeremy's favorite show even though he himself would not have chosen that program. He follows the tactical rule of maintaining relational harmony with his partner.

Overall, a rules approach instructs researchers to discover the rules that govern particular communication contexts and construct theoretical statements around these rules. The rules perspective offers a theory-generating option that aims for a satisfying explanation of a specific communication situation. The theorist would normally begin with a typology of the rules that govern the situation and move from those to statements connecting the rules and specifying the conditions affecting the rules.

Systems Approach

Systems thinking in communication is derived from General Systems Theory (GST), which is both a theory of systems in general—"from thermostats to missile guidance computers, from amoebas to families" (Whitchurch & Constantine, 1993, p. 325)—and a program of theory construction. Systems thinking captured the attention of communication researchers because it changed the focus from the individual to an entire family, a small group, or an organization. This shift reconceptualized communication for scholars and helped them to think innovatively about experience and interaction in groups. Further, systems thinking replaced the stringent assumptions of covering law with more realistic ones. Systems theorists (Monge, 1973) agreed with the rules assertion that "human communication is not characterized by universal patterns" (p. 9). Systems thinking requires systemic, nonuniversal generalizations, does not depend on inductive reasoning, separates the logical from the empirical, allows alternative explanations for the same phenomenon, and permits partial explanations (Monge, 1973).

Systems thinking rests on several properties, including wholeness, interdependence, hierarchy, boundaries, calibration/feedback, and equifinality. We will explain each of these properties briefly.

wholeness
a fundamental property of systems theory stating that systems are more than the sum of their individual parts

Wholeness   The most fundamental concept of the systems approach is **wholeness**. It refers to the idea that a system cannot be fully comprehended by a study of its individual parts in isolation from one another. In order to understand the system, it must be seen as a whole. Wholeness suggests that we learn more about a couple, for example, by analyzing their interactions together than we do by simply analyzing one partner's motivations or statements alone.

interdependence
a property of systems theory stating that the elements of a system affect one another

Interdependence   Because the elements of a system are interrelated, they exhibit **interdependence**. This means that the behaviors of system members co-construct the system, and all members are affected by shifts and changes in the system. Virginia Satir (1988) compares the family to a mobile to illustrate how this principle applies to families. We might expect that when elderly parents decide to sell the family home and move to a small condo, their decisions will affect all of their children.

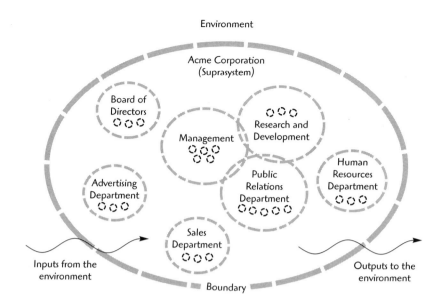

Environment

Acme Corporation
(Suprasystem)

Board of
Directors

Research and
Development

Management

Advertising
Department

Public
Relations
Department

Human
Resources
Department

Sales
Department

Inputs from the
environment

Outputs to the
environment

Boundary

Hierarchy   All systems have levels, or **subsystems**, and all systems are embedded in other systems, or **suprasystems**. Thus, systems are a **hierarchy**, a complex organization. Each of the subsystems can function independently of the whole system, but each is an integral part of the whole. Subsystems generally shift and change over time, but they may potentially become extremely close and turn into alliances or coalitions that exclude others. For example, if one parent confides a great deal in a son whereas the other talks to one of their daughters, two coalitions may form in the family, making interactions more strained and troubled. This property is mapped in Figure 3.1.

Boundaries   Implicit in the preceding discussion about hierarchy and complexity is the notion that systems develop **boundaries** around themselves and the subsystems they contain. Because human systems are open systems (it is not possible to completely control everything that comes into or goes out from them), these boundaries are relatively permeable: They have **openness**. Thus, although the managers of a General Motors plant in Ohio may wish that their employees did not know about the strike at a General Motors plant in Michigan, they will be unable to prevent information and communication from passing through the boundary around their organizational system.

Calibration/Feedback   All systems need stability and constancy within a defined range (Watzlawick, Beavin, and Jackson, 1967). **Calibration**, or checking the scale, and subsequent **feedback** to change or stabilize the system, allow for control of the range. The thermostat provides a common example illustrating this process. Home heating is usually set at a certain temperature, say 65 degrees. The thermostat will allow a temperature range around 65 before changing anything. Therefore, if the thermostat is set for 65 and the temperature is 65 plus or minus 3 degrees, nothing happens. If the temperature drops below

subsystems
smaller systems that
are embedded in
larger ones

suprasystems
larger systems that
hold smaller ones
within them

hierarchy
a property of systems
theory stating that
systems consist of
multiple levels

boundaries
a property of systems
theory stating that
systems construct
structures specifying
their outer limits

openness
the acknowledgment
that within all human
systems the boundaries
are permeable

calibration
a property of systems
theory stating that
systems periodically
check the scale of
allowable behaviors
and reset the system

feedback
a subprocess of
calibration;
information allowing
for change in the
system

62 degrees, the heat goes on; if it rises above 68 degrees, the furnace shuts off. In this way, the heating system remains stable. However, if conditions change in the house (for example, the family insulates the attic), the thermostat may need to be recalibrated or set at a slightly lower temperature to accommodate the change. After insulating, the house may feel comfortable if the temperature is set at 63 degrees.

Changing the standard (moving the temperature from 65 to 63 degrees) is accomplished through feedback. Feedback, in systems thinking, is positive when it produces change (the thermostat is set differently) and negative when it maintains the status quo (the thermostat remains at 65). When systems change they are called **morphogenic**, and when they stay the same they are called **homeostatic.**

Equifinality   Open systems are characterized by the ability to achieve the same goals through different means, or **equifinality** (von Bertalanffy, 1968). This principle applies to human groups in two ways. First, a single group can achieve a goal through many different routes. For example, if a manager wants to increase productivity, he can raise wages, threaten the workers with firing, hire a consultant, or do some combination of these. There are several ways the manager can reach the goal. Additionally, equifinality implies that different groups can achieve the same goal through multiple pathways. For instance, PK Computer Systems may achieve profitability by adopting a casual organizational culture, whereas Western Communication Systems may achieve profitability by demanding a more formal workplace.

Overall, a systems approach instructs researchers to search for holistic explanations for communication behavior. Systems offers a theory-generating option that aims to model the phenomenon as a whole, admitting the possibility for change from a variety of outside influences.

The Research Process

In the example at the beginning of the chapter, we illustrated how interrelated theory and research processes are. Now we'll briefly discuss the research process. Our discussion will necessarily be brief here; we know many of you will take an entire class devoted to the study of research methods, so here we simply give you an idea of how important theory and research are to one another. At the beginning of this chapter, Dr. Stevens's study illustrated the theory-then-research model. Rolanda's transcripts are used to test what Communication Accommodation Theory predicts about communication behaviors in the workplace. Dr. Stevens will see if the speculations she made based on the theory's logic hold true in the conversations that Rolanda taped. This traditional process, known as the **scientific method**, follows **deductive logic** in that Stevens moved from the general (the theory) to specific instances (the actual conversations gathered in two workplaces). If Stevens had used **inductive logic**, she would have asked Rolanda to record many more conversations. Stevens would have refrained from hypothesizing, or guessing, about what she might find in advance of the data collection. Then she and Rolanda would

morphogenic
a term for when a system recalibrates (or changes)

homeostatic
a term for a stable system that isn't changing

equifinality
a property of systems theory stating that systems can achieve the same goals through different means

scientific method
the traditional method for doing research involving controlled observations and analysis to test the principles of a theory

deductive logic
moving from the general (the theory) to the specific (the observations)

inductive logic
moving from the specific (the observations) to the general (the theory)

have listened to their tapes, trying to find some type of pattern that best explained what they heard. Finally, Stevens would have generalized based on her observations.

After Stevens has hypothesized about what she will find in the workplace regarding accommodations between workers and managers based on the theory, she then must **operationalize** all the concepts. This means she needs to specify how she will measure the concepts that are important to her study. In this process, Dr. Stevens turns the abstract concepts of the theory into concrete variables that can be observed and measured. For example, status difference is a critical notion in the theoretical framework, so Stevens specifies to Rolanda how she should measure this. In this case, measurement will be based on job title. Rolanda has to discover the job title for each of the people she observes and then compare those titles to a chart Stevens has given her classifying job titles into the two categories of "supervisor" and "subordinate." This seems like a fairly straightforward means to operationalize the notion of status, but there may be instances where it is not a perfect operationalization. For instance, a lower-level employee who has worked for the company for many years might hold more status than a middle manager who has only recently arrived and is just learning the corporate culture. Additionally, women managers often report some problems with achieving the status expected from their job title. You can see how concepts that are more complex and abstract, such as love and intimacy, would be even more difficult to operationalize than occupational status.

The next step in the traditional scientific model sends Rolanda into the two organizations to make **observations** and collect **data** (in this case, the conversations and the job titles). When Rolanda returns with the tapes, Dr. Stevens will have to **code** the conversations, again using operationalizations for terms such as *convergence* (making your speech patterns similar to your partner's) and *divergence* (making your speech patterns dissimilar to your partner's). Some types of data do not need extensive coding to analyze. For example, if Dr. Stevens operationalized status based on income and then provided respondents with a survey asking them to indicate the category for their salary, these data would not need the same type of coding required in the taped conversations. The income categories could simply be numbered consecutively. In contrast, the conversations have to be listened to repeatedly to determine whether a given comment converges with or diverges from the comment preceding it.

The deductive approach allows Stevens to test a specific prediction, or hypothesis, generated from a generalization, or theory. The results of this testing allow modifications and corrections to the theory.

The inductive approach operates in the opposite direction and enables Stevens first to gather many specific instances in the hopes of then being able to generalize, or create, theory. This approach is called **grounded theory**. The grounded theory approach does not seek to test hypotheses to support theory; instead, theory "is discovered, developed, and provisionally verified through systematic data collection and analysis of data" (Young, 1998, p. 26) relating to the phenomenon of interest. In this manner, the components of the research process (theory, data collection, and data analysis) are in reciprocal relationship with one another.

operationalize
making an abstract idea measurable and observable

observations
focused examination within a context of interest; may be guided by hypotheses or research questions

data
the raw materials collected by the researcher to answer the questions posed in the research or to test a hypothesis

code
converting raw data to a category system

grounded theory
theory induced from data and analysis

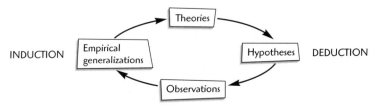

Figure 3.2 The Wheel of Science

Source: Loosely adapted from several conceptual drawings and reduced from the concept on page 18 of Walter L. Wallace, THE LOGIC OF SCIENCE IN SOCIOLOGY (New York: Aldine de Gruyter, 1971). Copyright © 1971 by Walter L. Wallace. Renewed 1999. Reprinted by permission of Transaction Publishers.

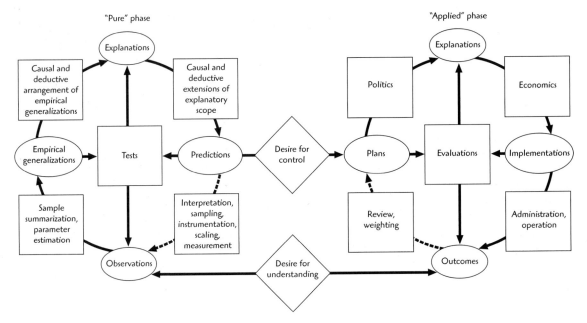

Figure 3.3 The Procedures of Scientific Analysis

Source: From Walter L. Wallace, PRINCIPLES OF SCIENTIFIC SOCIOLOGY (New York: Aldine de Gruyter, 1983), page 359. Copyright © 1983 by Walter L. Wallace. Reprinted by permission of Transaction Publishers.

Although some researchers approach their work strictly as hypothesis testers and some approach it more as theory generators, in practice most weave back and forth between the two. Walter Wallace (1971) suggests that the research process is circular, moving continuously between induction and deduction. Researchers refer to this as the wheel of science (Figure 3.2). Additionally, as Wallace (1983) noted elsewhere, this process is endless: "Each step presupposes that all the others have been taken before it—presumably at lower levels of understanding and control. Thus, although one may *consciously* start a given analysis by making certain predictions, one always has in mind (as largely unconscious background assumptions) certain prior explanations, empirical generalizations, tests, outcomes, implementations, and so on" (p. 358).

Furthermore, Wallace (1983) has expanded this wheel of science to include two types of research: pure and applied (Figure 3.3). In **pure research,** researchers

pure research
research to generate knowledge

are guided by knowledge-generating goals. They are interested in testing or generating theory for its own sake and for the sake of advancing our knowledge in an area. In **applied research,** researchers wish to solve specific problems with the knowledge they or other researchers have generated. Figure 3.3 illustrates the relationship between these two types of research goals and processes. In our example of Dr. Stevens's research, we see her performing pure research. If a specific organization hired Dr. Stevens to consult with them to improve employee morale, however, her research would become applied. Theory and practice are intertwined, and pure and applied research are not unrelated processes. As Larry Frey and his colleagues observe (2000), "the interrelationship of theory and application is especially important in a 'practical discipline' such as communication that has enormous potential to make a difference in people's lives" (p. 36). In Figure 3.2, you can see the arrows running between the two types of research showing this interrelationship.

applied research research to solve a problem or create a policy

In the example of Rolanda and Dr. Stevens, we have seen how Rolanda's job utilizes theory and how theory and research relate in Dr. Stevens' study. In addition, Rolanda operates as an intuitive or naïve scientist in her daily life. An intuitive scientist follows many of the same processes and reasoning patterns that trained scientists do, just not in as explicit or rigorous a fashion. Usually, intuitive scientists follow inductive logic: They experience something and then generalize from that. So when Rolanda concludes that all men are untrustworthy, she is inducing a general statement about all men from her experiences with one man, Anton. This is similar to the process a researcher might follow; however, a social scientist would not make hasty generalizations, or move to theory, on the basis of one observation. Intuitive science proceeds on the basis of deductive logic as well, as Rolanda's theory about cities demonstrates. She believes that larger cities are more diverse than smaller ones. As she moves from Sheridan to Chicago, she will test that theory with her observations about life in Chicago. Here again, the issue of numbers of observations is important. How long does Rolanda have to live in Chicago before she can be satisfied that her theory is correct? Does she have to sample life in other large cities to substantiate her theory, or is Chicago alone a sufficient observation? This is very similar to Dr. Stevens's concerns in her study. When Rolanda wonders about the number of conversations that she is collecting for Dr. Stevens, she focuses on a key point: How many instances do you need to observe before you can come to a conclusion? There are no absolute answers to this question, although there are some standards that are often accepted by practicing researchers.

In conducting research, one key difference between professional researchers and naïve ones rests on the definition of two terms: reliability and validity. Researchers say that something has **reliability** when you can get the same results over time. For example, if Rolanda visited the organizations in two years and her observations there yielded the same results that they do now, her observations would be called reliable. You can imagine many reasons reliability is difficult to obtain. For instance, if there had been a big turnover in personnel at one of the organizations, reliability would be difficult. Professional researchers conduct statistical tests to judge reliability, or they may return to ask participants if they still feel the same way they did when they were first questioned or observed. Naïve scientists usually operate as though their observations are reliable without ever testing for it.

Reliability is important, but validity is even more critical to the research process. This is the case because observations can be reliable even if they are not valid, but the opposite is not true. To draw useful conclusions from research, observations must be both reliable and valid. **Validity** refers to the fact that the observation method actually captures what it is supposed to. For instance, Dr. Stevens is interested in communication accommodation, so she is having Rolanda listen to workplace conversations in hallways to find it. If people engage in extensive conversations where Rolanda can tape them, then probably the observations are able to measure the concept of interest. But what if people in these organizations don't talk much in the public spaces of the office? What if Rolanda tapes a lot of casual greetings that don't show much of anything important to the notion of communication accommodation? Would Dr. Stevens be correct in concluding that people do not accommodate their communication according to status? Maybe not, if a lot of accommodating is going on behind closed doors where Rolanda didn't go. In that case, the measurement (taped hallway conversations) was not valid because it didn't capture what the researcher was interested in. Again, professional researchers are concerned about the validity of their observations and work diligently to demonstrate validity. Naïve researchers don't think too much about validity unless they somehow discover that they have been basing their generalizations on a mistaken notion.

Overall, the research process is similar for naïve and professional researchers, but professional researchers are more rigorous at every step of the process. Both draw conclusions based on their findings, and ultimately we are convinced by the arguments each advances about the strength of their process. When we believe that the results are based on good (reliable and valid) observations and careful logic, we accept the findings.

reliability
the stability and predictability of an observation

validity
the truth value of an observation

Observations and logic combine in many patterns beyond the deductive and inductive that we have outlined here. There are almost as many research methods as there are researchers, and there is room for a great deal of creativity in the research process.

Conclusion

This chapter introduced the concepts of theory and research and discussed their usefulness for examining communication behaviors. We have provided an initial definition of *theory* as well as explored some of the goals of theory and the relationship between theory and experience. We discussed the frameworks for theories, or three approaches to knowing: empirical, interpretive, and critical. Each of these approaches answers questions about truth (ontology), gathering information (epistemology), and values (axiology) somewhat differently. Further, we discussed how theories can be created using three different guidelines: covering law, systems, and rules. We explained the research process briefly, discussing issues of induction (grounded theory) and deduction (scientific method) and we suggested that researchers differ from naïve theorists in their application of reliability and validity. As we seek to understand communication, we turn to theory to help us organize the information that research provides.

Yet we must realize the limitations of theory and research. Communication interactions consist of multiple perspectives. Theories are, at best, only partial explanations of the multiplicity of social life. Research methods are limited by the assumptions guiding them. We can overcome these limits to an extent by acknowledging the partiality of our theories and research and opening ourselves to diverse points of view. As Yerby (1995) states, our ability to listen to the perspectives of others while at the same time voicing our own perspectives ultimately contributes to our ability to understand how we are connected to others.

Discussion Starters

1. Do you think a theory can help us understand the communication behavior of subordinates and superiors in an organization? Why or why not? Use examples in your response.

2. Provide some examples of ways you think like a theorist in your daily life.

3. What is the difference between inductive and deductive logic? Give some examples of your everyday use of both induction and deduction.

4. Do you see communication behavior as being lawlike, like a system, or rule governed? Explain your answer.

5. How would you characterize your own intellectual traditions? How do these traditions affect your theoretical thinking? Be specific.

6. How do a researcher's belief's about the world actually affect the research process? Be specific.

7. How is a critical theory different from an empirical or humanistic theory? What do we learn about a theory by classifying it in terms of its approach to knowing?

Online Learning Center [www. mhhe.com/west4e]

Visit the Online Learning Center at www.mhhe.com/west4e for chapter-specific resources, such as story-into-theory and multiple-choice quizzes, as well as theory summaries and theory connection questions.

CHAPTER 4

As We Begin...

As you read the communication theories in the following chapters, we know you need some structures to help you understand them and some standards for judging their worth. As we have mentioned previously, understanding theory is complicated by the fact that the word "theory" describes so many different things. Two theories may approach communication from completely different points of view and be rooted in differing intellectual traditions. Robert Craig and Heidi Muller (2007) observe that "different theories are in essence written in different languages" (p. ix) and this is what makes the subject of communication theory complex. The material we discussed in Chapters 1, 2, and 3 is intended to help you read through these "different languages" and find what each theory is saying and evaluate how that contributes to our understanding of the communication behaviors the theory purports to describe, explain, predict, or change.

For Review

In Chapter 1, we framed our definition of communication, although we noted that it was a complicated task because different researchers approach communication very differently. We argued that communication is a social process in which individuals employ symbols to establish and interpret meaning in their environment. We use that definition to guide our choice of theories and you should keep it in mind as you read through the following twenty-five chapters in the text that describe specific theories. We chose theories that we think illuminate communication as we've interpreted it. As you read the theories, think about the extent to which they relate to you and others.

In Chapter 2, we explained how theories can be classified as growing out of one (or more) of the seven traditions identified by Robert Craig (1999): rhetorical (or seeing communication as the art of public address); semiotic (or seeing communication as a process conducted through signs); phenomenological (or seeing communication as existing in dialogue with others); cybernetic (or seeing communication as a process of information flow); socio-psychological (or seeing communication as interaction in a cause–effect model); socio-cultural (or seeing communication as the co-creation of social reality); and critical (or seeing communication as a means for critiquing and changing social injustice).

We also described how theories can be classified in an additional way—not based on the way communication is pictured, as in Craig's (1999) system, but rather by the situation, or context, to which the theory refers. As we explained in Chapter 2, some theories focus on communication in one of the following contexts: intrapersonal (or when people engage in internal dialogues); interpersonal (or when two [or more] people talk together socially); small group (or when a number of people work together to achieve the accomplishment of a task); organizational (or when people communicate within and among large, extended environments we call organizations); public (or when one person addresses a large group); mass (or when people communicate to a large audience via mass media such as TV, radio, the Internet, and so forth); and cultural (or when people whose cultural backgrounds vary engage in communication).

You can see there is a little overlap between the traditions and the contexts (i.e., the rhetorical tradition and the public context) and, as we pointed out in Chapter 2, the traditions and contexts are not completely discrete. Thus, it is possible to have a conversation with members of a small task group that begins as small group communication but becomes interpersonal as the members stop working on their task to talk about their plans for the holiday weekend. In addition, the Internet, a mass medium, may often be used for interpersonal communication in chat rooms, and social networking sites.

In Chapter 3, we reviewed three foundational approaches to the study of communication: empirical or positivistic, interpretive, and critical. These three approaches conform to the three perspectives (empiricism, hermeneutics, and critical theory) that Art Bochner (1985) reviewed while discussing the study of interpersonal communication. The positivistic, or empirical, approach assumes that objective truths can be uncovered and that the process of inquiry that discovers these truths can be, at least in part, value-neutral. The interpretive approach views truth as subjective and co-created by the participants, with the researcher clearly one of the participants. There is less emphasis on objectivity because complete objectivity is seen as impossible. The critical approach asserts that an understanding of knowledge relates to power. For critical researchers, it is generally important to change the status quo to resolve power imbalances and to give voice to those who have been silenced by the power structure.

Remember, as we mentioned in Chapter 3, these approaches are presented in extreme form, and many researchers would not identify themselves as subscribing to the extremes. Most people find a comfortable middle ground based on these approaches that represents their worldview. In addition, there are intellectual traditions we have not reviewed that entail different values, goals, and methods. Intellectual traditions influence how given researchers try to understand, explain, predict, or change communication. When researchers pick a theory to guide them that is rooted in one of these traditions, they also get all the intellectual trappings that come along with the tradition. These trappings provide people with a lens for seeing and making sense of the world they inhabit.

Our views of the world—answers to questions about what is the nature of humans, what is the best way to gather knowledge, and what is the relationship between values and knowledge—together form a foundation to guide us as we think about the questions of our lives and strive to discover the answers.

Something New

As you read the communication theories in the following chapters, you need some standards for judging their worth. Though we have chosen theories that are generally regarded as important in the communication field, they all have unique strengths and shortcomings. The following criteria are generally accepted as useful measures for evaluating communication theory: scope, logical consistency, parsimony, utility, testability, heurism, and the test of time. We will discuss each of them briefly.

Scope

Scope refers to the breadth of communication behaviors covered by the theory. Boundaries are the limits of a theory's scope. Although theories should explain enough of communication to be meaningful, they should also have clear boundaries specifying the limits of their scope. Some theories cover a relatively narrow range of behaviors, whereas others try for much larger scope. Uncertainty Reduction Theory (URT), for example, which we discuss in Chapter 9, originally was bounded by initial encounters between strangers. In some ways this suggests a rather limited scope for the theory. However, although the duration of initial encounters is short, it is true that people spend a great deal of time throughout their lives meeting and conversing with new people. Thus, the scope of the theory may seem a bit broader upon reflection. In addition, because URT was first proposed in 1975, other researchers have expanded the theory to include developed relationships such as dating and friendship (Planalp & Honeycutt, 1985; Planalp & Rivers, 1988; Planalp, Rutherford, & Honeycutt, 1988), marriage (Turner, 1992), and online romantic relationships (Anderson & Emmers-Sommer, 2006). As the theory has been used by researchers, its scope and boundaries have expanded.

scope
a criterion for evaluating theories; refers to the breadth of communication behaviors covered in the theory

Logical Consistency

Simply put, theories should make sense and have an internal **logical consistency** that is clear and not contradictory. Theories should provide us with good explanations that show us how the concepts work together and what results follow from their interactions. In addition, the claims made by the theory should be consistent with the assumptions of the theory. If a theory is constructed using the covering law approach, it would be inconsistent for the theory to focus on people's choices and idiosyncratic activities. Logical consistency means that the theory "hangs together" and doesn't contradict itself, either by advancing two propositions that are in conflict with each other or by failing to operate within the parameters of its assumptions.

logical consistency
a criterion for evaluating theories; refers to the internal logic in the theoretical statements

Parsimony

parsimony
a criterion for evaluating theories; refers to the simplicity of the explanation provided by the theory

Parsimony refers to the simplicity of the explanation provided by the theory. Theories should contain only the number of concepts necessary to explain the phenomenon under consideration. If a theory can explain a person's communication behavior satisfactorily by using one concept (such as expectancy violations), that may be more useful than having to use five or six concepts. However, because theories of communication and social behavior are dealing with complex phenomena, they may have to be complex themselves. Parsimony requires simplicity without sacrificing completeness.

Utility

utility
a criterion for evaluating theories; refers to the theory's usefulness or practical value

This criterion refers to the theory's usefulness, or practical value. A good theory has **utility** in that it tells us a great deal about communication and human behavior. It allows us to understand some element of communication that was previously unclear. It weaves together pieces of information in such a way that we are able to see a pattern that was previously unclear to us. In so doing, theories can shape and change our behavior.

Testability

testability
a criterion for evaluating theories; refers to our ability to test the accuracy of a theory's claims

Testability refers to our ability to investigate a theory's accuracy. One of the biggest issues involved in testability concerns the specificity of the concepts that are central to the theory. For example, as we discuss in Chapter 11, Social Exchange Theory is predicated on the concepts of costs and rewards. The theory predicts that people will engage in behaviors that they find rewarding and avoid behaviors that are costly to them. However, the theory does not clearly define costs and rewards. In fact, the terms are defined in a circular fashion: Behaviors that people engage in repeatedly are rewarding, and those that they avoid are costly. You can see how difficult it is to test the central prediction of Social Exchange Theory given this circular definition. This criterion is more useful in theories framed from an objectivist epistemology than those from a subjectivist epistemology.

Heurism

heurism
a criterion for evaluating theories; refers to the amount of research and new thinking stimulated by the theory

Heurism refers to the amount of research and new thinking that is stimulated by the theory. Theories are judged to be good to the extent that they generate insights and new research. Although not all theories produce a great deal of research, an effective theory prompts some research activity. For example, the theory we discuss in Chapter 21, Cultural Studies, came from many diverse disciplines and has stimulated research programs in English, anthropology, social psychology, and communication.

Test of Time

test of time
a criterion for evaluating theories; refers to the theory's durability over time

The final criterion, the **test of time**, can be used only after some time has passed since the theory's creation. Are these theories still generating research or have

Theory Into Practice
Ray

Before reading this chapter, I never thought that I could evaluate theory. It just seemed like theory was a given. It's interesting to think about some theories being better or worse than others. I guess that's why researchers argue. It's not exactly about the facts—those are probably not all that different—but it's about whose theory is a better explanation of those facts. It helps to have some criteria to use in evaluating theory. But I bet that even with those criteria, researchers with different paradigms will disagree. It's just hard to see things the same way if one person thinks there's absolute truth out there and another thinks that everyone has his or her own truth.

Table 4.1   Criteria for Evaluating Communication Theories

CRITERIA	QUESTIONS TO CONSIDER
Scope	What are the boundaries of the theory's explanation?
Logical consistency	Do the claims of the theory match its assumptions? Do the principles of the theory contradict each other?
Parsimony	Is the theory as simple as it can be to explain the phenomenon under consideration?
Utility	Is the theory useful or practical?
Testability	Can the theory be shown to be false?
Heurism	Has the theory been used in research extensively to stimulate new ways of thinking about communication?
Test of time	How long has the theory been used in communication research?

they been discarded as outmoded? Deciding whether a theory has withstood the test of time is often arbitrary. For instance, if a theory was conceptualized and tested in the 1970s but has remained dormant in the literature for over a decade and is now being reintegrated into research, has this theory satisfied the test of time? Judging this criterion is often a subjective process. Furthermore, it is not a criterion that can be used to assess a new theory (see Table 4.1 for a review of each of the seven criteria just discussed).

Conclusion

In this bridge chapter, we've distilled some of the most important parts of our initial three chapters and added new information for you about how to evaluate theory. We've done this to provide you with a guide for reading the twenty-five theory chapters that follow. We wanted you to have this guide for two reasons. First, as Leslie Baxter and Dawn Braithwaite (2008) observe,

> Researchers rarely articulate explicitly their [approaches to knowing] (and perhaps they should do so more than they do). Rather, scholars' philosophical alignments often float at a latent level, between the lines of their prose. The sophisticated reader needs to know how to interpret a given researcher's choices in order to infer what his or her [approaches to knowing] are in a given study. Once one knows what key signs to look for, it is possible to locate a given researcher's commitments. Why is this helpful and important? Because it tells the reader what the researcher values about theory and how theory should be used and evaluated in the given study. (p. 10)

So we've tried to help you look for the key signs to develop your sophistication as a consumer of research and as a researcher yourself.

Second, we have structured the text to provide a conclusion to each theory chapter based on the information provided in Chapters 2 and 3. This bridge chapter will help you use and understand the conclusions of all the theory chapters. At the end of each theory chapter, we identify the following points for the theory that has been profiled in the chapter: (1) what communication tradition the theory represents, (2) what communication context the theory refers to, (3) what approach to knowing is reflected in the theory, and (4) what evaluative criteria have been used to judge the theory. Each chapter will end with the following feature, and one or more of the terms listed in each box will be highlighted regarding the theory.

Communication Tradition	Rhetorical | Semiotic | Phenomenological | Cybernetic | Socio-Psychological | Socio-Cultural | Critical
Communication Context	Intrapersonal | Interpersonal | Small Group | Organizational | Public/Rhetorical | Mass/Media | Cultural
Approach to Knowing	Positivistic/Empirical | Interpretive/Hermeneutic | Critical
Evaluation Criteria	Scope | Logical Consistency | Parsimony | Utility | Testability | Heurism | Test of Time

When you reach the end of a theory chapter, you will see the answers we've provided, but you should be thinking about them yourself as you read about the theory. Some of the decisions regarding tradition or context are debatable and sometimes more than one context, for instance, is chosen. If you choose different terms than we have chosen, think about what ideas were guiding your choices.

Thinking about theory and research is a challenging yet exhilarating enterprise. You now have some tools to begin our journey together.

PART TWO

Understanding the Dialogue

The Self and Messages

ACHIEVING MEANING IS CRITICAL IN OUR LIVES. We can't get too far in our conversations unless we understand others and can make ourselves understood. Understanding messages is what the meaning-making process is all about. Meaning, therefore, requires us to assess our own thinking and also to be prepared to assess how others interpret our messages. Through our conversations with others, we gain a better sense of ourselves and a clearer understanding of the messages we and others send and receive.

How we process meaning is the cornerstone of our first section of theories, which we have labeled "The Self and Messages." Four theories highlight the prominent role of intrapersonal communication in meaning making. First, Symbolic Interaction Theory explores the interplay between the self and the society in which we live. Symbolic interactionists argue that people act toward other people or events on the basis of meaning they assign to them. The Coordinated Management of Meaning is also concerned with achieving meaning; however, the theory goes a bit further. It states that people will apply a personal set of rules to try to understand a social situation. Cognitive Dissonance Theory also looks at a person's ability to manage meaning and the need for people to avoid listening to views opposite their own. Expectancy Violations Theory looks specifically at what happens when someone violates our expectations. The theory suggests that we will judge a violation as either good or bad and act accordingly in the conversation.

The theories associated with the self and with messages deal with the ways people work toward gaining clarity and comprehension. Before and during conversations with others, we process things cognitively to determine how best to achieve meaning. As you read about these theories, you will encounter a number of important topics; namely, the influence of society on attitudes, communicator credibility, decision making, conversational rules, attraction, and liking.

CHAPTER 5

Symbolic Interaction Theory

*Based on the research of **George Herbert Mead***

Roger Thomas

Roger Thomas stared in the mirror and straightened his tie. He gave himself a last glance and decided that he looked as good as he could. He was a little apprehensive about the new job, but he was excited too. He had just graduated from Carlton Tech in Omaha, Nebraska, with a degree in engineering, and he had landed a terrific job in Houston. This made for a lot of changes in his life. It was a bit overwhelming. He was born and raised in central Nebraska, and he had never really been in a city bigger than Omaha until he went on his job interviews. Now he was living in Houston! It had all happened so quickly that Roger could almost feel his head spin.

Some of Roger's concern centered on the fact that he was the first person in his family to graduate from college. As far back as he could recall, his family had been farmers, and although he knew that engineering was something he loved and excelled at, he felt a little confused about how to behave off the farm and in a completely new life. It also didn't help that he was so far from home. Whenever he had felt stressed at Carlton, he had gone home to see his family. That had usually made him feel better. He remembered one day in his first year at Carlton when he felt impossibly out of place and uncomfortable. He really didn't know how to act as a college student. He went home for the weekend, and being in a familiar place with his family instantly gave him confidence. When he returned to Carlton on Monday, he felt much more self-assured.

Even though his parents had not attended college themselves, they respected education and communicated this to Roger. They expressed pride in him and his accomplishments. They also told him how his younger brothers looked up to him. This gave Roger confidence in himself, and he liked the idea that he was blazing a new trail for his family. Also, whenever he visited, he appreciated his parents' qualities; they were so calm and steady. As they went about their tasks, they demonstrated the peace and harmony that Roger wanted to find in his life's work. After seeing them, he always had a renewed sense of self.

Now Roger decided he would just have to carry their image in his mind, because he had to face his new office alone. Yet even thinking about his family made him feel a little stronger. He was smiling when he got to the office. He was greeted warmly by the office assistant, who showed him into the conference room. He waited there for the other new hires to join him. By 9:05 A.M. they were all gathered, and their boss came in to give them an orientation speech. While the boss was talking, Roger looked around at his colleagues.

There were ten new employees in all, and they could not have been more different. Roger was the youngest person in the room by at least five years. He was a bit alarmed when he realized that he must be the one with the least experience. He tried to calm himself down. He thought of his parents' pride in him and how his brothers looked up to him. Then he remembered his favorite teacher telling him that he was one of the best engineering students ever to go through Carlton. This helped Roger, and after the boss was finished speaking, he felt prepared to face the challenges of the job. During the break, he even had the confidence to begin talking to one of his new colleagues. He introduced himself and discovered that he didn't have less experience than she did. Helen Underwood explained that she had lived in a small Texas farming town, where she worked for the government. After working there for a couple of years, she decided to go back to school and get a degree. Roger was amazed to meet someone else who came from a farming background. Helen told Roger she was really impressed that he had graduated from Carlton. She knew it had a wonderful reputation, and its internship program was supposed to be the best in the country. Roger replied that he had been really lucky to go there and had loved working at his internship, where he had learned a great deal. Helen said she was nervous about starting out at this firm, and Roger smiled and nodded.

This conversation made him feel much better about the challenges that were ahead of him. Even though Helen was in her forties, they had a great deal in common, and they were in the same situation at the firm. Roger thought they would be friends.

As Roger goes through his preparations for the first day of his new job and as he speaks with his boss and his new colleague, he is engaging in the dynamic exchange of symbols. George Herbert Mead, who is credited with originating the Theory of Symbolic Interaction, was fascinated with humans' ability to use symbols; he proposed that people act based on the symbolic meanings that arise in a given situation. In Chapter 1 we defined *symbols* as arbitrary labels or representations for phenomena. And, in Chapter 2, we identified symbols as closely aligned with the semiotic tradition. Symbols form the essence of Symbolic Interaction Theory (SI). As its name suggests, Symbolic Interaction Theory centers on the relationship between symbols and interactions. Although Mead published very little during his academic career, after he died his students collaborated on a book based on his lectures. They titled the book *Mind, Self, and Society* (Mead, 1934), and it contains the foundations of Symbolic Interaction Theory. Interestingly, the name, "Symbolic Interaction," was not a creation of Mead's. One of his students, Herbert Blumer, actually coined the term, but it was clearly Mead's work that began the theoretical movement. Blumer published his own articles in a collection in 1969.

Ralph LaRossa and Donald C. Reitzes (1993) suggest that Symbolic Interaction is "essentially . . . a frame of reference for understanding how humans, in concert with one another, create symbolic worlds and how these worlds, in turn, shape human behavior" (p. 136). LaRossa and Reitzes reflect Mead's contention about the interdependency between the individual and society. In fact, Symbolic Interaction forms a bridge between theories focusing attention on individuals and theories attending to social forces. As Kenneth J. Smith and Linda Liska Belgrave (1994) note, Symbolic Interaction Theory argues that society is made "real" by the interactions of individuals, who "live and work to make their social world meaningful" (p. 253). Further, in this claim we can see Mead's belief in individuals as active, reflective participants in their social context.

The ideas of this theory have been very influential in communication studies. Judy Pearson and Shannon VanHorn (2004), for instance, found that Mead's theory framed older adults' sense of their gender identity; Gail McGregor (1995) employed the theory to critique gender representations in advertisements; Patricia Book (1996) examined family narrative influences on a person's ability to communicate about death. In addition, Daniel Flint (2006) found the theory useful in understanding marketing and Jan Fernback (2007) studied online social networking. Several researchers observe, however, that Symbolic Interaction is a community of theories, rather than simply one theory. Many theorists refer to the Chicago School and the Iowa School as the two main branches of the theory. Let's briefly examine the history of the theory to better understand Symbolic Interaction today.

History of Symbolic Interaction Theory

The intellectual ancestors of Symbolic Interaction Theory were the early-twentieth-century pragmatists, such as John Dewey and William James. The pragmatists believed that reality is dynamic, which was not a popular idea at that time. In other words, they had different ontological beliefs than many other leading intellectuals at the time. They advanced the notion of an emerging social structure and insisted that meanings were created in interaction. They were activists, or critical theorists, who saw science as a way to advance knowledge and improve society.

Symbolic Interaction had its genesis at two different universities: the University of Iowa and the University of Chicago. At Iowa, Manford Kuhn and his students were instrumental in affirming the original ideas of the theory and added to the theory as well. Additionally, the Iowa group was advancing some new ways of looking at the self, but their approach was viewed as eccentric; thus, most of SI's principles and developments stemmed from the Chicago School.

Both George Herbert Mead and his friend John Dewey were on the faculty at the University of Chicago (although Mead had never completed his doctorate). Mead had studied both philosophy and social science, and he lectured on the ideas that form the core of the Chicago School. As a popular teacher who was widely respected, Mead played a critical role in establishing the perspective of the Chicago School. He focused on an approach to social theory emphasizing the importance of communication to life and social encounters.

The two schools diverged primarily on methodology (or epistemology). Mead and his student at the University of Chicago, Herbert Blumer, contended that the study of human beings could not be conducted using the same methods as the study of other things. They advocated the use of case studies and histories and nondirective interviews. The Iowa School adopted a more quantitative approach to their studies. Kuhn believed that the concepts of SI could be operationalized, quantified, and tested. To this end, Kuhn developed a technique called the "Twenty-statements Self-attitudes" questionnaire. A research respondent taking the twenty-statements test is asked to fill in twenty blank spaces in answer to the question, Who am I? Some of Kuhn's colleagues at Iowa became disenchanted with this view of the self and broke away to form the "new" Iowa

School. Carl Couch was one of the leaders of this new school. Couch and his associates began studying interaction behavior through videotapes of conversations, rather than simply examining the twenty-statements test.

In addition to these main schools of Symbolic Interaction, there are many variations. Many other theories that emphasize slightly different aspects of human interaction owe some debt to the central concepts of SI. Despite a diversity in ideas, Mead's central concepts remain relatively constant in most interpretations of SI. Consequently, we will examine the basic assumptions and the key concepts that Mead outlined and later Blumer later elaborated.

Symbolic Interaction Theory • *Theory at a Glance*

People are motivated to act based on the meanings they assign to people, things, and events. These meanings are created in the language that people use both in communicating with others (interpersonal context) and in self-talk (intrapersonal context), or their own private thought. Language allows people to develop a sense of self and to interact with others in the community.

Themes and Assumptions of Symbolic Interaction Theory

Symbolic Interaction is based on ideas about the self and its relationship to society. Because this can be interpreted very broadly, we wish to spend some time detailing the themes of the theory and, in the process, reveal the assumptions framing the theory.

LaRossa and Reitzes (1993) have examined Symbolic Interaction Theory as it relates to the study of families. They note that seven central assumptions ground the theory and that these assumptions reflect three central themes:

- the importance of meanings for human behavior
- the importance of the self-concept
- the relationship between the individual and society

We'll describe each of these themes briefly and show how each one supports central assumptions of the theory.

The Importance of Meanings for Human Behavior

Symbolic Interaction Theory holds that individuals construct meaning through the communication process because meaning is not intrinsic to anything. It takes people to make meaning. In fact, the goal of interaction, according to the theory, is to create shared meaning. This is the case because without shared meaning communication is extremely difficult, if not impossible. Imagine trying

an indiv. character or quality

to talk to a friend if you had to explain your own idiosyncratic meaning for every word you used, and your friend had to do the same. Of course, sometimes we assume that we and our conversational partner agree on a meaning only to discover that we are mistaken ("I said get ready as fast as you can." "One hour was as fast as I could get ready." "But I meant for you to be ready in 15 minutes." "You didn't say that!"), but, frequently, we can count on people having common meanings in a conversation.

Lets give an example. In the United States, we generally associate wedding rings with love and commitment. The ring is a symbol of a legal and emotional bond, and thus most people invest the symbol with a positive connotation. However, some people see marriage as an oppressive institution. Those people will respond negatively to wedding rings and any other symbols of what they perceive as a degrading situation. The point that Symbolic Interaction theorists make is that the ring itself has no specific meaning; it takes on meaning as people interact and invest it with importance. According to LaRossa and Reitzes, this theme supports three main assumptions, which are taken from Herbert Blumer's (1969) work. These assumptions are as follows:

- Humans act toward others on the basis of the meanings those others have for them.
- Meaning is created in interaction between people.
- Meaning is modified through an interpretive process.

Humans Act Toward Others on the Basis of the Meanings Those Others Have for Them   This assumption explains behavior as a loop between stimuli and the responses people exhibit to those stimuli. Symbolic Interaction theorists such as Herbert Blumer were concerned with the meaning behind behavior. They looked for meaning by examining psychological and sociological explanations for behavior. Thus, as researchers study the behaviors of Roger Thomas (from our beginning scenario), they see him making meanings that are congruent with the social forces that shape him. For instance, Roger assigns meaning to his new work experience by applying commonly agreed-upon interpretations to the things he sees. When he sees the age of his co-workers, he believes that they have more experience than he does because in the United States, we often equate age with experience. Furthermore, SI researchers are interested in the meaning that Roger attaches to his encounter with Helen (for example, he is cheered up and believes they will become friends).

Meaning Is Created in Interaction Between People   Mead stresses the intersubjective basis of meaning. Meaning can exist, according to Mead, only when people share common interpretations of the symbols they exchange in interaction. Blumer (1969) explains that there are three ways of accounting for the origin of meaning. One approach regards meaning as being intrinsic to the thing. Blumer states, "Thus, a chair is clearly a chair in itself . . . the meaning

Research Notes

Forte, J. A. (2004). Symbolic interactionism and social work: A forgotten legacy, Part 2. *Families in Society, 85,* 521–530.

Forte presents the concepts of Symbolic Interactionism to the social work profession, noting that it is foundational to social work. He reviews the contributions the theory has made to social work in the areas of social policy and welfare, social work practice, research, and professional education. Forte cites Denzin (2002) who observed that some of the same conditions that plague contemporary society were present at the turn of the last century as well: Issues of consumerism and forces further marginalizing social work clients characterize both the early 20th and 21st centuries. Forte notes that in the early 20th century sociologists and social workers joined forces around the Chicago School of Symbolic Interaction Theory, and he suggests that same alliance might be practical for contemporary social workers. Forte notes that the important legacy of the theory to social work has been largely forgotten and explains why this is a mistake. He also discusses the contributions the theory can make to the practice of social work today.

Pearson, J. C., & VanHorn, S. B. (2004). Communication and gender identity: A retrospective analysis. *Communication Quarterly, 52,* 284–299.

This study posed four research questions grounded in Symbolic Interaction Theory and social constructivism approaches: (1) How do older adults define masculinity and femininity? (2) How did others' messages affect gender identity enactment? (3) How did circumstances affect gender identity enactment? and (4) How does one's development of life span affect gender identity enactment? To answer these questions, Pearson and VanHorn conducted thirteen focus groups including thirty-five older adults (from 67 to 97 years of age), audiotaped these groups, and transcribed the tapes. The tapes were coded inductively based on themes sounded by the participants about gender identity. The researchers found that Symbolic Interaction Theory grounded many of the stories people told in the focus groups. For example, when women reported receiving consistent messages from many sources about the appropriateness of a traditional feminine gender role, they abandoned behaviors defined as masculine (such as playing with tools) in favor of feminine behaviors.

emanates, so to speak, from the thing and as such there is no process involved in its formation; all that is necessary is to recognize the meaning that is there in the thing" (pp. 3–4).

A second approach to the origin of meaning sees it as "brought to the thing by the person for whom the thing has meaning" (Blumer, 1969, p. 4). This position supports the popular notion that meanings are in people, not in things. In this perspective, meaning is explained by isolating the psychological elements within an individual that produce a meaning.

Mead's theory takes a third approach to meaning, seeing it as occurring between people. Meanings are "social products" or "creations that are formed in and through the defining activities of people as they interact" (Blumer, 1969, p. 5). Therefore, if Roger and Helen did not share a common language and did not agree on denotations and connotations of the symbols they exchanged, no meaning would result from their conversation. Furthermore, the meanings created by Helen and Roger are unique to them and their relationship. A study of how police officers symbolically construct the meaning of their jobs (Innes, 2002) illustrates this assumption by showing how the police talk about murders to the public and among themselves.

Meaning Is Modified Through an Interpretive Process   Blumer notes that this interpretive process has two steps. First, communicators point out the things that have meaning. Blumer argues that this part of the process is different from a psychological approach and consists of people engaging in communication with themselves. Thus, as Roger gets ready for work in the morning, he communicates with himself about the areas that are meaningful to him. The second step involves communicators selecting, checking, and transforming the meanings in the context in which they find themselves. When Roger talks with Helen, he listens for her remarks that are relevant to the areas he hasdecided are meaningful. Further, in his interpretation process, Roger depends on the shared social meanings that are culturally accepted. Thus, Roger and Helen are able to converse relatively easily because they both come from similar co-cultures.

The Importance of the Self-Concept

self-concept
a relatively stable set of perceptions people hold about themselves

The second overall theme focuses on the importance of the **self-concept,** or the relatively stable set of perceptions that people hold of themselves. When Roger (or any social actor) asks the question "Who am I?" the answer relates to self-concept. The characteristics Roger acknowledges about his physical features, roles, talents, emotional states, values, social skills and limits, intellect, and so forth make up his self-concept. This notion is critical to Symbolic Interactionism. Furthermore, Symbolic Interaction is interested in the ways in which people develop self-concepts. The theory pictures individuals with active selves, grounded in social interactions with others (Figure 5.1). This theme suggests two additional assumptions, according to LaRossa and Reitzes (1993):

- Individuals develop self-concepts through interaction with others.
- Self-concepts provide an important motive for behavior.

Individuals Develop Self-Concepts Through Interactions With Others This assumption suggests that it is only through contact with others that we develop a sense of self. People are not born with self-concepts; they learn them through interactions. According to SI, infants have no sense of an individuated self. During the first year of life, children begin to differentiate themselves from their surroundings. This is the earliest development of the self-concept. Mead's theory contends that this process continues through the child's acquisition of language and the ability to respond to others and internalize the feedback he or she receives. Roger has a sense of self because of his contacts with his parents and his teachers and his colleagues. Their interactions with him tell him who he is. Early family researchers such as Edgar Burgess (1926) reflect this assumption when they discuss the importance of

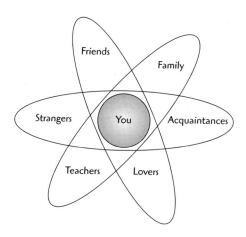

Figure 5.1
How the
Self-Concept
Develops

the family as a socializing institution. Furthermore, Burgess notes that children and parents might conflict over children's self-concept or image. Alicia Cast (2003) studied married couples' use of power, and her results support this assumption. She asserts that social context and interaction are critical when investigating the self.

Self-Concepts Provide an Important Motive for Behavior   The notion that beliefs, values, feelings, and assessments about the self affect behavior is a central tenet of the theory. Mead argues that because human beings possess a self, they are provided with a mechanism for self-interaction. This mechanism is used to guide behavior and conduct. It is also important to note that Mead sees the self as a process, not as a structure. Having a self forces people to construct their actions and responses, rather than simply expressing them. So, for instance, if you feel great about your abilities in your communication theory course, then it is likely that you will do well in the course. In fact, it is likely that you will feel confident in all of your courses. This process is often called the **self-fulfilling prophecy,** or the self-expectations that cause a person to behave in such a way that the expectations are realized. When Roger remembers his professor's praise of his engineering abilities, he is setting himself up to make a self-fulfilling prophecy about his performance at his new job.

self-fulfilling prophecy
a prediction about yourself causing you to behave in such a way that it comes true

The Relationship Between the Individual and Society

The final theme pertains to the relationship between individual freedoms and social constraint. Mead and Blumer took a middle position on this question. They tried to account for both order and change in social processes. Assumptions relating to this theme include the following:

• People and groups are influenced by cultural and social processes.
• Social structure is worked out through social interaction.

People and Groups Are Influenced by Cultural and Social Processes This assumption recognizes that social norms constrain individual behavior. For instance, when Roger gets ready for his first day at his new job, he selects a navy suit, a white oxford shirt, and a burgundy and blue striped tie. His preferred mode of dress would be jeans and a flannel shirt, but he chooses clothing that he feels will be socially appropriate in the job context. Furthermore, culture strongly influences the behaviors and attitudes that we value in our self-concepts. In the United States, people who see themselves as assertive are likely to be proud of this attribute and reflect favorably on their self-concept. This is the case because the United States is an individualistic culture that values assertiveness and individuality. In some Asian cultures, cooperation and community are highly valued, and the collective is more important than the individual. Thus, an Asian who sees herself as assertive might feel ashamed of such a self-concept.

As an example, Mary Roffers (2002) notes that a college assignment to design a personal website was very difficult for a Hmong student in her class. The student explained that talking about oneself was not approved of in his culture and putting information about himself on the website felt inappropriate.

Social Structure Is Worked Out Through Social Interaction This assumption mediates the position taken by the previous assumption. SI challenges the view that social structure is unchanging and acknowledges that individuals can modify social situations. For example, many U.S. workplaces have instituted "casual Fridays," when the employees wear casual clothing rather than the typical, socially prescribed office wear. In this way, the participants in the interaction modify the structure and are not completely constrained by it. In other words, SI theorists believe that humans are choice makers. In our opening scenario, Roger chooses to introduce himself to Helen; he is not bound

T∗I∗P

I liked the example about casual Fridays in the workplace. When I went to work at my current job there were a lot of rules I found difficult to follow. At first, it seemed like I was going to be constrained by the structure I found on the job. But then I started to talk to people and we were able to make a couple of changes that makes working there a lot better for me. So, I think that assumption of SI is true. People have some constraints on them because of social rules, but people also have free will and can change some of the rules. If I hadn't been able to change things, I probably would have quit—which would have been my choice, too.

to do so by forces outside his control. In making choices, Roger exerts his individuality and demonstrates that he is not completely constrained by culture or situation.

To review, we list the themes that ground the theory and the assumptions they support:

THEMES

- The importance of meanings for human behavior
- The importance of the self-concept
- The relationship between the individual and society

ASSUMPTIONS

- Humans act toward others on the basis of the meanings those others have for them.
- Meaning is created in interaction between people.
- Meaning is modified through an interpretive process.
- Individuals develop self-concepts through interaction with others.
- Self-concepts provide an important motive for behavior.
- People and groups are influenced by cultural and social processes.
- Social structure is worked out through social interaction.

Key Concepts

Earlier we stated that the book outlining Mead's thinking was titled *Mind, Self, and Society*. The title of the book reflects the three key elements of Symbolic Interaction. We describe each element here, noting how other important issues relate to these basic three. It will become clear that the three concepts overlap to some extent.

Mind

mind
the ability to use symbols with common social meanings

language
a shared system of verbal and nonverbal symbols

significant symbols
symbols whose meaning is generally agreed upon by many people

Mead defines **mind** as the ability to use symbols that have common social meanings, and Mead believes that humans must develop minds through interaction with others. Infants cannot really interact with others until they learn **language,** or a shared system of verbal and nonverbal symbols organized in patterns to express thoughts and feelings. Language depends on what Mead calls **significant symbols,** or those symbols that evoke basically the same meaning for many people. Let's use the infant as an example to illustrate the concept of significant symbols. When parents coo and talk to their baby, the infant may respond, but he does not really understand the meanings of the words his parents use. As he learns language, the infant exchanges shared or significant symbols and can anticipate the responses of others to the symbols she uses.

By using language and interacting with others, we develop what Mead calls *mind*, and this enables us to create an interior setting for the society that we see operating outside us. Thus, mind can be viewed as the way people internalize society. Yet mind does not just depend on society. Mead suggests that they have a reciprocal relationship: Mind reflects and creates the social world. As people learn language, they learn the social norms and cultural values that constrain them. But they also learn ways to shape and change that social world through interaction. When children learn to talk, they may learn to say "please" and "thank you" as cultural indicators of politeness. Yet they may also create unique, personal ways of expressing politeness, like saying "mayberry" and "yes you," that become accepted phrases within a specific relationship.

thought
an inner conversation

Closely related to the concept of mind is the notion of **thought,** which Mead conceives of as an inner conversation. While Roger, in our opening story, prepares for his new job, he reviews all the experiences that brought him to that time and place. He thinks about his family's example and support, he remembers a favorite teacher, and he tells himself that he will be successful at this challenge. Through this intrapersonal conversation, Roger sorts out the meaning of his new situation. Mead holds that without social stimulation and interaction with others, people would not be capable of holding inner conversations or sustaining thought.

role taking
the ability to put oneself in another's place

According to Mead, one of the most critical activities that people accomplish through thought is **role taking,** or the ability to symbolically place oneself in an imagined self of another person. This process is also called "perspective taking" because it requires that one suspend one's own perspective on an experience and instead view it from the imagined perspective of another. For example, if Helen thought about Roger after their meeting and reflected on how he must have felt to be newer and younger than most of the other employees, then she would be role taking. Whenever we try to imagine how another person might view something or when we try to behave as we think another would, we are role taking. Mead suggests that role taking is a symbolic act that can help clarify our own sense of self, even as it allows us to develop the capacity for empathy with others.

Mead defines **self** as the ability to reflect on ourselves from the perspective of others. From this you can see that Mead does not believe that self comes from introspection or from simply thinking on one's own. For Mead, the self develops from a particular kind of role taking—that is, imagining how we look to another person. Borrowing a concept originated by the sociologist Charles Cooley in 1912, Mead refers to this as the **looking-glass self,** or our ability to see ourselves in the reflection of another's gaze. Cooley (1972) believes that three principles of development are associated with the looking-glass self: (1) we imagine how we appear to others, (2) we imagine their judgment of us, and (3) we feel hurt or pride based on these self-feelings. We learn about ourselves from the ways others treat us, view us, and label us. For example, when Rachel participated in the Great Bike Ride Across Iowa, she rode a three-speed bike 523 miles, from one end of the state to the other. The ride took one week, and after about three days, she felt she could not pedal a minute longer. But just as she was about to give up, a man biked up beside her and said, "You are amazing, going on this bike ride on a three-speed bike. You are just great. Keep it up." As he pedaled off, she straightened up and thought to herself, "Well, I guess I *am* amazing. I can finish this ride!" The label the man gave her actually changed her feelings of exhaustion and made her see her accomplishments and herself differently and more positively.

Other researchers (e.g., Gecas & Burke, 1995; Ichiyama, 1993; Milkie, 1999) refer to the looking glass self as *reflected appraisals,* or people's perceptions of how others see them. Joanne Kaufman and Cathryn Johnson (2004) used the concept of reflected appraisals to examine how gay men and lesbians develop and manage their identities. They argue that SI is a much better framework for understanding identity construction than the stage models often applied to gay and lesbian identity development. Kaufman and Johnson found that gay men and lesbians who experienced positive reflected appraisals (in regard to homosexuality) had an easier time developing their identity than did those people who experienced negative reflected appraisals.

Mead's notion of the looking-glass self implies the power that labels have on self-concept and behavior. This power represents a second type of self-fulfilling prophecy. Earlier in the chapter we spoke of self-fulfilling prophecies as being self-expectations that affect behaviors. For example, Roger tells himself repeatedly that he will succeed at his job and then engages in behaviors that are congruent with his expectations of success. In turn, these behaviors will likely ensure that he will succeed. By the same token, negative self-talk can create situations where predictions of failure come true. The second type of self-fulfilling prophecy produced by labels is called the **Pygmalion effect,** and it refers to the expectations of others governing one's actions.

The name comes from the myth of Pygmalion, on which a play of the same name and the musical *My Fair Lady* were based. The main character, Eliza, states that the difference between an upper-class lady and a poor flower girl is not in her behavior but in how others treat her. This phenomenon was tested in a classic study by Robert Rosenthal and Lenore Jacobson (1968). In their study,

self
imagining how we look to another person

looking-glass self
our ability to see ourselves as another sees us

Pygmalion effect
living up to or down to another's expectations of us

Rosenthal and Jacobson told elementary-school teachers that 20 percent of their students were gifted. But the names of these "gifted" students were simply drawn at random. Eight months later these students showed significantly greater gains in IQ compared to the rest of the children in the class. Rosenthal and Jacobson concluded that this was the result of teachers' expectations (and behaviors based on these expectations) toward the "gifted" children.

As Mead theorizes about self, he observes that through language people have the ability to be both subject and object to themselves. As subject, we act, and as object, we observe ourselves acting. Mead calls the subject, or acting self, the **I** and the object, or observing self, the **Me**. The I is spontaneous, impulsive, and creative, whereas the Me is more reflective and socially aware. The I might want to go out and party all night, whereas the Me might exercise caution and acknowledge the homework assignment that should be done instead of partying. Mead sees the self as a process that integrates the I and the Me.

I
the spontaneous, impulsive, creative self

Me
the reflective, socially aware self

Theory Application in Groups (TAG)

Devise a study that could test an idea supported by the SI framework. Decide whether your study should use quantitative or qualitative methods. Discuss the reasons for your choices.

Society

Mead argues that interaction takes place within a dynamic social structure that we call culture or society. Mead defines **society** as the web of social relationships that humans create. Individuals engage in society through behaviors that they choose actively and voluntarily. Society thus features an interlocking set of behaviors that individuals continually adjust. Society exists prior to the individual, but is also created and shaped by the individual, acting in concert with others (Forte, 2004).

Society, then, is made up of individuals, and Mead talks about two specific parts of society that affect the mind and the self. Mead's notion of **particular others** refers to the individuals in society who are significant to us. These people are usually family members, friends, work colleagues, and supervisors. We look to particular others to get a sense of social acceptability and a sense of self. When Roger thinks of his parents' opinion of him, he is deriving a sense of self from particular others. The identity of the particular others and the context influence our sense of social acceptability and our sense of self. Often the expectations of some particular others conflict with those of others. For example, if Roger's family wants him to work hard and be successful, whereas his friends want him to party and ignore work, he is likely to experience conflict.

The **generalized other** refers to the viewpoint of a social group or the culture as a whole. It is given to us by society, and "the attitude of the generalized other is the attitude of the whole community" (Mead, 1934, p. 154). The

society
the web of social relationships humans create and respond to

particular others
individuals who are significant to us

generalized other
the attitude of the whole community

generalized other provides information about roles, rules, and attitudes shared by the community. The generalized other also gives us a sense of how other people react to us and of general social expectations. This sense is influential in developing a social conscience. The generalized other may help mediate conflicts generated by conflicting groups of particular others. So if your friends want you to party and your family wants you to study, your knowledge of the importance of a college degree in your culture may lead you to decide in favor of your parents' position.

Integration, Critique, and Closing

Symbolic Interaction Theory has been a powerful theoretical framework for over sixty years. It provides striking insights about human communication behavior in a wide variety of contexts. The theory is well developed, beginning with the role of the self and progressing to an examination of the self in society. Yet the theory is not without its critics. As you think about Mead's theory, consider three areas of evaluation: scope, utility, and testability.

Integration

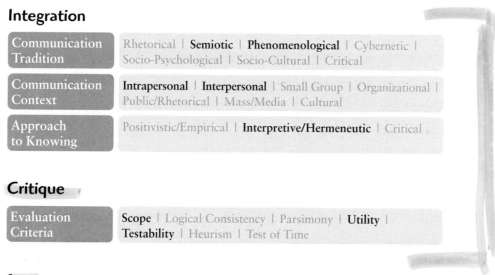

| Communication Tradition | Rhetorical | **Semiotic** | **Phenomenological** | Cybernetic | Socio-Psychological | Socio-Cultural | Critical |

| Communication Context | **Intrapersonal** | **Interpersonal** | Small Group | Organizational | Public/Rhetorical | Mass/Media | Cultural |

| Approach to Knowing | Positivistic/Empirical | **Interpretive/Hermeneutic** | Critical |

Critique

| Evaluation Criteria | Scope | Logical Consistency | Parsimony | **Utility** | **Testability** | Heurism | Test of Time |

Scope

Some critics complain that Symbolic Interaction Theory is too broad to be useful. This criticism centers on the evaluation criterion of scope. The theory covers too much ground, these critics assert, to fully explain specific meaning-making processes and communication behaviors. It is helpful to have a theory that explains a wide variety of human behavior, but when a theory purports to explain everything, it will be vague and difficult to apply. This is the criticism leveled against the theory: It tries to do too much, and its scope needs to be refined. In response to this criticism, proponents explain that Symbolic Interaction is not one unified theory; rather, it is a framework that can support many specific theories.

Utility

The second area of criticism concerns the theory's utility. Symbolic Interaction Theroy has been faulted as not as useful as it could be for two reasons. First, it focuses too much on the individual, and second, it ignores some important concepts that are needed to make the explanation complete. In the first case, critics observe that the theory's focus on the individual's power to create reality ignores the extent to which people live in a world not of their own making. Symbolic Interaction theorists regard a situation as real if the actors define it as real. But Erving Goffman (1974) comments that this notion, although true, ignores physical reality. For instance, if Roger and his parents agreed that he was an excellent engineer and that he was doing a wonderful job at his new firm, that would be reality for them. Yet it would not acknowledge the fact that Roger's boss perceived his skills as inadequate and fired him. Others counter by citing that they try to tread a middle ground between freedom of choice and external constraint. They recognize the validity of constraint, but they also emphasize the importance of shared meanings.

Related to this is the suggestion that the theory ignores important concepts such as emotions and self-esteem. Critics observe that it does not explain the emotional dimension of human interaction. Further, critics note that Symbolic Interaction discusses how we develop a self-concept, but it does not have much to say about how we evaluate ourselves. These deficiencies render the theory less useful than it should be in explaining the self. With reference to the lack of attention to the emotional aspects of human life, theorists respond that although Mead does not emphasize these aspects, the theory itself can accommodate emotions. In fact, some researchers have applied the theory to emotions with success. For instance, James Forte, Anne Barrett, and Mary Campbell (1996) used a Symbolic Interaction perspective to examine grief. Their study examined the utility of a Social Interaction perspective in assessing and intervening in a bereavement group. The authors found that Symbolic Interaction was a useful model. Regarding self-esteem, symbolic interactionists agree that it is not a focus of the theory. But they point out that this is not a flaw in the theory; it is simply beyond the bounds of what Mead chose to investigate.

Testability

With regard to testability, critics comment that the theory's broad scope renders its concepts vague. When so many core concepts are nominal (not directly observable), it is difficult to test the theory. Again, the response to this critique argues that Mead's theory is a general framework, not a single theory. In the more specific theories, such as Role Theory, for example, the concepts are more clearly defined and are capable of falsification, satisfying the criterion of testability.

In sum, Symbolic Interaction has critics, but it still remains an enduring theory. It supports research in multiple contexts, and it is constantly being refined and extended. Further, it is one of the leading conceptual tools for interpreting social interactions, and its core constructs provide the foundation for many other theories that we discuss in this book. Thus, because Symbolic Interaction Theory has stimulated much conceptual thinking, it has accomplished much of what theories aim to do.

Discussion Starters

1. Discuss Roger Thomas's initial reactions to his new job in Houston. How do they specifically relate to his sense of self?

2. Do you believe Mead's argument that one cannot have a self without social interaction? Would a person raised by an animal, for example, have no sense of self? Explain your answers.

3. Has there been a time in your life when your sense of self changed dramatically? If so, what contributed to the change? Did it have anything to do with others in your life?

4. Do you agree with the emphasis that Mead places on language as a shared symbol system? Is it possible to interact with someone who speaks a completely different language? Explain your position.

5. One of the criticisms of Symbolic Interaction Theory is that it puts too much emphasis on individual action and not enough emphasis on the constraints on individuals that they cannot think their way out of. What is your position on this criticism?

6. Explain the difference between the concepts self-fulfilling prophecy and Pygmalion effect. How are they similar? How are they different?

7. Do you agree that Mead's theory is too broad in scope to really be considered a theory? Explain your answer.

Online Learning Center (www. mhhe.com/west4e)

Visit the Online Learning Center at www.mhhe.com/west4e for chapter-specific resources, such as story-into-theory and multiple-choice quizzes, as well as theory summaries and theory connection questions.

CHAPTER 6

Coordinated Management of Meaning

Based on the research of **W. Barnett Pearce** *and* **Vernon Cronen**

The Taylor-Murphys

About four years ago, Jessie Taylor decided that she could not stay in her abusive marriage and left her husband, taking her two children—Megan, 13, and Melissa, 9—with her. They currently live in a small apartment, and Jessie knows that the place is too cramped for the three of them. Yet, with her upcoming marriage to Ben Murphy, Jessie realizes that her living situation will change very soon. Her work hours as a new law clerk, however, are quite long; at times, she must be in the office for twelve-hour days. As a result, Jessie's children frequently require adult supervision in the early evening. Although Jessie would rather be at home with her children, she realizes that she cannot count on her ex-husband's child support payments, and she must keep her job. She hopes that her approaching marriage to Ben will help ease the financial and familial challenges.

Ben Murphy's wife died a little over a year ago. He parents his 4-year-old son, Patrick, but gets a great deal of help from both his mother and his two sisters. He feels bad about leaving Patrick but is grateful that his family is there, because his job as a state trooper is frequently unpredictable. He never really knows when he is going to be called out for an emergency or when he will be asked to work overtime. Lately, however, his sisters have made some comments, and Ben worries that the baby-sitting may be turning into a burden for them

and his mom. Ben is hoping that his marriage to Jessie will ease his reliance upon his mother and sisters.

One evening, as Ben and Jessie are discussing final wedding plans, the two begin to talk about their future family. Ben is very excited about raising three children and looks forward to his son, Patrick, having new siblings. Jessie, however, is nervous about the logistics of bringing new people into her children's lives. Megan and Melissa are not pleased about their upcoming "blended" family. They have already had disagreements with Ben about a number of issues, including computer use and after-school activities.

As Ben and Jessie sit in front of the fireplace, they openly talk about the challenges, obstacles, and frustrations that they know they will experience in just a few months. Ben admits, "First, I need to tell you that I love you and that should be the most important thing right now. And I really think that the kids will come around in time—probably after we've been together for a while. A lot of families in our situation start out like this. There's a lot of chaos and then things begin to settle down. Hey, we're not all that unusual."

Jessie agrees. "Yeah, I know we're not the first family arranged this way. And I know things will work out. But when? And how are we all going to keep from screaming at each other while we work it all out? Adjusting can take some time." Her words are greeted by a warm hug from Ben.

Many people take their conversations for granted. When individuals speak to one another, they often fall into predictable patterns of talk and rely on prescribed social norms. To understand what takes place during a conversation, Barnett Pearce and Vernon Cronen developed Coordinated Management of Meaning (CMM). For Pearce and Cronen, people communicate on the basis of rules. Rules figure prominently in this theory; the theorists contend that rules help us not only in our communication with others but also in our interpretation of what others are communicating to us. CMM helps explain how individuals co-create the meaning in a conversation. Jessie Taylor and Ben Murphy, for instance, are beginning to forge rules and patterns that will govern their new family's interaction.

For our purposes, Coordinated Management of Meaning generally refers to how individuals establish rules for creating and interpreting meaning and how those rules are enmeshed in a conversation where meaning is constantly being coordinated. Human communication, therefore, is guided by rules. Cronen, Pearce, and Harris's (1982) summary of CMM is informative here: "CMM theory describes human actors as attempting to achieve coordination by managing the ways messages take on meaning" (p. 68). And it is important to note that Pearce (2007) succinctly underscores the transactional nature of communication we identified in Chapter 1 by noting: "CMM invites you to ask, of the passing moment, 'What are we making together?'" (p. xi). Clearly, the theory requires an understanding of the co-creation of "social worlds" that Pearce believes exist. Finally, Pearce (2004) notes, "CMM is a way of thinking about ourselves. Its ultimate questions are 'who are we?' and 'how shall we live?'" (p. 10). As we discuss this theory in this chapter, we will underscore a number of issues associated with it.

All the World's a Stage

To describe life experiences, Pearce and Cronen (1980) use the metaphor "undirected theater" (p. 120). They believe that in life, as in theater, a number of actors are following some sort of dramatic action and other actors are producing "a cacophonous bedlam with isolated points of coherence" (p. 121). Pearce (1989) describes this metaphor in eloquent detail:

> Imagine a very special kind of theater. There is no audience: everyone is "on stage" and is a participant. There are many props, but they are not neatly organized: In some portions of the stage are jumbles of costumes and furniture; In others, properties have been arranged as a set for a contemporary office; in yet another, they depict a medieval castle. . . . Actors move about the stage, encountering sets, would-be directors, and other actors who might provide a supporting cast for a production of some play. (p. 48)

The theorists believe that in this theatrical world, there is no one grand director, but rather a number of self-appointed directors who manage to keep the chaos in check.

Conversational flow is essentially a theater production. Interactants direct their own dramas, and, at times, the plots thicken without any script. For many people, how they produce meaning is equivalent to their effectiveness as communicators. To continue the metaphor, when actors enter a conversation, they rely on their past acting experiences to achieve meaning. How they perceive the play is their reality, but the roles they play in the production are not known until the production begins. To this end, the actors are constantly coordinating their scripts with one another.

The theatrical metaphor was later reconsidered by Pearce (2007). He noted that it was somewhat ineffective as he considered the ebb and flow of conversations and the unpredictability of dialogue. As you might imagine, conversations are frequently chaotic. Pearce and Cronen indicate that the actors who are able to read another's script will attain conversational coherence. Those who do not will need to coordinate their meaning. Of course, even agreeing upon what conversational script to follow can be difficult. Jessie and Ben, for example, may agree that achieving family harmony is essential but may not agree on how to achieve that harmony. As Pearce (1989) observes, people may battle it out with respect to what script they will enact and then continue to argue about it.

This notion of a creative theatrical production was in stark contrast to the perspective held by other researchers when CMM was conceptualized. Early discussions of CMM centered on the need to break away from the empirical tradition that characterized much theory building at that time. To shape their theory, Pearce and Cronen looked to a number of different disciplines, including philosophy (Wittgenstein), psychology (James), and education (Dewey). Before delving into the theory's central features, we first consider three assumptions of the Coordinated Management of Meaning.

Theory at a Glance • Coordinated Management of Meaning

In conversations and through the messages we send and receive, people co-create meaning. As we create our social worlds, we employ various rules to construct and coordinate meaning. That is, rules guide communication between people. CMM focuses on the relationship between an individual and his or her society. Through a hierarchical structure, people come to organize meaning of literally hundreds of messages received throughout the day.

Assumptions of Coordinated Management of Meaning

CMM focuses on the self and its relationship to others; it examines how an individual assigns meaning to a message. The theory is especially important because it focuses on the relationship between an individual and his or her society (Philipsen, 1995). Referring back to the theater metaphor, consider the fact that all actors must be able to improvise—using their personal repertoire of acting experiences—as well as reference the scripts that they bring into the drama.

Human beings, therefore, are capable of creating and interpreting meaning. There are a few other assumptions as well:

- Human beings live in communication.
- Human beings co-create a social reality.
- Information transactions depend on personal and interpersonal meaning.

The first assumption of CMM points to the centrality of communication. That is, human beings live *in* communication. Communication is, as noted in Chapter 1, a dynamic process that is more than talk; communication, according to CMM, is also a way creating and doing things (Pearce, 2007). Pearce (1989) claims that "communication is, and always has been, far more central to whatever it means to be a human being than had ever been supposed" (p. 3). That is, we live in communication. In adopting this claim, Pearce rejects traditional models of the communication process such as the linear model to which we referred in Chapter 1. Rather, CMM theorists propose a counterintuitive orientation: They believe that social situations are created by interactions. Because individuals create their conversational reality, each interaction has the potential to be unique. This perspective requires CMM adherents to cast aside their preexisting views of what it means to be a communicator. Further, CMM theorists call for a reexamination of how individuals view communication because "Western intellectual history has tended to use communication as if it were an odorless, colorless, tasteless vehicle of thought and expression" (Pearce, 1989, p. 17). Pearce and Cronen contend that communication must be reconfigured and contextualized in order to begin to understand human behavior. When researchers begin this journey of redefinition, they start investigating the consequences of communication, not the behaviors or variables that accompany the communication process (Cronen, 1995a).

To illustrate this assumption, consider our opening story. Although Jessie and Ben believe that they have covered most of the details associated with merging their families, many more issues will appear as the families come together. Family members will create new realities for themselves, and these realities will be based on communication. Conversations will frequently be determined by what the family knows as well as what the family does not know. That is, parents and children will work through unexpected as well as expected joys and sorrows. Like many families in their situation, they may stumble upon areas they never considered. The two families will be working from different sets of conversation rules and therefore may arrive at very different conclusions as they discuss important issues.

A second assumption of CMM is that human beings co-create a social reality. Although we implied this assumption earlier, it merits delineation. The belief that people in conversations co-construct their social reality is called **social constructionism.** Pearce (2007) is clear in his social construction advocacy. He observes: "Rather than 'What did you mean by that?' the relevant questions are 'What are we making together?' 'How are we making it?' and

social constructionism
belief that people co-construct their social reality in conversations

social reality
a person's beliefs
about how meaning
and action fit within
an interpersonal
interaction

'How can we make better social worlds?'" (pp. 30–31). These social worlds require an understanding of **social reality,** which refers to a person's beliefs about how meaning and action fit within his or her interpersonal encounters. When two people engage in a conversation, they each come with a host of past conversational experiences from previous social realities. Current conversations, however, elicit new realities because two people are arriving at the conversation from different vantage points. In this way, two people co-create a new social reality.

Sometimes, these communication experiences are smooth; at other times they are cumbersome. As Gerry Philipsen (1995) concludes, "Many interactions are more messy than clean and more awkward than elegant" (p. 19). Our opening example of Jessie and Ben illustrates this assumption. Although Jessie and Ben have been dating for some time and are preparing for their wedding, CMM theorists believe that they will continue to co-create a new social reality. For instance, the two will have to manage the issue of Jessie's daughters' reluctance to support the marriage. As Jessie and Ben discuss the matter in front of the fireplace, regardless of how they have previously discussed it, they create a new social reality. Perhaps some new issues will emerge—child support, Jessie's job, the age of the children, Jessie's ex-spouse, and so forth—or perhaps Jessie, Ben, or both will adopt new perspectives on their future family makeup. In any event, the social reality that the two experience will be a shared reality.

T*I*P

Theory Into Practice

Alejandro

I am not a "rules" person and I'm glad I work in a company where the people break all the rules. We don't have a "new employee" orientation and so there is no rule for how employees get introduced to our company. There are no rules for when and where we take our breaks. I just think that even though a lot of relationships have different kinds of rules, the place where I work simply forgets about the rules. Eventually, I'm sure, we'll have to change all that if a new owner takes over!

personal meaning
the meaning achieved
when a person brings
his or her unique
experiences to an
interaction

The third assumption guiding CMM relates to the manner in which people control conversations. Specifically, information transactions depend on personal and interpersonal meaning, as distinguished by Donald Cushman and Gordon Whiting (1972). **Personal meaning** is defined as the meaning achieved when a person interacts with another and brings into the interaction his or her unique experiences. Cushman and Whiting suggest that personal meaning is derived from the experiences people have with one another, and yet "it is improbable that two individuals will interpret the same experience in a similar manner . . . and equally improbable that they would select the same symbolic patterns to represent the experience" (p. 220). Personal meaning helps people in discovery; that is, it not only allows us to discover information about ourselves but also aids in our discovery about other people.

When two people agree on each other's interpretation, they are said to achieve **interpersonal meaning.** Cushman and Whiting (1972) argue that interpersonal meaning can be understood within a variety of contexts, including families, small groups, and organizations. They note that interpersonal meaning is co-constructed by the participants. Achieving interpersonal meaning may take some time because relationships are complex and deal with multiple communication issues. A family, for example, may be challenged with financial problems one day, child-raising concerns the next, and elderly care the next. Each of these scenarios may require family members to engage in unique communication pertaining to that particular family episode.

Personal and interpersonal meanings are achieved in conversations, frequently without much thought. Perceptive individuals recognize that they cannot engage in specialized personal meaning without explaining themselves to others. Cushman and Whiting tell us that interpersonal meaning must often be negotiated so that rules of meanings move from "in-house usage" to "standardized usage." Sharing meaning for particular symbols, however, is complicated by the fact that the meaning of many symbols is left unstated. For instance, consider a physician specializing in AIDS who discusses recent drug therapies with a group of college students. As the physician discusses AIDS, she must talk in laypersons' terms so that audience members will understand. However, despite honest efforts at avoiding jargon, it may be nearly impossible to avoid it completely. That is, as much as the physician tries, time may not permit her to fully explain the meaning of all specialized terms.

These three assumptions form a backdrop for discussing Coordinated Management of Meaning. As these assumptions indicate, the theory rests primarily on the concepts of communication, social reality, and meaning. In addition, we can better understand the theory by examining a number of other issues in detail. Among these issues is the manner in which meaning is categorized.

interpersonal meaning
the result when two people agree on each other's interpretations of an interaction

The Hierarchy of Organized Meaning

According to CMM theorists, human beings organize meanings in a hierarchical manner. This is one of the core features of CMM, so we will discuss this at length. First we examine the meaning behind this claim, and then we look at the framework associated with the assumption. We have highlighted the hierarchy in Figure 6.1.

Suggesting that people organize meaning implies that they are able to determine how much weight to give to a particular message. It is true that people are constantly being bombarded with stimuli and that they must be able to organize the stimuli for communication to occur. This thinking is relevant to CMM. Imagine, for instance, Ian arriving at his new job on Monday

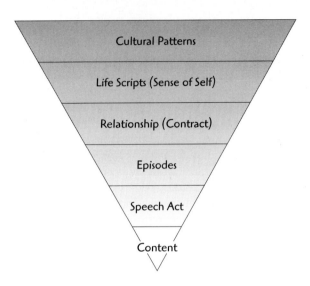

Figure 6.1
Hierarchy of Meaning
Source: Adapted from
Pearce & Cronen, 1980.

Cultural Patterns

Life Scripts (Sense of Self)

Relationship (Contract)

Episodes

Speech Act

Content

morning. Throughout the day he will be exposed to a number of messages. From understanding company policy on medical leaves to overtime pay to computer terminal safety, Ian must manage countless messages. As he returns home at the end of the day, he must organize the messages. In some way, he must try to coherently frame literally hundreds of messages from his day.

The process of organizing for Ian is similar to what many people experience when they speak to others. When people come together, they must try to handle not only the messages that are sent to them from others but also the messages that they send to others. This helps people understand the full meaning of the messages. Let's consider how Pearce and Cronen (1980) illustrate the management of meaning.

CMM theorists propose six levels of meaning: content, speech acts, episodes, relationship, life scripts, and cultural patterns. As you read about the levels, keep in mind that higher levels help us to interpret lower-level meanings. That is, each type is embedded in the other. In addition, Pearce and Cronen prefer to use this hierarchy as a model rather than as a true ordering system. They believe that no true ordering is appropriate because people differ in their interpretation of meaning at various levels. So, the theorists propose a hierarchy to help us understand the sequencing of meaning in different people.

Content

content
the conversion of raw
data into meaning

The **content** level specifies the first step of converting raw data into some meaning. For instance, during your break at work, you may convert the symbols being observed or sent into some sort of meaning by their content. You may group information you hear about the boss in one category, information about the workplace environment in a second category, and information about the pay scale in a third category. For Ben Murphy in our chapter's opening, the words "I love you" convey information about Ben's reaction to Jessie, but the content of his words requires this additional level of meaning. Imagine the content level as a message without a context (Pearce, Cronen, & Conklin, 1979).

Speech Act

In discussing the second level of meaning, Pearce (2007) describes **speech acts** as a "class of very familiar things, such as *promises, threats, insults, speculations, guesses,* and *compliments*" (p. 105). These are actions we perform by speaking. Speech acts communicate the intention of the speaker and indicate how a particular communication should be taken. Using our earlier example of Ben Murphy, when Ben states, "I love you," to Jessie, the phrase communicates more than an assertion. The phrase carries an affectional tone because of the speech act (Austin, 1975).

Furthermore, Pearce (1994) notes that "speech acts are not things; they are configurations in the logic of meaning and action of conversations, and these configurations are co-constructed" (p. 119). Therefore, we should be aware that two people co-create the meaning of the speech act, a belief we talked about in our earlier assumption of CMM. Frequently, the speech act is defined both by the sender and by the response to what others have said or done. As Pearce concludes, "You cannot be a 'victim' unless there is a 'victimizer'" (p. 119). In addition, the relational history must be taken into consideration when interpreting a speech act. It is difficult to figure out what a message means unless we have a sense of the dynamics between the participants. And, it's important to point out that speech acts don't always involve speech; Pearce acknowledges the importance of nonverbal communication, too.

speech act
action we perform by speaking (e.g., questioning, complimenting, or threatening)

Episodes

To interpret speech acts, Pearce and Cronen (1980) discuss **episodes**, or communication routines that have definable beginnings, middles, and endings. In a sense, episodes describe contexts in which people act. At this level, we begin to see the influence of context on meaning. Episodes vary tremendously—from picking up a hitchhiker to talking to your doctor about a diagnosis to having an affair with a co-worker to fighting with your roommate over dirty dishes. Pearce (2007) states that episodes are sequences of speech acts that are "linked together as a story" (p. 132). Individuals in a communication exchange may differ in how they **punctuate** an episode. Punctuation pertains to how interactions are organized into a meaningful pattern. Pearce and Conklin (1979) clearly note that "coherent conversation requires some degree of coordinated punctuation" (p. 78). Different punctuation, however, may elicit different impressions of the episode, thereby creating "inside" and "outside" perspectives of the same episode. For example, Ben Murphy and Jessie Taylor may have punctuated differently their previous discussions about their future together. Ben may believe that dealing with the children will be better left until after their wedding, whereas Jessie may believe that the issue should be dealt with beforehand. Their subsequent episodes, therefore, will be partly determined by the way they handle their punctuation differences. Pearce (1976) believes that

episodes
communication routines that have recognized beginnings, middles, and endings

punctuate
how individuals interpret or emphasize an episode

episodes are essentially imprecise because the actors in social situations find themselves in episodes that vary tremendously. He also notes that episodes are culturally based in that people bring to their interactions cultural expectations for how episodes should be executed.

Relationship

relationship
agreement and understanding between two people

The fourth level of meaning is the **relationship,** whereby two people recognize their potential and limitations as relational partners.

Pearce (2007) expands our traditional understanding of relationship. In addition to partnerships between and among friends, spouses, and family members, he also believes that relationships can include "larger, less personal relationships such as corporations, cities, religions, and tennis clubs" (p. 200). He asserts that, in a sense, we're all "related" because of genes, language, and the planet's forces on each of us. These all coalesce to connect us, willingly or unwillingly.

Relationships are like contracts, which set guidelines and often prescribe behavior. In addition, relationships suggest a future. Few people take the time to outline relational issues unless they are concerned about their future together.

enmeshment
extent to which partners identify themselves as part of a system

The relationship level suggests relational boundaries in that parameters are established for attitudes and behavior—for instance, how partners should speak to each other or what topics are considered taboo in their relationship. Pearce and Cronen (1980) note that boundaries distinguish between "we" and "they," or those people who are included in the contract and those who are not. The theorists use the term **enmeshment** to describe the extent to which people identify themselves as part of the relational system.

A relationship may prove invaluable as two people discuss issues that are especially challenging. For instance, there will certainly be some difficult discussions once the Murphy-Taylor family resides together. Knowing the relational boundaries and the expectations the family members hold for themselves as well as for one another will be important as they become a stepfamily. Although upcoming events will be trying for this family, they will be managed more effectively with an understanding of the contract.

Life Scripts

life scripts
clusters of past or present episodes that create a system of manageable meanings with others

Clusters of past and present episodes are defined as **life scripts.** Think of life scripts as autobiographies that communicate with your sense of self. You are who you are because of the life scripts in which you have engaged. And how you view yourself over your lifetime affects how you communicate with others. Imagine the differences between Ben Murphy's and Jessie Taylor's life scripts. Their past episodic experiences will be very informative as they try to deal with their future plans together. Ben comes from a very supportive and loving family, so he may expect conversations with Jessie to be characterized by these nurturing episodes. In fact, it is likely that his experiences as a single father and his perceptions of parenthood are less troubled because of past episodes co-created with his biological family. Jessie, however, did not have an affirming relationship with her ex-husband. Consequently, her past debilitating episodes influence how she now communicates with Ben. Moreover, in her interactions with Ben, she may expect something very different from what Ben expects from her. We should point out, though, that life scripts include those episodes that two people construct together. So, once Ben and Jessie begin to co-create their social world, they will simultaneously co-create a life script.

Cultural Patterns

When discussing cultural patterns, Pearce and Cronen (1980) contend that people identify with particular groups in particular cultures. Also, each of us behaves according to the actual values of our society. These values pertain to sex, race, class, and spiritual identity, among others. **Cultural patterns,** or archetypes, can be described as "very broad images of world order and [a person's] relationship to that order" (Cronen & Pearce, 1981, p. 21). That is, an individual's relationship to the larger culture is relevant when interpreting meaning. Speech acts, episode relationships, and life scripts are all understood within the cultural level. This is even more paramount when two people from two different cultures try to understand the meaning of each other's words. For instance, Larry Samovar, Richard Porter, and Edwin McDaniel (2007) point out that the U.S. culture puts a premium on **individualism,** or the notion that the interests of an individual are put before the interests of the group. Individualism focuses on independence and initiative. Other cultures (such as Colombia, Peru, and Taiwan) emphasize **collectivism,** or the notion that the interests of the group are put before the interests of the individual. Difficulty may arise when two people representing two different orientations interpret meaning from their particular vantage point. Culture, therefore, requires shared meanings and values.

The levels of meaning espoused by Pearce and Cronen are critical to consider when conversing with another. However, keep in mind that the theorists contend that their purpose is to model the way people process information, not to establish a true ordering. Also, remember that individuals vary in their past and present interactions. Therefore, some people will have highly complex hierarchies and others will have simplified hierarchies. In addition, some people are able to interpret complex meaning, while others are not as proficient. The hierarchy of meaning is an important framework in helping us understand how meaning is coordinated and managed.

Charmed and Strange Loops

The hierarchy of meaning presented earlier suggests that some lower levels can reflect back and affect the meaning of higher levels. Pearce and Cronen (1980) have termed this process of reflexivity a **loop.** Because the hierarchy cannot go on forever, the theorists propose that some levels reflect back. This supports their view that communication is an ongoing, dynamic, and ever-changing process, a topic we discussed in Chapter 1.

When loops are consistent throughout the hierarchy, Pearce and Cronen identify them as a **charmed loop.** Charmed loops occur when one part of the

cultural patterns
images of the world and a person's relationship to it

individualism
prioritizing personal needs or values over the needs or values of a group (I-identity)

collectivism
prioritizing group needs or values over the needs or values of an individual (we-identity)

loop
the reflexiveness of levels in the hierarchy of meaning

charmed loop
rules of meaning are consistent throughout the loop

Research Notes

Montgomery, E. (2004). Tortured families: A coordinated management of meaning analysis. *Family Process, 43,* 349–371.

The application of CMM is clearly evidenced in this research study. Looking at the difficult subject of torture in refugee families, Montgomery employs CMM principles and elements to understand families from the Middle East (fourteen individuals) whose father had been detained and tortured. Montgomery concludes by indicating that all families "placed their experiences in their own hierarchically built meaning systems" (p. 368). Furthermore, unwanted repetitive patterns of conflict often existed for spouses; at present, couples report no such conflicts. Finally, a discussion of the various life scripts held by family members is detailed.

Pearce, K. A., & Pearce, W. B. (2001). The Public Dialogue Consortium's school-wide dialogue process: A communication approach to develop citizenship skills and enhance school climate. *Communication Theory, 11,* 105–123.

Pearce and Pearce examined the nonprofit group, the Public Dialogue Consortium (PDC), and applied principles of CMM to ascertain the theory's utility and practical value. Looking specifically at a middle school and three high schools, the authors contend that their examination includes various conversations, underscoring a key feature in CMM. They believe that CMM has important value to community members associated with the PDC, practitioners, and other communication theorists. The researchers conceptualized the SHEDD model of public dialogue. SHEDD is an acronym for getting <u>S</u>tarted, <u>H</u>earing all voices, <u>E</u>nriching the conversation, <u>D</u>eliberating the options, and <u>D</u>eciding how to move forward together. Designing public dialogue and embracing the practicality of theories such as CMM are essential according to these authors.

hierarchy confirms or supports another level. Furthermore, the rules of meaning are consistent and agreed upon throughout the loop. Figure 6.2 illustrates a charmed loop. Note that there is consistency, or confirmation, in the loop. To illustrate, consider the following example. You hired a painter to repaint the first floor of your home. You agreed to pay the painter by the hour, and when you receive the bill you are shocked at the price. You confront the painter, stating that you observed a lot of "wasted" hours and that you are not going to pay the entire bill. The painter is prepared to challenge your judgment.

This encounter between painter and client exemplifies a charmed loop. In this case, the episode, or event, is the disagreement you both have over the costs of painting your home. Because your life script is your sense of self, your life script in this encounter is consistent with your passion to stand up for what you believe. In this example, the cultural pattern suggests that the two of you—painter and client—enter the conflict with two different views of the situation. The painter wants to get paid for a service and the client wants to feel satisfied with the service. In this brief example, the loop is charmed in that there is consistency among the levels (episode, life script, cultural pattern) in the hierarchy. In other words, the encounter makes sense in that your willingness to challenge the bill is *consistent* with who you are. And the way you communicate with

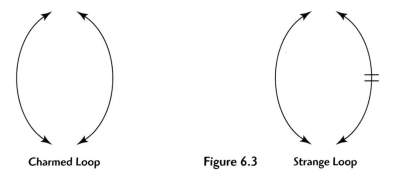

| Figure 6.2 | Charmed Loop | | Figure 6.3 | Strange Loop |

the painter is *consistent* with the cultural expectations of this type of relationship (i.e., you expect efficiency). The rules of meaning in this interaction are confirmed throughout the loop.

At times, however, some episodes are inconsistent with levels higher up in the hierarchy. Pearce and Cronen have called this a **strange loop.** Strange loops usually align with *intra*personal communication in that individuals engage in a sort of internal dialogue about their self-destructive behaviors. In a basic sense, if, for example, you thought you were a good student, but your professor gave you a "C" and a "D" on recent papers, your perception does not confirm the grade, and the grades do not confirm your perception. We illustrate strange loops in Figure 6.3.

To exemplify strange loops, the theorists offer the case of an alcoholic whose bouts with sobriety are followed by bouts of drinking. We present this strange loop in Figure 6.4. In this strange loop, confusion sets in. The life script of an alcoholic, for instance, suggests that drinking is out of control, so the alcoholic refuses to drink. But once the drinking stops, an alcoholic may feel a sense of control, so drinking begins again. In this example, the life script is the person's alcoholism, which manages meaning (or drinking) in particular episodes. The episodes are part of the alcoholic's life script. It's apparent, then, that the strange loop will continue to repeat itself. We call this a vicious cycle. With this background, we now turn our attention to the issue of coordination and examine its meaning in CMM.

strange loop
rules of meaning change within the loop

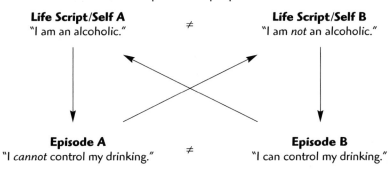

Cultural Pattern: It is important for people to control their behavior.

Life Script/Self A
"I am an alcoholic."

≠

Life Script/Self B
"I am *not* an alcoholic."

Episode A
"I *cannot* control my drinking."

≠

Episode B
"I can control my drinking."

Figure 6.4
Example of a Strange Loop
Source: Adapted from Pearce, 2004.

The Coordination of Meaning: Making Sense of the Sequence

In his discussion of coordination, Pearce believes that coordination is best understood by watching people interact on a daily basis. Underscoring the first assumption of CMM, Pearce (2007) concludes that "'coordination' is probably not the first word that leaps to your mind when someone says 'communication.' Perhaps it should be" (p. 83).

coordination
trying to make sense of message sequencing

Because people enter conversations with a variety of abilities and competencies, achieving coordination can be difficult at times. Coordination with others is challenging, in part because others try to coordinate their actions with ours. **Coordination** exists when two people try to make sense out of the sequencing of messages in their conversation. Three outcomes are possible when two people converse: They achieve coordination, they do not achieve coordination, or they achieve some degree of coordination (Philipsen, 1995). Gerry Philipsen reminds us that social reality is not perfectly coordinated, so the most likely outcome is partially achieved coordination.

Let's look at some examples of perfect coordination, no coordination, and partial coordination by borrowing the experiences of Jessie Taylor and Ben Murphy. They are discussing an upcoming camping trip:

BEN: We need to be straightforward with the girls now. I don't see any problem with sleeping in the same tent and letting the kids sleep in their tent. Patrick can sleep with us if he gets upset.

JESSIE: I think you're right. He should have fun with the girls.

BEN: Also, they love him, which makes it easier for all of us.

JESSIE: The weekend should be a great bonding time for the families.

The two have coordinated their meanings of what to do with their children on the first family trip. Although each is entering the conversation with different experiences, Ben and Jessie have created a completed episode of meaning. Perfect coordination is attained.

However, things are not usually this smooth when discussing such complex issues. For instance:

BEN: We need to be straightforward with the girls now. I don't see any problem with sleeping in the same tent and letting the kids sleep in their tent. Patrick can sleep with us if he gets upset.

JESSIE: My girls will not like that. Are you trying to say that our feelings are more important than our kids' feelings?

BEN: I didn't say that. . . .

JESSIE: Why would you even think that? Our first trip together shouldn't be spent trying to explain why Mom and Dad want their privacy.

BEN: All I was trying to do was to let the kids know that Mom and Dad need to have their own space.

JESSIE: And that they need to deal with their own problems?! Look, I may be overreacting here, but . . .

BEN: I'm sorry that I ever brought up the issue.

As you can see, this episode is quite different from the previous one. In fact, it appears that Ben and Jessie have different interpretations of what the other is saying, which prevents coordination from being achieved.

The following dialogue represents partial coordination of meaning:

BEN: We need to be straightforward with the girls now. I don't see any problem with sleeping in the same tent and letting the kids sleep in their tent. Patrick can sleep with us if he gets upset.

JESSIE: It's more complicated than that. This is the first time that we're all going to be together for a weekend.

BEN: Honey, if we don't try this right away, it'll be more difficult when we all move in together.

JESSIE: But the kids are still trying to get this situation all figured out. Separating things out this way may be more of a pain than we thought.

BEN: How about if we bought a larger tent and let the kids sleep on one side and we'll be on the other?

JESSIE: That should work.

This partially coordinated dialogue closes the episode between the two parents. Both appear to be satisfied with the compromised sleeping arrangements.

Influences on the Coordination Process

Coordination is influenced by several issues, including a sense of morality and the availability of resources. In this section, we examine both areas.

First, coordination requires that individuals be concerned with a higher moral order (Pearce, 1989). Many CMM theorists, like Pearce, explain morality as honor, dignity, and character. Moral order involves ethics, a topic we touched on in Chapter 1. Moral order is essentially an opportunity for individuals to assert an ethical stance in a conversation. CMM theorists contend that ethics is an inherent part of the conversational flow.

Each person brings various moral orders into a conversation to create and complete the episode. Pearce contends that people simultaneously perform various roles, such as sister, mother, lover, student, employee, friend, and citizen. He believes that each of these roles carries various rights and responsibilities that differ from one person to another. Difficulty arises, however, if inconsistent moral obligations exist in conversations. For instance, in some cultures, men are identified as the sole decision makers and chief protectors of their family. This may conflict with women's obligations and may affect the coordination process in their conversations. These value differences may play themselves out throughout a relationship.

In addition to morality, coordination can be influenced by the resources available to an individual. When CMM theorists discuss **resources**, they refer to "the stories, images, symbols, and institutions that persons use to make their world meaningful" (Pearce, 1989, p. 23). Resources also include perceptions, memories, and concepts that help people achieve coherence in their social realities.

resources
stories, symbols, and images that people use to make sense of their world

When resources in a conversation vary from one person to another, coordination is challenged. To better understand this notion, consider the experiences of Loran and Wil. As a nineteen-year employee of a local textile mill, Loran is respected by the seven employees he supervises. Although he does not have a college degree, he relishes his seniority in a company that almost shut down a few years ago. Wil, however, has a college degree and an MBA. Because the company is interested in energizing its employees with fresh perspectives on management, it is hiring college graduates with management savvy. As a result, Wil became a new supervisor in Loran's department. These changes were marked by heated discussions and a great deal of disagreement between Loran and Wil. Loran's resources—his historical understanding of the factory, his relationships with his employees, the stories shared with others, the perceptions he has of the company's goals, and so forth—seem to be secondary to Wil's resources. Wil's resources are limited, because he has little understanding of the company's history, but he does bring his college education to his job, a credential shared by few at the factory. Because an incompatibility between resources exists, Loran and Wil may have difficulty coordinating their meaning. Two important, but incompatible, sets of resources exist between Loran and Wil, and each may threaten conversation coordination.

Coordinating conversations is critical to communication. At times, coordinating with others is simple, but at other times it is quite challenging. People bring different resources into conversations, prompting individuals to respond to others based on their own management of meaning. In addition to resources, coordination relies on the rules that conversationalists follow. We now explore rules and their relationship to CMM.

Rules and Unwanted Repetitive Patterns

One way that individuals manage and coordinate meaning is through the use of rules. Earlier in the chapter we mentioned that CMM follows a rules perspective, "meaning that people enter into dialogues with a framework for how to behave." For CMM theorists, rules provide people opportunities to choose between alternatives. Once rules are established in a dialogue, interactants will have a sufficiently common symbolic framework for communication (Cushman & Whiting, 1972). CMM theorists argue that rule usage in a conversation is more than an ability to use a rule; it also requires "flexible expanding abilities that cannot be reduced to technique" (Cronen, 1995b, p. 224). Rules, therefore, are more than prescriptions for behavior. Interactants must understand the social reality and then incorporate rules as they decide how to act in a given situation.

Pearce and Cronen (1980) discuss two types of rules: constitutive and regulative. **Constitutive rules** refer to how behavior should be interpreted within a given context. In other words, constitutive rules tell us what types of behavior mean. We are able to understand another person's intention because of the constitutive rules in place. For example, saying "I love you" has different

constitutive rules organize behavior and help us to understand how meaning should be interpreted

"Let's stop this before we both say a lot of things we mean."

implications when you speak to a roommate, a lover, a family member, or even a co-worker. In each of these relationships, we adopt a rule that suggests that the relationship type (contract) and the episode will determine how the statement should be received. Constitutive rules, then, help individuals assign meaning.

A second type of rule assisting coordination is the regulative rule. Constitutive rules assist people in their interpretation of meaning, but they do not provide people with guidelines for behavior. That is the function of regulative rules. **Regulative rules** refer to some sequence of action that an individual undertakes, and they communicate what happens next in a conversation. There are, for instance, regulative rules for meeting a new co-worker. You generally introduce yourself, welcome your colleague to the workplace, and indicate that you're available to answer appropriate questions.

regulative rules
guidelines for
people's behavior

To understand the interfacing of constitutive and regulative rules, consider the following situation. A couple married twenty years is having a crisis. The wife has discovered her husband's extramarital affair and must now decide what constitutive and regulative rules to follow. She decides on a venting session because the constitutive rule tells her that such an affair is wrong in their marriage. In turn, her husband must determine how to interpret the venting (constitutive rule) and must construct some sequence of response (regulative rule). As the two engage in their discussion (and co-create their social reality), they will ultimately discover each other's rules systems. Although they have been married for two decades, this situation has not surfaced before, and consequently they may not know what the possibilities are in terms of constitutive and regulative rules. As this discovery takes place, it is likely that

unwanted repetitive patterns (URPs)
recurring, undesirable conflicts in a relationship

the coordination of the conversation will be jeopardized. That is, each person may enact different episodes along the way. They may not always agree on the rules enacted, but at least they are able to make sense out of their conversational experiences.

If the couple continue to have sustained conflict, they may engage in what Cronen, Pearce, and Linda Snavely (1979) identify as unwanted repetitive patterns (URPs). **Unwanted repetitive patterns** are sequential and recurring conflictual episodes that are considered unwanted by the individuals in the conflict. The researchers studied hostile workplace relationships and noted that although privately each worker communicated a genuine desire to be amicable and efficient, publicly their discussions were hostile and ego bruising. This verbal sparring seemed to be ripe for explanation using CMM. The researchers explained that URPs arise because two people with particular rules systems follow a structure that obligates them to perform specific behaviors, regardless of their consequences. It may seem peculiar that people believe they are obligated to act a certain way. Yet Pearce (1989) reminds us that "persons find themselves in URPs . . . in which they report, with all sincerity, that 'I had no choice; I had to act this way'" (p. 39). Why do two people continue to engage in URPs? First, they may see no other option. That is, the couple may not possess the skill to remove themselves from the conflict. Second, the couple may be comfortable with the recurring conflict. They know each other and know how the other generally communicates in conflictual situations. Finally, a couple may simply be too exhausted to work toward conflict resolution.

Integration, Critique, and Closing

Coordinated Management of Meaning is one of the few theories to place communication explicitly as a cornerstone in its foundation. Because communication is central to the theory, many scholars have employed the theory in their writings. Among the criteria for evaluating a theory, four seem especially relevant for discussion: scope, parsimony, utility, and heurism.

Integration

Communication Tradition	Rhetorical | Semiotic | **Phenomenological** | **Cybernetic** | Socio-Psychological | **Socio-Cultural** | Critical
Communication Context	**Intrapersonal** | **Interpersonal** | Small Group | Organizational | Public/Rhetorical | Mass/Media | Cultural
Approach to Knowing	**Positivistic/Empirical** | **Interpretive/Hermeneutic** | Critical (early research) (recent research)

Critique

Evaluation Criteria	**Scope** | Logical Consistency | **Parsimony** | **Utility** | Testability | **Heurism** | Test of Time

Scope

It is unclear whether CMM is too broad in scope. Some communication scholars (e.g., Brenders, 1987) suggest that the theory is too abstract and that imprecise definitions exist. Further, Brenders believes that some of the ideas espoused by Pearce and Cronen lack parameters and beg clarification. The introduction of personal language systems, argues Brenders, is problematic and "leaves unexplained the social nature of meaning" (p. 342). Finally, M. Scott Poole (1983), in his review of CMM, notes that the theory may be problematic in that it is difficult to "paint with broad strokes and at the same time give difficult areas the attention they deserve" (p. 224).

Yet CMM theorists contend that such criticisms do not take into account the evolution of the theory and its refinement over the years (Barge & Pearce, 2004). Pearce (1995) candidly admits that during "the first phase of the CMM project, [our writings] were confused because we *could not* say what we were doing in the language of social science" (pp. 109–110). Therefore, critics should interpret the theory within the spirit of change; even theorists change as they clarify the goals of their theory. Furthermore, Cronen (1995b) admits some early problems with the conceptualization of CMM by indicating that the way he and Pearce discussed the creation of meaning was originally confusing and "wrong-headed." Pearce, Cronen, and other CMM theorists believe that those who levy indictments regarding the scope of the theory should understand the time period in which the theory was developed.

Parsimony

The scope may be broad, but do not think that the theory has not undergone tests of parsimony. At first glance, one may conclude that the theory is too cumbersome because it "is better understood as a worldview and open-ended set of concepts and model" (Barge & Pearce, 2004, p. 25). However, illustrating difficult concepts with a visual and succinct way of looking at conversations (vis-à-vis the hierarchy of meaning), for instance, has resulted in making CMM a model that is efficient and available. They go on to say that "there is no reason why any research method could not be used in CMM research" (p. 25). One could argue, then, that Pearce and Cronen's illustration of the hierarchy of meaning is a visual and succinct way of looking at conversations. Therefore, even cumbersome and complex conversations can be analyzed and understood.

Utility

The application of this theory to individuals and their conversations is quite apparent. The practicality of looking at how people achieve meaning, their potential recurring conflicts, and the influence of the self on the communication process is admirable. CMM is one of the few communication theories that has been identified by both theorists and CMM scholars as a "practical theory" (Barge, 2004). In fact, Pearce's later writings (2007) on the theory underscore his desire to put "CMM in practice" (p. 224). As well, he is direct in calling CMM a practical theory and notes that the one question guiding CMM is "How can we make better social worlds?" (p. 45). Finally, Pearce observes that the theory has evolved along three stages: interpretive, critical, and *practical*" [emphasis added] (p. 52). Pearce (2006) further elaborates on his desire to sustain CMM's pragmatic legacy: "The orienting question for CMM as a practical theory is, "How can we make better social worlds?"" (p. 45).

Heurism

CMM is a very heuristic theory, spanning a number of different content areas, including examining community and municipal groups (Dillon & Galanes, 2002; Pearce & Pearce, 2000), childhood obesity (Bruss et al., 2005), child and adolescent health (Salmon & Faris, 2006), refugee families (Montgomery, 2004), consumer research technology (Buttle, 1994), and the Chinese culture (Jia, 2001). Furthermore, researchers have incorporated the theory and its tenets to understand conflict (Pearce & Littlejohn, 1997), managerial leadership (Barge, 2004), domestic violence (Sundarajan & Spano, 2004), and families who have been tortured or persecuted across cultures (Montgomery, 2004).

Thanks in large part to CMM, we have a deeper understanding of how individuals co-create meaning in conversations. The theory has aided us in understanding the importance of rules in social situations. It is clear that few can deny that CMM positioned communication at the core of human experience.

Discussion Starters

1. What types of coordination will our opener's Taylor-Murphy family experience as they begin a life together? Try to identify stages that the family may experience and specific episodes of coordination.

2. How would you explain the reasoning behind Pearce and Cronen's hierarchy of meaning?

3. Discuss enmeshment and its relationship to conversations in your family. Be sure to define the term and apply it to your family relationships.

4. Chess and poker are games requiring coordination. Discuss some of life's "games" and how they require coordination. Be creative and give specific examples.

5. What types of meaning breakdowns have you experienced in your conversations with others? Be specific and identify the context, the situation, and the conversation topic.

6. Identify and explain a strange loop that exists in popular culture or in your interpersonal relationships.

7. Discuss specific ways in which any component of CMM has practical value to you as a college student. Identify the part of the theory that has relevancy to you and reasons for its applicability.

Online Learning Center www. mhhe.com/west4e

Visit the Online Learning Center at www.mhhe.com/west4e for chapter-specific resources, such as story-into-theory and multiple-choice quizzes, as well as theory summaries and theory connection questions.

CHAPTER 7

Cognitive Dissonance Theory

Based on the research of **Leon Festinger**

Ali Torres

Ali Torres shuffled the papers on her desk and looked out the office window. She was really bored with this job. When she initially signed on to work with the Puerto Rican Alliance in Gary, Indiana, she was so excited. The job seemed to be a dream come true. First, it offered her a chance to give back to her community—both the city of Gary and the Puerto Rican community within the city. She had grown up in Gary, Indiana, and knew firsthand how difficult it was to get ahead for people of color, especially Latinos. Latinos were a minority among minorities in this city, and it was tough to make much progress. Despite that, Ali had gotten a lot from growing up in Gary. When she was in high school, a friendly guidance counselor had offered her a helping hand and suggested that Ali consider college. Without Ms. Martinez's support, she never would have thought about college, much less actually graduated. But Ali had finished college and now she felt strongly about giving something back. So the job had seemed perfect; it would be a way for her to give back to the community and at the same time use her major in public relations.

Yet, in the six months Ali had worked in the Alliance office, her sole responsibilities had centered on typing and running errands. She felt like a gofer, with no chance to do anything she considered important. Actually, she was beginning to question whether the Alliance itself was doing anything worthwhile. Sometimes she thought the whole operation was just a front so politicians could say something was being done to help the Latino population in the city.

Her co-workers didn't seem to mind that they didn't do much all day, so Ali wasn't getting much support from them. But it was her boss's attitude that bothered Ali the most. He was a respected leader in the Latino community; she remembered him from when she was growing up. When she found out she would be working for him, she had been delighted. But as far as Ali could tell, he hardly ever worked at all. He was rarely in the office, and when he did come in, he took long lunch hours and many breaks. He spoke to Ali very infrequently and never gave her assignments.

Ali was feeling extremely frustrated. She was on her own to develop projects or, more likely, simply to put in eight hours doing a lot of nothing. Ali had decided that she would quit this job and start looking for something where she could feel more useful, but she was having a hard time giving up on her dream of contributing to her community. She had begun this job with such high hopes. She had expected to work to persuade funding agencies to sponsor programs to strengthen opportunities for the Latino community. Ironically, now she found that the only person she was persuading was herself, as she wrestled with the decision of whether to keep working or give up on this job. Ali spoke to some of her friends, who encouraged her to do what she thought was right and quit the Alliance if she wanted to. That made her feel better, but she couldn't completely shake her memories of the auspicious beginning of the job and all her high hopes.

Suppose you are Ali Torres's friend and are interested in knowing how she feels about her job. You notice that she seems a little depressed when she talks about work, and lately she hasn't brought up the subject at all. Her silence about her work is especially obvious to you compared with how enthusiastically she spoke about the position when she first started at the Alliance. You could ask Ali directly how she feels, but you wonder how honest she will be with you. You know Ali doesn't want you to worry about her. You also know that Ali cares a great deal about the ideals of the Alliance and that she might not want to tell you if she is disappointed. Your problem in this situation is inferring Ali's attitudes.

The problem faced by Ali's friend is a common one because people's attitudes cannot be directly observed; yet attitudes are believed to be excellent predictors of people's behaviors (O'Neill & Arendt, 2008). As Susan Fiske and Shelley Taylor (1984) observe, "Attitudes have always been accorded star status in social explanations of human behavior by lay people and professionals alike" (p. 341). Because of their importance, many theories try to explain attitude formation, change, and the interlocking relationship among cognitions, attitudes, affect, and behavioral tendencies. Many psychologists (for example, Rydell, Hugenberg, & McConnell, 2006) assert that the most influential approaches to attitudes come from cognitive consistency theories.

Consistency theories in general posit that the mind operates as an intermediary between stimulus and response. These theories assert that when people receive information (a stimulus), their mind organizes it into a pattern with other previously encountered stimuli. If the new stimulus does not fit the pattern, or is inconsistent, then people feel discomfort. For example, people who supported Barack Obama in the 2008 Democratic primaries found his decision not to take public financing jarring once he had garnered the delegates needed to become the nominee in June 2008. People who supported Obama as an agent of change had to cope with cognitive discomfort when he did something that seemed like "politics as usual." Ali Torres also feels this type of discomfort as she reflects on the discrepancy between her desire to respect her boss and her observations of his seeming indifference to the job. In these cases, consistency theorists note that there is a lack of balance among your **cognitions,** or ways of knowing, beliefs, judgments, and so forth.

Leon Festinger called this feeling of imbalance **cognitive dissonance;** this is the feeling people have when they "find themselves doing things that don't fit with what they know, or having opinions that do not fit with other opinions they hold" (1957, p. 4). This concept forms the core of Festinger's Cognitive Dissonance Theory (CDT), a theory that argues that dissonance is an uncomfortable feeling that motivates people to take steps to reduce it (Figure 7.1). As Roger Brown (1965) notes, the basics of the theory follow rather simple principles: "A state of cognitive dissonance is said to be a state of psychological discomfort or tension which motivates efforts to achieve consonance. *Dissonance* is the name for a disequilibrium and *consonance* the name for an equilibrium" (p. 584). Further, Brown points out that the theory allows for two elements to have three different relationships with each other: They may be consonant, dissonant, or irrelevant.

cognitions
ways of knowing, beliefs, judgments, and thoughts

cognitive dissonance
feeling of discomfort resulting from inconsistent attitudes, thoughts, and behaviors

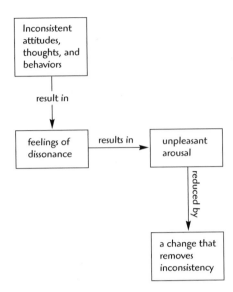

Figure 7.1
The Process
of Cognitive
Dissonance

Inconsistent attitudes, thoughts, and behaviors

result in

feelings of dissonance

results in

unpleasant arousal

reduced by

a change that removes inconsistency

consonant relationship
two elements in equilibrium with one another

dissonant relationship
two elements in disequilibrium with each other

irrelevant relationship
two elements that have no meaningful relation to each other

A **consonant relationship** exists between two elements when they are in equilibrium with one another. If you believe, for instance, that health and fitness are important goals and you work out three to five times a week, then your beliefs about health and your own behaviors would have a consonant relationship with one another. Ali would have a consonant relationship if she believed that the Alliance was really making a difference in the Latino community and that her work was meaningful. A **dissonant relationship** means that elements are in disequilibrium with one another. An example of a dissonant relationship would be if a practicing Catholic we'll call Rita also believes in a woman's right to choose abortion. In this case, Rita's religious beliefs are in conflict with her beliefs about abortion. In our opening story, Ali Torres is experiencing a dissonant relationship.

An **irrelevant relationship** exists when elements imply nothing about one another. This type of relationship is illustrated by believing that the speed limit should be raised to 65 miles per hour on all freeways and believing that women should have equal rights in the workplace. Although the two beliefs may indicate a general view endorsing individual freedoms, they basically have no relationship to each other. When beliefs are consonant or irrelevant, there is no psychological discomfort. However, if beliefs are dissonant, discomfort results.

The importance of cognitive dissonance for communication researchers rests on Festinger's assertion that the discomfort caused by dissonance motivates

Theory Application in Groups (TAG)

In small groups, create role plays that illustrate a consonant relationship, a dissonant relationship, and an irrelevant relationship.

change. As we see in our opening vignette, Ali Torres is feeling frustrated and uncomfortable in her job. Her initial belief about the opportunities for her to help others through this job and her prior high regard for her boss are inconsistent with her present situation. This is the point at which persuasion can occur. The theory suggests that to be persuasive, strategies should focus on the inconsistencies while providing new behaviors that allow for consistency or balance. Further, cognitive dissonance may motivate communication behavior as people seek to persuade others and as people strive to reduce their dissonant cognitions. For example, when Ali went to her friends to discuss her decision, she was seeking help in reducing dissonance. Her conversations with friends and her efforts at self-persuasion are examples of communication being used in the dissonance reduction process.

Cognitive Dissonance • Theory at a Glance

The experience of dissonance—incompatible beliefs and actions or two incompatible beliefs—is unpleasant, and people are highly motivated to avoid it. In their efforts to avoid feelings of dissonance, people will ignore views that oppose their own, change their beliefs to match their actions (or vice versa), and/or seek reassurances after making a difficult decision.

Assumptions of Cognitive Dissonance Theory

As we have indicated, Cognitive Dissonance Theory is an account of how beliefs and behavior change attitudes. Its focus is on the effects of inconsistency among cognitions. Our introductory material suggested a number of assumptions that frame CDT. Four assumptions basic to the theory include:

- Human beings desire consistency in their beliefs, attitudes, and behaviors.
- Dissonance is created by psychological inconsistencies.
- Dissonance is an aversive state that drives people to actions with measurable effects.
- Dissonance motivates efforts to achieve consonance and efforts toward dissonance reduction.

The first assumption portrays a model of human nature that is concerned with stability and consistency. When we discuss Uncertainty Reduction Theory in Chapter 9, you will see a similar conceptualization of human nature. Cognitive Dissonance Theory suggests that people do not enjoy inconsistencies in their thoughts and beliefs. Instead, they seek consistency. This is why Ali feels uncomfortable in her job and unhappy with her thoughts about quitting the job. She is seeking consistency, yet her perceptions of her job provide her with inconsistency.

The second assumption speaks to the kind of consistency that is important to people. The theory is not concerned with a strict logical consistency. Rather, it refers to the fact that cognitions must be psychologically inconsistent (as opposed to logically inconsistent) with one another to arouse cognitive dissonance. For example, if Ali Torres holds the cognition that "I want to contribute to my community," it is *not* logically inconsistent to also believe that the Alliance is not contributing much to the community. The two beliefs are not logically contradictory. Yet it is psychologically inconsistent for Ali to continue to work for the Alliance when she believes it is doing little to help Latinos in Gary, Indiana. That is, Ali will feel psychologically inconsistent by continuing to do nothing when she wishes to be of help. Ali also is stressed by her thoughts of quitting and her lingering hopes for what she might have accomplished in this job.

The third assumption of the theory suggests that when people experience psychological inconsistencies, the dissonance that is created is aversive. Thus, people do not enjoy being in a state of dissonance; it is an uncomfortable state. Festinger asserted that dissonance is a drive state possessing arousal properties. Since Festinger's initial conceptualization of the theory, a significant amount of research has supported this assumption (Rydell, McConnell, & Mackie, 2008; Zanna & Cooper, 1976). Another study (Elkin & Leippe, 1986) found that physiological arousal was related to dissonance. Cognitive Dissonance Theory would assume that Ali would feel uncomfortable as a result of the psychological dissonance that she is experiencing.

Finally, the theory assumes that the arousal generated by dissonance will motivate people to avoid situations that create inconsistencies and strive toward situations that restore consistency. Thus, the picture of human nature that frames the theory is one of seeking psychological consistency as a result of the arousal caused by the aversive state of inconsistent cognitions (Figure 7.2).

Figure 7.2
Consistency in
Beliefs, Attitudes,
and Behaviors

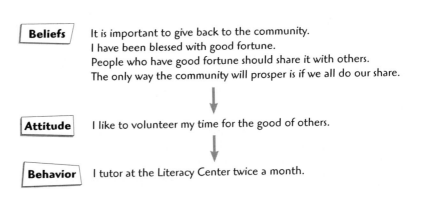

Beliefs
It is important to give back to the community.
I have been blessed with good fortune.
People who have good fortune should share it with others.
The only way the community will prosper is if we all do our share.

Attitude
I like to volunteer my time for the good of others.

Behavior
I tutor at the Literacy Center twice a month.

Concepts and Processes of Cognitive Dissonance

As the theory developed over the years, certain concepts were refined. For example, the following scenario illustrates a situation where dissonance would arise: If Juan believes that relationships should be completely harmonious (a cognition) and yet he argues a great deal with his partner (a conflicting cognition), the theory predicts that Juan will become tense and suffer discomfort. When dissonance theorists seek to predict how much discomfort or dissonance Juan will suffer, they invoke many concepts, which we will discuss in some detail.

Magnitude of Dissonance

The first concept is **magnitude of dissonance,** which refers to the quantitative amount of dissonance a person experiences. Magnitude of dissonance will determine actions people may take and cognitions they may espouse to reduce the dissonance. The theory differentiates between situations producing more dissonance and those producing less dissonance.

Three factors influence the magnitude of dissonance a person will feel (Zimbardo, Ebbesen, & Maslach, 1977). First, the degree of **importance,** or how significant the issue is, affects the degree of dissonance felt. If, for example, Juan has many friendships and activities outside his relationship and his partner is not critically important to him, the theory predicts that his magnitude of dissonance will be small. But if Juan finds much of his identity and social interaction in his relationship with his partner, then the magnitude of dissonance should be greater. The same could be said for Ali Torres. If she does a great deal of volunteer work in the community and her job is not the main source of her identity, then the magnitude of her dissonance is not as great as if her job is critically important to her.

Second, the amount of dissonance is affected by the **dissonance ratio,** or the amount of dissonant cognitions relative to the amount of consonant cognitions. Given Juan's propensity to argue with his partner, he probably has many cognitions that are relevant to that behavior. Some of these cognitions are consistent with his behavior; for example, "It is good to get feelings out in the open." "It is positive to feel you can really be yourself with your partner." "Sometimes arguing allows you both to see problems in a creative way." Several of his cognitions are dissonant with conflict behavior, however. For example, consider: "If we really loved each other, we wouldn't argue so much." "We spend so much time fighting, we never have any fun." "Our fights are so repetitive, we never solve anything." "My parents never argued with each other; we must not be very sensitive to each other." "I didn't picture my relationship like this." Because Juan has more dissonant cognitions than consonant ones, the ratio is negative. Thus, Juan is likely to feel that there is inconsistency, and dissonance will result. If the ratio were more balanced, Juan would feel less dissonance.

Finally, the magnitude of dissonance is affected by the rationale that an individual summons to justify the inconsistency. The **rationale** refers to the

magnitude of dissonance
the quantitative amount of discomfort felt

importance
a factor in determining magnitude of dissonance; refers to how significant the issue is

dissonance ratio
a factor in determining magnitude of dissonance; the amount of consonant cognitions relative to the dissonant ones

rationale
a factor in determining magnitude of dissonance; refers to the reasoning employed to explain the inconsistency

reasoning employed to explain why an inconsistency exists. The more reasons one has to account for the discrepancy, the less dissonance one will feel. For instance, if Juan and his partner have just moved, changed or lost a job, purchased a home, or experienced any other stressor, Juan may be able to justify the conflicts as being a result of the stress he is feeling and thus probably a temporary situation. In this case, it is likely that the dissonance he feels will be much less than if he is unable to come up with any rationale explaining his behaviors (Matz & Wood, 2005).

Coping With Dissonance

Although Cognitive Dissonance Theory explains that dissonance can be reduced through both behavioral and attitudinal changes, most of the research has focused on the latter. Many ways to increase consistency are cognitively based, and the theory suggests several methods Juan may use to reduce his dissonance. First, Juan could add or subtract cognitions to change the ratio of consonant to dissonant cognitions. In Juan's case, this might mean adding the fact that his friends Jeff and Don fight a lot but seem to be happy, and subtracting the idea that he didn't picture his relationship as full of conflict. Alternatively, Juan might try to reduce the importance of the dissonant cognitions. He might think about the fact that children do not know much about their parents' relationship, so the fact that he did not think his parents fought a lot might not weigh too heavily in the equation. Finally, Juan could seek out information that advocates conflict in relationships and stresses the benefits of open communication between partners. He might discredit the information that suggests conflict is not good for a relationship by believing that it comes from an unrealistic, overly optimistic point of view. In sum, we can cope with dissonance by (1) adding to our consonant beliefs, (2) reducing the importance of our dissonant beliefs, or (3) changing our beliefs to seemingly eliminate the dissonance in some way.

Cognitive Dissonance and Perception

As Juan engages in any of these strategies to change his cognitions and reduce his feelings of dissonance, perceptual processes come into play. Specifically, Cognitive Dissonance Theory relates to the processes of selective exposure, selective attention, selective interpretation, and selective retention because the theory predicts that people will avoid information that increases dissonance. These perceptual processes are basic to this avoidance.

selective exposure
a method for reducing dissonance by seeking information that is consonant with current beliefs and actions

Selective exposure, or seeking consistent information not already present, helps to reduce dissonance. CDT predicts that people will avoid information that increases dissonance and seek out information that is consistent with their attitudes and behavior. In the example of the conflictual relationship, Juan might seek friends who also fight a great deal yet seem to be happy in their relationships.

selective attention
a method for reducing dissonance by paying attention to information that is consonant with current beliefs and actions

Selective attention refers to looking at consistent information once it is there. People attend to information in their environment that conforms to their attitudes and beliefs while ignoring information that is inconsistent. Thus, Ali

Torres might read favorable articles about the Alliance in the newspaper while overlooking articles that suggest contrary views.

Selective interpretation involves interpreting ambiguous information so that it becomes consistent. Utilizing selective interpretation, most people interpret close friends' attitudes as more congruent with their own than is actually true (Berscheid & Walster, 1978). Elaine Showalter (1997) discusses the seeming inconsistency of being a feminist critic while also loving to shop and wear feminine clothing and accessories. She interprets advice given to her by an academic about dressing conservatively as actually agreeing with her position that we should put "the *femme* back into feminist" (p. 80). People use selective interpretation to avoid potential dissonance.

Finally, **selective retention** refers to remembering and learning consistent information with much greater ability than we do inconsistent information. Cognitive Dissonance Theory predicts that if a couple were arguing about whether to spend a vacation camping or on a cruise, the partner who wished to camp would not remember the details of the cruise package and the one desiring the cruise would not remember much about the camping plans. If Juan heard a lecture once about how important conflict can be in close relationships, he may well remember that in his current situation of frequent fighting with his partner. Similarly, Ali might focus on stories she heard in the past about good works that the Alliance has done.

Attitudes seem to organize memory in this selective retention process (Lingle & Ostrom, 1981). When thinking about someone as your teacher, you will remember her ability to lecture, her command of the subject, her ability to get a discussion started, and her accessibility to help you with assignments. If, on the other hand, you were thinking about the same person as an actor, you would recall her ability to project a character and to gain your interest. Once you have formed an attitude about someone as a teacher rather than an actor, that influences your recall about that person.

Minimal Justification

One of the interesting and counterintuitive assertions that Festinger advances in this theory has to do with what he calls minimal justification. **Minimal justification** has to do with offering only the minimum incentive required to get someone to change. Festinger (1957) argues that "if one wanted to obtain private change in addition to mere public compliance, the best way to do this would be to offer just enough reward or punishment to elicit compliance" (p. 95).

The experiment that Festinger and his colleague James Carlsmith performed that established the principle of minimal justification is the now-famous one dollar/twenty dollars study. Festinger and Carlsmith (1959) recruited male students at Stanford University and assigned them to do a boring, repetitive task consisting of sorting spools into lots of twelve and giving square pegs a quarter turn to the right. At the end of an hour of this monotonous assignment, the experimenter asked the research participants to do him a favor. The researcher explained that they needed another person to continue doing this task and offered to pay the participants to recruit a woman in the waiting room by telling

selective interpretation
a method for reducing dissonance by interpreting ambiguous information so that it becomes consistent with current beliefs and actions

selective retention
a method for reducing dissonance by remembering information that is consonant with current beliefs and actions

minimal justification
offering the least amount of incentive necessary to obtain compliance

Theory Into Practice

Nancy

I certainly have experienced buyer's remorse. And I think I probably handled it in the way Cognitive Dissonance Theory predicts. When my husband and I bought our first house, I was a nervous wreck and the only way I calmed myself down was to think about how bad our other choices were and to spend time talking with Neil about how great this house was. We kind of talked ourselves into believing we made a fabulous choice.

her how enjoyable the task was. This woman was actually a research assistant also, and she was helping the researchers examine how the men tried to persuade her. Some of the men were offered one dollar to recruit the woman, whereas others were offered twenty dollars for the same behavior. Remember, this was 1959, and both these sums were worth a great deal more than they are now. Festinger and Carlsmith found that the men engaged in this study differed in their attitudes at the end. Those who received twenty dollars for recruiting the woman said that they really thought the task was boring, whereas those who received only one dollar stated that they really believed the task was enjoyable.

From these results came the notion of minimal justification. Festinger and Carlsmith argue that doing something a person does not believe in for a minimal reward sets up more dissonance than doing that same thing for a larger reward. If people engage in deception for a lot of money, they will acknowledge that they did it for the money. If they engage in deception for only one dollar, they do not have a ready explanation that will make their attitudes and behaviors form a consonant relationship. To reduce their dissonance, they have to make some type of change to bring consistency to their cognitions. Therefore, they may change their opinion of the task to make sense of why they told the woman in the waiting room that it was fun. Now they believe they told her it was fun because, in fact, it *was* enjoyable. Thus, minimal justification sets up more cognitive dissonance and requires more change to reduce it than a more substantial justification would.

Cognitive Dissonance Theory and Persuasion

Much of the research following from Festinger's work focuses on persuasion, especially with regard to decision making. A large amount of research concentrates on cognitive dissonance as a postdecision phenomenon. Several studies examine **buyer's remorse**, which refers to the dissonance people often feel after deciding on a large purchase. An interesting study about buyer's remorse related to automobile purchases (Donnelly & Ivancevich, 1970). In their study,

buyer's remorse
postdecision dissonance related to a purchase

they located people who were waiting for delivery of cars they had signed contracts to buy. These people were divided into two groups. One group was contacted twice to reassure them about the wisdom of their purchase. Another group was not contacted between the contract signing and the delivery of the car. About twice as many in the group that was not contacted canceled the order for the car. This finding supported the theory that dissonance may be activated after making a large purchase. Further, the study showed that providing people with information about the wisdom of their decision can reduce the dissonance. This finding speaks to the importance of the decision and to manipulating the dissonance ratio, factors we discussed earlier in the chapter.

Another study (Knox & Inkster, 1968) investigated this regret period after a decision in a different context. This study had experimenters approach people either shortly before or shortly after they had placed a two-dollar bet at a Canadian racetrack. The bettors were asked how confident they felt about their horse's chances. Their findings indicated that people were more confident that their horse would win after they had placed the bet than they were before they placed the bet. They interpreted these findings as consistent with CDT because they reasoned that after the bet has been placed, people feel dissonance. The decision to choose one particular horse is dissonant with the belief that the horse has flaws that could prevent it from winning the race. A simple coping mechanism for reducing this dissonance is to increase the beliefs about the attractiveness of the horse that you bet on, or the chosen alternative. Thus, the theory would predict, and Knox and Inkster found, bettors expressing more confidence after making their decision than before. As Robert Wicklund and Jack W. Brehm (1976) point out, when a decision is irrevocable, as in a bet placed, people have to work quickly to reduce the inevitable dissonance that results.

A more recent study (Brownstein, Read, & Simon, 2004) also looked at cognitive dissonance at the racetrack. Participants were given information about horses and then were asked to rate each horse's chance of winning the race. The respondents rated the horses three times before placing their bets and one time afterward. Consistent with Cognitive Dissonance Theory's predictions, the researchers found that the ratings of the chosen horse increased after the choice had been made.

Vani Simmons, Monica Webb, and Thomas Brandon (2004) studied whether cognitive dissonance principles could help college students stop smoking. They tested an experimental learning intervention based on the theory. One hundred forty-four college students who smoked were asked to create educational videos about the risks of smoking or about quitting smoking. They found that intentions to quit smoking were increased by making the videos.

Festinger and two colleagues also examined postdecision dissonance in a pioneering case study (Festinger, Riecken, & Schachter, 1956). Festinger and his colleagues joined a doomsday cult based in Chicago in the 1950s. The group was led by a middle-aged man and woman. The woman, whom the researchers named Mrs. Keech, began to receive messages from spiritual beings who seemed to be predicting a great disaster, a flood that would end the world. Then the spiritual beings transmitted information to Mrs. Keech that the members of the cult would be saved before the flood. The group was instructed that spacemen would arrive and transport the believers to safety on another planet. The believers began to make preparations for the end of their world and their departure to another world. The appointed time for departure was midnight, and the group gathered in Mrs. Keech's living room to await the spaceship that would take them to safety. As the moments slipped by, it became apparent that no one was coming to rescue the believers, and, in fact, they did not need to be rescued because the world was not under water. At first, the cult seemed on the verge of disintegration as a result of the extreme dissonance everyone was feeling. Yet the group was so committed to their beliefs that they found ways to reconcile the dissonance.

The group reconciled their dissonance in two specific ways. First, Mrs. Keech claimed a new message came from the spiritual beings telling the group that their faith had caused God to save the world from destruction. Thus, the group used selective interpretation and allowed new information through selective attention. Second, Mrs. Keech said she had received an additional message telling the group to publicize the situation. The group became energized again, reduced their dissonance, and confirmed themselves in their decision to be members of the group.

Some researchers have observed the relationship of dissonance and communication strategies in situations other than decision making. Patrice Buzzanell and Lynn Turner (2003) examined family communication in families where the major wage earner had lost his or her job within the past eighteen months. Buzzanell and Turner interviewed family members to assess the communication issues created by the job loss.

Buzzanell and Turner found that job loss did create feelings of dissonance in most family members, and the researchers argued that family members reduced their dissonance about job loss by using three interesting strategies. First, families adopted a tone of normalcy, telling the interviewers that nothing had really changed after the job loss. Second, families deliberately foregrounded positive themes and backgrounded negative ones. Finally, families maintained gendered identity construction, working to assure the man who had lost his job that he was still the man of the family. In all of these strategies, family members worked to reduce the dissonance created by job loss.

In yet another context, Patricia Sullivan and Lynn Turner (1996) examined strategies used by female politicians to cope with assumptions about women in the public domain. Sullivan and Turner profiled several women in public life in the 1990s. One of their case studies was of Lani Guinier, who was nominated by President Clinton to be the Assistant Attorney General for Civil Rights. Guinier withdrew her nomination before the confirmation hearings after suffering scathing treatment in the press concerning her views on affirmative action and voting rights. Sullivan and Turner argue that Guinier did not speak out during this time because she believed that the truth would vindicate her. Sullivan and Turner imply that Guinier sought to play by the rules, because to do otherwise would have caused her too much dissonance. Her strategy for coping and keeping consistency ultimately cost her the chance to defend herself in confirmation hearings.

Research Notes

DeSantis, A. D., & Morgan, S. E. (2003). Sometimes a cigar [magazine] is more than just a cigar [magazine]: Pro-smoking arguments in *Cigar Aficionado*, *1992–2000. Health Communication, 15*, 457–480.

This study examines the magazine *Cigar Aficionado* from a rhetorical approach to analyze the pro-smoking arguments it advances. The authors analyzed the forty-one issues of the magazine from its inception in 1992 to the last issue of the 2000 calendar year. They found more than 380 pro-smoking arguments, which they defined as "any assertion made in the periodical that defended smoking against anti-smoking health claims" (p. 461).

Each of the arguments was organized into one of the following seven categories:

1. Cigars are not cigarettes.
2. Life is dangerous.
3. Cigars have health benefits.
4. The moderation argument
5. The old-smokers argument
6. The bad-science argument
7. The good-science argument

After a brief review of the evidence, the authors assert that cigar smoking is quite hazardous to health, and they note that many health professionals and nonsmokers cannot understand why people continue to smoke cigars. They argue that the reason, at least in part, may be that these pro-smoking arguments offered by *Cigar Aficionado* provide a major source of cognitive dissonance reduction.

They note that people can experience cognitive dissonance from a variety of sources, such as inconsistency (saying smoking is no problem, but experiencing a hacking cough), cultural mores (noticing the many places where a person can no longer smoke in public), opinion generality (believing oneself to be logical but continuing to smoke in the face of evidence that says it's harmful), or past experience (knowing someone who died from a disease attributed to smoking). They observe that smokers likely feel dissonance from all of these sources.

The authors proceed to illustrate each of the seven arguments advanced in the magazine as methods offered to readers to reduce this dissonance. For instance, in detailing the cigars are not cigarettes argument, the authors note that the magazine creates a "cognitive buffer" between the established health risks of cigarettes and cigar smoking.

The authors conclude with suggestions for countering these pro-smoking arguments based on an understanding of the cognitive processes detailed in Cognitive Dissonance Theory. They note that "until prevention agencies begin to take *Cigar Aficionado* more seriously, view the magazine as a diligent pro-smoking force, and become more strategic and dynamic in their message construction, cigar smokers will continue to light up, dissonance-free" (p. 479).

Matz, D. C., & Wood, W. (2005). Cognitive dissonance in groups: The consequences of disagreement. *Journal of Personality and Social Psychology, 88*, 1–22.

This article begins with the premise, adopted from Festinger's work, that social groups are both vehicles for reducing cognitive dissonance and sources for generating it. The authors conduct three studies demonstrating group-generated dissonance. Their findings are consistent with the predictions of Cognitive Dissonance Theory. Participants in groups with others who disagreed with them experienced more dissonance than those in groups with others who agreed with them. Participants who believed they had little to no choice in the group they were in experienced less dissonance from disagreements than those who thought they had chosen their group.

(continued)

Sun, C. F., & Scharrer, E. (2004). Staying true to Disney: College students' resistance to criticism of *The Little Mermaid*. *The Communication Review*, *7*, 35–55.

This article reviews a media literacy program employed in a college classroom. The program included an extended analysis and critique of the Disney movie, *The Little Mermaid,* combined with a reading of the Hans Christian Andersen tale on which the movie was based. One hundred three written samples from the final project for the class were analyzed for this study.

The authors found that students resisted a critical analysis of the Disney film. In the end, the media literacy program was largely unsuccessful in getting students to be more critical consumers of media that challenge the dominant ideology surrounding the mediated images and messages. To explain this result, the authors draw on Cognitive Dissonance Theory stating that this theory provides important insights into students' resistance. The authors argue that dissonance was created when the students had to weigh their past favorable experience with Disney against the material of the class, which was largely negative and pointed out the problematic issues in the film. Therefore, the students were motivated to reduce their dissonance. Their written work at the end of the program revealed several strategies aimed at doing just that.

As this brief review indicates, CDT has been employed in countless studies examining decision making. Recent studies have explored the processes of dissonance and dissonance reduction in contexts such as family (Buzzanell & Turner, 2003), friendships (G. B. White, 2006), business (Shinnar, Young, & Meana, 2004), political communication (Sullivan & Turner, 1996), and the classroom (Boysen, 2008; Sun & Scharrer, 2004). Thus, CDT continues to be a theoretical force for explaining communication behaviors.

Integration, Critique, and Closing

Although researchers have been using and revising Festinger's theory since 1957, and some scholars point to the theory as the primary achievement of social psychology (Aron & Aron, 1989), the theory does have weaknesses and detractors. Most of the criticisms have to do with the utility and testability of the theory.

Integration

Communication Tradition	Rhetorical	Semiotic	Phenomenological	Cybernetic	**Socio-Psychological**	Socio-Cultural	Critical
Communication Context	**Intrapersonal**	Interpersonal	Small Group	Organizational	Public/Rhetorical	Mass/Media	Cultural
Approach to Knowing	**Positivistic/Empirical**	Interpretive/Hermeneutic	Critical

Critique

| Evaluation Criteria | Scope | Logical Consistency | Parsimony | **Utility** | **Testability** | Heurism | Test of Time |

Utility

One concern of CDT relates to critics' complaints that that the theory may not possess utility because other theoretical frameworks can explain the attitude change found in the one dollar/twenty dollars experiment better than cognitive dissonance.

Irving Janis and Robert Gilmore (1965) argue that when people participate in an inconsistency, such as arguing a position they do not believe in, they become motivated to think up all the arguments in favor of the position while suppressing all the arguments against it. Janis and Gilmore call this process biased scanning. This biased scanning process should increase the chances of accepting the new position—for example, changing one's position from evaluating the spool-sorting task as dull to the position that it really was an interesting task.

Janis and Gilmore (1965) note that when a person is overcompensated for engaging in biased scanning, suspicion and guilt are aroused. Thus, they are able to explain why the large incentive of twenty dollars does not cause the students in Festinger and Carlsmith's (1959) experiment to have an increased attitude change.

Other researchers (Cooper & Fazio, 1984) argue that the original theory of cognitive dissonance contains a great deal of "conceptual fuzziness." Some researchers note that the concept of dissonance is confounded by self-concept or impression management. Impression management refers to the activities people engage in to look good to themselves and others. For example, Elliot Aronson (1969) argues that people wish to appear reasonable to themselves and suggests that in Festinger and Carlsmith's (1959) experiment, if "dissonance exists, it is because the individual's behavior is inconsistent with his self-concept" (p. 27). Aronson asserts that the Stanford students' dissonance resulted from seeing themselves as upright and truthful men contrasted with their behavior of deceiving someone else because they were being paid to do so.

In the study we discussed earlier by Patrice Buzzanell and Lynn Turner (2003) concerning family communication and job loss, we could conceive of the strategies the families adopted as employing impression management rather than reducing dissonance. When fathers reported that nothing had changed in their family despite the job loss, they may have been rationalizing to continue to seem reasonable to themselves, just as Aronson suggests.

In the preceding critiques, researchers disagree about what cognitive state is at work: dissonance, biased scanning, or impression management. Daryl Bem (1967) argues that the central concept of importance is not *any* type of cognition but, rather, is behavioral. Bem states that rather than dissonance in cognitions operating to change people, self-perception is at work. Self-perception simply means that people make conclusions about their own attitudes the same way others do—by observing their behavior. Bem's alternative explanation allows more simplicity in the theory as well.

In Bem's conceptualization, it is not necessary to speculate about the degree of cognitive dissonance that a person feels. People only need to observe what they are doing to calculate what their attitudes must be. For instance, if I am not working out regularly, but I believe fitness and health are important goals, I must not really believe working out is so important to good health. In our chapter opening story about Ali Torres, Bem would argue that the longer Ali works at the Alliance, the more likely she is to come to believe that she is doing something worthwhile. Bem's argument suggests that if Ali's mother asks her if she likes her job, she might reply, "I guess I do. I am still there."

Claude Steele's work (Steele, 1988; Steele, Spencer, & Lynch, 1993) also offers a behavioral explanation for dissonance effects: self-affirmation. However, unlike Bem, Steele and his colleagues argue that dissonance is the result of behaving in a manner that threatens one's sense of moral integrity. You can see how this explanation might work quite well in Ali Torres's situation. Her discomfort might not be because she holds two contradictory beliefs but because she doesn't respect herself for staying in a job where she is not accomplishing anything of significance.

Other scholars believe that Cognitive Dissonance Theory is basically useful and explanatory but needs some refinements. For example, Wicklund and Brehm (1976) argue that CDT is not clear enough about the conditions under which dissonance leads to change in attitudes. They believe that choice is the missing concept in the theory. Wicklund and Brehm posit that when people believe they have a choice about the dissonant relationship, they will be motivated to change that relationship. If people think they are powerless, then they will not be bothered by the dissonance, and they probably will not change. Regarding our beginning scenario about Ali Torres, Wicklund and Brehm would argue that we could predict whether she will leave her job based on how much choice she believes she has in the matter. If, for instance, she is tied to Gary, Indiana, because of family responsibilities or if she believes she would have trouble locating a new job in the city, she may not be motivated to act on her dissonant cognitions. On the other hand, if nothing really ties her to Gary, or there are plenty of other job opportunities, she will be motivated to change based on those same cognitions.

Another refinement is suggested by the work of Joel Cooper and Jeff Stone (2000). Cooper and Stone point out that in the more than 1,000 studies using CDT, only rarely has the group membership of the person experiencing dissonance been considered. Cooper and Stone believe that group membership plays an important role in how people experience and reduce dissonance. For example, they found that social identity derived from religious and political groups had an impact on how people responded to dissonance.

Other critics note that CDT is not as useful as it should be because it does not provide a full explanation for how and when people will attempt to reduce dissonance. First, there is what has been called the "multiple mode" problem. This problem exists because, given a dissonance-producing situation, there are multiple ways to reduce the dissonance. As we discussed earlier in the chapter, there are several ways to bring about more consonance (such as changing your mind or engaging in selective exposure, attention, interpretation, or retention). The weakness in the theory is that it doesn't allow precise predictions.

This prediction problem is also apparent in the fact that the theory does not speak to the issue of individual differences. People vary in their

Theory Into Practice

Amelia

T*I*P

This theory makes so much sense, and I can apply it to my own struggle to quit smoking. I know smoking isn't good for me, and I have tried to quit. Everyone tells me I should; and I know it's true. It makes me feel like an idiot that I continue to do something that's harmful to my health. But it's so hard to quit. I have noticed that I use some of the ways to reduce dissonance that the theory talks about. Like I've said that everyone has to die of something, so I've tried to reduce the importance of the dissonance. And I've also mentioned that I smoke low tar cigarettes, and I don't smoke as much as some of my friends—trying to add to the consonant beliefs. The only technique I haven't actually used is to quit, which would remove the dissonance completely!

tolerance for dissonance, and the theory fails to specify how this factors in to its explanation.

Testability

Another weakness that scholars point out relates specifically to our criterion of testability. As you recall, testability refers to the theory's likelihood of ever being proven false. Theories that have a seeming escape clause against being falsified are not as strong as those that do not. Researchers have pointed out that because Cognitive Dissonance Theory asserts that dissonance will motivate people to act, when people do not act, proponents of the theory can say that the dissonance must not have been strong enough, rather than concluding that the theory is wrong. In this way it is difficult to disprove the theory.

Although Cognitive Dissonance Theory has its shortcomings, it does offer us insight into the relationship among attitudes, cognitions, affect, and behaviors, and it does suggest routes to attitude change and persuasion. Social cognition researchers as well as communication scholars continue to use many of the ideas from CDT. As Steven Littlejohn and Karen Foss (2008) observe, Festinger's theory is not only the most important consistency theory, it is one of the most significant theories in social psychology. CDT has been the framework for over a thousand research studies (Perloff, 1993), most of which have supported the theory. Additionally, numerous critiques and interpretations have refined and revised the theory. And some researchers (Harmon-Jones, 2000) believe that continuing to refine the theory by examining cognitions more specifically, for example, will yield rich theoretical insights.

Cognitive Dissonance Theory has contributed greatly to our understanding of cognitions and their relationship to behaviors. The concept of dissonance remains a powerful one in the research literature, informing studies in psychology, cognitive psychology, communication, and other related fields.

Discussion Starters

1. Explain the relationship of selective attention, exposure, interpretation, and retention to cognitive dissonance. Provide examples where appropriate. How do you think Ali Torres might use these processes, given her situation?

2. Give an example of two attitudes you hold that have an irrelevant relationship to each other. Cite two consonant attitudes you hold. Do you have any attitudes that are dissonant with each other? If so, have you done anything about them? Explain how your actions fit with the theory.

3. What do you think about the problem of CDT's testability suggested in this chapter? Could the theory be revised to make it testable?

4. Suppose you want some friends to change their drinking and driving behaviors. How could you apply the theory in persuading your friends?

5. Do you agree with the minimal justification notion? Provide an example in which minimal justification seemed to work to persuade someone.

6. How do you think group membership affects dissonance and what role do you believe it plays in dissonance reduction?

7. Besides persuasion, what other communication applications might you have for CDT?

Online Learning Center (www. mhhe.com/west4e)

Visit the Online Learning Center at www.mhhe.com/west4e for chapter-specific resources, such as story-into-theory and multiple-choice quizzes, as well as theory summaries and theory connection questions.

CHAPTER 8

Expectancy Violations Theory

*Based on the research of **Judee Burgoon***

Margie Russo

As she prepared for her interview with Ingraham Polling, Margie Russo felt confident that she would be able to handle any questions posed to her. As a 44-year-old mother of three young children, she felt that her life experiences alone would help her respond to any of the more difficult questions. She was a Girl Scout leader, served as treasurer of the Parent Teacher Association at the middle school, and worked part-time as an executive assistant. She knew these experiences would be invaluable as she answered questions in her interview.

Despite her confidence, Margie suddenly felt anxious about her interview with Janet Mueller, the polling company's human resources representative. When told by the office assistant that Ms. Mueller was ready to see her, Margie approached Janet's office, knocked on her door, and went into the room. When she was still more than 10 feet away from the big desk, Janet looked up and asked, "Are you Ms. Russo?" Margie responded, "I am." Janet replied, "Well, c'mon over here and sit down and let's chat a bit."

As Margie approached her interviewer, an uneasy feeling fell over her, a nervousness that she had never experienced before and had certainly not expected. Janet could sense Margie's anxiety and asked if she could get her some coffee or tea. "No, thank you," said Margie. "Well, why don't you sit down?" asked Janet.

Margie really wanted this job. She had been preparing for the interview with her husband, who asked her a number of different kinds of questions the night before. She didn't want to lose her chance at getting this job.

As the two sat and discussed the job and its responsibilities, Margie's mind began to wander. Why was she so nervous? She had been around people, and she knew that she had expertise for the job. Yet Margie was very nervous, and she had butterflies in her stomach.

Janet focused on the duties Margie would be responsible for and to whom she would report. As she spoke, Janet walked around her office a bit, at times leaning on the side of her desk in front of Margie's chair. Janet had a number of different questions remaining but wanted Margie to speak. She asked her whether she had seen a good movie recently. "Oh, sorry, Janet," Margie replied. "I just don't have time for movies."

"I guess I should have figured that out," said Janet. "You really are a busy person. I'm very impressed by how you seem to manage so many things at one time. Your children are very lucky. How does your family do when you're so busy?"

"Oh, they're fine, thanks. I do get some free time, but I try to spend as much time as I can with my children." Margie was feeling more relaxed as she began to talk about how busy she was helping her two daughters sell Girl Scout cookies. She then talked about her ability to juggle several things at once.

Janet responded, "That's great! Let's talk some more about how you handle deadlines."

It was apparent that as the two talked Margie became more comfortable speaking to Janet. Eventually, she dismissed her nervousness and felt that she was well on her way to becoming employed with Ingraham Polling.

◼

An important part of any discussion of communication is the role of nonverbal communication. What we do in a conversation (or how we say something) can be more important than what we actually say (Knapp & Hall, 2010; Richmond, McCroskey, & Hickson, 2008). To understand nonverbal communication and its effects on messages in a conversation, Judee Burgoon developed Expectancy Violations Theory (1978). Since that time, Burgoon and a number of her associates have studied various messages and the influence of nonverbal communication on message production. Burgoon (1994) discusses the intersection of nonverbal communication and message production when she states that "nonverbal cues are an inherent and essential part of message creation (production) and interpretation (processing)" (p. 239). The theory, following a positivistic, covering law approach, was originally called the Nonverbal Expectancy Violations Theory, but Burgoon later dropped the word *nonverbal* because the theory now examines issues beyond the domain of nonverbal communication, something that we will explore a bit later in the chapter. Nonetheless, from its early beginnings in the late 1970s, Expectancy Violations Theory (EVT) has been a leading theory in identifying the influence of nonverbal communication on behavior.

Our opening story of Margie Russo and Janet Mueller represents the nature of the theory. Margie entered the conversation with her interviewer with a sense of trepidation, and once their brief interaction was under way, she began to feel uneasy about the manner in which the space between them changed. Janet moved closer to Margie during the interview, causing Margie to feel uncomfortable. However, once the conversation centered on Margie's children, she did not view Janet or her closeness as a threat to her confidence.

Expectancy Violations Theory (EVT) suggests that people hold expectations about the nonverbal behavior of others. Burgoon contends that unexpected changes in conversational distance between communicators are arousing and frequently ambiguous. Interpreting the meaning behind an expectancy violation depends on how favorably the "violator" is perceived. Returning to our opening scenario, in many interviews, the interviewer is not expected to lean on a desk in front of the job candidate. When this occurred, Margie became uncomfortable. It was only after Janet began to talk about the movies that Margie began to feel more at ease. In other words, she started to view Janet in a more favorable light.

In our discussion thus far, we have been using examples from nonverbal communication, primarily distance. Burgoon's (1978) early writing on EVT integrated specific instances of nonverbal communication; namely, personal space and people's expectations of conversational distance. Because personal space is a core concept of the theory, we will explore it in more detail. Also, because spatial violations constitute a primary feature of the theory, it is important to understand the various spatial distances before we delve further into the theory. Finally, examining the spatial framework undergirding EVT will give you an historical understanding of the theory.

Space Relations

The study of a person's use of space is called **proxemics**. Proxemics includes the way people use space in their conversations as well as perceptions of another's use of space. Many people take spatial relations between communicators for granted, yet, as Dale Leathers and Michael Eaves (2008) conclude, people's use of space can seriously affect their ability to achieve desired goals. Spatial use can influence meaning and message, and people's spaces have intrigued researchers for some time. Burgoon began her original work on EVT by studying interpretations of space violations.

Burgoon (1978) starts from the premise that humans have two competing needs: affiliation and personal space. **Personal space,** according to Burgoon, can be defined as "an invisible, variable volume of space surrounding an individual which defines that individual's preferred distance from others" (p. 130). Burgoon and other Expectancy Violations writers believe that people simultaneously desire to stay in close proximity to others but also desire some distance. This is a perplexing but realistic dilemma for most of us. Few people can exist in isolation, and yet people prefer their privacy at times.

Proxemic Zones

Burgoon's Expectancy Violations Theory has been informed by the pioneering and classic work of anthropologist Edward Hall (1992, 1996). After studying North Americans (in the Northeast), Hall claimed that four proxemic zones exist—intimate, personal, social, and public—and each zone is used for different reasons. Hall includes ranges of spatial distance and the behaviors that are appropriate for each zone. We have highlighted the proxemic zones in Figure 8.1.

Intimate Distance   This zone includes behaviors that exist in a range encompassing 0 to 18 inches. Hall (1966) notes that this includes behaviors that range from touch (for instance, making love) to being able to observe a person's facial characteristics. Whispers, for instance, carried out in this **intimate distance** range have the ability to become extremely powerful. Hall finds it interesting that when U.S. citizens find themselves in intimate surroundings but are not with intimate partners, they often attempt to create a nonintimate experience. Consider what happens in an elevator. People usually fix their eyes on the ceiling, the buttons, or the door as the elevator passes floor after floor. People keep their hands at their side or grasp some object. Hall finds it amusing that many people expend so much energy extracting themselves from

proxemics
study of a person's use of space

personal space
individual's variable use of space and distance

intimate distance
very close spatial zone spanning 0–18 inches

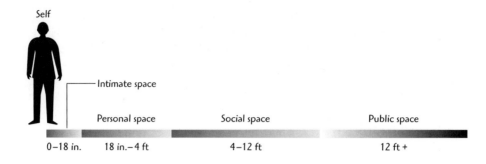

Figure 8.1
Proxemic Zones

Self

Intimate space

Personal space　　Social space　　Public space

0–18 in.　　18 in.–4 ft　　4–12 ft　　12 ft +

intimate distances. Margie Russo in our opening story seems to be troubled by the intimate distance created by Janet. If she wasn't in an interview, she'd likely remove herself from the situation. It's important to point out that some invasions of personal space may be construed as sexual harassment, regardless of the intent. For this reason, we need to remain sensitive to the various perceptions of intimate distance.

Personal Distance   This zone includes those behaviors that exist in an area ranging from 18 inches to 4 feet. According to Hall (1966), **personal distance** encompasses being as close as holding another's hand to keeping someone at arm's length. You may find that most, if not all, of the intimate relationships you have are within the closest point of the personal distance zone. Personal distance is likely to be used for your family and friends. The farthest point—4 feet—is usually reserved for less personal relationships, such as sales clerks. Hall indicates that in the personal distance zone, the voice is usually moderate, body heat is detectable, and breath and body odor may be perceptible.

personal distance
spatial zone of 18 inches to 4 feet, reserved for family and friends

Social Distance   With a proxemic range spanning 4 to 12 feet, the **social distance** category characterizes many conversations in U.S. culture, for instance, between and among co-workers. Hall (1966) contends that the closer social distance is usually reserved for those in a casual social setting, for example, a cocktail party. Although the distance seems a bit far, Hall reminds us that we are able to perceive skin and hair texture in the close phase of this category. The far phase is associated with individuals who have to speak louder than those in the close phase. In addition, the far phase can be considered to be more formal than the close phase. The far phase of social distance allows people to carry on simultaneous tasks. For instance, receptionists are able to carry on with their work while they converse with approaching strangers. It is possible, therefore, to monitor another person while completing a task.

social distance
spatial zone of 4–12 feet, reserved for more formal relationships such as those with co-workers

Public Distance   The range encompassing 12 feet and beyond is considered to be **public distance.** The close phase of public distance is reserved for fairly

public distance
spatial zone of 12 feet and beyond, reserved for very formal discussions such as between professor and students in class

formal discussions, for instance, in-class discussions between teachers and students. Public figures usually are at the far phase (around 25 feet or more). As you may have determined, it is difficult to read facial reactions at this point, unless media enhancements (for instance, large-screen projection) are used in the presentation. Whereas the close phase characterizes teachers in a classroom, the far phase includes teachers in a lecture hall. Also, actors use public distance in their performances. Consequently, their actions and words are exaggerated. Teachers and actors, however, are just two of the many types of people who use public distance in their lives.

Territoriality

Before we close our discussion of personal space, we explore an additional feature: **territoriality,** or a person's ownership of an area or object. Frequently, we lay claim to various spatial areas that we want to protect or defend. People decide that they want to erect fences, put on nameplates, or designate spaces as their own (for example, Marissa's room, Mom's car, and so forth). Three types of territories exist: primary, secondary, and public (Altman, 1975; Lyman, 1990). **Primary territories** signal an individual's exclusive domain. For instance, one's own workshop or computer are primary territories. In fact, many people put their names on their primary territories to further signify ownership. **Secondary territories** signal some sort of personal connection to an area or object. Secondary territories are not exclusive to an individual, but the individual feels some sort of association to the territory. For instance, many graduate students feel that a campus library is their secondary territory; they don't own the building, but they frequently occupy a space in the building. **Public territories** involve no personal affiliations and include those areas that are open to all people—for example, beaches, parks, movie theaters, and public transportation areas.

Territoriality is frequently accompanied by prevention and reaction (Knapp & Hall, 2010). That is, people may either try to prevent you from entering their territory or will respond once the territory is invaded. Some gangs use territorial markers in a neighborhood to prevent other gangs from invading their turf. Knapp and Hall note that if prevention does not work in defending one's territory, a person may react in some way, including getting both physically and cognitively aroused. In sum, humans typically stake out their territory in four primary ways: markers (marking our spot), labels (identification symbols), offensive displays (demonstrating aggressive looks and behaviors), and tenure (being there first and staying the longest) (Knapp, 1978).

Our elaborated discussion of space has relevance to Expectancy Violations Theory not only because the theory is rooted in proxemics, but also because it has direct application to the distances previously discussed. EVT assumes that people will react to space violations. To this end, our expectations for behavior will vary from one distance to another. That is, people have a sense of where they want others to place themselves in a conversation. For

territoriality
person's ownership of an area or object

primary territories
signal a person's exclusive domain over an area or object

secondary territories
signal a person's affiliation with an area or object

public territories
signal open spaces for everyone, including beaches and parks

Expectancy Violations Theory is concerned primarily with the structure of nonverbal messages. It asserts that when communicative norms are violated, the violation may be perceived either favorably or unfavorably, depending on the perception the receiver has of the violator. Violating another's expectations is a strategy that may be used rather than conforming to another's expectations.

instance, consider Margie and Janet from our opening story. Just as Margie has expectations for Janet's behavior in an interview, Janet, too, expects Margie to behave in a predictable way. Janet expects Margie to maintain a comfortable distance as well. She does not expect Margie to come into the office, put her briefcase on the desk, and pull a chair up next to Janet. According to EVT, if Margie's behavior is unexpected and Janet evaluates her behavior negatively, Janet may become more concerned with the expectancy violation than with Margie's credentials. The proxemic zones proposed by Hall, then, are important frameworks to consider when interpreting another's behavior.

Thus far, we have introduced you to how personal space is associated with Expectancy Violations Theory. The theory has evolved over the years, with Burgoon and other EVT proponents clarifying their original findings and concepts. Although we provide her pioneering theory in detail in this chapter, we also integrate updates and revisions of the theory where appropriate. To further explore the theory, we will first provide the basic assumptions of the theory and then examine a number of issues associated with the theory.

Assumptions of Expectancy Violations Theory

Expectancy Violations Theory is rooted in how messages are presented to others and the kinds of behaviors others undertake during a conversation. In addition, three assumptions guide the theory:

- Expectancies drive human interaction.
- Expectancies for human behavior are learned.
- People make predictions about nonverbal behavior.

The first assumption states that people carry expectancies in their interactions with others. In other words, expectancies drive human interaction. **Expectancies** can be defined as the cognitions and behaviors anticipated and prescribed in a conversation with another person. Expectancies, therefore, necessarily include individuals' nonverbal and verbal behavior. In her early

expectancies
thoughts and behaviors anticipated in conversations

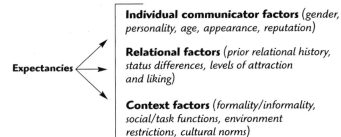

Expectancies

Individual communicator factors (*gender, personality, age, appearance, reputation*)

Relational factors (*prior relational history, status differences, levels of attraction and liking*)

Context factors (*formality/informality, social/task functions, environment restrictions, cultural norms*)

Figure 8.2
Influences on Expectancies
Adapted from Burgoon & Hale, 1988.

writings of EVT, Burgoon (1978) notes that people do not view others' behaviors as random; rather, they have various expectations of how others should think and behave. Reviewing the research by Burgoon and her associates, Tim Levine and his colleagues (2000) suggest that expectancies are a result of social norms, stereotypes, hearsay, and the idiosyncrasies of communicators. Consider, for instance, our story of Margie Russo and Janet Mueller. If you were the interviewer, what sort of expectations would you have for the nonverbal and verbal behavior of the interviewee? Many people conducting the interview would certainly expect a specific level of confidence, manifested by a warm handshake, a give-and-take conversational flow, and active listening skills. Interviewees would also be expected to keep a reasonable distance from the interviewer during the interview process. Many people in the United States do not want people whom they do not know to stand either too close or too far away from them. Whether it is in an interview situation or even a discussion between two people who have a prior relationship, Burgoon and other EVT writers argue that people enter interactions with a number of expectations about how a message should be delivered and how the messenger should deliver it. See Figure 8.2 for factors that influence a person's expectations.

Judee Burgoon and Jerold Hale (1988) contend that two types of expectations exist: pre-interactional and interactional. **Pre-interactional expectations** include the types of interactional knowledge and skills the communicator possesses *before* he or she enters a conversation. People do not always understand what it takes to enter and maintain a conversation. Some conversationalists may be very argumentative, for example, and others may be extremely passive. Most people do not expect such extreme behavior in their dialogues with others. **Interactional expectations** pertain to an individual's ability to carry out the interaction itself. Most people expect others to maintain appropriate conversational distance. In addition, in communicating with others, listening behaviors such as prolonged eye contact are frequently expected. These and a host of other behaviors are important to consider when examining the role of expectations before and during an interaction.

Of course, depending on the cultural background of communicators, these behaviors can vary tremendously from one person to another. In addition, whether our expectations are met will usually be influenced by the culture in

pre-interactional expectations
the knowledge or skills a communicator brings to an interaction

interactional expectations
an individual's ability to carry out the interaction

which we live and by whether we have internalized cultural patterns for conversation expectations.

This leads us to our second assumption of EVT—that people learn their expectations from both the culture at large and the individuals in that culture. For instance, the U.S. culture teaches that a professor–student relationship is underscored by professional respect. Although not explicitly stated in most college classrooms, professors have more social status than students, and therefore certain expectations exist in their relationships with their students. For instance, we expect teachers to be knowledgeable about subject matter, to present it to students in a clear manner, and to be available if students are concerned or confused about a topic. We also expect professors to recognize, acknowledge, and affirm students in the classroom who offer their thoughts (Schrodt et al., 2008). The teacher–student relationship is just one example of a culture teaching its citizens that expectations exist in a particular relationship. Most discussions between teachers and students, therefore, are laden with cultural expectations of how the two should relate to each other. A number of societal institutions (the family, the media, business and industry, and so forth) are central in prescribing what cultural patterns to follow. These at-large cultural prescriptions ultimately may be followed by individuals in conversation with each other.

Individuals within a culture are also influential in communicating expectations. Burgoon and Hale (1988) remark that differences based on our prior knowledge of others, our relational history with them, and our observations are important to consider. For instance, Janet Mueller's past experiences with prospective employees influence how she perceives an interaction and her expectations of job candidates in an interview (relational history). In addition, expectations result from our observations. In one family, for instance, standing very close to one another is a family norm, and yet this norm is not shared in other families. Interesting scenarios occur in conversations between individuals with different norms; expectations for conversational distance vary and may influence perceptions of the interaction or have other consequences.

The third assumption pertains to the predictions people make about nonverbal communication. Later in this chapter we note that EVT theorists have applied the notion of expectancies to verbal behavior. Nonetheless, the original statement of EVT related specifically to nonverbal behavior. To this end, it's important to point out a belief inherent in the theory: People make predictions about another's nonverbal behavior.

In later writings of EVT, Judee Burgoon and Joseph Walther (1990) expanded the original understanding of EVT via personal space to other areas of nonverbal communication, including touch and posture. They suggest that the attractiveness of another influences the evaluation of expectancies. In conversations, people do not simply attend to what another is saying. As you will learn in this chapter, nonverbal behavior affects the conversation, and this behavior prompts others to make predictions.

Let's use an example to explain this assumption a bit further. Suppose someone whom you feel is attractive starts to make direct eye contact with you at a grocery store. At first, you may feel a bit odd with the prolonged stare. But because you are attracted to the person, that initial awkwardness may melt into comfort. Then you may begin to surmise that the person is interested in you because you see a decrease in physical distance between the two of you. This example illustrates the fact that you were making predictions (e.g., the person is attracted to you) based on his or her nonverbal behavior (e.g., eye contact and personal space). Before you begin to believe your own projection of attractiveness, however, keep in mind that your reaction may be either misguided or simply wrong. Despite your level of confidence, nonverbal communication is frequently ambiguous and is open to multiple interpretations (Hickson, Stacks, & Moore, 2007).

Burgoon and her colleagues caution us that not all violations are clear, and consequently we employ a communicator reward valence. If a violation is ambiguous or has multiple meanings, EVT predicts that "communicator valence" will influence how the violation is interpreted and evaluated (more on this later in the chapter). Communicators interpret the violation using communicator reward valence. If the person is someone we like, we will positively evaluate the violation; if it is someone we do not like, we will view the violation negatively. We now turn our attention to additional concepts and features of EVT: arousal, threat threshold, violation valence, and communicator reward valence.

Arousal

Burgoon originally felt that deviations from expectations have consequences. These deviations, or violations, have what is called "arousal value" (Burgoon, 1978, p. 133). By this she means that when a person's expectations are violated, the person's interest or attention is aroused, and he or she uses a particular mechanism to cope with the violation. When **arousal** occurs, one's interest or attention to the deviation increases and one pays less attention to the message and more attention to the source of the arousal (LaPoire & Burgoon, 1996). Burgoon and Hale (1988) later termed this "mental alertness" or an "orienting response," in which attention is diverted toward the source of the deviation.

A person may be both cognitively and physically aroused. **Cognitive arousal** is an alertness or an orientation to a violation. When we are cognitively aroused, our intuitive senses become heightened. **Physical arousal** includes those behaviors that a communicator employs during an interaction—such as moving out of uncomfortable speaking distances, adjusting one's stance during an interaction, and so forth. Most EVT studies have investigated cognitive arousal (via self-report inventories), yet little research has examined physiological arousal. One interesting study that examined physical arousal in conversation was undertaken by Beth LaPoire and Judee Burgoon (1996). Specifically, they asked college students to engage in a practice medical interview. During the interaction, the researchers studied heart rate, skin temperature, and pulse volume changes every 5 seconds while they assessed expectancy violations. Only heart rate and pulse volume demonstrated any statistical significance. Results indicated that after subjects registered cognitive arousal to a violation, they first experienced heart rate decreases and pulse volume increases. This was followed by pulse volume decreases. In sum, people

arousal
increased interest or attention when deviations from expectations occur

cognitive arousal
mental awareness of deviations from expectations

physical arousal
bodily changes as a result of deviations from expectations

Theory Application in Groups (TAG)

Among the many concepts in Expectancy Violations Theory is the notion that each of us has a threat threshold that may vary tremendously, depending on the person with whom we are interacting. In a small group, identify how threat threshold can vary over a number of conversations. Be sure to include how distance functions and how conversation topic might play a role in the threat thresholds.

notice when others are not adhering to interaction expectations. Arousal remains a complicated but important part of EVT; as you can see, arousal is more than simply recognizing when someone commits a violation.

Threat Threshold

threat threshold
tolerance for distance violations

Once arousal exists, threats may occur. A second key concept associated with EVT is **threat threshold,** which Burgoon (1978) defines as the "distance at which an interactant experiences physical and physiological discomfort by the presence of another" (p. 130). In a sense, the threat threshold is a tolerance for distance violation. Burgoon maintains that "when distance is equated with threat, closer distances are perceived as more threatening and farther distances as less threatening" (p. 134). In this sense, distance is interpreted as a statement of threat from a communicator. People may either reward or punish a threat. Burgoon arrives at this conclusion by consulting the research on liking and attraction. This research suggests that closer distances are reserved for people we like or to whom we are attracted. Some people don't mind when others stand close to them; their threat threshold, therefore, is high. Others become very uncomfortable around those who stand too close; for them, the threat threshold is low. So, for instance, if you are attracted to a person you see each morning at Starbucks, your threat threshold will likely be high as he or she talks to you and comes closer to you as your conversation progresses. During this same interaction, however, you may discover that this is not the sort of person you want to hang out with, and you may find your threat threshold getting smaller. Burgoon notes that the size of the threshold is based on how we view the initiator of the threat, which we discussed earlier as the communication reward valence. Once a violation occurs, however, we again interpret the violation. Although Burgoon later decided that the threat threshold is not necessarily associated with the other communicator, the concept remains important to consider as you understand EVT.

Violation Valence

Throughout this chapter, we have emphasized that when people speak to others they have expectations. Many of these expectations are based on social norms of the other person. When expectations are violated, however, many people evaluate the violation on a valence. **Violation valence** refers to the positive or negative assessment of an unexpected behavior. Violation valence focuses on the deviation of an expectation.

violation valence
perceived negative
or positive assessment
of an unexpected
behavior

Violation valence requires making sense of a violation through interpretation and evaluation (Burgoon & Hale, 1988). Quite simply, communicators try to interpret the meaning of a violation and decide whether they like it. If, for instance, a professor is speaking very close to you, you may interpret the behavior as an expression of superiority or intimidation. Consequently, the violation valence would be negative. Or you may view the violation as something positive; you might think the professor is demonstrating a sense of connection. Your violation valence, then, would be positive. Most of the research in the area of violations suggests that violations are likely to have a negative impact on close relationships (e.g., Cohen, 2007).

To better understand the violation valence, consider two situations between co-workers Noland and Rick. Standing in the break room, Noland begins to talk about his phone call to his wife this morning. As he discusses his conversation about where they decided to go for vacation, Noland begins to close this distance between him and Rick. Rick feels very uncomfortable with the distance in that his expectations for spatial distance between co-workers is violated. In other words, Rick is negatively aroused by Noland's distance behavior. A different situation, however, might prompt a different reaction. Imagine that Noland corners Rick to tell him that he heard that the company was laying off 20 percent of its workers within two months. Because Rick was recently hired by the company, he might be positively aroused and allow Noland to violate his personal space. Most likely, he will positively evaluate Noland and allow the violation to take place.

It may be perplexing to think that violations can be viewed positively. Yet there are many such examples. For instance, in a job interview, the candidate who is able to convince the interviewer that he or she is the most qualified is usually the person who gets the job. Most job interviews are very structured and have an agreed-on informal process. Most job candidates follow the interview script and do not violate anyone's expectations. At times, though, candidates do not follow the script; they violate expectations. Although some interviewers may think these candidates are too independent, others may see them as creative, bold, and original. These may be the qualities that ultimately get the person the job. Thus, violations may yield positive effects.

Communicator Reward Valence

What happens when our expectations are not met in a conversation with another? Burgoon believes that when people depart, or *deviate,* from expectations, how that deviation is received depends on the reward potential of others. Let's explain this a bit further. Burgoon, along with Deborah Coker and Ray Coker (1986), notes that not all violations of expected behavior necessarily yield negative perceptions. Specifically, the researchers offer the following: "In cases where behaviors are ambiguous or have multiple interpretations, acts committed by a high-reward communicator may be assigned positive meanings, and the same acts committed by a low-reward communicator may be assigned negative meanings" (p. 498). Communicators can offer each other a number of rewards, including smiles, head nods, physical attractiveness, attitude similarity, socioeconomic status, credibility, and competence. In our opening story, Janet Mueller's demeanor in asking about Margie's children was apparently viewed as reward behavior because Margie's nervousness immediately subsided. Burgoon thinks people have the potential to either reward or punish in conversations and maintains that people bring both positive and negative characteristics to an interaction. She terms this **communicator reward valence**.

communicator reward valence the sum of the positive and negative characteristics of a person and the potential for him or her to carry out rewards or punishments

Burgoon holds that the concept of reward includes a number of characteristics that allow a person to be viewed favorably or unfavorably. According to Expectancy Violations Theory, interpretations of violations frequently depend on the communicator and his or her value. So, for instance, Margie Russo may not view Janet's close proximity as a positive deviation from expected behavior in an interview. Yet Janet's behavior was more positively received because of other characteristics; namely, her courteous manner and interest in Margie's children.

Let's apply this idea to eye behavior in a number of different contexts. A prolonged stare from a person on public transportation is probably not going to be received favorably, but it may be received favorably from one's romantic partner. If a keynote speaker at a dinner banquet looked above the listeners' heads, many people would be bewildered by this lack of eye contact. But when strangers pass on the street, lack of eye contact is expected. Or think about your response to receiving a constant stare from your supervisor or a co-worker. Finally, cultural differences influence perceptions of eye contact. A wife who avoids eye contact while telling her husband that she loves him may elicit a different evaluation than if she had direct eye contact, but this interpretation varies across cultural groups. Some (e.g., Irish Americans) would expect another to look directly at them when saying something very personal, such as "I love you." Others (e.g., Japanese Americans), however, do not place such value on eye contact. In each of these contexts, violations of expected eye behavior may be interpreted differently according to how we receive the communicator.

Integration, Critique, and Closing

Expectancy Violations Theory is one of the few theories specifically focusing on what people expect—and their reactions to others—in conversations. The assumptions and core concepts clearly demonstrate the importance of nonverbal messages and information processing. EVT also enhances our understanding of how expectations influence conversational distance. The theory uncovers what takes place in the minds of communicators and how communicators monitor nonverbal (and verbal) behavior during their conversations. Among the criteria for evaluating a theory, three seem especially relevant for discussion: scope, utility, and testability.

Integration

Communication Tradition	Rhetorical | Semiotic | Phenomenological | Cybernetic | **Socio-Psychological** | Socio-Cultural | Critical
Communication Context	**Intrapersonal** | **Interpersonal** | Small Group | Organizational | Public/Rhetorical | Mass/Media | Cultural
Approach to Knowing	**Positivistic/Empirical** | Interpretive/Hermeneutic | Critical

Critique

Evaluation Criteria	Scope | Logical Consistency | Parsimony | **Utility** | **Testability** | Heurism | Test of Time

 Research Notes

Floyd, K., & Voloudakis, M. (1999). Affectionate behavior in adult platonic friendships: Interpreting and evaluating expectancy violations. *Human Communication Research, 25,* 341–369.

This study examined affection as a key part of communication in close relationships. Affectionate communication research suggests that affection is influenced by expectancies. Looking specifically at nonromantic (platonic) relationships, the research team studied forty pairs of adults. The researchers told the couples that they would be involved in two conversations about their thoughts and feelings pertaining to their friendship with each other. Results showed that unexpected increases in affectionate communication resulted in positive expectancy violations. By contrast, unexpected negative increases in affectionate communication resulted in negative expectancy violations. Floyd and Voloudakis discuss these findings in light of the central principles and concepts of EVT.

Lannutti, P. J., Laliker, M., & Hale, J. L. (2001). Violations of expectations and social-sexual communication in student/professor interactions. *Communication Education, 50,* 69–82.

Expectancy Violations Theory was utilized as a framework to understand the influence of touch in professor–student interactions. The researchers studied nearly 400 undergraduate students who were asked to imagine that they were a student in a particular scenario. After reading the scenario, students were asked to complete a series of questions involving touch behavior and professor credibility. Location of touch, reward value of professor, and participant sex were analyzed in relation to an office visit to a professor. Overall, results showed that a professor who uses more expected touch behavior is associated with more positive evaluations. An interesting gender difference emerged: The more the unexpected touch by the professor, the more negative the assessment of the professor by female participants. Lannutti and her colleagues posit that there appears to be a threat threshold to the acceptance of touch in these types of interactions. Partial support for EVT was confirmed with calls for future research and cautions pertaining to professor touch provided.

Theory Into Practice

Ashley

Talking about space differences got me thinking about how people use it. I remember a time where a vendor at a ball park got pretty close to me as I bought some popcorn. As I gave him the money, I could tell he was standing way too close to me. As a matter of fact, he was what I would call (using Hall's category) "intimate" in his space. Really, though, I didn't mind it all that much. He was cute, I was single, and we were both kind of bored, I think!

Scope

At first glance, the scope of this theory may appear to be too broad; nonverbal communication is an expansive area. Yet Burgoon's theory has parameters in that she originally conceptualized one category of nonverbal communication as she articulated her theory: personal space. She has investigated and expanded her research to include other nonverbal behaviors such as eye gaze, yet her original work was clear in scope.

Utility

The practicality of EVT is apparent. Burgoon's theory presents advice on how to elicit favorable impressions and discusses the implications of space violations, a topic that affects countless conversations. From the early writings (Burgoon & Jones, 1976) to more recent work (McPherson & Liang, 2007), research employing an EVT framework has fulfilled the criterion of utility.

Testability

Some scholars (e.g., Sparks & Greene, 1992) have criticized the clarity of concepts in Burgoon's theory, suggesting that testability may be problematic. Sparks and Greene comment that self-perceptions of arousal are not valid measures. They specifically note that Burgoon and her associates failed to establish valid indices of observers' ratings and believe "we should not accept the claim about the validity of any nonverbal index until that validity has been demonstrated" (p. 468). This intellectual debate may appear trivial to you, yet recall that arousal is a key component of EVT. LaPoire and Burgoon (1992) thoughtfully responded to this criticism by first claiming that Sparks and Greene did not fairly reflect the objectives of Burgoon's research. Additionally, LaPoire and Burgoon (1996) contend that because arousal is such a complicated and layered concept, their approach to defining arousal remains valid.

Generally speaking, EVT is a testable theory. In Chapter 3, we noted that testability requires that theorists be specific in their concepts. In fact, Burgoon (1978) is one of a few theorists who clearly defines her terms; as she refined her theory, she also clarified past ambiguities. In doing so, she presents a foundation from which future researchers might continue to draw and replicate her claims.

Expectancy Violations Theory is an important theory because it offers a way to link behavior and cognitions. It is one of the few communication theories that offers us a better understanding of our need for both other people and personal space. For that, Burgoon's work continues to be critical and groundbreaking in the communication discipline.

Discussion Starters

1. In addition to distance behaviors, what other nonverbal behaviors are present in interview situations like the one between Margie and Janet?

2. Explain how EVT might inform research and thinking on touch behavior. For instance, does the theory help us to understand the difference between appropriate and inappropriate touch? Explain with examples.

3. Provide some nonverbal expectations that you have learned from your culture. Discuss what similarities and differences exist.

4. How do you suppose arousal manifests itself in conversations between supervisors and employees? Identify a few arousal mechanisms.

5. Suppose you want to study expectancy violation in school. How might you begin to investigate violations? Be as specific as possible, and identify some methods for studying expectations.

6. Employing at least two examples, differentiate between communicator reward valence and violation valence.

7. Discuss the application of any component of EVT to a job/interview.

Online Learning Center (www. mhhe.com/west4e)

Visit the Online Learning Center at www.mhhe.com/west4e for chapter-specific resources, such as story-into-theory and multiple-choice quizzes, as well as theory summaries and theory connection questions.

Relationship Development

MILLIONS OF DOLLARS HAVE BEEN MADE BY authors of self-help books that promote ways to begin, develop, and maintain our interpersonal relationships. The sad reality is that the vast majority of these books are written by people who don't understand that there are no easy steps associated with relationship development. As we all can testify, our various relationships with friends, family, partners, co-workers, religious leaders, and others are filled with dynamics that are not explained in these books. This becomes especially important as we think about the millions of people seeking out these resources, which are pretty much void of theory.

This is precisely why the theories under this section called "Relationship Development" are important to consider. They represent scholarship that has examined all types of interpersonal relationships and the numerous patterns and processes involved in relationship development. In sum, the theories address how and why relationships develop and are maintained.

Five theories are discussed in this section. Uncertainty Reduction Theory suggests that when strangers meet, their focus is on reducing levels of uncertainty about each other and about their relationship. Social Penetration Theory examines how a person's decision to reveal personal information to another influences the direction of that relationship. In Social Exchange Theory, people add up their costs and benefits of being in a relationship and arrive at a net outcome. They also compare their current relationships with others. As relationships progress, they are likely to experience conflicting pulls. Managing these tensions is the essence of Relational Dialectics Theory. Communication Privacy Management Theory states that people in relationships constantly manage boundaries between thoughts and feelings they are willing to share and those they are not.

Relational life is interesting, challenging, complex, entertaining, and exhausting. The theories we present help unravel the reasons we continue to be part of other people's lives and why they stay with us. When you encounter these theories, you will also become familiar with a number of engaging topics. You will read about trust, vulnerability, intimacy, nonverbal warmth, interpersonal roles, and attraction. As you read the next five chapters, pay attention to the different ways each theory conceptualizes and explains relational life.

CHAPTER 9

Uncertainty Reduction Theory

Based on the research of **Charles Berger** *and* **Richard Calabrese**

Edie Banks and Malcolm Rogers take the same philosophy class at Urban University and are enrolled in the same section. Until today, they really had not spoken together, although they had seen each other in the class every Monday, Wednesday, and Friday for the past three months. Malcolm had noticed Edie and found her attractive. Today, as Edie was leaving class, she noticed Malcolm staring at her from the corner of the room where he sat with his friends. Edie felt a little uncomfortable about being on the receiving end of Malcolm's gaze, and she hurried to get out of the classroom.

Unfortunately, her friend Maggie stopped her at the doorway with a question about the assignment for next week, and so Edie and Malcolm reached the hallway at the same time. There was an awkward pause as they smiled uncertainly at each other. Malcolm cleared his throat and said, "Hi. That was a pretty interesting lecture in class today, wasn't it?" Edie shrugged, smiled back, and replied, "I'm not sure I get what's going on in there. I'm majoring in engineering, and this is just an elective for me. Sometimes I think I should have taken bowling instead." Malcolm smiled and said, "I've been pretty happy since I decided to major in philosophy. But I guess I'd have the same reaction you're having if I got stuck in an engineering class! I probably couldn't engineer my way out of a paper bag." The two laughed for a minute. Then Edie said, "Gotta run. Catch you later," and hurried off down the hall.

Malcolm walked to his next class wondering if they would talk again, if Edie was putting down his major, if she thought he had been rude about her major, if she liked him, if he liked her, or if he cared.

Sometimes called Initial Interaction Theory, Uncertainty Reduction Theory (URT) was originated by Charles Berger and Richard Calabrese in 1975. It continues to be an important theory, because, as Leanne Knobloch (2008) states, "everyday life is infused with uncertainty" (p. 133). Berger and Calabrese's goal in constructing this theory was to explain how communication is used to reduce uncertainties between strangers engaging in their first conversation together. Berger and Calabrese believe that when strangers first meet, they are primarily concerned with increasing predictability in an effort to make sense out of their communication experience. As we discussed in Chapter 3, people act as naïve researchers. Berger and Calabrese think that as naïve researchers we are motivated both to predict and to explain what goes on in initial encounters. **Prediction** can be defined as the ability to forecast the

prediction
the ability to forecast one's own and others' behavioral choices

explanation
the ability to interpret
the meaning of
behavioral choices

behavioral options likely to be chosen from a range of possible options available to oneself or to a relational partner. Explanation refers to attempts to interpret the meaning of past actions in a relationship. These two concepts—prediction and explanation—make up the two primary subprocesses of uncertainty reduction.

Our opening example of Malcolm and Edie illustrates Berger and Calabrese's basic contentions about meeting someone for the first time. Because Malcolm does not know Edie, he is not sure how to interpret her comments to him. Nor is he certain about what will happen the next time they see each other. There are so many possible explanations for what was said that Malcolm's uncertainty level is high. This is consistent with the ideas of theorists Claude E. Shannon and Warren Weaver (1949), who note in their information theory that uncertainty exists whenever the number of possible alternatives in a given situation is high and the likelihood of their occurrence is relatively equal. Conversely, they say, uncertainty is decreased when the alternatives are limited in number and/or there is an alternative that is usually chosen. Berger and Calabrese used Shannon and Weaver's work as a foundation for URT.

For example, when Teresa walks into her Spanish I classroom on the first day of class and the person sitting nearest the door smiles at her, Teresa has a few alternative explanations for this behavior. The person could be friendly, trying to get to know her, squinting in the sunlight, or mistaken in thinking she knows Teresa. Because a college classroom is often governed by a norm of friendliness and because the alternative explanations are few in number, Teresa will probably decide the smile was one of friendly welcoming, reducing her uncertainty fairly easily. But if Teresa walked into a job interview and found another candidate in the waiting room with her who glanced her way and smiled, the alternative explanations would be more numerous. They would contain all of the above possibilities and others, including that the person is sizing her up as competition, the person thinks she's weak competition, the person is trying to get her to let her guard down, and so forth. These increased alternatives will increase uncertainty, causing Teresa to attempt to reduce it. Berger and Calabrese theorize that communication is the vehicle by which people reduce their uncertainty about one another. In turn, reduced uncertainty creates conditions ripe for the development of interpersonal relationships.

After Berger and Calabrese (1975) originated their theory, it was later slightly elaborated (Berger, 1979; Berger & Bradac, 1982). The current version of the theory suggests that there are two types of uncertainty in initial encounters: cognitive and behavioral. Our cognitions refer to the beliefs and attitudes that we and others hold. Cognitive uncertainty, therefore, refers to the degree of uncertainty associated with those beliefs and attitudes. When Malcolm wonders whether Edie was ridiculing his major and whether he really cares, he experiences cognitive uncertainty. Behavioral uncertainty, on the other hand, pertains to "the extent to which behavior is predictable in a given situation" (Berger & Bradac, 1982, p. 7). Because we have cultural rituals for small talk, Edie and Malcolm probably know how to behave during their short conversation. If one of them had violated the ritual by either engaging in inappropriate self-disclosure (revealing private information about oneself to another) or

cognitive
uncertainty
degree of uncertainty
related to cognitions

behavioral
uncertainty
degree of uncertainty
related to behaviors

self-disclosure
personal messages
about the self disclosed to another

totally ignoring the other, their behavioral uncertainty would have increased. People may be cognitively uncertain, behaviorally uncertain, or both before, during, or following an interaction.

Berger (1987) speaks about the nature of behavioral uncertainty in this passage: "To interact in a relatively smooth, coordinated, and understandable manner, one must be able both to predict how one's interaction partner is likely to behave, and, based upon these predictions, to select from one's own repertoire those responses that will optimize outcomes in the encounter" (p. 41). In our opening example, if Malcolm is able to predict that Edie will be an affectionate individual who is willing to ask questions and reveal personal information to him, then he must be prepared to offer responses so that he and Edie will have a satisfying encounter.

Furthermore, Berger and Calabrese (1975) argued that uncertainty reduction has both proactive and retroactive processes. Proactive uncertainty reduction comes into play when a person thinks about communication options before actually engaging with another person. When Edie attempted to avoid Malcolm at the classroom door, she was trying to deal with her uncertainty proactively. If Malcolm preplanned what he might say to Edie, he was also using proactive processes. Retroactive uncertainty reduction consists of attempts to explain behavior after the encounter itself. Thus, Malcolm's questions to himself about what Edie did and said and his own reactions are part of the retroactive process.

In addition, Berger and Calabrese suggest that uncertainty is related to seven other concepts rooted in communication and relational development: verbal output, nonverbal warmth (such as pleasant vocal tone and leaning forward), information seeking (asking questions), self-disclosure, reciprocity of disclosure, similarity, and liking. Each of these works in conjunction with the others so that interactants can reduce some of their uncertainty.

URT posits a dynamic movement of interpersonal relationships in their initial stages. This theory has been described as an example of original theorizing in the field of communication (Miller, 1981) because it employs concepts (such as information seeking, self-disclosure) that are specifically relevant to studying communication behavior. URT attempts to place communication as the cornerstone of human behavior, and to this end a number of assumptions about human behavior and communication underlie the theory.

Uncertainty Reduction Theory · Theory at a Glance

When strangers meet, their primary focus is on reducing their level of uncertainty in the situation because uncertainty is uncomfortable. People can be uncertain on two different levels: behavioral and cognitive. They may be unsure of how to behave (or how the other person will behave), and they may also be unsure of what they think of the other person and what the other person thinks of them. High levels of uncertainty are related to a variety of verbal and nonverbal behaviors.

Assumptions of Uncertainty Reduction Theory

As we have mentioned in earlier chapters, theories are frequently grounded in assumptions that reflect the worldview of the theorists. Uncertainty Reduction Theory is no exception. The following assumptions frame this theory:

- People experience uncertainty in interpersonal settings.
- Uncertainty is an aversive state, generating cognitive stress.
- When strangers meet, their primary concern is to reduce their uncertainty or to increase predictability.
- Interpersonal communication is a developmental process that occurs through stages.
- Interpersonal communication is the primary means of uncertainty reduction.
- The quantity and nature of information that people share change through time.
- It is possible to predict people's behavior in a lawlike fashion.

We will briefly address each assumption. First, in a number of interpersonal settings, people feel uncertainty. Because differing expectations exist for interpersonal occasions, it is reasonable to conclude that people are uncertain or even nervous about meeting others. As Berger and Calabrese (1975) state, "When persons are unable to make sense out of their environment, they usually become anxious" (p. 106). Consider Malcolm's anxiety, for instance, as he meets Edie after class. Berger and Calabrese contend that he experiences uncertainty when meeting Edie, a classmate to whom he is attracted. Although there are a great many cues in the environment that can help Malcolm make sense out of his interaction with Edie, there are complicating factors as well. For example, Malcolm may have noticed Edie hurrying to leave the room. There may be several alternative explanations for this behavior, including another class that is a distance away, a general predisposition toward hurrying, having to go to the bathroom, feeling faint and wanting fresh air, wanting to avoid meeting Malcolm at the door, and so forth. Given all these alternatives, it is likely that Malcolm (or anyone in his situation) feels uncertain about how to interpret Edie's behavior.

The second assumption suggests that uncertainty is an aversive state. In other words, it takes a great deal of emotional and psychological energy to remain uncertain. When Miguel met his new boss, Sandra, for the first time he was highly uncertain. He'd never worked for a woman before or for someone his own age, as Sandra was. He had a million questions that occupied his cognitive and psychological energy. The longer he worked for Sandra, the more he resolved his uncertainty. Miguel was free, then, to think about other things beyond his questions about what Sandra might do or say and how he should respond.

The next assumption underlying URT advances the proposition that when strangers meet, two concerns are important: reducing uncertainty and increasing predictability. At first glance, this may sound commonsensical, yet, as

Research Notes

Hargie, O., Tourish, D., & Wilson, N. (2002). Communication audits and the effects of increased information: A follow-up study. *Journal of Business Communication, 39,* 414–436.

This study examined communication audits performed in an organization to determine how effective they actually are. Although audits have been discussed for fifty years, the authors observe that no reports of the impact of an audit on communication performance in the organization exist in the literature. Contrary to the view that employees really don't want more information and if more information is provided it will never be judged enough, this study found that employees in the organization responded as URT would predict: Receiving information from the audit reduced uncertainty and increased satisfaction with communication processes in the organization.

Knobloch, L. K., & Solomon, D. H. (2003). Responses to changes in relational uncertainty within dating relationships: Emotions and communication strategies. *Communication Studies, 54,* 282–305.

This article examines how emotions affect the communication strategies of dating couples. But it is relevant to a discussion of URT because it examines emotions based on the context of a change in the certainty levels people experience in their relationship. One hundred forty-one participants filled out questionnaires asking about their emotional experiences relative to changes in relational certainty level and their subsequent communicative responses. The researchers found the following: Increases in relational certainty were beneficial whereas increases in relational uncertainty were detrimental; the communicative responses to both increases in certainty and uncertainty may not be all that different in that respondents indicated using integrative behaviors for dealing with both; and happiness, anger, and sadness were the salient emotions people reported.

Berger (1995) concludes, "There is always the possibility that one's conversational partner will respond unconventionally to even the most routine message" (pp. 2–3). Uncertainty Reduction Theory suggests that these concerns are often dealt with through information seeking. Information seeking usually takes the form of asking questions in order to gain some predictability. Politicians often ask questions when meeting their constituents. They spend time with the voters in their district and ask them questions to gain a sense of their needs. This process can be quite engaging, and many people do this unconsciously.

The fourth assumption of URT suggests that interpersonal communication is a process involving developmental stages. According to Berger and Calabrese, generally speaking, most people begin interaction in an **entry phase,** defined as the beginning stage of an interaction between strangers. The entry phase is guided by implicit and explicit rules and norms, such as responding in kind when someone says, "Hi! How are you doing?" Individuals then enter the second stage, called the **personal phase,** or the stage where the interactants start to communicate more spontaneously and to reveal more idiosyncratic information. The personal phase can occur during an initial encounter, but it is more likely to begin after repeated interactions. The third stage, the **exit phase,** refers to the stage during which individuals make decisions about whether they wish

entry phase
the beginning stage of an interaction between strangers

personal phase
the stage in a relationship when people begin to communicate more spontaneously and personally

exit phase
the stage in a relationship when people decide whether to continue or leave

to continue interacting with this partner in the future. Although all people do not enter a phase in the same manner or stay in a phase for a similar amount of time, Berger and Calabrese believe that a universal framework exists that explains how interpersonal communication shapes and reflects the development of interpersonal relationships.

The fifth assumption states that interpersonal communication is the primary means of uncertainty reduction. Because we have identified interpersonal communication as the focus of URT, this assumption should come as no surprise. Uncertainty Reduction Theory draws on the interpersonal context that we discussed in Chapter 2: You may recall that interpersonal communication requires a host of preconditions—among them listening skills, nonverbal response cues, and a shared language. Most of us presume that these and other conditions are present in our conversations, yet Berger (1995) warns that there are a number of situations where "these preconditions for carrying out face-to-face encounters may not be met" (p. 4). For instance, he notes the inherent challenges in communicating with hearing-impaired or visually impaired interactants who do not have full sensory capabilities. Or you may have had some experience communicating with someone who does not speak your language. Challenges such as these affect the uncertainty reduction process and relational development.

The next assumption underscores the nature of time. It also focuses on the fact that interpersonal communication is developmental. Uncertainty reduction theorists believe that initial interactions are key elements in the developmental process. To illustrate this assumption, consider the experiences of Rita, who spent a few minutes by herself before entering the YWCA to attend her first meeting of Parents, Family, and Friends of Lesbians and Gays (PFLAG). She immediately felt more comfortable when Dan, another newcomer, came over to introduce himself and welcome her to the group. As the two exchanged information about their anxieties and uncertainties, they both felt more confident. As they talked, Rita and Dan reduced their uncertainties about what the other members of the support group would be like. Charles Berger and Kathy Kellermann (1994) believe that Rita and Dan are goal directed and therefore will employ a number of communication strategies to acquire social information. Reducing uncertainty is key for both Rita and Dan. A bit later in the chapter, we will discuss some of these strategies.

The final assumption indicates that people's behavior can be predicted in a lawlike fashion. Recall from Chapter 3 that theorists have some guidelines to help them in the job of theory construction. One of the guidelines we reviewed was covering law, which assumes that human behavior is regulated by generalizable principles that function in a lawlike manner. Although there may be some exceptions, in general people behave in accordance with these laws. The goal of a covering law theory is to lay out the laws that will explain how we communicate. As you might imagine, covering law theories have a difficult task. Although some aspects of the natural world may operate under laws, the social world is much more variable. That is why covering laws in the social science are called "lawlike." A pattern is outlined, but the deterministic notion implied with natural laws is relaxed a bit. Still, even to approach the goal of lawlike statements is daunting. Thus, theories like URT begin with what may seem like commonsense observations in order to establish regularities that govern people's behaviors. Covering law theories are constructed to move from statements that are presumed to be true (or axioms) to statements that are derived from these truisms (or theorems).

Axioms of Uncertainty Reduction Theory

Uncertainty Reduction Theory is an axiomatic theory. This means that Berger and Calabrese began with a collection of **axioms, or truisms drawn from past research and common sense**. These axioms, or what some researchers might call propositions, require no further proof than the statement itself. Berger and Calabrese extrapolated this axiomatic thinking from earlier researchers (Blalock, 1969), who concluded that causal relationships should be stated in the form of an axiom. Axioms are the heart of the theory. They have to be accepted as valid because they are the building blocks for everything else in the theory. Each axiom presents a relationship between uncertainty (the central theoretical concept) and one other concept. URT originally posited seven axioms. To understand each, we refer back to our opening example of Edie and Malcolm.

axioms
truisms drawn from past research and common sense

> **Axiom 1:** Given the high level of uncertainty present at the onset of the entry phase, as the amount of verbal communication between strangers increases, the level of uncertainty for each interactant in the relationship decreases. As uncertainty is further reduced, the amount of verbal communication increases. This asserts an inverse or negative relationship between uncertainty and verbal communication.

Regarding Malcolm and Edie's situation with reference to this axiom, the theory maintains that if they talk more to each other, they will become more certain about each other. Furthermore, as they get to know each other better, they will talk more with each other.

> **Axiom 2:** As nonverbal affiliative expressiveness increases, uncertainty levels decrease in an initial interaction situation. In addition, decreases in uncertainty level will cause increases in nonverbal affiliative expressiveness. This is another negative relationship.

If Edie and Malcolm express themselves to each other in a warm nonverbal fashion, they will grow more certain of each other, and as they do this, they will increase their nonverbal affiliation with each other: They may be more facially animated, or they may engage in more prolonged eye contact. The two might even touch each other in a friendly fashion as they begin to feel more comfortable with each other.

> **Axiom 3:** High levels of uncertainty cause increases in information-seeking behavior. As uncertainty levels decline, information-seeking behavior decreases. This axiom sets forth a positive relationship between the two concepts.

This axiom, which we will discuss later, is one of the more provocative propositions associated with URT. It suggests that Edie will ask questions and otherwise engage in information seeking as long as she feels uncertain about Malcolm. The more certain she feels, the less information seeking she will do. The same would apply to Malcolm.

Axiom 4: High levels of uncertainty in a relationship cause decreases in the intimacy level of communication content. Low levels of uncertainty produce high levels of intimacy. This axiom poses a negative relationship between uncertainty and levels of intimacy.

Because uncertainty is relatively high between Edie and Malcolm, they engage in small talk with no real self-disclosures. The intimacy of their communication content is low, and their uncertainty level remains high. The fourth axiom asserts that if they continue to reduce the uncertainty in their relationship, then their communication will consist of higher levels of intimacy.

Axiom 5: High levels of uncertainty produce high rates of reciprocity. Low levels of uncertainty produce low levels of reciprocity. A positive relationship is advanced here.

According to URT, as long as Edie and Malcolm remain uncertain about each other, they will tend to mirror each other's behavior. **Reciprocity** suggests that the people involved in these initial encounters will tend to mirror each other's communication behaviors. For example, after Edie shares that she is lost in the class and that she is an engineering major, Malcolm reveals his major to her and admits that he would probably have troubles in engineering classes. Immediate reciprocation of that sort (I tell you where I am from and you tell me where you are from) is a hallmark of initial encounters. The more people talk to each other and develop their relationship, the more they trust that reciprocity will be made at some point. If I don't tell you something that mirrors your communication today, I will probably do so the next time we talk or the time after that. With this in mind, strict reciprocity is replaced by an overall sense of reciprocity in our relationship.

Axiom 6: Similarities between people reduce uncertainty, whereas dissimilarities increase uncertainty. This axiom asserts a negative relationship.

Because Edie and Malcolm are both college students at Urban University, they may have similarities that reduce some of their uncertainties about each other immediately. Yet they are different sexes and have different majors— dissimilarities that may contribute to their uncertainty level.

Axiom 7: Increases in uncertainty level produce decreases in liking; decreases in uncertainty produce increases in liking. Another negative relationship is posited in this axiom.

As Edie and Malcolm reduce their uncertainties, they typically will increase their liking for each other. If they continue to feel highly uncertain about each other, they probably will not like each other very much. This axiom has

reciprocity
communication that mirrors the previous communication behavior

Table 9.1 Axioms of Uncertainty Reduction Theory

AXIOM	MAIN CONCEPT	RELATIONSHIP	RELATED CONCEPT
1.	↑ Uncertainty	Negative	↓ Verbal Communication
2.	↑ Uncertainty	Negative	↓ Nonverbal Affiliative Expressiveness
3.	↑ Uncertainty	Positive	↑ Information Seeking
4.	↑ Uncertainty	Negative	↓ Intimacy Level of Communication
5.	↑ Uncertainty	Positive	↑ Reciprocity
6.	↓ Uncertainty	Negative	↑ Similarity
7.	↑ Uncertainty	Negative	↓ Liking

received some indirect empirical support. In a study examining the relationship between communication satisfaction and uncertainty reduction, James Neuliep and Erica Grohskopf (2000) found that participants playing interviewers in an organizational role play were more likely to feel positively toward the participants playing the job seekers (and more likely to hire them) when their uncertainty was low.

The seven axioms and their relationships are summarized in Table 9.1. Berger and Calabrese combined the axioms to deduce a number of **theorems,** or theoretical statements. Axiomatic theories are constructed by pairing two axioms to produce a theorem. The process follows deductive logic: If *A* is related to *B* and *B* is related to *C*, then *A* is related to *C*.

Berger and Calabrese combined all seven axioms in every possible pair combination to derive twenty-one theorems (Table 9.2). For instance, if the amount of verbal communication is negatively related to uncertainty (Axiom 1) and uncertainty is negatively related to intimacy levels of communication (Axiom 4), then verbal communication and intimacy levels are positively related (Theorem 3, see Table 9.2). You can generate the other twenty theorems by combining the axioms using the deductive formula above. You need to use the rule of multiplication for multiplying positives and negatives. For example, if two variables have a positive relationship with a third, they are expected to have a positive relationship with each other. If one variable has a positive relationship with a third whereas the other has a negative relationship with the third, they should have a negative relationship with each other. Finally, if two variables each have a negative relationship with a third, they should have a positive relationship with each other. This process allows URT to be a comprehensive theory.

theorems
theoretical statements derived from axioms, positing a relationship between two concepts

Expansions of Uncertainty Reduction Theory

As we discussed in Chapter 4, one evaluative criterion for theories is heurism, or how much the theory generates discussion and stimulates research. In many ways URT satisfies this criterion very well. Many researchers have tested URT

Table 9.2 Theorems of Uncertainty Reduction Theory Deduced from Axioms

1.	↑ Verbal Communication	Positive	↑ Nonverbal Affiliative Expressiveness
2.	↑ Verbal Communication	Negative	↓ Information Seeking
3.	↑ Verbal Communication	Positive	↑ Intimacy Level of Communication
4.	↑ Verbal Communication	Negative	↓ Reciprocity
5.	↑ Verbal Communication	Positive	↑ Similarity
6.	↑ Verbal Communication	Positive	↑ Liking
7.	↑ Nonverbal Affiliative Expressiveness	Negative	↓ Information Seeking
8.	↑ Nonverbal Affiliative Expressiveness	Positive	↑ Intimacy Level of Communication
9.	↑ Nonverbal Affiliative Expressiveness	Negative	↓ Reciprocity
10.	↑ Nonverbal Affiliative Expressiveness	Positive	↑ Similarity
11.	↑ Nonverbal Affiliative Expressiveness	Positive	↑ Liking
12.	↑ Information Seeking	Negative	↓ Intimacy Level of Communication
13.	↑ Information Seeking	Positive	↑ Reciprocity
14.	↑ Information Seeking	Negative	↓ Similarity
15.	↑ Information Seeking	Negative	↓ Liking
16.	↑ Intimacy Level	Negative	↓ Reciprocity
17.	↑ Intimacy Level	Positive	↑ Similarity
18.	↑ Intimacy Level	Positive	↑ Liking
19.	↑ Reciprocity	Negative	↓ Similarity
20.	↑ Reciprocity	Negative	↓ Liking
21.	↑ Similarity	Positive	↑ Liking

and based their studies on the tenets of the theory. Furthermore, Berger and several colleagues continue to refine and expand the theory, taking into account research findings. URT has been expanded and modified in a few areas. These areas include additional axioms, antecedent conditions, strategies, developed relationships, and context.

Additional Axioms

Based on further research, Berger and Gudykunst (1991) added an eighth axiom, which then provided seven new theorems.

> **Axiom 8:** Uncertainty is negatively related to interaction with social networks. The more people interact with the friends and family members of their relational partner, the less uncertainty they experience.

The research that Berger and Gudykunst based this axiom on pertained to relationships beyond the entry stage; they were actually considering romantic relationships.

James Neuliep and Erica Grohskopf (2000) suggested a ninth axiom based on their work correlating uncertainty and communication satisfaction.

> **Axiom 9:** There is an inverse, or negative, relationship between uncertainty and communication satisfaction.

They define communication satisfaction similarly to Hecht (1978, cited in Neuliep & Grohskopf, 2000) as "an affective response to the accomplishment of communication goals and expectations" (p. 69). After conducting two studies, Neuliep and Grohskopf found that "during initial interaction encounters, as individuals reduce uncertainty they experience more communication satisfaction than in situations where uncertainty remains high" (p. 74). The researchers agreed that this is an important axiom because it relates uncertainty to a specific communication outcome variable.

Antecedent Conditions

Berger (1979) has suggested that three antecedent (prior) conditions exist when seeking uncertainty reduction. The first condition occurs when the other person has the *potential* to reward or punish. If Edie is a very popular, charismatic figure on campus, her attention may be seen as a reward by Malcolm. Likewise, Malcolm might experience a rejection by her as punishing. If Malcolm finds out that a friend thought Edie was boring and unattractive or if he discovers she has a bad reputation on campus, he will not see her attention as rewarding or her rejection as punishing. Thus, according to Berger, Malcolm will be more motivated to reduce his uncertainty the more attractive Edie appears to him.

A second antecedent condition exists when the other person behaves contrary to expectations. In the case of Edie and Malcolm, Berger theorizes that Malcolm expects a superficial response to his comment about the class exercise. That is, his expectation may be that Edie will smile and agree with his assessment of the class activities. When Edie disagrees and comments that she might be happier in a different class, Malcolm's expectations are violated, and thus his desire to reduce his uncertainty increases.

The third and final condition exists when a person expects future interactions with another. Malcolm knows that he will continue to see Edie in class for the rest of the semester. Yet, because he has discovered that she is an engineering major, he may feel that he can avoid her in the future. In the first case, Berger would expect Malcolm's desire to increase predictability to be high—he knows he'll be seeing Edie often; in the second case, Malcolm's desire level is lower because Edie has a different major, and they can avoid each other after this class ends.

Strategies

A third area of expansion pertains to strategies. Berger (1995) suggests that people—in attempting to reduce uncertainty—use tactics from three categories of strategies: passive, active, and interactive. At the core of each is the goal of acquiring information. First, there are **passive strategies,** whereby an individual assumes the role of unobtrusive observer of another. **Active strategies** exist when an observer engages in some type of effort other than direct contact to find out about another person. For instance, a person might ask a third party for information about the other. Finally, **interactive strategies** occur when

passive strategies
reducing uncertainties by unobtrusive observation

active strategies
reducing uncertainties by means other than direct contact

interactive strategies
reducing uncertainties by engaging in conversation

Theory Into Practice

Max

It was so funny when I read about the strategies to reduce uncertainty. When I first moved here to go to school I am sure I used all of these strategies. I spent a lot of time at the union, kind of just watching what everyone was doing, and I remember asking someone I knew a little bit from high school to tell me more about someone else I'd just seen in passing, but who looked really nice. And, finally, of course, I got up the nerve to actually talk to her and we went through a lot of small talk before things got going.

the observer and the other person engage in direct contact or face-to-face interaction—that is, conversation that may include self-disclosures, direct questioning, and other information-seeking tactics. Although these strategies are critical to reducing uncertainty, Berger believes that certain behaviors, such as asking inappropriately sensitive questions, may increase rather than decrease uncertainty, and people may need additional reduction strategies.

To briefly illustrate these strategies, consider Malcolm and Edie. The time they spend in class covertly observing each other falls into the passive category. When Malcolm observes how Edie reacts to jokes the professor tells in lecture, he is utilizing a particular passive strategy called **reactivity searching**, or observing Edie doing something. A different passive strategy, called **disinhibition searching**, would require Malcolm to observe Edie in more informal settings outside the classroom to see how she behaves when her inhibitions are down. If either one of them engages friends to find out information about the other, he or she will be using an active strategy. When they speak after class, they use an interactive strategy to find out about each other and to reduce their uncertainties.

Tara Emmers and Dan Canary (1996) argue that in established relationships an additional strategy is employed. They call this strategy "uncertainty acceptance," and it includes responses such as simply trusting your partner. Emmers and Canary suggest that accepting or trusting your partner even when you are not completely certain about what is happening is a viable strategy for coping with uncertainty in developed relationships.

reactivity searching
a passive strategy involving watching a person doing something

disinhibition searching
a passive strategy involving watching a person's natural or uninhibited behavior in an informal environment

Developed Relationships: Beyond the Initial Encounter

When Berger and Calabrese conceived their theory, they were interested in describing the initial encounters between strangers. They stated a clear and narrow boundary around their theoretical insights. In the intervening years, however, the theory has been expanded to include developed relationships, as the acceptance strategy discussed previously indicates. Berger (1982, 1987) has updated his theory since its inception. First, he comments that uncertainties are ongoing in relationships, and thus the process of uncertainty reduction is relevant in *developed* relationships as well as in *initial* interactions. This conclusion broadens earlier claims by Berger and Calabrese that specifically limited URT to initial encounters.

The inclusion of the three antecedent conditions discussed previously (potential for reward or punishment, deviation from expectations, and anticipation of future interactions) points us toward an examination of uncertainty in developed relationships. Specifically, we will expect rewards from, be surprised by, and anticipate future interactions with those with whom we have ongoing relationships.

Uncertainty in developed relationships may be different than it is in initial encounters. It may function dialectically within relationships; that is, there may be a tension between reducing and increasing uncertainty in developed relationships (Baxter & Wilmot, 1985). Berger and Calabrese (1975) observe, "While uncertainty reduction may be rewarding up to a point, the ability to completely predict another's behavior might lead to boredom. Boredom in an interpersonal relationship might well be a cost rather than a reward" (p. 101). Gerald R. Miller and Mark Steinberg (1975) mention a similar belief, noting that people have a greater desire for uncertainty when they feel secure than they do when they feel insecure. This suggests that as people begin to feel certain about their relationships and their partners, the excitement of uncertainty becomes desirable. Neuliep and Grohskopf (2000) agree, stating that the linear relationship between uncertainty and other communication variables may not hold in stages beyond initial interaction.

We return to the notion of dialectics again in Chapter 12, but let's examine this certainty-uncertainty dialectic a bit further with an example. In our opening vignette, Malcolm and Edie met for the first time after class. If their subsequent conversations evolve into a relationship, then their relationship will involve a level of predictability—that is, both will be able to predict certain things about the other because of the time they spend together. Yet this predictability (certainty) may get tedious after a time, and they may feel their relationship is in a rut. At this point, the need for uncertainty, or novelty, will become high, and the couple might try to build some variety into their routine to satisfy this need. Yet Leanne Knobloch and her colleagues (2007) observe that uncertainty is undesirable in marriage because it leads the partners to be more negative in evaluating conversations with each other.

Uncertainty and uncertainty reduction processes operate in dating relationships in somewhat the same ways that Berger and Calabrese theorize they do in initial interactions. One study (Mongeau, Jacobsen, & Donnerstein, 2007) found that reducing uncertainty was cited as a primary goal in dating. Research conducted by Sally Planalp and her colleagues (Planalp, 1987; Planalp & Honeycutt, 1985; Planalp, Rutherford, & Honeycutt, 1988) discovered that dating couples found that at times their uncertainty increased. When this happened, the individuals were motivated to reduce it through their communication behaviors. In a study of forty-six married couples, Lynn Turner (1990) reached similar conclusions. Therefore, according to these researchers, we must not assume that once relationships begin, uncertainty disappears.

Another example of how Uncertainty Reduction Theory has been extended into developed relationships is found in the research of Malcolm Parks and Mara Adelman (1983). Parks and Adelman studied the social networks (friends and family members) of an individual and indicate that these third-party networks can be quite important information sources about a romantic partner. They note that network "members may comment on the partner's past actions and behavioral tendencies. They may supply ready-made explanations for the partner's behavior or serve as sounding boards for the individual's own explanations" (p. 57). They conclude that the more partners communicate with their social networks, the less uncertainty they will experience. Furthermore, the researchers found that the less uncertainty people feel, the less likely they will be to dissolve a relationship with another.

Based on this expansion into established relationships, Berger and Gudykunst (1991) posited an eighth axiom and seven resulting new theorems, which we discussed previously. As we mentioned, the new axiom asserted that romantic partners who interact with their partner's social network experience less uncertainty about their partner than do those who do not have this interaction. The more interaction with the social network, the less uncertainty there will be.

Some researchers who were interested in how URT applied to established relationships suggested that people in this stage experienced a different type of uncertainty than did those in initial encounters. This uncertainty was labeled **relational uncertainty** and defined as lack of certainty about the future and the status of the relationship. Berger (1987) discussed this new uncertainty type and noted that it mars relational stability. More recent research (e.g., Ficara & Mongeau, 2000; Knobloch & Solomon, 2003) established that relational uncertainty is distinct from the individual uncertainty that Berger and Calabrese originally theorized about. Relational uncertainty is found to be different from individual uncertainty because it exists at a higher level of abstraction (Knobloch & Solomon, 2003).

Marianne Dainton and Brooks Aylor (2001) examined how relational uncertainty operated in three different types of relationships: long-distance relationships with no face-to-face interaction, long-distance relationships with some face-to-face interaction, and geographically close relationships. The researchers were interested to see how relational uncertainty, jealousy, maintenance, and trust interacted in these three types of relationships. This is an important investigation because, as they note, 25 to 40 percent of romantic relationships between college students are long distance.

They found overall, as URT would predict, that the more uncertainty existed in a relationship the more jealousy, the less trust, and the fewer maintenance behaviors also existed. Dainton and Aylor also found support for trust as "a potent means for reducing relational uncertainty" (p. 183). The researchers also found that face-to-face contact is critical to reducing relational uncertainty. The people in long-distance relationships with no face-to-face interaction suffered from significantly more relational uncertainty. However, those who were geographically close did not differ significantly from those in long-distance relationships with some face-to-face interaction, which is not

relational uncertainty
a lack of certainty about the future and status of a relationship

exactly what URT would predict. The researchers conclude that this is a fruitful line for further research into the utility and heurism of URT.

Context

Thus far, our examples clearly relate to the interpersonal context. However, Uncertainty Reduction Theory has been applied to other contexts. Most of the work has been done in the context described in Chapter 2, and we will discuss that first. Berger (1987) points out that uncertainty varies across cultures, and a number of research studies illustrate the cultural applicability of URT.

William Gudykunst and his colleagues are credited with adapting URT to communication between Americans and Asians (Gudykunst, Chua, & Gray, 1987; Gudykunst & Nishida, 1984; Gudykunst, Yang, & Nishida, 1985). Gudykunst has extended Berger and Calabrese's formulation of URT into a new theory that deals specifically with culture, which he calls Anxiety-Uncertainty Management (Gudykunst, 1995). These researchers conclude that in Japan, Korea, and the United States, being attracted to another most likely reduces some uncertainty in acquaintance, friend, and dating relationships. However, the researchers add that reduced uncertainty may not lead to increased attraction.

Gudykunst and Tsukasa Nishida (1986a) discovered differences in low- and high-context cultures. According to Edward T. Hall (1977), **low-context cultures** are those in which meaning is found in the explicit code or message. Examples of low-context cultures are the United States, Germany, and Switzerland. In these cultures, plain, direct speaking is valued. Listeners are supposed to be able to understand meaning based merely on the words a speaker uses. In **high-context cultures**, nonverbal messages play a more significant role, and most of the meaning of a message is internalized by listeners or resides in the context. Japan, Korea, and China are examples of high-context cultures. These cultures value indirectness in speech because listeners are expected to ignore much of the explicit code in favor of understood meanings cued by nonverbals and context.

low-context cultures
cultures, like the United States, where most of the meaning is in the code or message

high-context cultures
cultures, like Japan, where the meaning of a message is in the context or internalized in listeners

With respect to research on low- and high-context cultures, Gudykunst and Nishida (1986b) found that frequency of communication predicts uncertainty reduction in low-context cultures but not in high-context cultures. The researchers also discovered that people use direct communication (asking questions) to reduce their uncertainty in individualistic cultures. In collectivistic cultures, more indirect communication is used with individuals who are not identified as members of the cultural in-group. Based on this research, then, people from different cultures engage in different kinds of communication to reduce their uncertainty.

Gudykunst and Mitchell Hammer (1987) undertook an additional study examining URT and culture. Instead of studying cultures outside the United States, however, they focused their research on African Americans. Interestingly, they found that URT did not apply to their African American respondents. Specifically, African Americans were not more confident in their impressions of others after asking them questions, and they were not attracted to people about

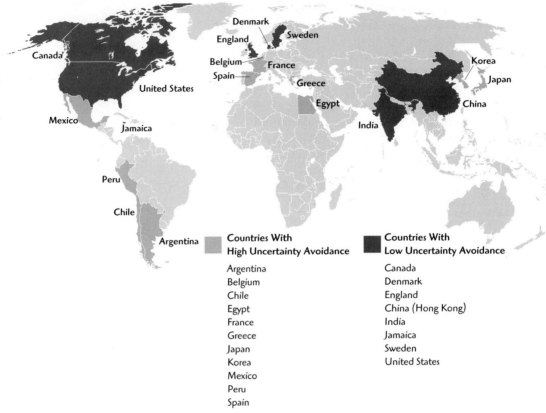

Countries With High Uncertainty Avoidance	Countries With Low Uncertainty Avoidance
Argentina	Canada
Belgium	Denmark
Chile	England
Egypt	China (Hong Kong)
France	India
Greece	Jamaica
Japan	Sweden
Korea	United States
Mexico	
Peru	
Spain	

Figure 9.1 Countries and Uncertainty Avoidance

Theory Application in Groups (TAG)

In small groups, debate whether URT presents an accurate view of relationship development and maintenance. Some of you should defend the social scientific, objectivist epistemology of the theory, while others should question it.

uncertainty avoidance
an attempt to avoid ambiguous situations

whom they could make predictions. Consequently, uncertainty reduction may not be applicable in all cultural communities.

A concept similar to uncertainty reduction is **uncertainty avoidance,** which is an attempt to shun or avoid ambiguous situations (Hofstede, 1991). In other words, uncertainty avoidance refers to a person's tolerance for uncertainty. Geert Hofstede believes that the perspective of people in high uncertainty avoidance cultures is "What is different is dangerous," whereas people in low uncertainty avoidance cultures subscribe to "What is different is curious" (1991, p. 119). Gudykunst and Yuko Matsumoto (1996) point out that a number of cultures differ in their uncertainty avoidance (Figure 9.1), and understanding that these differences exist can help us understand communication behaviors in other countries.

Although not as developed as Anxiety-Uncertainty Management, researchers have begun to cast the principles of URT into other contexts beyond the interpersonal. One such example is Michael Boyle and his colleagues' (2004) work examining people's information-seeking behaviors in the United States after the terrorist attacks of September 11, 2001. Boyle and his co-researchers argue that "although uncertainty reduction theory has primarily been used in interpersonal communication research [its] basic logic can be applied to mass communication research" (p. 157). In addition, some work has set uncertainty reduction principles in the context of the workplace (Hargie, Tourish, & Wilson, 2002; Morrison, 2002) and through computer-mediated communication (Flanagin, 2007; Tidwell & Walther, 2002).

Integration, Critique, and Closing

Over a decade after the publication of the original theory, Berger (1987) admitted that Uncertainty Reduction Theory "contains some propositions of dubious validity" (p. 40). Other writers concur. Although URT has stimulated a great deal of discussion and research, it also has been criticized. As you think about how useful URT is, keep the following criteria in mind: utility and heurism.

Integration

Communication Tradition	Rhetorical	Semiotic	Phenomenological	Cybernetic	**Socio-Psychological**	Socio-Cultural	Critical
Communication Context	**Intrapersonal**	**Interpersonal**	Small Group	Organizational	Public/Rhetorical	Mass/Media	Cultural
Approach to Knowing	**Positivistic/Empirical**	Interpretive/Hermeneutic	Critical

Critique

Evaluation Criteria	Scope	**Logical Consistency**	Parsimony	**Utility**	Testability	**Heurism**	Test of Time

Utility

Some researchers believe that the major assumptions of the theory are flawed. Michael Sunnafrank (1986) argues that reducing uncertainty about the self and another in an initial encounter is not an individual's primary concern. Instead, Sunnafrank argues, "a more primary goal is the maximization of relational outcomes" (p. 9). Sunnafrank calls for a reformulation of URT that takes into account the importance of predicted outcomes during initial interactions. This has come to be known as predicted outcome value (POV).

Drawing on our chapter's opening, Sunnafrank would contend that Malcolm will be more concerned with maximizing rewards in a potential relationship with Edie than in figuring out what she might do and why she is doing it. Actually, Sunnafrank suggests that URT might kick in after Malcolm decides what the predicted outcomes of talking with Edie will be.

Berger's (1986) response to Sunnafrank is that outcomes cannot be predicted without knowledge and reduced uncertainty about oneself, one's partner, and one's relationship. It is Berger's contention that uncertainty reduction is independent of as well as necessary to predicted outcome values. In fact, he believes that if one remains highly uncertain, there really are no predicted outcome values. Furthermore, Berger responds to Sunnafrank's critique by noting that the act of predicting an outcome serves as a means to reduce uncertainty. Thus, Berger concludes that Sunnafrank has simply expanded the scope of URT rather than offering an alternative to it.

A second problem with URT's utility has to do with its validity. Recall that even Berger (1987) has admitted some validity problems, yet he is not willing to give up on the theory. Some of his more skeptical colleagues, however, assert that given the tight logical structure of an axiomatic theory, if one building block is wrong, then much of the resulting theory is suspect. Kathy Kellermann and Rodney Reynolds (1990) point to Axiom 3, which suggests that high uncertainty causes high levels of information-seeking behavior, as problematic.

Their study of over a thousand students failed to find support for the third axiom. Instead, they found that "*wanting* knowledge rather than *lacking* knowledge is what promotes information-seeking in initial encounters with others" (p. 71 [emphasis added]). Kellermann and Reynolds point out that many times we may be uncertain about another but because we have no interest in the other, we are not motivated to reduce our uncertainties by information-seeking behaviors. People engage in communication, therefore, not to reduce uncertainty but because they care about the other, are interested in the other, or both. In a different vein, Dale Brashers (2001) also questions the validity of Axiom 3. He notes with reference to post–September 11 anxieties that sometimes more information results in a greater sense of uncertainty. Interestingly, however, Dell McKinney and William Donaghy (1993) found some empirical support for Axiom 3, so the debate on this issue undoubtedly will continue concerning URT's usefulness.

Heurism

Despite these shortcomings, Uncertainty Reduction Theory remains the only communication theory to specifically examine initial interactions. Reflecting on our criteria for theory evaluation from Chapter 4, this theory is highly heuristic. For instance, URT has been integrated into research examining small groups (Booth-Butterfield, Booth-Butterfield, & Koester, 1988) as well as research in mass communication (Dimmick, Sikand, & Patterson, 1994) and computer-mediated communication (Walther & Burgoon, 1992). It is clear from our earlier discussions that URT has been expanded into many contexts, making it highly heuristic.

Finally, URT, like all theoretical thinking, can be considered to be tentative in that the theorists originally claimed that "there are other relevant constructs which might be explicitly incorporated into the model" (Berger & Calabrese, 1975, p. 111). Obviously, the writers were qualifying their original assumptions and conclusions, which paved the way for others to apply the theory variously. Uncertainty Reduction Theory has made a very important contribution to the field of communication, even as it has generated controversy and theoretical disputes. Although this theory may be somewhat linear in nature (recall our discussion on communication models in Chapter 1), it has provoked a great deal of commentary and research, and it places communication in a central position. It marks the beginning of communication researchers focusing on their own discipline for theoretical explanations rather than borrowing theories from other disciplines. In addition, it provides an ongoing dialogue as researchers continue to debate the validity of uncertainty reduction as a primary issue in relationship development.

Discussion Starters

1. Why is examining initial interactions like that of Edie and Malcolm an important undertaking for communication theorists? Provide at least one example to support your view.

2. Uncertainty reduction is the process of using communication to increase our ability to explain and predict others' behaviors. How do we use new media such as e-mail, pagers, palm pilots, and so forth in this process?

3. Are there times when asking questions in initial encounters with others only results in more uncertainty? Give examples. Has reducing your uncertainty about someone ever led to you liking the person less? Describe how this occurs.

4. Do you agree with Berger and Calabrese's assumption about the developmental process of interpersonal relationships? Give examples that support or contest the notion that relationships use communication to pass through entry, personal, and exit phases.

5. What additional factors or events exist—other than those presented in this chapter—when two people meet for the first time? Be sure to be specific and provide appropriate examples.

6. If you could talk with Berger or Calabrese, what would you say to either one of them about the utility of their theory in your life? Apply the theory to any aspect or relationship type in your life today in answering this question.

7. How useful is URT when it comes to examining communication across cultures? What do you think of the extensions that have been made to URT to make it apply to intercultural Communication?

Online Learning Center (www. mhhe.com/west4e)

Visit the Online Learning Center at www.mhhe.com/west4e for chapter-specific resources, such as story-into-theory and multiple-choice quizzes, as well as theory summaries and theory connection questions.

CHAPTER 10

Social Penetration Theory

*Based on the research of **Irwin Altman** and **Dalmas Taylor***

Jason LaSalle

About three years ago, Jason LaSalle's wife, Miranda, died in a car accident, leaving Jason a single parent of 8-year-old twins. Since his wife's death, he has struggled both financially and emotionally. He has worried about making his rent and van payments and about meeting his children's needs. For the past three years, Jason has worked odd jobs around the neighborhood to supplement his modest income as custodian for a local cinema complex. In addition, Jason has been lonely. He is shy around others, especially women. Miranda was the only woman he really felt comfortable with, and he misses her a great deal.

Jason's sister, Kayla, is always trying to get Jason out of the house. One night, she hired a baby-sitter and picked him up to go out. This evening was especially important to Kayla because she had also invited her friend Elise Porter, who was recently divorced. Kayla thought that Elise might be a good match for her brother. She was hoping that Elise's easygoing nature and her great sense of humor would appeal to Jason. Throughout the evening, Jason and Elise talked about a variety of things, including their experiences as single parents, her divorce, and the two children they were each raising. Much of their night was spent dancing or talking to each other. The evening ended with Jason and Elise promising to get together again soon.

As Jason drove home to his apartment he couldn't help but think about Miranda. He was lonely; it had been three years since he had shared any intimacy with an adult. When he arrived home, his sadness increased as he caught sight of a family picture taken at Disney World shortly before Miranda's death. He wasn't sure if it was a good time to pursue an intimate relationship, and yet he wanted a chance to see what kind of person Elise was. He knew that future dates would inevitably require him to talk about Miranda, and he felt that such conversations would be very difficult. He would have to open up emotionally to Elise, and the thought of being placed in such a vulnerable position seemed challenging.

After he paid the baby-sitter and closed the door behind her, he walked into the twins' room and gave each a kiss on the forehead. Sitting drinking his tea in the living room, Jason felt that he was embarking upon something new, exciting, and a bit frightening.

When we say we're close to someone, we often act as though others understand precisely what we mean. That is not always the case, however. Saying that you are close or intimate with someone may not be universally understood.

social penetration
process of bonding
that moves a
relationship from
superficial to more
intimate

To understand the relational closeness between two people, Irwin Altman and Dalmas Taylor (1973) conceptualized Social Penetration Theory (SPT). The two conducted extensive study in the area of social bonding among various types of couples. Their theory illustrates a pattern of relationship development, a process that they identified as social penetration. Social penetration refers to a process of relationship bonding whereby individuals move from superficial communication to more intimate communication. According to Altman and Taylor, intimacy involves more than physical intimacy; other dimensions of intimacy include intellectual and emotional, and the extent to which a couple share activities (West & Turner, 2009). The social penetration process, therefore, necessarily includes verbal behaviors (the words we use), nonverbal behaviors (our body posture, the extent to which we smile, and so forth), and environmentally oriented behaviors (the space between communicators, the physical objects present in the environment, and so forth).

Altman and Taylor (1973) believe that people's relationships vary tremendously in their social penetration. From husband–wife to supervisor–employee to golf partners to physician–patient, the theorists conclude that relationships "involve different levels of intimacy of exchange or degree of social penetration" (p. 3). The authors note that relationships follow some particular trajectory, or pathway to closeness. Furthermore, they contend that relationships are somewhat organized and predictable in their development. Because relationships are critical and "lie at the heart of our humanness" (Rogers & Escudero, 2004, p. 3), Social Penetration theorists attempt to unravel the simultaneous nature of relational complexity and predictability. And, although many individuals may have established online relationships, Altman and Taylor did not conceptualize this development in their writing.

The opening story of Jason LaSalle and his arranged date illustrates a central feature of Social Penetration Theory (SPT). The only way for Jason and Elise to understand each other is for them to engage in personal conversations; such discussion requires each sharing personal bits of information. As the two become closer, they will move from a nonintimate relationship to an intimate one. In addition, each person's personality will influence the direction of the relationship. So Jason and Elise's relationship will be influenced by Jason's shyness and Elise's easygoing manner. The future of Jason's relationship with Elise is based on a multiplicity of factors—factors that we will explore throughout this chapter.

Early discussions of SPT began during the 1960s and 1970s, an era when opening up and talking candidly was highly valued as an important relational strategy. Now, however, researchers have acknowledged that cultures can vary tremendously in their endorsement of openness as a relational skill, and some question the initial enthusiasm for relational openness in general (Stafford, 2005). Therefore, as you read this chapter, keep in mind that we are discussing a theory that is rooted in a generation for which speaking freely was a highly valued characteristic. Nevertheless, much of the theory remains relevant today as we live in a society where openness is still a valued personal characteristic.

Simply look at daytime television talk shows such as Oprah or Dr. Phil for evidence of this.

To begin, we outline several assumptions of Social Penetration Theory. We then identify the catalyst for the theory.

Assumptions of Social Penetration Theory

Social Penetration Theory (called a "stage theory" by Mongeau & Henningsen, 2008), has enjoyed widespread acceptance by a number of scholars in the communication discipline. Part of the reason for the theory's appeal is its straightforward approach to relationship development. Although we alluded to some assumptions earlier, we will explore the following assumptions that guide SPT:

- Relationships progress from nonintimate to intimate.
- Relational development is generally systematic and predictable.
- Relational development includes depenetration and dissolution.
- Self-disclosure is at the core of relationship development.

First, relational communication between people begins at a rather superficial level and moves along a continuum to a more intimate level. On their date arranged by Kayla, Jason and Elise no doubt talked about trivial issues related to being single parents. They probably shared how difficult it is to have enough time in the day to do everything, but they probably did not express how desperate they feel at 3 A.M. when they awake from a nightmare, for example. These initial conversations at first may appear unimportant, but as Jason discovers, such conversations allow an individual to size up the other and provide the opportunity for the early stages of relational development. There is little doubt that Jason feels awkward, but this awkwardness can pass. With time, relationships have the opportunity to become intimate.

Not all relationships fall into the extremes of nonintimate or intimate. In fact, many of our relationships are somewhere in between these two poles. Often, we may want only a moderately close relationship. For instance, we may want a relationship with a co-worker to remain sufficiently distant so that

Theory Application in Groups (TAG)

This chapter attempts to demonstrate that relationships are predictable and somewhat routine in their development. There are, however, many times when relationship development is messy. In small groups, discuss those times when relationship development wasn't so predictable. Try to account for all types of relationships and include how self-disclosure functioned during those times.

we do not know what goes on in her house each night or how much money she has in the bank. Yet we need to know enough personal information to have a sense of whether she can complete her part of a team project.

The second assumption of Social Penetration Theory pertains to predictability. Specifically, Social Penetration theorists argue that relationships progress fairly systematically and predictably. Some people may have difficulty with this claim. After all, relationships—like the communication process—are dynamic and ever-changing, but even dynamic relationships follow some acceptable standard and pattern of development.

To better understand this assumption, again consider Jason LaSalle. Without knowing all the specifics of his situation, we could figure out that if he pursues a relationship with Elise, he will have to work through his emotions about Miranda. In addition, he must inevitably reconcile how their families might merge if the relationship progresses into more intimacy. We could probably predict that the relationship will move slowly at first while both Jason and Elise work out their feelings and emotions.

These projections are grounded in the second assumption of the theory: Relationships generally move in an organized and predictable manner. Although we may not know precisely the direction of a relationship or be able to predict its exact future, social penetration processes are rather organized and predictable. We can be fairly sure, for instance, that Jason and Elise will not introduce each other to important people in their families before they date a few more times. We would also expect that neither would declare his or her love for the other before they exchanged more intimate information. Of course, a number of other events and variables (time, personality, and so forth) affect the way relationships progress and what we can predict along the way. As Altman and Taylor (1973) conclude, "People seem to possess very sensitive tuning mechanisms which enable them to program carefully their interpersonal relationships" (p. 8).

The third assumption of SPT pertains to the notion that relational development includes depenetration and dissolution. At first, this may sound a bit peculiar. Thus far, we have explored the coming together of a relationship. Yet relationships do fall apart, or **depenetrate**, and this depenetration can lead to relationship dissolution. Elise, for example, may be unprepared for Jason's past and may wish to depenetrate and ultimately dissolve the relationship.

depenetrate
slow deterioration of relationship

Addressing depenetration and dissolution, Altman and Taylor liken the process to a film shown in reverse. Just as communication allows a relationship to move forward toward intimacy, communication could move a relationship back toward *non*intimacy. If the communication is conflictual, for example, and this conflict continues to be destructive and unresolved, the relationship may take a step back and become less close. And Social Penetration theorists think that depenetration—like the penetration process—is often systematic.

If a relationship depenetrates, it does not mean that it will automatically dissolve or terminate. At times, relationships experience **transgressions**, or the violation of relational rules, practices, and expectations. These transgressions may seem unworkable and, at times, they are. In fact, Tara Emmers-Sommer (2003) points out that various relational transgressions can aid in the breakdown of relationships. In Chapter 6, we discussed unwanted repetitive patterns of conflict in couples. We noted that recurring conflicts characterize a number of different relationship types and that couples generally learn to live with these conflicts. You may believe conflict or relational transgressions will inevitably lead to dissolution, but depenetration does not necessarily mean that the relationship is doomed.

transgression
a violation of relational rules, practices, and expectations

The final assumption contends that self-disclosure is at the core of relationship development. **Self-disclosure** can be generally defined as the purposeful process of revealing information about yourself to others. Usually, the information that makes up self-disclosure is of a significant nature. For instance, revealing that you like to play the piano may not be all that important; revealing a more personal piece of information, such as that you are a practicing Catholic and are pro-life, may significantly influence the evolution of a relationship.

self-disclosure
purposeful process of revealing information about oneself

According to Altman and Taylor (1973), nonintimate relationships progress to intimate relationships because of self-disclosure. This process allows people to get to know each other in a relationship. Self-disclosure helps shape the present and future relationship between two people, and "making [the] self accessible to another person is intrinsically gratifying" (p. 50). Elise will understand the challenges that lie ahead for her in a relationship with Jason by hearing Jason reveal his feelings about his wife's death and his desire to begin dating again. In turn, because social penetration requires a "gradual overlapping and exploration of their mutual selves by parties to a relationship" (p. 15), Elise, too, would have to self-disclose her thoughts and feelings.

Finally, we should note that self-disclosure can be strategic or nonstrategic. That is, in some relationships, we tend to plan out what we will say to another person. In other situations, our self-disclosure may be spontaneous. Spontaneous self-disclosure is widespread in our society. In fact, researchers have used the phrase "**stranger-on-the-train** (or plane or bus) phenomenon" to refer to those times when people reveal information to complete strangers in public places. Think about how many times you have been seated next to a stranger on a trip, only to have that person disclose personal information throughout the journey. Interpersonal communication researchers continue to investigate why people engage in this activity.

stranger-on-the-train
revealing personal information to strangers in public places

Research Notes

Dindia, K. (2003). Definitions and perspectives on relational maintenance communication. In D. J. Canary & M. Dainton (Eds.), *Maintaining relationships through communication* (pp. 1–28). Mahwah, NJ: Lawrence Erlbaum.

This chapter sets the stage for one of the few books in communication that specifically examines relationship maintenance. Dindia defines relational maintenance and further elaborates on communication behaviors, strategies, and routines individuals use to maintain their relationships with others. Reviewing research that looks at non-voluntary relationships, such as those with people whom we dislike and work relationships, Dindia provides an important backdrop from which the chapters are written. She concludes with some forecasts for directions of future research in the area of relational maintenance.

Johnson, A. J., Wittenberg, E., Haigh, M., Wigley, S., Becker, J., Brown, K., & Craig, E. (2004). The process of relationship development and deterioration: Turning points in friendships that have terminated. *Communication Quarterly, 52,* 54–68.

The researchers use social penetration principles to look at friendships that have ended. Using what are called "turning points" (perceptions of significant points in the friendship), Johnson and her colleagues examined 163 undergraduate students' beliefs about why their friendships terminated. The most frequently reported reasons include less affection, friend or self changed, stopped participating in activities or spending time together, and increase in distance. They also discovered that gender differences in breakups were apparent. Female same-sex friendships reported "conflict" as a turning point in the friendship, whereas male same-sex friendships were likely to report "common interests" (doing things together) as their turning point in friendship termination. The authors posit that both sets of friendships undergo both traditional and nontraditional models of relationship development, partially supporting early claims by Social Penetration theorists.

"Tearing Up" the Relationship: The Onion Analogy

Earlier we discussed the importance of revealing information about oneself of which others are unaware. In their discussion of SPT, Altman and Taylor incorporate an onionskin structure (Figure 10.1). They believe that a person like Jason LaSalle can be compared to an onion, with the layers (concentric circles) of the onion representing various aspects of a person's personality. The outer layer is an individual's **public image**, or that which is available to the naked eye. Jason's public image is an African American male in his mid-forties who is slightly balding. Elise Porter is also an African American but is significantly taller than Jason and has very short hair. A layer of the public image is removed, however, when Jason discloses to his date his frustrations with being a single father.

As the evening evolves for the two of them, Jason and Elise no doubt begin to reveal additional layers of their personalities. For instance, Elise may reveal that she, too, experiences single-parent anxieties. This **reciprocity**, or the process whereby one person's openness leads to the other's openness, is a primary component in SPT. Reciprocity has been shown to be significant in both established

public image
outer layer of a person; what is available to others

reciprocity
the return of openness from one person to another

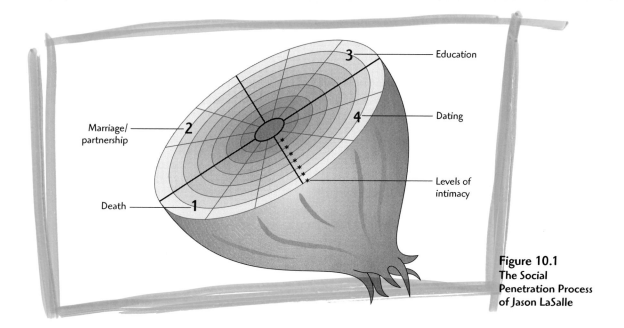

Figure 10.1
The Social
Penetration Process
of Jason LaSalle

and new relationships, such as Jason and Elise's. Lawrence Rosenfeld and Gary Bowen (1991), for example, found that marital satisfaction was highest when spouses reciprocated mutual levels of self-disclosure. The researchers point out that these relationships are "probably less distressed and more stable" (p. 80). Altman and Taylor believe intimacy cannot be achieved without such reciprocity.

Before leaving the discussion of self-disclosure, we need to point out that penetration can be viewed along two dimensions: breadth and depth. **Breadth** refers to the number of various topics discussed in the relationship; **breadth time** pertains to the amount of time that relational partners spend communicating with each other about these various topics. **Depth** refers to the degree of intimacy that guides topic discussions. In the initial stages, relationships can be classified as having narrow breadth and shallow depth. For Jason LaSalle, it is feasible that his first date with Elise was characterized this way. Most likely, the two did not discuss many topics, and what they did discuss probably lacked intimate overtones. As relationships move toward intimacy, we can expect a wider range of topics to be discussed (more breadth), with several of those topics marked by depth.

A few conclusions are important with respect to the breadth and depth of self-disclosure. First, shifts or changes in central layers (of the onion) have more of an impact than those in outer, or peripheral, layers. Because an individual's public image, or outer layer, represents those things that others can see, or the superficial, we expect that if there are changes in the outer layer, the consequence is minimal. For example, if Elise changed her hairstyle, her relationship with Jason would be less affected than if she changed her opinion about premarital sex.

Second, the greater the depth, the more opportunity for a person to feel vulnerable. Imagine that Jason reveals some inadequacy about himself to

breadth
number of topics discussed in a relationship

breadth time
amount of time spent by relational partners discussing various topics

depth
degree of intimacy guiding topic discussion

Table 10.1 Guidelines for Self-Disclosure

ASK YOURSELF	SUGGESTION
Is the other person important to you?	Reveal significant pieces of information about yourself to those people with whom you have developed a personal relationship.
Is the risk of disclosing reasonable?	Try not to reveal significant information about yourself if there is great risk associated with it. Assess the risk potential of your disclosure.
Are the amount and type of disclosure appropriate?	Discern whether you are revealing too much or too little information. Examine the timing of the disclosure.
Is the disclosure relevant to the situation at hand?	Constant disclosure is not typically useful in a relationship. Don't share everything.
Is the disclosure reciprocated?	Unequal self-disclosure creates an imbalanced relationship. Wait for reciprocity.
Will the effect be constructive?	If not employed carefully, disclosure can be used in destructive ways. Use care in disclosing information that may be perceived as damaging.
Are cultural misunderstandings possible?	Maintain cultural sensitivity as people disclose to you and you disclose to others.

Elise—for instance, the fact that he was on welfare for two years after his wife's death. When he reveals this personal information to Elise, she can respond in several different ways. She can simply say, "Wow," and not venture further into the discussion. Or she can reply, "That must have been very hard for you," communicating compassion. A third possible response is "I don't see anything wrong with that. Millions of people need some help at some point in their lives." The latter response demonstrates even more compassion and an effort to diffuse the possible anxiety that Jason is feeling. How Elise responds influences how vulnerable Jason feels. As you can see, the first response may elicit a high degree of vulnerability, whereas the third response may invoke little vulnerability.

As you reflect on the topic of self-disclosure, keep in mind that an individual should be judicious in using self-disclosure. Although self-disclosure generally moves a relationship toward more closeness, if people disclose too much during the early stages of a relationship, they may actually end the relationship. Some partners may be ill equipped and underprepared to know another so intimately. Also note that trust is an inherent part of the disclosure and reciprocity processes. Mark Knapp and Anita Vangelisti (2000), for example, note that "self-disclosure of intimate information is based on trust" (p. 240). They go on to say that if we desire reciprocity in disclosure, we must try to gain the trust of the other person and, similarly, feel trustful of the other person. One goal in self-disclosure, then, is to be thoughtful and appropriate. We have included other guidelines for self-disclosure in Table 10.1.

A Social Exchange: Relational Costs and Rewards

Social Penetration Theory is grounded in several principles of Social Exchange Theory (Thibaut & Kelley, 1959). As we will discuss in Chapter 11, this theory suggests that social exchanges "entail services that create unspecified obligations in the future and therefore exert a pervasive influence on social relations" (Blau, 1964, p. 140). Altman and Taylor based some of their work on social exchange processes; that is, an exchange of resources between individuals in a relationship. Specifically, rewards and costs relate to Social Exchange Theory.

Taylor and Altman (1987) argue that relationships can be conceptualized in terms of rewards and costs. Rewards are those relational events or behaviors that stimulate satisfaction, pleasure, and contentment in a relational partner, whereas costs are those relational events or behaviors that stimulate negative feelings. Quite simply, if a relationship provides more rewards than costs, then individuals are more likely to stay in that relationship. However, if an individual believes that there are more costs to being in a relationship, then relationship dissolution is probable. For instance, Jason LaSalle will most likely regulate the closeness of his relationship with Elise by assessing a **reward/cost ratio,** which is defined as the balance between positive and negative relationship experiences. If Jason believes he is deriving more pleasure (nurturance, supportive teasing, and so forth) than pain (frustration, insecurity, and so forth) from being in his relationship with Elise, then it is likely that he is fairly satisfied at the moment. His own expectations and experiences must also be taken into account in the reward/cost ratio. As Taylor and Altman point out, "rewards and costs are consistently associated with mutual satisfaction of personal and social needs" (1987, p. 264).

To understand this a bit better, consider the following two conclusions observed by Taylor and Altman: (1) Rewards and costs have a greater impact early on in the relationship than later in the relationship, and (2) relationships with a reservoir of positive reward/cost experiences are better equipped to handle conflict effectively. We will examine each of these briefly.

The first conclusion suggests that there are relatively few interpersonal experiences in the early stages, resulting in individuals focusing more on a single reward or a single cost. So, for instance, it is probable that Jason will be impressed with Elise if she is willing to give Jason space during the early stages of their relationship; for Jason, rushing into a relationship may be a bit overwhelming, and Elise's patience may be viewed as an important relational reward. Elise, however, may view Jason's early ambivalence as an indicator of things to come. She may, therefore, decide that his uncertainty is simply too much of a cost to endure and want to dissolve the relationship sooner than Jason does.

With respect to the second conclusion regarding costs and rewards, Taylor and Altman note that some relationships are better able to manage conflict than others. As relational partners move on in a relationship, they may experience a number of disagreements. Over the years, couples become accustomed to managing conflict in various ways, creating a unique relational culture that allows them to work through future issues. There may be more trust in handling a conflict in established relationships. In addition, the relationship is not

reward/cost ratio
balance between positive and negative relationship experiences

likely to be threatened by a single conflict because of the couple's stockpile of experiences in dealing with conflict.

In sum, then, relationships often depend on both parties assessing the rewards and costs. If partners feel that there are more rewards than costs, chances are that the relationship will survive. If more costs are perceived than rewards, the relationship may depenetrate or dissolve. However, keep in mind that both partners may not see an issue similarly; a cost by one person may be viewed as a reward by the other.

The Social Exchange perspective relies on both parties in a relationship to calculate the extent to which individuals view the relationship as negative (cost) or positive (reward). According to Social Exchange thinking, as relationships come together, partners ultimately assess the possibilities within a relationship as well as the perceived or real alternatives to a relationship. These evaluations are critical as communicators decide whether the process of social penetration is desirable. In the following section, we identify the stages of the social penetration process.

Stages of the Social Penetration Process

The decision about whether a potential relationship appears satisfying is not immediate. As we mentioned earlier, Social Penetration Theory is viewed as a "Stage" theory. Furthermore, relationship development occurs in a rather systematic manner, and decisions about whether people want to remain in a relationship are not usually made quickly. Not all relationships go through this process, and those that do are not always romantic relationships. To demonstrate how each stage functions in relationships that are *not* romantic, we provide a scenario for you to think about. We then talk about each stage and refer back to the example. Figure 10.2 outlines the four stages of the social penetration process.

Consider the relationship between Cathy and Barbra, first-year students at Upton University, who were randomly placed as roommates in Blackstone Hall, an all-female residence on campus. The two hail from different parts of the state; Cathy is from the city, and Barbra was raised on a farm. They also differ in family makeup in that Cathy is an only child and her roommate has four siblings. Finally, both of Cathy's parents have graduate degrees, whereas Barbra is the first in her family to attend college. They have only met each other once (at new student orientation) and are now about to have their first breakfast together.

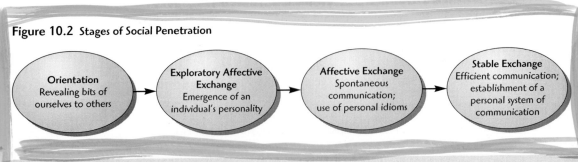

Figure 10.2 Stages of Social Penetration

Orientation
Revealing bits of ourselves to others

Exploratory Affective Exchange
Emergence of an individual's personality

Affective Exchange
Spontaneous communication; use of personal idioms

Stable Exchange
Efficient communication; establishment of a personal system of communication

Theory Into Practice
GK

The romantic relationship I have been in went through some pretty predictable stages. We actually had a third party introduce the two of us to each other. After that, we dated for a few months—disclosing a lot of private information along the way. I mean, I've never told anyone in my life the kinds of things I told her. She obviously knows me better than anyone after two years. We're now trying to figure out our "final commitment" (marriage) but we both want to wait till we graduate before that happens. I'm broke!

T*I*P

Orientation: Revealing Bit by Bit

The earliest stage of interaction, called the **orientation stage,** occurs at the public level; only bits of ourselves are revealed to others. During this stage, comments are usually on the cliché level and reflect superficial aspects of individuals. People usually act in socially desirable ways and are cautious of disturbing any societal expectations. Individuals smile pleasantly and react politely in the orientation stage.

Taylor and Altman (1987) note that people tend not to evaluate or criticize during the orientation stage. This behavior would be perceived as inappropriate by the other and might jeopardize future interactions. If evaluation does occur, the theorists believe that it will be couched in soft overtones. In addition, both parties actively avoid any conflict so that they have further opportunity to size up each other.

The orientation stage can be understood by examining the dialogue between Cathy and Barbra during their breakfast:

CATHY: I must admit that I was wondering what kind of roommate I'd have. It's kind of strange; we're picked by a computer, and we have to live with each other for a year.

BARBRA: I agree. [awkward silence]

CATHY: But, hey, it's cool that we both love lacrosse, and maybe we'll both make the team. I think this campus . . . [Barbra interrupts]

BARBRA: I love to study near . . . Sorry. You go ahead.

CATHY: No, you go.

BARBRA: I was going to say that I hope that we have some chances to go off campus and go to the lake. I love to study near the water. I also used to swim at a lake near my house. I haven't had time this past summer, though, because I was working too much.

CATHY: Believe it or not, I don't know how to swim! I tried to learn, but I just don't seem to be coordinated.

BARBRA: Hey! I'm a good swimmer. I'll teach ya when we get some time.

CATHY: Great!

orientation stage
stage of social penetration that includes revealing small parts of ourselves

As you can see, both women engage in a rather superficial and sometimes awkward conversation, and neither one appears to be judging the other. In fact, Barbra has an opportunity to tell Cathy how strange it is that she doesn't know how to swim, but she chooses to stay supportive.

Exploratory Affective Exchange: The Self Emerges

exploratory affective exchange stage
stage of social penetration that results in the emergence of our personality to others

In the orientation stage, interactants are cautious about revealing too much about themselves to each other. The **exploratory affective exchange stage,** however, is an expansion of the public areas of the self and occurs when aspects of an individual's personality begin to emerge. What was once private now becomes public. The theorists note that this stage is comparable to the relationships we have with casual acquaintances and friendly neighbors. Like other stages, this stage includes both verbal and nonverbal behaviors. People might begin to use some catch phrases that are idiosyncratic to the relationship. There is a small amount of spontaneity in communication because individuals feel more relaxed with each other, and they are not as cautious about blurting out something that they may later regret. Also, more touch behavior and more affect displays (such as facial expressions) may become part of the communication repertoire with the other person. Taylor and Altman tell us that many relationships don't proceed beyond this stage.

To gain a clearer picture of the exploratory affective exchange stage, think again about Cathy and Barbra. This time, however, consider that the two have been roommates for about eight weeks, and each is getting a better idea about the personality of the other. And like many roommates, they have decided to take a class together and are preparing for their midterm history exam:

> BARBRA: Hey, Cath, d'ya hear about what kind of tests Kading [the professor] gives in class?
>
> CATHY: At my [sorority] rush last month, I heard that they are mostly "recall", and we don't have to know dates. Ahhhh, I'm ready to scream because I can't remember all of this stuff from Chapter 3!
>
> BARBRA: Chill. . . . Breathe!
>
> CATHY: Chill! It's easy for a straight A student to say that.
>
> BARBRA: I *was* going to say—that I thought I'd do badly on my psych exam, and I got a B+ on it. Anyway, he may curve.
>
> CATHY: I can't rely on a curve. I'm just too removed from this stuff to understand it. My parents will kill me if I flunk this course.
>
> BARBRA: OK, I get why you're so nervous!

Clearly, Barbra and Cathy are starting to feel more comfortable around each other. In fact, Barbra's "Chill" reflects the sort of catchphrase to which Taylor and Altman refer. Furthermore, Cathy is slowly revealing more personal information about her parents' expectations and her ability to understand the material. Their exploratory affective exchange is relatively supportive, although their anxiety level gets the best of them at times.

Affective Exchange: Commitment and Comfortability

This stage is characterized by close friendships and intimate partners. The **affective exchange stage** includes those interactions that are more "freewheeling and casual" (Taylor & Altman, 1987, p. 259) in that communication is frequently spontaneous and individuals make quick decisions, often with little regard for the relationship as a whole. The affective exchange stage represents further commitment to the other individual; the interactants are comfortable with each other.

The stage includes those nuances of a relationship that make it unique; a smile may substitute for the words "I understand," or a penetrating gaze may translate into "We'll talk about this later." We might also find individuals using **personal idioms** (Hopper, Knapp, & Scott, 1981), which are private ways of expressing a relationship's intimacy through words, phrases, or behaviors. Idiomatic expressions—such as "sweetie" or "bubbles"—carry unique meaning for two people in a relationship. These idioms are different from the catchphrases we discussed in the exploratory affective exchange in that idioms usually characterize more established relationships, whereas catchphrases may develop at any point in an initial interaction. We should add that this stage may also include some criticisms. As the theorists contend, these criticisms, hostilities, and disapprovals may exist "without any thought of threat to the relationship as a whole" (Altman & Taylor, 1973, p. 139). Consequently, barriers to closeness may be broken down, but many people still protect themselves from becoming too vulnerable.

Returning to our example, Cathy and Barbra have been together for a little more than 12 weeks. They have had ample opportunity to understand a number of idiosyncrasies about each other; living with someone usually does that to people. Their conversation centers around a date that Barbra had on Saturday night:

BARBRA: He's a pig! All I could think about during the whole night is that someday, some woman will be with him! I pity her.

CATHY: He couldn't have been all that bad.

BARBRA: Oh yeah? He tried telling me that all I ever do is talk and that I don't listen enough. Give me a break!

CATHY: Well, Barb, to be truthful, you don't seem to listen as much as you talk.

BARBRA: What does that even mean?

CATHY: I'm simply saying that sometimes I can't get a word in edgewise in this friendship. Every time I want to say something, all you ever do is shut me up.

BARBRA: Okay, I can take the criticism, Cathy.

CATHY: Maybe we should just not talk about our dates to each other!

BARBRA: Fine.

CATHY: Fine.

As you can sense, there is noticeable tension in the relationship right now. Altman and Taylor would argue that although it appears that the two are very

affective exchange stage
stage of social penetration that is spontaneous and quite comfortable for relational partners

personal idioms
private, intimate expressions stated in a relationship

angry with each other at the moment, they will probably be able to move along. Many people have been in this sort of conflict before, and it seems that because a relationship carries significance and partners have emotionally invested in it, they are not prepared to end it because of a spontaneous statement. Yet we should not forget that Cathy and Barbra are ready to offer each other criticisms, and to that extent their comments sound somewhat nasty. Nonetheless, we hope you can see that their barriers are down, and both are comfortable sharing very personal comments about each other. To review, affective exchanges may include both positive and negative exchanges.

Stable Exchange: Raw Honesty and Intimacy

stable exchange stage
stage of social penetration that results in complete openness and spontaneity for relational partners

The fourth and final stage, stable exchange, is ultimately attained in many relationships. The **stable exchange stage** pertains to an open expression of thoughts, feelings, and behaviors that results in a high degree of spontaneity and relational uniqueness. During this stage, partners are highly intimate and synchronized; that is, behaviors between the two sometimes recur, and partners are able to assess and predict the behavior of the other fairly accurately. At times, the partners may tease each other about topics or people. This teasing, however, is done in a friendly manner.

Social Penetration theorists believe that there are relatively few misinterpretations in communication meaning at this stage. The reason for this is simple: Both partners have had numerous opportunities to clarify any previous ambiguities and have begun to establish their own personal system of communication. As a result, communication, according to Altman and Taylor, is efficient.

We return to our example of Cathy and Barbra. It is now final exam week, and obviously the two are very tense. Yet they both realize that this week must not be complicated by unnecessary conflict, and each realizes that after this week, they will not see each other for a month. The stable exchange stage is very apparent when we listen to their conversation:

CATHY: I was going down the hall to Anuka's to get coffee. Want any?

BARBRA: I'm too jittery right now. What I need is Sleepytime tea! [the two laugh]

CATHY: Do ya think you're ready for all the tests this week?

BARBRA: No, but that's okay. I know you have pushy parents, and they need to know that you're doin' your best.

CATHY: Yeah, I guess.

BARBRA: Ya' know, we're off the team if we don't get good grades.

CATHY: Think positive!

BARBRA: Maybe we can call some psychic hotline and ask how we're going to do on the tests. [again, the two laugh]

CATHY: Thanks for making me laugh. I needed that.

BARBRA: We'll do fine.

The stable exchange stage suggests that meanings are clear and unambiguous. The dialogue between Cathy and Barbra is very clear, and if we read between the lines we can see that the two do care about each other. Their communication suggests support and closeness. The women appear to be willing to allow each other some breathing room, and each sounds ready to help out the other. Although our earlier example suggested a conflicted relationship, there is now what Altman and Taylor (1973) call **dyadic uniqueness,** or distinctive relationship qualities such as humor and sarcasm.

dyadic uniqueness
distinctive relationship qualities

As we mentioned earlier, this stage approach to intimacy can get convoluted with periodic spurts and slowdowns along the way. In addition, the stages are not a complete picture of the intimacy process. There are a number of other influences, including a person's background and values and even the environment in which the relationship exists. The social penetration process is a give-and-take experience whereby both partners continue to work on balancing their individual needs with the needs of the relationship.

Integration, Critique, and Closing

Social Penetration Theory has been appealing since its inception almost 40 years ago. Altman and Taylor have proposed an intriguing model by which to view relational development. The theory had its beginnings during a time of openness in society. As you think about the theory and its value, consider the following criteria: scope and heurism.

Integration

Communication Tradition	Rhetorical | Semiotic | Phenomenological | Cybernetic | **Socio-Psychological** | Socio-Cultural | Critical
Communication Context	Intrapersonal | **Interpersonal** | Small Group | Organizational | Public/Rhetorical | Mass/Media | Cultural
Approach to Knowing	**Positivistic/Empirical** | Interpretive/Hermeneutic | Critical

Critique

Evaluation Criteria	**Scope** | Logical Consistency | Parsimony | Utility | Testability | **Heurism** | Test of Time

Scope

One could argue that the scope of SPT is limited. In fact, the scope of the theory "makes it difficult to adequately test it as a whole" (Mongeau & Henningsen, 2008, p. 370). Some scholars contend, for instance, that self-disclosure in particular may be too narrowly interpreted. For instance, Valerian Derlega,

Sandra Metts, Sandra Petronio, and Stephen Margulis (1993) believe that self-disclosure depends on a number of factors, not simply the need to reveal to people over time. Because people are constantly changing, they argue that what is considered to be self-disclosure often depends on the attitudes of a relational partner. Further, Derlega and his colleagues indicate that self-disclosure is not always a linear event, as suggested by SPT. Derlega and colleagues conclude that "self-disclosure and close relationships do not necessarily develop over time in a parallel, incremental, and continuous fashion" (p. 26).

The scope appears to be challenged by others. Mark Knapp and Anita Vangelisti (2009) reject the notion that relationship development is so linear. They believe relationships are embedded in other relationships, and in turn, these relationships affect the communication between partners. Therefore, other people may influence the direction of a relationship. In addition, the linearity of the theory suggests that the reversal of relational engagement (recall that Altman and Taylor likened relationship disengagement to a film shown in reverse) is relational disengagement. Leslie Baxter and Erin Sahlstein (2000) assert that the concept of information openness and closedness cannot be understood in isolation; there is much more going on in a relationship than simple self-disclosure. Baxter (1984) further discovered that several elements exist in relationship breakups, undercutting the linearity of relationship disengagement.

To be fair, Altman later revisited the social penetration processes and amended his original thinking with Taylor. Altman explained that being open and disclosive should be viewed in conjunction with being private and withdrawn (Altman, Vinsel, & Brown, 1981; Taylor & Altman, 1987). In a sense, Altman proposes what Baxter and Montgomery articulate in their theory on Relational Dialectics (Chapter 12). C. Arthur VanLear (1991) underscored this thinking by concluding that there are two competing cycles of openness and closedness in both friendships and romantic relationships. Jason LaSalle and Elise Porter from our opening story will surely experience this push and pull of self-disclosure as their relationship progresses. It is likely that as both of them share pieces of information, each will also remain private about other issues.

Heurism

There can be no doubt that Social Penetration Theory and the concept of self-disclosure has yielded literally hundreds of studies. Therefore, we believe SPT is a highly heuristic theory. Researchers have studied and written about the effects of self-disclosure, for example, on various types of relationships and across a variety of populations. Families (Turner & West, 2006), teachers (Mottet, Beebe, Raffeld, & Medlock, 2004; Russ, Simonds, & Hart, 2002), marriages (Caughlin & Petronio, 2004), and physician–patient relationships (Duggan & Parrott, 2001) have all been investigated. Furthermore, the effects of culture on the penetration process (e.g., Chen, 2006) have also been investigated. Scholars in the area of relationship development and its ancillary areas, including relational control (Rogers & Escudero, 2004), friendships (Johnson

Theory Into Practice

Sam

We talked about reciprocity in relationships. My own relationship with my boyfriend has a lot of reciprocity. He and I are constantly revealing parts of ourselves to each other, and we also talk about our emotional reactions to the other's self-disclosure. It's weird to be romantically involved with someone who's willing to return the same kind of intimacy I give. In the past, my relationships have been anything but reciprocal. Now, I think I've found someone who can let me know his reactions to what I say and how I feel.

T∗I∗P

et al., 2004), and relational maintenance (Dindia, 2003) owe much of their thinking to social penetration writings. Finally, HIV status (Moskowitz & Roloff, 2007) and Internet dating (Gibbs, Ellison, & Heino, 2006) and their relationship to self-disclosure have also been studied.

Despite its critics, Social Penetration Theory remains an integral theory pertaining to relationship development and has generated scholarly interest. In particular, the theory has resonated with interpersonal communication scholars. Relationship development can be challenging at times, and SPT helps people understand those challenges.

Discussion Starters

1. If their relationship develops further, what do you think Jason and Elise will talk about as the two get to know each other better? Will there be any risk involved as they disclose to each other? Explain with examples.

2. When self-disclosing to another person, several things can go wrong. Explain the consequences of poorly planned or inappropriate self-disclosure. Provide examples along the way.

3. What similar patterns cut across escalating relationships? Discuss marital relationships, relationships between friends, and parent–child relationships as individuals move toward intimacy.

4. Some critics have charged that Social Penetration Theory focuses too much on self-disclosure. Others, however, contend that self-disclosure forms the basis of most intimate relationships. What do you think? Is there a compromise between the two views?

5. If you outlined the stages of a past romantic relationship of yours, would it follow the sequencing that Altman and Taylor suggest? What

similarities are there to the social penetration process? What differences are there? Provide examples.

6. Apply SPT principles to workplace relationships you have encountered.

7. Other than an onion, what additional analogies can you think of that would apply to SPT?

Online Learning Center (www. mhhe.com/west4e)

Visit the Online Learning Center at www.mhhe.com/west4e for chapter-specific resources, such as story-into-theory and multiple-choice quizzes, as well as theory summaries and theory connection questions.

CHAPTER 11

Social Exchange Theory

*Based on the research of **John Thibaut** and **Harold Kelley***

Meredith Daniels and LaTasha Evans

Meredith Daniels and LaTasha Evans have been best friends since they served as hall monitors together in the fourth grade. After elementary school they moved on together to Collins High School. There they suffered through homework, dating dilemmas, and other typical high school concerns. In addition, they coped with racial issues because Meredith is European American and LaTasha is African American. In their hometown of Biloxi, Mississippi, the heritage of racism formed a barrier to their friendship. Although Biloxi is now fairly progressive, Meredith's grandfather was very uncomfortable about her friendship with LaTasha. Also, LaTasha's Uncle Benjamin had participated in Freedom Marches in the 1960s and had formed some unfavorable opinions about Whites. For a short time, her uncle had been a member of a Black separatist organization. He had some difficulty with LaTasha and Meredith's friendship too. Both of the young women had worked hard to maintain their relationship despite their family members' objections.

When LaTasha and Meredith were together, they often wondered why race was such a big deal. They seemed like sisters to each other, closer than many sisters they knew. They had the exact same sense of humor, and they could always cheer each other up with a goofy look or some silly joke about their past. They enjoyed the same movies (horror/thrillers) and the same subjects in school (English and French) and had similar taste in clothes (baggy pants) and boyfriends (intellectual guys).

But at home they often had to defend their friendship to their families. Meredith's parents said that they did not object to their friendship but that they were unhappy when Meredith socialized with African American boys and went to parties where she might be one of only two or three White girls in attendance. LaTasha's parents also had no problem with Meredith; they liked her and understood the friendship. But they drew the line when it came to dating White boys. LaTasha's parents were very proud of their African American heritage, and they told all their children how important it was to maintain their traditions and way of life. For them this meant that the family must stay African American: no dating or marriage with someone of another race. LaTasha's cousin had married a Japanese woman, and the whole family was having a great deal of difficulty accepting the couple.

Now that LaTasha and Meredith were entering their senior year at Collins, things had become even more difficult. LaTasha's parents were definite that she would be attending a historically Black college after graduation. Meredith's family wanted her to go to a small college in southern California because both her parents had graduated from this school, and they had many relatives living near the college. Both LaTasha and Meredith wanted to go to college together or at least be somewhat near each other. In addition, they resented how much time and energy all the discussions about college seemed to take up. It was almost ruining their senior year!

When they were together, they could usually forget about all the hassle and just have fun as usual, but the pressure was taking a toll on their friendship. Although they tried not to think about it, they both were concerned about the future. It was hard not to be able to tell each other everything, as they always had in the past, but Meredith and LaTasha found that talking to each other about college was stressful, so they mainly avoided the subject. Privately, each wondered what was going to happen and how she would get along next year without her best friend.

A Social Exchange theorist examining Meredith and LaTasha's relationship would predict that it might be heading for some trouble because the relationship currently seems to be costing the two more than it is rewarding them. Social Exchange Theory (SET) is based on the notion that people think about their relationships in economic terms. People tally up the costs of being in a relationship and compare them to the rewards that are offered by being in that relationship. **Costs** are the elements of relational life that have negative value to a person, such as the effort put into a relationship and the negatives of a partner. For example, the stress and tension that LaTasha and Meredith feel about the issue of college are now costs of their relationship. Their relationship always had the cost of generating conflict in their respective families. **Rewards** are the elements of a relationship that have positive value. In Meredith and LaTasha's case, the fun they have together, the loyalty they show for each other, and the sense of understanding they share are all rewards.

costs
elements of relational life with negative value

rewards
elements of relational life with positive value

Social Exchange theorists argue that people assess their relationships in terms of costs and rewards (Stafford, 2008). All relationships require some time and effort on the part of their participants. When friends spend time with each other, which they must do to maintain the relationship, they are unable to do other things with that time, so in that sense the time spent is a cost. Friends may need attention at inopportune times, and then the cost is magnified. For instance, if you had to finish a term paper and your best friend just broke up with her boyfriend and needed to talk to you, you can see how the friendship would cost you something in terms of time. Yet relationships provide us with rewards, or positives, too. Families, friends, and loved ones generally give us a sense of acceptance, support, and companionship. Some friends open doors for us or provide us with status just by being with us. Friends and families keep us from feeling lonely and isolated. Some friends teach us helpful lessons.

The Social Exchange perspective argues that people calculate the overall worth of a particular relationship by subtracting its costs from the rewards it provides (Monge & Contractor, 2003):

$$worth = rewards - costs$$

Positive relationships are those whose worth is a positive number; that is, the rewards are greater than the costs. Relationships where the worth is a negative number (the costs exceed the rewards) tend to be negative for the participants. Social Exchange Theory goes even further, predicting that the worth of a relationship influences its **outcome,** or whether people will continue with a relationship or terminate it. Positive relationships are expected to endure, whereas negative relationships will probably terminate.

outcome
whether people continue in a relationship or terminate it

Although, as we will explore in this chapter, the situation is more complicated than this simple equation, it does give the essence of what exchange theorists argue. John Thibaut and Harold Kelley say, for example, that "every individual voluntarily enters and stays in any relationship only as long as it is adequately satisfactory in terms of his [*sic*] rewards and costs" (1959, p. 37). As Ronald Sabatelli and Constance Shehan (1993) note, the Social Exchange approach views relationships through the metaphor of the marketplace, where each person acts out of a self-oriented goal of profit taking. However, Laura Stafford (2008) qualifies that economic exchanges and social exchanges have some differences: Social exchanges involve a connection with another person; social exchanges involve trust, not legal obligations; social exchanges are more flexible; and social exchanges rarely involve explicit bargaining.

We have been talking in general about exchange theories and the perspective of Social Exchange; this is because there are several theories of social exchange. Michael Roloff (1981) discusses five specific theories. Roloff observes that these theories are tied together by a central argument that "the guiding force of interpersonal relationships is the advancement of both parties' self-interest" (p. 14). Furthermore, Roloff notes that these theories do not assume that self-interest is a negative thing; rather, when self-interest is recognized, it will actually enhance a relationship. Yet Roloff also argues that there are significant differences among these five theories—some of which derive from the fact that they were developed by researchers in different disciplines (for example, psychology, social psychology, and sociology). It is beyond our purposes here to differentiate among all the theories of social exchange. We will concentrate on explicating what may be the most popular theory, John Thibaut and Harold Kelley's (1959) Theory of Interdependence. Although Thibaut and Kelley called their theory the Theory of Interdependence, it is often referred to as Social Exchange Theory because it fits into the exchange framework. We will use the two titles interchangeably here.

Social Exchange Theory • *Theory at a Glance*

Social Exchange Theory posits that the major force in interpersonal relationships is the satisfaction of both people's self-interest. Self-interest is not considered necessarily bad and can be used to enhance relationships. Interpersonal exchanges are thought to be analogous to economic exchanges where people are satisfied when they receive a fair return for their expenditures.

Assumptions of Social Exchange Theory

All Social Exchange theories are built upon several assumptions about human nature and the nature of relationships. Some of these assumptions should be clear to you after our introductory comments. Because Social Exchange Theory is based on a metaphor of economic exchange, many of these assumptions flow from the notion that people view life as a marketplace. In addition, Thibaut and Kelley base their theory on two conceptualizations: one that focuses on the nature of individuals and one that describes the relationships between two people. They look to drive reduction, an internal motivator, to understand individuals and to gaming principles to understand relationships between people. Thus, the assumptions they make also fall into these two categories.

The assumptions that Social Exchange Theory makes about *human nature* include the following:

- Humans seek rewards and avoid punishments.
- Humans are rational beings.
- The standards that humans use to evaluate costs and rewards vary over time and from person to person.

The assumptions Social Exchange Theory makes about the *nature of relationships* include the following:

- Relationships are interdependent.
- Relational life is a process.

We will look at each of these assumptions in turn.

The notion that humans seek rewards and avoid punishment is consistent with the conceptualization of drive reduction (Roloff, 1981). This approach assumes that people's behaviors are motivated by some internal drive mechanism. When people feel this drive, they are motivated to reduce it, and the process of doing so is a pleasurable one. If George feels thirsty, he is driven to reduce that feeling by getting a drink. This whole process is rewarding and, thus, "To be rewarded means that a person had undergone drive reduction or need fulfillment" (p. 45). This assumption helps Social Exchange theorists understand why LaTasha and Meredith enjoy each other's company: They feel a need for understanding and companionship, and this need (or drive) is fulfilled (or reduced) by spending time together.

The second assumption—that humans are rational—is critical to Social Exchange Theory. The theory rests on the notion that within the limits of the information that is available to them, people will calculate the costs and rewards of a given situation and guide their behaviors accordingly. This also includes the possibility that, faced with no rewarding choice, people will choose the least costly alternative. In the case of LaTasha and Meredith, it is costly to continue their friendship in the face of all the stress and family objections. Yet both young women may believe that it is less costly than ending their friendship and denying themselves the support and affection that they have shared for the past nine years.

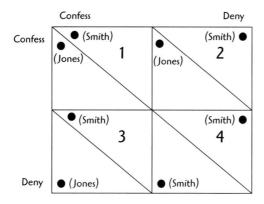

Figure 11.1
The Prisoner's Dilemma

James White and David Klein (2002) point out that assuming rationality is not the same as saying that people engage in rationalization. By assuming that people are rational beings, Social Exchange Theory asserts that people use rational thinking to make choices. But when we rationalize, we "attempt to provide an apparently rational justification for [our] behavior after the behavior occurred" (p. 37). Thus, rationalizing provides a fabricated attempt to make a choice look rational after the fact. This distinction becomes important when we discuss some of the criticisms of Social Exchange Theory at the end of this chapter.

The third assumption—that the standards people use to evaluate costs and rewards vary over time and from person to person—suggests that the theory must take diversity into consideration. No one standard can be applied to everyone to determine what is a cost and what is a reward. Thus, LaTasha may grow to see the relationship as more costly than Meredith does (or vice versa) as their standards change over time. However, Social Exchange Theory is a lawlike theory, as we described in Chapter 3, because SET claims that although individuals may differ in their definition of rewards, the first assumption is still true for all people: We are motivated to maximize our profits and rewards while minimizing our losses and costs (Molm, 2001).

As we mentioned earlier in this chapter, Thibaut and Kelley take those three assumptions about human nature from drive reduction principles. In their approach to relationships, they developed a set of principles that they call *game theory*. The classic game they developed that illustrates their first assumption about relationships is called the Prisoner's Dilemma (Figure 11.1). This game supposes that two prisoners are being questioned about a crime they deny committing. They have been separated for the questioning, and they are given two choices: They can confess to the crime, or they can persist in their denials. The situation is further complicated by the fact that the outcome for them is not completely in their own hands, individually. Instead, each prisoner's outcome is a result of the combination of their two responses. The configuration of their possible choices is called a 2 × 2 matrix because there are two of them and they each have two choices: confess or deny.

Theory Into Practice

Parker

I don't see how Social Exchange Theory could really work to predict something. How would you ever be able to make all the complicated feelings you have about a friend and your relationship with him turn into a number? Or how would you be able to predict what your friend would do like in the Prisoner's Dilemma? Although, I guess I do make predictions about what my friends will do or say and those do affect how I'll behave. When I wanted to sell my car to my friend, Mike, I did think about how he'd react to the price I wanted and then I adjusted it a little to what I thought he'd go for. Selling a car to a friend is both an economic and a social exchange—but in my experience it's not a very good idea!

If we call one of the prisoners Jones and the other Smith, we can see their choices and outcomes:

1. Jones confesses and Smith confesses = they both receive a life sentence.
2. Jones confesses and Smith denies = Jones goes free and Smith is executed.
3. Jones denies and Smith confesses = Smith goes free and Jones is executed.
4. Jones denies and Smith denies = they both serve a short jail term.

It is clear that the outcomes for Smith and Jones are interdependent. The outcome in each case depends on the relationship between Smith's and Jones's answers, not on one answer alone. This concept is so central to Thibaut and Kelley that they named their theory the Theory of Interdependence rather than Social Exchange or Game Theory. They did so because they wished to avoid the notion of win–lose in Game Theory, and they wished to stress that social exchange is a function of interdependence.

When we think of LaTasha and Meredith's situation, we can see that if Meredith decides to cut back on her friendship with LaTasha, LaTasha will inevitably be affected. Her own decisions about the costs and rewards of the relationship are contingent on Meredith's decision. Thus, whenever any one member of a relationship acts, both the other and the relationship as a whole are influenced. In a study of family members who care for elderly relatives (Raschick & Ingersoll-Dayton, 2004), the authors found there was interdependency in the care-giving and care-receiving relationship.

The second assumption that Thibaut and Kelley make is that relational life is a process. In stating this, the researchers are acknowledging the importance of time and change in relational life. Specifically, time affects exchanges because past experiences guide judgments about rewards and costs, and these judgments impact subsequent exchanges. For example, if Kathy dislikes school and has a very low opinion of teachers and then takes a class that exceeds her expectations, and she finds that she really likes this particular teacher, their relationship and Kathy's expectations about future relationships with teachers will be shaped by the process. Further, the notion of process allows us to see that relationships constantly change and evolve.

Given these assumptions about humans and relationships, we are ready to examine two of the major parts of the theory: evaluation of a relationship and exchange patterns.

Evaluation of a Relationship: Why We Stay or Go

As we mentioned earlier, SET is more complex than the simple equation of worth that we initially presented. Social exchange includes "both a notion of a relationship, and some notion of a shared obligation in which both parties perceive responsibilities to each other" (Lavelle, Rupp, & Brockner, 2007, p. 845). When people calculate the worth of their relationships and make decisions about staying in them, a few other considerations surface. One of the most interesting parts of Thibaut and Kelley's theory is their explanation of how people evaluate their relationships with reference to whether they will stay in them or leave them. Thibaut and Kelley claim that this evaluation rests on two types of comparisons: comparison level and comparison level for alternatives. The **comparison level (CL)** is a standard representing what people feel they should receive in the way of rewards and costs from a particular relationship. Thus, Meredith has a subjective feeling about what she should give and what she should get, in return, from a friendship. Her CL has been shaped by all her past friendships, by family members' advice, and by popular culture such as TV and film representations of friendships that give her an idea of what is expected from this relationship.

Comparison levels vary among individuals because they are subjective. Individuals base their CL, in large part, on past experiences with a specific type of relationship. Because individuals have very different past experiences with similar types of relationships, they develop different comparison levels. For example, if Suzanne has had many friendships that required her to do a great deal of listening and empathizing, her CL will include this. If Andrew has not experienced friends requiring this listening behavior from him, he will not expect to encounter this cost in friendship. Because we often interact with people from our own culture, we share many relational expectations due to messages we have received from popular culture (Rawlins, 1992). Thus, we overlap somewhat in our expectations for relationships, and our CLs may not be totally different from one another's.

Thibaut and Kelley argue that our satisfaction with a current relationship derives from comparing the rewards and costs it involves to our CL. If our current relationship meets or exceeds our CL, the theory predicts we will be satisfied with the relationship. Yet people sometimes leave satisfactory relationships and stay in ones that are not so satisfying. Thibaut and Kelley explain this seeming inconsistency with their second standard of comparison, the **comparison level for alternatives (CLalt).** This refers to "the lowest level of relational rewards a person is willing to accept given available rewards from alternative relationships or being alone" (Roloff, 1981, p. 48). In other words, the CLalt measures how people evaluate a relationship compared to the realistic alternatives to that relationship. For example, Michael Kramer (2005) studied community theater participation.

comparison level (CL)
a standard for what a person thinks he or she should get in a relationship

comparison level for alternatives (CLalt)
how people evaluate a relationship based on what their alternatives to the relationship are

Table 11.1 How Outcome, CL, and CLalt Affect the State of a Relationship

RELATIVE VALUE OF OUTCOME, CL, CLALT	STATE OF THE RELATIONSHIP
Outcome > CL > Clalt	Satisfying and stable
Outcome > CLalt > CL	Satisfying and stable
CLalt > CL > Outcome	Unsatisfying and unstable
CLalt > Outcome > CL	Satisfying and unstable
CL > CLalt > Outcome	Unsatisfying and unstable
CL > Outcome > Clalt	Unsatisfying and stable

> means greater than; < means less than
Source: Adapted from Roloff, 1981, p. 48. Reprinted by permission of Sage Publications, Inc.

He notes that people who live in towns where there is only one community theater are likely to stay with fewer rewards than those who have other options in their town. He observes that this emphasizes the importance of CLalt.

CLalt provides a measure of stability rather than satisfaction—that is, the CLalt suggests how likely it is that Meredith would leave her relationship with LaTasha, even though it is a satisfying one, for something she thinks would be better. If we further examine LaTasha and Meredith's relationship using CL and CLalt, we might speculate that Meredith finds her friendship with LaTasha very satisfying in general. She might give it an 8 out of a 10-point ranking where 1 is horrible and 10 is perfect. The 8 would be Meredith's outcome score for her relationship with LaTasha. If Meredith's expectations of friendship, or her CL, is only a 6, then Meredith should be satisfied with her friendship with LaTasha. Furthermore, if Meredith thinks that by being alone now as she decides about college she would rate herself at a 3, and she has few other friends that could even come close to her relationship with LaTasha, then her CLalt will be low. Her 8 outcome with LaTasha will exceed it, and Social Exchange Theory predicts that Meredith will want to remain friends with LaTasha.

If we calculate these numbers based on the format specified in Table 11.1, Meredith's outcome, 8, is greater than her CL (6), and her CL is greater than her CLalt, which is 3. Thus, her pattern fits the first example in the table and the theory predicts that the state of her relationship is satisfying and stable.

This kind of calculation—although perhaps a little unrealistic in turning a relationship into a single number—suggests why some people remain in relationships that are abusive. If people see no alternative and fear being alone more than being in the relationship, Social Exchange Theory predicts they will stay. Some have written about women in abusive relationships, using this theoretical reasoning to explain why women stay with violent men (Walker, 1984). Other researchers (Cox & Kramer, 1995) note that managers in organizations use these calculations to help them make decisions about dismissing employees. And Bishop, Dow, Goldsby, and Cropanzano (2005) investigate how employees use social exchange in forming commitments to their jobs. Table 11.1 summarizes six possible combinations among the outcome, the CL, and the CLalt and the resulting state of the relationship predicted by the theory.

Exchange Patterns: SET in Action

In addition to studying how people calculate their relational outcomes, Thibaut and Kelley were interested in how people adjust their behaviors in interaction with their relational partners. Thibaut and Kelley suggest that when people interact, they are goal directed. This is congruent with their assumption that human beings are rational. People, according to Thibaut and Kelley, engage in **behavioral sequences,** or a series of actions designed to achieve their goal. These sequences are the heart of what Thibaut and Kelley conceptualize as social exchange. As Thibaut and Kelley note in Game Theory, when people engage in these behavioral sequences they are dependent to some extent on their relational partner. For instance, if one person wishes to play gin rummy, cooperation from a partner is required. This interdependence brings up the concept of **power**—the dependence a person has on another for outcomes. If LaTasha depends more on Meredith for rewards than vice versa, then Meredith has greater power than LaTasha in their relationship. Some researchers (Bienenstock & Bianchi, 2004) observe that certain exchanges, such as gift-giving, bestow status and power on the giver. Other researchers (Trussell & Lavrakas, 2004) suggest there is probably an optimal amount a giver can give before status and power might begin to decline.

There are two types of power in Thibaut and Kelley's theory: fate control and behavior control. **Fate control** is the ability to affect a partner's outcomes. For example, if Meredith withholds her friendship from LaTasha, she affects LaTasha's outcome. If LaTasha cannot replace Meredith as a friend, Meredith's behavior gives her fate control over LaTasha. This presumes that Meredith does not care about the relationship. If she does, then withholding her friendship is a punishment for her as well, which gives LaTasha a certain amount of fate control in the relationship too.

Behavior control is the power to cause another's behavior to change by changing one's own behavior. If Meredith calls LaTasha on the phone, it is likely that LaTasha will stop whatever else she is doing and talk to Meredith. If LaTasha is with Meredith and falls silent, Meredith will probably change her behavior in response. She might stop talking too, or she might question LaTasha to find out if something is wrong.

Thibaut and Kelley state that people develop patterns of exchange to cope with power differentials and to deal with the costs associated with exercising power. These patterns describe behavioral rules or norms that indicate how people trade resources in an attempt to maximize rewards and minimize costs. Thibaut and Kelley describe three different matrices in social exchange to illustrate the patterns people develop. These matrices include the given matrix, the effective matrix, and the dispositional matrix.

The **given matrix** represents the behavioral choices and outcomes that are determined by a combination of external factors (the environment) and internal factors (the specific skills each interactant possesses). When two people engage in an exchange, the environment may make some options more difficult than others. LaTasha's and Meredith's families, for instance, are part of the environment that is making their friendship more difficult. A scarcity of money would

behavioral sequences
a series of actions designed to achieve a goal

power
the degree of dependence a person has on another for outcomes

fate control
the ability to affect a partner's outcomes

behavior control
the power to change another's behavior

given matrix
the constraints on your choices due to the environment and/or your own skill levels

Research Notes

Bishop, J. W., Dow, S. K., Goldsby, M. G., & Cropanzano, R. (2005). A construct validity study of commitment and perceived support variables. *Group & Organization Management, 30,* 153–180.

This study uses the social exchange principles of interdependence and direct exchange structures to investigate employee commitment. The researchers hypothesized that employees have different levels of commitment to their organizations and work teams and perceive that the organization and their work teams support them to varying degrees. They also posit that how much an individual employee perceives support from the organization and work team varies based on the employee's level of commitment to each.

To test these hypotheses, the researchers surveyed employees from four different organizations: an apparel manufacturer (485 participants), an automotive outsource air bag manufacturer (144 participants), a Benedictine community employing both Roman Catholic nuns and lay workers (166 participants), and a large public sector organization (136 participants). Each participant filled out a survey consisting of several instruments geared to measure the variables of interest.

After analysis, both of the hypotheses received support. The researchers conclude that "the results of this study support the notion that social exchange relationships and reciprocity attitudes and behaviors can exist between an individual and multiple entities simultaneously and independently within an organization" (p. 174). They suggest that their findings are especially important given the diversity of the organizations they sampled.

Timmer, S. G., Sedlar, G., & Urquiza, A. J. (2004). Challenging children in kin versus nonkin foster care: Perceived costs and benefits to caregivers. *Child Maltreatment, 9,* 251–262.

This study uses the social exchange framework to examine the costs and benefits in foster care situations. The authors note that foster care has both a cost (impermanence) and a benefit (a better home environment) for the children placed in it. In addition, there are costs and benefits for the foster caregivers. When a foster child has severe emotional and/or behavioral problems, the researchers state that the costs in terms of disruption to family life are high. They suggest that if the foster family perceives that the child is attached to them or if family members feel they are fulfilling an important family or social obligation (i.e., rewards), then the costs may be offset. Specifically, this study compares kin and nonkin foster parents' perceptions of their foster children, the relationship they have with them, and their own functioning as foster parents.

One hundred two kin foster parents and 157 nonkin foster parents filled out a packet of standardized measures and a demographic questionnaire to provide the data for this study. All of the participants were fostering children who had been referred for treatment based on behavior problems. Interestingly, although the researchers had not planned it this way, the two groups (kin and nonkin) were very similar on demographic variables. The data were analyzed in a variety of ways to compare kin and nonkin groups.

The researchers found that nonkin caregivers thought their foster children's behavior problems were more severe than did kin foster parents, but they rated themselves as less stressed than did the kin foster parents. Also, kin caregivers were more likely than nonkin caregivers to complete the treatment program with their foster children. They conclude, consistent with the principles of SET, that mental health providers need to reduce the costs and increase the benefits of treatment for both kin and nonkin foster families.

be another aspect of the given matrix that would make some alternatives less likely for some relationships. Furthermore, the given matrix depends on the skills people bring to the social exchange. If people lack skills for ballroom dancing, for example, it is unlikely that they will spend time dancing together. To a certain degree, the given matrix represents "the hand you are dealt."

People may be restricted by the given matrix, but they are not trapped by it. They can transform it into the **effective matrix,** "which represents an expansion of alternative behaviors and/or outcomes which ultimately determines the behavioral choices in social exchange" (Roloff, 1981, p. 51). If a man does not know how to tango, he can take lessons in this dance and learn it, transforming the given matrix into the effective matrix. If Meredith and LaTasha think their families are bothering their friendship too much, they can engage in conflict with them until they change their families' minds. Or they can stop talking about each other at home and keep their friendship secret so that they can avoid their families' negative sanctions.

The final matrix, the **dispositional matrix,** represents the way two people believe that rewards ought to be exchanged between them. If Meredith and LaTasha think that friends ought to stick together no matter how much outside interference they receive from family members, that will affect their dispositional matrix. Some people view exchanges as competition, and this belief will be reflected in their dispositional matrix.

Thibaut and Kelley assert that if we know the kinds of dispositions a person has (the dispositional matrix) and the nature of the situation in which he or she is operating (the given matrix), then we will know how to predict the transformations the person will make (the effective matrix) to impact the social exchange. Thus, if we understand that LaTasha expects great loyalty from her friends, and from herself as a friend, and we know that her family's opposition to her friendship to Meredith is not too strong, we might predict that LaTasha will defend Meredith to her family and attempt to change their beliefs. If her family has a stronger opposition, we might predict that LaTasha will simply remain friends with Meredith without trying to change her family's beliefs. The dispositional matrix guides the transformations people make to their given matrix; these transformations lead to the effective matrix, which determines the social exchange.

In their theory, Thibaut and Kelley do not explicitly deal with communication behaviors, such as self-disclosure, a topic we discussed in Chapter 10 in conjunction with Social Penetration Theory. Yet some of their discussion about the three matrices implies that self-disclosure does play an important role in social exchange. As Roloff (1981) observes,

> Self-disclosure would seem to imply the communication of two things: (1) the dispositions one has, and (2) the transformations (strategy) one is going to employ in this exchange. Since dispositions affect a person's strategy, we might assume that knowledge of dispositions might well allow us to predict the transformations. (p. 77)

This self-disclosure, like all disclosures about the self, contains risks. It could provide the relational partner with information that could be used against the discloser. If people know how another transforms the given matrix, they have an

effective matrix
the transformations you are able to make to your given matrix, by learning a new skill, for example

dispositional matrix
the beliefs you have about relationships

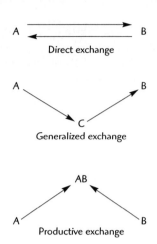

Figure 11.2
Exchange Structures

edge in social exchanges. For example, if LaTasha knows that Meredith tries to resolve problems in a cooperative fashion, she can use Meredith's cooperative nature against her to get what she wants in an exchange. An understanding of how the matrices affect communication behavior is one reason communication researchers are interested in Social Exchange Theory.

Exchange Structures

Exchanges may take several forms within these matrices. These include direct exchange, generalized exchange, and productive exchange (Figure 11.2). In a **direct exchange**, reciprocation is confined to the two actors. For instance, when Brad washes his father's car and then his dad lets him use the car on Saturday night, the exchange is direct. One social actor provides value to another and the other reciprocates. In a longtime friendship like Meredith and LaTasha's, they consistently participate in direct exchanges. It isn't necessary to reciprocate immediately, but when LaTasha does a favor for Meredith, she knows that Meredith will eventually respond in kind.

A **generalized exchange** involves indirect reciprocity. One person gives to another and the recipient responds but not to the first person. Generalized exchanges occur, for example, when someone moves away from the neighborhood and friends and neighbors help pack up the moving van. Because the person has moved away, he or she won't help any of those neighbors move when they are ready to relocate. The favor is reciprocated by helping someone else, in the new neighborhood. Generalized exchanges involve the community or social network rather than simply two specific people as in the examples we have discussed with LaTasha and Meredith.

Finally, exchanges may be productive, meaning that both actors have to contribute for either one of them to benefit. In a direct or generalized exchange, one person is the beneficiary of another's provision of value. One receives a reward and the other incurs a cost. In a **productive exchange**, both people incur benefits and costs simultaneously. If LaTasha and Meredith do a project

direct exchange
an exchange where two people reciprocate costs and rewards

generalized exchange
an exchange where reciprocation involves the social network and isn't confined to two individuals

productive exchange
an exchange where both partners incur costs and benefits simultaneously

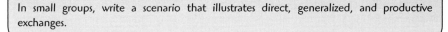

Theory Application in Groups (TAG)

In small groups, write a scenario that illustrates direct, generalized, and productive exchanges.

together for their senior English class, they engage in productive exchange. Both of them have to do the work, and they both share equally in the grade they receive.

Integration, Critique, and Closing

Social Exchange Theory has generated a great deal of research and has been called "one of the major theoretical perspectives in the field of social psychology" (Cook & Rice, 2003, p. 53). However, it does have its detractors. As you reflect on SET, the criteria of scope, utility, testability, and heurism are important to address.

Integration

Communication Tradition	Rhetorical	**Semiotic**	**Phenomenological**	Cybernetic	**Socio-Psychological**	Socio-Cultural	Critical

Communication Context	**Intrapersonal**	**Interpersonal**	Small Group	Organizational	Public/Rhetorical	Mass/Media	Cultural

Approach to Knowing	**Positivistic/Empirical**	Interpretive/Hermeneutic	Critical

Critique

Evaluation Criteria	Scope	Logical Consistency	Parsimony	**Utility**	Testability	**Heurism**	Test of Time

Scope

When examining SET on the basis of scope, some critics comment that it fails to explain the importance of group solidarity in its emphasis on individual need fulfillment (England, 1989). This critique combines some of the issues raised previously and argues that "the exchange framework can be viewed as valuing the separative self to the extent that rationality and self-interest are emphasized" (Sabatelli & Shehan, 1993, p. 397). By prioritizing this value, the

Theory Into Practice
Brittany

Thinking about Social Exchange Theory helped me understand my friend Lindsay's relationship with her boyfriend, Stan. I never could get what she saw in him at all until I read about CLalt. Then a lightbulb went on. Even though I think Lindsay is great, she has very low self-esteem, and Stan is her first real boyfriend. She's never said so, but I bet she thinks that if she leaves Stan she won't be able to get another boyfriend. We go to a rather conservative school, and Lindsay is a liberal person. Stan is less conservative than most of the other guys we know, so I am guessing that Lindsay thinks there aren't a lot of other guys around for her—because of both her low self-esteem and her political views. Now that I understand it a little better, I might try talking to Lindsay. She could do a lot better than Stan, and I hope she sees that.

connected self is overlooked and undervalued. In some ways, this objection has ontological considerations as well, but it also suggests that the scope of the theory is too narrow. SET only considers the individual as a unique entity without focusing on the individual as a member of a group. Because of this, SET cannot account for relationships in cultures that prioritize connection over individuality, for example.

Utility

The criterion of utility suggests that if the theory doesn't present an accurate picture of people, it will be faulted as not useful. SET has been criticized for the conceptualization of human beings it advances. In the theory, humans are seen as rational calculators, coming up with numerical equations to represent their relational life. Many people object to this understanding of humans, asking whether people really rationally calculate the costs and rewards to be realized when in a relationship. Social Exchange assumes a great deal of cognitive awareness and activity, which several researchers have questioned (Berger & Roloff, 1980). Researchers have not come to a definitive answer about how much people calculate their relational life, but this calculation probably ebbs and flows according to many factors. First, some contexts may make people more self-aware than others. As LaTasha and Meredith receive more pressure to decide about college, they may think about their relationship more than they did when they were younger. Second, some individual differences might affect how people process information. Some people are more self-aware than others (Snyder, 1979). As researchers continue to work with this theory, they must account for these and other factors relative to this calculation

In addition, critics wonder if people are really as self-interested as Social Exchange Theory assumes. Steve Duck (1994) argues that applying a marketplace mentality to the understanding of relational life vastly misrepresents what goes on in relationships. He suggests that it is wrong to think about personal relationships in the same way that we think about business transactions, like buying a house or a car. This suggestion relates to the approaches to knowing one brings to the theory, as we discussed in Chapter 3. For some people, the analogy of the marketplace is appropriate, but for others it is not and may be highly offensive. Perhaps it is no surprise that scholars of organizational communication and marketing find the Social Exchange perspective very useful. For example, Senthil Muthusamy and Margaret White (2005) use Social Exchange Theory to explain the process of strategic alliances among corporations, and Clara Agustin and Jagdip Singh (2005) drew from Social Exchange Theories to examine consumer loyalty.

Testability

A common criticism of Social Exchange Theory is that it's not testable. As we discussed in Chapter 4, one important attribute of a theory is that it is testable and capable of being proven false. The difficulty with social exchange is that its central concepts—costs and rewards—are not clearly defined. As Sabatelli and Shehan (1993) note,

> It becomes impossible to make an operational distinction between what people value, what they perceive as rewarding, and how they behave. Rewards, values, and actions appear to be defined in terms of each other (Turner, 1978). Thus, it is impossible to find an instance when a person does not act in ways so as to obtain rewards. (p. 396)

When the theory argues that people do what they can to maximize rewards and then also argues that what people do is rewarding behavior, it is difficult, to disentangle the two concepts. This issue relates to the difference between rationalization and rationality that we discussed earlier in the chapter. As long as Social Exchange Theory operates with these types of circular definitions, it will be untestable and, thus, unsatisfactory. However, Roloff (1981) observes that some work has been done to create lists of rewards in advance of simply observing what people do and labeling that as rewarding because people are doing it. Edna Foa and Uriel Foa (1974, 1976) began this work of clearly defining rewards. Roloff further argues that despite this problem, there has been a great deal of empirical work using Social Exchange theories.

Heurism

People who support SET point out that it has been heuristic. Studies in many diverse areas, from corporations (Muthusamy & White, 2005) to foster care (Timmer, Sedlar, & Urquiza, 2004) have been framed using the tenets of Social Exchange. Researchers have also examined communication in romantic relationships (Markey & Markey, 2007), theater groups (Kramer, 2005), and online (Metzger, 2004) using SET. Furthermore, the emphasis that Thibaut and Kelley placed on interdependence is congruent with many researchers' notions of interpersonal relationships.

As a theory that examines human relationships, Social Exchange Theory has resonated with a number of scholars. Undoubtedly, the theory has attracted some criticisms. However, it has lasting appeal in the field of communication and will continue to intrigue both researchers and practitioners.

Discussion Starters

1. Discuss Meredith and LaTasha's given matrix, transformational matrix, and dispositional matrix.

2. Explain the problem with Social Exchange Theory regarding testability. Is there anything that Social Exchange theorists could do to make the theory more testable? Use examples in your response.

3. Choose a current relationship of yours and perform a cost-benefit analysis on it. Assess whether the relationship meets, fails to meet, or exceeds your comparison level.

4. How does Social Exchange Theory explain the unselfish things that people do that do not seem calculated to gain rewards for themselves?

5. Have you ever stayed in a relationship because you thought you did not have any other alternatives? Explain.

6. How realistic do you think gaming principles like those used to develop the Prisoner's Dilemma are? Give examples that support or contest the use of a 2×2 matrix to model human choices.

7. Do you believe that SET is too culture-specific and can't account for communication in cultures that aren't individualistic?

Online Learning Center (www. mhhe.com/west4e)

Visit the Online Learning Center at www.mhhe.com/west4e for chapter-specific resources, such as story-into-theory and multiple-choice quizzes, as well as theory summaries and theory connection questions.

CHAPTER 12

Relational Dialectics Theory

*Based on the research of **Leslie Baxter** and **Barbara Montgomery***

Eleanor Robertson and Jeff Meadows

Eleanor Robertson and Jeff Meadows worked together to clean up the mess left from the dinner party they had just given for their friend Mary Beth's thirty-fifth birthday. They both agreed that the party had been a great success and that everyone had had a wonderful time. They were having fun talking about their friends—who was breaking up and who was getting together.

Eleanor smiled as she thought about how much she and Jeff had learned about each other and their relationship in the two years they had lived together. Eleanor used to get upset when Jeff wanted to be with friends and not spend all his time with her alone. Now she thought she understood Jeff's desire for others in their lives. She also found that the more she was able to let go of her possessive feelings and behaviors, the more Jeff wanted to be close.

Jeff came over and hugged Eleanor. He said, "Honey, that was a great party. The food was perfect—I'm glad we decided to do Italian. Thanks for all your help to make everything go so well. Mary Beth really appreciated it, I know. And since she and I have been friends forever, it really means a lot to me."

Eleanor pulled away and laughed at Jeff. "I didn't do too much, sweetheart," she said to Jeff. "You were the one who was busy in the kitchen. But I am glad Mary Beth had fun. I really like her a lot too."

Jeff and Eleanor finished cleaning up and started talking about what they would do tomorrow. They decided they would take a picnic to Golden Gate Park and then maybe go to a movie. It sounded like a fun Sunday—they had a plan, but they could change their minds and skip the movie if picnicking in the park was too inviting.

Eleanor was very happy and thought about telling Jeff how much she loved and needed him, but she decided to keep quiet about the depth of her feelings for now. Jeff probably knew how she felt, and she was a little afraid of revealing all her feelings to him right now. It had been a perfect day, and she didn't want to spoil it by making herself completely open to him. She wasn't sure she wanted to be so vulnerable to Jeff at this point in their relationship, even though when they first started going out together, she had told him she loved him repeatedly. Now she found herself being a bit more guarded and self-protective.

When researchers examine the story of Eleanor and Jeff, they might speculate that their relationship is moving through stages. Researchers who work within the framework of Social Penetration Theory (see Chapter 10), for example, would point to the fact that Jeff and Eleanor have worked through some of their earlier issues and now interact with each other at a deeper level of intimacy than they once did. These researchers might point to the fact that the relationship between Eleanor and Jeff is more coordinated and less conflictual than it once was as an indication that they have moved to a more intimate stage of relational development. Yet other researchers would look at Jeff and Eleanor and see their story as best explained by a different theoretical position, called Relational Dialectics Theory.

Relational Dialectics Theory (RDT) maintains that relational life is characterized by ongoing tensions between contradictory impulses (Baxter & Braithwaite, 2008). Although that may sound confusing and messy, researchers who assert the dialectical position believe it accurately depicts the way that life is for people. People are not always able to resolve the contradictory elements of their beliefs, and they can hold inconsistent beliefs about relationships. For example, the adage "absence makes the heart grow fonder" seems to coexist easily with its opposite, "out of sight, out of mind."

In the communication discipline, Leslie Baxter and Barbara Montgomery (1996) formulated the most complete statement of the theory in their book *Relating: Dialogues and Dialectics,* although both of them had been writing about dialectical thinking for several years prior to that book's publication. Other researchers, notably William Rawlins (1992) and Sandra Petronio (2000), were also influential in bringing the framework of dialectics to the study of communication in relationships. Baxter and Montgomery's work was directly influenced by Mikhail Bakhtin, a Russian philosopher who developed a theory of personal dialogue. Social life for Bakhtin was an open dialogue among many voices, and its essence was the "simultaneous differentiation from yet fusion with another" (Baxter & Montgomery, 1996, p. 24). According to Bakhtin, the self is only possible in context with another. Bakhtin notes that human experience is constituted through communication with others. And, as Baxter (2006) notes, the concept of a relationship for Bakhtin is only possible by maintaining two distinct voices. In some ways, Bakhtin's notions relate to Mead's theory of Symbolic Interactionism (see Chapter 5) because he focuses on the importance of interaction with others for meaning making.

From Bakhtin's thinking, Baxter and Montgomery shaped the notion of the dialectical vision. We can best explain this vision of human behavior by contrasting it to two other common approaches: monologic and dualistic approaches. The **monologic approach** pictures contradictions as either/or relationships. For instance, monologic thinking would lead to the belief that Jeff and Eleanor's relationship was either close or distant. In other words, the two

monologic approach
an approach framing contradiction as either/or

Theory Application in Groups (TAG)

In small groups, discuss the differences among the monologic, dualistic, and dialectic approaches to relational life. Try to come to a consensus about what the dialectic approach offers that the other two do not.

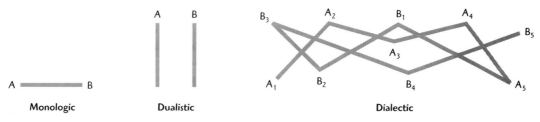

Figure 12.1 Monologic, Dualistic, and Dialectic Approaches to Relational Contradictions

parts of a contradiction are mutually exclusive in monologic thinking, and as you move toward one extreme, you retreat from the other. See Figure 12.1 for a visual representation of this notion.

In contrast, the **dualistic approach** sees the two parts of a contradiction as two separate entities, somewhat unrelated to each other. In our example of Eleanor and Jeff, dualistic thinkers might choose to evaluate them separately, rating how close each one feels compared to the other. Furthermore, dualism allows for the idea that relationships may be evaluated differently on these scales at different times (Figure 12.1).

Thinkers with a **dialectic approach** maintain that multiple points of view play off one another in every contradiction. Although a contradiction involves two opposing poles, the resulting situation expands beyond these two poles. As Baxter and Montgomery (1996) observe, "Dialectical thinking is not directed toward a search for the 'happy mediums' of compromise and balance, but instead focuses on the messier, less logical, and more inconsistent unfolding practices of the moment" (p. 46).

As Eleanor and Jeff interact, many voices contribute to their sense of their relationship: their memories of their past conflicts about Jeff's friends, their current sense of confidence in their relationship, their concerns about their future, their friendships with others, and so forth. Dialectic theory holds that it is not

dualistic approach
an approach framing contradiction as two separate entities

dialectic approach
an approach framing contradiction as both/and

Relational Dialectics Theory • *Theory at a Glance*

Relational Dialectics Theory pictures relational life as constant progress and motion. People in relationships continue to feel the push and pull of conflicting desires throughout the life of the relationship. Basically, people wish to have both/and, not either/or, when talking about opposing goals. For instance, people in relationships want to be both connected and autonomous, open and self-protective, and to have both predictability and spontaneity in their interactions. As people communicate in relationships, they attempt to reconcile these conflicting desires, but they never eliminate their need for both parts of the opposition.

accurate to say that only one or two positions exist in relational contradictions. Leslie Baxter and Dawn Braithewaite (2008) give the example of a college student saying, "Well, I'm kinda like, seeing him, but we're not, ya know, serious" (p. 349) to illustrate a struggle in meaning with voices of both closeness and distance competing with each other.

We now turn our attention to the assumptions underlying RDT.

Assumptions of Relational Dialectics Theory

RDT is grounded in four main assumptions that reflect its contentions about relational life:

- Relationships are not linear.
- Relational life is characterized by change.
- Contradiction is the fundamental fact of relational life.
- Communication is central to organizing and negotiating relational contradictions.

The most significant assumption that grounds this theory is the notion that relationships do not exist in a linear fashion. Rather, relationships consist of oscillation between contradictory desires. In fact, Baxter and Montgomery (1996) suggest that we should rethink our language and our metaphors about relationships. They note that the phrase "relational development" connotes some linear movement or forward progress. Progress contains either/or thinking. Relationships that progress are pictured as having more of certain elements such as intimacy, self-disclosure, certainty, and so forth. Thus, relationships may be imagined as on a continuum of more or less intimate, open, and certain. The either/or thinking frames the relationship as *either* intimate, open, certain *or* not. In the dialectic perspective, complexity is viewed as an *alternative* to progress. The dialectic notion of complexity introduces the concept of *both/and*.

The second assumption of RDT promotes the notion of process or change, although not necessarily framing this process as linear progress. Baxter and Montgomery observe that "relationship process or change . . . refers to quantitative and qualitative movement through time in the underlying contractions around which a relationship is organized" (1996, p. 52). Thus, Jeff and Eleanor are different now than they were a year ago. But that difference is not a linear move toward intimacy as much as it is a difference in the way they express their togetherness and their independence.

The third assumption stresses that contradictions or tensions between opposites never go away and never cease to provide tension. People manage these tensions and oppositions in different ways, but they are present continuously in relational life. The push and pull represented by dialectics constructs relational life, and one of our main communication tasks is managing these tensions. This approach differs from other types of relational theories in that it considers homeostasis to be unnatural: Change and transformation are the hallmarks of relational interaction in this perspective (Montgomery, 1992; Sahlstein, 2004).

The final assumption of RDT pertains to communication. Specifically, this theory gives a central position to communication. As Baxter and Montgomery (1996) observe, "From the perspective of relational dialectics, social actors give life through their communicative practices to the contradictions that organize their relationships. The social reality of contradictions is produced and reproduced by the communicative action of social actors" (p. 59). When Jeff praises Eleanor for the party, for example, he is expressing affection and negotiating closeness. When Eleanor keeps silent instead of saying, "I love you," to Jeff, she is protecting herself and keeping herself from being too open with him. As Eleanor and Jeff plan their picnic for the next day, they are discussing how much predictability and how much novelty they wish to have. Planning initially provides predictability, but the couple's stated willingness to be flexible in their plan allows for spontaneity as well. Thus, Jeff and Eleanor's communication practices organize the three basic dialectics we will discuss later in the chapter: autonomy and connection, openness and protection, and novelty and predictability.

Elements of Dialectics: Building the Tension

The following elements are basic to the dialectical perspective: totality, contradiction, motion, and praxis (Rawlins, 1992). **Totality** suggests that people in a relationship are interdependent. This means that when something happens to one member of a relationship, the other member(s) will be affected as well. For example, if Jeff gets a promotion at work that entails more travel than his former position, Eleanor will have to deal with his absences. She may compensate by making more friends outside their relationship, and this will affect Jeff somewhat when he is home. He will have to meet new friends and share Eleanor's time, for example.

totality
acknowledges the interdependence of people in a relationship

In addition, totality means that the social and cultural context affects the process; communicating in relationships "involves the constant interconnection and reciprocal influence of multiple individual, interpersonal, and social factors" (Rawlins, 1992, p. 7). For instance, Eleanor and Jeff's relationship is affected by their social circle, by their location in San Francisco, and by the historical moment in which they live.

Contradiction refers to oppositions—two elements that contradict each other. As such, contradiction is the central feature of the dialectic approach. Dialectics are the result of oppositions. When Eleanor desires to tell Jeff that she loves him but also wishes to withhold that information to protect herself, she is experiencing contradiction.

contradiction
the central feature of the dialectic approach; refers to oppositions

Motion refers to the processual nature of relationships and their change over time. When Eleanor reflects on how different her relationship with Jeff is now compared to what they had two years ago, she is experiencing motion. Think back to one of your own relationships. Compare how you relate now to how you did when you first met. No doubt you will see motion at work also.

motion
refers to the processual nature of relationships

praxis
refers to the choice-making capacity of humans

Finally, **praxis** means that humans are choice makers. Although we do not have completely free choice in all instances and are restricted by our previous choices, by the choices of others, and by cultural and social conditions, we are still conscious and active choice makers. For example, Eleanor chooses to be with Jeff, and this choice restricts other choices she might make. She must get along with Jeff's parents and siblings when they get together for the holidays. She might not ever have chosen to be with these people on her own, but because she is in love with Jeff, she must spend time with them. On a more basic level, Jeff and Eleanor did not choose the time in which they live, but the culture shapes some of their choices. If they lived in the 1950s, for instance, they would be less likely to be unmarried and living together.

Basic Relational Dialectics

Many different specific dialectics have been discussed with reference to relational life. As we mentioned earlier, the three most relevant to relationships are the dialectics of autonomy and connection, openness and protection, and novelty and predictability (Baxter, 1990). Other researchers have also found that these dialectics are common to relational life. For example, in one study (Erbert, 2000) marital couples were interviewed to determine how they perceived relational dialectics with reference to conflicts. Autonomy and contradiction and openness and closedness were perceived as the most important contradictions, and predictability and novelty were deemed important for some specific conflict types.

Autonomy and Connection

autonomy and connection
an important relational tension that shows our conflicting desires to be close and to be separate

The dialectic between **autonomy and connection** refers to our simultaneous desires to be independent of our significant others and to find intimacy with them. As our story of Eleanor and Jeff illustrates, relational life involves the conflicting desires to be both close to and separate from relational partners. Jeff appreciates Eleanor's efforts on the dinner party, which makes him feel

close to her. Yet the reason for the party in some sense celebrates his separateness from Eleanor. The fact that Jeff has a long-standing friendship with Mary Beth illustrates his autonomy. Seeing both autonomy and closeness as constants in relational life is a hallmark of RDT, which makes it unique from many other theories of communication in relationships.

For example, as Baxter and Montgomery observe, Social Penetration Theory advances a rather static view of closeness; partners move toward closeness or away from it. From this vantage point, Eleanor and Jeff may be seen as growing closer and closer as they share more experiences and affection. Dialectic theory holds that contradictions are inherent in all relationships and that the dynamic interplay between autonomy and closeness is important to understanding a relationship. So Jeff and Eleanor are seen by RDT as moving between closeness and distance throughout their relationship. They are not understood as moving toward or moving away from either of these two competing needs.

Communication researchers are interested in dialectic thinking because of the communication implications of the theory. Baxter and Montgomery (1996) discuss how couples' private communication codes illustrate the presence of both connection and autonomy in relationships. For instance, nicknames celebrate something inherently individual in that they are usually highlighting an individual trait (such as Shorty, Chief, or Sweetness). Yet they also indicate a relational closeness in that distant friends do not invoke pet names for one another. In the simple practice of calling someone by a nickname, we are coding individuation and closeness.

Openness and Protection

openness and protection
an important relational tension that shows our conflicting desires to tell our secrets and to keep them hidden

A second critical tension in relational life has to do with openness and protection. The **openness and protection** dialectic focuses on our conflicting desires first to be open and vulnerable, revealing personal information to our relational partners, and second to be strategic and protective in our communication. As Eleanor mulls over how much to tell Jeff about her feelings, she is wrestling with the tension between disclosure and silence, or the openness and protection dialectic.

The dialectic position features both/and with respect to candor and concealment. For instance, Leslie Baxter and Erin Sahlstein (2000) mention how gossiping can accomplish a balancing of both openness and privacy as gossipers simultaneously disclose about others while keeping silent about themselves. With reference to disclosing highly personal information, Katherine Dindia (1994) argues for what she calls an "intrapersonal dialectic" of disclosure. This involves a gradual and incremental process of disclosure ranging from concealment to full revelation. However, we do not have much research focusing on the actual communication practices that allow relational partners to simultaneously disclose to each other and protect themselves.

One exception to this is the research of Angela Hoppe-Nagao and Stella Ting-Toomey (2002) who discovered that married couples communicate in a variety of ways to manage the tension between openness and closedness. They found six ways that couples communicated around this tension: (1) topic selection, (2) time alternation, (3) withdrawal, (4) probing, (5) antisocial strategies, and (6) deception.

Topic selection involved making some topics taboo, or off limits for discussion, thereby guarding privacy while assuring openness on all other topics.

Time alternation meant blocking out specific times to talk about sensitive topics. Withdrawal and probing were either leaving the conversation or asking for more information from the partner. Yelling, crying, or pouting were examples of antisocial communication. Deception involved small distortions of the truth or omissions to keep some things private and to avoid conflict in the relationship.

Novelty and Predictability

The dialectic between **novelty and predictability** refers to the conflict between the comfort of stability and the excitement of change. The dialectic position sees the interplay of certainty and uncertainty in relationships. Jeff and Eleanor's planning behavior illustrates this interplay. When they make a plan together, they are accomplishing at least two things with reference to predictability about themselves and their relationship. First, their plan defines them as in a relationship, because planning is a relational activity. It also establishes a routine so they know what they will be doing in the short-term future. Yet they leave the plan a bit open-ended to allow for creativity and novelty. With their plan for Sunday, Eleanor and Jeff have dealt simultaneously with their contradictory needs for routine and spontaneity.

novelty and predictability
an important relational tension that shows our conflicting desires to have stability and change

Contextual Dialectics

What we have just discussed are **interactional dialectics** in that they are located within the relationship itself—they are part of the partners' interaction with each other (Rawlins, 1992). Researchers have also discussed other dialectics that affect relational life. William Rawlins calls these **contextual dialectics,** which means that they derive from the place of the relationship in the culture.

Contextual dialectics are formed from the tension between the public definitions of a given relationship—friendship, for example—and the private interactions within a specific friendship. Rawlins discusses two contextual dialectics—between the public and the private and between the real and the ideal. Although perhaps a little less important to us than interactional dialectics, these two do affect interpersonal communication in relationships. The **public and private dialectic** refers to the tension between the two domains—a private relationship and public life. Rawlins discusses the fact that in the public realm friendship occupies a rather marginal position. Lillian Rubin (1998) makes the same observation, noting that public expectations favor kin relationships over friendships even when individuals may value their friends more highly than their kin. Rubin argues that people tend to prioritize commitments to their friends as less important than those to their family members. Rawlins notes that friendship suffers in comparison to other relationships because there is no institution to sanction it. Eleanor and Jeff's cohabiting relationship may have the same marginal status because, unlike marriage, it is not legally sanctioned.

interactional dialectics
tensions resulting from and constructed by communication

contextual dialectics
tensions resulting from the place of the relationship within the culture

public and private dialectic
a contextual dialectic resulting from a private relationship and public life

Rawlins (1992) argues that tension arises in a close friendship between this marginal public status and the friendship's deep private character. Rawlins states that this dialectic results in friendships (and by implication, other unsanctioned relationships) acting with what he calls double agency. By this he means that these relationships fulfill both public and private functions. Rawlins observes that sometimes the public functions constrain the private ones. For instance, people who form friendships in the workplace may encounter negative feedback from their significant others who see the friendships as a threat to their relationship. When Jeff and Eleanor first became serious, Eleanor felt threatened by Jeff's female friends. The public aspects of friendships and love relationships provide tension.

The dichotomy of the public and the private is obvious when we think about political figures. Politicians live a public life but have private lives as well. Dialectical thinking shows us that private, relational life is intertwined with public life. Although the two spheres can be separated to an extent, in many meaningful ways Dialectic Theory shows us that they are interwoven.

real and ideal dialectic
a contextual dialectic resulting from the difference between idealized relationships and lived relationships

This public and private dialectic interacts with the dialectic of the real and the ideal. The tension of the **real and ideal dialectic** is featured when we think of television shows like *Leave It to Beaver:* We receive an idealized message of what family life is like, and then when we look at the families we live in, we have to contend with the troublesome realities of family life. The tension between these two images forms this dialectic. If Eleanor reads a lot of romance novels emphasizing complete openness between romantic partners, she may feel a tension between that vision and her lived experience with Jeff, which involves some sharing but not complete openness.

In addition, this dialectic contrasts all the expectations one has of a relationship with its lived realities. Generally, expectations about relationships are lofty and idealized. Friendships are seen as sites of affection, loyalty, and trust. Families are pictured as havens in a troubled world. Loved ones are believed to provide unconditional affection and support. Yet we know that interpersonal relationships are not always pleasant and can have a dark side that contrasts starkly with these ideals. Dialectic Theory attempts to explain how people live with and manage this contradiction.

Finally, cultural and contextual factors influence these two dialectics. In cultures where friends are elevated to the status of family (some Middle Eastern cultures, for example), the tension will be experienced quite differently than in Rawlins's description, if it is felt at all. In addition, social mores and expectations vary over time, and the dialectics are influenced by these changes. For example, Ernest Burgess and Harvey Locke (1953) distinguish between an institutional and a companionate marriage. Prior to the 1950s, marriage was expected to be an economic institution, critical to the survival of the human race. More recently in the United States, marriage has been viewed as a love relationship where one's partner functions as one's best friend. Obviously, the tensions between the ideal and the real will shift depending on the contours of the socially prescribed ideal. See Table 12.1 for a summary of the basic relational dialectics.

Table 12.1 Interactional and Contextual Dialectics

TRADITIONAL INTERACTIONAL DIALECTICS	CONTEXTUAL DIALECTICS
Autonomy–Connection desiring a separate identity and wanting a bond between partners	Public–Private contrasting the public and private aspects of a relationship
Openness–Protection wanting to tell personal information while seeking privacy	The Real–The Ideal Comparing a lived relationship to a fantasy of that relationship
Novelty–Predictability wanting change while desiring stability	

Beyond Basic Dialectics

The basic dialectic tensions we have just reviewed characterize many inter-personal relationships, but a growing body of research is uncovering additional tensions and questioning whether autonomy–connection, openness–protection, and novelty–predictability permeate relationships in all contexts (Braithwaite & Baxter, 1995). For instance, Rawlins (1992) did not find evidence of the novelty–predictability dialectic in his study of friendship. Instead, he found a dialectic focusing on the tensions between judgment and acceptance. This dialectic emerges in the tension between judging a friend's behaviors and simply accepting them. In studying friendships in the workplace, Ted Zorn (1995) found the three main dialectics, but he also found some additional tensions that were specific to the workplace context.

Julie Apker, Kathleen Propp, and Wendy Zabava Ford (2005) note that the workplace is a relatively unexplored context for applying RDT. When they studied nurses working in health-care team interactions, they found several dialectics related to how the nurses negotiated their status and identity. They called these *role dialectics* because they spoke to the tensions nurses experienced relative to being equal to and subordinate to the physicians on the health-care team.

In examining people's participation in a community theater group, Michael Kramer (2004) advanced eleven dialectic tensions ranging from commitment to group and commitment to other life activities to tolerance and judgment (of the other members). Kramer organized these tensions into four main categories of dialectics: group–individual, ordered activities–emergent activities, inclusion–exclusion, and acceptable behaviors–unacceptable behaviors. Kramer suggests that dialectic tensions can frame a communication theory of group behavior.

Michaela Meyer (2003) examined the relationship between two characters in the television show *Dawson's Creek* and found the dialectic of connection–autonomy and a new dialectic, informing–constituting identity formation. Meyer was interested to discover how the show defined adolescent sexual identity, and she found the dialectic approach explained the process well. Meyer conducted a narrative analysis of the show, focusing on the character of Jack McPhee—who came out as gay in the second season—and his relationship with

Table 12.2 New Dialectics

INTERACTIONAL DIALECTIC	CONTEXT WHERE FOUND
Judgment–Acceptance	Friendship
Subordinate–Equal	Workplace
Group–Individual	Community group
Ordered activities–Emergent activities	Community group
Inclusion–Exclusion	Community group
Acceptable behavior–Unacceptable behavior	Community group
Presence–Absence	Families/Stepfamilies
Joy–Grief	Families
Informing–Constituting identity	Televised friendship
One parent–Two parent authority	Stepfamilies
Control–Restraint	Stepfamilies

another character, Jen Lindley, who is straight. Meyer argues that through their relationship Jack works through "the formation of his new sexual identity—gay adolescent" (p. 265).

It is possible that relational context makes a difference in the dialectics; these new dialectics were discovered in friendships, the workplace, a community group, and a televised friendship. But other researchers (Baxter, Braithwaite, Golish, & Olson, 2002; Bryant, 2003; Toller, 2005) examined issues of illness and death in the context of the family and also uncovered additional dialectics. They found that the dialectic of presence–absence was an important consideration for families dealing with Alzheimer's patients (Baxter et al., 2002), for those experiencing the death of a parent and becoming part of a stepfamily (Bryant, 2003), or for parents losing a child (Toller, 2005). Tamara Golish and Kimberly Powell (2003) advanced a further dialectical tension, that of joy–grief. They noted that parents experiencing a premature birth experienced the contradictory emotions of joy and grief and needed to find communication strategies for managing this contradiction. A study in stepfamilies' communication (Baxter, Braithwaite, Bryant, & Wagner, 2004) found the dialectic of one parent versus two parents in authority to be important to children. The children experience a tension between wanting their biological parent to have all the authority and wanting their stepparent to share authority with their biological parent. And, also in the context of stepfamilies, other researchers (Braithwaite, Toller, Daas, Durham, & Jones, 2008) found children voicing the dialectic of control and restraint. See Table 12.2 for a summary of these new dialectics.

Responses to Dialectics

Although the dialectic tensions are ongoing, people do make efforts to manage them. Some research (Jameson, 2004) examined politeness as a general method for managing dialectic tensions. Baxter (1988) identifies four specific

Research Notes

Braithwaite, D. O., & Baxter, L. A. (1995). "I do" again: The relational dialectics of renewing marriage vows. *Journal of Social and Personal Relationships, 12,* 177–198.

This study uses a dialectic framework to examine the renewal of marriage vows, a ceremony providing a public relationship ritual in the United States. The authors note that marriage vow renewal is a recent phenomenon that holds considerable appeal for North Americans according to contemporary media reports. Braithwaite and Baxter argue that this study responds to scholars' observations that the public enactment of a private relationship is an important area of study. As they say, "the web of others in which a relationship is embedded is a significant factor in pair stability" (p. 179).

They solicited respondents through multiple means, including the snowball technique and following up on marriage renewal announcements in local papers. They conducted twenty-one in-depth interviews with twenty-five people representing sixteen married couples who had participated in marriage renewal ceremonies. The researchers describe this process as follows: "Ten interviews were conducted separately with the husbands and wives who comprised five couples; four interviews were conducted jointly with husband–wife pairs; two interviews were conducted with husbands only; and five interviews were conducted with wives only" (p. 181).

Three dialectics were discovered in these interviews: public–private, stability–change, and conventionality–uniqueness. The authors discuss each of these tensions in turn, concluding that participants used marriage renewals as a ritual "to cope simultaneously with a variety of dialectical oppositions" (p. 193).

Sahlstein, E. M. (2004). Relating at a distance: Negotiating being together and being apart in long-distance relationships. *Journal of Social and Personal Relationships, 21,* 689–710.

This study used RDT to examine long-distance romantic relationships (LDRs) and explore the contradictions partners experience as they negotiate the distance and togetherness that mark the very definition of their relationship. Although not the norm in the United States, Sahlstein notes that LDRs are increasing in frequency, yet they remain understudied. This study is an attempt to remediate that problem. Sahlstein asked three research questions: (1) How does being together work with and against being apart within LDRs? (2) How does being apart work with and against being together within LDRs? (3) Does a contradiction exist between being together and being apart in LDRs? If so, what are some of the themes of this contradiction?

Twenty long-distance heterosexual couples audiotaped a couple interview (interviewing each other without the researcher present) based on questions the researcher provided. After completing the couple interview, they each answered a questionnaire independently. The audiotapes were transcribed, and the researcher coded and analyzed them. Sahlstein found that LDRs were both enabled and constrained by their situation. Being apart simultaneously works with and against their time together by providing refreshment and pressure for high-quality time, for instance.

strategies for this purpose: cyclic alternation, segmentation, selection, and integration (Table 12.3). **Cyclic alternation** occurs when people choose one of the opposites to feature at particular times, alternating with the other. For instance, when sisters are very young, they may be inseparable, highlighting the closeness pole of the dialectic. As adolescents, they may favor autonomy in their relationship, seeking separate identities. As adults, when they are perhaps living in the same town, they may favor closeness again.

cyclic alternation
a coping response to dialectical tensions; refers to changes over time

Table 12.3 Responses to Dialectic Tensions

RESPONSE	DESCRIPTION
Cyclic alternation	Choosing different poles for different times. Being close when young and more distant with age, for example.
Segmentation	Choosing different poles for different contexts. Being close at home and more distant at work, for example.
Selection	Choosing one pole and acting as though the other does not exist. Being an extremely close family, for example.
Integration	Synthesizing the oppositions in dialectic tensions; composed of three substrategies.
Neutralizing	A substrategy of integration; involves choosing a compromise between the oppositions. Being moderately close, for example.
Disqualifying	A substrategy of integration; involves exempting certain issues from the general pattern. Deciding to be open on all topics except sex, for example.
Reframing	A substrategy of integration; involves transforming the oppositions so they no longer appear to oppose one another. Deciding that closeness can only be achieved if there's a little distance too, for example.

segmentation
a coping response to dialectical tensions; refers to changes due to context

selection
a coping response to dialectical tensions; refers to prioritizing oppositions

integration
a coping response to dialectical tensions; refers to synthesizing the opposition; composed of three substrategies

neutralizing
a substrategy of integration; refers to compromising between the oppositions

disqualifying
a substrategy of integration; refers to exempting certain issues from the general pattern

Segmentation involves isolating separate arenas for emphasizing each of the opposites. For example, a husband and wife who work together in a family business might stress predictability in their working relationship and novelty for times they are at home. The third strategy, **selection**, refers to making a choice between the opposites. A couple who choose to be close at all times, ignoring their needs for autonomy, use selection.

Finally, **integration** involves some kind of synthesis of the opposites. Integration can take three forms: neutralizing, disqualifying, or reframing the polarities. **Neutralizing** involves compromising between the polarities. People who choose this strategy try to find a happy medium between the opposites. Jeff and Eleanor may decide they cannot really be as open as Eleanor would like, yet they cannot be as closed as Jeff might want either. Thus, they forge a moderately open relationship.

Disqualifying neutralizes the dialectics by exempting certain issues from the general pattern. A family might be very open in their communication in general yet have a few taboo topics that are not discussed at all, such as sex and finances.

Reframing refers to transforming the dialectic in some way so that it no longer seems to contain an opposition. Julia Wood and her colleagues (1994) discuss how couples reframe by defining connection as including differences. Thus, the dialectic between autonomy and connection is redrawn as a unity rather than as an opposition. If Eleanor and Jeff begin to see their closeness as a function of their ability to also be separate from each other, they are reframing, or redefining, what it means to be close.

Baxter and Montgomery (1996) review these and other techniques for dealing with dialectical tensions. They argue that any techniques that people use share three characteristics: They are improvisational, they are affected by time, and they are possibly complicated by unintended consequences. Let's look at these three characteristics in turn.

Improvisational, according to Baxter and Montgomery, means that whatever people do to deal with a particular tension of relational life, they do not alter the ongoing nature of the tension. For example, Jeff and Eleanor have come to a moderately open relationship to neutralize the dialectical tension, but they have not changed the fact that openness and protectiveness continue to be an issue in their relationship.

The aspect of time refers to the notion that, when dealing with dialectics, communication choices made by relational partners are affected by the past, enacted in the present, and filled with anticipation for the future. When Jeff praises Eleanor for the party they gave for Mary Beth, he does so knowing that they have argued about his friends in the past and hoping that these arguments will not continue in the future. In speaking about applying the dialectical approach to friendship, Rawlins (1992) comments that "configurations of contradictions compose and organize friendships throughout an ongoing process of change across the life course" (p. 8). He further observes that the way friends coordinate and manage their tensions over time is a key factor in dialectical analysis. The conclusion he draws is that "dialectical inquiries are intrinsically historical investigations" (p. 8), concerned with developmental processes over time.

Finally, Baxter and Montgomery point out that relational partners may enact a strategy for coping with a tension, yet it may not work out as they intended. For example, the husband and wife who work together and employ segmentation as we described earlier may feel they are coping with the novelty and predictability tension. But they may become dissatisfied because they spend a lot of time at work and so do not get enough novelty in their relationship.

Integration, Critique, and Closing

Dialectical process thinking adds a great deal to our explanatory framework for relational life. First, we can think specifically about issues around which relational partners construct meaning. Second, we can remove a static frame and put our emphasis on the interplay between change and stability. We do not have to choose between observing patterns and observing unpredictability because we recognize the presence of both within relationships. Likewise, dialectical thinking directs people to observe the interactions within a relationship, among its individual members, as well as outside a relationship, as its members interact with the larger social and cultural systems in which they are embedded. This approach helps us focus on power issues and multicultural diversity.

In general, scholars have been excited about the promise generated by Relational Dialectics Theory, and their responses to it have been positive. As you think about RDT, parsimony and utility are two evaluative criteria to consider.

Integration

Communication Tradition	Rhetorical	Semiotic	Phenomenological	Cybernetic	Socio-Psychological	**Socio-Cultural**	Critical

Communication Context	Intrapersonal	**Interpersonal**	Small Group	Organizational	Public/Rhetorical	Mass/Media	Cultural

Approach to Knowing	Positivistic/Empirical	**Interpretive/Hermeneutic**	Critical

Critique

Evaluation Criteria	Scope	Logical Consistency	**Parsimony**	**Utility**	Testability	Heurism	Test of Time

Parsimony

A few questions have been raised about the theory, however. One concerns parsimony. Some researchers question whether the dialectics of autonomy and connection, openness and protection, and novelty and predictability are the only dialectics in all relationships. In some ways, dialectics may be too parsimonious. For instance, many of the studies we have cited have generated additional dialectics, which raise questions about how well the theory does on the criterion of parsimony. Endless lists of new dialectic tensions would be problematic. Yet it's possible that some of these newer tensions may be subsumed under a few categories, which would enable RDT to explain relational life in a relatively parsimonious fashion. Furthermore, as Leslie Baxter (2006) observes, the most important criterion for a theory like RDT is heurism because the theory's goal is to shed light on the "complex and indeterminate process of meaning-making" (p. 130). As such, we might not judge it so stringently on the criterion of parsimony.

Utility

Perhaps the most positive appeal of the theory is that it seems to explain the push and pull people experience in relationships much better than some of the other, more linear, theories of relational life. Most people experience their relationships in ebb-and-flow patterns, whether the issue is intimacy, self-disclosure, or something else. That is, relationships do not simply become more or less of something in a linear, straight-line pattern. Instead, they often seem to be both/and as we live through them. Dialectics offers a compelling explanation for this both/and feeling, making the theory score well on utility.

Baxter and Montgomery (1996) observe that dialectics is not a traditional theory in that it offers no axioms or propositional arguments. Instead, it describes

Theory Into Practice
Martin

I can believe that dialectics is a useful theory because it definitely opened my eyes about my relationship with my brother. The push–pull idea says it all. When we were younger, we couldn't stand each other. But I did notice that if he went away for a while or I just didn't see him, I'd start to miss him. When he got back, I went back to hating him again. Now that we're older, I wouldn't say we hate each other, but we still react negatively if one gets too close. Yet we can't get too far apart either or that's bad. If we haven't talked in a couple of days, one of us will surely call the other just to check in. I always thought we had an odd relationship. It helps to see that we're struggling with what everyone else does in relationships with others—wanting connection and independence at the same time.

T*I*P

a set of conceptual assumptions. Thus, it does not offer us good predictions about, for example, what coping strategies people might use to deal with the major dialectic tensions in their relationships. This lack of predictive ability may be the result of the relative youth of dialectics as a theoretical frame for relational life, but more likely, it results from differing goals: An empirical or positivistic theory seeks prediction and final statements about communication phenomena; dialectics is a more interpretative theory and it operates from an open-ended, ongoing viewpoint. Baxter and Montgomery end their 1996 book with a personal dialogue between themselves about the experience of writing about a theory that encourages conversation rather than provides axiomatic conclusions. They agree that in some ways it is difficult to shake the cultural need for consistency and closure.

Many researchers agree that the dialectic approach is an extremely exciting way to conceive of communication in relational life. Expect to see more refinements of this theory and more studies testing its premises.

Discussion Starters

1. Can you think of other dialectic tensions that will pervade the relational life of Eleanor and Jeff besides those discussed in the chapter?

2. Do you think relationships are better explained through stage theories or dialectics? Why? Provide examples.

3. How do you think communication is used to deal with conflicting desires within a relationship? How does RDT help us understand communication behaviors?

4. Can two contradictory things both be true? Provide at least one example.

5. Provide an example of a dialectical tension that was managed through cyclic alternation.

6. Provide an example of how you could use segmentation do resolve a dialectical tension.

7. Provide an example of how you could use reframing to resolve a dialectical tension.

Online Learning Center   www. mhhe.com/west4e

Visit the Online Learning Center at www.mhhe.com/west4e for chapter-specific resources, such as story-into-theory and multiple-choice quizzes, as well as theory summaries and theory connection questions.

CHAPTER 13

Communication Privacy Management Theory

*Based on the research of **Sandra Petronio***

Lisa Sanders

Lisa Sanders knew that she would have a tough time making it through her workday without being sidetracked by someone. She rushed around the office, keeping her eyes down, trying to avoid getting sucked into a conversation with anyone. She enjoyed her work and loved her co-workers, but the downside was that somebody always wanted to chat and she simply had no time to waste today. She had already used too much precious work time going through her e-mail. She had thrown out about sixty-five pieces of junk, which was really getting to be a problem. The worst was that somehow she was on a porn list, and she kept getting solicitations for all sorts of nasty things. Lisa couldn't figure out what site she'd visited that had given her e-mail address to these low-lifes. She just hoped that the office didn't have some type of surveillance to observe all the porn messages she got. It made her feel vaguely uneasy.

She was thinking about ways to reduce or eliminate all that spam when she went into the break room for a cup of coffee. That was a mistake. Yolanda and Michael were there, and they wanted to ask her opinion about a change the front office was making in how they did the billing. One thing led to another, and soon the three were talking about Yolanda's concerns about going on maternity leave next month. Lisa found herself enjoying the conversation even though she knew she had to get back to work.

After work, Lisa went to Central State to take a night class so that someday she could finish her B.A. She was hopeful that she'd finish within the year, and she had her eye on a management position that she expected would be vacant by then. During the break, she visited with her friend Doug Banda, who was also finishing up his degree. She confided in Doug that she didn't think she was doing very well balancing work, school, and her personal life. It was a continual challenge, and today it was getting the better of her. She almost surprised herself with how emotional she got while talking to Doug. She could feel tears welling up in her eyes, and she felt her hands tremble. Doug was a good friend; he just listened and offered a friendly hug of support. She felt better after talking with him.

Finally, class was over and Lisa went home. The phone rang, and it was one of those annoying telemarketers. She got rid of him as soon as possible and then listened to the messages on her answering machine. Most weren't very important; Lisa's mother had called with the usual gossip about the family. Most of the message had to do with Lisa's sister-in-law, Margo. Lisa's mom didn't get along very well with Margo, and she often called Lisa to let off steam about something her daughter-in-law had done (or hadn't done). Today it was the fact that Ed's wife was taking the kids on a vacation and Lisa's mom wouldn't get to see them for two weeks. Of course, her mom was also interested in Lisa's life. While she was listening to her mother ask her if she had plans for the weekend, her roommate, Amanda Torelli, came home.

Lisa liked Amanda and she certainly couldn't afford the apartment without a roommate, but sometimes it felt like she didn't have a moment to herself. Amanda had an overpowering personality, and she filled the apartment to the extent that Lisa often felt crowded. Amanda always had something to say, and she didn't seem very sensitive to Lisa's mood for listening.

Tonight was no exception. Amanda wanted to tell Lisa all about her most recent fight with her boyfriend, Joel. Amanda and Joel were always fighting, and Lisa privately thought Amanda should dump the guy. But then she realized that Amanda liked playing the drama queen role, so she stopped telling Amanda any of her true reactions to Amanda's sagas. Lisa grabbed a glass of wine and some crackers as she settled on the couch to listen to Amanda's latest tale of woe. ∎

As Lisa encounters the various people in her life—co-workers, classmates, family members, roommates, and so forth—she engages in a complex negotiation between privacy and disclosure. This chapter presents the theory of Communication Privacy Management (CPM), which helps us sort through and explain the complexities of this process. Sandra Petronio (2002) states that CPM is a practical theory designed to explain the "everyday" issues described in Lisa's activities. As Petronio and Durham (2008) observe, the question of whether to tell someone something we are thinking is a complicated one, yet it's one we face frequently in our daily lives.

Examining Lisa's day, we can see at least five instances when Lisa is occupied with questions of disclosure: (1) She worries about someone at work finding out about the pornographic e-mails, (2) she engages in conversation with co-workers without telling them that she's feeling harried, (3) she confides in a friend about feeling unbalanced in her work and personal life, (4) she listens to her mother's voice-mail-recorded complaints, and (5) she hears her roommate's disclosures without telling her what she really thinks about her boyfriend.

All of these examples illustrate Petronio's contention that deciding what to reveal and what to keep confidential is not a straightforward decision but rather a continual balancing act. Both disclosure and privacy have potential risks and rewards for Lisa in all of the situations she encounters.

Lisa has to think about the possible risks and rewards her decisions may create for those with whom she interacts. How would Amanda feel if Lisa told her that she thought her boyfriend was a loser? The act of revealing or withholding personal information has effects on relationships as well as on individuals. What happens to the relationship between Lisa and Doug as she confides in him about her feelings? All these concerns, relational and individual, create the complicated process of balance that Petronio addresses with Communication Privacy Management Theory.

As Petronio (2002) observes:

> We try to weigh the demands of the situation with our needs and those of others around us. Privacy has importance for us because it lets us feel separate from others. It gives us a sense that we are the rightful owners of information about us. There are risks that include making private disclosures to the wrong people, disclosing at a bad time, telling too much

about ourselves, or compromising others. On the other hand, disclosure can give enormous benefits. . . . [We may] increase social control, validate our perspectives, and become more intimate with our relational partners when we disclose. . . . The balance of privacy and disclosure has meaning because it is vital to the way we manage our relationships. (pp. 1–2)

Thus, there was a need for a theory like CPM that attempts to do what few other theories have done: Explain the process that people use to manage the relationship between concealing and revealing private information.

Communication Privacy Management Theory is unlike most of the other theories presented in this text because it is so recent. For example, our discussion in Chapter 18 on Aristotle's *Rhetoric* centers on a theoretical approach to public address and persuasion that goes back thousands of years. Of course, not all of the theories in this text have the history of Aristotle's *Rhetoric,* but most have been in use for at least twenty years. The ideas in CPM are also more than twenty years old (Petronio, 1991), but the first formal statement of the mature version of the theory didn't appear until Petronio published *Boundaries of Privacy* in 2002.

This recency is notable for three reasons. First, it is exciting because it indicates the currency of thought in the communication discipline. It indicates that fresh, new thinking continues to illuminate questions of communication behavior. Having new theories illustrates the vibrancy of communication as a field. In case you were tempted to dismiss theory as something from musty tomes about dead Greeks, Petronio's CPM Theory shows that theorizing is alive and well in our own century.

Second, and related to the excitement generated by its recency, is the fact that CPM grows specifically from a focus on communication. This also shows the maturing and growth of the field of communication. Some of the other theories in this text, you will remember, originated in other disciplines. Communication researchers found them useful for some reason and borrowed them for their own work. For example, Symbolic Interaction Theory (Chapter 5), comes from sociology. Communication researchers appreciate the theory because it places a great deal of emphasis on the importance of interaction in developing a sense of self. Cognitive Dissonance Theory (Chapter 7) originated in psychology, yet communication scholars found it useful for the insights it sheds on persuasive practices. Communication researchers have found these and other theories extremely useful for framing their studies examining communication behaviors. Even so, it may be more helpful to have theories that place communication concepts centrally in the explanation process. CPM Theory does just that, allowing researchers to be more focused in their examinations of the communication process and specific communication practices.

Evolution of Communication Privacy Management Theory

Twenty years ago, Petronio and her colleagues published some studies outlining principles that would eventually become part of CPM (e.g., Petronio & Martin, 1986; Petronio, Martin, & Littlefield, 1984). In these studies, the researchers were interested in criteria for rule development in a rule management system for disclosure. They noted that men and women have different criteria for judging when to be open and when to stay silent. These criteria lead to differing rules for men and women on the subject of disclosure. The notion of gender differences and the concept of disclosure as rule governed are now parts of CPM Theory.

In 1991, Petronio published her first attempt to codify all the principles of the theory. Her work then differed from her later (Petronio, 2002) conceptualization in two ways. First, the theory had more limited boundaries in 1991. At that time, Petronio referred to it as a **microtheory** because its boundaries were confined to privacy management within a marital dyad. Now, as we explain in this chapter, the theory is less restricted and attempts to explain privacy and disclosure in many more contexts than marriage. Petronio now refers to CPM as a **macrotheory** because its boundaries include a large variety of interpersonal relationships, including groups and organizations.

The second change in the theory was a name change. In 1991 Petronio called the theory Communication Boundary Management. When she published the fuller statement of the theory in her 2002 book, she renamed it Communication Privacy Management Theory. Petronio explained the new name as better "reflecting the focus on private disclosures. Though the theory uses a boundary metaphor to explain the management process, the name change underscores that the main thrust of the theory is on private disclosures" (2002, p. 2). Although the book represents Petronio's current thinking about CPM, she notes that she expects (and hopes) that the theory will continue to grow and evolve as it is applied to practical questions of disclosure in relationships.

microtheory
a theory with limited boundaries

macrotheory
a theory with extensive boundaries

Theory at a Glance • Communication Privacy Management Theory

Disclosure in relationships requires managing private and public boundaries. These boundaries are between those feelings that one wants to reveal and those one wants to keep private. Disclosure in relationship development is more than revealing private information to another, however. Negotiation and coordination of boundaries is required. Decisions regarding disclosure require close monitoring.

Assumptions of CPM

Communication Privacy Management Theory is rooted in assumptions about how individuals think and communicate as well as assumptions about the nature of human beings. First, CPM adheres to aspects of both rules and systems

Table 13.1 Assumptions of CPM

CPM THEORY	ALL DIALECTIC THEORIES
Human choice	Relational life characterized by change
Human-made rules	Contradiction as the fundamental fact of relational life
Social concerns	

approaches that we discussed in Chapter 3. The theory makes three assumptions about human nature congruent with rules and systems:

- Humans are choice makers.
- Humans are rule makers and rule followers.
- Humans' choices and rules are based on a consideration of others as well as the self.

Petronio (2002) notes that people make choices and rules about what to tell and what to withhold from others based on a "mental calculus" grounded in criteria such as culture, gender, and context, among other things. These criteria include considerations about the other person(s) involved as well as the self. Therefore, Petronio uses the terms *disclosure* and *private disclosure* rather than *self-disclosure* as identified in Social Penetration Theory (Chapter 10).

In addition, CPM Theory is a dialectic theory. As a dialectic theory, CPM subscribes to assumptions similar to those that ground Relational Dialectics Theory (Chapter 12), including:

- Relational life is characterized by change.
- Contradiction is the fundamental fact of relational life.

These assumptions, taken together, represent an active perception of human beings and a picture of humans as engaged in relational life to the extent that self and other are intertwined (Table 13.1). The notion of being intertwined is important to CPM. Not only are the self and the other in an engaged relationship, but disclosure is also intertwined with the concept of privacy. As Petronio and Caughlin (2006) observe, privacy is only understood in a dialectical tension with disclosure. If we disclosed everything, we wouldn't have a concept of privacy. Conversely, if all information were private, the idea of disclosure wouldn't make sense. It's only by pairing them that each concept can be defined.

Basic Suppositions of CPM

As we have noted, CPM is concerned with explaining people's negotiation processes around disclosing private information. Our first task, then, is defining **private information.** Some researchers have stated that "what makes things private is in large part their importance to our conceptions of ourselves and to our

private information
information about things that matter deeply to a person

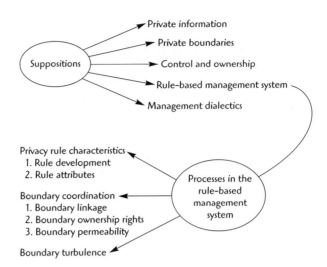

Figure 13.1
Overview of CPM
Basic Suppositions
Source: Adapted from
Petronio, 2002.

relationships with others" (Schoeman, 1984, p. 406). Petronio (2000) commented that people define private information as information about things that matter deeply to them. Thus, the process of communicating private information in relationships with others becomes **private disclosures.** As we have stated previously, CPM focuses on private disclosures rather than self-disclosures.

private disclosures
the process of communicating private information to another

The emphasis away from self-disclosure marks a distinction between CPM's definition of disclosure and that of traditional research on openness (e.g., Jourard, 1971). CPM views the definition differently in three ways. First, private disclosure puts more emphasis on the personal content of the disclosure than does traditional self-disclosure literature. In doing this, CPM gives more credence to the substance of disclosures, or that which is considered private. In addition, CPM examines how people disclose through a rule-based system. Finally, CPM does not consider that disclosures are only about the self. Disclosures are a communicative process. As Petronio (2002) observes, "to fully understand the depth and breadth of a disclosure, CPM does not restrict the process to only the self, but extends it to embrace multiple levels of disclosure including self and group. Consequently, CPM theory offers a privacy management system that identifies ways privacy boundaries are coordinated between and among individuals" (p. 3).

Communication Privacy Management Theory accomplishes this goal by proposing five basic suppositions: private information, private boundaries, control and ownership, rule-based management system, and management dialectics (see Figure 13.1). We will explain each of these basic suppositions of the theory in turn.

Private Information

The first supposition, private information, reiterates a traditional way to think about disclosure: It is the revealing of private information. However, Petronio (2002) observes that focusing on the content of disclosures allows us to disentangle the concepts of privacy and intimacy and examine how they are related. Many researchers have conflated self-disclosure with intimacy as though the two are essentially the same thing even though they are two distinct concepts (Parks, 1982). Petronio argues that "**intimacy** is the feeling or state of knowing someone deeply in physical, psychological, emotional, and behavioral ways because that person is significant in one's life. Private disclosure, on the other hand, concerns the *process* of telling and reflects the *content* of private information about others and us" (p. 5). When Lisa tells her friend Doug about her feelings, she is engaging in private disclosure, which may be increasing the intimacy of their relationship. However, when Amanda tells Lisa about her boyfriend problems, their intimacy is probably not deepening despite the disclosures.

intimacy
the feeling state of knowing someone deeply in all ways because that person is significant in one's life

Private Boundaries

The second supposition is **private boundaries.** CPM relies on the boundary metaphor to make the point that there is a line between being public and being private. On one side of the boundary, people keep private information to themselves (Petronio, Ellemers, Giles, & Gallois, 1998); on the other side, people reveal some private information to others in social relationship with them. When private information is shared, the boundary around it is called a **collective boundary,** and the information is not only about the self; it belongs to the relationship. When private information remains with an individual and is not disclosed, the boundary is called a **personal boundary** (Figure 13.2). When Lisa and her mother talk about Lisa's brother's wife, that information belongs to them as a dyad, and neither one of them reveals it to Margo or Lisa's brother, creating a collective boundary. When Lisa privately holds her opinion of Joel, Amanda's boyfriend, that information has a personal boundary.

private boundaries
the demarcation between private information and public information

collective boundary
a boundary around private information that includes more than one person

personal boundary
a boundary around private information that includes just one person

Boundaries can vary in other ways as well. They may be relatively permeable (easy to cross) or relatively impregnable (rigid and difficult to cross). Boundaries also may change related to life-span issues. As Figure 13.3 illustrates, children in the United States maintain relatively small privacy boundaries. The boundaries increase as children grow into adolescence and adulthood and cultivate a more developed sense of privacy. As people enter old age, their boundaries begin to shrink. As Petronio and Kovach (1997) discovered, issues of caregiving for the elderly—such as their need for others to bathe them or manage their finances—causes the boundary for the elderly to diminish.

Control and Ownership

Supposition 3 relates to control and ownership. This supposition relies on the notion that people feel they own private information about themselves. As owners of this information, they believe they should be in a position to control who else (if anyone) is allowed to gain access to it. When Lisa finds herself inundated with unwanted e-mails and telephone calls, she feels she has lost control over access to her personal space. She has not told the senders of the pornographic e-mails or the telemarketers how to contact her, but they do so regardless, violating Lisa's sense of control over information she believes she owns.

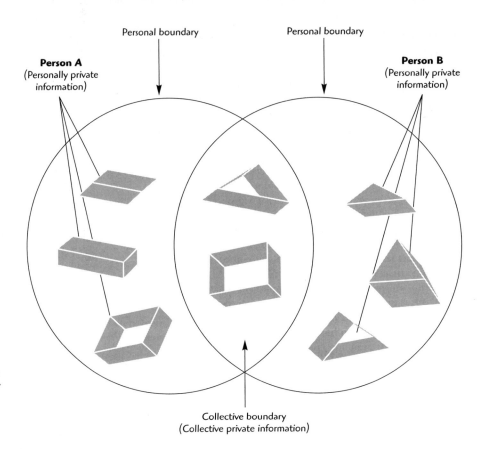

Person A
(Personally private
information)

Personal boundary

Personal boundary

Person B
(Personally private
information)

Collective boundary
(Collective private information)

Figure 13.2
Boundary Types
Source: Reprinted
by permission from
Boundaries of Privacy:
Dialectics of Disclosure
by Sandra Petronio, the
State University of New
York Press. © 2002
State University of
New York. All Rights
Reserved.

John Caughlin and Tamara Afifi's (2004) research speaks to the issue of ownership. They found that avoiding disclosures or maintaining private ownership of information can sometimes be helpful to relationships between parents and their college-student children as well as between boyfriends and girlfriends. Specifically, when study participants thought topic avoidance was motivated by a desire to protect their relationship, they were less likely to be unhappy about the avoidance. If, on the other hand, participants thought the avoidance was motivated by the other person's incompetence, they were very dissatisfied. In sum, Caughlin and Afifi concluded that it is possible to be too open in a relationship and that more restricted boundaries are helpful in some situations.

Rule-Based Management System

The fourth supposition of CPM Theory is a rule-based management system. This system is the framework for understanding the decisions people make about private information. The rule-based management system allows for management on the individual and collective levels and is a complex arrangement consisting of three processes: privacy rule characteristics, boundary coordination,

Theory Into Practice

Aleah

T*I*P

I was thinking about the part in the chapter that talked about topic avoidance. I know I like to keep a lot of information private. Topic avoidance is really how I get along with my father. We don't agree on much of anything and if he knew all my personal beliefs he would be arguing with me all the time. It works pretty well to keep those boundaries in place and my dad and I can talk about the weather, sports, and our dog—we get along just great that way.

and boundary turbulence. Because many subprocesses are involved in each of these three, we will describe them in a separate section.

Management Dialectics

The fifth supposition, privacy management dialectics, focuses on the tensions between the forces advocating for revealing private information and those advocating concealing it. Petronio (2002) states that "the basic thesis of the theory is grounded in the unity of dialectics" (p. 9), which refers to the tensions

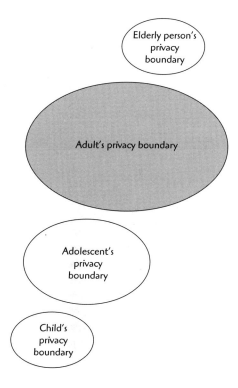

**Figure 13.3
Boundaries and the Life Span**

Source: Reprinted by permission from *Boundaries of Privacy: Dialectics of Disclosure* by Sandra Petronio, the State University of New York Press. © 2002 State University of New York. All Rights Reserved.

people experience due to opposites and contradictions. When Lisa is drawn into the conversation with her co-workers, she experiences conflicting desires. She is enjoying the visit and wants to support Yolanda as much as she can, yet she needs to work and disclosing is taking away time from working.

These five suppositions form the heart of CPM Theory. In the next section we detail the fourth supposition, concerning the privacy rule management system, to explicate the theory further.

Research Notes

Afifi, T. D. (2003). "Feeling caught" in stepfamilies: Managing boundary turbulence through appropriate communication privacy rules. *Journal of Social and Personal Relationships, 20,* 729–755.

This study used CPM to examine communication in stepfamilies. Specifically, Afifi was interested in how stepfamily members use communication patterns to forge alliances among small groups of the extended family (including the custodial and noncustodial parents). Furthermore, she sought to understand how these alliances might affect patterns of power resulting in better or worse adjustment to the new family form.

Afifi conducted ninety in-depth interviews with members from thirty stepfamilies (thirty stepchildren, twenty-nine stepparents, and thirty-one parents). The stepchildren participated in face-to-face interviews, and the parents were interviewed over the phone. Participants were asked to describe the stepfamily's history and development and to reflect on the communication patterns that characterized their stepfamily. These interviews were transcribed, yielding 1,015 single-spaced pages. Afifi analyzed the transcripts to discern themes.

She discovered that 80 percent of the participants expressed a theme she called "being caught" to describe a sense of being pulled between the stepfamily and the members of their biological family. She notes that these feelings seemed to result from enmeshed privacy boundaries that themselves were the result of revealing too much personal information. She further argues that "these enmeshed

boundaries fostered dialectical tensions that comprised family members' feelings of being caught, which could be viewed as a form of boundary turbulence" (p. 742). The dialectic tensions she found were labeled loyalty–disloyalty and revealment–concealment. The results of her analysis also revealed that the participants exhibited a variety of strategies to try to reduce the turbulence and coordinate privacy boundaries.

Afifi concludes that her study extends CPM into the context of stepfamilies and also shows the utility of examining the communication strategies displayed to manage privacy boundaries.

Petronio, S., Sargent, J., Andea, L., Reganis, P., & Cichocki, D. (2004). Family and friends as health-care advocates: Dilemmas of confidentiality and privacy. *Journal of Social and Personal Relationships, 21,* 33–52.

This study used CPM to examine the practice of bringing a family member or friend to a doctor's visit to act as a health-care advocate for the patient. The authors begin by noting that a health-care advocate's role is inherently fraught with privacy dilemmas. Health-care advocates are present during what is essentially a private matter between a physician and a patient, and they are expected to participate to a degree in interpreting, clarifying, and perhaps translating private information. It may be difficult to know how to define the limits of confidentiality and privacy in this role, and physicians are often confused about the role informal advocates play. Yet past research has shown

(continued)

many benefits to the patient in having such an advocate present.

In this study, a preliminary attempt was made to understand the privacy management process occurring in the context of physician visits with informal advocates present. One hundred twenty-three people who had served as health-care advocates for a friend or family member participated in the study. They filled out a questionnaire asking them about this role. Some of the questions were closed-ended, and others were open-ended. The open-ended questions were analyzed to see what themes recurred throughout.

Four main themes emerged from the analysis: (1) privacy versus well-being, (2) the altruistic supporter, (3) information seeking by the physician, and (4) shared responsibility. The first theme reflected the participants' management strategy for the tension between privacy and openness. The researchers note that "the advocates seemed to use their own privacy rules to make decisions to interfere or intervene" (pp. 42– 43). In the second theme the respondents indicated that they saw themselves as helpful and supportive to the patient by playing this role. The third theme indicates that physicians saw the advocates as sources of information about the patient in addition to their role as supporters of the patient. Occasionally, this placed the advocate in a tricky position when physicians asked them to reveal information they knew from a dyadic privacy boundary with the patient. The final theme suggests that the advocates saw their increased knowledge of private information as requiring them to take on more responsibility for helping make medical decisions with the patient and the physician.

The authors conclude that CPM provides some insight into the ways that the sometimes confusing role of health-care advocate can be enacted.

Privacy Rule Management Processes

The fourth supposition, a rule-based management system, depends on three privacy rule management processes: privacy rule characteristics, boundary coordination, and boundary turbulence (see Figure 13.1). The theory proposes that these regulate the process of revealing and concealing private information. We will discuss each of the three processes to illustrate how the theory explains the overall rule-based management system.

Privacy Rule Characteristics

Privacy rule characteristics have two main features: development and attributes. **Rule development** is guided by people's decision criteria for revealing or concealing private information. CPM Theory states that five decision criteria are used for developing privacy rules: cultural criteria, gendered criteria, motivational criteria, contextual criteria, and risk-benefit ratio criteria. In describing how she came to develop and refine CPM, Sandra Petronio (2004) observes that it was very important to explicate how privacy rules developed by proposing these five criteria. She notes that this was key because privacy rules are a foundational principle of the theory (Table 13.2).

Cultural criteria depend on the norms for privacy and openness in a given culture. Individuals are guided in their own expectations for privacy by the values they learn in their cultures. Thus, we might understand Amanda's desire to be transparent to Lisa in our opening story by noting that she is Italian American, a culture that generally values openness of expression.

privacy rule characteristics
one of the processes in the privacy rule management system; describes the nature of privacy rules

rule development
one of the features of privacy rule characteristics; describes how rules come to be decided

Table 13.2 Privacy Rule Development Criteria

DECISION CRITERIA	EXAMPLE
Cultural criteria	The United States favors more openness in relational communication than does Japan.
Gendered criteria	American women are socialized to be more disclosive than men.
Motivational criteria	If you have disclosed a great deal to me, because of reciprocity I might be motivated to disclose to you.
Contextual criteria	If we're in a traumatic situation (e.g., we've survived an earthquake together), we'll develop new rules.
Risk–benefit criteria	Our rules are influenced by our assessment of the ratio of risks to benefits of disclosing.

Gendered criteria refer to differences that may exist between men and women in drawing their privacy boundaries (Petronio & Martin, 1986). Although these differences are not unchangeable, men and women seem to be socialized to develop different rules for how privacy and disclosure operate.

A third set of criteria revolves around motivation. People make decisions about disclosing based on their motivations. Some people may have such motives as control, manipulation, and power for disclosing or concealing private information. Others may be motivated by self-clarification or relational closeness. In addition, there may be individual differences in people's motivations. Lisa may have a lower motivation for disclosing in general than Amanda has, for example.

Contextual criteria also have an influence on decisions people make about privacy. Petronio (2002) discusses two elements that make up context: social environment and physical setting. The social environment involves the special circumstances that might prompt a disclosure or a decision not to disclose. For example, Lisa's mother's disclosures might have been prompted by a recent conflict with Margo. Lisa's disclosure to Doug was stimulated by her circumstances that day, which made her feel particularly stressed and needy. The physical environment has to do with the actual location, issues of crowding, and physical space. Certain environments invite disclosures whereas others caution against them. When Lisa is in the break room at work, she may not find the physical setting conducive to disclosing because it reminds her of how busy she is and because there is the constant possibility that someone else could come in during the conversation. On the other hand, being in her apartment on the couch with a glass of wine might be a very inviting setting for disclosure.

Finally, rules are developed based on risk-benefit ratio criteria. This means that people evaluate the risks relative to the benefits of disclosing or keeping quiet. This is similar to the contentions of Social Exchange Theory (Chapter 11) except in this case it is applied to the notion of disclosing behavior rather than relationship development.

The five decision criteria help explain the process of rule development, which is one element of privacy rule characteristics. The second aspect of privacy rule characteristics concerns **privacy rule attributes.** Attributes are further divided into the ways people acquire rules and the properties of the rules. Generally, the theory suggests that people learn rules through socialization processes or by negotiation with others to create new rules.

For example, Lisa was socialized in her company through informal networks that taught her it was important to spend time nurturing relationships with her co-workers. The organization often invoked the metaphor of a family, hosted many social events for the workers, and tried in several other ways to impress on employees that close relationships were an important part of the organizational culture. When learned rules are inadequate or need modifying, then people collaborate to forge new rules. For instance, if the company determined that its workers were disclosing to one another to the detriment of productivity, they might work to renegotiate the rules. This example also speaks to the concept of **rule properties,** which refers to the characteristics of rules. Characteristics index how stable or changeable a rule is.

Boundary Coordination

The second process under the rule-based management system is **boundary coordination,** which refers to how we manage information that is co-owned. For example, when Lisa and her mother talk about Margo, Lisa's sister-in-law, it is clear that the information is to be kept from Margo and Lisa's brother. Boundary coordination is the process through which that decision is made and through which Lisa and her mother become co-owners of private information. Petronio (2002) notes that people "regulate private information through rules that moderate boundary linkage, boundary ownership rights, and boundary permeability" (pp. 26–27).

Boundary linkage refers to the connections that form boundary alliances between people. For example, when Lisa tells private information to Doug, they are linked in a privacy boundary. Physicians form linkages with their patients because the medical profession stresses patient confidentiality. If you overhear a piece of private information that wasn't intended for you, you are technically linked; however, the linkage is weak because you know you weren't the intended recipient of the information.

Boundary ownership refers to rights and privileges accruing to co-owners of private information. For boundary ownership to be exercised accurately, the rules need to be clear. For instance, if your friend tells you private information, are you allowed to share it with someone else (Petronio, Sargent, Andea, Reganis, & Cichocki, 2004)? If your friend has told you explicitly not to tell anyone her secret, then the boundary is clear and unambiguous. However, if she just told you the secret without specifying whether you could tell anyone else, you might feel unsure about your co-ownership. You could suspect you aren't supposed to tell, but without instructions you feel uncertain.

Yet boundaries are dynamic and may be redrawn over time. For example, when Rachel Norton was eighteen, her brother had an accident with the family

privacy rule attributes
one of the features of privacy rule characteristics; describes how people acquire rules and the properties of rules

rule properties
the characteristics of a rule that reveal how stable or changeable it is

boundary coordination
one of the processes in the privacy rule management system; describes how we manage private information that is co-owned

boundary linkage
the connections forming boundary alliances between people

boundary ownership
rights and privileges accruing to co-owners of private information

car. Together, she and her brother had the car repaired and paid for the repairs without telling their parents. Now that they are both adults, they have told their parents about the incident. Thus, the boundary broadened to include the whole family. It may also be the case that co-owners do not agree about boundary issues. For example, Amanda might think that her tales about Joel, her boyfriend, link Lisa into a boundary that Lisa, herself, would rather not be included in.

Finally, boundary coordination is accomplished through **boundary permeability,** which refers to how much information is able to pass through the boundary. When access to private information is closed, boundaries are said to be **thick boundaries;** when access is open, people have **thin boundaries** in place. As Petronio (2002) observes:

> Although we do have secrets and people may be very open, more typically, people regulate the permeability to varying degrees through an array of access and protection rules. For example, people may completely hide health concerns from others for a period of time, cautiously expose flaws they find in themselves to certain others, use discretion in commenting on another's behavior, or be completely open with one other person. In each case, the permeability, that is how much information is allowed to pass through the boundary, varies depending on the rules for access and protection. (p. 29)

Boundary Turbulence

Boundary turbulence exists when the rules of boundary coordination are unclear or when people's expectations for privacy management come into conflict with one another. Boundary regulation is not always a smooth operating system, and the people involved can experience clashes that Petronio labels turbulence. For example, if Lisa refused to listen to Amanda's problems one evening, they might come into conflict. If you discovered that a friend told another about some private information you had shared and meant for that friend to keep private, boundary turbulence would ensue. CPM Theory asserts that when individuals experience boundary turbulence, they will try to make adjustments so that they can reduce the turbulence and achieve coordination (Afifi, 2003).

Boundary turbulence can occur for a number of different reasons. In writing about CPM in relation to HIV disclosures, Kathryn Greene and her colleagues (Greene, Derlega, Yep, & Petronio, 2003) observed that one reason for a boundary disturbance might be when a discloser attempts to draw another into a privacy boundary but the other person rejects this attempt. The researchers cite many instances of people trying to tell their immediate family members about their HIV status only to be ignored or cut off. For example,

> I said, "Well, I need to tell you something that's kind of serious" and she said, "What are you talking about?" I said, "Well, it has to do with my health" and she said, "What's wrong with your health?" I said, "Well, this isn't easy to say, but I need to say it." I basically told her that I'm HIV positive, and she didn't say anything. Just looked at me. I didn't get a whole lot of feedback from her at all. (pp. 31–32)

boundary permeability
how much information is able to pass through a boundary

thick boundaries
closed boundaries allowing little or no information to pass through

thin boundaries
open boundaries allowing all information to pass through

boundary turbulence
conflicts about boundary expectations and regulation

Greene and her colleagues conclude that when people invite others into their privacy boundaries they expect an appropriate response. When this is violated, people experience hurt and boundary turbulence.

Integration, Critique, and Closing

Communication Privacy Management Theory, although relatively new to the communication field, has enjoyed significant attention from scholars across many areas. The theory appears to resonate because its boundaries and boundary rules guide all sorts of behaviors in all types of relationships. As you think about the merits of CPM, three criteria for theory evaluation are relevant: logical consistency, utility, and heurism.

Integration

Communication Tradition	Rhetorical	Semiotic	Phenomenological	Cybernetic	Socio-Psychological	**Socio-Cultural**	Critical

Communication Context	Intrapersonal	**Interpersonal**	Small Group	Organizational	Public/Rhetorical	Mass/Media	Cultural

Approach to Knowing	Positivistic/Empirical	**Interpretive/Hermeneutic**	Critical

Critique

Evaluation Criteria	Scope	**Logical Consistency**	Parsimony	**Utility**	Testability	**Heurism**	Test of Time

Logical Consistency

One criticism of the theory that Petronio (2002) has discussed relates to its logical consistency. Some critics have observed that CPM uses the term *dialectic* inaccurately, claiming to be dialectic in nature when it's really based on dualistic thinking. The basis for the criticism stems from Baxter and Montgomery's (1996) distinctions among monologic, dualistic, and dialectic approaches (see Chapter 12). Using these distinctions, Baxter and Montgomery have argued

Theory Into Practice

Cleo

One of the biggest issues that this theory made me think about was the health-care system. I feel that there is a lot of boundary turbulence going on in that. Also, the whole idea of my ownership of my private information is a big issue with health care. I mean, are they really keeping it private? Also, the theory kind of helps explain why I don't like it when the school calls to tell me something on the phone about my son's health. The phone seems like the wrong way for me to hear that Nathan had a seizure. I know they have to use the phone, but I remember how lonely and impersonal it felt when the school called with that news. It was the first we knew that Nathan had a problem. Now that he's been diagnosed, I keep in contact with the school all the time. I have gotten to know the nursing staff at his school, and it doesn't feel so bad to talk to them now.

that CPM takes a dualistic approach, treating privacy and disclosure as independent of one another and able to coexist in tandem.

Petronio (2002) responds to this criticism by noting that perhaps the accusation of dualistic thinking comes from the use of the terms *balance* and *equilibrium* in the early versions of CPM Theory. Petronio argues that CPM is not focused on balance in the psychological sense. "Instead, [CPM] argues for coordination with others that does not advocate an optimum balance between disclosure and privacy. As an alternative, the theory claims there are shifting forces with a range of privacy and disclosure that people handle by making judgments about the *degrees* of privacy and publicness they wish to experience in any given interaction" (pp. 12–13 [emphasis in original]). Thus, Petronio argues that it is legitimate to call CPM Theory dialectical in nature.

Utility

Communication Privacy Management Theory has much promise of utility. It offers an explanation for the delicate process of coordination disclosing and concealing that people perform continually in their relationships with others. Furthermore, CPM may provide insights as that process of coordination becomes even more complex. CPM is needed to explain those daily intrusions into our lives due to technological advances. As technology moves more and more of what we have considered private information into the public realm, we will need to understand the rule-based management system underlying this trend.

Heurism

Communication Privacy Management Theory seems to be heuristic because it has been utilized as a framework in a variety of situations, including child sexual abuse (Petronio, Reeder, Hecht, & Ros-Mendoza, 1996), disclosure of

HIV or AIDS status (Cline & McKenzie, 2000), medical mistakes (Allman, 1998), and in the disclosures of voluntarily child-free couples (Durham, 2008). The heuristic nature of the theory and its evaluation on the other criteria all argue for CPM's success as a theoretical framework for communication questions.

As we continue to understand the decision to reveal private information to others, Communication Privacy Management Theory will be an important and valuable reference. Our conversations and relationships with others are complex, as we evidenced in Chapter 2. To this end, CPM provides us a critical framework as we seek to unravel the many and varied communication practices we undertake in our lives.

Discussion Starters

1. Apply CPM Theory to Lisa Sanders's case. How might it help Lisa to understand her situation?

2. Do you think CPM will stand the test of time? Why or why not?

3. What approach to theory building does Petronio take in CPM Theory (laws, rules, systems, or some combination)? Explain your answer.

4. What topics of interest can you use CPM Theory to investigate?

5. Can CPM Theory explain technological disclosures and privacy attempts such as those encountered in online conversations? Explain your answer.

6. Explain the concept of control with reference to communication boundaries. The chapter mentioned a study about medical mistakes that focused on control. Think of other contexts besides health care where control might be an issue. Explain your choices.

7. Give an example of how boundary turbulence affects communication privacy management processes.

Online Learning Center www. mhhe.com/west4e

Visit the Online Learning Center at www.mhhe.com/west4e for chapter-specific resources, such as story-into-theory and multiple-choice quizzes, as well as theory summaries and theory connection questions.

Groups and Organizations

THE UNITED STATES IS A SOCIETY THAT RELIES ON groups and organizations in order to function. Small group and organizational communication has a rich tradition in communication studies. A number of articulate theoretical developments are occurring in this field. One reason we have seen such attention in this area is that most of us will work for some sort of a company or corporation at some point in our lives. Further, global, political, social, and economic changes have prompted groups and organizations to look at their roles across the globe.

Companies and organizations are undergoing significant changes in the twenty-first century. These changes are a result of the corporate scandals of the early 2000s, the need to work together in more culturally diverse work environments, the increased accountability as a result of the 2008 federal bailout, and the fact that very few jobs these days can be accomplished at work without the help of others. As Bob Dylan once sang, "The times they are a-changin'."

The four theories we present in this section of the book consider the influence that changing times have on groups and organizations. Each theory looks at the role of a group member or employee in a different way. For instance, Groupthink views group members as capable of being so connected that they fail to question the group's goals or tasks. Structuration Theory sees individuals and teams as being both constrained and encouraged by the structure of an organization. Employees can either be bound by the rules or norms of a company or transcend these existing structures and tap into personal creativity. In Organizational Culture Theory, employees are perceived as part of a company's culture, positioned to develop and sustain a company's principles and values. Trying to make sense out of vague, misleading, or ambiguous information is at the heart of Organizational Information Theory. This theory examines how organizational members extract themselves from confusing situations while at work.

These theories view groups and organizational members as being both active and passive. Group and organizational life is precisely like that. At times we are consumed with getting the task accomplished and may be unaware of our eagerness to get things done. We actively work toward clarity and toward becoming part of a company. At other times, though, we may simply allow others to engage. The theories in this section help us understand a number of interesting areas, including decision making, social influence, rules, corporate climate, and employee satisfaction.

CHAPTER 14

Groupthink

*Based on the research of **Irving Janis***

Melton Publishing Board of Directors

As they sat in the seminar room at Melton Publishing, the seven men and women privately wondered when they would find their next superstar author. Last week the board heard the bad news: Their profits were down significantly, and they needed a best-seller to counter some of the company's financial loss. Elizabeth Hansen, the board's chairperson, suggested that the group review at least two books that they felt could reverse the company's losses. From early reviews of one of the books—*Red Warnings,* a science fiction novel—she felt that here was an opportunity to turn around the downward spiral and give the small press a promising future against the megapresses. She knew that employee and board morale was down and felt that something had to be done quickly.

As chairperson for the past few years, Elizabeth knew that, in a way, her own credibility was on the line. She was chairing a board of literary people, for the most part; only one member previously had been on a board. She knew that the similarity among the members would likely result in them agreeing to a quick and reasonable solution to the company's financial circumstances. Although no clear solution was obvious at this difficult time in the company, Elizabeth felt that something had to be done.

The seven gathered around the table as they reviewed their financial future. Elizabeth opened the discussion with an upbeat message: "We can beat this downward spiral," she said. She reminded the group that the 9-year-old company had a history of surviving rough times. "This is just another bump in the road," she reported.

The discussion soon turned to the book *Red Warnings,* which had been reviewed favorably in a national book magazine. Since the review's publication, orders for the book had skyrocketed. Elizabeth felt that the best way to generate more money for the small company, thereby resulting in more publicity, was to market *Red Warnings* aggressively: through the media, on college campuses, at science fiction conventions across the country, and, hopefully, on *Oprah*! The book could bring in hundreds of thousands of dollars in profits, but Elizabeth knew that this would require tireless marketing. Melton Publishing is small, she thought, but not too small to promote a best-seller. The Internet will help, she believed to "spread the message."

Randy Miles, another board member, disagreed with Elizabeth's plans. He thought that there was simply too much risk in concentrating so much time and money on one book. Randy's way to improve the financial situation of the company could be summed up in one word: cutbacks. After looking over the company's financial records of the past few years, he had discovered that far too many people had been hired, resulting in overspending on salary, benefits, and book production. He knew that cutting back was not a popular strategy but felt that this wasn't the time for being popular.

Their meeting dragged on, from an anticipated 2 hours to approaching 5 hours. Elizabeth and Randy continued to explain and defend their viewpoints. At times, there was heated arguing; the two would frequently raise their voices to make their points. During their arguments, the remaining board members would try to be agreeable. They knew that they weren't all that knowledgeable about how to turn the company around, and for the most part, they sat silently while the two leaders squared off against each other.

Finally, as the afternoon sun began to set, Tina, a writer from the Boston area, said, "Look, we've all been very patient while the two of you decide what's best for this company. And maybe we've learned for the future that we need to get more financial expertise on this board. But, for now, I have to speak. We need to make a decision. A hard decision. Whether a decision can be made today is iffy. I recommend that we postpone our decision until our next meeting so that we can all think about our options."

Randy interrupted, "Look, Tina, I appreciate your honesty, but this is not about whether we should build another bathroom! This is the company's future. I recommend that we hash this out now."

Elizabeth agreed, as did the other board members. It occurred to Tina that their "lunch meeting" was turning into a "working dinner." As evening came, it was clear that Elizabeth and Randy were getting tired. "Listen, Randy, we're running low on energy and time. I think we should just get the two motions out and have the board vote." The other members soon agreed. It was obvious that they were all tired.

Randy reminded the group that they shouldn't rush their decision, but Tina reminded him that he was the one who hadn't wanted to postpone a decision. Although Randy tried to attack Tina's tone, the other group members began clamoring for a vote. Each member openly expressed support for Elizabeth's aggressive marketing plan. Because the group was small and he could sense the overwhelming support for Elizabeth, Randy decided to give in. He left the meeting feeling that he had been silenced by the group at the end of their discussion.

■

Participating in small groups is a fact of life. Whether people are at school or at work, they frequently spend significant working hours in groups. To understand the nature of decision making in small groups, Irving Janis, in his book *Victims of Groupthink* (1972), explains what takes place in groups where group members are highly agreeable with one another. Studying foreign policy decision making, Janis contends that when group members share a common fate, there is great pressure toward conformity. He labels this pressure *groupthink*, a term cleverly patterned after vocabulary found in George Orwell's *1984* (for example, *doublethink*).

groupthink
a way of group
deliberation that
minimizes conflict
and emphasizes, the
need for unanimity

Groupthink is defined as a way of deliberating that group members use when their desire for unanimity overrides their motivation to assess all available plans of action. Janis contends group members frequently engage in a style of deliberating in which consensus seeking (need for everyone to agree) outweighs good sense. You may have participated in groups where the desire to achieve a goal or task was more important than developing reasonable solutions to problems. Janis believes that when highly similar and agreeable groups fail to consider fully any dissenting opinions, when they suppress conflict just so they get along, or when the group members do not consider all solutions, they are prone to groupthink. He argues that when groups are "in" groupthink,

Highly cohesive groups frequently fail to consider alternatives to their course of action. When group members think similarly and do not entertain contrary views, they are also unlikely to share unpopular or dissimilar ideas with others. Groupthink suggests that these groups make premature decisions, some of which have lasting and tragic consequences.

they immediately engage in a mentality to "preserve group harmony" (Janis, 1989, p. 60). To this end, making peace is more important than making clear and appropriate decisions.

Our example of the board of directors at Melton Publishing exemplifies the groupthink phenomenon. The board members are a group of people who apparently get along. The members are essentially connected by their literary backgrounds, making them more predisposed to groupthink. The group is under a deadline to come up with a thoughtful and financially prudent decision about the financial future of the company. As the chapter unfolds, we will tell you more about how this group becomes susceptible to groupthink.

Before we identify the assumptions guiding the theory, we first need to point out that Janis looked at "small elite groups at critical junctures in the foreign policy process" (Yetiv, 2003, p. 420). The individuals comprising these groups were usually considered the "inner circle" of those in charge; namely, the president of the United States. Using principles from small group research, Janis (1982) explains why several foreign policy decisions are flawed.

In the development of groupthink, Janis analyzed five matters of significant national importance: (1) the preparedness policies of the U.S. Navy at Pearl Harbor in 1941, (2) the decision to pursue the North Korean Army on its own territory by President Eisenhower, (3) the decision by President Kennedy to invade Cuba at the Bay of Pigs shortly after Fidel Castro established a communist government, (4) the decision to continue the Vietnam War by President Johnson, and (5) the Watergate cover-up by President Nixon. Janis argues that each of these policy decisions was made by both the president and his team of advisors and that, because each group was under some degree of stress, they made hasty and what amounted to inaccurate decisions. He interviewed a number of people who were part of these teams and concluded that each of these policy fiascoes occurred because of groupthink. It was discovered that in each of these cases, the presidential advisors did not thoroughly test information before making their decisions.

According to Janis, the group members failed to consider forewarnings, and their biases and desire for harmony overshadowed critical assessments of their own decisions. Usually, the decision-making process underscoring groupthink is historical. Randy Hirokawa, Dennis Gouran, and Amy Martz (1988), for instance, came to the conclusion that faulty decision making characterized the disaster of the space shuttle *Challenger*. Furthermore, John Schwartz and Matthew Wald (2003) comment that groupthink principles were at work when the *Columbia*, another shuttle, broke up. A "quick analysis" by aviation giant Boeing and their engineers showed that "smart people working collectively can be dumber than the sum of their brains" (p. 4). We address the application of groupthink principles in more depth later in the chapter.

Assumptions of Groupthink

Groupthink is a theory associated with small group communication. In Chapter 2 we noted that small groups are a part of virtually every segment of U.S. society. In fact, emphasizing the importance of small groups, Marshall Scott Poole (1998) argues that the small group should be "THE basic unit of analysis" (p. 94). Janis focuses his work on **problem-solving groups** and **task-oriented groups,** whose main purpose is to make decisions and give policy recommendations. Decision making is a necessary part of these small groups. Other activities of small groups include information sharing, socializing, relating to people and groups external to the group, educating new members, defining roles, and telling stories (Engleberg & Wynn, 2007; Harris & Sherblom, 2008). With that in mind, let's examine three critical assumptions that guide the theory:

problem-solving groups
sets of individuals whose main task is to make decisions and provide policy recommendations

task-oriented groups
sets of individuals whose main goal is to work toward completing jobs assigned to them

- Conditions in groups promote high cohesiveness.
- Group problem solving is primarily a unified process.
- Groups and group decision making are frequently complex.

The first assumption of Groupthink pertains to a characteristic of group life: cohesiveness. Conditions exist in groups that promote high cohesiveness. Ernest Bormann (1996) observes that group members frequently have a common sentiment or emotional investment, and as a result they tend to maintain a group identity. This collective thinking usually guarantees that a group will be agreeable and perhaps highly cohesive.

T*I*P

Theory Into Practice

Missy

I know that Groupthink will apply to almost any job. For example, I want to get a job in Human Resources. I think virtually everything from the theory will help me as I make decisions. From understanding personnel to understanding the company's hierarchy, I know this theory will be useful for me. To think that he [Janis] wrote in the 1970s and it's still related to today is incredible.

What is cohesiveness? You probably have heard of groups sticking together or having a high esprit de corps. This phrase essentially means that the group is cohesive. **Cohesiveness** is defined as the extent to which group members are willing to work together. It is a group's sense of togetherness. Cohesion arises from a group's attitudes, values, and patterns of behavior; those members who are highly attracted to other members' attitudes, values, and behaviors are more likely to be called cohesive.

cohesiveness
the extent to which group members are willing to work together

Cohesion is the glue that keeps a group intact. You may have been a member of a cohesive group, although it can be difficult to measure cohesiveness. For instance, is a group cohesive if all members attend all meetings? If all members communicate at each meeting? If everyone seems amiable and supportive? If group members usually use the word *we* instead of the word I? All of these? You know if you have been in a cohesive group, but you may not be able to tell others precisely why the group is cohesive.

Our second assumption examines the process of problem solving in small groups: It is usually a unified undertaking. By this, we mean that people are *not* predisposed to disrupting decision making in small groups. Members essentially strive to get along. Dennis Gouran (1998) notes that groups are susceptible to **affiliative constraints**, which means that group members hold their input rather than risk rejection. According to Gouran, when group members do participate, fearing rejection, they are likely "to attach greater importance to preservation of the group than to the issues under consideration" (p. 100). Group members, then, seem more inclined to follow the leader when decision-making time arrives. Taking these comments into consideration, the board of directors at Melton may simply be a group who recognizes the urgency associated with their financial dilemma. Listening to two board members, Elizabeth and Randy, therefore, is much easier than listening to seven. The two become leaders, and the group members allow them to set the agenda for discussion.

affiliative constraints
refers to when members withhold their input rather than face rejection from the group

The third assumption underscores the nature of most problem-solving and task-oriented groups to which people belong: They are usually complex. In discussing this assumption, let's first look at the complexity of small groups and then at the decisions emerging from these groups. First, small group members must continue to understand the many alternatives available to them and be able to distinguish among these alternatives. In addition, members must not only understand the task at hand but also the people who provide input into the task. Nearly fifty years ago, social psychologist Robert Zajonc (1965) studied what many people have figured out for themselves: The mere presence of others has an effect on us. He offered a very simple principle regarding groups: When others are around us, we become innately aroused, which helps or hinders the performance of tasks. Nickolas Cottrell and his research team (Cottrell, Wack, Sekerak, & Rittle, 1968) later clarified the findings of Zajonc and argued that what leads people to task accomplishment is knowing that an individual will be evaluated by other individuals. Cottrell and his colleagues believe that group members may be apprehensive or anxious about the consequences that other group members bring to the group. In our opening, for instance, the board members are eager to listen to others with ideas because they do not offer ideas themselves. If any of the five nonspeakers were to openly challenge the ideas of either Elizabeth or Randy, they would be asked for their own ideas. Accordingly, they simply yield the floor to those who have a specific plan.

Marvin Shaw (1981) and Randy Fujishin (2007) discuss additional issues pertaining to groups. They note that a wide range of influences exist in a small group—age of group members, competitive nature of group members, size of the group, intelligence of group members, gender composition of the group, and leadership styles that emerge in the group. Further, the cultural backgrounds of individual group members may influence group processes. For instance, because many cultures do not place a premium on overt and expressive communication, some group members may refrain from debate or dialogue, to the surprise of other group members. This may influence the perceptions of both participative and nonparticipative group members.

If group dynamics are both complex and challenging, why are people so frequently assigned to group work? Clearly, the answer rests in the maxim "Two heads are better than one." John Brilhart, Gloria Galanes, and Katherine Adams (2001) effectively argue this point:

> Groups are usually better problem solvers, in the long run, than solitary individuals because they have access to more information than individuals do, can spot flaws and biases in each other's thinking, and then think of things an individual may have failed to consider. Moreover, if people participate in planning the work of solving the problem, it is more likely that they will work harder and better at carrying out the plans. Thus, participation in problem solving and decision making helps guarantee continued commitment to those decisions and solution. (p. 6)

Groups and group decisions, therefore, may be difficult and challenging, but through group work, people can achieve their goals more expeditiously and efficiently.

The relationship of this assumption to Groupthink should not escape you. Two issues merit attention. First, groups whose members are similar to one another are groups that are more conducive to groupthink (Myers & Anderson, 2008). We term this group similarity **homogeneity**. So, as we mentioned earlier, the board of directors at Melton is homogeneous in its backgrounds—they are all part of literary inner circles. This similarity is one characteristic that can foster groupthink.

Second, group decisions that are not thoughtfully considered by everyone may facilitate groupthink. The quality of effort and the quality of thinking are essential in group decision making (Hirokawa, Erbert, & Hurst, 1996). For example, in our opening story, Elizabeth and Randy clearly offer opinions on what they think is the best course of action for the company. Their charisma, their ability to communicate their vision, and their willingness to openly share their ideas with the group may be intoxicating to a board that is under pressure to resolve a financial dilemma. It's important to note that the two group leaders have clear ideas about how to proceed next, failing to identify alternative and additional ways of looking at the problem.

homogeneity
group similarity

What Comes Before: Antecedent Conditions of Groupthink

Janis (1982) believes that three conditions promote groupthink: (1) high cohesiveness of the decision-making group, (2) specific structural characteristics of the environment in which the group functions, and (3) stressful internal and external characteristics of the situation.

Group Cohesiveness

We have already discussed cohesiveness and its effects in relation to the three assumptions that guide Groupthink. Cohesiveness is also an antecedent condition. You may be wondering how cohesiveness can lead to groupthink. One reason this may be perplexing is that cohesion differs from one group to another, and different levels of cohesion produce different results. In some groups, cohesion can lead to positive feelings about the group experience and the other group members. Highly cohesive groups also may be more enthusiastic about their tasks and feel empowered to take on additional tasks. In sum, greater satisfaction is associated with increasing cohesiveness.

Despite the apparent advantages, highly cohesive groups may also bring about a troubling occurrence: groupthink. Janis (1982) argues that highly cohesive groups exert great pressure on their members to conform to group standards. Janis believes that as groups reach high degrees of cohesiveness, this euphoria tends to stifle other opinions and alternatives. Group members may be unwilling to express any reservations about solutions. And members even censor their own comments without being provoked (Adams & Galanes, 2007). High-risk decisions, therefore, may be made without thinking about consequences. The risks involved in decisions pertaining to war, for instance, are high. The 2003 bombings in Iraq entailed high risks for the soldiers, for the refugees who left the country, and for those who stayed. However, the risks associated with the decision pertaining to where a homecoming committee should hold its meetings, for instance, are minimal in comparison to the bombing decision. You can see that risk varies across settings, and assessing risk is critical to the groupthink phenomenon.

Although people may feel confident that they will recognize groupthink when they see it, often they don't. Too much cohesion may be seen as a virtue, not a shortcoming. Imagine sitting around a conference table where everyone is smiling, affirming one another, and wanting to wrap things up. Would you be willing to stop the head nodding and slaps on the back and ask, "But is this the best way to approach this?" To paraphrase the words from a famous fairy tale, who wants to tell the emperor that he has no clothes? Cohesiveness, therefore, frequently leads to conformity, and conformity is a primary route to groupthink.

Before moving on, let's make sure we're clear. We are not suggesting that cohesion automatically leads to groupthink. Rather, when the effectiveness or consequences of a group's decision remains secondary to a group's cohesion, Janis contends that the group is *prone* to groupthink.

Structural Factors

Janis notes that specific structural characteristics, or faults, promote group-think. They include insulation of the group, lack of impartial leadership, lack of clear procedures for decisions, and homogeneity of group members' backgrounds. **Group insulation** refers to a group's ability to be unaffected by the outside world. Many groups meet so frequently that they become immune from what takes place outside of their group experience. In fact, they may be discussing issues that have relevance in the outside world, and yet the members are insulated from its influence. People outside the group who could help with the decision may even be present in the organization but not asked to participate.

group insulation
a group's ability to remain unaffected by outside influences

A **lack of impartial leadership** means that group members are led by people who have a personal interest in the outcome. An example of this point can be found in Janis's appraisal of President Kennedy's Bay of Pigs episode. When the president presided over the meetings on the Cuban invasion, Janis observes the following:

lack of impartial leadership
when groups are led by individuals who put their personal agenda first

> [At] each meeting, instead of opening up the agenda to permit a full airing of the opposing considerations, he allowed the CIA representatives to dominate the entire discussion. The president permitted them to refute immediately each tentative doubt that one of the others might express, instead of asking whether anyone else had the same doubt or wanted to pursue the implications of the new worrisome issue that had been raised. (1982, p. 42)

The deference of group members to their leader can be observed in the words of Arthur Schlesinger Jr., a member of Kennedy's policy group: "I can only explain my failure to do more than raise a few timid questions by reporting that one's impulse to blow the whistle on this nonsense was simply undone by the circumstances of the discussion" (cited in Janis, 1982, p. 39). It is apparent that Kennedy considered other opinions to be detrimental to his plan, and alternative leadership was suppressed.

lack of decision-making procedures
failure to provide norms for solving group issues

A final structural fault that can lead to groupthink is a **lack of decision-making procedures** and similarity of group members. First, some groups have few, if any, procedures for decision making; failing to have previously established norms for evaluation of problems can foster groupthink. Dennis Gouran and Randy Hirokawa (1996) suggest that even if groups recognize that a problem exists, they still must figure out the cause and extent of the problem. Groups, therefore, may be influenced by dominant voices and go along with those who choose to speak up. Other groups may simply follow what they have observed and experienced in previous groups. In fact, when independent analyses of the *Columbia* space shuttle disaster were undertaken after the craft's breakup, John Schwartz (2005) reports that NASA management was influential in decisions to launch on the fateful day in 2003. Schwartz quotes a former shuttle commander at the Johnson Space Center in Houston: "Managers 'ask for dissenting opinion because they know they are supposed to ask for them,' but the managers 'are either defending their own position or arguing against the dissenting opinion' without seriously trying to understand it" (p. A17). In other words, group members may try to challenge management, but their words are either muted or dismissed.

A second structural fault is the homogeneity of members' backgrounds. Janis (1982) notes that "lack of disparity in social background and ideology among the members of a cohesive group makes it easier for them to concur on whatever proposals are put forth by the leader" (p. 250). We alluded to this fault earlier in the chapter. Without diversity of background and experience, it may be difficult to debate critical issues.

Group Stress

The final antecedent condition of groupthink pertains to the stress on the group—that is, **internal and external stress** on the group may evoke groupthink. When decision makers are under great stress—whether imposed by forces outside the group or within the group—they tend to break down.

When stress is high, groups usually rally around their leaders and affirm their beliefs. Suppose you have only two weeks left before your class presentation. You and your group have been working on the project for about three months, and the project is worth about 25 percent of your final grade. The professor assigned the project during the first week of class and is expecting a top-notch presentation. Your group has a lot more work to do, however, and you know that other groups in the class seem to be much more prepared for their presentations. According to Janis, then, your group members may begin to feel the pressure to finish the project, may look to one another for moral support during this crisis time, and may be inclined to agree with ideas in order to get the project completed. Your group, we're sorry to say, is likely on its way to groupthink.

As you can see, groups frequently insulate themselves from outside criticism, form what ostensibly are close bonds, seek consensus, and ultimately develop groupthink. To get a clearer picture of what groupthink looks like, Janis (1982) identifies eight symptoms that can be assigned to three categories. We turn to these symptoms next.

> **internal and external stress** pressure exerted on the group by issues and events both inside and outside of the group

Symptoms of Groupthink

Preexisting conditions lead groups to concurrence seeking. **Concurrence seeking** occurs when groups try to reach consensus in their final decision. Consider the interpretation of consensus seeking from Andrea Hollingshead and her colleagues (2005): "Groupthink teams place such a high priority on supporting each other emotionally that they choose not to challenge one another" (p. 30). When concurrence seeking goes too far, Janis contends, it produces symptoms of groupthink. Janis (1982) observes three categories of symptoms of groupthink: overestimation of the group, closed-mindedness, and pressures toward uniformity. Figure 14.1 presents one model of the antecedent conditions and symptoms of groupthink.

> **concurrence seeking** efforts to search out group consensus

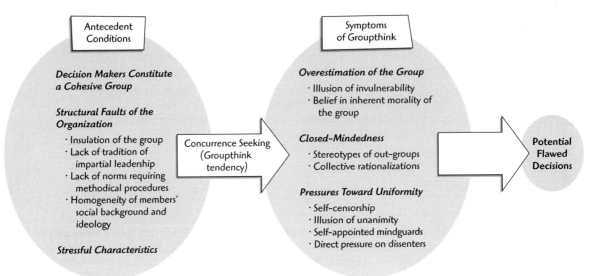

Figure 14.1 Antecedent Conditions and Symptoms of Groupthink

Source: Adapted with the permission of The Free Press, a Division of Simon & Schuster, Inc., from DECISION MAKING: *A Psychological Analysis of Conflict, Choice, and Commitment* by Irving L. Janis and Leon Mann. Copyright © 1977 by The Free Press. All rights reserved. And from Janis, GROUPTHINK, Second Edition. Copyright © 1982 Wadsworth, a part of Cengage Learning, Inc. Reproduced by permission. www.cengage.com/permissions.

To illustrate these symptoms and to give you a sense of how Janis conceptualized groupthink, we examine a policy decision that continues to resonate in the United States today: the Vietnam War. During the height of the war, polls showed that most people felt that the objectives for going to Vietnam were ambiguous and ill-founded. War protestors were prominent in the 1960s and early 1970s, arguing that the country had no clear reason (that is, policy) for entering the war. The controversy associated with Vietnam parallels the controversies surrounding current U.S. involvement in Iraq and Afghanistan.

We present Janis's (1982) interpretation of what took place when President Lyndon Johnson's foreign policy advisors examined decisions about bombing North Vietnam. Janis's comments are based on extensive discussions with individuals who were presidential advisors, and many of their comments are contained in the following analysis.

Overestimation of the Group

overestimation of the group
erroneous belief that the group is more than it is

An **overestimation of the group** includes those behaviors that suggest the group believes it is more than it is. Two specific symptoms exist in this category: illusion of invulnerability and a belief in the inherent morality of the group.

illusion of invulnerability
belief that the group is special enough to overcome obstacles

Illusion of Invulnerability The **illusion of invulnerability** can be defined as a group's belief that they are special enough to overcome any obstacles or setbacks. The group believes it is invincible. With respect to the Vietnam War, Janis explains that President Johnson's foreign policy group wanted to avoid peace negotiations because they did not want to be viewed as having little bargaining power. The group, therefore, was willing to take a risk and believed that selecting bombing targets in North Vietnam was a wise course of action. The group members based their decision to bomb on four issues: the military advantage, the risk to American aircraft, the potential to widen the conflict to other countries, and civilian casualties. Janis asks whether the group members shared the illusion that they were invulnerable when they confined their attacks to bombing targets.

Belief in the Inherent Morality of the Group   When group members have a **belief in the inherent morality of the group,** they are said to adopt the position that "we are a good and wise group" (Janis, 1982, p. 256). Because the group perceives itself to be good, they believe that their decision making must, therefore, be good. By embracing this belief, group members purge themselves of any shame or guilt, although they ignore any ethical or moral implications of their decision. Janis found it interesting that Johnson and his advisors were not concerned with bombing villages in North Vietnam; for them, the moral consequences did not outweigh the perception that the United States might be weak or fearful. In fact, the foreign policy council continued to encourage bombing of Hanoi (North Vietnam) even though peace initiatives were concurrently under way in Poland. A sense of moral certitude prevailed because the president and his advisors felt that North Vietnam would not negotiate a surrender.

belief in the inherent morality of the group assumption that the group members are thoughtful and good; therefore the decisions they make will be good

Closed-Mindedness

When a group is **closed-minded,** it ignores outside influences on the group. The two symptoms discussed by Janis in this category are stereotypes of out-groups and collective rationalization.

closed-mindedness a group's willingness to ignore differences in people and warnings about poor group decisions

Out-Group Stereotypes   Groups in crisis frequently engage in **out-group stereotypes,** which are stereotyped perceptions of rivals or enemies. These stereotypes underscore the fact that any adversaries are either too weak or too stupid to counter offensive tactics. For Johnson's advisors, *enemy* meant Communist. It was this stereotype that kept the advisors from seeing the enemy as people. Janis (1982) reasons that because the North Vietnamese were considered to be Communist enemies, this embodiment of evil justified the "destruction of countless human lives and the burning of villages" (p. 111).

out-group stereotypes stereotyped perceptions of group enemies or competitors

Collective Rationalization   The fourth symptom of groupthink, **collective rationalization,** refers to the situation in which group members ignore warnings that might prompt them to reconsider their thoughts and actions before they reach a final decision. President Johnson and his staff were given a number of forewarnings—from intelligence agencies, among others—about the implications of bombing North Vietnam. Some in the intelligence community felt that bombing sites such as oil facilities would do nothing to erode Communist operations. Nonetheless, Johnson's group maintained its unified position on escalating the bombing. Janis (1982) observed that the men in Johnson's inner circle were very convinced of the importance of the Vietnam War to the United States. Therefore, revisiting any strategies to exit the war was out of the question.

collective rationalization situation in which group members ignore warnings about their decisions

pressure toward uniformity
occurs when group members go along to get along

The **pressure toward uniformity** can be enormous for some groups. Janis believed that some groups who go along to get along may be setting themselves up for groupthink. The four symptoms in this category are self-censorship, an illusion of unanimity, the presence of self-appointed mindguards, and direct pressure on dissenters.

self-censorship
group members minimize personal doubts and counterarguments

Self-Censorship Earlier we discussed self-censorship. **Self-censorship** refers to group members' tendency to minimize their doubts and counterarguments. They begin to second-guess their own ideas. For those in President Johnson's foreign policy group, self-censorship was exhibited when group members dehumanized the war experience. These advisors would not allow themselves to think of the innocent people being killed because such thinking would only personalize the war. Janis argues that silencing one's own opposing views and using in-group rhetoric further bolster the decisions of the group.

illusion of unanimity
belief that silence equals agreement

Illusion of Unanimity The sixth symptom of groupthink is an **illusion of unanimity**, which suggests that silence is consent. Although some advisors in Johnson's inner circle felt differently about the Vietnam intervention, they were silent. This silence prompted others around the table to believe that there was consensus in planning and execution.

self-appointed mindguards
individuals who protect the group from adverse information

Self-Appointed Mindguards Groups in crisis may include **self-appointed mindguards**—group members who shield the group from adverse information. Mindguards believe that they act in the group's best interest. Walt Rostow, White House assistant, effectively played the role of mindguard in Johnson's group. Janis relates the following: "Rostow cleverly screened the inflow of information and used his power to keep dissident experts away from the White House. This had the intended effect of preventing the President and some of his advisers from becoming fully aware of the extent of disaffection with the war and the grounds for it" (1982, p. 119). Ironically, within the group, keeping the peace at the White House was more important than maintaining it in Vietnam.

pressures on dissenters
direct influence on group members who provide thoughts contrary to the group's

Pressures on Dissenters The final symptom involves pressuring any group member who expresses opinions, viewpoints, or commitments that are contrary to the majority opinion. Janis calls this **pressures on dissenters.** In his interviews with those within President Johnson's inner circle, Janis discovered that the group members formed a gentlemen's club, where mutual respect and congenial talk pervaded. Janis also later realized that these men often turned to one another for support, and they were loyal to one another. Is it any wonder, then, that group members believed that everyone agreed to the course of action? This attitude would prevail, of course, considering that those who openly disagreed frequently resigned or were replaced (Janis, 1982). Robert McNamara, secretary of defense under President Johnson, was a dissenter who believed that bombing North Vietnam was the wrong way to get the enemy to the negotiation

Hollingshead, A. B., Wittenbaum, G. M., Paulus, P. B., Hirokawa, R. Y., Ancona, D. G., Peterson, R. S., Jehn, K. A., & Yoon, K. (2005). A look at groups from the functional perspective. In M. S. Poole & A. B. Hollingshead (Eds.), *Theories of small groups: Interdisciplinary perspectives* (pp. 21–62). Thousand Oaks, CA: Sage.

Looking at the Persian Gulf crisis (1990–1991), sometimes called the first Gulf war, Yetiv applied groupthink principles to decision making pertaining to President George H. W. Bush's inner circle of advisors. The researcher looked at group cohesiveness and four structural conditions that may lead to groupthink: group insulation, lack of impartial leadership, lack of norms for procedures, and homogeneity in group members' backgrounds. Yetiv suggests that many of these conditions were present during decisions regarding the crisis. He further posits that failure was avoided in the Persian Gulf because the ground war was easier than anticipated and because of the president's past military and government background.

Yetiv, S. A. (2003). Groupthink and the Gulf crisis. *British Journal of Political Science, 33,* 419–442.

This chapter, from a collection of readings on small groups, introduces the notion of the functional perspective and its four primary assumptions: (1) groups are goal-oriented, (2) group behavior and performance vary in quality and quantity and can be evaluated, (3) interaction processes have utility and can be regulated, and (4) internal and external factors influence group behavior and performance via interaction. The authors believe that Groupthink illustrates these four core assumptions of the functional perspective. The chapter is comprehensive in its approach to understanding the intersection of the functional perspective of groups and several important areas in small group theory and research.

table. However, he was under much pressure to avoid disagreeing with the gentlemen's club.

(Group)Think About It: It's All Around U.S.

Thomas Jefferson once said that "difference of opinion leads to inquiry, and inquiry to truth." His words are still relevant, especially in foreign policy. Yet, considering that Janis studied national policy decisions, his research may leave you with the impression that groupthink cannot "hit home." As we've tried to illustrate in this chapter, however, groupthink is everywhere. In addition to the large-scale decisions we identified earlier, groupthink decision making can be seen pertaining to Watergate, the Hubble telescope, the *Columbia* and *Challenger* tragedies, the Gulf War, Hurricane Katrina, and the decision to invade Iraq in 2003.

On a smaller scale, and as we alluded to earlier, groupthink occurs all around us in "less critical" small groups. Decisions such as whether you will attend college, for instance, may have been prone to groupthink. If your parents went to college, your grandparents were college graduates, and you read literature stating that a college graduate will make twice as much money in a lifetime as a high school graduate, your decision to attend college may have been made without completely examining any alternatives to college attendance. Presumably, your group is a cohesive group. Your family rationalized your attendance, and most likely, you didn't raise any objections. In other words, your small group was susceptible to groupthink.

This is but one example of the many episodes of groupthink in our daily lives. We may find conditions for groupthink with staff behind the deli counter at the grocery store; on a construction site with architects, contractors, and skilled laborers; or even at an investment club meeting where a group of people make decisions about what stocks to invest in during difficult economic times.

Think Before You Act: Ways to Prevent Groupthink

It bears repeating: Our discussion of Groupthink and the issues that accompany this theory may have given you the impression that all cohesive groups will be prone to groupthink. This is not true; Janis (1982) notes that cohesiveness is a necessary but not sufficient condition of groupthink. Nonetheless, frequently, when groups find themselves in highly cohesive situations and when decision makers are under great stress, groupthink may materialize.

How can group members learn to avoid groupthink, or at least work toward more healthy interactions? Janis (1989; Herek, Janis & Huth, 1987) suggests that groups engage in vigilant decision making, which involves (1) looking at the range of objectives group members wish to achieve, (2) developing and reviewing action plans and alternatives, (3) exploring the consequences of each alternative, (4) analyzing previously rejected action plans when new information emerges, and (5) having a contingency plan for failed suggestions. Janis offers additional recommendations, but critics such as Paul 't Hart (1998) question whether Janis's recommendations inadvertently erode collegiality and foster group factionalism.

To avoid oversimplifying the groupthink problem, 't Hart (1990) has proposed four general recommendations for groups who may be prone to groupthink: (1) Require oversight and control, (2) embrace whistle-blowing in the group, (3) allow for objection, and (4) balance consensus and majority rule. We will look at each recommendation (Table 14.1).

First, 't Hart believes that one way to enhance group decision making is to impose some external oversight and control. He argues that groups need to hold key decision makers accountable for their actions; this should be done *before* groups begin their deliberations about issues. Accountability may take the form of a committee that serves to enforce control (vis à vis rules, governance procedures, decorum, and so forth). 't Hart theorizes that such committees prompt group members to challenge collective rationalizations and inaccurate perceptions. Reflecting on our example of President Johnson and his foreign policy group, 't Hart proposes that the inner circle of advisors was insulated from external oversight. As well, there were inadequate intragroup measures to improve the group's decisions on North Vietnam.

whistle-blowing process in which individuals report unethical or illegal behaviors or practices to others

In addition to accountability, 't Hart proposes that **whistle-blowing** be embraced in a group's culture. That is, group members "should be encouraged

Table 14.1 Preventing Groupthink

RECOMMENDATION	ACTION
Require Oversight and Control	*Establish a parliamentary committee:* Develop resources to proactively monitor ongoing policy ventures; establish incentives to intervene; link personal fate to fate of group members.
Embrace Whistle-Blowing	*Voice doubts:* Avoid suppressing concerns about group processes; continue to disagree and debate when no satisfactory answers are given; question assumptions.
Allow for Objection	*Protect conscientious objectors:* Provide for group members' exits; do not play down the moral implications of a course of action; acknowledge private concerns about ethical issues in the group.
Balance Consensus and Majority Rule	*Alter rules governing choice:* Relieve pressure on groups in minority positions; dissuade the development of subgroups; introduce a multiple advocacy approach to decisions.

Source: Adapted from 't Hart, 1990.

Theory Application in Groups (TAG)

Groupthink is primarily concerned with how group members balance their need for cohesiveness with the need for arriving at a decision. In this chapter, we have presented symptoms of groupthink and identified some ways to prevent it. However, we have not addressed ways to help a group member out of groupthink once it's under way. As a group, identify possible remedies for assisting group members out of a groupthink situation. You may include a number of different group scenarios in your response.

to voice concerns rather than to voluntarily suppress them, to question assumptions rather than to accept them at face value, and to continue to disagree and debate when no satisfactory answers to their concerns are given by the rest of the group" (p. 385). Anna Mulrine (2008) writes that the U.S. Army is attempting to bring about internal whistle-blowing. She notes that the 2003 Iraq invasion has brought about great chaos in the planning and execution of decision making by the Army. To that end, the Army has developed a "cadre of devil's advocates" (p. 30) who are charged with "questioning prevailing assumptions to avoid getting sucked into that groupthink" (p. 30) which can happen in stressful times. Embracing whistle-blowing in this way results in looking at a decision from alternate point of view. 't Hart advocates that groups protect these sorts of whistle-blowers because groups usually need dissenting voices when decisions have lasting and significant consequences.

A third suggestion by 't Hart is that groups allow **conscientious objectors,** or group members who refuse to participate in the decision-making process because it would violate their conscience. He reasons that groupthink causes groups to downplay the moral implications of their decisions, and if conscientious objectors know that they can exit a conversation based on moral or ethical grounds, then they may be more likely to speak up. Thus, these objectors may be able to raise doubts about the decision or even to protest it. President Johnson's decision to continue bombing Vietnam, therefore, may have been different if conscientious objectors had been allowed to introduce the moral implications of killing innocent people.

Finally, 't Hart advocates that groups not require consensus but work instead toward a majority of support. Because consensus demands that every group member agree on a decision, group members often feel pressured to consent (illusion of unanimity). 't Hart believes that groups should strive toward consensus but be prepared for majority support. If groups adopt this orientation, 't Hart believes, they will function more like teams. Janis (1982) discusses the fact that several members of President Johnson's inner circle of advisors (McNamara, Rusk, Bundy) wanted to temporarily halt the Hanoi bombings; we can only speculate how the passion for consensus affected both the United States and the Vietnamese people.

Integration, Critique, and Closing

Groupthink is a theory dedicated to understanding the decision-making process in small groups. Janis believes that groups frequently make decisions with profound consequences, and although he focused his efforts on foreign policy groups, the application of Groupthink terminology resonates in many other decision-making groups. Among the criteria for evaluating a theory, four are especially relevant for discussion: scope, testability, heurism, and test of time.

Integration

Communication Tradition	Rhetorical	Semiotic	Phenomenological	Cybernetic	**Socio-Psychological**	**Socio-Cultural**	Critical
Communication Context	Intrapersonal	Interpersonal	**Small Group**	**Organizational**	Public/Rhetorical	Mass/Media	Cultural
Approach to Knowing	**Positivistic/Empirical**	Interpretive/Hermeneutic	Critical

Critique

Evaluation Criteria	Scope	Logical Consistency	Parsimony	Utility	**Testability**	**Heurism**	**Test of Time**

Scope

Despite the fact that many groupthink principles can be applied to several types of groups, Janis was clear in his original conceptualization in applying Groupthink solely to decision-making groups in crisis periods; he does not readily apply his thinking to every group type. Although the theory has been applied to groups as diverse as presidential advisors and citizen juries (van Assche, 2007), the focus has been in those groups that are *decision-making* groups. Therefore, the scope of the theory could be defined as narrow.

Testability

Group scholars have pointed to some validity problems with the theory, calling into question its testability. For instance, Jeanne Longley and Dean Pruitt (1980) criticize the validity of the theory. They argue that half of the symptoms of groupthink are not associated with concurrence seeking—a key feature of the theory. They charge that "a theory should be a logical progression of ideas, not a grab-bag of phenomena that were correlated with each other in a sample of six cases" (p. 80). Further, they note that Janis incorporates self-esteem in discussions of groupthink, but failed to mention it in his theory. In later writings, however, Janis (1982) addresses self-esteem as an antecedent to groupthink.

Heurism

The theory of Groupthink is a heuristic undertaking; the theory and many of its elements have been employed in a number of studies and have enjoyed the attention of many communication and social psychology scholars (e.g., Cline, 1990; Courtright, 1978; Huitema, van de Kerkhov, & Pesch, 2007; Pavitt & Johnson, 2002). In addition to foreign policy decisions, researchers have studied Groupthink and applied its concepts and tenets to Hurricane Katrina, the

1937 Japanese massacre of Nanking, and even *Mensa*, the society of the so-called highly intelligent (Garnett & Kouzmin, 2007; Matthews, 2003). The theory has also generated a number of assumptions about group behavior, and Groupthink remains an important part of the literature on group decision making (Myers & Anderson, 2008).

Test of Time

The theory of Groupthink has withstood the test of time. Scholars continue to investigate many of its fundamental features, and the theory continues to be discussed in the popular media (Ginnett, 2005). On the thirtieth anniversary of Groupthink, Schwartz and Wald (2003) called Janis a "pioneer in the study of social dynamics" (p. 4). Finally, given that government policy decisions will always exist, the likelihood of future instances of groupthink is rather high.

Groupthink may be more intuitively appealing than empirically driven. The theory, however, continues to receive attention in research as well as in the popular press. In fact, Janis's thinking on groupthink has been quite influential in several fields of study, including communication, cognitive and social psychology, anthropology, and political science. Few would debate the failure of the foreign policy fiascoes outlined by Janis: massive violence and casualties, loss of confidence in governmental decisions, and policymaking gone wrong. For these reasons alone, Janis is credited with helping us identify and examine one type of group decision-making problem.

Discussion Starters

1. What advice would you give the Melton Publishing board of directors before they meet to discuss their financial situation? Frame your advice with Groupthink in mind.

2. Janis and 't Hart have proposed a number of ways to prevent Groupthink. Provide at least two additional ways to avoid groupthink. Be specific and provide examples.

3. Have you ever been in a small group with too much cohesiveness? If so, did Groupthink develop? If so, how did you know? If not, what prevented Groupthink from occurring?

4. In his book, *Groupthink*, Janis asks if a little knowledge of Groupthink is a dangerous thing. Why do you think Janis asks this question, and what are the consequences of knowing about Groupthink? Incorporate examples into your response.

5. How widespread is Groupthink? Do you believe society is aware of the problem? Discuss your response using examples.

6. Apply principles of Groupthink to recent domestic and foreign policy decisions made by the United States.

7. Discuss the application of any principle of Groupthink to your workplace, family, or college life.

Online Learning Center (www. mhhe.com/west4e)

Visit the Online Learning Center at www.mhhe.com/west4e for chapter-specific resources, such as story-into-theory and multiple-choice quizzes, as well as theory summaries and theory connection questions.

CHAPTER 15

Structuration Theory

*Based on the research of **Anthony Giddens**, **M. Scott Poole**, **David R. Seibold**, and **Robert D. McPhee***

Tim Vondrasek and Bayside City Tire Company

Bayside City Tire Company (BCT) is a multinational company with many employees. One of the employees, Tim Vondrasek, is a new production shift manager. Jeremy has been a production floor supervisor for twenty-five years. He has been assigned the task of showing Tim, his new boss, around for a couple of weeks.

On the first day, Jeremy takes Tim around the production floor to introduce him to the workers on his shift. When approached, all of the workers call Tim by his last name: "Good morning, Mr. Vondrasek." "It's great having you onboard, Mr. Vondrasek." Tim responds to the workers by saying, "Mr. Vondrasek is my father. Please, call me Tim."

As Tim and Jeremy walk away, Tim asks, "Why is everyone so formal?"

Jeremy responds, "That's company policy. We believe that addressing one another in this way establishes a sense of respect for our supervisors at Bayside City Tire."

Tim comes back with, "This is my shift, and I would really prefer if we do things my way."

Jeremy pauses, "Well, sure, this is your shift, but this is the way they have been taught to communicate with one another. After all, think of how confused they will be if they are allowed to address you by your first name, and other managers expect to be addressed as 'Mr.' or 'Ms.'"

"You're right. I guess I'll have to get used to the workers calling me Mr. Vondrasek until I can get this straightened out. Besides, I don't want them to think that I am going against company rules or that I want to change things," Tim answers reluctantly.

Later that day, Tim talks to Angela Griffith, the human relations coordinator for BCT, about changing the policy to allow employees and staff to address one another less formally. Angela listens to Tim's ideas and agrees to call a meeting of the production shift managers to discuss the potential change.

At the meeting, the six production shift managers all voice their opinions about the change in policy. Janette, a fifteen-year veteran with BCT, points out, "Personally, I like having the workers address me more formally. It's tough enough being a female in this type of work environment, and I think this encourages respect in the workplace."

Darnell, who joined BCT only three years ago after graduating with his M.B.A. from Marden, counters by stating that he thinks the workers don't feel comfortable coming to him to discuss problems because of the formality and rules that are in place at BCT. "I think Tim's onto something here," Darnell says. "We might be able to establish a friendlier work environment if we were less formal in how we address one another."

Wayne, who is a third-generation employee of BCT, argues, "You don't mess around with tradition.

This is the way it's always been, and it's worked just fine for the past thirty years."

Angela listens to all their opinions, but the managers are split 50–50 on the policy change issue. She says, "Please, let's try to arrive at some sort of closure on this. Let's take a vote and see what you all think we should do." After voting numerous times, it is obvious that the issue will not be resolved. "Okay," says Angela, "I guess we'll keep the rule in place as it is for right now since you can't agree on this."

■

Just as a contractor uses a blueprint as a guide in building a structure, members of an organization use rules to state expectations of behavior and communication within the organization. As we learned in Chapter 9 (Uncertainty Reduction Theory), people tend to be uncomfortable with uncertainty. Consider the need for structure in your own life. Usually, students want to know the structure or rules so they will understand what is expected of them in class. If a professor were simply to announce, "This term we'll have a couple of tests, a few quizzes, and you'll need to do a project," students would likely be uncomfortable with such limited information. They would want more specific instructions, or rules, regarding page-length requirements of any papers, due dates, expectations for exams, and so on. Thus, the school and the instructor provide students with a course syllabus, a *blueprint* of the rules for the class, in which the structure is created and maintained. However, we can also change the structure of an institution by adapting rules or creating new ones. Feedback from student evaluations, for instance, may guide a professor to alter the syllabus or the exam criteria in the future.

Sociologist Anthony Giddens believes that social institutions are produced, reproduced, and transformed through the use of rules. David Seibold and Karen Kroman Myers (2006) contend that social institutions are "organized around members' interactional processes and practices: disseminating information, allocating resources, accomplishing tasks, making choices, managing disagreements, and the like" (p. 143). The structure of these institutions is the focus of Structuration Theory.

Recall from our discussion in Chapter 3 that rules indicate how things are to be done; they suggest a course of action in a setting. In Structuration Theory, rules in a social institution go beyond telling employees what they can and cannot do. In interactions among people, the rules guiding these conversations allow employees to maintain or alter an organization. An instance in which this would apply would involve a company's talking about poor customer service to make changes in the customer service policy. The rules governing these conversations might pertain, for instance, to hierarchy (for example, the extent to which an employee can share a candid opinion with superiors). We return to a more detailed examination of rules later in the chapter.

In the opening example, the employees involved in the managers' meeting could potentially influence the structure of the organization by decisions made during their debate. If they had voted to change the rule of formally addressing one another, the entire organizational structure may have had to be altered. Communication is what allows for an organization to change.

Giddens (1979, 1993) views social structures as a double-edged sword. The structures and the rules that we create restrict our behavior. However, these same rules also enable us to understand and interact with others. We need rules to guide our decisions about how we are expected to behave. These rules may be either explicitly stated (such as grievance procedures that are outlined in an employee manual) or implicitly learned (such as respecting one another by providing each member of the group an opportunity to voice his or her opinion).

Groups and organizations are coordinated around various social interactions—for example, socializing new members through new employee receptions, arriving at decisions during conference calls, conducting meetings in person or via videoconference, or teaching new skills in employee training sessions. Giddens (1984) points out that the key to making sense of the communication that occurs in these groups and organizations is to examine the structures that serve as their foundation. He makes a distinction between the concepts of system (as we discussed in Chapter 3) and structure. The term **system**, in this sense, refers to the group or organization itself and the behaviors and practices that the group engages in to pursue its goals. Organizations may engage in many behaviors and practices that result in diverse events including new employee assimilation processes and performance appraisals (Seibold & Myers, 2006). The term **structure** refers to the rules and resources members use to create and sustain the system, as well as to guide their behaviors.

In the opening scenario, both the BCT organization and the group meeting of the shift managers can be viewed as a system. Their goal is to discuss the problem of using formal names to address one another, as well as to conduct the daily operations of the organization. To assist them in accomplishing their goals in an efficient manner, both of these systems have a formal set of rules that includes guidelines for how employees are expected to address one another at BCT as well as guidelines for allowing everyone to voice their opinion during the group meeting. These represent the structures of the group and organization. Tim Vondrasek is frustrated by the structure that restricts his employees from communicating with him informally. The rules for interactions between supervisors and subordinates contradict what he has learned about building relationships from his past experiences as a supervisor. Angela employs rules for conducting open discussions about issues before any decisions about changes are made. Thus, BCT is created and guided by structures—rules that explain how to demonstrate respect for one another.

Marshall Scott Poole (1990) and his colleagues (Poole & DeSanctis (1990); Poole & McPhee, 2005; Poole, Seibold, & McPhee, 1986; 1996) have studied the application of structuration principles to the communication field. Their theory has been called *adaptive* structuration theory to explain how task groups use information technology (Poole & McPhee, 2005). For our purposes, however, we retain the original thinking of Giddens and discuss Structuration Theory as a perspective with appeal to many areas in the study of communication.

To begin, it's important to define structuration. In a general sense, structuration allows people to understand their patterns of behavior—the structures of their social system. Specifically, **structuration** is described as "the process by which systems are produced and reproduced through members' use of rules

system
a group or organization and the behaviors that the group engages in to pursue its goals

structure
the rules and resources used to sustain a group or organization

structuration
the production, reproduction, and transformation of social environments through rules and resources in relationships

and resources" (Poole, Seibold & McPhee, 1996, p. 117). For structuration theorists, organizational structures are produced and replicated by people who interact on a daily basis, trying to accomplish personal and company goals (Modaff, DeWine, & Butler, 2008).

Structuration allows people to understand their patterns of behavior—the structures of their social system. Poole et al. conclude that the key to understanding groups is through an analysis of the structures that underlie them. Rules and resources for communicating and arriving at decisions are typically learned from the organization itself and from members' past experiences and personal rules. These same rules and resources are reaffirmed as a result of their application or use; the group may decide to keep them in their existing format or alter them to meet the changing needs of the group.

In arriving at a decision on whether BCT should change its rule about having employees address one another formally, Angela enacts a rule of decision making that requires the group to discuss their viewpoints before making changes. BCT may also have a rule for company meetings in which the majority vote decides the action that should be taken. If Angela fails to call a meeting of the managers to solicit their opinions, many of them might be displeased. Or, if Angela doesn't give everyone the opportunity to state an opinion on the rule while the rest of the group observes an unspoken rule to respect others' opinions (that is, challenge ideas but do not attack people), some of the group's members will be dissatisfied with the outcome of the meeting. Janette, for one, depends on the rule to maintain her credibility and authority when interacting with her male employees. The fact that Angela follows the rule of calling a meeting to discuss the issue reaffirms the belief that this is a good guideline to follow in making decisions in the organization. However, some of the group's members may not be pleased with the decision to keep the rule in its current form, and they may invoke a new rule among their own teams in which they permit subordinates to address them in a less formal manner. Thus, the rule will be altered from its original state.

Structuration provides a useful foundation for examining the impact that rules and resources have on group decisions and organizational communication. In addition, it helps describe how these rules are altered or confirmed through interactions. Finally, structuration is communicative: "Talk is action. If structure is truly produced through interaction, then communication is more than just a precursor to action; it is action" (Modaff et al., 2008, p. 121).

Structuration Theory • *Theory at a Glance*

Organizations create structures, which can be interpreted as an organization's rules and resources. These structures, in turn, create social systems in an organization. Organizations achieve a life of their own because of the way their members use their structures. Power structures guide the decision making that takes place in these organizations.

Assumptions of Structuration Theory

To understand Structuration Theory, let's first consider some of the basic assumptions that guide this theory:

- Groups and organizations are produced and reproduced through the use of rules and resources.
- Communication rules serve as both the medium for, and an outcome of, interactions.
- Power structures are present in organizations and guide the decision-making process.

fresh act
something new
developed from
action or behavior

Underscoring the first assumption, Giddens proposes that every action or behavior results in the production of something new—a **fresh act**. Each of the actions or behaviors in which a group or organization engages is influenced and affected by the past. This history serves as a reference for understanding what rules and resources are required to operate within the system. Consider, for instance, when a group leader decides to conduct a vote using an anonymous ballot. If past voting using the ballot has proven to be effective for group members, history is influencing the rules for operation within that system.

It is important to remember that every time we communicate with someone, we are establishing a new beginning by (a) creating a new rule or expectation, (b) altering an existing rule, or (c) reaffirming rules that have been used in the past. In establishing these new beginnings, we still rely on past rules and expectations to guide our behaviors. Thus, we never escape our history—it continually influences our decisions for behavior in groups and organizations. It also influences changes that may take place in the system.

All of our communicative actions exist in relationship to the past. Angela may have learned in past group meetings that members are not supportive of others' thoughts and opinions. She may have decided simply to state the problem and have group members vote on a potential solution without first soliciting the advice and opinions of group members. In this instance, historical rules would have been used as a reference for altering the group's rules in future interactions.

Recall the interaction between Tim and Jeremy. According to Structuration Theory, each interaction that takes place between Tim and Jeremy is new and creates something unique in the structure of their future interactions. At the same time, Jeremy and Tim each bring to the interaction a set of rules (based on their history) and expectations that will guide and shape their communication with each other. In other words, as we observed in Chapter 1, their fields of experience become critical in their communication with one another. Jeremy addresses Tim by his last name, Mr. Vondrasek, the first time they meet. Tim responds by saying, "Please, call me Tim." Tim creates something new in the social structure by establishing a precedent (a new norm) of asking his subordinate to call him by his first name. This precedent is influenced by the past expectations that each man brings to the interaction. In other words, the experiences that Tim and Jeremy bring to the interaction affect their expectations for the structure that will guide their future communication. Tim believes that an open and relaxed communication style works, whereas Jeremy operates under a very different set of rules for interaction—formal address works best. In this case, Jeremy's rules for conversing serve the dual function of guiding his current behavior and setting expectations for future behavior.

The second assumption of Structuration Theory is the notion that rules simultaneously provide a guideline and constrain a group's behavior. The structure of a group includes a network of rules and resources that are used by its members in making decisions about what communication behaviors are expected. Katherine Miller (2005) succinctly notes the importance of rules in organizations: "Rules act as recipes for social life, in that they are generalizable procedures about how to get things done" (p. 215). Some rules take precedence over others, and history influences the action that is enacted. That is, if a rule worked well in the past, it's likely to be retained; if not, it's likely to be modified or abandoned. The challenge lies in determining which rule will be the most efficient or productive in achieving the goals of the group or organization. We return to a discussion of rules later in the chapter.

Let's take a moment to examine this issue a little more closely. Giddens (1979) asserts that a rule can only be truly understood "in the context of the historical development" as a whole (p. 65). So, Structuration Theory assumes that to understand the rules of a social system, individuals need to know some of the background resources that led to the rule. Perhaps if Tim from our opening scenario were to investigate the origins of the rule for addressing superiors, he would have a better understanding of why this rule is currently enforced. There may have been a past incident when employees showed a blatant disregard for their supervisors by substituting nicknames for the informal first names that they were permitted to use in addressing their superiors. For example, Tim may discover that Wayne was called "Wayne the Pain" by his employees years earlier when the rule was not in existence. The company subsequently developed more formal rules to help Wayne enhance his credibility and gain the respect of his employees. However, if after conducting his research, Tim does not discover a satisfactory reason for the structure or rules that are in place, he may try to alter this particular rule. Not only may his refusal to attend meetings demonstrate a personal rule, but it may also be an attempt to exert his power in the group.

The third assumption guiding Structuration Theory posits that power is an influential force in arriving at decisions in organizations. In this theory, **power** is perceived as the ability to achieve results—it enables us to accomplish our goals. Giddens believes that power is a two-way street; any time two people are engaged in communication with each other, both sources have a certain level of power that they bring to the interaction. Even subordinates have some power over superiors. Giddens adds, "subordinate positions in social systems are frequently adept at converting whatever resources they possess into some degree of control" (p. 6). In other words, we all have power, but some have more than others. It is important to consider the role that rules play in this discussion of power. Based on the history of an organization, typically rules have been established to grant some members a particular form of power over other

power
imposition of personal will on others

members. In BCT, a rule of the group is that Angela has the power to call a meeting of the members.

Tim wants his employees to call him "Tim" and not "Mr. Vondrasek," but the structure—in this case a company norm—does not allow production floor workers to communicate informally. However, Tim's personal communication rule is that his workers should call him by his first name. His rule is based on his training, which taught him that in this situation it would be better for worker morale if subordinates were permitted to call him "Tim." Tim's decision to tell Jeremy to support keeping things the way they are for the time being is based not solely on one rule, but also on Tim's power as a supervisor in this organization. In convincing Angela to call a meeting of shift managers to discuss the feasibility of adopting this rule at BCT, Tim is once again able to exert a sense of power that is granted to him as a member of the group and as a shift manager. However, we see that all of the shift managers bring power in one form or another to the group decision-making process. Darnell brings the power associated with his knowledge of managerial techniques as a result of his M.B.A. Wayne's extensive background and knowledge of the organization's history afford him a different type of power to bring to the discussion. Angela contributes the power associated with her position as human resources coordinator at BCT.

To summarize, when it comes to decision making, no one power structure in the web of organizational rules is more important than the other. Giddens views power as a two-way street, and the fact that an actor is even invited to participate in discussions and decision making indicates that he or she has a certain amount of power over others.

Elements of Structuration Theory

To better understand Structuration Theory, let's break it down into its component parts. We'll also look at the various elements that are central to understanding the complexity of rules and the influence they have on communication within systems. The elements we will discuss include agency and reflexivity, duality of structure, and social integration.

Agency and Reflexivity

agency
behaviors or activities
used in social
environments

agent
a person engaging in
behaviors or activities
in social environments

Structuration Theory is based on the simple notion that human activity is the source that creates and re-creates the social environment in which we exist. Thus, **agency** is defined as the specific behaviors or activities that humans engage in and that are guided by the rules and contexts in which interactions take place. **Agent** refers to the person who engages in these behaviors. For example, students serve as the agents who engage in the agency of attending classes at a college or university. The context of the classroom provides a template of rules that the agents (students) are expected to follow. If the context of the class is a large lecture setting, the rules might dictate that the particular agency (behaviors) to be performed in asking a question be formal in nature (for example, raising one's hand to ask a question).

Poole, Seibold, and McPhee (1986, 1996) apply the notion of agency to their examination of small groups by proposing that a group's members are aware of and knowledgeable about the events and activities that take place around them. This awareness guides their decision to engage in particular behaviors (agency). According to structuration theorists, organizations (and groups) engage in a process known as reflexivity. **Reflexivity** refers to the actors' ability to monitor their actions and behaviors. In essence, members of an organization are able to look into the future and make changes in the organization's structure if it appears as if things are not going to work according to plan. An important element in agency and reflexivity is the ability of an individual to articulate the reasons for his or her choices of behavior. When an instructor asks a student why she didn't ask the question during class time, the student may respond that the number of questions being asked was too overwhelming for her to receive personal attention at that time. Thus, the agent has a level of consciousness about his or her behavior and can explain why a particular behavior was chosen over another.

reflexivity
a person's ability to monitor his or her actions or behaviors

In employing agency and reflexivity, organizations reflect on the structures and systems that are in place, and members have the ability to explain the reasons for the behaviors as well as the ability to identify their goals. This awareness occurs on two levels. **Discursive consciousness** refers to the ability of a person to state his or her thoughts in a language that can be shared with other members of the organization. Put another way, this consciousness pertains to knowledge that can be expressed through words to others. **Practical consciousness** refers to those actions or feelings that cannot be put into words. Modaff et al. (2008) state that "some activities and/or feelings are easily explained by individuals (discursive consciousness), while other experiences, behaviors, and feelings are not as easily put into words (practical consciousness)" (p. 118).

discursive consciousness
a person's ability to articulate personal goals or behaviors

practical consciousness
a person's inability to articulate personal goals or behaviors

To understand these terms, let's look at our chapter-opening scenario. Tim may be able to explain the reasons he proposed the change in BCT's rule for supervisor–subordinate communication. It is likely that he will engage in reflexivity by describing his past supervisory experiences and the success that he had in relating to his former employees. Thus, he is using a level of discursive consciousness. What Tim may not be able to articulate is the practical consciousness, or the internal feelings, that he experiences in a formal work environment. Tim might find it difficult to explain the warm, familial feelings that emerge when his employees address him by first name. He also might not realize the fact that when they address him as "Mr. Vondrasek," he feels as though they are addressing his father or grandfather—maybe he does not perceive himself as being old enough to be addressed as "Mr." The agency, Tim's decision to address the issue, is based on his ability to reflect on previous experience.

Reflexivity also enables Tim to make a prediction about how these behaviors will impact employer–employee relationships in the future. Tim's ability to articulate his reasons for his attitudes and actions provides others with an understanding of why he pursues these goals. Both personal and organizational rules are influencing the decision of how employees should address supervisors in the organization. The task Tim faces is in deciding whether to maintain the organizational rule or alter it to accommodate his personal rules.

Duality of Structure

Rules and resources fulfill dual functions in organizations. According to the principle of **duality of structure**, members of an organization depend on rules and resources to guide their decisions about the behaviors or actions that they will employ in their communication. However, the fact that the individual has chosen either to follow a rule or to alter it will result in a change in that rule or resource in future communication interactions.

To better understand this relationship, let's explore the distinction between rules and resources. In Structuration Theory, the term **rules** is used to refer to general routines that the organization has or follows in accomplishing its goals. Rather than viewing rules as strictly guidelines for *why* something must be done, it is more useful to view them as an instruction manual for *how* a goal may be accomplished. As was stated earlier in this chapter, and as referred to in Chapter 3, these rules may be explicitly stated or implicitly learned.

At BCT, Tim realizes that it would not be effective simply to change the communication expectations for his team without first consulting the other managers in the organization. He employs a personal rule that states that he should respect his colleagues and their reasons for organizational protocol. He accomplishes that goal by implementing this rule; he requests a meeting with the human resources coordinator. Next, a group meeting is called to give all shift managers the opportunity to express their opinions. The group's rule of giving every member equal voice in arriving at decisions is employed. Finally, a vote is taken to decide the preferred action of the majority of the group's members. Tim could initially decide simply to invoke his own rules and disregard the rules of the organization, but he decides to discuss the issue with his colleagues and supervisors to arrive at a decision. A vital element in understanding why some rules are enforced over others lies in understanding the power that certain agents have in the decision-making process.

Resources refers to the power that individuals bring to the group or organization. This power is influential because it leads an individual to take action or initiate change. An organization can employ two types of resources. **Allocative resources** refers to the material assistance generated by an organization to help the group in accomplishing its goal. Suppose a group of university students wants to have access to a facility where they can work out during their breaks between classes or during their "off" time. Some of the group's members decide to write a proposal to the administrators of the university and to provide them with a list of activities that they are willing to undertake to raise some of the money if the university will match the funds that are collected. Thus, a plan for providing allocative, or material, resources has been established.

Authoritative resources refers to the interpersonal characteristics that are employed during communication interactions. Recall from Chapter 2 that interpersonal communication pertains to the dynamic between two people. In Structuration Theory, interpersonal communication is viewed as the ability to

Table 15.1 Power Type as a Resource in an Organization

TYPE OF POWER	DEFINITION
Reward	Chris has the ability to provide something of value to Pat.
Coercive	Chris can deliver punishment to Pat.
Referent	Chris achieves agreement or compliance because Pat respects Chris and desires to be like Chris.
Legitimate	Chris exerts control over Pat because of Chris's title or position.
Expert	Chris possesses special knowledge or expertise that Pat needs.

influence others. Put another way, authoritative resources allow a person to execute power in an organization. Every person possesses a degree of power and influence on the operations of an organization (Modaff et al., 2008).

One key point about power in this theory is how agents can employ power to get what they want in a social system (Poole & McPhee, 2005). To understand better what we mean by power, consider one model of social power (French & Raven, 1959; Raven, 1993) that has had lasting appeal. These bases of power can be thought of as the various authoritative resources employed in organizations. As Giddens suggests (1984), when individuals are oppressed, they still have resources (such as power) available to overcome the status quo. Each power type is explained next and in Table 15.1.

Reward Power   **Reward power** is based on a person's perception that another has the ability to provide positive reinforcements. These rewards may come in the form of praise, material rewards, or simply removal of negative aspects of the system. Tim's employees may decide to accommodate his request to address him by his first name because they perceive him as having power to promote them or give them raises. If this is the case, reward power is a resource that is affecting communication in the organization.

reward power
perception that another person has the ability to provide positive outcomes

Coercive Power   If Tim's employees fear that they will be demoted or fired as a result of failing to comply with his wishes to establish relationships on a first-name basis, coercive power may be influencing decisions and communication. **Coercive power** is based on the expectation that an individual has the ability to exact punishment. A person may comply with another's request simply to avoid negative consequences such as losing credibility in front of one's co-workers or getting a rotten work schedule.

coercive power
perception that another person has the ability to enact punishment

Referent Power   Perhaps Tim's employees choose to address him by his first name primarily because he is a friendly, likable person who demonstrates a genuine interest in his workers. Then, the resource guiding the communication decisions is due to **referent power,** or the ability of an individual to engage compliance based on the fact that personal relationships have been established between the two interactants.

referent power
perception that another person has the ability to achieve compliance because of established personal relationships

Theory Into Practice

Gretchen

I want to write about how power dominates the organization. I worked for a company where no one other than the supervisor had a college degree. He loved that he was the only college graduate, and put the rest of the employees down. He'd do it in a pretty subtle way by saying things like, "I know you all haven't gone to college to know the latest. . ." The irony about what he'd say was that his college degree did not really qualify him to oversee us (you didn't have to have a college degree to work on painting luminous decorations on alarm clocks!), but he had what we learned was reward power: He made out the schedule. If you needed to have a day off because you couldn't get a babysitter or if you wanted a day off to go watch the Red Sox, he was in a (powerful) position to allow (or not allow) that. The guy certainly tried to wield his power at times and it really destroyed the morale in our work unit.

legitimate power
perception that another person has the ability to exert influence because of title or position

expert power
perception that another person has the ability to exert influence because of special knowledge or expertise

Legitimate Power   Recall Tim's comment to Jeremy: "This is my shift, and I would really prefer if we do things my way." The influence a person exerts on the basis of his or her position or title is called **legitimate power**. If shift managers decide to retain the current communication rules simply because they respect Wayne and his tenure with the company, legitimate power is a resource guiding their decision. This type of power is associated with one's right to exert influence.

Expert Power   **Expert power** refers to one's ability to exert influence over others based on the knowledge or expertise that one possesses. In the opening scenario, we learned that Darnell holds an M.B.A. from Marden and has extensive knowledge about effective managerial communication strategies in the workplace. If the shift managers decide to base their decision to adopt a less formal environment in the workplace on Darnell's knowledge, his expert power serves as a resource in the decision.

If we were to view power as a resource, as defined in Structuration Theory, duality of structure could be applied to explain how power was used in generating action in the group as well as in determining if power was altered or changed as a result of the action that was taken. For example, many students have assigned expert power to a teacher based on their previous experiences in classes with knowledgeable instructors. However, if an instructor were to enter a classroom and employ profanity or only provide examples based on supermarket tabloids, those same students might alter their personal rule that all teachers possess expert power; they might decide to employ a rule in the future that requires them to be tentative in their decision to assign power to an instructor. This is an example of duality of structure.

Social Integration

social integration
reciprocity of communication behaviors in interaction

The third concept, **social integration,** refers to the reciprocity of communication behaviors among persons in interactions. This is an ongoing process whereby members of an organization become acquainted with one another and form expectations based on previous impressions or information that is learned. If members are interacting with one another for the first time, their knowledge of one another will be quite limited, and the process of social integration will be much more extensive. However, as members become acquainted with one another, the social integration process relies heavily on structures that are recalled from past interactions.

Each interactant brings his or her own background, experiences, and expectations to a communication event, a conclusion we addressed in Chapter 1. However, as a member of an organization, an individual brings knowledge to the situation that is subject to change based on the influence of both internal and external sources. As we gain a sense of how we and others fit into the group, we begin to communicate and act in ways that indicate the roles we expect each member to fulfill. Expectations for patterns of behavior are established, but these expectations could potentially change as the members of the group interact and evolve. Recall the meeting of the shift managers. Because Tim is the newest member of the group, the other shift managers may be uncertain about what type of power to attribute to him as he presents his ideas. The same applies to Tim's interactions with his subordinates. As Tim and the others engage in subsequent interactions, his view of himself and others' views of Tim will evolve.

Application of Time and Space

We now examine the role of time and space in organizations. Structuration theorists believe that all social interaction in an organization is composed of temporal (time) and spatial (space) dimensions. The actual communication or interaction that takes place in the organization can be examined as existing in real time and as taking place in real space.

We hear a message as it occurs in a context. For instance, think about a conversation that your supervisor has with you about company layoffs while the two of you are walking to your cars at the end of the workday. The supervisor's decision to talk about this topic, in this place (parking lot), and at this particular time would be of interest to structuration theorists. However, researchers would likely need to look more deeply to determine the factors that motivated your boss to communicate this message to you. Furthermore, does your boss make reference to *past experiences* with company layoffs? Does she look ahead to potential consequences if such a layoff was to happen? And, especially relevant to many communication researchers, if a layoff were to be announced, how would it be communicated to employees? Telephone? E-mail? Public posting? How would the conversation, as Poole and McPhee (2005) express it, "bind" (p. 180) space and time in the discussion of company layoffs?

Essentially, space is viewed as a contextual element that has meaning for the various members of a group or organization. The elements of time and space are factors that enable us to engage in communication. One's view of his or her tenure in a group spans both time and space and influences the decisions

Theory Application in Groups (TAG)

In small groups, talk about how you would describe Structuration Theory to a family member. What would you tell that person to demonstrate the importance of the theory in everyday life? What is especially critical to talk about in a society plagued by ethical lapses by organizational leaders?

that are made. For example, it is not likely that a single event or a single location has solely influenced Tim's action to request a change in the company's policy. Rather, it is a series of experiences and references that are the result of his own managerial history—and perhaps even his own experience as an employee in an organization—that have influenced his choice of action.

In addition to understanding the influence that space and time have on the structures employed in an organization, we can also consider the dynamics of group interaction. How do first impressions affect the rules and resources (structures) that are implemented by members in their communication with others? The concept of social integration allows us to consider this element in comprehending yet another dimension of the complex activity of group decision making.

Integration, Critique, and Closing

Organizations are a central part of our lives. It is estimated that company employees spend almost 90 percent of their time in group or team meetings. Structuration Theory provides an important framework for understanding these communication opportunities. Among the criteria relevant to evaluating theory, we identify two for our discussion: scope and parsimony.

Integration

Communication Tradition	Rhetorical	Semiotic	Phenomenological	**Cybernetic**	Socio-Psychological	Socio-Cultural	Critical
Communication Context	Intrapersonal	Interpersonal	Small Group	**Organizational**	Public/Rhetorical	**Mass/Media**	Cultural
Approach to Knowing	**Positivistic/Empirical**	Interpretive/Hermeneutic	Critical

Critique

Evaluation Criteria	**Scope**	Logical Consistency	**Parsimony**	Utility	Testability	Heurism	Test of Time

Scope

Structuration Theory can be applied to almost all social settings (Mumby & May, 2005) and virtually every communication interaction. As noted previously, the areas of communication that have applied the theory with the most theoretical success are organizational communication and group decision making. By now, you can see that the application of structuration principles is appropriate in both the organizational and small group context. Our focus has been on the organizational environment, namely, how the structures created in organizations influence communication and decisions. At first glance, you may view the theory as too expansive, resulting in too broad a scope. With a discussion of rules, resources, power, and discourse, it would seem that the theory is trying to do too much at one time.

Parsimony

Recall that this criterion pertains to the simplicity of a theory: Is the theory easy to understand or cumbersome? Stephen Banks and Patricia Riley (1993) point out that Structuration Theory is difficult to read and understand: "Structuration lacks certain characteristics that communication researchers and other social science scientists often find appealing: It is not quickly read, immediately intuitive, or parsimonious" (p. 178). Banks and Riley present many concepts as they examine the intricate process of how organizations and groups structure their communication and arrive at decisions. Their advice to those who are researching this theory in an attempt to understand organizations and groups is to "begin at the beginning" (p. 181). This requires insight and understanding of the historical rules brought into an organization by each member—and this is an extremely difficult task to accomplish. Furthermore, Banks and Riley suggest that scholars resist the temptation to apply preestablished categories in explaining how organizations (and groups) are developed and how they experience change.

Research Notes

Kirby, E., & Krone, K. (2002). "The policy exists but you can't really use it": Communication and the structuration of work–family policies. *Journal of Applied Communication Research, 30,* 50–77.

This research looks at work–family policies enacted at the local, state, and federal level. The variety of policies (e.g., flextime, family, and medical leave) and the number of people who use them in their workplace justified this study. Kirby and Krone use a Structuration framework to understand how workers used the policies. Interestingly, the research team find wide variability in how the policies were utilized and embraced. In trying to explain the work–family policies, Kirby and Krone note that many of the policies were seen as inequitable; they were more often used by those employees with children than by those without children. Furthermore, the researchers discovered that some employees felt they were picking up the slack of those out on "leave," resulting in some perceiving a use and abuse of the policies. In fact, the organizational communication scholars observe that there was a "system of peer pressure [that encouraged employees] not to utilize work–family programs" (p. 67). The results are interpreted with Structuration principles in mind.

Ogden, D., & Rose, R. A. (2005). Using Giddens's Structuration Theory to examine the waning of participation of African Americans in baseball. *Journal of Black Studies, 35,* 225–245.

This provocative research explores the evolution of African Americans in baseball using such Structuration principles as rules, resources, and identity. Ogden and Rose appear to be the first organizational communication researchers to apply Structuration Theory to leisure activities. The scholars embark on a chronological understanding of Negro league teams and their opportunities to fulfill identity needs in the African American community. Furthermore, Ogden and Rose suggest that Giddens's notion that unintended consequences result from others' behaviors is illustrated by a "pattern of segregation" (p. 233). Structures were in place during the 1940s that allowed African Americans to have their own baseball league, but the success of the league necessitated the integration of such baseball players as Jackie Robinson into "America's past time." Ogden and Rose note that "structures that facilitated the operation of the Negro leagues also developed and put the skills of Negro league stars on display" (p. 234). In other words, baseball stars were willing to use discursive consciousness to undermine the routines found in the Negro league (and major league) baseball teams. The analysis concludes with a discussion of how baseball routines have been shifted to basketball routines, with nearly 80 percent of NBA players identifying as African American. The researchers note, "In drawing on structures to produce/reproduce basketball routines and identities, the roles of family and friends, access to facilities, and social messages delivered through mass media and other communication forms should not be underestimated" (p. 240).

The challenge for communication scholars in studying Structuration Theory is to continue their study on the dynamics of the theory and its applicability to real-life situations. As applied to the group context, the theory was renamed *Adaptive* Structuration Theory, thereby avoiding confusion with Giddens's original thinking. In other words, the theory allows us to unravel the complexities of organizational life and does so with an appropriate theoretical framework. Although the theory is a bit intimidating because of the complexity of the elements that must be considered, it is an important theory to consider as we explore the complexities involved in organizational life.

Discussion Starters

1. Recall a time when you were involved in a group similar to the Bayside City Tire Company—a time when a decision had to be made. What were some of the rules that influenced the process of decision making? Were the rules changed as a result of the decision that was reached or the process that was followed in arriving at that decision? If so, how?

2. One of the assumptions of this theory is that power structures are present in groups and guide the decision-making process by providing us with information on how to best accomplish our goals. Discuss the potential positive and negative implications of power as an element of structuration.

3. Giddens proposes that structure (rules and resources) should not be viewed as a barrier to interaction but as a necessary part of the creation of the interaction. Do you agree or disagree with this position? Defend your answer.

4. Identify elements of other communication theories that are evident in the Structuration approach to groups and organizations.

5. Structuration Theory proposes that structures themselves should be viewed as being nontemporal and nonspatial. Discuss the significance of this idea. Provide an example from your own experience of the influence of time and space in a group or organization.

6. How would you explain your family using any of the principles of Structuration Theory?

7. Structuration theorists state that the theory has the potential to provide real-world applications. Discuss your reaction to this claim.

Online Learning Center [www. mhhe.com/west4e]

Visit the Online Learning Center at www.mhhe.com/west4e for chapter-specific resources, such as story-into-theory and multiple-choice quizzes, as well as theory summaries and theory connection questions.

CHAPTER 16

Organizational Culture Theory

*Based on the research of **Clifford Geertz**, **Michael Pacanowsky**, and **Nick O'Donnell-Trujillo***

Fran Callahan

As an employee of Grace's Jewelers, Fran Callahan knew that her job was unlike those of her friends. The company employed about 150 people throughout its twenty stores in the southeastern United States and targeted primarily teenage girls who frequented malls. Its founder, Grace Talmage, made it a point to visit employees like Fran each week, helping them to feel good about working in such a small company.

Fran's relationship with Grace had always been quite cordial. Why wouldn't it be? She received excellent commission rates and a reasonable health-care package (including dental and vision care) and got along superbly with her supervisor. In addition, Fran and the other employees were able to wear casual clothing to work, which made them the envy of other workers in the mall. All of this may explain why Fran had worked for the company for almost nine years and why she had no plans to leave—until now.

After thirty-three years in the business, Grace decided it was time to sell the business and retire. Because of the profits that Grace has shown over the years, Jewelry Plus, a large retail jewelry store, decided to bid for the small chain. Although Grace did not want to sell to such a retail giant, their bid was simply too good to pass up. In the end, she decided to sell her business, much to the disappointment of her employees. Fran was especially concerned after hearing gossip about the larger company's treatment of its employees and its way of handling day-to-day operations. She privately wondered how much would change once Grace sold the stores. She needed the job, though, and decided to stay on.

Fran's instincts were right. Once the company's transition was completed, she had to undergo a "new employee" orientation, which meant standing in front of all of the new employees and explaining why she had applied to the company. Among the new company policies were new dress codes and a new policy for store exchanges. Fran could no longer wear casual clothing; instead, she had to wear a company uniform and black shoes with low heels.

With respect to store exchanges, company policy changed from "complete satisfaction or 100% money-back guarantee" to "product must be returned within 10 days with register receipt." Although Fran felt that this new policy would turn many customers away, the success of Jewelry Plus was proof enough that it had worked in the past.

Finally, with the new company, her health benefits no longer included dental or vision coverage. This lack of coverage was grist for the gossip mill. The story that Fran heard during her orientation was that an employee actually lost two back teeth because she couldn't afford the dental bills!

With all the changes in store policies, dress codes, and company philosophies, Fran and a number of her co-workers felt overwhelmed. In fact, many of Fran's co-workers, with whom she had worked over the past nine years, quit their jobs. As a single parent, however, Fran felt that she couldn't resign.

On top of all that, her new boss was a disaster! Fran and her co-workers nicknamed him "The Shadow" because he was right behind them as they waited on and rang up their customers. Having her supervisor watch everything she did was annoying and seemed pointless to Fran, especially considering the fact that most of her customers were teenagers and that they were fickle in their purchasing behaviors.

Despite these concerns, Fran went to the company's first picnic. She didn't really want to, but she felt that she had to give the company a chance. As she and her old and new co-workers drank ice tea and ate hot dogs, they seemed to bond. Former employees of Grace's Jewelers told the workers of the retail giant about the way things used to be. They seemed to be genuinely interested in hearing about people like Gabby, the 70-year-old retiree who wouldn't stop talking to customers. There was a great deal of laughing about the old times.

The day ended quite differently from the way Fran had envisioned it. She made a few friends, reminisced about the past, and felt a bit more comfortable with her future. Although she knew that her boss would be difficult to deal with, Fran decided that she would try to make the most out of her job. At the very least, she thought, she had some people in whom to confide.

Once you graduate from college, it's likely that many of you will work for an organization. Organizational life is characterized as much by change as it is by anything else. Change is frequently marked by excitement, anxiety, uncertainty, frustration, and disbelief. These emotions are especially acute during stressful times; for example, when companies lay off their employees.

Go to any bookstore on campus or at the mall and you're sure to see a number of books on organizational life. This pop culture approach to the world of corporate America is everywhere. Some authors tell us that there are *10 Easy Ways to Get a Raise* or that there are *8 Safe Steps to Being Promoted*. Other authors have made millions touting the importance of *Communicating With Difficult People* and *Working to Live and Living to Work*. Most of these books center on what people can do to make their lives easier in the workplace. The problem, however, is that organizational life is very complex. It's safe to say that there are few "easy ways" to anything in organizations.

To understand organizational life beyond pop culture—including an organization's values, stories, goals, practices, and philosophies—Michael Pacanowsky and Nick O'Donnell-Trujillo (1982, 1983, 1990) conceptualized Organizational Culture Theory (OCT). Pacanowsky and O'Donnell-Trujillo feel that organizations can best be understood using a cultural lens, an idea originally proposed by anthropologist Clifford Geertz. They believe researchers are limited in their understanding of organizations when they follow the scientific method, a process we outlined in Chapter 4. According to Pacanowsky and O'Donnell-Trujillo, the scientific method is constrained by its task of measuring, rather than discovering. Pacanowsky and O'Donnell-Trujillo (1982) argue that Organizational Culture Theory invites all researchers "to observe, record, and make sense of the communicative behavior of organizational members" (p. 129). They embrace the "totality or lived experience within organizations" (Pacanowsky, 1989, p. 250). The theorists paint a broad stroke in their understanding of organizations by stating that "culture is not something an

"I don't know how it started, either. All I know is that it's part of our corporate culture."

organization has; a culture is something an organization *is*" (Pacanowsky & O'Donnell-Trujillo, 1982, p. 146). Culture is communicatively constructed by organizational practices, and culture is distinct to each organization. For the theorists, understanding individual organizations is more important than generalizing from a set of behaviors or values across organizations. These thoughts form the backdrop of the theory.

Think about the types of organizations to which you now belong. They may vary in scope and size and may contain a number of practices that are unique to the organization. For instance, one organization that we all have in common is an academic one—a college or university. You've heard and perhaps shared stories about certain professors and classes to take or to avoid. There are various rites of passage in college, such as freshman orientation, fraternity or sorority rush, and cafeteria food. Practices such as advising and internships also characterize most institutions of higher education.

It is clear that the essence of organizational life is found in its culture. In this sense of the word, *culture* does not refer to the variety of races, ethnicities, and backgrounds of individuals, a perspective we discussed in Chapter 2. Rather, according to Pacanowsky and O'Donnell-Trujillo (1983), culture is a way of living in an organization. Organizational culture includes the emotional and psychological climate or atmosphere. This may involve employee morale, attitudes, and levels of productivity (Belasen, 2008). Organizational culture also includes all the symbols (actions, routines, conversations, and so forth) and the meanings that people attach to these symbols. Cultural meaning and understanding are achieved through the interactions employees and

People are like spiders who are suspended in webs that they created at work. An organization's culture is composed of shared symbols, each of which has a unique meaning. Organizational stories, rituals, and rites of passage are examples of the culture of an organization.

management have with one another. Joann Keyton (2005) states the following about organizational culture: "Although difficult to describe, as an employee we *know* what it's like in our organization" (p. 1). We begin our discussion of Organizational Culture Theory by first interpreting culture and then presenting three assumptions of the theory.

The Cultural Metaphor: Of Spider Webs and Organizations

The origin of the word *culture* is interesting. Culture originally referred to preparing the ground for tending crops and animals. It was interpreted as fostering growth. Pacanowsky and O'Donnell-Trujillo (1982) believe that organizational culture "indicates what constitutes the legitimate realm of inquiry" (p. 122). In other words, **organizational culture** is the essence of organizational life. As we mentioned earlier, they apply anthropological principles to construct their theory. Specifically, they adopt the Symbolic-Interpretive approach articulated by Clifford Geertz (1973) in their theoretical model. Geertz remarks that people are animals "suspended in webs of significance" (p. 5). He adds that people spin webs themselves. Pacanowsky and O'Donnell-Trujillo (1982) comment on Geertz's metaphor:

organizational culture
the essence of organizational life

> The web not only exists, it is spun. It is spun when people go about the business of construing their world as sensible—that is, when they communicate. When they talk, write a play, sing, dance, fake an illness, they are communicating, and they are constructing their culture. The web is the residue of the communication process. (p. 147)

A primary goal of researchers, then, should be to think about all possible web-like configurations (features) in organizations.

Geertz invokes the image of a spider web deliberately. He believes that culture is like the webs spun by a spider. That is, webs are intricate designs, and each web is different from all others. Furthermore, webs "represent strength, life, and cohesion, but they are also things that need constant maintenance . . ." (Modaff, DeWine, & Butler, 2008, p. 95). For Geertz, cultures are like this as well. Basing his conclusions on various cultures around the world, Geertz argues that cultures are all different and that their uniqueness should be celebrated. To understand a culture, Geertz believes that researchers should begin to focus on the meaning shared within it. We examine more of Geertz's beliefs later.

Pacanowsky and O'Donnell-Trujillo (1983) apply these basic principles to organizations. Employees and managers alike spin their webs. People are critical in the organization, and therefore, it is important to study their behaviors in conjunction with the overall organization. Pacanowsky and O'Donnell-Trujillo claim that members of organizations engage in a number of communication behaviors that contribute to the culture of the company. They may do this through gossiping, joking, backstabbing, or becoming romantically involved with others.

The organizational culture at Jewelry Plus will be revealed in a number of ways. You will recall that Fran learned of the new owner through gossip and that the company picnic was a way for her to learn more about the new company culture. No doubt she will experience an organizational culture with her new job that is very different from what she experienced with Grace's Jewelers. The company has changed, the faces are new, and the rules reflect new ownership. Fran also contributes to the spinning of the organizational web by both responding to company stories and passing them on to others. In sum, the web of organizational culture has been spun. This broad perspective underscores why Pacanowsky and O'Donnell-Trujillo argue that organizational culture "is not just another piece of the puzzle; it is the puzzle" (p. 146).

Assumptions of Organizational Cultural Theory

Three assumptions guide Organizational Culture Theory. As you work through these assumptions, keep in mind the diversity and complexity of organizational life. Also, understand that these assumptions emphasize the process view of organizations that Pacanowsky and O'Donnell-Trujillo advocate:

- Organizational members create and maintain a shared sense of organizational reality, resulting in a better understanding of the values of an organization.
- The use and interpretation of symbols are critical to an organization's culture.
- Cultures vary across organizations, and the interpretations of actions within these cultures are diverse.

The first assumption pertains to the importance of people in organizational life. Specifically, individuals share in creating and maintaining their reality. These

Table 16.1 Symbols of an Organizational Culture

GENERAL CATEGORY	SPECIFIC TYPES/EXAMPLES
Physical Symbols	art/design/logo buildings/decor dress/appearance material objects
Behavioral Symbols	ceremonies/rituals traditions/customs rewards/punishments
Verbal Symbols	anecdotes/jokes jargon/names/nicknames explanations stories/myths/history metaphors

individuals include employees, supervisors, and employers. At the core of this assumption is an organization's values. **Values** are the standards and principles within a culture that have intrinsic worth to a culture. Values inform organizational members about what is important. Pacanowsky (1989) notes that values derive from "moral knowledge" (p. 254) and that people display their moral knowledge through narratives, or stories. The stories that Fran hears and shares, for example, will result in her understanding the organization's values.

values
standards and principles in a culture

People share in the process of discovering an organization's values. Being a member of an organization requires active participation in that organization. The meanings of particular symbols—for instance, why a company continues to interview prospective employees when massive layoffs are under way—are communicated by both employees and management. The symbolic meaning of hiring new people when others are being fired will not escape savvy workers; why dedicate money to new personnel when others are losing their jobs? Pacanowsky and O'Donnell-Trujillo (1982) believe that employees contribute to the shaping of organizational culture. Their behaviors are instrumental in creating and ultimately maintaining organizational reality.

The reality (and culture) of an organization are also determined in part by the symbols, the second assumption of the theory. Earlier we noted that Pacanowsky and O'Donnell-Trujillo adopted the Symbolic-Interpretive perspective of Geertz. This perspective underscores the use of symbols in organizations, and, as we mentioned in Chapter 1, symbols are representations for meaning. Organizational members create, use, and interpret symbols every day. These symbols, therefore, are important to the company's culture. Mary Jo Hatch (2006) extends the notion of symbols in her discussion of the categories of symbolic meaning (Table 16.1).

Symbols include the verbal and nonverbal communication in an organization (Hatch, 2006). Frequently, these symbols communicate an organization's values. Symbols may take the form of slogans that carry meaning. For example, several companies have slogans—past and present—that symbolize their values, including State Farm Insurance ("Like a good neighbor, State Farm is there"), the *New York Times* ("All the News That's Fit to Print"), and Disneyland ("The Most Magical Place on Earth"). The extent to which these symbols are effective relies not only on the media but also on how the company's employees enact them. For example, Disneyland's belief that it is the most magical place on earth would be quite odd if its employees didn't smile or if they were rude.

For evidence of verbal symbols in an organization, consider this story. A supervisor named Derrick communicates a great deal about values in casual conversation with his employees. Derrick frequently tells long stories about how he handled a particular issue at a previous workplace. He often launches into detailed accounts of how, for instance, he managed to get his employees a bonus at the end of the year. His stories inevitably begin with a short vignette about his upbringing in Arkansas and end with a moral. At first, employees were unsure how to handle this type of communication. As time went on, however, they soon realized that Derrick was trying to demonstrate a connection with his employees and to indicate that although problems may seem insurmountable, he knows ways to handle them. Through many of his stories, he communicates that he cares about the issues of the company and the workers; he also communicates a new view of what he thinks the organizational culture should be.

Our third assumption of OCT pertains to the variety of organizational cultures. Simply put, organizational cultures vary tremendously. The perceptions of the actions and activities within these cultures are just as diverse as the cultures themselves. Consider what it is like for Fran as she moves from Grace's Jewelers to Jewelry Plus. We have already provided a number of examples that underscore the various cultural issues within each company. Her perceptions, however, and her participation in the culture may differ from those of others. Some people might appreciate a cultural change after working nine years for the same small company.

As an employee in a small jewelry store, Fran knew that a store's problems could readily be resolved and that any suggestions for changes were welcomed and enacted. The culture was such that employees were empowered to make quick decisions, often without supervisor approval. Exceptions to the store return policy, for instance, were handled by all employees. The store's founder felt that employees were in the best position to deal with difficult problems needing quick resolutions. In addition, employee rewards for customer service were routine, and conflict mediation and anger management programs were available for both employees and management. These organizational practices communicate the importance of a shared sense of organizational reality among employees. Employees at Grace's Jewelers got together regularly for F.A.C.—Friday Afternoon Club—at a local restaurant. These activities communicated the esprit de corps in the company. The employees of Grace's were members of an organizational culture who "constitute and reveal their culture to themselves and to others" (Pacanowsky & O'Donnell-Trujillo, 1982, p. 131).

Research Notes

Rosenfeld, L. B., Richman, J. M., & May, S. K. (2004). Information adequacy, job satisfaction, and organizational culture in a dispersed-network organization. *Journal of Applied Communication Research, 32,* 28–54.

This research examines a number of themes and variables pertaining to the organizational environment. Exploring a dispersed-network organizational structure where employees are placed in offices that are geographically separated, Rosenfeld and his colleagues analyzed one company's information adequacy on the job satisfaction of its employees and the overall organizational culture. A number of concepts and principles explained by OCT are presented in this research. The researchers sent out a packet to more than 400 employees of a health-care company; the return rate was over 50 percent. Contained in the packets were a number of surveys that looked at the work environment, job satisfaction, and information adequacy. After carefully examining the survey responses and conducting focus group interviews, Rosenfeld and his research team found that in relationship to organizational culture, lower amounts of information adequacy reported by those working in an office were associated with lower perceptions of the culture of a company (clarity, supervisor support, and innovation). In addition, those office personnel who were not given sufficient information regarding the company were also less likely to know what was expected of them on the job. The researchers also found that field workers (those outside the office setting) were likely to view the organizational culture as high in involvement and work pressure and low in task orientation and physical comfort when information adequacy was achieved. The study concludes with a discussion of limitations and some practical applications of the findings.

Schrodt, P. (2002). The relationship between organizational identification and organizational culture: employee perceptions of culture and identification

in a retail sales organization. *Communication Studies, 53,* 189–202.

This research looks at employee perceptions of organizational culture. For this study, organizational culture was defined along six dimensions: teamwork, morale, information flow, involvement, supervision, and meetings. Organizational culture was predicted to influence the perception of identification that employees have with their organizations. The identification process is "related to all of the social aspects of an organization . . . [and] fundamental in an employee's decision-making premises" (p. 193). Two research questions guided this study. The first question looked at the relationship between employee perceptions of organizational culture and employee perceptions of organizational identification. A second question examined how employees' perception of culture contributed to perceptions of organizational identification.

Participants for the study were seventy-six employees from different store locations of a large retail company. For purposes of the study, this store was called "SalesCo," and the study included participants from both the sales force and upper management. Participants completed questionnaires on organizational identification and organizational culture.

Analyses of the results of the surveys showed that each dimension of the organizational culture survey was positively and significantly related to organizational identification. In particular, Schrodt discovered that perceptions of morale, information flow, involvement, supervision, and meetings were more closely related to organizational identification than were perceptions of teamwork and supervision. The results of the second question found that employee morale emerged as the only significant predictor of employee perceptions of organizational identification. The study concludes with a brief discussion of the limitations of the research and calls for future studies that might help us better understand the complex relationship between organizational culture and organizational identification.

The organizational culture of Jewelry Plus is very different from that of Grace's, and Fran's experiences with Jewelry Plus are very different from hers with Grace's Jewelers. The corporate giant has no exception to its policy on store returns, and any suggestions for store improvement must be placed in the employee suggestion box or e-mailed to the national headquarters. A sense of community is not encouraged at Jewelry Plus because tasks clearly promote autonomy. There are some efforts to ensure that employees have time together—through breaks, lunch, or holiday gatherings—but these opportunities are too limited to foster collegiality. Without collegiality, stories, rituals, and rites of passage are restricted. Obviously, significant differences exist in the organizational cultures of Grace's and Jewelry Plus.

We have presented three assumptions of Organizational Culture Theory. Each is grounded in the belief that when researchers study organizational cultures, they will uncover a complex and intricate web. Pacanowsky and O'Donnell-Trujillo believe that the Symbolic-Interpretive perspective provides a realistic picture of the culture of a company. To gain a better sense of how they went about studying organizations, we turn our attention to the primary methodology employed in their work and the work of their predecessor, Clifford Geertz: ethnography.

Ethnographic Understanding: Laying It On Thick

Communication and performance studies researcher Dwight Conquergood (1992, 1994) studied one of the most provocative of all research topics in communication: gang communication. In an effort to understand gang communication, Conquergood moved into a run-down building in Chicago known at the time as "Big Red." He lived in the building for nearly two years, observing and participating in virtually all parts of life occupied by gang members. Through observing, participating, and taking notes, Conquergood's research offered a view of gang communication virtually ignored in the media. He uncovered many private rituals and symbols, and his work enabled the gang population to have a "voice" never written about in the communication discipline. His efforts in revealing gang-related stories to others is part of ethnography, the underlying methodology of Organizational Culture Theory.

You will recall that Pacanowsky and O'Donnell-Trujillo based much of their work on Geertz's. Because Geertz's work was ethnographic in nature, let's briefly discuss the ethnographic orientation of Geertz and explain its relationship to the theory.

Geertz (1973) argues that to understand a culture one must see it from the members' points of view. In order to do this, Geertz believes researchers should become ethnographers. Ethnography is a qualitative methodology that uncovers and interprets artifacts, stories, rituals, and practices to reveal meaning in a culture. Ethnographers frequently refer to their study as naturalistic research in that they believe that the manner in which they study cultures is much more natural than, say, that of quantitative researchers. In this spirit, Geertz remarked that ethnography is not an experimental science but rather a

methodology that uncovers meaning. Discovering meaning, then, is paramount to ethnographers. Geertz, and later Pacanowsky and O'Donnell-Trujillo, primarily subscribe to direct observation, interviews, and participant observation in finding meaning in culture.

As an ethnographer, Geertz spent many years studying various cultures. His writings have addressed a number of diverse subjects, from Zen Buddhism to island life in Indonesia. During his stay in some of these places, he relied heavily on field notes and kept a **field journal,** recording his feelings and ideas about his interactions with members of a specific culture. In his writings, Geertz (1973) concludes that ethnography is a kind of **thick description,** or an explanation of the intricate layers of meaning underlying a culture. Ethnographers, therefore, strive to understand the thick description of a culture and "to ferret out the unapparent import of things" (p. 26). Interestingly, Geertz believes that any cultural analysis is incomplete because the deeper one goes, the more complex the culture becomes. Therefore, it is not possible to be completely certain of a culture and its norms or values.

Geertz (1983) points out that this qualitative methodology is not equivalent to walking a mile in the shoes of those studied. This thinking only perpetuates "the myth of the chameleon fieldworker, perfectly self-tuned to his [her] exotic surroundings, a walking miracle of empathy, tact, patience, and cosmopolitanism" (p. 56). Geertz suggests that a balance must be struck between naturally observing and recording behavior and integrating a researcher's values into the process. He states that "the trick is to figure out what the devil they think they are up to" (p. 58). This, as you might imagine, can be quite difficult for ethnographers.

Pacanowsky and O'Donnell-Trujillo were drawn to Geertz's ethnographic experiences and his articulation of the importance of observation, analysis, and interpretation. Their own research experiences with different co-cultures within a larger culture proved invaluable. For instance, Pacanowsky (1983) observed police in the Salt Lake [Utah] valley, and Trujillo (1983) studied a new and used car dealership. The diversity of their experiences in these smaller cultures in the United States prompted them to acknowledge that cultural performances, or what

field journal
personal log to record feelings about communicating with people in a different culture from one's own

thick description
explanation of the layers of meaning in a culture

we call storytelling, are instrumental in communicating about an organization's culture. We return to the topic of performance a bit later in this chapter.

Organizational Culture Theory is rooted in ethnography, and organizational culture should be viewed by adopting ethnographic principles. Let's explore ethnography by using our example of Fran Callahan. If ethnographers were interested in studying the culture of her new job at Jewelry Plus, they might begin by examining several areas: For instance, what sort of new corporate rules are in place? What do new employees like Fran think about them? What types of strategies are used to ease the transition for employees like Fran? Are there any corporate philosophies or ideologies? Are there morale problems? How are they resolved? Has the company responded to employee complaints? If so, how? If not, why not? These and a host of other questions would begin the ethnographic process of understanding the organizational culture of Jewelry Plus.

We could never fully capture the excitement of ethnography in this limited space. Yet we hope that you have grounding in the basic processes associated with ethnography and an understanding of why Pacanowsky and O'Donnell-Trujillo embrace such a methodology in their work on organizational culture. We now wish to expand on the topic of performance, which is a key component in OCT.

The Communicative Performance

performance
metaphor suggesting that organizational life is like a theatrical presentation

Pacanowsky and O'Donnell-Trujillo (1982) contend that organizational members act out certain communication performances, which result in a unique organizational culture. **Performance** is a metaphor that suggests a symbolic process of understanding human behavior in an organization. Organizational performances frequently mimic the theater, in that both supervisor and employees choose to take on various roles, or parts, in their organization.

Although the category system is not necessarily exclusive, you will get an idea about the extent to which organizations vary in terms of how human behavior can be understood. The theorists outline five cultural performances: ritual, passion, social, political, and enculturation. In Table 16.2, we identify these performances. As you read this material, keep in mind that these performances may be enacted by any member of the organization.

ritual performances
regular and recurring presentations in the workplace

personal rituals
routines done at the workplace each day

task rituals
routines associated with a particular job in the workplace

Ritual Performances

Communication performances that occur on a regular and recurring basis are termed **ritual performances**. Rituals include four types: personal, task, social, and organizational. **Personal rituals** include things that you routinely do each day at the workplace. For instance, many organizational members regularly check their voicemail or e-mail when they get to work each day. **Task rituals** are routinized behaviors associated with a person's job. Task rituals get the job done. For instance, task rituals of employees of the Department of Motor Vehicles include issuing eye and written examinations, taking pictures of prospective drivers, administering driving tests, verifying car insurance, and

Table 16.2 Cultural Performances in Organizations

Ritual Performances	personal rituals—checking voicemail and e-mail; task rituals—issuing tickets, collecting fees; social rituals—happy-hour gatherings; organizational rituals—department meetings, company picnics
Passion Performances	storytelling, metaphors, and exaggerated speech—"this is the most unappreciative company," "follow the chain of command or it'll get wrapped around your neck"
Social Performances	acts of civility and politeness; extensions of etiquette—customer thank-yous, water cooler chat, supporting another's "face"
Political Performances	exercising control, power, and influence—"barking" bosses, intimidation rituals, use of informants, bargaining
Enculturation Performances	acquired competencies over organizational career—learning/teaching roles, orientations, interviews

collecting fees. **Social rituals** are the verbal and nonverbal routines that normally take into consideration the interactions with others. For instance, some organizational members get together for a happy hour in bars on Fridays, celebrating the week's end. With respect to your own social rituals, consider the social routines you experience in your classes. Many of you arrive early to catch up with your classmates on what has happened since the last time you spoke and continue the social ritual either during a class break or after class. Social rituals may also include nonverbal behaviors in an organization, including casual Fridays and employee-of-the-month awards. Finally, **organizational rituals** include frequently occurring company events such as division meetings, faculty meetings, and even company picnics like the one Fran Callahan attended.

Passion Performances

The organizational stories that members enthusiastically relate to others are termed **passion performances.** Many times, people in organizations become fervent in their storytelling. Consider, for instance, the experience of Adam, who works at a national retail store. Adam and his co-workers hear and retell stories about their department supervisor. The story goes that the boss walks the perimeter of their department every thirty minutes to get an expanded view of the workers and customers. If the supervisor sees something that he feels is peculiar, he calls the employee into the back room, reviews a videotape of the event, and asks the employee what he or she will do to improve any future problems. Adam relates that all of his co-workers passionately tell this story over and over to both new and seasoned employees. In fact, even after six years, Adam's passion for sharing the story is the same as when he told it for the first time.

social rituals
routines that involve relationships with others in the workplace

organizational rituals
routines that pertain to the organization overall

passion performances
organizational stories that employees share with one another

Social Performances

Whereas passionate performances, like Adam's, appear to have little regard for the butt of the story, **social performances** are the common extensions of civility, politeness, and courtesy used to encourage cooperation among organizational members. The adage that "a little goes a long way" relates directly to this performance. Whether with a smile or a "good morning" greeting, establishing some sense of collegiality is frequently part of an organization's culture.

Yet it is often difficult to be polite. When the mood is tense, it is both trying and somewhat insincere to smile or to wish another a "good morning." Most organizations wish to maintain a professional decorum, even in difficult times, and these social performances help to accomplish this.

Political Performances

When organizational cultures communicate **political performances**, they are exercising power or control. Acquiring and maintaining power and control is a hallmark of U.S. corporate life. In fact, some might argue that power and control pervade organizational life. Nonetheless, because by their nature most organizations are hierarchical, there must be someone with the power to accomplish things and with enough control to maintain the bottom line.

When organizational members engage in political performances, they essentially communicate a desire to influence others. That is not necessarily a bad thing. Consider the experiences of a group of nurses, for instance, at Spring Valley Hospital. For years, the nurses were quiet regarding their second-class status relative to the hospital's physicians. Recently, however, the nurses decided to speak out about their treatment. They talked to physicians, other medical staff, and patients. In this instance, they were exercising more control over their jobs. Their cultural political performances centered on being recognized for their competency as medical professionals and for their commitment to the mission of the hospital. Their goal was to be legitimized in the hospital by the physicians, their co-workers, and the patients. Their performances, no doubt, were critical in establishing a modified organizational culture.

Enculturation Performances

The fifth type of performance identified by Pacanowsky and O'Donnell-Trujillo is termed enculturation performance. **Enculturation performances** refer to how members obtain the knowledge and skills to be contributing members of the organization. These performances may be bold or subtle, and they demonstrate a member's competency within an organization. In the chapter opening scenario, for example, a number of performances will be enacted to enculturate Fran into her new position. She will watch and listen to her colleagues "perform" their thoughts and feelings on a number of issues: work hours, employee discounts, and the company newsletter, among others. In sum, Fran will begin to know the organization's culture.

As we mentioned earlier, these performances may overlap. It is possible, therefore, to have social performances considered ritual performances. Think about, for instance, greeting one co-worker with "Good morning" or fetching coffee for another each day. In this example, the acts of politeness are considered to be a personal (and even task) ritual. Therefore, the performance may be both a social and a ritual performance.

Furthermore, performances may arise from a conscious decision to act out thoughts and feelings about an issue, as in our example of the nurses at Spring Valley Hospital. Or the performances may be more intuitive, as in our example of Fran Callahan. It is clear that Pacanowsky and O'Donnell-Trujillo believe that communicative performances are critical to an organization's culture.

Integration, Critique, and Closing

Organizational Culture Theory, as articulated by Pacanowsky and O'Donnell-Trujillo, remains an important influence on organizational communication theory and research. To evaluate the effectiveness of the theory, we discuss three criteria: logical consistency, utility, and heurism.

Integration

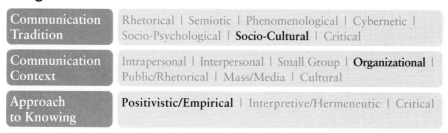

Communication Tradition	Rhetorical | Semiotic | Phenomenological | Cybernetic | Socio-Psychological | **Socio-Cultural** | Critical
Communication Context	Intrapersonal | Interpersonal | Small Group | **Organizational** | Public/Rhetorical | Mass/Media | Cultural
Approach to Knowing	**Positivistic/Empirical** | Interpretive/Hermeneutic | Critical

Critique

Evaluation Criteria	Scope | **Logical Consistency** | Parsimony | **Utility** | Testability | **Heurism** | Test of Time

Logical Consistency

The logical consistency of the model should not go unnoticed. Recall that logical consistency refers to the notion that theories should follow a logical arrangement and remain consistent. From the outset, Pacanowsky and O'Donnell-Trujillo tried to remain true to their belief that the organization's culture is rich and diverse; they felt that listening to the communicative performances of organizational members was where we must begin in understanding "corporate culture." This is the basis from which much of the theory gained momentum.

Still, some believe consistency is lacking. Eric Eisenberg, H. L. Goodall, and Angela Tretheway (2006), for instance, observe that Organizational Culture Theory relies heavily on shared meaning among organizational members. They comment that stories, for example, are not shared similarly across employees because

Theory Into Practice

Nola

I remember working for a company that had the worst corporate culture you could imagine. I worked for a telemarketer, and even during our breaks we felt very uncomfortable. We never dared talk about other employees, share stories of our families, or even try to give ideas to the company. Without doubt, there was a lot of tension in the workplace. One time, my sister had to stop at work to get my car keys. Even she couldn't believe it. She said that no one should be forced to work in that environment. If I didn't need the money, I would have quit after one day on the job!

different organizational stories are told by different organizational narrators. That is, although the theory posits that stories are told and retold and contribute to the culture of an organization, the stories may not have shared meaning.

Utility

The theory is useful because the information is applicable to nearly every employee in an organization. The approach is useful because much of the information from the theory (e.g., symbols, stories, rituals) has direct relationship to how employees work and their identification with their work environment (Schrodt, 2002). Because the theorists' work is based on real organizations with real employees, the researchers have made the theory more useful and practical.

Heurism

The appeal of Organizational Culture Theory has been far and wide, resulting in a heuristic theory. Researchers have focused several of the theory's fundamental themes in research examining college campus facilities (Harris & Cullen, 2008) and gender roles (Lester, 2008). Organizational Culture has framed research examining Muslim employees (Alkhazraji, 1997), law enforcement officers (Frewin & Tuffin, 1998), student discipline (van der Westhuizen, Oosthuizen, & Wolhuter, 2008), and pregnant employees (Halpert & Burg, 1997). It has influenced scholars to consider organizational culture in how they teach their classes (Morgan, 2004). And relevant to us in the educational arena, the theory has been used to study the stories of undergraduate students and their perceptions of "fitting in" at college (Kramer & Berman, 2001).

Pacanowsky and O'Donnell-Trujillo were among the first communication scholars to examine organizational life by looking at both employees and their behaviors. Perhaps looking at organizational culture in this way will enable researchers to appreciate the importance of connecting with the people and their performances at work.

Discussion Starters

1. How can employees like Fran Callahan ease into a new and different organizational culture? What advice would you give her as she begins her new job with Jewelry Plus?

2. Consider some of the organizations to which you belong. Identify the cultural performances that you have either observed or shared. How could you use these performances in your work?

3. Geertz has compared culture to a spider web. What other metaphors can you think of that could represent organizational cultures?

4. Explain how organizational culture can vary within a large organization. Use examples in your response.

5. Imagine that you're an ethnographer who has been assigned to study your school's culture. How might you go about studying it? What sort of cultural artifacts or rituals would you find?

6. Based on your job experiences, explain the frequency of the various cultural performances identified by Pacanowsky and O'Donnell-Trujillo.

7. How would you apply principles of OCT to your family?

Online Learning Center www. mhhe.com/west4e

Visit the Online Learning Center at www.mhhe.com/west4e for chapter-specific resources, such as story-into-theory and multiple-choice quizzes, as well as theory summaries and theory connection questions.

CHAPTER 17

Organizational Information Theory

*Based on the research of **Karl Weick***

Dominique Martin

The year was 1999 and Dominique Martin could feel the stress build as the year progressed. She was an expert on computer conversion to Y2K (year 2000) and was very busy as companies continued to call for her assistance in converting their systems. In fact, she became even busier as media coverage caused many people to question the ability of companies to adapt their systems to the year 2000. The task was not an easy one, and many organizations developed special project teams to deal with the challenge of bringing their systems up-to-date.

As she approached the door of the conference room, Dominique thought about how happy and relieved she would be once the year was over. But, for now, she had to deal with NowBank's Year 2000 Conversion Team. She had been appointed project manager, and today she would meet for the first time with members of various teams via a videoconference. Employees from Dallas, Denver, and Phoenix offices would take part. The Y2K project goal involved the conversion of all NowBank computer systems so that they would be compatible for the changes that would take place in the new millennium. The Y2K project team consisted of approximately eighty people who would be responsible for various aspects of the conversion. Dominique was used to managing a team of twelve employees who were all located in the same city, so this was a new challenge.

As Dominique began the meeting, she asked each team leader in the various cities to introduce their team members and to share their overall goals for the project. As they went around to the various locations, Dominique became overwhelmed. There were so many different areas to manage in this project: maintaining communication with the computer technicians, coordinating information with the federal regulatory agencies regarding their rules for computer configurations, providing updates to and obtaining feedback from the bank's customers to monitor their awareness and concerns about NowBank's readiness for Y2K, keeping the other divisions within the bank informed of changes that were being made to the computer systems and how those changes would affect their departments . . . and that was only the beginning! Each of the teams needed to be kept informed about the others' progress in order to meet their deadlines.

As the meeting progressed, Dominique realized that the success of this project would depend on effective communication. The team from Phoenix insisted that they needed more support staff to collect information from NowBank customers in a timely manner. The Dallas team leader pointed out that her team needed this customer information in order to develop a promotion strategy to gain public confidence. Denver's team argued that they would need to provide federal regulatory information to the computer technicians to ensure that their changes met the government's standards.

After the meeting, Dominique consulted with her team leaders via a telephone conference call.

They developed a communication strategy to help keep the teams in the different offices across the country informed of the events associated with the project. The plan included hiring an internal communication coordinator to manage all the messages that would be sent about Y2K computer conversions. Next, they decided that a company electronic chat area would be established so that all project members could communicate about the information needed to complete the project. Also, an electronic newsletter would be distributed weekly to update all members of NowBank about the progress that was being made. In addition, survey questionnaires were included in the monthly statements sent to all NowBank customers to gain insight about their attitudes and concerns regarding Y2K. Finally, they decided that they would use computer software to record the goals, resources, deadlines, and accomplishments associated with the project.

Although several years have passed since that time, Dominique continues to wonder whether she facilitated the Y2K project effectively. She knew that she was a good team leader, but even today, she thinks about whether her thoughts, actions, and activities were the most appropriate at the time. She felt confident that everyone had a voice in the matter and that their conversations helped move the project along. Still, she couldn't rid herself of a nagging doubt about whether she managed the events to the best of her ability.

The task of managing vast amounts of information is a typical challenge for many organizations. As our options for new communication channels increase, the number of messages that we send and receive, as well as the speed at which we send them, increases as well. Not only are organizations faced with the task of decoding the messages that are received, but they are also challenged with determining which people need to receive the information to help achieve the organization's goals. New media are enabling companies to accomplish their goals in ways never before seen. Videoconferencing, teleconferencing, e-mail chat areas, and podcasting allow people like Dominique to provide teams with the opportunity to share and react to great amounts of information simultaneously. Each of the teams was given the opportunity to decide what information was essential to its tasks or to request additional information that would be needed in the future. Clearly, the introduction of new technologies into organizations is reshaping existing structures and an organization's function (Mars & Ginter, 2007).

Sometimes the information an organization receives is ambiguous. In the case of the Y2K project, each team depended on the others to provide information so that it could complete its portion of the project. Teams needed the information to be presented in a way that they could understand. After all, the customer service team had little knowledge of computer jargon, so they depended on the technicians to clarify the information and present it to them in a way that they could then communicate to their customers. Without this exchange and management of information, several gaps would exist and NowBank's computer conversion would probably fail.

Some organizational communication theorists have used the metaphor of a living system to describe organizations. Just as living systems engage in a process of activities to maintain their functioning and existence, an organization must have a procedure for dealing with all the information it needs to send

and receive to accomplish its goals. Much like systems, organizations are made up of people and teams that are interrelated. They depend on one another to complete their goals.

Consider the process that colleges and universities go through to recruit new students. The publications office conducts research to find out what criteria matter to potential students. Are graduation rates and job placement something high school students are looking for in deciding where to pursue their education? Is the diversity of the student body an important factor in making a decision? Will the recent rating by *The Princeton Review* have an impact on student decisions? Or are students attracted to a campus that has superior computer facilities? After collecting these data, the publications office will use this information to develop publicity materials that appeal to potential students. Recruitment fairs may be held in major cities to provide parents and students with the opportunity to ask admissions counselors about the school. While this process is taking place, the school collects feedback and monitors the reactions of potential students and their parents in order to make changes in their current recruitment strategies. The admissions office reduces uncertainty about what qualities are attractive to students while at the same time assisting students in making their decision by providing information about the school.

Karl Weick developed an approach to describe the process by which organizations collect, manage, and use the information that they receive. Rather than focusing his attention on the *structure* of the organization in terms of the roles and rules that guide its members, Weick emphasizes the *process* of organizing. In doing so, the primary focus is on the exchange of information that takes place within the organization and how members take steps to understand this material. Weick (1995) believes that "organizations talk to themselves" (p. 281). To this end, organizational members are instrumental in the creation and maintenance of message meaning.

Weick sees the organization as a system taking in confusing or ambiguous information from its environment and making sense out of it. Therefore, organizations will evolve as they try to make sense out of themselves and their environment. Rather than focusing on Dominique's role as project manager or on the specific communication rules for sending messages between superiors and subordinates, Weick's Organizational Information Theory (OIT) directs our attention to the steps that are necessary to manage and use the information for the NowBank project. As it becomes more difficult to interpret the information

> The main activity of organizations is the process of making sense of equivocal and ambiguous information. Organizational members accomplish this sensemaking process through enactment, selection, and retention of information. Organizations are successful to the extent that they are able to reduce equivocality through these means.

that is received, an organization needs to solicit input from others (often multiple sources) to make sense of the information and to provide a response to the appropriate people or departments.

The Only Constant Is Change (in Organizations)

Weick first presented his theoretical approach explaining how organizations make sense of, and use, information in his book *The Social Psychology of Organizing* (1969), with a later clarification of the theory (1995). The theory focuses on the process that organizations undergo in their attempt to make sense out of all the information that bombards them on a daily basis. Often the process results in changes in the organization and its members. In fact, Weick states, "Organizations and their environments change so rapidly that it is unrealistic to show what they are like now, because that's not the way they're going to be later" (1969, p. 1). According to this approach, it would be unrealistic to try to depict what a college or university and its surrounding environment look like today because it is likely that they will change. The major fields of study chosen by students may change as organizations' needs for employees change. Consider, for instance, the early 1990s. To assist them in making changes in their computer systems, many companies were seeking graduates in the fields of computer technology and management information systems. Today, however, as a result of the "dot com" bust in the late 1990s, many of these same individuals are either underemployed or employed in an area outside their major field of study. As you can see, once a problem is solved, the hiring needs of organizations frequently change.

The focus of Organizational Information Theory is on the communication of information that is vital in determining the success of an organization (Eisenberg, 2007). It is quite rare that one person or one department in an organization has all the information necessary to complete a project. This knowledge typically comes from a variety of sources. However, the task of information processing is not completed simply by attaining information; the difficult part is in deciphering and distributing the information that is gained. To understand this process better, we will discuss how two major perspectives influenced OIT: General Systems Theory and the Theory of Sociocultural Evolution.

General Systems Theory

To explain the influence of information from an organization's external environments and to understand the influence that an organization has on its external environments, Weick applied General Systems Theory in the development of his approach to studying how organizations manage information. As you recall from Chapter 3 in our discussion on General Systems Theory, Ludwig von Bertalanffy is most frequently associated with the systems approach. von Bertalanffy believed that patterns and wholes exist across different types of phenomena. To this end, he proposed that when there is a disruption in one part of a system, it affects the entire system. In sum, systems theorists argue that there are complex patterns of interaction among the parts of a system, and understanding these interactions will help us understand the entire system.

Systems thinking is especially useful in understanding the interrelationships that exist among various organizational units. Organizations are usually made up of different departments, teams, or groups. Although these units may focus on independent tasks, the goals of the organization as a whole typically require sharing and integrating the information that each of the teams has to arrive at a solution or conclusion. Organizations depend on combined information so that they can make any necessary adjustments in order to reach their goal. They may need additional information, they may need to send information to other departments or people within the organization, or they may need outside consultants to make sense of the information. If one team fails to address the information needed to fulfill its obligation in the completion of the project, achieving the final goal will probably be delayed for the entire organization.

In the opening scenario, we learned that the Phoenix team was responsible for collecting information from NowBank customers in order to identify their level of knowledge about the Y2K conversion. The team from Dallas was responsible for developing a publicity plan to gain public confidence that NowBank's computers would be compatible for the year 2000. However, the Dallas team could not begin to develop its campaign until it received information about the issues that concerned the customers. If the Phoenix team was not efficient in providing this information, the entire process would be delayed.

An important component of General Systems Theory, and one that is essential to making sense of information in an organization, is feedback, which is information that is received by an organization and its members. It's important to remember that this information can be either positive or negative. The organization and its members can then choose to use the information to maintain the current state of the organization or can decide to initiate some changes in accordance with the goals that the system is trying to accomplish. It is through feedback that units are able to determine if the information that is being transmitted is clear and sufficient to achieve the desired goals.

In the NowBank example, the Dallas team needs to provide feedback to Phoenix that the Dallas team needs the customer information by a specific deadline. If the deadline is not possible, Phoenix will provide feedback to request a later date. This process is likely to continue until a deadline is agreed on that is feasible for both teams. It is apparent that both teams are dependent on each other for feedback that is essential to meeting their project deadlines.

The decision of the organization to request or provide feedback reflects a selective choice made by the group in an effort to accomplish its goals. If an organization hopes to survive and accomplish its goals, it will continue to engage in cycles of feedback to obtain necessary information and reduce its uncertainty about the best way to accomplish its goals. This process reflects a Darwinian approach to how organizations manage information, as we discuss next.

Darwin's Theory of Sociocultural Evolution

A second perspective that has been used to describe the process by which organizations collect and make sense out of information is the **theory of sociocultural evolution.** You may have heard of the "survival of the fittest," which is an apt phrase to describe the theory. The eventual goal of any organization is survival, and, like humans, it works to discover the best strategies for getting by. Although this approach is used to describe the social interactions that take place in an organization with regard to making sense out of information, its origins are in the field of biology.

theory of sociocultural evolution
Darwin's belief that only the fittest can survive challenging surroundings

The theory of evolution was originally developed to describe the adaptation processes that living organisms undergo in order to thrive in a challenging ecological environment. Charles Darwin (1948) explained these adaptations in terms of mutations that allow organisms to cope with their various surroundings. Some organisms could not adapt and died, whereas others made changes and prospered. Taking the example of Dominique Martin and the Y2K computer challenge, it has been suggested that companies that took steps to manage the information and convert their systems to accommodate the new millennium have a greater chance to prosper and thrive. Those who did not make the attempt to adapt to the changing environment may be faced with severe consequences.

Campbell (1965) extends this theory to explain the processes by which organizations and their members adapt to their social surroundings. The sociocultural theory of evolution examines the changes people make in their social behaviors and expectations to adapt to changes in their social surroundings.

Consider the scenario at the beginning of this chapter. Suppose that Dominique had a team of representatives from NowBank's offices in Japan involved in this project. If she wanted to make a quick decision on how to address the Y2K changes in the Japanese offices, her first tendency would likely be to employ a communication style that U.S. employees would perceive as efficient. However, she would soon realize that the Japanese approach to business is quite different from that practiced in the United States. Instead of quickly presenting the facts and signing on the dotted line, Japanese bank employees prefer an approach that emphasizes the development of rapport. Only after the relationship has been developed would the issue of signing an agreement have been presented. Dominique must engage in the process of sociocultural evolution to adapt to the norms and expectations of her overseas team.

Weick adapts sociocultural evolution to explain the process that organizations undergo in adjusting to various information pressures. These pressures may be the result of information overload or ambiguity. Although the evolutionary approach is useful in describing the adaptations that are necessary to process information, General Systems Theory is also an essential piece in this puzzle because it highlights the interrelatedness among organizational teams, departments, and employees in the processing of information. We now continue our discussion of Organizational Information Theory and identify its underlying assumptions.

Assumptions of Organizational Information Theory

Organizational Information Theory is one way of explaining how organizations make sense out of information that is confusing or ambiguous. It focuses on the process of organizing members of an organization to manage information rather than on the structure of the organization itself. A number of assumptions underlie this theory:

- Human organizations exist in an information environment.
- The information an organization receives differs in terms of equivocality.
- Human organizations engage in information processing to reduce equivocality of information.

The first assumption states that organizations depend on information in order to function effectively and accomplish their goals. Weick (1979) views the concept of information environment as distinct from the physical surroundings in which an organization is housed. He proposes that these information environments are created by the members of the organization. They establish goals that require them to obtain information from both internal and external sources. However, these inputs differ in terms of their level of understandability.

Consider the university admissions office example. A school can use numerous channels to gain information about student needs: It may develop a website to answer prospective students' questions and to solicit student feedback; it may conduct surveys at high school academic fairs to gain more information about student desires; it may host focus group interviews with current students to find out their needs and concerns; or it may ask alumni to provide examples from their educational experiences to attract future students. Once it has received messages from all of these external sources, the university must decide how to communicate messages internally to establish and accomplish its goals for current and future students. The possibilities for information are endless, and the university must decide how to manage all the available potential messages.

The second assumption proposed by Weick focuses on the ambiguity that exists in information: Messages differ in terms of their understandability. An organization needs to determine which of its members are most knowledgeable or experienced in dealing with particular information that is obtained. A plan to make sense of the information needs to be established.

At NowBank, it is likely that the publicity team will be able to comprehend and make sense out of the information that is provided by the customer survey team. However, when they receive messages from the computer technician team, the publicity team may not understand the content of the messages and how it applies or relates to their portion of the project. Messages, according to Weick's theory, are frequently equivocal. **Equivocality** refers to messages that are complicated, uncertain, and unpredictable. Equivocal messages are often sent in organizations. Because these messages are not clearly understood, people need to develop a framework or plan for reducing their ambiguity about the message.

equivocality
the extent to which organizational messages are uncertain, ambiguous, or unpredictable

You may be tempted to think that equivocality is ineffectual in an organization. Yet, as Eric Eisenberg (2007) thoughtfully reminds us, equivocality is not necessarily problematic. He states that rather than viewing equivocality as difficult, "Weick turned this idea on its head, arguing instead that equivocality is *the* engine that motivates people to organize" (p. 274). Eisenberg further clarifies that equivocality may "make coordinated action possible" (p. 274). When individuals in an organization reduce equivocality, they engage in a process that tries to make sense out of excessive information received by the organization. We delve further into equivocation a few more times later in the chapter.

In an attempt to reduce the ambiguity of information, the third assumption of the theory proposes that organizations engage in joint activity to make information that is received more understandable. Weick (1979) sees the process of reducing equivocality as a joint activity among members of an organization. It is not the sole responsibility of one person to reduce equivocality. Rather, this is a process that may involve several members of the organization. Consider the NowBank example. Each department needs to use information from other departments, but they also need to provide information to these same departments to accomplish the tasks necessary to meet the organization's Y2K goal. This illustrates the extent to which departments in an organization may depend on one another to reduce their ambiguity. An ongoing cycle of communicating feedback takes place in which there is a mutual give-and-take of information.

Key Concepts and Conceptualizing Information

Weick's theory of Organizational Information contains a number of key concepts that are critical to an understanding of the theory. They include information environment, rules, and cycles. We now explore each in detail.

Information Environment: The Sum Total

Information environment is an integral part of Weick's theory. Information environment is a core concept in understanding how organizations are formed as well as how they process information. Every day, we are faced with literally thousands of stimuli that we could potentially process and interpret. However, it is unrealistic to think that an organization or its members could possibly

Research Notes

Miller, K. M., Joseph, L., & Apker, J. (2000). Strategic ambiguity in the role development process. *Journal of Applied Communication Research, 28,* 193–214.

This is a case analysis of a hospital system and how the roles of its nurses have been defined. Believing that the health-care system is undergoing a significant transformation in the twenty-first century, the research team examined the "care coordinator role," which was instituted in a "strategically ambiguous way" (p. 207). The role required sense making, a key element in Weick's theory. The nurses in this research were not only care coordinators but also tried to make sense of the ambiguous nature of their role and were "grounded in identity construction" (p. 207). The nurses noted that there was insufficient training for the role and not enough ongoing learning opportunities as they encountered professional changes. Miller and her colleagues provide theoretical implications of their findings and offer several suggestions for future research.

Taylor, J. R., & Van Every, E. J. (2000). *The emergent organization: Communication as its site and surface.* Mahwah, NJ: Erlbaum.

This book is an articulate foundation from which to understand Organizational Information Theory. The authors provide readers with the fundamental belief that organizations are realized through rules and routines.

The book is organized into two parts, and each chapter delves deeply into both relevant and ancillary topics related to Organizational Information Theory. Of particular interest, Taylor and Van Every argue that an organization is a "site . . . [as a result] of the sensemaking activities of its members, endlessly renegotiated" (p. 33). To this end, the authors spend the remainder of the book trying to make sense of organizational life and the frequent layers of meaning pertaining to the discourses occurring every day.

Taylor and Van Every believe that there is a "profound ambiguity in Weick's thinking" (p. 244) and try to clarify some portions of Organizational Information Theory. In particular, they point out some deficiencies with the notion of enactment, a key stage in reducing equivocality.

The book attempts to remain communicative in focus, with continued linkage to the communication discipline and communication theory specifically. The book provides those who study organizational life with an understanding of how influential the communication process is in organizations.

---

information environment
the availability of all stimuli in an organization

process all the information that is available. Thus, we are faced with the tasks of selecting information that is meaningful or important and focusing our senses on processing those cues. The availability of all stimuli is considered to be the **information environment**. Organizations are composed of information that is vital to their formation and continues to be essential to their existence. For example, the Y2K project team was formed as a result of information about concerns over the capacity of computers to deal with the date change at the start of the new millennium. There was enough information received by the NowBank organization that a smaller organization (the project team) was formed to manage this knowledge. Now the Y2K organization depends on additional information to solve the problem and reach its goal.

Essentially, organizations have two primary tasks to perform in order to successfully manage these multiple sources of information: (1) They must interpret the external information that exists in their information environment, and (2) they must coordinate that information to make it meaningful for the

members of the organization and its goals. These interpretation processes require the organization to reduce the equivocality or ambiguity of the information to make it meaningful.

Rules: Guidelines to Analyze

Weick (1979) proposes two communication strategies that are essential if the organization hopes to reduce message equivocality. The first strategy requires that organizations determine the rules for reducing the level of equivocality of the message inputs as well as for choosing the appropriate response to the information received. In Organizational Information Theory, **rules** refer to the guidelines that an organization has established for analyzing the equivocality of a message as well as for guiding responses to information. For example, if any of the Y2K team leaders experience ambiguity over the information that is provided to them from the computer technicians, they are instructed to contact the technician team leader for clarification. If they were to contact Dominique first, an additional step would be added to the process of reducing equivocality because she would have to contact the technicians and then report back to the team leaders. Recall the example of the university admissions office, which conducted research in order to design materials that appeal to students. As a result, when it receives information from students inquiring about the university, the rule that it applies in dealing with the information environment is to respond to that message by sending out their informational brochure. Both organizations have rules for determining the equivocality of the information and for identifying the appropriate way in which they should respond to the messages.

Weick provides examples of rules that might cause an organization to choose one cycle of information or feedback over another for reducing the equivocality of messages. These rules include duration, personnel, success, and effort. Examples of duration and personnel rules guiding communication can be seen in our opening story. **Duration** refers to a choice made by an organization to engage in communication that can be completed in the least amount of time. For example, NowBank has rules that state who should be contacted to clarify

rules
guidelines in organizations as they review responses to equivocal information

duration
organizational rule stating that decisions regarding equivocality should be made in the least amount of time

technical information. These rules prevent people from asking those who are not knowledgeable on the topic. In establishing these rules, NowBank increases its efficiency by having employees go directly to the person who can provide the necessary information, thus eliminating delays that might result from having to channel questions through several different people. In doing so, NowBank is also guided by the rule of **personnel.** This rule states that people who are the most knowledgeable should emerge as key resources to reduce equivocality. Computer technicians, not human resources personnel, are consulted to reduce equivocality of technical information associated with the Y2K project.

When an organization chooses to employ a plan of communication that has been proved effective in the past at reducing equivocality of information, **success** is the influential rule that is being applied. A university knows that many of its potential students' questions and concerns can be answered via a well-researched brochure. It has proved to be a successful recruiting tool in the past, as the enrollment figures of the school have increased by 4 percent per year over the past five years. Thus, the university knows that this is a successful way of reducing information ambiguity for students.

Effort is also a rule that influences the choice to use a brochure to promote the university. This rule guides organizations in choosing an information strategy that requires the least amount of effort to reduce equivocality. Rather than fielding numerous phone calls from potential students asking the same questions about the school, the university's decision to print a brochure that answers frequently asked questions is the most efficient means of communicating all the university has to offer. The decision made by many companies to implement automated telephone customer service is another example of how organizations reduce equivocality of information. Rather than requiring a customer to explain the reason for the call multiple times, as the customer is connected to various employees, the customer chooses a number that best matches the problem or concern. This directs the customer directly to the appropriate department.

Cycles: Act, Respond, Adjust

If the information that is received is highly equivocal, the organization may engage in a series of communication behaviors in an attempt to decrease the level of ambiguity. Weick labels these systems of behavior **cycles.** The more equivocal the message, the more cycles needed to reduce equivocation (Herrmann, 2007). The cycle of communication behaviors used to reduce equivocality includes three stages: act, response, and adjustment. An **act** refers to the communication statements and behaviors used to indicate one's ambiguity. For example, Dominique may say to the computer technician, "The customer research team wants to know if the compatibility of customers' personal computers could potentially impact their ability to effectively conduct transactions online." In deciding to share her ambiguity with the computer technician directly, Dominique is employing the rule of personnel.

A second step in the communication cycle is response. **Response** is defined as a reaction to the act. That is, a response that seeks clarification in the equivocal message is provided as a result of the act. The technician might reply, "It

---

personnel
organizational rule stating that the most knowledgeable workers should resolve equivocality

success
organizational rule stating that a successful plan of the past will be used to reduce current equivocality

effort
organizational rule stating that decisions regarding equivocality should be made with the least amount of work

cycles
series of communication behaviors that serve to reduce equivocality

act
communication behaviors indicating a person's ambiguity in receiving a message

response
reaction to equivocality

is essential that customers contact their computer manufacturer to see if their machines are Y2K compatible. If they're not, they may experience difficulty in using our online banking services even though our computers are compatible."

As a result of the response, the organization formulates a response in return as a result of any **adjustment** that has been made to the information that was originally received. If the response to the act has reduced the equivocality of the message, an adjustment is made to indicate that the information is now understood. If the information is still equivocal, the adjustment might come in the form of additional questions designed to clarify the information further. Dominique's response to the technician—"I'll contact the publicity department immediately so they can inform our customers of this new information"— indicates that the equivocality of the original message has been decreased.

adjustment
organizational responses to equivocality

Feedback is an essential step in the process of making sense of the information that is received. Weick uses the term double interact loops to describe the cycles of act, response, and adjustment in information exchanges. **Double interact loops** refer to multiple communication cycles that are used to assist the organization's members in reducing the equivocality of information. These communication cycles are essential for reducing the equivocality of information so that organizational members can make sense of and apply the information to attain their goals. Because these cycles require members in the organization to communicate with one another to reduce the level of ambiguity, Weick suggests that the relationships among individuals in the organization are more important to the process of organizing than the talent or knowledge that any one individual brings to the team. Hence, the General Systems Theory philosophy— "the whole is greater than the sum of its parts"—is apparent.

double interact loops
cycles of an organization (e.g., interviews, meetings) to reduce equivocality

The Principles of Equivocality

By now, we're sure that you are able to see that one central feature of Organizational Information Theory is equivocality. Indeed, it is a critical theme woven throughout the theory, even as the theory has been revisited and refined by scholars (Salem, 2007). In this section, we discuss equivocality by looking at three guiding principles of equivocality and also at ways to reduce this communication process in organizational life.

Organizations use three principles when dealing with equivocality. First, an organization must analyze the relationship among the equivocality of information, the rules the organization has for removing the equivocality, and the cycles of communication that should be used. When analyzing the relationship among these three variables, a few conclusions are possible. If a message is highly equivocal, chances are that the organization has few rules for dealing with the ambiguity. As a result, the organization has to employ a greater number of cycles of communication to reduce the level of equivocality of the information. The organization will examine the degree of equivocality of the information (inputs) it receives and determine if it has sufficient rules that will be of assistance in guiding the cycle of communication that should be employed to reduce the ambiguity.

To exemplify, a technical question is highly equivocal to those who are not trained in the field of expertise. Thus, the organization may not have a set of rules to guide communication responses and may rely solely on one rule (that is, personnel) to guide the cycles of communication. If inputs are easily understood by many members of the organization (for example, a customer may ask, "Is NowBank doing anything to prepare for the Y2K computer problems?"), more rules (that is, success, effort, duration) can be employed in reducing the equivocality. The more equivocal the message, the fewer rules that are available to guide cycles of communication; the less equivocal the message, the more rules that are available to assist the organization in reducing equivocality, thus reducing the number of cycles that are needed to interpret the information.

A second principle proposed by Weick (1979) deals with the association between the number of rules that are needed and the number of cycles that can be used to reduce the equivocality. If the organization has only a few rules available to assist it in reducing equivocality, a greater number of cycles will be needed to filter out the ambiguity. In our chapter-opening example, a majority of the members in the organization view technical information as highly equivocal. The only rule that many of them have for dealing with this equivocality is to communicate with a person who is knowledgeable in the area of technology (personnel). Thus, more cycles of information exchange will be employed between the technician and the organization's employees to reduce the ambiguity of the information. If a large number of rules are available for an organization's members to choose from in reducing equivocality, there is less need for using communication cycles to reduce the ambiguity of an input that is already understood. When there are fewer rules for an organization to use, it must increase the number of cycles it uses to reduce equivocality of information.

The third principle proposed by Weick regards a direct relationship between the number of cycles used and the amount of equivocality that remains. The more cycles that are used to obtain additional information and make adjustments, the more equivocality is removed. Weick proposes that if a larger number of cycles are used, it is more likely that equivocality can be decreased than if only a few cycles are employed.

Although NowBank has increased the potential for equivocality of information by providing its employees with multiple resources for obtaining information about the project's status (videoconferences, telephone conferences, chat areas), it has also provided its employees with a larger number of potential cycles that can be employed to reduce this equivocality. Employees can engage in online dialogues in an attempt to answer their questions and concerns about the project. They can download database files that track the progress of the project and inquire if other teams will be meeting various deadlines that are crucial to their success in the project's completion. And they have the benefit of having an internal communication team to manage all the messages they receive from various sources. Thus, there is the potential for a greater number of cycles that can be used to reduce the equivocality of information.

Reducing Equivocality: Trying to Use the Information

The process of reducing equivocality can be complex. According to Weick (1995), organizations evolve through three stages in an attempt to integrate the rules and cycles so the information can be easily understood and is meaningful. The process of equivocality reduction is essentially an interpersonal process and occurs through the following stages: enactment, selection, and retention.

Enactment: Assigning Message Importance

Enactment refers to how information will be received and interpreted by the organization. Andrew Herrmann (2007) posits that "Enactment starts with the bracketing or framing of a message in the environment by an individual" (p. 18). During this stage, the organization must analyze the inputs it receives to determine the amount of equivocality that is present and to assign meaning to the information. Existing rules are reviewed in making decisions about how the organization will deal with the ambiguity. If the organization determines that it does not have a sufficient number of rules for reducing the equivocality, various cycles of communication must be analyzed to determine their effectiveness in assisting the organization in understanding the information. Weick believes that this action stage is vital to the success of an organization. If a university made no effort to interpret information from potential students, it would not be able to address their concerns and desires in choosing a college to attend effectively. Eric Eisenberg and H. L. Goodall (2004) observe that enactment may be Weick's most "revolutionary" concept (p. 109).

Weick believes that one affiliate of enactment is **sensemaking**, or the attempt to create understanding in situations that are complex and uncertain. For Weick (1995), sensemaking includes "the placement of items into frameworks, comprehending, redressing surprise, constructing meaning, interacting in pursuit of mutual understanding, and patterning" (p. 6). Sensemaking covers many forms of communication, including stories, routines, arguments, symbols, commitments, and other actions and behaviors (Salem, 2007). Although Weick finds sensemaking activities in all three stages (enactment, selection, retention), enactment is most appropriately identified with sensemaking (Eisenberg, 2007).

Selection: Interpreting the Inputs

Once the organization has employed various rules and cycles to interpret the new inputs in its information environment, it must analyze what it knows and choose the best method for obtaining additional information to further reduce the level of equivocality. This stage is referred to as **selection**. In this stage of organizing, the group is required to make a decision about the rules and cycles that will be used. If the information is still ambiguous, the organization has to look into the resources that it has available and determine if it has any additional rules that could help in reducing the ambiguity.

enactment
interpretation of the information received by the organization

sensemaking
creating awareness and understanding in situations that are complex or uncertain

selection
choosing the best method for obtaining information

For instance, imagine Jake is overwhelmed with a task that was assigned to him by his boss. As he considers all the inputs required of him, Jake becomes visibly agitated and anxious. He has one week to report back to his supervisor and he is entering a time period at work during which he is constantly interrupted by colleagues seeking his assistance. His perception of being inundated has resulted in his dealing with a project that has a high degree of equivocality. As he oversees the project, he has to attend several meetings, which, interestingly, result in additional information and additional ambiguity. If Jake is to reduce his feeling of being overwhelmed, he will have to develop a plan to obtain information and disseminate it appropriately in order to finish the task. Reviewing organizational rules regarding communication channels may assist Jake as he manages the inputs. In this case, his selection process will be instrumental in his reduction of equivocality. As an organizational member, his expertise will also be quite important in the equivocality decline (Weick & Sutcliffe, 2007).

Retention: Remember the Small Stuff

retention
collective memory allowing people to accomplish goals

Once the organization has reviewed its ability to deal with ambiguity, it analyzes the effectiveness of the rules and cycles of communication and engages in **retention.** In the retention stage, the organization stores information for later use. This stage requires organizations to look at what to deal with and what to ignore or leave alone. If a particular rule or cycle was beneficial in assisting the organization in reducing the equivocality of information, it's likely that it will be used to guide the organization in future decisions of a similar nature. Suppose that Dominique found the videoconferences to result in even more confusion among the team members because they were bombarded with more information than was either desired or required to complete various tasks in the project. She will retain that valuable insight and likely refrain from using the technology as a means of sharing project information in the future. Instead, she may choose to use online discussions to allow team members to choose the information essential to their portion of the task and skip over information that is of little relevance to them. If strategies for dealing with equivocality are deemed to be useful, they will be retained for future use.

Integration, Critique, and Closing

Karl Weick's Organizational Information Theory has been identified as a powerful theoretical framework for explaining how organizations make sense of the information they receive for their existence. The theory draws from other theoretical perspectives that explain the processes that organizations undergo to receive input from others. Weick emphasizes the importance of human interaction in information processing, thus, centralizing communication as a key focus of the "theoretical latticework" (Herrmann, 2007, p. 18) associated with OIT.

T*I*P

Integration

| Communication Tradition | Rhetorical | Semiotic | Phenomenological | **Cybernetic** | Socio-Psychological | Socio-Cultural | Critical |

| Communication Context | Intrapersonal | Interpersonal | Small Group | **Organizational** | Public/Rhetorical | Mass/Media | Cultural |

| Approach to Knowing | **Positivistic/Empirical** | Interpretive/Hermeneutic | Critical |

Critique

| Evaluation Criteria | Scope | **Logical Consistency** | Parsimony | **Utility** | Testability | **Heurism** | Test of Time |

Logical Consistency

Recall that theories must make sense and make clear the concepts under discussion. Weick's theory seems to fail the test of logical consistency. One prevailing criticism pertains to the belief that people are guided by rules in an organization. Yet organizational scholars note that "we puzzle and mull over, fret and stew over, and generally select, manipulate, and transform meaning to come up with an interpretation of a situation" (Daniels, Spiker, & Papa, 2008, p. 114). In other words, some organizational members may have little interest in the communication rules in place at work. Individuals are not always so conscious or precise in their selection procedures, and their actions may have more to do with their intuition than with organizational rules. As employees become more immersed in the organizational milieu, they may be guided more by instinct if that instinct is accurate, ethical, and thoughtful.

An additional criticism underscoring the problems of logical consistency is that Organizational Information Theory views organizations as static units in society (Taylor & Van Every, 2000). These researchers challenge Weick's view by noting that "at no point are inherent contradictions in organizational structure and process even remotely evoked" (p. 275) in his research. Organizations have ongoing tensions, and these need to be identified and examined in light of Weick's claims. Furthermore, given the dynamic changes in organizations due to corporate mergers, downsizing, offshore outsourcing of employee work, and the evolution of technology, static or frozen assessments of organizations are shortsighted.

With his model of organizational organizing, Karl Weick has provided communication scholars an understanding of how decisions are made and the key processes pertaining to those decisions. As individuals encounter an organization, they need to understand the communication processes taking place. As OIT continues to be refined, centralizing communication will be instrumental. As Eric Eisenberg (2007) states, "Weick's most valuable contributions have been his insistence on the centrality of language and communication in the construction of organizational reality, and his sustained focus on communication as a site for improving our understanding of cognition, culture, and social interaction (p. 284).

Utility

The theory's utility is underscored by its focus on the communication process. Organizational Information Theory focuses on the *process* of communication rather than on the role of communicators themselves. This is of great benefit in understanding how members of an organization engage in collaborative efforts with both internal and external environments to understand the information they receive. Rather than attempt to understand the people in an organization—and their unpredictability—Weick decides to unravel the complexities of information processing, which makes this a rather useful theoretical undertaking.

Heurism

Organizational Information Theory is heuristic and has prompted considerable scholarly discussion. The theory has inspired thinking in research on a variety of topics, including environmental flooding (Ulmer, Sellnow, & Seeger, 2007), nomadic work (Bean & Eisenberg, 2006), online financial communities (Herrmann, 2007), and cohesion in the U.S. Army (Van Epps, 2008). Charles Bantz (1989) observes that in terms of Weick's influence on research overall, "it is not surprising that a variety of scholars picked up the organizing concept directly from Weick or integrated it into their on-going research" (p. 233). Weick clearly was influential in the work of organizational communication scholars.

Karl Weick has centralized the notion of organizational ambiguity and his theory resonates today. Organizational Information Theory continues to attract theorists and practitioners interested in the intersection of organizations, messages, and people. To that end, the theory will have even more importance as the United States prepares itself for significant corporate changes in the twenty-first century.

Discussion Starters

1. Based on your understanding of the concepts of Organizational Information Theory, what additional avenues could Dominique engage in to facilitate a solution to the Y2K problem in NowBank? Respond using at least two concepts discussed in the chapter.

2. Recall an organization in which you are or were a member. Can you remember an incident when you or the organization received ambiguous information? If so, what rules did you or the organization use in dealing with this equivocality?

3. Weick describes the process of enactment, selection, and retention to understand how organizations deal with information inputs. Provide an example of how your school has employed these strategies in making sense of information on your campus.

4. Discuss the importance of the principle of requisite variety in dealing with ambiguity. Do you think that highly equivocal information requires more complex communication processes in order to make sense of the input? Defend your answer.

5. Does your college or university solicit feedback from students regarding its promotion of the organization? Discuss the methods that your school uses.

6. Discuss how organizational rules function in OIT.

7. Apply equivocality to an organization with which you are familiar.

Online Learning Center   www. mhhe.com/west4e

Visit the Online Learning Center at www.mhhe.com/west4e for chapter-specific resources, such as story-into-theory and multiple-choice quizzes, as well as theory summaries and theory connection questions.

The Public

WHEN WE LISTEN TO A SPEECH, WATCH A PLAY, participate in a conversation, or consume media, we are members of an audience. We are the public. As audience members, we act out the transactional nature of communication discussed in Chapter 1. We simultaneously serve as both sender and receiver of messages. Both verbal and nonverbal communication, therefore, are important in audience-centered messages.

The public is at the core of the three theories we selected for this section of the book. As one of the classic works of the Western world, the *Rhetoric* is an attempt to show speakers that to be persuasive with their audiences, they should follow some suggestions. This advice includes looking at the speech, considering the speaker, and analyzing the audience. Dramatism pertains to the important role that the public plays in persuasion. Dramatists believe that unless the audience identifies with the speaker, persuasion is not possible. The Narrative Paradigm proposes to look at the audience as participants in a storytelling experience. Narrative theorists contend that a person's stories are effective when they appeal to a listener's values.

The public in communication theory refers to how we—as listeners, consumers, and audiences—play a role in deciding the extent to which others will affect us. Reading about the theories in this section will introduce you to several noteworthy topics related to the audience, including audience analysis, speech effectiveness, speaker integrity, credibility, and character.

CHAPTER 18

The *Rhetoric*

Based on the writings of **Aristotle**

Camille Ramirez

Camille Ramirez knew that she would have to take a public speaking course for her major. Although she had been active in high school—serving as treasurer for the student council and playing on the lacrosse team—she had never done any public speaking. Now that she was in her second semester at the university, she wanted to get the required course out of the way, so she had enrolled in Public Speaking 101.

The class seemed to be going quite well. She felt fairly confident about her speaking abilities; she had received two As and one B on her speeches so far. The final speech, however, would be her most challenging. It was a persuasive speech, and she decided that she would speak on the dangers of drinking and driving. The topic was a personal one for Camille because she would talk about her Uncle Jake, a wonderful man who had died last year in an accident with a drunk driver. As she prepared for the speech, she thought that she would blend both emotion and logic into her presentation. Camille also thought that she would have to identify both sides of the drinking issue—the desire to let loose and the need to be responsible.

On the day of her speech, Camille took several deep breaths before the class started; it was a strategy that had worked before her previous speeches. As she approached the lectern, she could feel the butterflies well up in her stomach. She reminded herself about the topic and its personal meaning. So, as planned, she began with a short story about her favorite time with Uncle Jake—the time they went to Philadelphia to see the Liberty Bell. Camille then talked about the night—two weeks after her trip—that her uncle died; he was driving home from his daughter's soccer game, and a drunk driver slammed his car from behind, forcing Jake to the embankment. His car then slid into a pond where he drowned.

The room was silent as Camille finished the story. She proceeded to identify why she was speaking on the topic. She told the group that considering their classroom was filled with people under the age of 25, it was important that they understand how fragile life is. Her words resonated with the group. For the next five minutes, Camille mentioned her Uncle Jake several times as she repeated the importance of not drinking and getting behind the wheel of a car.

Camille felt relieved as she finished her speech. She thought that she had done a decent job with her assignment, and she also felt that it helped her to be able to talk about her uncle again. After class, several of Camille's classmates came up and congratulated her. They told her that it took a lot of guts to talk about such a personal subject in front of so many people. A few of them also commented that they felt her topic was perfect for the audience; in fact, one of her classmates said that he wanted Camille to give the same speech to his fraternity brothers. As Camille walked to her dorm, she couldn't help but think that she had made a difference and that the speech was both a personal and a professional success.

Modern life is filled with opportunities to speak in front of others. Politics and education, in particular, are areas where people spend much of their time speaking to others. Studying public speaking and communication in general is important in U.S. society for several reasons. First, The National Association of Colleges and Employers (2008) notes that communication skills are paramount to securing and maintaining a job. Second, public speaking, by definition, suggests that as a society we are receptive to listening to views that may conflict with our own. Third, when one speaks before a group, the information resonates beyond that group of people. For instance, when a politician speaks to a small group of constituents in southwest Missouri, what she says frequently gets told and retold to others. When a minister consoles her congregation after a fatal shooting at a local middle school, the words reverberate even into the living rooms of those who were not present at the service. Finally, effective communication is identified as paramount in communication among individuals from various parts of the globe (Rudd, 2007). Clearly, public speaking has the ability to affect individuals beyond the listening audience, and it is a critical skill in a democratic society.

Despite the importance of public speaking in our lives, it remains a dreaded activity. In fact, some opinion polls state that people fear public speaking more than they fear death! Comedian Jerry Seinfeld reflects on this dilemma: "According to most studies, people's number one fear is public speaking. Number two is death. Death is number two. Does that seem right? This means to the average person, if you have to go to a funeral, you're better off in the casket than doing the eulogy" (Seinfeld, 1993, p. 120).

Public speaking is not so funny to people like Camille Ramirez. She must work through not only her anxiety about speaking before a group but also her anxiety about discussing a very personal topic. For Camille, having a sense of what to speak about and what strategies to adopt are foremost in her mind. Based on her classmates' reactions, her speech is quite effective. Camille may not know that the reasons for her success may lie in the writings of Aristotle, published more than twenty-five centuries ago.

Aristotle is generally credited with explaining the dynamics of public speaking. The *Rhetoric* consists of three books—one primarily concerned with public speakers, the second focusing on the audience, and the third attending to the speech itself. His *Rhetoric* is considered by historians, philosophers, and communication experts to be one of the most influential pieces of writing in the Western world. In addition, many still consider Aristotle's works to be the most significant writing on speech preparation and speech making. In a sense, Aristotle was the first to provide the "how to" for public speaking. Lane Cooper (1932) agrees. More than seventy-five years ago, Cooper observed that "the rhetoric of Aristotle is a practical psychology, and the most helpful book extant for writers of prose and for speakers of every sort" (p. vi). According to Cooper, people in all walks of life—attorneys, legislators, clergy, teachers, and media writers—can benefit in some way when they read Aristotle's writings. That is some accolade for a man who has been dead for over 2,500 years!

To understand the power behind Aristotle's words, it's important first to understand the nature of the *Rhetoric*. In doing so, we will be able to present the simple eloquence of rhetorical theory. First, we present a brief history of life in Aristotle's day followed by a discussion of his definition of rhetoric.

The Rhetorical Tradition

The son of a physician, Aristotle was encouraged to be a thinker about the world around him. He went to study with his mentor, Plato, at the age of 17. Aristotle and Plato had conflicting worldviews; therefore, their philosophies differed as well. Plato was always in search of absolute truths about the world. He didn't care much whether these truths had practical value. Plato felt that as long as people could agree on matters of importance, society would survive. Aristotle, however, was more interested in dealing with the here and now. He wasn't as interested in achieving absolute truth as he was in attaining a logical, realistic, and rational view of society. In other words, we could argue that Aristotle was much more grounded than Plato, trying to understand the various types of people in Athenian society.

Because he taught diverse groups of people in Greek society, Aristotle became known as a man committed to helping the ordinary citizen—at the time, a land-owning male. During the day, common citizens (men) were asked to judge murder trials, oversee city boundaries, travel as emissaries, and defend their property against would-be land collectors (Golden, Berquist, Coleman, Sproule, & Golden, 2007). Because there were no professional attorneys at that time, many citizens hired **Sophists,** teachers of public speaking, to instruct them in basic principles of persuasion. These teachers established small schools where they taught students about the public speaking process and where they produced public speaking handbooks discussing practical ways to become more effective public speakers. Aristotle, however, believed that many of these handbooks were problematic in that they focused on the judicial system to the neglect of other contexts. Also, he thought that authors spent too much time on ways to arouse judges and juries: "It is not right to pervert the judge by moving him to anger or envy or pity—one might as well warp a carpenter's rule before using it," Aristotle observes (cited in Rhys & Bywater, 1954, p. 20).

Sophists
teachers of public speaking (rhetoric) in ancient Greece

Aristotle reminds speakers not to forget the importance of logic in their presentations.

The *Rhetoric* could be considered Aristotle's way of responding to the problems he saw in these handbooks. Although he challenges a number of prevailing assumptions about what constitutes an effective presentation, what remains especially important is Aristotle's definition of rhetoric: the available means of persuasion. For Aristotle, however, availing oneself of all means of persuasion does not translate into bribery or torture, common practices in ancient Greece, where slavery was institutionalized. What Aristotle envisions and recommends is for speakers to work beyond their first instincts when they want to persuade others. They need to consider all aspects of speech making, including their audience members. When Camille prepared for her speech by assessing both her words and her audience's needs, she was adhering to Aristotle's suggestions for successful speaking.

For some of you, interpreting rhetoric in this way may be unfamiliar. After all, the word has been tossed around by so many different types of people that it may have lost Aristotle's original intent. For instance, Jasper Neel (1994) comments that "the term *rhetoric* has taken on such warm and cuddly connotations in the postmodern era" (p. 15) that we tend to forget that its meaning is very specific. For people like Neel, we must return to Aristotle's interpretation of *rhetoric* or we will miss the essence of his theory. Politicians often indict their opponents by stating that their "rhetoric is empty" or that they're all "rhetoric, with little action." These sorts of criticisms only trivialize the active and dynamic process of rhetoric and its role in the public speaking process.

Assumptions of the *Rhetoric*

To this end, let's examine two primary assumptions of Rhetorical Theory as proposed by Aristotle. You should be aware that Rhetorical Theory covers a wide range of thinking in the communication field, and so it is nearly impossible to capture all of the beliefs associated with the theory. Nonetheless, Aristotelian theory is guided by the following two assumptions:

- Effective public speakers must consider their audience.
- Effective public speakers use a number of proofs in their presentations.

The first assumption underscores the definition of communication that we presented in Chapter 1: Communication is a transactional process. Within a public speaking context, Aristotle suggests that the speaker–audience relationship must be acknowledged. Speakers should not construct or deliver their speeches without considering their audiences. Speakers should, in a sense, become audience-centered. They should think about the audience as a group of individuals with motivations, decisions, and choices and not as some undifferentiated mass of homogeneous people. The effectiveness of Camille's speech on drinking and driving derived from her ability to understand her audience. She knew that students, primarily under the age of 25, rarely think about death, and, therefore, her speech prompted them to think about something that they normally would not consider. Camille, like many other public speakers, engaged in **audience analysis,** which is the process of evaluating an audience and its background (such as age, sex, educational level, and so forth) and tailoring one's speech so that listeners respond as the speaker hopes they will.

Aristotle felt that audiences are crucial to a speaker's ultimate effectiveness. He observes, "Of the three elements in speech-making—speaker, subject, and person addressed—it is the last one, the hearer, that determines the speech's end and object" (cited in Roberts, 1984, p. 2159). Each listener, however, is unique, and what works with one listener may fail with another. Expanding on this notion, Carnes Lord (1994) observes that audiences are not always open to rational argument. Consider Camille's speech on drinking and driving. Her speech may have worked wonderfully in the public speaking classroom, but she might have different results with a group of alcohol distributors. As you can see, understanding the audience is critical before a speaker begins constructing his or her speech.

The second assumption underlying Aristotle's theory pertains to what speakers do in their speech preparation and their speech making. Aristotle's proofs refer to the means of persuasion, and, for Aristotle, three proofs exist: ethos, pathos, and logos. **Ethos** refers to the perceived character, intelligence, and goodwill of a speaker as they become revealed through his or her speech. Eugene Ryan (1984) notes that *ethos* is a broad term that refers to the mutual influence that speakers and listeners have on each other. Ryan contends that Aristotle believed that the speaker can be influenced by the audience in much the same way that audiences can be influenced by the speaker. Interviewing ethicist Kenneth Andersen, Pat Arneson (2007) relates Andersen's thoughts about Aristotle and ethos. Ethos, according to Andersen, is "something you create on the occasion" (p. 131). To that end, a speaker's ethos is not simply something that is brought into a speaking experience; it *is* the speaking experience.

Aristotle felt that a speech by a trustworthy individual was more persuasive than a speech by an individual whose trust was in question. Michael Hyde (2004) contends that Aristotle felt that ethos is part of the virtue of another and, therefore, "can be trained and made habitual" (p. xvi). **Logos** is the logical proof that speakers employ—their arguments and rationalizations. For Aristotle, logos involves using a number of practices, including using logical claims and clear language. To speak in poetic phrases results in a lack of clarity and naturalness. **Pathos** pertains to the emotions that are drawn out of listeners. Aristotle argues that listeners become the instruments of proof when emotion is stirred in them; listeners judge differently when they are influenced by joy, pain, hatred, or fear. Let's return to our example of Camille to illustrate these three Aristotelian proofs.

The ethos that Camille evokes during her presentation is important. Relating a personal account of her relationship with her Uncle Jake and describing his subsequent death at the hands of a drunk driver bolster perceptions of her credibility. Undoubtedly, her audience feels that she is a credible speaker by

audience analysis
an assessment and evaluation of listeners

ethos
the perceived character, intelligence, and goodwill of a speaker

logos
logical proof; the use of arguments and evidence in a speech

pathos
emotional proof; emotions drawn from audience members

virtue of her relationship with Jake and her knowledge of the consequences of drinking and driving. Logos is evident in Camille's speech when she decides to logically argue that although drinking is a part of recreation, mixing it with driving can be deadly. Using examples to support her claims underscores Camille's use of logical proof. The pathos inherent in the speech should be apparent from the subject matter. She chooses a topic that appeals to her college listeners. They most likely will feel for Camille and reflect on how many times they or their friends have gotten behind the wheel after having a few drinks. The proofs of Aristotelian theory, therefore, guide Camille's effectiveness.

Each of these three—ethos, logos, and pathos—is critical to speech effectiveness. But each, alone, may not be sufficient. Keep in mind Kenneth Burke's belief that according to Aristotle, "an audience's confidence in the speaker is the most convincing proof of all" (Burke, 2007, p. 335). We look more at Burke's thinking in Chapter 19.

Aristotle delineates logos much further. In his discussion, he notes that speakers who consider logos must necessarily consider syllogisms. We now turn our attention to this critical Aristotelian principle.

Syllogisms: A Three-Tiered Argument

We noted that logos is one of the three proofs that, according to Aristotle, create a more effective message. Nestled in these logical proofs is something called syllogisms. The term requires clarification because there is some debate among scholars on its precise meaning.

Communication scholars have studied the *Rhetoric* and its meaning for years and have attempted to untangle some of Aristotle's words. We look here at the term **syllogism,** defined as a set of propositions that are related to one another and draw a conclusion from the major and minor premises. Typically, syllogisms contain two premises and a conclusion. A syllogism is nothing more than a deductive argument, a group of statements (premises) that lead to another group of statements (conclusions). In other words, premises are starting points or beginners used by speakers. They establish justification for a conclusion. In a syllogism, both major and minor premises exist. Symbolically, a syllogism looks like this:

syllogism
a set of propositions that are related to one another and draw a conclusion from the major and minor premises

$$A \rightarrow B$$

$$B \rightarrow C$$

$$\text{Therefore, } A \rightarrow C$$

Consider this classic example of a syllogism:

Major Premise:	All people are mortal.
Minor Premise:	Aristotle is a person.
Conclusion:	Therefore, Aristotle is mortal.

Let's use the beginning story about Camille and construct a syllogism that she might employ in her speech:

Major Premise:	Drunk driving can kill people.
Minor Premise:	College students drink and drive.
Conclusion:	Therefore, college students can kill others (by drinking and driving).

As a speaker, you might (unwittingly) incorporate syllogisms to persuade your audience. However, in an often complex and convoluted society, drawing such a clear conclusion from preliminary premises may not be appropriate. Syllogistic reasoning may undercut a point you're making. For example, it is usually difficult to draw a clear conclusion when dealing with the behaviors of close friends or family members. Personality, relational history, and timing all intersect to make drawing a simple conclusion quite difficult.

Syllogisms are a critical part of the speaking process for Aristotle. Speakers use them to enhance effectiveness in their speeches. In addition, speakers also incorporate other techniques that are labeled *canons*.

Canons of Rhetoric

Aristotle was convinced that, for a persuasive speech to be effective, speakers must follow certain guidelines or principles, which he called canons. These are recommendations for making a speech more compelling. Classical rhetoricians have maintained Aristotle's observations, and to this day, most writers of public speaking texts in communication follow canons for effective speaking that early Greeks and Romans advocated.

Although his writings in the *Rhetoric* focused on persuasion, these canons have been applied in a number of speaking situations. Five prescriptions for effective oratory exist and we now discuss these canons, which are highlighted in Table 18.1.

Invention

invention
a canon of rhetoric that pertains to the construction or development of an argument related to a particular speech

The first canon is invention. This term can be confusing because invention of a speech does not mean invention in a scientific sense. **Invention** is defined as the construction or development of an argument that is relevant to the purpose of a speech. Invention is discovering all the proofs a speaker plans to use. Invention is broadly interpreted as the body of information and knowledge that a speaker brings to the speaking situation. This stockpile of information can help a speaker in his or her persuasive approaches.

Suppose, for instance, you are presenting a speech on DNA testing. Invention associated with this speech would include appeals woven throughout your speech (for example, "DNA helps living organisms pass along information to their offspring," "DNA is the fundamental blueprint for all life," or "DNA testing has proven to be instrumental in capturing rapists"). In constructing your arguments, you may draw on all these examples.

Table 18.1 Aristotle's Canons of Rhetoric

CANON	DEFINITION	DESCRIPTION
Invention	Integration of reasoning and arguments in speech	Using logic and evidence in speech makes a speech more powerful and more persuasive.
Arrangement	Organization of speech	Maintaining a speech structure—Introduction, Body, Conclusion—bolsters speaker credibility, enhances persuasiveness, and reduces listener frustration.
Style	Use of language in speech	Incorporating style ensures that a speech is memorable and that a speaker's ideas are clarified.
Delivery	Presentation of speech	Effective delivery complements a speaker's words and helps to reduce speaker anxiety.
Memory	Storing information in speaker's mind	Knowing what to say and when to say it eases speaker anxiety and allows a speaker to respond to unanticipated events.

Aids to invention are identified as topics. **Topics,** in this sense, refer to the lines of argument or modes of reasoning a speaker uses in a speech. Speakers may draw on these invention aids as they decide which speaking strategy will persuade their audiences. Topics, therefore, help speakers enhance their persuasiveness.

Speakers look to what are called **civic spaces,** or the metaphorical locations where rhetoric has the opportunity to effect change, "where a speaker can look for 'available means of persuasion'" (Kennedy, 1991, p. 45). Recall, for instance, Camille's decision to talk about drinking and driving in her public speaking class. As she speaks, she defines her terms, looks at opposing arguments, and considers ideas similar to her own. That is, she identifies a "location" in her speech where she is able to adapt to an audience that may be losing attention. Camille does whatever it takes to ensure that she has the chance to persuade her audience.

Arrangement

A second canon identified by Aristotle is called arrangement. **Arrangement** pertains to a speaker's ability to organize a speech. Aristotle felt that speakers should seek out organizational patterns for their speeches to enhance the speech's effectiveness. Artistic unity among different thoughts should be foremost in a speaker's mind. Simplicity should also be a priority because Aristotle believed that there are essentially two parts to a speech: stating the subject and

topics
an aid to invention that refers to the arguments a speaker uses

civic spaces
a metaphor suggesting that speakers have "locations" where the opportunity to persuade others exists

arrangement
a canon of rhetoric that pertains to a speaker's ability to organize a speech

Theory Application in Groups (TAG)

Considering the canon of arrangement, construct a speech on why your school should keep tuition as it is and not raise it. Develop the structure of the speech and specify why you chose your particular arrangement.

finding the proof, or what he calls "demonstrating it" (Kennedy, 1991, p. 258). At the time, he felt that speakers were organizing their speeches haphazardly, making them less effective speakers.

Aristotle, however, is very clear in his organizational strategy. Speeches should generally follow a threefold approach: introduction, body, and conclusion. The **introduction** should first gain the audience's attention, then suggest a connection with the audience, and finally provide an overview of the speech's purpose.

Introductions can be quite effective in speeches that are intended to arouse emotionally. Gaining attention by incorporating emotional wording is an effective persuasive technique. Consider Camille's introductory words. She obviously captures the audience's attention by personalizing a very difficult subject. She then suggests her relationship with the topic, followed by an overview of her speaking purpose:

> Jake McCain was killed by someone he didn't know. Jake was a wonderful man and the person who killed him never knew that. Yet, Jake's death could have been prevented. You see, he was killed by someone who was drunk. The driver may have a future, but Jake will never have a chance to see his grandchild grow up or see his sister get married. I know about Jake McCain: He's my uncle. Today, I wish to discuss the dangers of drunk driving and identify how you can avoid becoming one of the many thousands who get behind a wheel after drinking too much.

Arrangement also includes the body and conclusion of the speech. The **body** includes all of the arguments, supporting details, and necessary examples to make a point. In addition to the entire speech being organized, the body of the speech also follows some sort of organizational structure. Aristotle states that audiences need to be led from one point to another.

Finally, the **conclusion** or epilogue of a speech is aimed at summarizing the speaker's points and arousing emotions in the audience. Conclusions should be arrived at logically and should also attempt to reconnect with listeners. Camille's conclusion clearly demonstrates her desire to leave her listeners with a message:

> So I leave you today after examining the prevalence of drunk driving, the current laws associated with this behavior, and what you and I can personally do to help rid our society of this terrible and overlooked part of being a college student. The next time you go and have a drink, don't

introduction
part of an organizational strategy in a speech that includes gaining the audience's attention, connecting with the audience, and providing an overview of the speaker's purpose

body
part of an organizational strategy in a speech that includes arguments, examples, and important details to make a point

conclusion
part of an organizational strategy in a speech that is aimed at summarizing a speaker's main points and arousing emotions in an audience

forget to give your keys to a friend. Or get a cab. I'm sure your family will thank you. Do it for me. Do it for my Uncle Jake.

We can feel Camille's passion for a topic that is both personal and personally difficult.

Style

The use of language to express ideas in a certain manner is called **style.** In his discussion of style, Aristotle includes word choice, word imagery, and word appropriateness. He believes that each type of rhetoric has its own style, yet style is often overlooked. He notes that strange words or **glosses** (outdated words and phrases, such as "colored person" or "girl Friday") should be avoided. Speaking in terms that are too simplistic will also turn off an audience. To bridge this gap between the unfamiliar and the too familiar, Aristotle introduces the notion of **metaphor,** or a figure of speech that helps to make the unclear more understandable. Metaphors are critical devices to employ in speeches, according to Aristotle, because they have the capacity to "alter the content and activities of one's mind" (Moran, 1996, p. 391).

Style can be better understood through an example from Camille's speech on drunk driving. If Camille were concentrating on style, her speech would have the following passage:

> Drinking is often looked at as a means to release. After a very long day at work or at school, there is nothing as soothing as a cold beer. So they say. Yet too often one beer turns into two, which by the end of a few hours, has turned into a six-pack. And the result can be tragic: How many times have you watched your friend or family member get into a car after a six-pack? This person can be as dangerous as a bullet, unleashed from a gun that is randomly pointed at someone. If you must drink, it's not only your business; but, now, it's our business, too.

Camille's words evoke some strong imagery; mentally, we can re-create the scene that she has laid out. Her word choice is unmistakable in that she uses familiar words. Finally, she uses the compelling metaphor of a bullet.

Memory

Storing invention, arrangement, and style in a speaker's mind is **memory.** In contrast to the previous four canons, Aristotle does not spend significant time delineating the importance of memory in speech presentation. Rather, he alludes to memory in his writings. Throughout the *Rhetoric,* for instance, Aristotle reminds us to consider a number of issues prior to the presentation (such as examples, signs, metaphors, delivery techniques, and so on). He further notes that to speak persuasively a speaker has to have a basic understanding of many of these devices when constructing and presenting a speech. In other words, speakers need to have memorized a great deal before getting up to speak.

style
a canon of rhetoric that includes the use of language to express ideas in a speech

glosses
outdated words in a speech

metaphor
a figure of speech that helps to make the unclear more understandable

memory
a canon of rhetoric that refers to a speaker's effort in storing information for a speech

Research Notes

Behnke, R. R., & Sawyer, C. R. (2004). Public speaking anxiety as a function of sensitization and habituating processes. *Communication Education, 53,* 164–173.

This study examines the role of communication apprehension in public speaking. Habituation is defined as the moment "when anxiety decreases with time due to repeated or prolonged exposures to a stimulus" (p. 165). Sensitization "reflects an increase in responsiveness produced by highly potent stimuli" (p. 165). Specifically, the researchers looked at beginning public speakers in an undergraduate class; 109 students made up this study. An inventory examining anxiety was given, which was based on four periods ("anxiety milestones") in the speaking process: anticipation (one minute before speech), confrontation (first minute of speech), adaptation (last minute of speech), and release (the minute immediately following the speech). Participants delivered a 5-minute informative speech about a hobby or favorite activity to a group of classmates.

Those called upon to speak first showed quite a bit of anxiety. Only after the confrontational stage was under way did habituation processes allow for a reduction in anxiety. In fact, the findings show that the last few minutes of the speech-making process were not related to overall level of performance anxiety.

These results prompted Behnke and Sawyer to comment that "communication teachers should be enjoined to minimize the anxiety students experience during 'the moment of truth'" (p. 170). Furthermore, they believe that the way public speaking is taught needs to be altered to include, for instance, an opportunity for students to present practice speeches to small groups of classmates (graduated exposure experiences). In sum, the researchers call for more classroom speaking assignments that attempt to reduce the performance anxiety of students.

Neel, J. (1994). *Aristotle's voice: Rhetoric, theory, & writing in America.* Carbondale: Southern Illinois University.

This classic book on Aristotle is geared to teachers of writing, but its application to students of communication theory is apparent. Neel looks at writing by invoking the writings of Aristotle and points out the relationship between such theories as the *Rhetoric* and the contemporary college classroom. Neel calls himself a sophist and interestingly claims that "I truly do not understand 'Aristotle': I truly do not know 'rhetoric'" (p. 1). Clearly, the remainder of the book demonstrates a comprehensive understanding of both areas, making Neel's opening assertion quite provocative.

The book is organized in a way that helps readers understand the intersection between writing and rhetoric. Many of the principles contained in Aristotle's theory are consistently woven throughout the book. Neel admits that the *Rhetoric* is a "here's how you do it textbook" (p. 156), and in that spirit Neel explains both the strengths and weaknesses of such an approach. The book is written from the vantage point of an English professor, yet the information contained suggests a clear application to those interested in Aristotle and his rhetorical principles.

Today, people interpret memory in speech making differently from Aristotle. Memorizing a speech often means having a basic understanding of material and techniques. Although other rhetoricians like Quintilian made specific recommendations on memorizing, Aristotle felt that familiarizing oneself with the speech's content was understood. When Camille presents her speech on drinking and driving, for example, she has some parts of her speech committed to memory and other parts overviewed on notes.

Delivery

Thus far we have concentrated on how a speech is constructed. Aristotle, however, was also interested in how a speech is delivered. In this case, **delivery** refers to the nonverbal presentation of a speaker's ideas. Delivery normally includes a host of behaviors, including eye contact, vocal cues, pronunciation, enunciation, dialect, body movement, and physical appearance. For Aristotle, delivery specifically pertains to the manipulation of the voice. He especially encouraged speakers to use appropriate levels of pitch, rhythm, volume, and emotion. He believed that the way in which something is said affects its intelligibility.

Aristotle felt that delivery could not be easily taught, yet it is crucial for a speaker to consider. He also believed that speakers should strive to be natural in their delivery. Speakers should not use any vocal techniques that may detract from the words and should strive to capture a comfortable presence in front of an audience.

The canons of rhetoric are incorporated into a number of different persuasive speeches. Our exploration of Aristotle's Rhetorical Theory concludes with a discussion of the three types of rhetoric.

delivery
a canon of rhetoric that refers to the nonverbal presentation of a speaker's ideas

Types of Rhetoric

You will recall that during Aristotle's time citizens were asked to take part in a number of speaking activities—from judge to attorney to legislator. It was in this spirit that Aristotle identified different speaking situations for citizens to consider when conversing on trade, finance, national defense, and war. He denoted three types of rhetoric, or what he called three types of oratory: forensic, epideictic, and deliberative. **Forensic rhetoric** pertains to establishing a fact; at the core of forensic rhetoric is justice. **Epideictic rhetoric** is discourse related to praise or blame. **Deliberative rhetoric** concerns speakers who must determine a course of action—something should or should not be done. The three types refer to three different time periods: forensic to the past, epideictic to the

forensic rhetoric
a type of rhetoric that pertains to speakers prompting feelings of guilt or innocence from an audience

epideictic rhetoric
a type of rhetoric that pertains to praising or blaming

deliberative rhetoric
a type of rhetoric that determines an audience's course of action

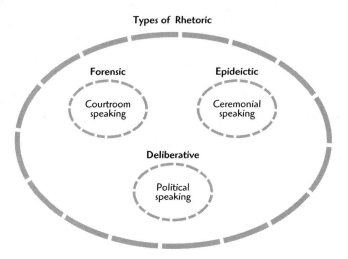

Types of Rhetoric

Forensic

Courtroom speaking

Epideictic

Ceremonial speaking

Deliberative

Political speaking

Figure 18.1
Types of Rhetoric

present, and deliberative to the future. We discuss these three rhetorical types next and illustrate them in Figure 18.1.

Forensic oratory, or judicial rhetoric, specifically refers to speaking in courtrooms. Its intent is to establish guilt or innocence; in Aristotle's day, forensic speakers directed their presentation to courtroom judges. Aristotle examined forensic rhetoric within a legal framework, and thus many of his beliefs on the law are found in the *Rhetoric*. Amelie Rorty (1996) notes that forensic speaking requires focusing on arguments that tap into judges' psyches, including their beliefs about why certain criminals act the way they do and which types of circumstances tempt people to break the law. Because past actions are frequently indicative of a person's current behavior, forensics orators rely on previous behaviors.

Aristotle recognized that a person's character is critical in forensic rhetoric. He interprets character as both status (that is, whether a person is young or old, rich or poor, fortunate or unfortunate) and morality (whether a person is just or unjust, reasonable or unreasonable). If people act voluntarily, Aristotle argued, the choices they make have consequences. To establish guilt, the forensic speaker needs to establish motivation for doing wrong. In speaking before an audience, then, speakers will invoke what Aristotle called the "moral habits" of a person.

Examples of forensic rhetoric abound in our society. Forensic speakers have played prominent roles in U.S. courtrooms. Attorneys, in particular, have effectively and persuasively used their forensic rhetoric over the years. One of the most memorable forensic presentations took place in the closely watched trial of football star O. J. Simpson. Prosecutors tried to implicate Simpson's morals by playing a tape recording of a 911 call in which Simpson could be heard yelling at his wife and by showing pictures of her beaten body to the jury. More recent forensic efforts by prosecutors include the legal proceedings of corporate executives accused of stealing hundreds of millions of dollars from company profits. In all these cases, forensic speaking was used to undercut the moral integrity of the defendant and to establish guilt.

The second type of rhetoric, epideictic, is also called ceremonial speaking. Speeches during Aristotle's time were given in public arenas with the goal of praising, honoring, blaming, or shaming. Epideictic rhetors include people, events, organizations, or nations in their speeches. These speeches usually focus on social issues because—according to Aristotle—people are interested in the here and now. Epideictic speaking cannot be separated from ethos, Aristotle stated. He believed that by understanding the need to praise or blame, epideictic speakers understand the importance of their own character. For instance, a speech criticizing prison conditions may not resonate deeply with an audience if the speaker is on death row for rape and murder.

Epideictic speaking is greatly informed by the study of virtues or values—a theme that Aristotle borrowed from Plato. The epideictic speaker must be able to relate the virtues of the topic to a diverse audience. Aristotle felt that courage and justice ranked above all virtues, but virtue is defined according to the law of the land.

Epideictic rhetoric is exemplified in funeral practices in our country. Eulogies, which are commonplace at many funerals, usually laud the life of the deceased. Commenting on contemporary values, the epideictic speaker at a funeral frequently compares the virtues of the dead person with those of society. For instance, after the death of his grandmother, one of your authors was asked to give the eulogy at the funeral. During his speech, he talked about his grandmother's uplifting spirit and how she rarely complained about her ailments or about her financial situation. He evoked images of contemporary society in his speech, noting how unusual it is today for someone to refrain from self-centered complaining. His speech centered on a prevailing virtue of his grandmother—her selflessness—and also commented on society as a whole.

The third type is deliberative rhetoric, also called political rhetoric, and it was the focus of much of Aristotle's comments on rhetorical discourse. Aristotle believed that although many writers fail to discuss this rhetorical form, it deserves attention because it has the potential to elicit the most change in an audience.

As we mentioned earlier, deliberative rhetoric is associated with the future—what an audience will do or think as a result of a speaker's efforts. Deliberative speaking, then, requires the speaker to be adept at understanding how his or her thoughts are aligned with those of the audience. The deliberative speaker should be prepared to consider subjects that are relevant to the audience and to which the speaker can personally relate. Aristotle identified five subjects on which people deliberated in his day: revenue, war and peace, the defense of the country, commerce, and legislation (Arnhart, 1981). Today's list of deliberative topics might include health insurance, taxes, relationships, education, and civil rights. Deliberative speakers might try to raise interest in these topics, and once interest is piqued, they might find that listeners are more prone to being persuaded.

Larry Arnhart (1981) comments that the deliberative rhetorician needs to know not only the actual subject of deliberation but also the elements of human nature that influence deliberation. There are a number of topics, therefore, which are suited for deliberation and others that are not. Aristotle focused on what deliberative speakers can say to an assembly (a body of legislators, for example), and today this deliberative oratory continues. Consider the following example. When asked to give a short presentation to her state's legislative committee on health insurance, Beverly, a 64-year-old mother of four, spoke about the health insurance of elderly people. As the caretaker of her 90-year-old mother-in-law, a patient in a local nursing home, Beverly knew precisely the kinds of persuasive strategies to use with the group of politicians. Her speech focused on the difficulties of being old and how these problems are amplified by not having enough insurance. She asked the legislators to consider their own aging parents in their discussions. She outlined five "points of action" for the committee to follow. Three of the points could be undertaken immediately: establishing a task force, interviewing elderly citizens, and setting up a toll-free number to solicit citizen concerns and complaints. The remaining two required funding from the legislature. At the conclusion of her brief speech, Beverly was satisfied that her suggestions would not be ignored.

Aristotle would have approved of Beverly's rhetoric. Her recommendations were doable (the committee enacted three of the five), and she made her experiences relevant to her audience by asking the group to think about their own parents. This approach elicited personal identification, which is an important tactic in deliberative speaking. By eliciting these feelings, Beverly knew that she would be able to get her audience to agree with her thinking.

Integration, Critique, and Closing

Aristotle's *Rhetoric* remains an influential theoretical foundation in communication studies. You can pick up any public speaking text (e.g., Griffin, 2009) and find discussions on delivery, organization, and style. Students of public speaking have benefited greatly from the words and values of Aristotle, and for this reason the theory will resonate deeply for years to come. The evaluative criteria for communication we wish to discuss center on three primary areas: logical consistency, heurism, and test of time.

Integration

Communication Tradition	**Rhetorical**	Semiotic	Phenomenological	Cybernetic	Socio-Psychological	Socio-Cultural	Critical
Communication Context	Intrapersonal	Interpersonal	Small Group	Organizational	**Public/Rhetorical**	Mass/Media	Cultural
Approach to Knowing	**Positivistic/Empirical**	**Interpretive/Hermeneutic**	Critical

Critique

Evaluation Criteria	Scope	**Logical Consistency**	Parsimony	Utility	Testability	**Heurism**	**Test of Time**

Logical Consistency

Critics of Aristotle's theory have taken issue with some tenets of the theory. For instance, Aristotle has been criticized for contradiction and incoherence. Charles Marsh (2006), for instance, reports on one critic who undercut the notion of ethos as proposed by Aristotle: "In a society so small, where everyone knew one another, how could [Aristotle] think—was he really that dumb—that a person of bad character could hoodwink the other leaders of society?" (p. 339). Lord (1994) contends that in developing his theory, Aristotle blasts his contemporaries for focusing too much on the audience's emotions. Although Aristotle encourages speakers to avoid focusing on emotions while making their points, he proceeds to do just that when he stresses the importance of presenting emotions and invoking audience passions (pathos) during a speech. This makes the theory somewhat inconsistent.

John Cooper (1996) challenges Lord's critique. He argues that Aristotle was simply responding to the Sophists' messages of the day. Because most of the speeches in ancient Greece were directed to judges and rulers, Aristotle felt that speakers should try to elicit feelings of pity in the courtroom. To do that, Aristotle felt that speakers should try to view judges in congenial ways.

Further criticism of the logical consistency of the theory has been offered. First, scholars agree that the *Rhetoric* is a rather unorganized undertaking; in fact, the theory is assembled from Aristotle's lecture notes (Kennedy, 1991; Sokolon, 2005). It is not surprising, then, that Aristotle seems to discuss topics in a random and arbitrary manner. At times, Aristotle introduces a topic and then drops it, only to return to it later. His terminology is especially problematic for some scholars. You may not find this too earth-shattering, but recall that researchers need clear foundations of terms before they can embark upon testing or clarifying theory. Larry Arnhart (1991) concludes that Aristotle defined his terms in less than precise ways so that audiences (readers) would have a broader understanding of his words and ideas. Arnhart believes that this conscious decision to remain unclear does not mean that Aristotle's thoughts should be discarded.

Finally, the logical consistency is further challenged by an examination of how Aristotle views the audience. Critics charge Aristotle with ignoring the critical nature of listeners. For instance, Jasper Neel (1994) states, "Aristotle makes clear that the introduction [of a speech] has nothing to do with the 'speech itself.' It exists only because of the hearer's weak-minded tendency to listen to what is beside the point" (p. 156). Eugene Ryan (1984) is more blunt: "Aristotle is thinking of listeners who have some difficulty keeping their minds on the speaker's business, are easily distracted, tend to forget what has gone on before, [and] are not absorbed with abstract ideas" (p. 47). From these writers, we get the impression that Aristotle perceived audiences to be incapable of being discriminating listeners or critical thinkers. It's important to note, though, that Aristotle was writing at a time when people were rather passive listeners; they did not watch the evening news and did not have access to information about world events. Furthermore, when one considers that the *Rhetoric* is based on lecture notes and that students back then were not accustomed to openly challenging their mentors, Aristotle's view of the audience is not so implausible.

Theory Into Practice

Ned

When I gave my first speech in public speaking, I was pretty amazed that the three proofs of Aristotle worked so well. I gave my speech on physician-assisted suicide. My aunt wanted her doctor to help her commit suicide, and my whole family was against it. I was, too. So I was trying to persuade the class that we should never allow this to happen anywhere. I had credibility because it was right in my family (ethos), I used emotion and caused emotion in my speech (pathos), and I offered some statistics on how many people try to get their doctors to help in suicides (logos). I had a lot of students come up to me after the speech and tell me how effective my speech was. And all of that was thanks to Aristotle!

Heurism

Few would argue that Aristotle's *Rhetoric* is one of the most heuristic theories found in communication. Scholars in political science, medicine, English composition, and philosophy have studied Rhetorical Theory and incorporated Aristotelian thinking in their research. The theory has spawned a number of subareas in the communication discipline, such as communication apprehension, and has generated research. Some interesting research has discussed the deliberative rhetoric of an African American activist (McClish, 2007), the application of Aristotelian proofs to umbilical cord blood banking (White, 2006), and the use of pathos in letters sent by nonprofit charities (Myers, 2007). Aristotle's theory will continue to resonate with scholars across disciplines.

Test of Time

No other theory in the communication discipline has withstood the test of time as well as Aristotle's *Rhetoric*. With more than 2000 years behind it and public speaking textbooks, teachers, and researchers communicating Aristotelian principles, it's hard to believe that any other theory in the field of communication will ever achieve such longevity!

As the twenty-first century continues, we are in an informed position to reflect upon some of the greatest written works of all time. The *Rhetoric* is clearly such a work. Aristotle's words continue to resonate in a society that is far different from his day. Some people may reject his thoughts as outdated in an age in which multiple ways of knowing are embraced. Nonetheless, a theory focusing on how speakers use and engender emotions, logic, and trustworthiness cannot be ignored.

Discussion Starters

1. In the chapter-opening scene, Camille Ramirez relied on Aristotle's view of public speaking. Do you believe that she could have been more effective? In what way? Use examples in your response.

2. Aristotle's critics have focused on the fact that his theory is simply a collection of lecture notes that are contradictory, vague, and often narrow. Do you agree or disagree, based on the information in this chapter? What examples can you point to for support?

3. Employ syllogistic reasoning for and against each of the following topics: physician-assisted suicide, abortion, and medicinal marijuana use.

4. Discuss what canon of rhetoric is most important when politicians speak to their constituents. Use examples to defend your view.

5. If Aristotle were alive today and you were his student, what additional suggestions would you offer him for a new edition of the *Rhetoric*? Why do you believe your suggestions are important to address in public speaking? Incorporate examples in your response.

6. Aristotle spent a great deal of time discussing the role of the audience. If you were giving a speech on safety to a group of convenience store employees, what sort of audience analysis would you undertake?

7. Explain how principles from the *Rhetoric* relate to job interviews.

Online Learning Center [www. mhhe.com/west4e]

Visit the Online Learning Center at www.mhhe.com/west4e for chapter-specific resources, such as story-into-theory and multiple-choice quizzes, as well as theory summaries and theory connection questions.

CHAPTER 19

Dramatism

*Based on the research of **Kenneth Burke***

Karl Nelson

Karl Nelson really looked forward to this part of his morning routine. He settled down with his first cup of coffee and the morning paper. He allowed himself an hour to read all the news of the day and savor his caffeine fix. In many ways this was his favorite part of the day, and he got up extra early to make sure he would have enough time for it after his workout and before he left for the office. But today he was not happy. He looked at the headlines with disgust. He was so sick of reading about politicians who had no common sense. Today he was reading about Evan Spector, the mayor of Elmhurst, New Mexico, where Karl lived. The article was about the fact that Spector had campaigned on a "clean" platform, claiming that he would make government respectable again, and now he'd been caught with a prostitute!

Karl looked up from his paper just as his partner, Max, came into the breakfast room. Karl asked, "Max, have you read about Evan Spector? That man is such an incredible low-life hypocrite. How could he pretend to be Mr. Clean during his campaign, talking all about family values when he's cheating on his wife with a prostitute?"

Max just shrugged and laughed. He was used to seeing Karl getting worked up over current events. It didn't seem all that important to him, but Karl certainly cared about this stuff. Max grabbed a cup of coffee and left to go to work. Karl went back to reading the paper.

The article described the sting that had caught Spector and a few other local politicians who were clients at a high priced call girl ring. Spector wasn't admitting anything and his family was defending him, but Karl thought the evidence in the paper was pretty damaging. He didn't see how Spector could get out of this. At least, he hoped Spector wouldn't be able to escape punishment.

Karl noticed that it was getting late, so he put the rest of the newspaper in his briefcase and left for work. When he got to the office, a couple of people were talking about Evan Spector. His colleague Diane agreed with him, saying that Spector was a hypocrite. But another colleague, Randy, disagreed, saying that we are always forgiving people for mistakes, and that the United States was a country of second chances. Randy said that this was really between Spector and his wife anyway.

As Karl drove home from work that night, he listened to the local news on the radio. A commentator said that people in the United States loved to build up public figures and then they loved even more to see them fall. The commentator agreed with Karl's co-worker, Randy. She said that we are a nation that loves a comeback and maybe Spector would be back in political life someday. Karl disagreed. He thought Spector deserved disapproval because he'd done the wrong thing, and because he'd been so judgmental about other people who made mistakes in the past. This Spector case was disgusting, Karl thought, and he hoped the guy never got into public office again.

Some rhetoricians might analyze Evan Spector's problems and Karl's responses to them using Dramatism, a theoretical position seeking to understand the actions of human life as drama. Kenneth Burke is known as the originator of Dramatism, although he did not initially use that term himself. Burke, who died in 1993 at the age of 96, was a fascinating person, and he was unlike many of the other theorists covered in this book. Burke never earned an undergraduate degree, much less a Ph.D. He was self-taught in the areas of literary criticism, philosophy, communication, sociology, economics, theology, and linguistics. He taught for almost twenty years at several universities, including Harvard, Princeton, and the University of Chicago. His breadth of interests and perhaps his lack of formal training in any one discipline made him one of the most interdisciplinary theorists we will study. His ideas have been applied widely in various areas including literature, theater, communication, history, and sociology. No doubt one reason Burke is so widely read and applied has to do with his focus on *symbol systems*—the primary means of intellectual exchange and scholarly effort for most researchers working in the humanities. Dramatism provides researchers with the flexibility to scrutinize an object of study from a variety of angles.

Dramatism, as its name implies, conceptualizes life as a drama, placing a critical focus on the acts performed by various players. Just as in a play, the acts in life are central to revealing human motives. Dramatism provides us with a method that is well suited to address the act of communication between the text (how Karl perceives and relates to what he learns about Spector) and the audience for that text (Karl), as well as the inner action of the text (Spector's motives and choices). As C. Ronald Kimberling (1982) notes, "Dramatism assuredly provides critical insights that cannot be generated by any other method" (p. 13). When Karl reads about Spector's case, it is as if he sees him as an actor. In Burke's terms, Karl understands Spector as an actor in a scene, trying to accomplish purposes because of certain motives. Thus, he comments on his motives as he evaluates his act of going to a prostitute. Burke's theory of Dramatism allows us to analyze both Spector's rhetorical choices in this situation (how he framed his case) and Karl's responses to his choices.

Drama is a useful metaphor for Burke's ideas for three reasons: (1) Drama indicates a grand sweep, and Burke does not make limited claims; his goal is to theorize about the whole range of human experience. The dramatic metaphor is particularly useful in describing human relationships because it is grounded in interaction or dialogue. In its dialogue, drama both models relationships and illuminates relationships. (2) Drama tends to follow recognizable types or genres: comedy, musical, melodrama, and so forth. Burke feels that the very way we structure and use language may be related to the way these human dramas are played out. As Barry Brummett (1993) observes, "Words string out into patterned discourses at the macroscopic level of whole texts or discourses. Burke argues that recurring patterns underlying texts partially account for how those texts move us" (p. xiv). (3) Drama is always addressed to an audience. In this sense, drama is rhetorical. Burke views literature as "equipment for living," which means that literature or texts speak to people's lived experiences and problems and provide people with responses for dealing with these

Burke's theory compares life to a play and states that, as in a theatrical piece, life requires an actor, a scene, an action, some means for the action to take place, and a purpose. The theory allows a rhetorical critic to analyze a speaker's motives by identifying and examining these elements. Furthermore, Burke believes, guilt is the ultimate motive for speakers, and Dramatism suggests that rhetors are most successful when they provide their audiences with a means for purging their guilt.

experiences. In this way, Dramatism studies the ways in which language and its usage relate to audiences.

Assumptions of Dramatism

Assumptions provide a sense of a theorist's beliefs. As we discussed in Chapters 3, some ontological issues concern how much choice and free will humans possess. The assumptions we make about human nature are articles of faith about basic reality. Kenneth Burke's thinking is so complex that it is difficult to reduce it to one set of assumptions or to a specific ontology. Some of the assumptions that follow illustrate the difficulty of labeling Burke's ontology. Researchers such as Brummett (1993) have called Burke's assumptions a symbolic ontology because of his emphasis on language. Yet, as Brummett cautions, "The best one can do, in searching for the heart of Burke's thought, is to find a partial ontology, a grounding-for-the-most-part. For Burke, people *mainly* do what they do, and the world is *largely* the way it is, because of the nature of *symbol systems themselves*" (p. xii; emphasis in original). Brummett's comment prefigures the following three assumptions of Burke's Dramatism theory:

- Humans are animals who use symbols.
- Language and symbols form a critically important system for humans.
- Humans are choice makers.

The first assumption speaks to Burke's realization that some of what we do is motivated by our animal nature and some of what we do is motivated by symbols. Recall the semiotic tradition from Chapter 2 to understand this notion. For example, when Karl drinks his morning coffee, he is satisfying his thirst, an animal need. When he reads the morning paper and thinks about the ideas he encounters there, he is being influenced by symbols. The idea that humans are animals who use symbols represents a tension in Burke's thought. As Brummett (1993) observes, this assumption "teeters between the realizations that some of what we do is motivated by animality and some of it by symbolicity" (p. xii). Of all the symbols that humans use, language is the most important for Burke.

In the second assumption (the critical importance of language), Burke's position is somewhat similar to the concept of linguistic relativity known as the Sapir-Whorf hypothesis (Sapir, 1921; Whorf, 1956). Edward Sapir and Benjamin Whorf noted that it is difficult to think about concepts or objects without words for them. Thus, people are restricted (to an extent) in what they can conceive by the limits of their language. For Burke, as well as for Sapir and Whorf, when people use their language, they are used by it as well. When Karl tells Max that Spector is a hypocrite, he is choosing the symbols he wishes to use, but at the same time his opinions and thoughts are shaped by hearing himself use these symbols. Furthermore, when a culture's language does not have symbols for a given motive, then speakers of that language are unlikely to have that motive. Thus, because English does not have many symbols that express much nuance of opinion about Spector's behavior and motivations, our discussions are often polarized. When Karl talks with his colleagues Diane and Randy, the discussion is focused on whether Spector was right or wrong. There is not much choice in between, and Burke would argue that this is a direct result of our symbol system. Think back to other controversies you have talked about (such as the moral implications of cloning, stem cell research, dealing with North Korea, invading Iraq, and so forth). You may remember the discussions as either/or propositions—positions were cast as either right or wrong. Burke's response is that symbols shape our either/or approach to these complex issues.

Burke asserts that words, thoughts, and actions have extremely close connections with one another. Burke's expression for this is that words act as "terministic screens" leading to "trained incapacities," meaning that people cannot see beyond what their words lead them to believe (Burke, 1965). For example, despite educational efforts, U.S. public health officials still have difficulty persuading people to think of the misuse of alcohol and tranquilizers when they hear the words "drug abuse." Most people in the United States respond to "drug abuse" as the misuse of illegal drugs, such as heroin and cocaine (Brummett, 1993). The words "drug abuse" are "terministic screens," screening out some meanings and including others. For Burke, language has a life of its own, and "anything we can see or feel is already *in* language, given to us *by* language, and even produced *as us* by language" (Nelson, 1989, p. 169; emphasis in original). This explanation is somewhat at odds with the final assumption of Dramatism.

The second assumption suggests that language exerts a determining influence over people (Melia, 1989), but the final assumption states that human beings are choice makers. Burke persistently suggests that behaviorism has to be rejected because it conflicts with human choice. Thus, as Karl reads about Evan Spector, he forms his opinions about his behavior through his own free will.

Much of what we discuss in the rest of the chapter rests on the conceptualization of agency, or the ability of a social actor to act out of choice.

As Charles Conrad and Elizabeth Macom (1995) observe, "The essence of agency is choice" (p. 11). Yet, as Conrad and Macom go on to discuss, Burke grappled with the concept of agency throughout his career, largely because of the difficult task of negotiating a space between complete free will and complete determinism. Burke's thinking continued to evolve on this point, but he always kept agency in the forefront of his theorizing. To understand Burke's scope in this theory, we need to discuss how he framed his thinking relative to Aristotelian rhetoric.

Dramatism as New Rhetoric

In his book *A Rhetoric of Motives* (1950), Burke is concerned with persuasion, and he provides an ample discussion of the traditional principles of rhetoric articulated by Aristotle (see Chapter 18). Burke maintains that the definition of rhetoric is, in essence, persuasion, and his writings explore the ways in which persuasion takes place. In so doing, Burke proposes a new rhetoric (Nichols, 1952) that focuses on several key issues, chief among them being the notion of identification. In 1952, Marie Nichols said the following about the difference between Burke's approach and Aristotle's: "The difference between the 'old' rhetoric and the 'new' rhetoric may be summed up in this manner: whereas the key term for the 'old' rhetoric was *persuasion* and its stress was upon deliberate design, the key term for the 'new' rhetoric is *identification* and this may include partially 'unconscious' factors in its appeal" (p. 323; emphasis in original). Yet Burke's purpose was not to displace Aristotle's conceptualizations but rather to supplement the traditional approach.

Identification and Substance

substance
the general nature of something

Burke asserts that all things have **substance**, which he defines as the general nature of something. Substance can be described in a person by listing demographic characteristics as well as background information and facts about the present situation, such as talents and occupation. Thus, from our opening scenario, we may understand Karl's substance by noting he is a 38-year-old Polish American male, high school math teacher, collector of rare coins, tennis player, and crossword puzzle enthusiast. In addition, Karl has been in a relationship with Max for seven years and lives in Hartford, Connecticut. Of course, many other pieces of information make up Karl's substance as well, but these facts give us a starting point.

identification
when two people have overlap in their substances

division
when two people fail to have overlap in their substances

Burke argues that when there is overlap between two people in terms of their substance, they have **identification**. The more overlap that exists, the greater the identification. The opposite is also true, so the less overlap between individuals, the greater the **division** that exists between them. For instance, the fact that Evan Spector is a wealthy, Jewish, married man who is the mayor of Elmhurst, Indiana and appears in the media frequently provides little in terms of identification between him and Karl. They are both professionals who live in the United States, but they overlap on little else.

T * I * P

However, it is also the case that two people can never completely overlap with each other. Burke recognizes this and notes that the "ambiguities of substance" dictate that identification always rests on both unity and division. Individuals will unite on certain matters of substance but at the same time remain unique, being "both joined and separated" (Burke, 1950, pp. 20–21). Furthermore, Burke indicates that rhetoric is needed to bridge divisions and establish unity. Thus, potentially, Evan Spector could have made some rhetorical appeals that convinced Karl that the divisions between them could be bridged. Burke refers to this process as **consubstantiation**, or increasing their identification with each other.

consubstantiation
when appeals are made to increase overlap between people

The Process of Guilt and Redemption

Consubstantiality, or issues of identification and substance, are related to the guilt/redemption cycle because guilt can be assuaged as a result of identification and divisions. Patricia Sullivan and Lynn Turner (1993) argued that Zoe Baird, President Clinton's first, unsuccessful, nominee for U.S. attorney general, acted as a sacrificial vessel for the country to expiate our feelings of guilt about inadequate child care. Using Burke, Sullivan and Turner argue that Baird was consubstantial with many Americans because the problems of adequate child care are widespread. Yet her uncommon wealth separated her from most, allowing people to blame her without condemning themselves.

For Burke, the process of guilt and redemption undergirds the entire concept of symbolizing. **Guilt** is the central motive for all symbolic activities, and Burke defines guilt broadly to include any type of tension, embarrassment, shame, disgust, or other unpleasant feeling. Central to Burke's theory is the notion that guilt is intrinsic to the human condition. Because we are continuously feeling guilt, we are also continuously engaging in attempts to purge ourselves of guilt's discomfort.

guilt
tension, embarrassment, shame, disgust, or other unpleasant feeling

This process of feeling guilt and attempting to reduce it finds its expression in Burke's cycle, which follows a predictable pattern: order (or hierarchy), the negative, victimage (scapegoat or mortification), and redemption.

Order or Hierarchy   Burke suggests that society exists in the form of an **order,** or **hierarchy,** which is created through our ability to use language. Language enables us to create categories like richer and more powerful—the haves and the have-nots. These categories form social hierarchies. Often we feel guilt as a result of our place in the hierarchy. If we are privileged, we may feel we have power at the expense of those with less wealth and power. This feeling prompts guilt.

The Negative   The **negative** comes into play when people see their place in the social order and seek to reject it. Saying no to the existing order is both a function of our language abilities and evidence of humans as choice makers. When Burke penned his often-quoted definition of Man, he emphasized the negative:

> Man is
> the symbol-using inventor of the negative
> separated from his natural condition by instruments
> of his own making
> goaded by the spirit of hierarchy
> and rotten with perfection. (1966, p. 16)

When Burke coined the phrase "rotten with perfection," he meant that because our symbols allow us to imagine perfection, we always feel guilty about the difference between the real state of affairs and the perfection that we can imagine.

Victimage   **Victimage** is the way in which we attempt to purge the guilt that we feel as part of the human condition. There are two basic types of victimage, or two methods to purge our guilt. Burke calls the type of victimage that we turn in on ourselves **mortification.** When we apologize for wrongdoing and blame ourselves, we engage in mortification. Had Evan Spector said he did the wrong thing he would have attempted mortification. In 1998, Republican leaders said they would have felt more sympathetic about President Clinton's sex scandal if he had admitted he was wrong and had not perjured himself. Clinton refused to engage in mortification. Instead he turned to another purging technique called scapegoating.

In **scapegoating,** blame is placed on some sacrificial vessel. By sacrificing the scapegoat, the actor is purged of sin. Clinton attempted to scapegoat the Republicans as deserving the real blame for the country's problems after confessing to an inappropriate relationship with Monica Lewinsky. When the news of the sex scandal first broke in 1998, before Clinton admitted his relationship with Lewinsky, Hillary Rodham Clinton appeared on television suggesting that the rumors about her husband were the result of a complex "right-wing conspiracy" that was out to get her and her husband. This type of rhetoric illustrates Burke's concept of scapegoating. In the aftermath of the 9/11 tragedy, President Bush also engaged in scapegoating. When Bush spoke of the "Axis of Evil" and used stark contrasts between good and evil, he operated within Burke's concept of scapegoating. People who objected to this rhetoric pointed out that the United States itself had some responsibility for the fact that people from developing countries harbored resentments against the United States.

Redemption   The final step in the process is **redemption**, which involves a rejection of the unclean and a return to a new order after guilt has been temporarily purged. Inherent in the term *redemption* is the notion of a Redeemer. The Redeemer in the Judeo-Christian tradition is the Savior (Christ) or God. When politicians blame problems on the media or on the opposing party, they offer themselves as potential Redeemers—those who can lead the people out of their troubles. A key in the redemption phase is the fact that guilt is only temporarily relieved, through the Redeemer or any other method. As any order or hierarchy becomes reestablished, guilt returns to plague the human condition.

redemption
A rejection of the unclean and a return to a new order after guilt has been temporarily purged

The Pentad

In addition to devising the theory of Dramatism, Burke (1945) created a method for applying his theory toward an understanding of symbolic activities. He called his method the **pentad** because it consists of five points for analyzing a symbolic text like a speech or a series of articles about Martha Stewart, for instance. The pentad may help determine why a speaker selects a particular rhetorical strategy for identifying with an audience. The five points that make up the pentad include the act, the scene, the agent, agency, and purpose. Almost twenty years after creating this research tool, Burke (1968) added a sixth point, attitude, to the pentad, making it a hexad, although most people still refer to it as the pentad (Figure 19.1). We will examine each of the points in turn.

pentad
Burke's method for applying Dramatism

The Act   Burke considered the **act** to be what is done by a person. In the case of Evan Spector, the act would be getting caught with a prostitute.

act
one prong of the pentad; that which *is* done by a person

The Scene   The **scene** provides the context surrounding the act. In Spector's case, the scene would include a time period in which America is under fire for corruption and hypocrisy. We don't have much information about the way Evan Spector would contextualize the scene because he has provided very limited information publicly about any contributing factors to the act.

scene
one prong of the pentad; the context surrounding the act

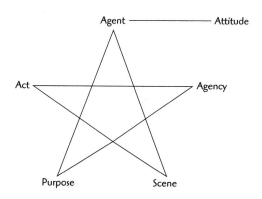

Figure 19.1
Burke's Pentad

Research Notes

Fox, C. (2002). Beyond the "Tyranny of the Real": Revisiting Burke's pentad as a research method for professional communication. *Technical Communication Quarterly, 11,* 365–388.

In this article Fox reports on observations she made during a case study of technical writers who were employed in the transportation industry. Specifically, Fox spent eight weeks observing the technical writers at work and in negotiations with the engineers in the company as they worked together to edit a manual about concrete cracking in pavements. The manual was already written, and the goal of these negotiations was to produce a shortened version to respond to the request of the client who funded the manual.

Fox uses the pentad to explicate what was going on in the negotiations and as a tool to explain to technical writing students how to interact with their coworkers. Fox concludes that the dramatistic ratios she constructed using Burke's theory and method "enabled [her] to see the ways in which power, authority, and agency were negotiated, rather than fixed and finalized as the dominant dichotomy between engineer and technical writer often suggests" (pp. 382–383). Fox observes that using the pentad as a way of "seeing differently" about negotiations in the workplace has pedagogical implications as well. She notes that her analysis (and others like it)

could be the basis for meaningful case studies to use with students. Furthermore, she argues that using pentadic analysis allows students to see power relations in the workplace more completely and with a more nuanced understanding.

Smudde, P. M. (2004). Implications on the practice and study of Kenneth Burke's idea of a "public relations counsel with a heart." *Communication Quarterly, 52,* 420–432.

In this article, Smudde advances that Burke's perspective can help public relations practitioners "reveal important dimensions at both the micro- and the macro-levels about the symbolic action of public relations" (p. 424). Specifically, Smudde shows how the context for public relations is illuminated by describing it in the progression of order, guilt, purification, and redemption. Through this description, Smudde states that public relations practitioners should conceptualize their tasks and nurture identification with their desired audiences.

Smudde states that "examining public relations texts dramatistically reveals public relations officials' use of language to structure publics' thinking about issues" (p. 429). In short, Smudde believes that public relations practitioners are dramatists, and when they acknowledge this by utilizing Burke's perspective, they are able to visualize their work more clearly and more ethically.

---

agent
one prong of the pentad; the person performing the act

The Agent   The **agent** is the person or persons performing the act. In the case of Evan Spector, he is the agent. However, if a researcher wished to analyze Karl's act of deciding he did not support Spector, then Karl would be the agent.

agency
one prong of the pentad; the means used to perform the act

Agency   **Agency** refers to the means used by the agent to accomplish the act. Possible forms of agency include message strategies, storytelling, apologies, speech making, and so forth. In Spector's case, the agency included the justifications he made.

purpose
one prong of the pentad; the goal the agent had for the act

Purpose   The **purpose** refers to the goal that the agent had in mind for the act—that is, why the act was done. In Spector's case, the purpose was unclear. He provided no reasons. Karl believed he did it because he was weak.

Attitude   **Attitude** refers to the manner in which an actor positions himself or herself relative to others. Again, in Spector's case, this is a contested point. Karl might say that he acted from an attitude of superiority. Many of the articles he read commented that Spector's believed himself to be above the law.

When using the pentad to analyze a symbolic interaction, the analyst first determines all the elements of the pentad and identifies what occurred in a particular act. After labeling the points of the pentad and fully explicating each, the analyst then examines the **dramatistic ratios**, or the proportions of one element relative to another. By isolating any two parts of the pentad and examining their relationship to each other, we determine a ratio. An agent:act ratio, for instance, is at issue when we attempt to understand how a good person might do a bad thing. In analyzing the ratios in this manner, the researcher is able to discover a dominant element. Is the agent emphasized more than the situation or vice versa? An examination of the dramatistic ratio suggests something about point of view and rhetorical strategies (Meisenbach, Remke, Buzzanell, & Liu, 2008). Steven Hunt (2003) calls dramatistic ratios the "interaction effects of two or more elements" (p. 379) and argues that observing these interactions is one criterion by which to judge the worth of a piece of rhetorical criticism.

Integration, Critique, and Closing

There is no question that Kenneth Burke has made an immeasurable contribution to the field of communication with his theory of Dramatism. Various researchers have praised Burke in the following terms: "He has become the most profound student of rhetoric now writing in America" (Nichols, 1952, p. 331); "Kenneth Burke is more than a single intellectual worker; he is the ore for a scholarly industry" (Brummett, 1993, p. xi); "Few critics have revealed the scope, imagination, insights, and dazzling concern for symbol using which Kenneth Burke possesses" (Chesebro, 1993, p. xii); and in 1981, the *New York Times* recognized Burke as a leading American critic, saying he was "the strongest living representative of the American critical tradition, and perhaps the largest single source of that tradition since its founder, Ralph Waldo Emerson" (cited in Chesebro, 1993, p. xi). Burke's work is widely praised and frequently cited. In fact, the National Communication Association, one of the main organizations for communication teachers, researchers, and professionals, has an entire division devoted to Burkean criticism. Several of the regional associations also have interest groups that focus on Burkean analysis. No other single theorist is similarly represented in our associations.

attitude
a later addition to the pentad; the manner in which the agent positions himself or herself relative to others

dramatistic ratios
the proportions of one element of the pentad relative to another element

As we analyze Dramatism, four criteria become relevant: scope, parsimony, utility, and heurism.

Integration

| Communication Tradition | **Rhetorical** | **Semiotic** | Phenomenological | Cybernetic | Socio-Psychological | Socio-Cultural | **Critical** |

| Communication Context | Intrapersonal | Interpersonal | Small Group | Organizational | **Public/Rhetorical** | Mass/Media | Cultural |

| Approach to Knowing | Positivistic/Empirical | **Interpretive/Hermeneutic** | **Critical** |

Critique

| Evaluation Criteria | **Scope** | Logical Consistency | **Parsimony** | **Utility** | Testability | **Heurism** | Test of Time |

Scope

Dramatism has been criticized for being too wide in scope. Burke's goal is no less than to explain the whole of human experience with symbolic interaction. This is an extremely broad and ambitious goal, and some critics believe it renders the theory too broad to be meaningful. When you contrast Dramatism with a theory like Uncertainty Reduction Theory, which we discussed in Chapter 9, you can see the two extremes of theoretical scope. URT seeks to explain the first few minutes of an initial encounter between strangers. Dramatism encompasses all human symbolic interaction. Some critics might suggest that when a theory attempts such a lofty goal it is doomed to be overly complex and obtuse. Whether or not you see the range of Dramatism's goal as a weakness is somewhat subjective. Interestingly, for Burke and many who followed him, the wide scope of Dramatism is part of its appeal.

Parsimony

Some critics complain that Burke's theory is too unclear and obtuse to be useful. Dramatism is seen by some as overly complex and confusing (Foss, Foss, & Trapp, 1991). Even proponents of Burke acknowledge that he is difficult to read. Marie Hochmuth Nichols concluded her 1952 essay on Burke's Dramatistic Theory of Rhetoric by saying,

> Burke is difficult and often confusing. He cannot be understood by casual reading of his various volumes. In part the difficulty arises from the numerous vocabularies he employs. His words in isolation are usually simple enough, but he often uses them in new contexts. To read one of his volumes independently, without regard to the chronology of publication, makes the problem of comprehension even more difficult because of the specialized meaning attached to various words and phrases. (p. 330)

However, Nichols also provides a rebuttal to some of these criticisms by concluding that some of the difficulty arises from "the compactness of his writing, the uniqueness of his organizational patterns, the penetration of his thought, and the breadth of his endeavor" (p. 330). In other words, Burke is a genius and worth the effort it requires to understand his original thinking. When a student is diligent, Burke's theory repays the hard work with many rewards.

Utility

Some researchers (Condit, 1992; Murray, 2003) observe that Dramatism falls short on the criterion of utility. This critique is lodged mainly because of what Burke leaves out of the theory. For example, Celeste Condit (1992) argues that the theory would be more useful if it addressed gender and culture more expansively. Condit observes that although Burke was supportive of feminism, his support came mainly in the form of including women under the sign of "man." She notes that given the historical context in which Burke wrote, his support for women was not inconsequential. Many writers in Burke's generation completely ignored women, so Burke was making a contribution by including women at all. Condit maintains, however, that today the scene has altered, and it is inappropriate to subsume women under the word *man*. Here Condit is talking both about the use of the generic *man* to represent all people and about our ability as a society to begin to think in new ways about sex and gender.

As Condit notes, "We must extend our language beyond duality to a broad 'humanity' and to 'human beings,' discovering ways to speak that emphasize human plurality" (p. 351). Condit says the definition of man that Burke provides, which we discussed earlier in the chapter, is not adequate to include woman. She recasts the definition from the perspective of a radical feminist who would see the following as descriptive of man's woman:

> Woman is
> the symbol-receiving (hearing, passive) animal
> inventor of nothing (moralized by priests and saints)
> submerged in her natural conditions by instruments of man's making
> goaded at the bottom of hierarchy (moved to a sense of orderliness)
> and rotted by perfection. (p. 351)

Then she recasts the definition to move beyond an essentialism defining men and women as opposite to each other and essentially the same as others of the same sex:

> People are
> players with symbols
> inventors of the negative and the possibility of morality
> grown from their natural condition by tools of their collective making
> trapped between hierarchy and equality (moved constantly to reorder)
> neither rotten nor perfect, but now and again lunging down both paths.
> (p. 352)

Condit's argument is that Burke's approach needs to be broadened both to include women and to move past a focus on one sex or the other to be truly inclusive of both. But she asserts that merely broadening the language of "man/his" to include "people/their" will not in itself be sufficient to challenge the hold that language exerts as a terministic screen against women in the United States. We need to change both our language and our thinking about women, men, gender, and inclusivity for significant progress to occur.

Condit also suggests that Burke emphasizes universality among cultures at the expense of particularity. For Condit, this is especially the case in the matter of Burke's contention that victimage is a transcultural experience—a method for purging guilt in all cultures. She argues that cultures other than Western Christian ones (from which Burke draws almost exclusively) might not see victimage as the dominant motive for human conduct. For example, Buddhism might provide different motives than Christianity does. Furthermore, if we examine trickster tales from Native American or African American cultures, we might see victimage characterized in a strikingly different fashion from what Burke describes. The trickster is in a low power position relative to the rest of the society but is able to triumph through wits and cleverness. The trickster is not a victim in the Christian sense that we see in Dramatism; rather, the trickster emerges victorious by turning the rules of the system against those in power.

In sum, Condit's critique does not deny the enormous contribution made by Burke's theory. Instead, she simply suggests some extensions and modifications for improving the theory. Jeffery Murray (2003) agrees with Condit, asserting that although Burke's theory continues to be widely used, it is necessary to expand it to include the voices of those who have been marginalized. Murray uses what he calls an "Other-Burkean" frame to analyze Nazi propaganda and a speech Ted Kennedy made after the 1969 death of Mary Jo Kopechne, a passenger in his car who died when he drove off a bridge in Massachusetts. In both cases, Murray argues that paying attention to what was omitted in the rhetoric and to "Others" whose concerns are not highlighted by the pentad (such as the Jews in relationship to the Nazis, and Mary Jo Kopechne) provides a rich analysis.

Heurism

With regard to heurism, most critics agree that Dramatism is very successful. For instance, Dramatism was originally used in rhetorical analyses of speeches, but now the focus has widened to other discourse in the public sphere such as "editorials, pamphlets and monographs, books, docudramas, radio and television news, movies, music, and even the Internet" (Hunt, 2003, p. 378). Furthermore, Catherine Fox (2002) finds Dramatism to be a useful frame for application to professional communication, specifically technical writing in a transportation organization. And Peter Smudde (2004) advocates applying Dramatism to the practice of public relations.

Gregory Clark (2004) uses the theoretical framework of Dramatism and the pentad, specifically Burke's concept of scene, to explore how tourism in the United States creates a sense of national identity. Clark argues that Dramatism shows us how sharing particular places in the landscape through tourism

Theory Into Practice
Amber

I can see applying Dramatism for real. When I look at President Bush's speeches about invading Iraq, I see how he's the agent and the U.S. public is the audience. The act would be invading Iraq itself—although there are a lot of subacts involved, like going after (and capturing) Saddam Hussein. I am pretty sure Bush had a lot of purposes going on there too. For one thing, there are the purposes he stated in his speeches. First he said that Iraq harbored terrorists and so had something to do with 9/11, and that they were hiding weapons of mass destruction. Now he's changed the purpose to how bad Hussein was and how cruel he was to the people of Iraq. Then there are all the reasons that other people say are going on. Like, maybe he wanted to do it for oil or to get revenge for his father's problems with Saddam. This whole situation is pretty confusing, but I think using Dramatism to sort it out might really help clarify it. I guess we'll never really know why public figures like the president do what they do, but a rhetorician can really go to town trying to figure it out.

T*I*P

accomplishes the identification of a common culture. Furthermore, he notes that these sites have already accomplished the work of differentiation by showing tourists how they are uniquely American and unlike any other culture. Meisenbach, Remke, Buzzanell, & Liu (2008) illustrate that the pentad can be applied to interview data in their study of women's talk about taking maternity leave.

Thus, there is general consensus that Burke's theory provides us with imaginative and innovative insights into human motives and interaction. Dramatism provides us with a theory that models the big picture. It allows an analysis of human motivations and behavior, and its focus on language as the critical symbol system makes it especially attractive to communication researchers.

Discussion Starters

1. How could Karl talk about Evan Spector's situation in a less polarized fashion? What are the linguistic barriers to such a discussion? Does a feminist critique of Burke's theory enable you to think of less polarized language? Explain your answer.

2. Use the pentad to analyze a public figure and the discourse surrounding some current controversy involving this figure.

3. How do you understand the use of the pentad as a method relative to Dramatism as a theory? Do all theories have specific methods that are used only with them? Why or why not?

4. Do you agree with Burke that guilt is the primary human motive? If not, what do you think is the primary human motive?

5. Burke believes that symbols, and language, in particular, are critical in life. When he says that symbolic action is more than mere physical or material reality, what do you think he means?

6. Do you agree with Condit that Burke's theory is culture specific rather than universal? Explain your answer.

7. Apply any element of Dramatism to classroom life.

Online Learning Center [www. mhhe.com/west4e]

Visit the Online Learning Center at www.mhhe.com/west4e for chapter-specific resources, such as story-into-theory and multiple-choice quizzes, as well as theory summaries and theory connection questions.

CHAPTER 20

The Narrative Paradigm

*Based on the research of **Walter Fisher***

Miles Campbell

Miles Campbell rolled over in bed and turned off his screaming alarm. He burrowed under the covers for a minute before he realized he'd better get up or he would miss his chem lab. He was tempted to sleep in, but a vision of his mother's face flashed before him, and he thought about how hard she had worked to help him get to college. He didn't want to disappoint her by not doing his very best now that he was here. So Miles sighed and shrugged off the covers. He slipped out of bed and splashed cold water on his face. By the time he was dressed and headed for the kitchen, he felt better about his day and his life in general.

In the kitchen he heard his housemates, Robert and Carlos, arguing about something. Seems like a normal morning, Miles thought. Those two can never get along. "What has got you guys up and yelling so early in the morning?" Miles asked as he began making his breakfast. Both Robert and Carlos looked up and grinned at Miles. "You won't think it's a big deal, Miles," Carlos said, "but we are discussing the candidates who are running for president of the Student Multicultural Association." "Yeah, you're right, Carlos," Miles laughed. "That doesn't seem like something worth arguing about to me!"

Robert handed Miles a copy of two campaign flyers. "Well, you might not think it's all that big a deal, but look at the difference between these two and tell me that Laura Huyge doesn't make more sense than Jorge Vega." Miles glanced at the two

flyers that Robert had given him. Huyge was an Asian American graduate student, and she had presented a list of ten points that represented her platform. She claimed to be interested in promoting cultural sensitivity and appreciation for diversity within the student body. Her flyer also listed a few ways that she planned to accomplish her goals. Her first big initiative, if she was elected, would be to sponsor a workshop with outside speakers and several hands-on activities to get students of different ethnicities talking to one another about difference and respect.

Miles looked up at Robert and Carlos and said, "Well, Laura sounds reasonable enough." Robert clapped Miles on the back, smiling broadly. Carlos interrupted, saying, "Hey, man, you haven't even looked at what Jorge has to say. Keep reading, man."

Miles put Laura's flyer aside and took up Jorge's. Jorge had chosen a completely different presentation style for his campaign flyer. Instead of laying out a specific platform point by point as Laura had, Jorge's flyer told a series of short stories. In the first one, Jorge related an incident in class when an African American woman could not get the professor's attention for anything she had to say. Every time she tried to contribute in class, the professor ignored her and asked a European American's opinion. Because she was the only Black person in the class, this woman believed the professor was prejudiced, but she wasn't sure what she could do about it. Another story in the flyer described a classroom situation in which the only two Latino students believed that they were called on to give the "Latin perspective" on every issue the professor raised. They were both really tired of being tokens. A third story talked about how certain bars on campus were considered "Black" and others were "Latino" and others were "White." This story told of two African American students who went to a White bar and felt really isolated.

As Miles read these stories, he thought that Jorge had it down cold. His description of life at the university was totally accurate. He himself had been ignored in classes and wondered if it had been because of his race. He'd also experienced being asked for the "Black" opinion, and he really resented that. Also, his social life rarely included people outside his own race, except for Carlos and a couple of Carlos's friends who were also Latinos. He never socialized with the Whites on campus. Jorge had given Miles a lot to think about, and, if he voted, he would vote for Jorge.

Throughout this book we have begun each chapter with a story about a person or several people who experience something through which we can illustrate the chapter's theory. The reason we have made this choice may be found within the theory of narration that Walter Fisher calls the Narrative Paradigm. The Narrative Paradigm promotes the belief that humans are storytellers and that values, emotions, and aesthetic considerations ground our beliefs and behaviors. In other words, we are more persuaded by a good story than by a good argument. Thus, Fisher would explain Miles's decision to vote for Jorge on the basis of the stories Jorge presented in his campaign flyer. Fisher asserts that the essence of human nature is storytelling.

Fisher is not alone in this belief. Robert Rowland (1989) comments that the idea that people are essentially storytellers has been adopted by many different disciplines including history, biology, anthropology, sociology, philosophy, psychology, and theology. Communication studies has also been influenced by the interest in narration. John Lucaites and Celeste Condit (1985) assert "the growing belief that narrative represents a universal medium of human consciousness" (p. 90). Kirsten Theye (2008) agrees, arguing that "narratives are crucial in human communication as a way of explaining the world" (p. 163).

It is notable that Fisher calls his approach a paradigm rather than a theory. Fisher uses the term to signal the breadth of his vision because a paradigm is considered broader than a theory. Fisher states that "there is no genre, including technical communication, that is not an episode in the story of life" (1985, p. 347). Thus, Fisher has constructed an approach to theoretical thinking that is more encompassing than any one specific theory. Fisher states that his use of the term *paradigm* refers to an effort to formalize and direct our understanding of the experience of all human communication (Koenig Kellas, 2008).

Furthermore, the use of the term *paradigm* indicates that Fisher's thinking represents a major shift from the thinking that had supported most previous theories of communication. Fisher believes that he is capturing the fundamental nature of human beings with the insight that we are storytellers and that we experience our lives in narrative form. He contrasts his approach with what he calls the rational paradigm, which characterized previous Western thinking. In this way, Fisher presents what can be called a **paradigm shift,** or a significant change in the way people think about the world and its meanings.

Fisher (1987) explains the paradigm shift by recounting a brief history of paradigms that have guided Western thinking. He notes that originally logos meant a combination of concepts including story, rationale, discourse, and thought. Fisher explains that this meaning held until the time of Plato and Aristotle, who distinguished between logos as reason and mythos as story and emotion. In this split, mythos, representing poetical discourse, was assigned a negative status relative to logos, or reason. The concept of rhetoric fell somewhere between the lofty logic of logos and the inferior status of poetics or mythos. Ranking mythos, logos, and rhetoric in this way reinforced the concept that not all discourse is equal. In fact, according to Aristotle (Chapter 18), some discourse is superior to others by virtue of its relationship to true knowledge. Only logos, Aristotle asserted, leads to true knowledge because it provides a system of logic that can be proved valid. Logos was found in the discourse of philosophy. Other forms of discourse lead to knowledge, but the knowledge they produce is probabilistic, not *true* in an absolute, invariable sense.

This Aristotelian distinction did not prevent Aristotle himself from valuing all the different forms of communication equally, but it did provide a rationale for later theorists in preferring logic and reason over mythos, or story, and rhetoric. Much subsequent scholarship has focused on a struggle over these major forms of discourse. The scientific revolution dethroned philosophy as the source of logic, placing logic instead within science and technology. But Fisher contends that this change was not a far-reaching one because both philosophy and science privilege a formal system of logic that continues to leave poetics or rhetoric in a devalued position. The mind-set of logic as primary that scholars employ is what Fisher calls the **rational world paradigm.**

Struggles among these different branches of knowledge continue today, but Fisher asserts that the Narrative Paradigm finds a way to transcend these struggles. Fisher argues that "acceptance of the narrative paradigm shifts the controversy from a focus on who 'owns' logos to a focus on what specific instances of discourse, regardless of form, provide the most trustworthy, reliable, and desirable guides to belief and to behavior, and under what conditions" (1987, p. 6). Thus, the Narrative Paradigm represents a different way of thinking about the world than that posited by the rational world paradigm. With narrative, Fisher suggests, we move away from an either/or dualism toward a more unified sense that embodies science, philosophy, story, myth, and logic. The Narrative Paradigm presents an alternative to the rational world paradigm without negating traditional rationality.

Fisher argues that the Narrative Paradigm accomplishes this shift through recognizing that "some discourse is more veracious, reliable, and trustworthy in respect to knowledge, truth, and reality than some other discourse, but no *form* or *genre* has final claim to these virtues" (1987, p. 19; emphasis in original). In asserting this, Fisher lays the groundwork for reclaiming the importance of the narrative, or story, without denigrating logic and reason, and he establishes a new way of conceptualizing rhetoric. Furthermore, Fisher asserts

paradigm shift
a significant change in the way most people see the world and its meanings

rational world paradigm
a system of logic employed by many researchers and professionals

This approach is founded on the principle that humans are storytelling animals. Furthermore, narrative logic is preferred over the traditional logic used in argument. Narrative logic, or the logic of good reasons, suggests that people judge the credibility of speakers by whether their stories hang together (have coherence) and ring true (have fidelity). The Narrative Paradigm allows a democratic judgment of speakers because no one has to be specially trained in persuasion to be able to draw conclusions based on the concepts of coherence and fidelity.

that story, or mythos, is imbued in all human communication endeavors (even those involving logic) because all arguments include "ideas that cannot be verified or proved in any absolute way. Such ideas arise in metaphor, values, gestures, and so on" (1987, p. 19). Fisher thus attempts to bridge the divide between logos (rational argument) and mythos (story, or narrative).

Assumptions of the Narrative Paradigm

Despite Fisher's attempt to show the Narrative Paradigm as a fusion of logic and aesthetic, he does point out that narrative logic is different from traditional logic and reasoning. We will discuss how these two differ throughout the chapter because this is an important distinction for Fisher and one that he continually refined as his thinking about the Narrative Paradigm evolved. An important aspect of the assumptions of the Narrative Paradigm is that they contrast with those of the rational world paradigm, just as the two logics differ. Fisher (1987) stipulated five assumptions:

- Humans are naturally storytellers.
- Decisions about a story's worth are based on "good reasons."
- Good reasons are determined by history, biography, culture, and character.
- Rationality is based on people's judgments of a story's consistency and truthfulness.
- We experience the world as filled with stories, and we must choose among them.

We can see how these clearly contrast to the parallel assumptions Fisher highlights in the rational world paradigm. This contrast is revealed in Table 20.1. We will briefly discuss each of the assumptions of the Narrative Paradigm, comparing them with their opposites in the rational world paradigm.

First, the Narrative Paradigm assumes that the essential nature of humans is rooted in story and storytelling. As our opening example of Miles illustrates,

Table 20.1 Contrast Between Narrative and Rational World Paradigms

NARRATIVE PARADIGM	RATIONAL WORLD PARADIGM
1. Humans are storytellers.	1. Humans are rational beings.
2. Decision making and communication are based on "good reasons."	2. Decision making is based on arguments.
3. Good reasons are determined by matters of history, biography, culture, and character.	3. Arguments adhere to specific criteria for soundness and logic.
4. Rationality is based in people's awareness of how internally consistent and truthful to lived experience stories appear.	4. Rationality is based in the quality of knowledge and formal reasoning processes.
5. The world is experienced by people as a set of stories from which to choose among. As we choose, we live life in a process of continual re-creation.	5. The world can be reduced to a series of logical relationships that are uncovered through reasoning.

stories persuade us, move us, and form the basis for our beliefs and actions. Miles had not heard much about the election for the president of the Multicultural Student Association on campus. In fact, Miles was rather apathetic about the election and had no real interest in, or opinions about, either candidate. Yet, after reading the compelling stories that Jorge included in his campaign literature, Miles decided to vote for Jorge. Miles found Laura's campaign material interesting but not nearly as involving as Jorge's. If the assumption of the rational world paradigm held true, we would expect the more rational argument to hold sway over Miles, and he should have decided to vote for Laura. The Narrative Paradigm explains his preference for Jorge.

Fisher also believes in this first assumption because he observes that narrative is universal—found in all cultures and time periods. Fisher asserts that "Any ethic, whether social, political, legal, or otherwise, involves narrative" (1984, p. 3). This universality of narrative prompts Fisher to suggest the term *Homo narrans* as the overarching metaphor for defining humanity. Fisher was influenced in his approach by reading moral theory espoused by Alasdair MacIntyre (1981). MacIntyre observes that "man [*sic*] is in his actions and practice, as well as in his fictions, essentially a story-telling animal" (p. 201). Fisher used MacIntyre's ideas as the foundation for the Narrative Paradigm. James Elkins (2001) agrees with Fisher's assumption about the centrality of stories for humans. Elkins observes that

> we use stories in virtually every aspect of our everyday lives—to pass the time, convey information, to let someone know who we are (or at least who we want to be), to locate ourselves in a place, family, and community. We turn to stories to both survive and to imagine, as well as for a host of instrumental purposes, for pleasure, and because we must. Stories are part of our human inheritance. (p. 1)

Research Notes

Barker, R. T., Rimler, G. W., Moreno, E., & Kaplan, T. E. (2004). Family business members' narrative perceptions: Values, succession, and commitment. *Journal of Technical Writing and Communication, 34,* 291–320.

The authors note that in the next forty years people in the United States will experience a historic transfer of wealth from one generation to another as retirements change the leadership of family-owned businesses. Their study focused on the "values related to the succession process in small family business" (p. 292) in order to understand how these values might affect family conflict.

The researchers frame their study in the Narrative Paradigm because it offers a good way to analyze the organizational culture in family businesses and because the logic of good reasons stresses the importance of values in persuasion. Stories can be interpreted to discover the values that persuaded a listener to take action.

Fifty-four participants representing twenty-six family-owned businesses were involved in the study. They were asked to respond to a questionnaire soliciting their reactions to two stories created by the researchers, demographic questions, and an organizational commitment scale.

The researchers conclude that the process of sharing values and a positive organizational culture are keys to minimizing conflict in family businesses. Furthermore, the narrative analysis supports "the notion of value congruity and theme awareness in family business success" (p. 309).

Roberts, K. G. (2004). Texturing the narrative paradigm: Folklore and communication. *Communication Quarterly, 52,* 129–142.

In this article, Kathleen Roberts advocates taking an interdisciplinary approach to narratives. She argues that the Narrative Paradigm and narrative in folklore can complement each other and enrich the contributions that each is able to make separately. Roberts comments that U.S. culture has moved away from public narratives, or those we all hold in common as a society. This, she notes, makes narrative even more important because "creating the story of one's life and becoming embedded in it—becoming a person rather than an 'individual'—informs one's ethical decisions and binds one in a moral duty to other persons in the narrative" (p. 131).

Roberts argues that the performance paradigm contributes four principles to the Narrative Paradigm (pp. 138–140):

1. The performance paradigm provides data for evaluating narrative fidelity.

2. The performance paradigm underscores historicity with an understanding of emergent structures and adds the element of "relevance" to the Narrative Paradigm.

3. The performance paradigm democratizes communication even further, continuing the work of the Narrative Paradigm.

4. The performance paradigm highlights "personhood," shifting the ontology of narrative to an epistemological frame.

Roberts concludes by noting that combining the two paradigms offers a method for evaluating narrative coherence and fidelity as well as enhancing Fisher's focus on ethics.

The second assumption of the Narrative Paradigm asserts that people make decisions about which stories to accept and which to reject on the basis of what makes sense to them, or good reasons. We will discuss what Fisher means by good reasons later in the chapter, but he does not mean strict logic or argument. This assumption recognizes that not all stories are equally effective; instead, the deciding factor in choosing among stories is personal rather than

THE DYING ART OF STORYTELLING

an abstract code of argument, or what we traditionally call reason. From Fisher's point of view, in our beginning vignette, Laura has told a story in her campaign flyer too. Miles simply chooses to reject her story and accept Jorge's because it is more personally involving to him. Recent events—ranging from the tragic events of September 11, 2001, to the U.S. war in Iraq to the controversies over gay marriage to the floods in Louisiana, Mississippi, and the Midwest—show us the reality of competing stories.

As people listen to these conflicting stories, they choose among them. Their choices do not stem from traditional logic but from narrative logic. When people shift from traditional logic to narrative logic, Fisher believes their lives will be improved because narrative logic is more democratic than formal logic. As Fisher (1984) asserts, "All persons have the capacity to be rational in the narrative paradigm" (p. 10). Whereas formal logic calls for an elite trained in the complexities of the logical system, the Narrative Paradigm calls on the practical wisdom that everyone possesses.

The third assumption deals with what specifically influences people's choices and provides good reasons for them. The rational world paradigm assumes that argument is ruled by the dictates of soundness (Toulmin, 1958). For Stephen Toulmin, the anatomy of an argument is the movement from data to a conclusion. This movement needs to be judged by soundness, or an examination of the formal logic that guides the conclusion. In contrast, the Narrative Paradigm suggests that soundness is not the only way to evaluate good reasons. In

fact, soundness may not even be an accurate way of describing how people make this judgment. The Narrative Paradigm assumes that narrative rationality is affected by history, biography, culture, and character. Thus, Fisher introduces the notion of context into the Narrative Paradigm. People are influenced by the context in which they are embedded. Therefore, the material that appears persuasive to Miles is the material that is specifically relevant to him personally. It is not material that adheres to a code of formal logic and persuasion.

The fourth assumption forms a core issue of the narrative approach. It asserts that people believe stories insofar as the stories seem internally consistent and truthful. We will discuss this further in the next section when we describe the concept of narrative rationality.

Finally, Fisher's perspective is based on the assumption that the world is a set of stories, and as we choose among them, we experience life differently, allowing us to re-create our lives. Miles's choice to support Jorge may cause him to cast his own life story differently. He may no longer see himself as a loner. He may change his sense of political action based on his choice of Jorge's story. You can see how the Narrative Paradigm contrasts with the rational world paradigm, which tends to see the world as less transient and shifting and which discovers truth through rational analysis, not through narrative logic's emotional responses to compelling stories.

A study illustrating these assumptions in a courtroom context examined the Narrative Paradigm's utility for professional communication. Christine Kelly and Michele Zak (1999) assert that former football player O. J. Simpson's acquittal was due to the triumph of narrative argument over rational argument. The defense was victorious because it framed Simpson's story in a manner that resonated with the jury whereas the prosecution relied on the rational world paradigm, directed more toward the judge and the opposing lawyers. Kelly and Zak note that the prosecutors "drew on the language of technical expertise and took responsibility for presenting a careful case in a court of law without reference to the lives of the jury" (p. 301).

Key Concepts in the Narrative Approach

Tracing the assumptions of the Narrative Paradigm leads us to a consideration of some of the key concepts that form the core of the theoretical framework: narration, narrative rationality (which includes coherence or probability and fidelity), and the logic of good reasons.

Narration

Narration is often thought of simply as a story, but for Fisher, narration is much more than a plotted story with a beginning, middle, and end. In Fisher's perspective, **narration** includes any verbal or nonverbal account with a sequence of events to which listeners assign a meaning. Specifically, Fisher states, "When I use the term 'narration,' I do not mean a fictive composition whose propositions may be true or false and have no necessary relationship to the message of that composition. By 'narration,' I mean symbolic actions—words and/or deeds—that have sequence and meaning for those who live, create, or interpret them" (1987, p. 58). This definition implies the need for a storyteller and a listener.

Fisher's definition is extremely broad and parallels what many people think of as communication itself. This, of course, is Fisher's point: All communication is narrative. He argues that narrative is not a specific genre (stories as opposed to poems, for example), but rather it is a mode of social influence. Furthermore, it is his contention that all life is composed of narratives. When you listen to a class lecture, when you give an excuse to a professor for not turning in a paper on time, and when you read the newspaper, watch television, talk to your friends, you are hearing and shaping narratives.

Narrative Rationality

Given that our lives are experienced in narratives, we need a method for judging which ones to believe and which to disregard. This standard can be found in **narrative rationality**, which provides us with a means for judging narratives that is quite different from the traditional methods found in the rational world paradigm. As we mentioned previously, traditional tests of rationality include whether claims correspond to actual facts, whether all relevant facts have been considered, whether arguments are internally consistent, and whether the reasoning used conforms to standards of formal and informal logic (Fisher, 1978). Narrative rationality, in contrast to traditional logic, operates on the basis of two different principles: coherence and fidelity.

Coherence The principle of coherence is an important standard for assessing narrative rationality, which will ultimately determine whether or not a person accepts a particular narrative or rejects it. Coherence refers to the internal consistency of a narrative. When judging a story's coherence, the listener would ask whether the narrative seemed to hang together in a consistent manner. Narratives possess coherence when all the pieces of the story are present; we do not feel that the storyteller has left out important details or contradicted elements of the story in any way. Beginning in 2004, when many in the United States heard about the prisoner abuse at Abu Ghraib, they felt a lack of coherence. It didn't seem possible that enlisted soldiers could have participated in this torture without some official sanction. Coherence is the standard of sensemaking applied to a given narrative. This sensemaking is usually obtained when the characters in a story behave in relatively consistent ways.

When Miles read the narratives contained in Jorge's campaign literature, he saw a consistent thread running through them: His university has racial problems. If Jorge had presented some problems based on race and then shaped the narrative to conclude that all was well with race relations at the university, Miles would have rejected the story for being inconsistent.

Coherence is often measured by the organizational and structural elements of a narrative. When a storyteller skips around and leaves out important information, interrupts the flow of the story to add elements forgotten earlier, and generally is not smooth in structuring the narrative, the listener may reject the narrative for not possessing coherence. Coherence is based on three specific types of consistency: structural coherence, material coherence, and characterological coherence.

structural coherence
a type of coherence referring to the flow of the story

STRUCTURAL COHERENCE   The type of consistency Fisher calls **structural coherence rests** on the degree to which the elements of the story flow smoothly. When stories are confusing, when one part does not seem to lead to the next, or when the plot is unclear, then they lack structural coherence.

material coherence
a type of coherence referring to the congruence between one story and other related stories

MATERIAL COHERENCE   **Material coherence** refers to the degree of congruence between one story and other stories that seem related to it. For example, you may have heard several stories about why two friends of yours have stopped speaking to each other. If all the stories but one attribute the problem to one friend having misled the other, causing an embarrassing situation, you are unlikely to believe the one unique story. You would believe that the different story lacked material coherence.

characterological coherence
a type of coherence referring to the believability of the characters in the story

CHARACTEROLOGICAL COHERENCE   **Characterological coherence** refers to the believability of the characters in the story. For instance, you may have a professor whom you dislike a great deal. This professor ridicules you and other students in the class whenever anyone contributes to class discussions. In addition, the professor makes racist, homophobic, and sexist jokes in class. Your impression is that this professor is a thoroughly objectionable person. Given this background, you would be unlikely to accept a story in which this professor was shown in an admirable or even heroic light. You would reject the story for not possessing characterological coherence.

fidelity
a principle of narrative rationality judging the credibility of a story

Fidelity   The other critical standard for assessing narrative rationality is fidelity, or the truthfulness or reliability of the story. Stories with fidelity ring true to a listener. When Miles reads the stories that Jorge has in his campaign literature, he thinks to himself that those events have happened to him at the university. Miles wonders if Jorge has been following him around campus, watching what goes on in his life. This makes the stories powerful to Miles. They possess a great deal of fidelity for him. Fisher (1987) notes that when the elements of a story "represent accurate assertions about social reality" (p. 105), they have fidelity.

THE LOGIC OF GOOD REASONS   Related to Fisher's notion of fidelity is the primary method that he proposes for assessing narrative fidelity: the logic

of **good reasons.** Fisher asserts that when narratives possess fidelity, they constitute good reasons for a person to hold a particular belief or take an action. For example, Miles sees Jorge's stories as possessing fidelity, which makes the stories persuasive; the stories form good reasons for Miles to vote for Jorge.

good reasons
a set of values for accepting a story as true and worthy of acceptance; provides a method for assessing fidelity

Fisher (1987) explains his concept of logic by saying that it means "a systematic set of procedures that will aid in the analysis and assessment of elements of reasoning in rhetorical interactions" (p. 106). Thus, logic for the narrative paradigm enables a person to judge the worth of stories. The logic of good reasons presents a listener with a set of values that appeal to her or him and form warrants for accepting or rejecting the advice advanced by any form of narrative. This does not mean that any good reason is equal to any other; it simply means that whatever prompts a person to believe a narrative is bound to a value or a conception of what is good.

As Fisher describes it, this logic is a process consisting of two series of five questions that the listener asks about the narrative. The first five questions are the following:

1. Are the statements that claim to be factual in the narrative really factual?

2. Have any relevant facts been omitted from the narrative or distorted in its telling?

3. What are the patterns of reasoning that exist in the narrative?

4. How relevant are the arguments in the story to any decision the listener may make?

5. How well does the narrative address the important and significant issues of this case?

These questions constitute a logic of reasons. To transform this into a logic of *good* reasons, there are five more questions that introduce the concept of values into the process of assessing practical knowledge. These questions are as follows:

1. What are the implicit and explicit values contained in the narrative?

2. Are the values appropriate to the decision that is relevant to the narrative?

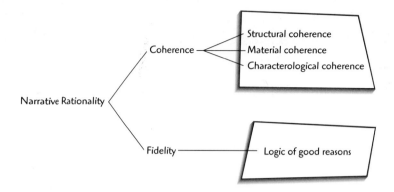

Figure 20.1
Elements of Narrative Rationality

Narrative Rationality
- Coherence
  - Structural coherence
  - Material coherence
  - Characterological coherence
- Fidelity
  - Logic of good reasons

3. What would be the effects of adhering to the values embedded in the narrative?
4. Are the values confirmed or validated in lived experience?
5. Are the values of the narrative the basis for ideal human conduct?

Fisher illustrates the logic of good reasons with a book written by Jonathan Schell (1982). *The Fate of the Earth,* which was very popular in the 1980s, argues that the nuclear weapons race must cease. Fisher asserts that even though experts found the book inaccurate on technical grounds, the narrative it espouses was extremely popular with the general public. Fisher argues that this was because the book tells a story that meets the criteria of coherence and fidelity. It focuses on a set of values that many people found relevant at that point in history. As the Narrative Paradigm predicts, the well-told story—consisting of narrative rationality—was more compelling to readers than the expert testimony that refuted the factual accuracy of the narrative. The relationship among the elements making up narrative rationality is illustrated by Figure 20.1.

Integration, Critique, and Closing

Fisher's Narrative Paradigm offers new insights into communication behavior and directs our attention to democratic processes in the area of rhetorical criticism. Fisher contributes the idea that people's lived experiences make them capable of analyzing rhetoric. Furthermore, the Narrative Paradigm helps us to see the nature of multiple logics at work in our communication encounters. Thus, the Narrative Paradigm has made a substantial contribution to our understanding of human communication and human nature in general.

As you think about the Narrative Paradigm, consider the criteria of scope, logical consistency, utility, testability, and heurism.

Integration

| Communication Tradition | Rhetorical | Semiotic | Phenomenological | Cybernetic | Socio-Psychological | Socio-Cultural | Critical |

Theory Into Practice

Colin

I understand exactly what Fisher meant with the terms *coherence* and *fidelity*. I have a friend named Marco who constantly tells crazy stories, and I spend a lot of time trying to figure out whether to believe him or not. And I do use coherence and fidelity to decide if he's being truthful or just trying to get me to fall for a bunch of bull. When he told me about how he got trapped in his car the other day in a parking ramp—I guess the locks froze and he couldn't open the doors—I first thought about the stories he's told me before (which I believed) to see if this one fit with those. Then I considered him as a character and whether this was something likely to happen to him. I also tried to judge how well the story hung together—I asked him a bunch of questions to see if he'd contradict himself or anything. Finally, I decided to believe him. It was a pretty funny story.

Fisher's logic of good reasons focuses on prevailing values and fails to account for the ways in which stories can promote social change. In some ways, both Kirkwood and Fisher agree that this observation is more of an extension to the theory than a punishing critique. Fisher (1987) claims that humans are inventive and that we can accept new stories when they appeal to us. In this process we can change our values rather than demand that stories simply confirm our existing values. To a degree, Miles changed his values regarding the importance of voting and involvement in student life as a result of Jorge's narratives.

Afsheen Nomai and George Dionisopoulos (2002) imply the same critique in their study of how the media advance the narrative of the American Dream. Nomai and Dionisopoulos analyze the story of Joe Cubas, an American sports agent who has brought more than twenty Cuban defectors to the United States to play baseball. They call this the "Cubas Narrative" and argue that the media coverage of Cubas and the ballplayers "illuminates a most benign and inviting myth of American capitalism . . . [while obscuring] the uncomfortable reality that the needs of the capitalist system bifurcate the Cuban refugees into two classes" (p. 109). The Narrative Paradigm may not easily allow access to marginalized or less popular stories in the culture.

Kirsten Theye (2008) argues that her analysis of Vice President Dick Cheney's apologies, after shooting his friend in a hunting accident in 2006, shows that Fisher's distinction between narrative coherence and narrative fidelity is not useful. She states that it's impossible to separate the two. Her suggestion is to forget the two components as separate concepts and instead focus on the basic question underlying narrative rationality: "whether a story rings true to the audience based on their experiences" (p. 174).

Communication Context	Intrapersonal | Interpersonal | Small Group | Organizational **Public/Rhetorical** | Mass/Media | Cultural
Approach to Knowing	Positivistic/Empirical | **Interpretive/Hermeneutic** | Critica

Critique

Evaluation Criteria	Scope | **Logical Consistency** | Parsimony | **Utility** | **Testability** | **Heurism** | Test of Time

Scope

The critique that the Narrative Paradigm is too broad mainly focuses or Fisher's claim that all communication is narrative. Researchers object to tha claim for two reasons: First, some have questioned the utility of a definitior that includes everything. How meaningful is the definition of narrative i it means all communication behavior? Second, some researchers, notably Robert Rowland (1987, 1989), suggest that some forms of communication are not narrative in the way that Fisher maintains. According to Rowland, science fiction and fantasy do not conform to most people's values. Rather, these genres often challenge existing values. Rowland also questions the utility of considering a novel (such as Arthur Koestler's *Darkness at Noon*) and a political pamphlet (such as one produced by the Committee on the Present Danger) both as narratives as Fisher does. Although both tell stories about the repressive character of the Soviet system, they do so in such different ways that Rowland believes it does a disservice to both writings to place them in the same category. Furthermore, it complicates our understanding of the definition of narrative when two such disparate examples can both be labeled as narrative.

Logical Consistency

The Narrative Paradigm has been faulted for failing to be consistent with some of the claims that Fisher makes about it. For instance, Rowland (1987) finds that the narrative approach does not actually provide a more democratic structure compared with the hierarchical system espoused by the rational world paradigm, nor does it completely offer an alternative to that paradigm. Rowland says that Fisher overstates the problem of domination of the public by the elite, or by the expert, in the rational world paradigm. In addition, Rowland argues that "there is nothing inherent in storytelling that guarantees that the elites will not control a society" (p. 272).

Utility

The Narrative Paradigm has critics who find it less than useful due to what they consider its conservative bias. William Kirkwood (1992) observes that

Testability

The criticism concerning the overly broad scope of the theory leads to another issue. How testable is a theory that is so broad and inclusive? For instance, how are we to discriminate stories from other types of communication if virtually all communication is narrative? The Narrative Paradigm offers little guidance for structuring our studies, making it difficult to prove whether an assertion is incorrect. Is there value in treating a ritual greeting ("Hi, how was your day?") and an involved narrative explaining one's desire for a divorce in the same way?

Heurism

Despite criticisms, which primarily urge refinements of the theory, not its abandonment, Fisher's Narrative Paradigm has contributed a great deal to the study of human communication. For one thing, the idea of people as storytellers has proved captivating and heuristic. Storytelling seems an apt metaphor for understanding how humans use communication to make sense of the world (Barker, Rimler, Moreno, & Kaplan, 2004; Fiese, 2003; Langellier & Peterson, 2004; Roberts, 2004). Fisher has provided a new paradigm for understanding human nature, squarely located in the symbolic realm of communication.

Future scholarship will extend the framework of the Narrative Paradigm to remediate its shortcomings and capitalize on its strengths. In constructing the Narrative Paradigm, Fisher has provided a rich framework for such scholarship to take place.

Discussion Starters

1. Can you think of any other explanations besides the Narrative Paradigm for Miles's preference for Jorge's candidacy after he read the campaign flyers?

2. Do you agree with Fisher that humans are storytellers? What does that mean to you in a practical sense?

3. When you listen to others' stories, do you evaluate them based on coherence and fidelity? Can you think of any other criteria that you use to evaluate the stories that you hear?

4. What support does Fisher have for his contention that all communication is narration? Can you think of some communication that is not narrative in nature? If all communication is narration, can the theory be tested?

5. The Narrative Paradigm suggests that when an expert argument is compared to a good story, the expert argument will fail because it will lack the coherence and the fidelity that a narrative possesses. Do you agree or disagree

with this claim? Give an example where expert testimony failed to persuade you. Give an example of a good story that failed to persuade you.

6. Choose a story that has been in the news recently and analyze it for narrative rationality.

7. If Fisher discards the rational world paradigm, why does he advocate narrative rationality? How are they different?

Online Learning Center (www. mhhe.com/west4e)

Visit the Online Learning Center at www.mhhe.com/west4e for chapter-specific resources, such as story-into-theory and multiple-choice quizzes, as well as theory summaries and theory connection questions.

The Media

ARGUABLY, VERY FEW INSTITUTIONS IN OUR LIVES affect us more than the media. Their presence almost invades us. Radio, television, film, DVDs, VCRs, cell phones, answering machines, and fax machines seem to be our technological friends. And we're all "virtually" followed by the Internet. Media have become part of our lives, and it's apparent we'll never be able to reverse this fact.

It is in this spirit that we offer the four theories in this section called "The Media." Each theory places various media as central to our lives, and these respective media theorists believe that we respond in different ways to the barrage of electronic technology. In "exposing" the media for their role in maintaining power relationships in society, Cultural Studies highlights the influence that mediated structures have on culture. Cultural theorists aim to unravel the power relationships in society in order to provide marginalized populations more voice. Cultivation Analysis focuses on the role of television in our lives. This theory is concerned with the effects of long-term exposure to television on people's perceptions of the world. Uses and Gratifications Theory, however, suggests that the viewer/listener is able to discriminate in media consumption. It concerns itself with what people do with particular media. The central feature of the Spiral of Silence Theory pertains to the influence of media on whether people will speak out about an issue. Examining how technology has ruled our lives, Media Ecology Theory argues that the primary media of the age (currently the Internet, for instance) usually take precedence over the content of the message.

We will continue to be affected by media throughout our lives. Technology continues to develop, and even as we write these words, new ways of bringing messages to people are being conceptualized. While learning about the theories in this section, you will encounter a number of timely topics pertaining to the media: dominance, patriarchy, personal needs and values, and the ethics associated with media reporting.

CHAPTER 21

Cultural Studies

*Based on the research of **Stuart Hall***

Lisa and John Petrillo have lived in the same trailer park for four years, and, with two young children, they realize that the wages they earn as migrant workers will probably never permit them to own their own home. They appreciate that Mr. DeMoss, the owner of the egg farm where they work, has provided housing for them, but they wish that they could have more privacy so that their neighbors would not be able to hear every word they say in the evening. The Petrillos do not have any desire to leave their tiny city because they realize that jobs are not that plentiful in New England. So they get by in the trailer park, and they dream about a big backyard where their two kids and their dog, Scooter, can play.

The Petrillos' dream often unfolds on the television shows they watch at night. Even though cable TV is expensive and not a necessity, they both love to watch shows that help them escape their daily routines. Watching TV, Lisa and John are bombarded with messages about the low home prices. They both know that the housing market is taking a dive, yet they keep seeing the same commercial over and over again promoting home ownership as the "American Dream." They watch the infomercials that promote "Ten Ways to Get Your American Dream." They look at each other, wondering why they continue to live the way they do—two children, two bedrooms, and a common bathing area in the migrant camp. They both know that they don't have the money to purchase a home, but they also know that they aren't happy with the way things are.

Recently, Mr. DeMoss's farm was investigated by the government for unsanitary living and working conditions. DeMoss was told to clean up the place and was threatened with stiff fines unless he improved the situation. As a result, he had authorized spending a lot of money for individual lavatory facilities and was talking to the local grocery chain to ask for their help in granting discounts to employees at the egg farm. As a gesture of goodwill, and to avoid a media attack, DeMoss was also prepared to increase each worker's paycheck by 15 percent by the end of the month. He also promised to help relocate families with children to more suitable accommodations.

The Petrillos were ecstatic. They dreaded the "communal" bathing area and welcomed more privacy for their children and themselves. They were very excited about the opportunity to save money on food, and, of course, they were thrilled that their paychecks would increase almost immediately. This, they thought, was the beginning of saving for their American Dream. They knew that they made just enough money to pay all of their bills, and now with the raise, the extra money would go into a rainy day fund that could eventually be used to purchase a home.

Lisa wrote to her brother in South America to tell him the good news. She wrote about how relatively easy it is to get a home in the United States. She quoted the commercials she saw so frequently on television: "Good sense, good money, and a good deal," she related. She had watched the evening news reports about the low interest rates and had even gone to the library to read up on mortgages. She thought that if they saved their extra money, within a year, she and her family could be living in a new home. For now, though, Lisa was excited about the chance to move to what DeMoss called "suitable" housing. "It has to be better than this," she thought. Lisa was starting to think that her luck was changing.

We cannot overstate how much the U.S. culture relies on the media. Each day, for instance, millions of homes tune in to dozens of different "news" programs on television. In fact, Stanley Baran and Dennis Davis (2009) conclude that "the media have become a primary means by which many of us experience or learn about many aspects of the world around us" (p. 215). However, the manner in which the media report events can vary significantly. Some journalists take pride in their fact finding. Others rely on personal testimony. Still others seek out experts to comment on events and topics as they unfold, whether they pertain to celebrity trials, natural disasters, refugees' plight, war, terrorist attacks, or school shootings. A consistent process for following a school shooting, for instance, resulted from the coverage of the 1999 Columbine school shooting in which twelve students and a teacher were killed. It is now predictable: First, the tragedy is usually reported in "real time," that is, as it happens. Next, reporters interview witnesses to get firsthand accounts of the shootings. Finally, journalists gather experts on both sides of the gun control issue to assess whether gun control laws are sufficiently tough. This last activity involving experts seems to beg other questions about the media's role in such events: Are they trying to convey a larger message about society in general? Is the reporting of images and stories done thoughtfully and conscientiously? Do the media have hidden agendas?

Reporting events with a hidden agenda has several implications. When the media fail to report all aspects of a story, someone or some group is inevitably affected. Nowhere is this more apparent than in the early coverage of AIDS, which was first diagnosed in the gay community. Edward Alwood (1997) notes that because most news editors did not consider gay deaths to be newsworthy, major news outlets (including the *New York Times*) failed to provide coverage of the disease. In fact, the disease was killing far more people than the thirty-four who died from Legionnaires' disease in 1976 and the eighty-four women who died of toxic shock syndrome in 1980. Yet it wasn't until the death of actor Rock Hudson in 1985 that major news stories were devoted to the subject of AIDS. By that time, however, more than 6,000 people had died from the disease. Again, the media's message is implied but significant: The deaths of gay men are not newsworthy.

Theorist Stuart Hall questioned the role of the media and their frequently false and misleading images. Unlike other communication theorists, however, Hall focused on the role of the media and their ability to shape public opinions of marginalized populations, including people of color, the poor, and others who do not reflect a White, male, heterosexual (and wealthy) point of view.

For Hall, the personal is the political. A former high school teacher who taught English, math, and geography, Hall's background influenced his conceptualization of cultural studies. He speaks of doing graduate work and, as a Jamaican, of "trying to understand what my relationship was to Jamaican culture, and what Jamaican culture was about because, basically, I'd left it behind and then it came to meet me" (cited in MacCabe, 2008, p. 13). This kind of philosophical thinking resonates throughout Cultural Studies.

This orientation underscores his work in Cultural Studies. Cultural Studies is a theoretical perspective that focuses on how culture is influenced by powerful, dominant groups. Cultural studies is clearly rooted in politics, but "too often, the politics pervades the body of work, where we are supposed to be figuring out what is going on, in all of its complexity" (cited in Cho, 2008, p. 103). Unlike several other theoretical traditions in this book, Cultural Studies does not refer to a single doctrine of human behavior. In fact, Stuart Hall (1992) persuasively argues that "Cultural Studies has multiple discourses; it has a number of different histories. It is a whole set of formations; it has its own different conjunctures and moments in the past. . . . I want to insist on that!" (p. 278). Although Hall and other theorists in Cultural Studies have applied many of the theory's concepts to the media, Cultural Studies extends beyond the media and has often been referred to as "audience studies" (Angus, Jhally, Lewis, & Schwichtenberg, 1989). Cultural Studies concerns the attitudes, approaches, and criticisms of a culture. Culture and media are the principle features of the theory, and it has provided an intellectual framework that has prompted scholars to discuss, disagree, challenge, and reflect. In fact, John Hartley (2003) observes that researchers have come to "little agreement about what counts as cultural studies, either as a critical practice or an institutional apparatus . . . the field is riven by fundamental disagreements about what cultural studies is for, in whose interests it is done, what theories, methods and objects of study are proper to it, and where to set its limits" (p. 2).

Cultural Studies has its background and its beginnings in Britain, although the United States has also taken a lead in understanding Cultural Studies (e.g., Grossberg, 1997). As a cultural theorist and the former director of the Center for Contemporary Cultural Studies (CCCS) at the University of Birmingham in England, Stuart Hall (1981, 1989) contends that the media are powerful tools of the elite. Media serve to communicate dominant ways of thinking, regardless of the efficacy of such thinking. Cultural Studies emphasizes that the media keep the powerful people in control while the less powerful absorb what is presented to them. Our Lisa and John Petrillo, for instance, exemplify a marginalized group (the poor) who have been taken in by the American Dream of owning a home. Of course, cultural theorists would argue that the media—in this case, the infomercial sponsors—are taking advantage of a couple who will probably never have enough money to own a home. Yet the message from the popular media is that it is possible. All that is needed, according to the message, is good sense and good money.

Cultural Studies is a tradition rooted in the writings of German philosopher Karl Marx. Because Marxist principles form the foundation of the theory,

Cultural Studies • *Theory at a Glance*

> The media represent ideologies of the dominant class in a society. Because media are controlled by corporations (the elite), the information presented to the public is consequently influenced and targeted with profit in mind. The media's influence and the role of power must be taken into consideration when interpreting a culture.

let's look further into this theoretical backdrop. We then examine two assumptions of Cultural Studies.

The Marxist Legacy: Power to the People

Philosopher Karl Marx (1818–1883) is generally credited with identifying how the powerful (the elite) exploit the powerless (the working class; 1963). He believed that being powerless can lead to **alienation,** or the psychological condition whereby people begin to feel that they have little control over their future. For Marx, though, alienation is most destructive under capitalism. Specifically, when people lose control over their own means of production (as happens in capitalism) and must sell their time to some employer, they become alienated. Capitalism results in a profit-driven society, and workers in a capitalistic society are measured by their labor potential.

Marx believed that the class system—a monolithic system that pervades all society—must be unearthed by the collective working class, or *proletariat*. He felt that laborers were often subjected to poor working and living conditions because the elite were unwilling to yield their control. As with Lisa and John Petrillo, laborers across society are constantly relegated to secondary status. The elite, or ruling, class's interests become socially ingrained, and therefore people become enslaved in society. One of Marx's principal concerns was ensuring that some revolutionary action of the proletariat be undertaken to break the chains of slavery and ultimately to subvert alienation under a capitalistic society. The capitalistic society, according to Marxist tradition, shapes society and the individuals within it (Weedon, 2004).

Marxist thinkers who believed the working class was oppressed because of corporate-owned media have been called the **Frankfurt School theorists.** These thinkers and writers believed that the media's messages were constructed and delivered with one goal in mind: capitalism. That is, although the media might claim that they are delivering information for the "common good," the bottom line (money) frames each message. Those affiliated with the Frankfurt School felt that the media could be considered an "authoritarian personality," which meant that they were opposed to the male-centered/male-owned media. In fact,

alienation
perception that one has little control over his or her future

Frankfurt School theorists
a group of scholars who believed that the media were more concerned with making money than with presenting news

Herbert Marcuse, a Frankfurt thinker, was the leader of a group of social revolutionaries whose goal was to break down this patriarchal system.

    The application of Marxist principles to Cultural Studies is more subtle than direct. This has prompted some scholars to consider the theory to be more **neo-Marxist,** which means the theory diverges from classical Marxism to some extent. First, unlike Marx, those in Cultural Studies have integrated a variety of perspectives into their thinking, including those from the arts, the humanities, and the social sciences. Second, theorists in Cultural Studies expand the subordinate group to include additional powerless and marginalized people, not just laborers. These groups include gay men and lesbians, ethnic minorities, women, and even children. Third, everyday life for Marx was centered on work and the family. Writers in Cultural Studies have also studied recreational activities, hobbies, and sporting events in seeking to understand how individuals function in society. In sum, Marx's original thinking may have been appropriate for post–World War II populations, but his ideas now require clarification, elaboration, and application to a diverse society. Cultural Studies moves beyond a strict, limited interpretation of society toward a broader conception of culture.

    Now that you have a brief understanding of how theorists in Cultural Studies were influenced by the writings of Marx, we examine two primary assumptions of Cultural Studies.

neo-Marxist
limited embracement of Marxism

Assumptions of Cultural Studies

Cultural Studies is essentially concerned with how elite groups such as the media exercise their power over subordinate groups. The theory is rooted in a few fundamental claims about culture and power:

- Culture pervades and invades all facets of human behavior.
- People are part of a hierarchical structure of power.

    The first assumption pertains to the notion of culture, a concept we addressed in Chapter 2. To review, we identified culture as a community of meaning. In Cultural Studies, we need a different interpretation of the word, one that underscores the nature of the theory. The various norms, ideas, values, and forms of understanding in a society that help people interpret their reality are part of a culture's ideology. According to Hall (1981), **ideology** refers to "those images, concepts and premises which provide the frameworks through which we represent, interpret, understand, and 'make sense' of some aspect of social existence" (p. 31). Hall believes that ideologies include the languages, the concepts, and the categories that different social groups collect in order to make sense of their environments.

ideology
framework used to make sense of our existence

To a great extent, cultural practices and institutions permeate our ideologies. We cannot escape the cultural reality that, as a global community, actions are not performed in a vacuum. Graham Murdock (1989) emphasizes the pervasiveness of culture by noting that "all groups are constantly engaged in creating and remaking meaning systems and embodying these meanings in expressive forms, social practices, and institutions" (p. 436). Interestingly and predictably, however, Murdock notes, being part of a diverse cultural community often results in struggles over meaning, interpretation, identity, and control. These struggles, or **culture wars,** suggest that there are frequently deep divisions in the perception of the significance of a cultural issue or event. Individuals often compete to help shape a nation's identity. For example, both pro-life and pro-choice groups want to define the "product" of conception. One wants to define it as a "fetus" and the other as a "baby." Both groups strive to make their meanings dominant. This struggle takes place not only in the courts but also in the media and in the classroom.

culture wars
cultural struggles over meaning, identity, and influence

In addition to the various ideologies, Dreama Moon (2008) notes that culture includes a number of diverse activities of a population. In the United States, there are many behaviors, some done daily and others less frequently. For instance, it is common for people to date within their ethnicity, for families to visit one another during holidays, and for people to attend religious services at least once a week. There are also more mundane behaviors, such as getting your driver's license renewed, running on the treadmill, pulling weeds from your garden, or listening to public radio while driving home from work. For those interested in Cultural Studies, it is crucial to examine these activities to understand how the ideology of a population is maintained. Paul du Gay, Stuart Hall, Linda Janes, Hugh Mackay, and Keith Negus (1997) explain that these practices intersect to help us understand the production and dissemination of meaning in a culture. At the same time, the meaning of a culture is reflected by such practices. Culture, then, cannot be separated from meaning in society. In fact, uncovering prevailing cultural meanings is one important aim of researchers in Cultural Studies.

Meaning in our culture is profoundly sculpted by the media. The media could simply be considered the technological carrier of culture, but as this chapter will point out, the media are so much more. Consider the words of Michael Real (1996) regarding the media's role in U.S. culture: "Media invade our living space, shape the taste of those around us, inform and persuade us on products and policies, intrude into our private dreams and public fears, and in turn, invite us to inhabit them" (pp. xiii–xiv). No doubt, for example, that the media contain messages—intentional or unintentional—that get the Petrillos to accept the goals, dreams, and standards of success portrayed in the media.

**"Power corrupts, but not like it did
when I was younger."**

A second assumption of cultural theory pertains to people as an important part of a powerful social hierarchy. Power operates at all levels in society. However, power in this sense is not role based, as we considered it in our discussion of Structuration Theory in Chapter 15. Rather, Hall is interested in the power held by social groups or the power between groups. Meaning and power are intricately related, for as Hall (1989) contends, "Meaning cannot be conceptualized outside the field of play of power relations" (p. 48). In keeping with the Marxist tradition, power is something that subordinate groups desire but cannot achieve. Often there is a struggle for power, and the victor is usually the person at the top of the social hierarchy. An example of what we are discussing here can be observed in the U.S. culture's preoccupation with beauty. Theorists in Cultural Studies contend that because beauty is often defined as thin and good-looking, anyone not matching these qualities would be considered unattractive. Hall may believe that the attractive people—at the top of the social hierarchy— are able to wield more power than those at the bottom (the unattractive).

Perhaps the ultimate source of power in our society, however, is the media. Hall (1989) maintains that the media are simply too powerful. He is not shy in his indictment of the media's character by calling it dishonest and "fundamentally dirty" (p. 48). In a diverse culture, Hall argues, no institution should have the power to decide what the public hears. Gary Woodward (1997) draws a similar conclusion when he states that there is a tradition whereby journalists serve as guardians of the nation's cultural activities: If the media deem something to have importance, then something has importance; an otherwise unimportant event suddenly carries importance.

Let's revisit our story of Lisa and John Petrillo. Theorists in Cultural Studies would argue that as members of a minority population, the Petrillos have been inherently relegated to a subordinate position in society. Their work environment—as migrant workers on a large egg farm—is the product of a capitalistic society, one in which laborers work under difficult conditions. Although they will inevitably have difficulty owning their own home because of their low wages, writers in Cultural Studies would point to the media's barrage of images and stories touting the American Dream. Although the message may convey hope for the Petrillos, their dream of owning their own home might better be called a fantasy because the elite power structure (the media) does not honestly convey the reality of their circumstances. Perhaps unknown to the Petrillos, the media are a tool of the dominant class. The future of Lisa and John Petrillo, then, will overtly and covertly be influenced by the ruling class.

Hegemony: The Influence on the Masses

The concept of hegemony is an important feature of Cultural Studies, and much of the theory rests on an understanding of this term. Scott Lash (2007) contends that "from the beginnings of cultural studies in the 1970s, 'hegemony' has been perhaps *the* pivotal concept" (p. 55). **Hegemony** can be generally defined as the influence, power, or dominance of one social group over another. The idea is a complex one that can be traced back to the work of Antonio Gramsci, one of the founders of the Italian Communist Party who was later imprisoned by the Italian fascists. Writers in Cultural Studies have called Gramsci a "second progenitor Marxist" (Inglis, 1993, p. 74) because he openly questioned why the masses never revolted against the privileged class:

> The study of hegemony was for him [Gramsci], and is for us, the study of the question why so many people assent to and vote for political arrangements which palpably work against their own happiness and sense of justice. What on earth is it, in schools or on the telly, which makes rational people accept unemployment, killing queues [wards] in hospitals, ludicrous waste on needless weaponry, and all the other awful details of life under modern capitalism? (Inglis, 1993, p. 76)

Gramsci's notion of hegemony was based on **Marx's** idea of **false consciousness,** a state in which individuals are unaware of the domination in their lives. Gramsci contended that audiences can be exploited by the same social system they support (financially). From popular culture to religion, Gramsci felt the dominant groups in society manage to direct people into complacency. Consent is a principal component of hegemony. Consent is given by populations if they are given enough "stuff" (e.g., freedoms, material goods, and so forth). Ultimately, people will prefer to live in a society with these "rights" and consent to the dominant culture's ideologies.

The application of Gramsci's thinking on hegemony is quite applicable to today's society. Under a hegemonic culture, some profit (literally) while others lose out. What happens in hegemonic societies is that people become susceptible to a subtle imbalance in power. That is, people are likely to support tacitly the dominant ideology of a culture. The complexity of the concept is further discussed by Hall (1989). He notes that hegemony can be multifaceted in that the

hegemony
the domination of one group over another, usually weaker, group

false consciousness
Gramsci's belief that people are unaware of the domination in their lives

Research Notes

Ott, B. L. (2003). "I'm Bart Simpson, who the hell are you?" A study in postmodern identity (re)construction. *Journal of Popular Culture, 37,* 56–78.

Ott outlines his analysis of the longest-running comedy in television history, *The Simpsons.* He believes that "television furnishes consumers with the symbolic resources—the actual cultural bricks—with which to (re)construct identity" (p. 58). Ott argues that the television show has transformed the way viewers look at the family in society. After heavy doses of traditional images of the family for decades, Ott believes, *The Simpsons* models a new way to configure family identity. He zeroes in on Bart, the adolescent son, who, among others, emulates and looks up to Krusty the Clown. Sadly, Krusty is always getting into trouble with law enforcement, and, as Ott asserts, the clown provides a mediated example of a "countercultural image" (p. 63). Ott presents a number of examples from the series and assert that the show has

frequently influenced viewers and their perceptions and configurations of identity.

Weedon, C. (2004). *Identity and culture: Narratives of difference and belonging.* New York: Open University.

This book is an in-depth examination of the intersection of race, class, and gender and its relationship to Cultural Studies. The author presents both personal insights and research findings from Stuart Hall and his followers. Weedon looks primarily at the British "version" of Cultural Studies, although, to make his point, he articulates its relationship to U.S. Cultural Studies theorists. Weedon extrapolates from a number of examples, including the Bible, the Confederate flag, the Aboriginal people, and "Islamaphobia" in the Western world. The book provides readers with concrete examples of many of the themes inherent in Cultural Studies. Weedon gives a scholarly account of the ways in which identity is constituted for a number of different cultural communities.

dominant, or ruling, class is frequently divided in its ideologies. That means that during the subtle course of being influenced, the public may find itself pushed and pulled in several directions. Unraveling such complexity is one goal of researchers in Cultural Studies.

Hegemony can be further understood by looking at today's corporate culture, where—using Marx's thinking—ruling ideas are ideas of the ruling class. In most corporate cultures, where decision making is predominantly made by White, heterosexual males, we expect certain ideologies to be present that support this class of people. Hall questions whether this dominant way of thinking and relating is legitimate or whether it simply perpetuates the subordination of the masses. How is consciousness raised and how is new consciousness presented? Perhaps it is the language used in an organization, for as Hall (1997) states, "Language in its widest sense is the vehicle of practical reasoning, calculation and consciousness, because of the ways by which certain meanings and references have been historically secured" (p. 40). People must share the same way of interpreting language, however, to achieve meaning in a context, and Hall notes that meanings change from one culture or era to another. So what exists in one organizational setting may not exist in another.

What all this means is that there are multiple ideologies in a society as complex as the United States. This translates into what Hall calls a **theatre of struggle**, which means that various ideologies in society compete and are in temporary states of conflict. Thus, as attitudes and values on different topics shift in society, so do the various ideologies associated with these topics. For example, think about what it meant to be a woman before 1920 and what it means to be a woman today. Before 1920, women were unable to vote and were generally regarded as subordinate and subservient to men. Then in August 1920, the amendment giving women the right to vote was ratified. Today, of course, women not only vote but hold high political office. Although U.S. society still does not provide entirely equal opportunity for women, and women continue to be targets of discrimination, the culture and ideology pertaining to women's rights have changed with the times.

Hegemony is but one component of the intellectual currents associated with Cultural Studies. Although people (audiences) are frequently influenced by dominant societal forces, at times people will demonstrate their own hegemonic tendencies. We explore this notion further.

Counter-Hegemony: The Masses Start to Influence the Dominant Forces

We have noted that hegemony is one of the core concepts associated with Cultural Studies. Yet audiences are not always duped into accepting and believing everything presented by the dominant forces. At times, audiences will use the same resources and strategies of dominant social groups. To some extent, individuals will use the same practices of hegemonic domination to challenge that domination. This is what Gramsci called **counter-hegemony**.

Counter-hegemony becomes a critical part of Cultural Studies thinking because it suggests that audiences are not necessarily willing and compliant. In other words, we—as audience members—are not dumb and submissive! Danny Lesh in *Counter Heg* (a newsletter dedicated to the counter-hegemonic movement; www.lesstreet/com/dan/counterheg) observes that part of the goal of counter-hegemony "is to understand history from other lenses, particularly from women's, workers', and racial minorities' perspectives." That is, in counter-hegemony, researchers try to raise the volume on muted voices. Think of counter-hegemony as a point where individuals recognize their consent and try to do something about it.

Counter-hegemonic messages, interestingly enough, occur in television programming. In particular, two shows—*The Cosby Show* and *The Simpsons*—exemplify counter-hegemony. Both shows are effective examples of how television content challenges the priorities established by the dominant forces. With respect to *The Cosby Show,* the Number 1 show on TV in the 1980s and 1990s, Bishetta Merrit (1991) notes that, in an effort to defy social stereotypes, this television family featured two working parents, one a gynecologist and the other an attorney. Furthermore, instead of having five children who argued all the time, Herman Gray (1989) claimed that in almost every episode, the children were taught the values of honesty, respect, and responsibility. Finally, the show was an educational tool as well, referencing many historically Black colleges, playing music by Black artists (e.g., jazz and rap), and depicting symbols of African American heritage. To this end, the show was an effort to dispel the messages that the media elite were presenting on nightly news: the absent father, the uneducated family members, and the poverty-ridden living environment. Counter-hegemony, then, takes shape with the presentation of the Cosbys as "Black America."

The Simpsons, the longest running comedy on television, also contains satiric counter-hegemonic messages aimed at showing that individuals who are dominated use the same symbolic resources to challenge that domination. The relevance of *The Simpsons* to the lives of people has been persuasively argued. Tim Delaney (2008) succinctly notes that the show reveals so much about us because so much of the show intersects with the social institutions (family, school, jobs, houses or worship, etc.) to which we belong. The show has included references to such diverse topics as talk shows, Kafka, the Beatles, Tennessee Williams, gay marriage, the invention of television, and hormone therapy! The core cast of characters—Marge (mother), Homer (father), Bart (son), Lisa (daughter), and Maggie (infant daughter)—all present different counter-hegemonic messages. For Marge, although cultural representations of a homemaker/housewife suggest a doting and supportive wife and mother, she is arguably the most independent of all the characters. She has tried a number of other professions, from police officer to protester against handgun violence. Homer, an employee at a local nuclear power plant, shows that despite what the government may tell us about the safety of these facilities, bumbling, inept people like Homer continue to stay employed. Lisa, contesting societal expectations that a "child should be seen and not heard," shows that she is intellectually curious, artistically savvy, and environmentally aware.

One of the more central characters of the show is Bart Simpson. Interestingly, although society tends to shut down boys of Bart's age (and girls to some extent), Bart manages to shut down the same society that tries to subdue him. His pranks range from harassing a local bar with sophomoric phone calls to disrespecting his grade school principal to calling his father by his first name. In the end, however, despite the 20 minutes of chaos, the family members show that they have high regard for one another in personal ways. As Carl Matheson (2001) notes, the show advocates "a moral position of caring at the level of the individual, one which favors the family over the institution" (p. 4).

A closer look at the television series illustrates other counter-hegemonic tones. Brian Ott (2003), for example, calls *The Simpsons* the "anti-show show" (p. 58). He states that "*The Simpsons* has always represented a sort of anti-show, spoofing, challenging, and collapsing the traditional codes, structures, and formulas of network television" (p. 59). Ott contends that the characters of Bart, Homer, and Lisa help viewers understand "lessons about selfhood" (p. 61) and that the show is watched by a number of different

Find other examples of counter-hegemony in society. You may examine film, video, the Internet, or other types of communication. Further, identify the specific counter-hegemonic message in your discussions.

cultural communities, including Whites, African Americans, and Hispanics. Ott and other scholars contend that the show has managed to transcend traditional images of the family that demonstrated and embraced patriarchal control. Indeed, a close examination of the series shows that children are frequently viewed as subverting or overthrowing parental control and asserting dominance in their family. *The Simpsons* continues to challenge prevailing religious, political, and cultural notions that the family is weakening.

Audience Decoding

No hegemonic or counter-hegemonic message can exist without an audience's ability to receive the message and compare it with meanings already stored in their minds. This is called **decoding**, the final topic of Cultural Studies we wish to address. When we receive messages from others, we decode them according to our perceptions, thoughts, and past experiences. So, for instance, when Lisa Petrillo, from our opening story, interprets information on purchasing a home, she is relying on several mental behaviors. These include her desire to have a home, her conversations with people who have already purchased a home, her library visits, and the fact that she and her family have never owned a home. Lisa will store the information she receives pertaining to a new home and retrieve it when someone engages her in a conversation on the topic. All of this is done instantaneously; that is, she will make immediate decisions about how to interpret a message once she receives it.

decoding
receiving and comparing messages

Decoding is central to Cultural Studies. But before we delve further into this, let's review the gist of Cultural Studies up to this point. You will recall that the public receives a great deal of information from the elite and that people unconsciously consent to what dominant ideologies suggest. Theorists reason that the public should be envisioned as part of a larger cultural context, one in which those struggling for a voice are oppressed (Budd & Steinman, 1992). As we discussed previously, hierarchical social relations (between the elite bosses and the subordinate workers, for example) exist in an uneven society. This results in subordinate cultures decoding the messages of the ruling class. Usually, according to Hall, the media connote the ruling class in Western society.

Hall (1980a) elaborates on how decoding works in the media. He recognizes that an audience decodes a message from three vantage points, or positions:

dominant-hegemonic, negotiated, and oppositional. We explore each of these next.

Hall claims that individuals operate within a code that dominates and exercises more power than other codes. He terms this the **dominant-hegemonic position.** The professional code of television broadcasters, for instance, will always operate within the hegemony of the dominant code. Hall relates that professional codes reproduce hegemonic interpretations of reality. This is done with subtle persuasion. Consider John and Lisa Petrillo from our opener. The television images of owning a home prompt the Petrillos to believe that owning a home is within their reach. The selection of words, the presentation of pictures, and the choice of spokespeople in infomercials are all part of the staging in the professional code. Audiences, like the Petrillos, are prone to either misunderstanding a message or selectively perceiving only certain parts of a message. Why? Hall writes, "The viewer does not know the terms employed, cannot follow the complex logic of argument or exposition, is unfamiliar with the language, finds the concepts too alien or difficult or is foxed by the expository narrative" (1980a, p. 135). Television producers are worried that people like the Petrillos will not accept the intended and preferred media message of owning a home. They (the media) therefore place their professional code placed in the larger, dominant cultural code of meaning. This ensures that John and Lisa Petrillo will work toward buying a home.

The second position is a **negotiated position;** audience members are able to accept dominant ideologies but will operate with some exceptions to the cultural rule. Hall holds that audience members always reserve the right to apply local conditions to large-scale events. This happens frequently when the media report on laws that are enacted at the national level and interpreted at the state or community level. For example, Hall might argue that although audiences may accept the elite's interpretation of a welfare reform bill in Washington, D.C. ("All people should work if they are able to"), they may have to negotiate when it does not coincide with a local or personal principle ("Children need parents at home"). Hall notes that due to the difficulty of negotiations, people are prone to communication failures.

The final way in which audiences decode messages is by engaging in an oppositional position. An **oppositional position** occurs when audience members substitute an alternative code for the code supplied by the media. Critical consumers reject the media's intended and preferred meaning of the message and instead replace it with their own way of thinking about a subject. Consider, for instance, the manner in which the media communicate feminine images of beauty. To many, the media present feminine beauty as a way to serve the sexual desire of men (Schwichtenberg, 1987). Some consumers, however, reject this capitalistic message and substitute more realistic portrayals.

Hall accepts the fact that the media frame messages with the covert intent to persuade. Audience members have the capacity to avoid being swallowed up in the dominant ideology, yet, as with the Petrillo family, the messages the audience receives are often part of a more subtle campaign. Theorists in Cultural Studies do not suggest that people are gullible, but rather that they often unknowingly become a part of the agenda of others (Hall, 1980b).

dominant-hegemonic position
operating within a code that allows one person to have control over another

negotiated position
accepting dominant ideologies, but allowing for cultural exceptions

oppositional position
substituting alternative messages presented by the media

Integration, Critique, and Closing

Although Cultural Studies began at the CCCS in England, its influence on writers, researchers, and theorists in the United States has been profound. The theory has attracted the attention of critical theorists in particular because it is founded on the principles of criticism. Its Marxist influence has also drawn scholars from philosophy, economics, and social psychology, and its emphasis on underrepresented groups in society has enticed writers in sociology and women's studies to take notice (Long, 1989). For additional criticism, we discuss three criteria for evaluating a theory: logical consistency, utility, and heurism.

Integration

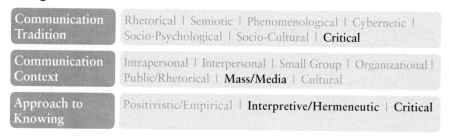

Communication Tradition	Rhetorical	Semiotic	Phenomenological	Cybernetic	Socio-Psychological	Socio-Cultural	**Critical**
Communication Context	Intrapersonal	Interpersonal	Small Group	Organizational	Public/Rhetorical	**Mass/Media**	Cultural
Approach to Knowing	Positivistic/Empirical	**Interpretive/Hermeneutic**	**Critical**

Critique

| Evaluation Criteria | Scope | **Logical Consistency** | Parsimony | **Utility** | Testability | **Heurism** | Test of Time |

Logical Consistency

Despite some glowing endorsements, the logical consistency of the theory has been challenged. This criticism relates to the audience. Even though some audiences resist the role of dupe, are they able to become interpretive and active resisters? In other words, to what extent can audiences be counter-hegemonic? Mike Budd, Robert Entman, and Clay Steinman (1990) suggest that some cultural and critical theorists overestimate the ability of oppressed and marginalized populations to escape their culture. For evidence of this thinking, reexamine our opening story of the Petrillos and assess the extent to which you believe they can "escape" their circumstances. Budd and colleagues believe that these communities frequently lack the skills, insights, and networks to be so political in their resistance. This dialogue is not likely to go away because "debates over the audience were once, and continue to be, a major field of contestation in cultural studies" (Kellner & Hammer, 2004, p. 79).

Utility

Cultural Studies "makes up a vehicle that can alter our self-image" (Carey, 1989, p. 94). Therefore, it's possible to translate some of the theory into daily

Theory Into Practice

Mirri

When someone said that Stuart Hall was concerned with oppression, I couldn't help but think of my own background in Haiti. The country is very poor, and we don't have a lot of resources like the United States. We rely on other countries a lot, which makes the dominance of the elites over ordinary people pretty common. The government acts like the people's voice is important, but everyone knows that simply is not the case. Media there are controlled by the government in a lot of ways and tells people both truthful and deceitful things. It's a perfect example of the dominance over the masses.

life, making it useful to some extent. Its utility can also be found in its dedication to studying the cultural struggles of the underprivileged. According to Hall (1997), these populations have remained subordinate for too long. By concentrating on these marginalized social groups, a number of subfields have emerged; namely, ethnic studies and gay, lesbian, bisexual, transgender studies (Surber, 1998). Hall's theory has been called "empirically elegant" (Carey, 1989, p. 31), and its usefulness beyond the written page has been widely articulated.

Heurism

Many of the principles and features of Cultural Studies have been investigated. Ideology has been examined (Lewis & Morgan, 2001; Soar, 2000), and the concept of hegemony has been applied to episodes of the long-running situation comedy *The Mary Tyler Moore Show* (Dow, 1990) and to the HBO series, *Sex in the City* (Brasfield, 2007). Research by Janice Radway (1984, 1986) focused on romance novels and the women who read them. She discovered that many women read these books silently to protest male domination in society. Lawrence Grossberg (1986) and Linda Steiner (1988) found oppositional coding with audiences in their research. Grossberg noted that punk music was an oppositional response to rock and roll music because rock and roll allowed for "new possibilities" (1986, p. 57). Steiner looked at a decade of the "No Comment" section of *Ms.* magazine, which is partly devoted to overt and covert male domination in society. Steiner claimed that the manner in which women read these sections is tantamount to oppositional decoding; they read the comments in a way that suits their own interests and not the superiority of males. Finally, counter-hegemony has been applied to Nike's Bode Miller Olympic Advertising campaign (Ryan, 2007) and to issues of globalization (de Sousa Santos, 2006).

Cultural Studies remains one of the few theoretical traditions that has attracted the attention of scholars from a variety of disciplines outside communication. Researchers interested in understanding the thinking, experiences, and activities of historically oppressed populations usually endorse Cultural Studies. Although some critics have faulted the theory for a number of reasons, Stuart Hall is credited with criticizing the elite and with drawing attention to oppressed voices in society. Hall's commitment to understanding the everyday acts and commonly accepted events is admirable.

Discussion Starters

1. Is the Petrillo family responsible for not trying to leave their current situation? If they are not able to achieve the American Dream of owning a home, should the media be blamed? Include examples when expressing your opinion.

2. Discuss how hegemony functions in world events. Now apply the concept to your campus. Identify any similarities and differences between the two applications. Use examples in your response.

3. What other cultural artifacts exist in our society that could be studied within a Cultural Studies framework?

4. British Cultural Studies is strongly focused on class differences. What do you think about applying the thinking of British Cultural Studies to Cultural Studies in North America? Do you believe that the concepts and principles are relevant to all countries? Why or why not?

5. Do you agree or disagree with the belief that oppressed populations have little voice in the United States? How does this view relate to how you feel about the theory?

6. How might Cultural Studies theorists view poverty in the United States?

7. Apply counter-hegemony to a contemporary television show.

Online Learning Center www. mhhe.com/west4e

Visit the Online Learning Center at www.mhhe.com/west4e for chapter-specific resources, such as story-into-theory and multiple-choice quizzes, as well as theory summaries and theory connection questions.

CHAPTER 22

Cultivation Analysis

Based on the research of **George Gerbner**

Joyce Jensen

Joyce Jensen was preparing to vote for the very first time. She had been looking forward to this privilege since she was 12 years old. She considered herself a news junkie, and she'd always devoured the morning newspaper, the local TV news, CNN, the national network news, *Time,* and *Newsweek.* She made it a point to watch C-SPAN, a cable station dedicated to the world of politics. She knew that she was one of only a handful in her class who could identify all of the U.S. Supreme Court justices. She was ready to take some flak as a news nerd because the world fascinated her. She always knew that when she turned 18, she'd be prepared for the right and responsibility of voting.

Now she was faced with a decision as she voted for her state's governor. Although undecided, she was leaning toward Roberta Johndrew, the tough-on-crime candidate. Johndrew favored greater use of the death penalty, limits on appeals by people convicted of crimes, and putting more police on the street. Yet Joyce thought that Frank Milnes, the education candidate, had some good ideas as well. Crime—in Joyce's state and in the country as a whole—was down for the sixth consecutive year. The statistics were most impressive, Milnes said, when considering violent crime. All types of violent crime had been in decline for nearly a decade. Milnes argued that money being spent for more police, more prisons, and more executions would be better spent on improving schools. After all, Milnes asserted, more dollars in the state were being spent on incarceration than

on educating young people. Better schools, he argued, would mean even less crime in the future. "What kind of state do we live in," he demanded in his campaign literature, "when we refuse to give raises to our teachers and pay our prison guards more than our teachers?"

Those were powerful arguments, thought Joyce. She regretted that teachers were not getting paid commensurate with their expertise and responsibilities. She knew that she wanted to have children eventually, and she wanted them to get the best education possible. She could see how paying teachers more might help achieve that.

But as a young, single woman, these arguments were secondary to safety considerations. There seemed to be so much crime in the city. Every night when she watched the news on television, there seemed to be more crimes reported. She was often uncomfortable when she was out at night. At times, she even felt uneasy being at home alone. Maybe it is an irrational fear, she thought to herself, but it's there and it feels real.

As Joyce pondered her vote in the booth, so much was going through her mind. She considered her present situation as a single woman as well as her desire for future children. She reflected on both Roberta Johndrew and Frank Milnes and their comments over the past several months. As she contemplated her options for another moment or two, she felt she would be able to make a good decision. So much depended on citizens making informed choices. Joyce was thrilled to exercise her right as a U.S. citizen.

Television is as much a part of the human experience in the United States as family. All across our country, people tune in to a variety of television programs, from soap operas to C-SPAN. We are a society reliant on TV and what it has to offer each day. Television has found its way into our living rooms, our conversations, and even our psyches. This invention from the 1940s has sustained itself well into the new millennium.

Responding to the pervasiveness of television in society over thirty years ago, George Gerbner and his colleague Lawrence Gross (1972) commented that people watch television as though they were attending church, except that they typically watch television more religiously. Focusing their work on the effects of television (a topic we return to later), Gerbner and Gross embarked on the Cultural Indicators Project, conducting regular, periodic examinations of television programming and the "conceptions of social reality that viewing cultivates in child and adult audiences" (p. 174). In initiating what would become known as Cultivation Analysis, they were making a **causal argument** (television cultivates—causes—conceptions of social reality). Cultivation Analysis is a theory that predicts and explains the long-term formation and shaping of perceptions, understandings, and beliefs about the world as a result of consumption of media messages. Gerbner's line of thinking in Cultivation Analysis suggests that mass communication, especially television, cultivates certain beliefs about reality that are held in common by mass communication consumers. As Gerbner observes, "most of what we know, or think we know, we have never personally experienced" (Gerbner, 1999, p. ix). We "know" these things because of the stories we see and hear in the media (Buffington & Fraley, 2008).

causal argument
an assertion of cause and effect, including the direction of the causality

Cultivation researchers can easily explain Joyce Jensen's voting quandary. Official statistics that indicate that violent crime is in steady decline are certainly real enough. But so, too, is Joyce's feeling of unease and insecurity when she is alone. Cultivation Analysis would refer to these feelings of insecurity as her social reality. Moreover, that reality is as real as any other for Joyce, and it is media fueled, if not media created and maintained.

Iver Peterson (2002) made a similar observation about the anthrax scares in the United States post–September 11, 2001. He notes that although the (media-fueled) fears about anthrax are very pervasive and real, the actual cases of anthrax contamination are rare. Peterson quotes Clifton R. Lacy, commissioner of the New Jersey Department of Health and Senior Services, as saying that the risks to the citizens of New Jersey by anthrax spores are "vanishingly small" (p. A21). Dr. Lacy also urged people to take to heart the message that there have been no new cases in the state since October 2001.

In the 1970s, Gerbner's view that media messages alter traditional notions of time, space, and social groupings was a direct challenge to the prevailing thought that media had little, if any, effect on individuals and on the culture. Like Uses and Gratifications Theory, which we discuss in Chapter 23, Cultivation Analysis was developed in response to the beliefs about the media's limited effects that were dominant at the time. More important, however, it reflects media theory's slow transformation from reliance on the transmissional perspective to greater acceptance of the ritual perspective of mass communication.

Calvin and Hobbes
by Bill Watterson

transmissional perspective
a position depicting the media as senders of messages across space

ritual perspective
a position depicting the media as representers of shared beliefs

The **transmissional perspective** sees media as senders of messages—discrete bits of information—across space. This perspective and limited effects theories are comfortable partners. If all media do is transmit bits of information, people can choose to use or not use that information as they wish. In the **ritual perspective,** however, media are conceptualized not as a means of transmitting "messages in space" but as central to "the maintenance of society in time" (Carey, 1975, p. 6). Mass communication is "not the act of imparting information but the representation of shared beliefs" (p. 6).

Developing Cultivation Analysis

Gerbner first used the term *cultivation* in 1969; however, Cultivation Analysis, as a discrete and powerful theory, did not emerge for a number of years. It evolved over time through a series of methodological and theoretical steps by Gerbner and his colleagues and, as such, reflects that development.

During the 1960s, interest in media effects, particularly effects of television, ran very high. The federal government was concerned about media's influence on society, especially media's possible contribution to rising levels of violence among young people. In 1967 President Lyndon Johnson ordered the creation of the National Commission on the Causes and Prevention of Violence. It was followed in 1972 by the surgeon general's Scientific Advisory Committee on Television and Social Behavior. Both groups examined media (especially television) and their impact (especially the effects of aggression and violence). Gerbner, a respected social scientist, was involved in both efforts.

Violence Index
a yearly content analysis of prime-time network programming to assess the amount of violence represented

Gerbner's task was to produce an annual **Violence Index,** a yearly content analysis of a sample week of network television prime-time content that would show, from season to season, how much violence was actually present on television. Its value to those interested in the media violence issue was obvious: If the link between television fare and subsequent viewer aggression was to be made, the presence of violence on television needed to be demonstrated. Moreover, observers would be able to correlate annual increases in the amount of violent television content with annual increases in the amount of real-world violent crime. But the index was immediately challenged by both media industry and limited effects researchers. How was violence defined? Was verbal aggression violence? Was obviously fake violence on a comedy counted the same as more realistically portrayed violence on a drama? Why examine only prime-time network television, because children's heaviest viewing occurs at other times of the day? Why focus on violence? Why not examine other social ills, such as racism and sexism?

Gerbner and his associates continuously refined the Index to meet the complaints of its critics, and what their annual counting demonstrated was that violence appeared on prime-time television at levels unmatched in the real world. The 1982 Index, for example, showed that "crime in prime time is at least 10 times as rampant as in the real world (and) an average of five to six acts of overt physical violence per hour involves over half of all major characters" (Gerbner, Gross, Morgan, & Signorielli, 1982, p. 106).

Cultivation Analysis • *Theory at a Glance*

Television and other media play an extremely important role in how people view their world. In today's society, most people get their information from mediated sources rather than through direct experience. Therefore, mediated sources can shape a person's sense of reality. This is especially the case with regard to violence. Heavy television viewing cultivates a sense of the world as a violent place, and heavy television viewers perceive that there is more violence in the world than there actually is or than lighter viewers perceive.

Assumptions of Cultivation Analysis

In advancing the position that mediated reality causes consumers to cultivate their own social reality, Cultivation Analysis makes a number of assumptions. Because it was and still remains primarily a television-based theory, these three assumptions speak to the relationship between that medium and the culture:

- Television is essentially and fundamentally different from other forms of mass media.
- Television shapes our society's way of thinking and relating.
- The influence of television is limited.

The first assumption of Cultivation Analysis underscores the uniqueness of television. Television is in more than 98 percent of all U.S. homes. It requires

Research Notes

Glascock, J., & Ruggerio, T. E. (2004). Representations of class and gender of primetime Spanish-language television in the United States. *Communication Quarterly, 52,* 390–402.

This study examines Spanish-language television available in the United States on three networks (Univision, Telemundo, and TV Azteca) through a content analysis. Six telenovelas and one drama were analyzed for gender roles, class, sexual talk, and physical and verbal aggression. The findings included that women were shown almost as often as men, and that they were more likely to play lead roles than men. Similar to U.S. television, women were depicted as having more household and child care responsibilities and having less job status. Gender-role stereotypes were more pronounced on the Spanish-language shows than on U.S. network prime-time programming, and men were more physically and verbally aggressive (although the overall amount of physical aggression was less than on U.S. TV).

The authors reflect on the sense of reality that is being cultivated in the minds of viewers by this type of programming.

Wilson, B. J., Martins, N., & Marske, A. L. (2005). Children's and parents' fright reactions to kidnapping stories in the news. *Communication Monographs, 72,* 46–70.

This study is based on a random telephone survey of 182 parents of children between the ages of 5 and 18 who were asked to report on their own, and their perception of their children's, fears about kidnapping. Respondents were also asked about their own and their children's exposure to television and other media. The phone interviews lasted approximately 20 minutes.

In general, they found that children's fears were reduced with age, as the parents reported that their older children had fewer fears about kidnapping than did their younger children. Parents also reported that they were more fearful than were their children. In terms of the relationship of media exposure and fear, the study revealed a pattern that "poses a challenge to cultivation theory . . . [because the] data suggest that heavy viewing of news can cultivate fear of abduction in children, but that TV viewing in general does not" (p. 63).

Partial support was obtained for CA in the parents' responses about their own fears and media habits. Parents who paid close attention to media reports about kidnapping were more afraid than those who did not, but the sheer amount of TV viewing did not predict parents' fear or perception of kidnapping. Further, the authors found that parents who read newspapers regularly "tended to estimate *fewer* child kidnappings each year and also tended to be less frightened by the kidnapping stories, even after controlling for education" (p. 65).

In conclusion, the authors observe that their study was conducted in a small town with a very low level of violent crime. Yet 30 percent of their respondents said the news stories about kidnapping had caused them to forbid their children to be outside alone, and 12 percent noted that they'd bought protection devices for their children as a result of the media reports. These results lend some support to Cultivation Analysis.

no literacy, as do print media. Unlike the movies, it can be free (beyond the initial cost of the set and the cost of advertising added to the products we buy). Unlike radio, it combines pictures and sound. It requires no mobility, as do church attendance and going to the movies or the theater. Television is the only medium ever invented that is ageless—that is, people can use it at the earliest and latest years of life, as well as all those years in between.

In small groups, research the actual number of violent crimes in your community from a governmental source. Compare that number to a night of prime-time television's representation of violent crimes. Use the following definition of violent crimes from the U.S. Department of Justice: murder, rape, robbery, and aggravated assault.

Because of this accessibility and availability to everyone, television is the "central cultural arm" of our society (Gerbner, Gross, Jackson-Beeck, Jeffries-Fox, & Signorielli, 1978, p. 178). Television draws together dissimilar groups and can show their similarities. For instance, during the initial attacks of the war in Iraq, television transmitted live signals from Baghdad. Those in support of the bombings pointed to the importance of hitting key military targets, whereas those opposed to the war noted the number of civilian casualties. It was television that allowed both sides to invoke disparate images of the war. In other words, television is the culture's primary storyteller and has the ability to gather together different groups. In addition, who can doubt the role that television has played in working through the nation's story about the tragedy of September 11, 2001? Hurricane Katrina? California brush fires?

The second assumption pertains to the influence of television. Gerbner and Gross (1972) comment that "the substance of the consciousness cultivated by TV is not so much specific attitudes and opinions as more basic assumptions about the 'facts' of life and standards of judgment on which conclusions are based" (p. 175). That is, television doesn't so much persuade us (it didn't try to convince Joyce Jensen that the streets are unsafe) as paint a more or less convincing picture of what the world is like. Gerbner (1998) observed that television reaches people, on average, more than seven hours each day. During this time, television offers "a centralized system of story-telling" (p. 177). Gerbner agrees with Walter Fisher, whom we discussed in Chapter 20, that people live in stories. Gerbner, however, asserts that most of the stories in modern society now come from television.

Television's major cultural function is to stabilize social patterns, to cultivate resistance to change. Television is a medium of socialization and enculturation. Gerbner and his cohorts eloquently state that

> the repetitive pattern of television's mass-produced messages and images forms the mainstream of the common symbolic environment that cultivates the most widely shared conceptions of reality. We live in terms of the stories we tell—stories about what things exist, stories about how things work, and stories about what to do—and television tells them all through news, drama, and advertising to almost everybody most of the time. (Gerbner et al., 1978, p. 178)

Where did Joyce Jensen's—and other voters'—shared conceptions of reality about crime and personal safety come from? Cultivation researchers would immediately point to television, where, despite a nationwide 20 percent drop in the homicide rate between 1993 and 1996, for example, the number of murder stories on the network evening news soared 721 percent (Kurtz, 1998). This distortion has continued in ways that the theory would predict. Barbara Wilson and her colleagues (Wilson, Martins, & Marske, 2005) found that parents who paid a great deal of attention to television news thought their children were more at risk for kidnapping than those parents who watched less TV. Yet the Bureau of Justice Statistics rates of violent crimes among 12- to 19-year-olds since 1973 does not support this belief. The findings indicate that in 1973 the rate of violent crimes against children ages 12–19 was approximately eighty cases per 1,000 children. Thirty years later, in 2003, the rate had dropped to approximately fifty per 1,000 youth (Bureau of Justice statistics, 2004). Further, kidnapping makes up less than 2 percent of all violent crimes against youth (Finklehor & Ormrod, 2000).

Based on this assumption, Cultivation Analysis supplies an alternative way of thinking about TV violence. Some theorics, like Social Learning Theory (Bandura, 1977), assume that we become more violent after being exposed to violence. Other approaches, like the notion of catharsis, would suggest that watching violence purges us of our own violent impulses and we actually become less violent. Cultivation Analysis does not speak to what we will do based on watching violent television; instead, it assumes that watching violent TV makes us feel afraid because it cultivates within us the image of a mean and dangerous world.

The third assumption of Cultivation Analysis states that television's effects are limited. This may sound peculiar, given the fact that television is so pervasive. Yet the observable, measurable, and independent contributions of television to the culture are relatively small. This may sound like a restatement of minimal effects thinking, but Gerbner uses an ice age analogy to distance Cultivation Analysis from limited effects. The **ice age analogy** states that "just as an average temperature shift of a few degrees can lead to an ice age or the outcomes of elections can be determined by slight margins, so too can a relatively small but pervasive influence make a crucial difference. The 'size' of an 'effect' is far less critical than the direction of its steady contribution" (Gerbner, Gross, Morgan, & Signorielli, 1980, p. 14). The argument is not that television's impact is inconsequential. Rather, although television's measurable, observable, and independent effect on the culture at any point in time might be small, that impact is nonetheless present and significant. Further, Gerbner and his associates argue that it is not the case that watching a specific television program causes a specific behavior (e.g., that watching *Without a Trace* will cause someone to kidnap another person) but rather that watching television in general has a cumulative and pervasive impact on our vision of the world.

ice age analogy
a position stating that television doesn't have to have a single major impact, but influences viewers through steady limited effects

Processes and Products of Cultivation Analysis

Cultivation Analysis has been applied to a wide variety of effects issues, as well as to different situations in which television viewers find themselves. In doing so, researchers have developed specific processes and products related to the theory.

The Four-Step Process

To empirically demonstrate their belief that television has an important causal effect on the culture, Cultivation researchers developed a four-step process. The first step, *message system analysis,* consists of detailed content analyses of television programming in order to demonstrate its most recurring and consistent presentations of images, themes, values, and portrayals. For example, it is possible to conduct a message system analysis of the number of episodes of bodily harm on such shows as *Laws & Order* and *CSI.*

The second step, *formulation of questions about viewers' social realities,* involves developing questions about people's understandings of their everyday lives. For example, a typical Cultivation Analysis question is, "In any given week, what are the chances that you will be involved in some kind of violence? About 1 in 10 or about 1 in 100?" Another is, "Of all the crime that occurs in the United States in any year, what proportion is violent crime like rape, murder, assault, and robbery?"

The third step, *surveying the audience,* requires that the questions from step two be posed to audience members *and* that researchers ask these viewers about their levels of television consumption.

Finally, step four entails *comparing the social realities of light and heavy viewers.* For Gerbner, a "cultivation differential" exists between light and heavy viewers and perceptions of violence. **Cultivation differential** can be defined as the percentage of difference in response between light and heavy television viewers. Gerbner (1998) explains that amount of viewing is used in relative terms. Thus, heavy viewers are those who watch the most in any sample of people that are measured, whereas light viewers are those who watch the least.

cultivation differential
the percentage of difference in response between light and heavy television viewers

Mainstreaming and Resonance

How does television contribute to viewers' conceptions of social reality? The process of cultivation occurs in two ways. One is mainstreaming. **Mainstreaming** occurs when, especially for heavier viewers, television's symbols dominate other sources of information and ideas about the world. As a result of heavy viewing, people's constructed social realities move toward the mainstream—not a mainstream in any political sense, but a culturally dominant reality that is more similar to television's reality than to any measurable, objective external reality. Heavy viewers tend to believe the mainstreamed realities that the world is a more dangerous place than it really is, that all politicians are corrupt, that teen crime is at record high levels, that African American families are all on welfare, that illegitimate births are skyrocketing, and so forth.

mainstreaming
the tendency for heavy viewers to perceive a similar culturally dominant reality to that pictured on the media although this differs from actual reality

Mainstreaming means that heavy television viewers of different co-cultures are more similar in their beliefs about the world than their varying group membership might suggest. Thus, African Americans and European Americans who are heavy television viewers would perceive the world more similarly than might be expected. As Gerbner (1998) states, "Differences that usually are associated with the varied cultural, social, and political characteristics of these groups are diminished in the responses of heavy viewers in these same groups" (p. 183).

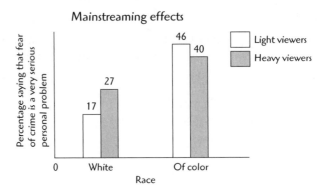

Mainstreaming effects

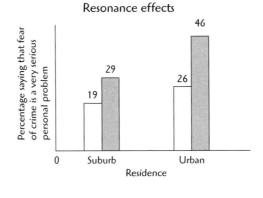

Resonance effects

Figure 22.1
Effects of
Mainstreaming
and Resonance
Source: Adapted from
"The Mainstreaming
of America: Violence
Profile No. 11" by
Gerber et al. in *Journal
of Communication,*
vol. 7 (1980), p. 16,
Figure 2. Reprinted by
permission of John
Wiley & Sons Ltd.

resonance
occurs when a
viewer's lived reality
coincides with the
reality pictured in the
media

The second way cultivation operates is through resonance. **Resonance** occurs when things on television are, in fact, congruent with viewers' actual everyday realities. In other words, people's objective external reality resonates with that of television. Some urban dwellers, for example, may see the violent world of television resonated in their deteriorating neighborhoods. As Gerbner (1998) notes, this provides "a 'double dose' of messages that 'resonate' and amplify cultivation" (p. 182). The social reality that is cultivated for these viewers may in fact match their objective reality, but its possible effect is to preclude the formation of a more optimistic social reality; it denies them hope that they can build a better life. See Figure 22.1 for a representation of the effects of mainstreaming and resonance.

first order effects
a method for cultiva-
tion to occur; refers
to learning facts from
the media

Cultivation, either as mainstreaming or as resonance, produces effects on two levels. **First order effects** refer to the learning of facts such as how many employed males are involved in law enforcement or what proportion of marriages end in divorce. For example, Joyce Jensen knew from candidate Milnes's television spots that the amount of crime in her state was in decline. **Second order effects** involve "hypotheses about more general issues and assumptions" that people make about their environments (Gerbner, Gross, Morgan, & Signorielli, 1986, p. 28). Questions like, Do you think people are basically honest? and Do you think police should be allowed to use greater force to subdue criminals? are aimed at these second order effects.

second order
effects
a method for cultiva-
tion to occur; refers
to learning values and
assumptions from the
media

The Mean World Index

A product of Cultivation Analysis is the Mean World Index (Gerbner, Gross, Morgan, & Signorielli, 1980), which consists of a series of three statements:

- Most people are just looking out for themselves.
- You can't be too careful in dealing with people.
- Most people would take advantage of you if they got the chance.

Cultivation Analysis predicts that agreement with these statements from heavy and light viewers will differ, with heavy viewers seeing the world as a meaner place than light viewers. It also predicts that the amount of television viewing is the best predictor of people's answers, overwhelming other kinds of distinctions among different people—for example, income and education.

Gerbner and his colleagues (1980) demonstrated the efficacy of their Mean World Index in a study that showed heavy viewers were much more likely to see the world as a mean place than were light viewers. Better-educated, financially better-off viewers in general saw the world as less mean than did those with less education and income. But in testing the power of television, the researchers demonstrated that heavy viewers from the better-educated, better-off groups saw the world as being as dangerous as did low-income and less-educated people. In other words, heavy viewers held a mainstreamed perception of the world as a mean place, regardless of factors such as education and income. Cultivation researchers see this as evidence that television content is a factor in the construction of social realities for heavy viewers, regardless of individual or social differences.

Gerbner and his associates identify a number of other areas where the two types of viewers might differ. They include their beliefs about the likelihood of involvement with a violent crime, their fear of walking at night, and their perceptions of law enforcement. The findings are intriguing. First, they found that people with light viewing habits believed that about 1 in 100 will be a victim of violence; heavy viewers of television predicted that about 1 in 10 will be involved in violence. Second, they found that more women than men were fearful of walking alone at night and that heavy viewers overestimated the amount of violent crime. Third, heavy viewers felt that 5 percent of the culture is involved in law enforcement, whereas light viewers felt that 1 percent is involved. Important to the logic of Cultivation Analysis is that the responses of the heavy viewers mirror quite accurately the results of content analyses of television, where violence is usually recorded in heavy doses: Because violence is so common on television, heavy viewers are more likely to be fearful or mistrustful of the real world. Given what we've presented here, Joyce Jensen's viewing habits may be influencing her thinking about her choice between Milnes and Johndrew.

Cultivation Analysis as Critical Theory

Cultivation Analysis has made an important contribution to contemporary thinking about mass communication. Horace Newcomb (1978), an early commentator about Cultivation Analysis, wrote of Gerbner and his colleagues:

Table 22.1 The Three Bs of Television

TERM	DEFINITION	EXAMPLE
Blurring	Traditional distinctions are blurred.	Educated people see the world similarly to those who have less education.
Blending	"Reality" is blended into a cultural mainstream.	We agree on what's real.
Bending	The mainstream reality benefits the elite.	We all want to buy more products.

"Their foresight to collect data on a systematic, long-term basis, to move out of the laboratory and away from the closed experimental model, will enable other researchers to avoid costly mistakes. Their material holds a wealth of information" (p. 281).

But just what is the role of television in our culture uncovered by the Cultivation Analysis researchers? Cultivation theorists would argue that Joyce Jensen's apprehension—and the vote for the tough-on-crime candidate it might produce—is based on a view of the world that is cultivated by television. Learning from television produces not only perceptions of a mean world (which researchers in Cultivation Analysis argue become a self-fulfilling prophecy as people's distrust of others breeds an atmosphere of further distrust) but also a warping of political, social, and cultural discourse. How many political candidates, they ask, have the courage to argue against the building of more prisons or against the death penalty? The issue is not the validity of these positions but the absence of meaningful, objective debate on them. The argument here is similar to that offered by Elizabeth Noelle-Neumann's Spiral of Silence Theory, which we discuss in Chapter 24: People may be less willing to speak out about alternative approaches to crime and crime prevention because the media, especially television, cultivate a dominant social reality that renders these conversations out of step with the voters.

How can television be so powerful a force if its influence occurs as slowly as the coming of the ice age? Gerbner answers this question with his 3 Bs of television. Television, he wrote, blurs traditional distinctions of people's views of their world, blends people's realities into television's cultural mainstream, and bends that mainstream to the institutional interests of television and its sponsors (Table 22.1). Television's power rests in its utilization by powerful industries and elites to meet their, rather than the culture's, interests. Cultivation Analysis is a critical theory, as we described it in Chapter 3, because it is concerned with the way that communication perpetuates the dominance of one group over another (Littlejohn & Foss, 2008). As James Shanahan and Victoria Jones (1999) argue,

> Cultivation is sometimes taken as a return to a strong "powerful effects" view of mass media. This view isn't completely incorrect, but it misses the point that cultivation was originally conceived as a *critical* theory, which

happens to address media issues precisely and only because the mass media (especially television) serve the function of storytelling. (p. 32)

Cultivation Analysis, as a critical theory, examines an important social institution (television) in terms of how it uses its storytelling function to serve ends other than the benefit of the larger society. In 1996, Gerbner helped found the worldwide Cultural Environment Movement to assist people in their struggle against powerful media industries. Its *Viewers' Declaration of Independence* reads, in part, "Let the world hear the reasons that compel us to assert our rights and take an active role in the shaping of our common cultural environment. . . . Humans live and learn by stories. Today they are no longer hand-crafted, home-made, community-inspired. They are no longer told by families, schools, or churches but are the products of a complex mass-production and marketing process" (Cultural Environment Movement, 1996, p. 1). Gerbner (1998) continues to be concerned with the effects created by stories told by agencies that do not aim to teach but rather aim to sell.

In addition, Cultivation Analysis shares another characteristic with other critical theories: It is political; that is, in accepting its assumptions, its proponents must commit to doing something about the situation.

George Gerbner has taken to heart the critical researcher's call to action. In the mid-1990s, he developed the PROD (Proportional Representation of Diversity) index. The goal of the index was to examine the distortion in representation of various co-cultures "across the demography of the media landscape" (Shanahan & Morgan, 1999, p. 223). The index determined how well or poorly groups were represented on television relative to their numbers in the population. The first index Gerbner produced surveyed broadcast network programming and major Hollywood films for 1995–1996. Almost every group (women, African Americans, Latinos, Asians, Native Americans, under age 18, over age 65, gay men and lesbians, disabled, and the poor or lower class) listed in the diversity index was grossly underrepresented in the media. The only group that was not was Native Americans, and this is probably explained by their relatively low population proportionally.

Gerbner took his critical role seriously and stated in a press release associated with the presentation of the index, "Far from being 'quotas' to be imposed on creative people, the Index reflects the limitations on creative freedom in the television and motion picture industries. This is a 'report card' of industry performance. We look forward to steady improvement in the diversity and equity of the cultural environment into which our children are born and in which they come to define themselves and others" (Gerbner, 1997, cited in Shanahan & Morgan, 1999, p. 223). Gerbner believed it is important to highlight how the media industries reflect the needs and perspectives of dominant groups. A more recent report analyzing the 2001 fall session of network programing came to similar conclusions (UCLA Center for African American Studies, 2002).

Integration, Critique, and Closing

Gerbner and his colleagues have been influential in identifying television as a shaping force in society. Cultivation Analysis helps explain the implications of viewing habits, and it has been a very popular theory in mass communication research. In a study conducted by Jennings Bryant and Dorina Miron (2004) surveying almost 2,000 articles published in the three top mass communication journals since 1956, the theory was the third most frequently utilized theory. As you think about Cultivation Analysis, the following criteria for evaluation are addressed: logical consistency, utility, heurism, and test of time.

Integration

Communication Tradition	Rhetorical	Semiotic	Phenomenological	Cybernetic	Socio-Psychological	**Socio-Cultural**	**Critical**
Communication Context	Intrapersonal	Interpersonal	Small Group	Organizational	Public/Rhetorical	**Mass/Media**	Cultural
Approach to Knowing	**Positivistic/Empirical**	Interpretive/Hermeneutic	Critical

Critique

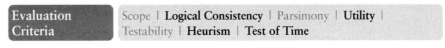

| Evaluation Criteria | Scope | **Logical Consistency** | Parsimony | **Utility** | Testability | **Heurism** | **Test of Time** |

Logical Consistency

Critics who fault the logical consistency of CA note that the methods employed by CA researchers do not match the conceptual reach of the theory. They note that the research supporting Cultivation Analysis employs social scientific methods typically identified with the transmissional perspective and limited effects findings. Yet Cultivation Analysis examines larger cultural questions most often raised by humanists. Horace Newcomb (1978) writes, "More than any other research effort in the area of television studies the work of Gerbner and Gross and their associates sits squarely at the juncture of the social sciences and the humanities" (p. 265). By asserting cultural effects, Cultivation Analysis offends many humanists, who feel that their turf has been improperly appropriated and misinterpreted. "The question," writes Newcomb, "'What does it all mean?' is, essentially, a humanistic question" (p. 266). Many humanists, quite at ease when discussing the relationship between literature (novels, art, music, theater) and culture, have great difficulty accepting television as the culture's new, dominant "literature."

Utility

Cultivation Analysis is also criticized because its claims are not always useful in explaining the phenomenon of interest: how people see the world. First, Newcomb (1978) argues that violence is not presented as uniformly on television as the theory assumes, so television cannot be reliably responsible for cultivating the same sense of reality for all viewers. In addition, Cultivation Analysis is criticized for ignoring other issues such as the perceived realism of the televised content, which might be critical in explaining people's understanding of reality (Minnebo & Van Acker, 2004). Furthermore, other researchers (Wilson, Martins, & Marske, 2005) found that attention to television might be more important to cultivating perceptions than simply the amount of TV viewing. The fact that the theory seems to ignore cognitive processes such as attention or rational thinking style renders it less useful than is desired (Berger, 2005).

Heurism

When we examine Cultivation Analysis against our criteria from Chapter 4, we find that it measures up quite well with regard to heurism. For example, the theory has been applied to crime (Signorielli, 1990), fear of victimization (Sparks & Ogles, 1990), attitudes toward racism (Allen & Hatchett, 1986), feelings of alienation (Morgan, 1986), anxiety (Zillman & Wakshlag, 1985), gender stereotyping (Carveth & Alexander, 1985; Preston, 1990), affluence (Potter, 1991), the aged (Gerbner et al., 1980), American stereotypes (Tan, 1982), civil liberties (Carlson, 1983), divorce (Potter, 1991), materialism (Reimer & Rosengren, 1990), values (Potter, 1993), health issues (Molitor, 1994; Potter, 1991), perceptions of adolescent drug use (Minnebo & Eggermont, 2007), and Spanish-language TV (Glascock & Ruggerio, 2004).

Test of Time

As we've noted, Cultivation Analysis is heuristic, but two issues may be working against it thirty years after its inception. First, studies based on its tenets are failing to find results consistent with the theory's predictions. Leo Jeffres, David Atkin, and Kimberly Neuendorf (2001), for instance, found that heavy television viewing seemed to be cultivating more diversity of opinion about public issues rather than mainstreaming people's perceptions as Cultivation Analysis predicts. In other words, the three Bs that Gerbner and his colleagues discussed did not obtain in Jeffres, Atkin, and Neuendorf's study. Jeffres and his colleagues called the effect they found "scatter-streaming" and noted that it provided weak support for Cultivation Analysis. Consistent with the Mean World Hypothesis, they did find that heavier users of TV expressed a greater need for gun control than did lighter users.

Second, as James Shanahan and Michael Morgan (1999) observe, times and media use are changing: "As more and more people grow up with TV, it is possible that it will become increasingly difficult to discern differences between light and heavy viewers" (p. 161). In addition, as TiVo, DVDs, digital cable, and other technologies alter our manner of TV viewing, it is likely that some of the theory's contentions will no longer hold true. For instance, if viewers can organize programming for themselves, it is unlikely that heavy viewing will mean the same thing for all viewers. Heavy viewing of cooking shows, for example, would be expected to cultivate a different reality from heavy viewing of soap operas or crime shows.

Cultivation offers responses to these criticisms. First, although there may be many more channels and people may have greater control over selectivity than they once had, television's dramatic and aesthetic conventions produce remarkably uniform content within as well as across genres. Second, because most television watching is ritual—that is, selected more by time of day than by specific program or the availability of multiple channels—heavy viewers will be exposed *overall* to more of television's dominant images. Further, most viewers, even with dozens of channels available to them, primarily select from only five or six, evidencing a very limited range of selection.

Criticism aside, Cultivation Analysis has been and remains one of the most influential mass communication theories of the last two decades. It is the foundation of much contemporary research and, as we've seen, has even become an international social movement. Another source of its influence is that it can be applied by anyone. It asks people to assess their own media use alongside the socially constructed reality of the world they inhabit. Imagine yourself as Joyce Jensen preparing to cast an important vote. You may well undergo the same mental debate as she. Yet think of how even a passing understanding of Cultivation Analysis might help you arrive at your decision and understand your motivations.

Discussion Starters

1. Are you like Joyce Jensen in that you do not feel safe walking in your neighborhood at night? How much television do you watch? Do you fit the profile offered by Cultivation Analysis? Why or why not?

2. Cultivation Analysis is a critical theory and demands action from its adherents. Do you believe researchers and theorists should become politically active in the fields they study? Why or why not?

3. Do you agree with the hypothesis concerning the Mean World Index? Why or why not?

4. How do you define violence on television? Do you think it is possible to calculate violent acts as Gerbner and his colleagues have done? Explain your answer.

5. Do you believe that the world is a mean place? What real-world evidence do you have that it is? What television evidence do you have that it is?

6. How do you respond to the criticism that more television channels and more divisions among viewers mean that the assumptions of Cultivation Analysis are no longer valid?

7. What other variables might affect people's perception of the world in addition to their amount of television viewing?

Online Learning Center www. mhhe.com/west4e

Visit the Online Learning Center at www.mhhe.com/west4e for chapter-specific resources, such as story-into-theory and multiple-choice quizzes, as well as theory summaries and theory connection questions.

CHAPTER 23

Uses and Gratifications Theory

*Based on the research of **Elihu Katz**, **Jay G. Blumler**, and **Michael Gurevitch***

Ryan Grant

It was a dreary Friday night and 16-year-old Ryan Grant was trying to figure out what he wanted to do. He worked for his father in a local hardware store, and without question, this was a rough week. He had to put in a lot of extra hours because it was inventory week and his dad had needed him to help catalog the merchandise. In addition, this morning he took an exam in his social studies class. Because he hadn't studied last week, Ryan crammed until 2 A.M. It was the end of the workweek, he thought, and time to escape both work and school.

Ryan felt exhausted and burned out. He wanted to be with others, but he knew he wouldn't be the best company. He considered two choices for the evening: He could stay at home and watch television, either with friends or alone, or he could try to get a group of friends together to go to the movies. He could see the value of going out with people who would help him loosen up. He could also appreciate being at home without having to exert any energy.

Ryan was faced with two opposing arguments. Here was the argument for watching television: First, he wouldn't have to spend a dime. He could dress and look how he wanted, and he could watch what he wanted when he wanted. And because it was Friday night, there were a couple of shows on that Ryan liked. At home, he could also command the best seat in the house. If he wanted to, he could invite over as many friends as he wished, making the night more social.

But the argument for going out to the movies seemed just as strong. He could see that new action/adventure movie he'd been waiting to see. Also, because Ryan was a "techie" who appreciated all technology, the movie theater's excellent fidelity THX system appealed to him. Finally, he could easily have fun in an evening out. Although he had never really thought about it too seriously, he enjoyed sitting with his friends in the dark, sharing the same experience. And Ryan loved movie popcorn!

Still, he was torn, so Ryan weighed the positives and negatives of each medium. If he chose television, he would have to deal with watching on a small screen. Also, if he did have friends over, he might have to endure fighting over what to watch. On the other hand, he could turn off the television if nothing good was on and simply hang out with his friends. The arguments for and against going to the movies seemed equivalent. He knew that first he'd have to drive to the cineplex and try to find a parking space. He also might have to stand in a long line, which he hated. To top it off, he would have to pay close to $15 for the movie ticket and popcorn. Yet he knew that watching a movie was a great escape from the real world, and he would be able to talk about the movie on Monday with his friends.

Ryan's decision about what to do came down to a simple question: What does a movie offer versus what television offers? As Ryan considered this question, a third alternative occurred to him: going to bed early.

Ryan is doing what we all do when dealing with the mass media: He is making choices. Most of us actively engage the media when making choices about what to do at different times in our lives. Consider how many times you have found yourself in a situation similar to Ryan's. You may have decided that you needed some relaxation and thought about all the options before making up your mind. The process may not have taken very long, but it was a process that required thinking about what was available.

In the early days of mass media (the era of the penny newspaper, radio, movies, and "talkies"), **Mass Society Theory**—the idea that average people are helpless victims of powerful mass media—defined the relationship between audiences and the media they consumed (see our discussion of the Spiral of Silence Theory in Chapter 24). This notion was eventually discredited, in large part because social science—and simple observation—could not confirm the operation of all-powerful media and media messages. Obviously, not only were most people not directly affected by media messages, but when they were influenced, they were not all influenced similarly.

In time, Mass Society Theory was replaced by what we now call the **limited effects** theories, conceptions of media influence that view it as minimized or limited by certain aspects of individual audience members' personal and social lives. Two approaches to the limited effects orientation have been identified. First, the **Individual Differences Perspective** sees media's power as shaped by personal factors such as intelligence and self-esteem. For example, smart people and more secure people are better able to defend themselves against unwanted media impact. A second limited effects approach, the **Social Categories Model**, views media's power as limited by audience members' associations and group affiliations. For example, Republicans tend to spend time with other Republicans, who help them interpret media messages in a consistent, Republican-friendly manner. This effectively limits any influence media messages alone might have.

A close reading of these few paragraphs illustrates that these views afford audience members little credibility. The former (Mass Society) suggests that people simply are not smart or strong enough to protect themselves against unwanted media effects. The latter (limited effects) suggests that people have relatively little personal choice in interpreting the meaning of the messages they consume and in determining the level of impact those messages will have on them. Eventually, in response to these unflattering views of typical audience members, theorists Elihu Katz, Jay G. Blumler, and Michael Gurevitch (1974) presented a systematic and comprehensive articulation of audience members' role in the mass communication process. They formalized their thinking and identified Uses and Gratifications Theory (UGT). The theory holds that people actively seek out specific media and specific content to generate specific gratifications (or results). Theorists in Uses and Gratifications view people as active because they are able to examine and evaluate various types of media to accomplish communication goals (Wang, Fink, & Cai, 2008). As we saw in our opening, Ryan not only identified the specific media that he was willing to consider but was also able to determine for himself the uses he could and would

Mass Society Theory
the idea that average people are the victims of the powerful forces of mass media

limited effects
the perspective replacing Mass Society Theory; holds that media effects are limited by aspects of the audience's personal and social lives

Individual Differences Perspective
a specific approach to the idea of limited effects; concentrates on the limits posed by personal characteristics

Social Categories Model
a specific approach to the idea of limited effects; concentrates on the limits posed by group membership

make of each and the personal values of those uses. Researchers in Uses and Gratifications Theory ask the question, What do consumers do with the media?

This audience-centered media theory underscores an active media consumer. Considering that this overarching principle contradicts the views offered by other media theorists and other theoretical perspectives, it is important to trace the theory's development. We present the beginnings of Uses and Gratifications Theory in the next section, followed by the assumptions of the theory.

Stages in Uses and Gratifications Research

Uses and Gratifications Theory is an extension of needs and motivation theory (Maslow, 1970). In needs and motivation theory, Abraham Maslow posited that people actively seek to satisfy a hierarchy of needs. Once they have achieved the goals they seek on one level of the hierarchy, they are able to move to the next level (Figure 23.1). This picture of humans as active seekers, out to satisfy specific needs, fits well with the ideas Katz, Blumler, and Gurevitch brought to their studies of how people consume mass communication.

People can and do actively participate in the mass communication process, as researchers had acknowledged before Katz, Blumler, and Gurevitch. Wilbur Schramm (1954), for example, developed a means of determining "which offerings of mass communication will be selected by a given individual" (p. 19). His **fraction of selection** visually represents precisely the process that Ryan goes through when he makes his choice of a movie or a television show:

$$\frac{\text{Expectation of reward}}{\text{Effort required}}$$

fraction of selection
Schramm's idea of how media choices are made: the expectation of reward divided by the effort required

Schramm sought to make clear that audience members judge the level of reward (gratification) they expect from a given medium or message against how much effort they must make to secure that reward—an important component of what would later become known as the Uses and Gratifications perspective.

Figure 23.1
Maslow's Hierarchy of Needs
Source: Adapted from *Motivation and Personality,* Second Edition, by Abraham Maslow. Copyright © 1970. Reprinted by permission of Pearson Education, Inc., Upper Saddle River, NJ

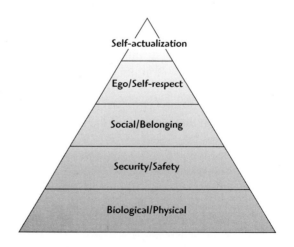

Self-actualization

Ego/Self-respect

Social/Belonging

Security/Safety

Biological/Physical

Even earlier, the classic and pioneering work of Herta Herzog (1944) began the first stage of Uses and Gratifications research. She sought to classify the reasons people engage in different forms of media behavior, such as newspaper reading and radio listening. Herzog studied the role of the audience's wants and needs, and she is sometimes credited with having originated UGT (although its label was to come much later).

Wanting to understand why so many women were attracted to radio soap operas, Herzog interviewed dozens of soap opera fans and identified three major types of gratification. First, some people enjoyed the dramas because of the emotional release they found in listening to the problems of others. Second, listeners seemed to engage in wishful thinking—that is, they gained a vicarious satisfaction from listening to the experiences of others. Finally, some people felt that they could learn from these programs because "if you listen to these programs and something turns up in your life, you would know what to do about it" (p. 25). Herzog's work was instrumental in the development of UGT because she was the first published researcher to provide an in-depth examination of media gratifications.

The second stage of Uses and Gratifications research began when researchers created typologies representing all the reasons people had for media use (Table 23.1). For example, Alan Rubin (1981) found that motivations for television use clustered into the following categories: to pass time, for companionship, excitement, escape, enjoyment, social interaction, relaxation, information, and to learn about a specific content. Other researchers (McQuail, Blumler, & Brown, 1972) asserted that media use could be categorized with only four basic divisions: diversion, personal relationships, personal identity, and surveillance.

Table 23.1 Uses and Gratifications Typologies

RESEARCHER	REASONS FOR MEDIA USE
Rubin (1981)	Passing time
	Companionship
	Excitement
	Escape
	Enjoyment
	Social interaction
	Relaxation
	Obtaining information
	Learning about a specific content
McQuail et al. (1972)	Diversion
	Personal relationships
	Personal identity
	Surveillance
Katz et al. (1973)	Connection with others
	Separation from others

Jay Blumler and another colleague, Denis McQuail (1969), began untangling reasons that people watch political programs. They found a number of motives for watching political broadcasts. This work formed an important foundation for researchers in Uses and Gratifications. Later work by McQuail, Blumler, and Joseph Brown (1972) and Katz, Gurevitch, and Hadassah Haas (1973) would begin to point out specifically how people see mass media. These teams of researchers found that there was a need either to connect with or to disconnect from others. Among the categories identified by individuals are needs associated with acquiring information or knowledge, pleasure, status, strengthening relationships, and escape. As you will recall, Ryan Grant was trying to work through two simultaneous needs: the need for strengthening friendships and the need to escape.

In the third and most recent stage, Uses and Gratifications researchers have been interested in linking specific reasons for media use with variables such as needs, goals, benefits, the consequences of media use, and individual factors (Faber, 2000; Greene & Kremar, 2005; Haridakis & Rubin, 2005; Rubin, 1994). In this effort, researchers are working to make the theory more explanatory and predictive. Alan Rubin and Mary Step (2000) conducted a study that exemplifies this stage of Uses and Gratifications research. Rubin and Step examined the relationship of motivation, interpersonal attraction, and **parasocial interaction** (the relationship we feel we have with people we know only through the media) to listening to public affairs talk radio. They found that a motivation for exciting entertainment and information acquisition interacted with perceptions of the parasocial relationship to explain why listeners tuned in to talk radio and why they found a host credible.

The gap between research such as Herzog's on audience use of media and the firm establishment of the perspective as an important and valuable theory some thirty years later was due to the dominance of the limited effects paradigm. A paradigm, as was discussed in Chapter 20, is an encompassing, organizing theoretical perspective, and because it was limited to effects that defined most mass communication theory and research at the time, attention was focused on what it was about media, messages, and audiences that limited media's influence. Little attention was paid to *how* audiences use media. The pioneering work of Katz, Blumler, and Gurevitch would change this state of affairs.

Uses and Gratifications Theory and its assumptions gained acceptance for a number of reasons. First, the limited effects researchers began to run out of things to study. Once all the variables that limited media influence were chronicled, what was left to say about the process of mass communication? Second, the limited effects perspective failed to explain why advertisers spend billions of dollars a year to place their ads in the media or why so many people spend so much time consuming the media. Third, some observers speculate that people often decide whether specific media effects are desirable and intentionally set out to achieve those effects. If this is so, researchers ask, what does this say about *limited* effects? Finally, those who do not live under the rules of the dominant paradigm were being neglected in the research. That is, psychologists—who were demonstrating on a regular basis the causal relationship between viewing mediated violence and subsequent aggressive behavior—were focusing too

parasocial interaction
the relationship we feel we have with people we know only through the media

> ### Uses and Gratifications Theory • *Theory at a Glance*
>
> People are active in choosing and using particular media to satisfy specific needs. Emphasizing a limited effects position, this theory views the media as having a limited effect because users are able to exercise choice and control. People are self-aware, and they are able to understand and articulate the reasons they use media. They see media as one way to gratify the needs they have. Uses and Gratifications Theory is primarily concerned with the following question: What do people do with media?

much attention on unintended negative effects. In the meantime, positive uses of media were left unexamined.

These factors produced a subtle shift in the focus of those researchers working within the limited effects paradigm. Their attention moved from the things media do *to* people to the things people do *with* media. If effects occur at all, either positive or negative, it is because audience members want them to happen, or at least let them happen.

Assumptions of Uses and Gratifications Theory

Uses and Gratifications Theory provides a framework for understanding when and how individual media consumers become more or less active and the consequences of that increased or decreased involvement.

Many of the assumptions of UGT were clearly articulated by the founders of the approach (Katz, Blumler, & Gurevitch, 1974). They contend that there are five basic assumptions of Uses and Gratifications Theory:

- The audience is active and its media use is goal oriented.
- The initiative in linking need gratification to a specific medium choice rests with the audience member.
- The media compete with other sources for need satisfaction.
- People have enough self-awareness of their media use, interests, and motives to be able to provide researchers with an accurate picture of that use.
- Value judgments of media content can only be assessed by the audience.

The theory's first assumption, about an active audience and goal-oriented media use, is fairly straightforward. Individual audience members can bring different levels of activity to their use of media. Audience members are also driven to accomplish goals via the media. As we mentioned previously, McQuail and colleagues (1972) identify several ways of classifying audience needs and gratifications. They include **diversion,** which is defined as escaping from routines or daily problems; **personal relationships,** which occurs when people

diversion
a category of gratifications coming from media use; involves escaping from routines and problems

Table 23.2 Needs Gratified by the Media

NEED TYPE	DESCRIPTION	MEDIA EXAMPLES
Cognitive	Acquiring information, knowledge, comprehension	Television (news), video ("How to Install Ceramic Tile"), movies (documentaries or films based on history, e.g., *The Other Boleyn Girl*)
Affective	Emotional, pleasant, or aesthetic experience	Movies, television (sitcoms, soap operas)
Personal integrative	Enhancing credibility, confidence, and status	Video ("Speaking With Conviction")
Social integrative	Enhancing connections with family, friends, and so forth	Internet (e-mail, chat rooms, Listservs, IM)
Tension release	Escape and diversion	Television, movies, video, radio, Internet

Source: Adapted from Katz, Gurevitch, & Haas, 1973.

personal relationships
a category of gratifications coming from media use; involves substituting media for companionship

personal identity
a category of gratifications coming from media use; involves ways to reinforce individual values

surveillance
a category of gratifications coming from media use; involves collecting needed information

substitute the media for companionship; **personal identity,** or ways to reinforce an individual's values; and **surveillance,** or information about how media will help an individual accomplish something. In Table 23.2 we present additional categories of needs that are fulfilled by the media.

In our opening, we saw Ryan choosing between two competing media—television and film. All of us have our favorite content within a given medium, and we all have reasons for selecting a particular medium. At the movies, for instance, many of us like love stories rather than historical war films; some of us prefer to be entertained at the end of a long day rather than be educated about a historical event (diversion). Some drivers prefer to talk on their cell phones over long trips; it not only passes the time but also allows people to stay connected with their family and friends (personal relationships). Truck drivers, for example, may prefer to listen to call-in radio talk shows rather than spend their long nights driving in silence (personal identity). Finally, there are people who enjoy watching home improvement shows on cable so that they can learn how to do projects around the house (surveillance). Audience members choose among various media, then, for different gratifications.

Uses and Gratifications' second assumption links need gratification to a specific medium choice that rests with the audience member. Because people are active agents, they take initiative. We choose shows like *The Simpsons* when we want to laugh and *CNN Newsroom* when we want to be informed, but no one decides for us what we *want* from a given medium or piece of content. We may well choose CNN because we want to be entertained by the anchors. The implication here is that audience members have a great deal of autonomy in the mass communication process.

The third assumption—that media compete with other sources for need satisfaction—means that the media and their audiences do not exist in a vacuum. Both are part of the larger society, and the relationship between media and audiences is influenced by that society. On a first date, for example, going out to the movies is a more likely use of media than is renting a video and watching it at home. Someone who is an infrequent consumer of media—who, for example, finds more gratification in conversations with friends and family—may turn to the media with greater frequency when seeking information during a national political election.

The fourth assumption of UGT relates to a methodological issue that has to do with researchers' ability to collect reliable and accurate information from media consumers. To argue that people are aware enough of their own media use, interests, and motives to be able to provide researchers with an accurate picture of that use reaffirms the belief in an active audience; it also implies that people are cognizant of that activity. In fact, the early research in Uses and Gratifications included questioning respondents about why they consumed particular media. This qualitative approach, which we explained in Chapter 3, included interviewing respondents and directly observing their reactions during conversations about media. The thinking surrounding this data collection technique was that people are in the best position to explain what they do and why they do it. Interestingly, as the theory evolved, the methodology also changed. Researchers began to abandon their qualitative analysis in favor of more quantitative procedures. Yet the questionnaires employed in these procedures emanated from many of the interviews and observations collected in the qualitative period.

The fifth assumption is also less about the audience than it is about those who study it. It asserts that researchers should suspend value judgments linking the audience's needs to specific media or content. Theorists in Uses and Gratifications argue that because it is individual audience members who decide to use certain content for certain ends, the value of media content can be assessed only by the audience. According to theorists in Uses and Gratifications, even tacky content found in such talk shows as *Jerry Springer* may be functional if it provides gratifications for the audience. People are critical consumers. According to researchers J. D. Rayburn and Philip Palmgreen (1984), "[A] person may read a particular newspaper because it is the only one available, but this does not imply that she is perfectly satisfied with that newspaper. Indeed, she may be dissatisfied enough to drop her subscription if an alternative paper becomes available" (p. 542).

Theory Application in Groups (TAG)

In small groups, create a typology of gratifications that a user might have for participating in an online chat group. Be prepared to discuss how these might differ (or not) from the gratifications sought from other media.

Some contemporary mass communication researchers (such as Turow, 2003) lament what they see as the negative, debasing influence of consumer product advertising on U.S. culture. The United States is fast becoming a nation of consumers: Love has been reduced to giving someone flowers; freedom now means the ability to buy a Big Gulp rather than a canned soda at 7-Eleven; a "good" mother is one who packs Lunchables in her child's lunchbox. Here we illustrate the influence of the limited effects paradigm. In the absence of hard evidence of the large-scale effect some critics fear, it's easier to assume that watching ads for these products—and the subsequent purchase of flowers, a Big Gulp, and Lunchables—is not only an individual choice, but a harmless one. (See our discussion of the intersection of media, culture, and individuals in Chapter 21 on Cultural Studies.)

The Active Audience

A theory that is based on the assumption that media consumers are active must delineate what it means by "the active audience." Mark Levy and Sven Windahl (1985) deal with the issue this way:

> As commonly understood by gratifications researchers, the term "audience activity" postulates a voluntaristic and selective orientation by audiences toward the communication process. In brief, it suggests that media use is motivated by needs and goals that are defined by audience members themselves, and that active participation in the communication process may facilitate, limit, or otherwise influence the gratifications and effects associated with exposure. Current thinking also suggests that audience activity is best conceptualized as a variable construct, with audiences exhibiting varying *kinds* and *degrees* of activity. (p. 110)

Jay G. Blumler (1979) offers several suggestions as to the kinds of audience activity in which media consumers could engage. They include utility, intentionality, selectivity, and imperviousness to influence.

utility
using the media to accomplish specific tasks

intentionality
occurs when people's prior motives determine use of media

selectivity
audience members' use of media reflects their existing interests

imperviousness to influence
refers to audience members' constructing their own meaning from media content

First, the media have uses for people, and people can put media to those uses. This is termed **utility**. People listen to the car radio to find out about traffic. They go online to buy CDs. They read fashion magazines to find out about the latest styles. **Intentionality** occurs when people's prior motivations determine their consumption of media content. When people want to be entertained, they tune in to comedy. When they want greater detail about a news story, it's Charlie Rose or *Nightline*. The third type of audience activity is termed **selectivity**, which means that audience members' use of media may reflect their existing interests and preferences. If you like jazz, you might listen to the jazz program on the local NPR station. If you regularly surf the Web, you are a likely reader of *Wired*. If you're interested in local politics, you probably subscribe to the local paper. Finally, an **imperviousness to influence** suggests that audience members construct their own meaning from content and that meaning influences what they think and do. They often actively avoid certain types of media influence. For example, some people buy products on the basis of quality and value rather than in response to advertising campaigns.

Or they exhibit no aggression against others, no matter how much they enjoy action/adventure films and television shows.

UGT also distinguishes between activity and activeness to understand better the degrees of audience activity. Although the terms are related, **activity** refers more to what the media consumer does (for example, she chooses to go online for news rather than read it in the newspaper). **Activeness** is closer to what really interests researchers in Uses and Gratifications: the audience's freedom and autonomy in the mass communication situation.

Activeness is relative. Some people are active participants in the mass communication process; others are more passive. We all know people who live their lives through talk shows or who follow every fad and fashion presented in the mass media. Terms like *couch potato* and *boob tube* developed from the idea that many folks simply sit back and suck up whatever is presented. On the other hand, we also know people who are quite adroit at consuming media. Your friend may listen to rap because of the beat. You may listen to rap not only for its rhythms, but also for its social commentary. For you, *Titanic* may have been a warm love story with great special effects. Your brother may have interpreted it as an allegory of class struggle.

Activeness is also individually variable. A person can be inactive at times ("I'll just turn on the television for background noise") and then become quite active ("The news is on! I'd better watch"). Our level of activeness often varies by time of day and type of content. We can be active users of the Internet by day and passive consumers of late-night talk shows on television.

Media Effects

We saw earlier that Uses and Gratifications Theory was developed in part to help solve a fairly important problem for mass communication theorists: How could they hold to notions of limited effects when there is so much evidence of media influence all around? Some researchers working in Uses and Gratifications believe its value lies in its ability to clarify how effects can and do happen.

Sven Windahl (1981) calls for the combination of the Uses and Gratifications Theory and the effects traditions into what he labels the "uses and effects" model. Similarly, Philip Palmgreen, Lawrence Wenner, and Karl Rosengren (1985) write that "a variety of audience gratifications [both sought and obtained] are related to a wide spectrum of media effects, including knowledge, dependency, attitudes, perceptions of social reality, agenda-setting, discussion, and various political effects variables" (p. 31). Blumler (1979) offers his suggestions on using Uses and Gratifications to predict and explain media effects:

> How might propositions about media effects be generated from . . . gratifications? First, we may postulate that cognitive motivation will facilitate information gain. . . . Second, media consumption for purposes of diversion and escape will favour audience acceptance of perceptions of social situations in line with portrayals frequently found in entertainment materials. . . . Third, involvement in media materials for personal identity reasons is likely to promote reinforcement effects. (pp. 18–19)

Research Notes

Kaye, B. K., & Johnson, T. J. (2004). A web for all reasons: Uses and gratifications of Internet components for political information. *Telematics and Informatics, 21,* 197–223.

The authors conducted an online survey during the 2000 presidential election to examine Internet users' motivations for using the following new media: the Web, bulletin boards/electronic mailing lists, and chat forums. The researchers were interested in people's desires for political information in their Internet use. Furthermore, they wanted to investigate whether political attitudes, Internet experience, and personal characteristics predict Internet use motivations. The survey was posted on the World Wide Web during the two weeks before and the two weeks after the 2000 presidential election. Notices about the survey were posted on a variety of sites geared to attract politically interested Internet users.

The study examined the 442 responses the researchers received. They found specific motives prompting these respondents to use the Web (guidance on how to vote, entertainment/social utility, convenience, and information seeking), message boards/electronic mailing lists (entertainment/social utility, information seeking, convenience, and guidance), and chat rooms (guidance/information seeking, entertainment/social utility, and convenience). The authors concluded that websites have become credible and so guidance/information seeking was a big motivating factor for using them; bulletin boards/mailing lists, perhaps because of their anonymity and lack of interpersonal contact, are still deemed less trustworthy and so are used less for guidance.

Lucas, L., & Sherry, J. L. (2004). Sex differences in video game play: A communication-based explanation. *Communication Research, 31,* 499–523.

In this study Lucas and Sherry investigated gender differences in video game use. They focused on "interpersonal needs for inclusion, affection, and control, as well as socially constructed perceptions of gendered game play" (p. 499). The authors used a Uses and Gratifications framework to examine these gender differences and posed the following hypotheses:

1. Young women will be less likely to be video game players than young men.

2. Young women will play video games for fewer hours than young men.

3. Young women will be less motivated by the gratification of social interaction than young men.

4. Young men and young women will be highly motivated to play video games by the ability to beat or control the game.

5. Young women will enjoy nonmental games more than mental games.

6. Young men will enjoy mental games more than nonmental games.

7. Young men will enjoy mental games more than young women will.

8. Young men will be motivated more by competition than young women.

9. Young women will be motivated more by the ability to beat or control the game than by competition.

Survey data were collected from 544 college students (313 women and 231 men). The results supported all the hypotheses posed by the researchers.

In other words, even when audience members are active—even when they determine for themselves the uses they wish to make of mass media and the gratifications they seek from those uses—effects can and do occur. The failure of researchers in traditional Uses and Gratifications to consider the possibility

of important media effects led the authors of the original work to chastise their colleagues eleven years later by noting that a "vulgar gratificationism" (Blumler, 1985, p. 259) should be purged from the theory. It was not their intention to imply that audience members are always totally free in either the uses they make of media or the gratifications they seek from them; the world in which media consumers live shapes them just as surely as they shape it, and content does have intended meaning.

These Uses and Gratifications theorists point to a second set of premises that make clear their belief that people's use of media and the gratifications they seek from it are inextricably intertwined with the world in which they live. Katz and his colleagues (1974) originally wrote that "social situations" in which people find themselves can be "involved in the generation of media-related needs" (p. 27) in five ways. First, social situations can produce tensions and conflicts, leading to pressure for their easement through the consumption of media. That is, we live in the world, and events in it can compel us to seek specific media and content. In 2005 nearly everyone was talking about Hurricane Katrina, the devastation in New Orleans, possible racism delaying the rescue efforts, and whether the people running FEMA were incompetent. It was a sizeable catastrophe in U.S. history, and all media provided a great deal of information about the natural disaster and the human problems that resulted. This was a social situation wrought with tension and conflict. Where did you go to ease the pressure?

Second, social situations can create an awareness of problems that demand attention, information about which may be sought in the media. Simply stated, the world in which we live contains information that makes us aware of things that are of interest to us, and we can find out more about those interests through the media. Everyone everywhere—work, school, virtually every social situation you entered—was talking about Katrina and the rescue efforts. This problem demanded your attention. You probably turned to the media—for information, perspective, and analysis.

Third, social situations can impoverish real-life opportunities to satisfy certain needs, and the media can serve as substitutes or supplements. In other words, sometimes the situations in which you find yourself make the media the best, if not the only, source possible. Your social situation—college student—made it difficult, if not impossible, for you to go to New Orleans to see for yourself how the rescue was proceeding. You weren't able to ask President Bush or other officials about available supplies and money or whether racism was involved. You needed to know what was going on in this historic crisis, but the reality of your position in society meant that you had little choice but to rely on the media to meet that need.

Fourth, social situations often elicit specific values, and their affirmation and reinforcement can be facilitated by the consumption of related media materials. Again, you are a college student. You are an educated person. The media offer an appropriate location for the affirmation and reinforcement of the knowledge and awareness that you value.

Finally, social situations demand familiarity with media; these demands must be met to sustain membership in specific social groups. As a college student, you are viewed as the future of our country. Not only should you have had an opinion about the government's response to Katrina, but you should have had something to say about the media's performance throughout that crisis. Lacking those opinions, you may have been regarded as out of it or uninformed.

In rejecting "vulgar gratificationism," Katz and his colleagues (1974) note that we should ask three things. First, are the mass media instrumental in creating this social situation? How, for instance, did we find out about possible racism in the aftermath of Katrina? What role did various media outlets play? Based on what information did we form our opinions? Second, are the mass media instrumental in making the satisfaction of this situation's related needs so crucial? Why, for instance, was it important to have an opinion at all? Who put this issue on the public's agenda? Who determined that it was more important than any of the myriad events that were happening in the world every day?

Uses and Gratifications and New Media

Many researchers (and mass media consumers) believe we will change the way we watch television and use media in general in the future. For example, Gilder (1994) talked about the way a hybrid of the television and the computer would affect our culture:

> Rather than exalting mass culture, the teleputer will enhance individualism. Rather than cultivating passivity, the teleputer will promote creativity. Instead of a master-slave architecture, the teleputer will have an interactive architecture in which every receiver can function as a processor and transmitter of video images and other information. The teleputer will usher in a culture compatible with the immense powers of today's ascendant technology. Perhaps most important, the teleputer will enrich and strengthen democracy and capitalism around the world. (p. 46)

In the years since Gilder's predictions, some of what he suggests has come to pass. Television viewing has changed somewhat and now must compete with multiple media, and many people watch videos on their computers, but much of what Gilder spoke of remains unrealized.

Although Gilder's predictions are not (yet) reality, almost everyone expects that new media will continue to change our future. In a study investigating that premise, Louis Leung and Ran Wei (2000) examined the uses and gratifications of the cell phone. Leung and Wei were interested in why people use cell phones and whether their reasons differed from why they used the old wired and "land-based" telephones. In addition, Leung and Wei observed, like Gilder, that "the new cellular phone represents a converged new technology hybrid as it dissolves boundaries between telecommunications and broadcast industries" (p. 318). However, in contrast to Gilder's conclusions, Leung and Wei's study indicated that Uses and Gratifications Theory, especially when combined with other theories, can explain cell phone use.

Leung and Wei's ability to apply Uses and Gratifications Theory to a new technology is explained by Shanahan and Morgan's (1999) observation that there is an "underlying consistency of the content of the messages we consume and the nature of the symbolic environment in which we live" (p. 199) even if the delivery technology changes. Shanahan and Morgan assert that new technologies have always developed by adopting the message content from the technology that was previously dominant. They argue, for example, that films took their content from serialized literature, radio did the same, and television simply repackaged radio programming. Marshall McLuhan (see Chapter 25) noted that new media merely provide new bottles for old wine.

The question for Uses and Gratifications researchers is whether the motivations people brought to their use of "old" media will apply to new media. Theorists are interested in finding out whether new media so alter the message and the experience that Uses and Gratifications Theory no longer applies or has to be radically modified. Access to new technologies has changed and extended our abilities for entertainment and information gathering, and media researchers require greater understanding of the personal and social reasons people have for using new media.

In a study investigating computerized video game playing, John Sherry and his colleagues (Sherry, Lucas, Rechtsteiner, Brooks, & Wilson, 2001) noted that video game playing is overwhelmingly popular among young people. The average number of hours that their female participants played per week was 9, whereas males played 14 hours a week on average. The authors took a Uses and Gratifications approach to this activity and found that video game playing satisfied the following motivations for their respondents: challenge, arousal, diversion, fantasy, competition, and social interaction.

The finding of social interaction was especially interesting because these types of games have often been assumed to be isolating and lacking in social presence (Perse & Courtright, 1993; Straus, 1997). Sherry and his colleagues found that adolescents played video games with friends and saw game playing as a time to gather and make connections with others. In addition to this interesting finding, the researchers concluded that although the medium is different, UGT still helps explain its appeal. In a study building on these findings (Lucas & Sherry, 2004), researchers found that a Uses and Gratifications framework also helped explain differences in how young adult women and men participated in video game play.

Likewise, Zizi Papacharissi and Alan Rubin's (2000) work predicting Internet use found a Uses and Gratifications perspective explanatory. Papacharissi and Rubin found that people had five primary motives for Internet use, and the most important was information seeking. They also found that people who felt valued interpersonally used the Internet primarily for information gathering and those who felt less secure in their face-to-face interactions turned to the Internet for social motives. Overall, they concluded that Uses and Gratifications Theory provided an important framework for studying new media.

Barbara Kaye and Thomas Johnson (2004) say that the growth of the Internet "has produced a renaissance in the uses and gratifications tradition as scholars are increasingly interested in going beyond discovering who uses the Internet to examine why they use this new medium" (p. 197). Robert LaRose and Matthew Eastin (2004) suggest that Uses and Gratifications Theory can explain Internet use, but the theory can also be enhanced by the addition of some new variables such as expected activity outcomes and social outcomes. *Expected activity outcomes* concern what people think they will obtain from the medium. LaRose and Eastin found that people expect that using the Internet will improve their lot in life. *Social outcomes* involve social status and identity. LaRose and Eastin speculate that people may enhance their social status by finding like-minded others through the Internet and expressing their ideas to them. They also suggest that "perhaps the Internet is a means of constantly exploring and trying out new, improved versions of our selves" (p. 373).

Finally, John Dimmick, Yan Chen, and Zhan Li (2004) observe that although the Internet is a relatively new medium, it overlaps the traditional media in terms of uses and gratifications. People seek out the Internet for news in the same way that they previously used other forms of media for that need. This finding has significance for possible displacement of older media by the Internet, but it shows that Uses and Gratifications is still useful and is applicable to new media.

Integration, Critique, and Closing

Uses and Gratifications, as a recognizable, discrete theory, had its greatest influence in the 1970s and 1980s. The limited effects paradigm held sway at the time, and media theorists needed a framework within which they could discuss the obvious presence of media effects without straying too far from disciplinary orthodoxy. This is not the reason that Katz, Blumler, and Gurevitch formalized the approach, but it is why the approach took on its particular character.

Two other factors shaped how it would be and is now used. The first is the simple nature of its development. Its founders were interested in how people use media in quite specific situations. They were political scientists and sociologists, so their focus was on political and informational campaigns. Therefore, researchers in traditional UGT studied how people used the *information* provided by media. They approached media as outlets of information rather than

Theory Into Practice

Mason

I thought the chapter-opening story about Ryan was so funny because I had the same internal debate last weekend. I was completely wiped, and I couldn't decide if I just wanted to veg out in front of the TV or hang out with my friends. I knew I would miss seeing my friends if I stayed home, but the idea of letting mindless TV wash over me was really appealing because I'd had such a hectic week. Frankly, I was kind of sick of talking to people, so sitting and watching something amusing sounded good. I definitely was looking for "tension release." But then my friends stopped by and convinced me to go to a movie with them. I guess I decided those "social integrative" needs were more important at that moment.

T*I*P

of symbols. It is only logical, then, that they envisioned the possibility—even the probability—of discerning, reflective audience members selecting the information they wanted and needed. Uses and Gratifications, therefore, is quite straightforward when discussing how people use newspapers (newspapers are made up of discrete sections, each aimed at a specific type of reader seeking specific types of information) or magazines (publications with very specific, demographically targeted readers) to come to some specific decision or judgment. As you think about this theory, consider the following criteria: logical consistency, utility, and heurism.

Integration

Communication Tradition	Rhetorical | Semiotic | Phenomenological | Cybernetic | **Socio-Psychological** | Socio-Cultural | Critical
Communication Context	Intrapersonal | Interpersonal | Small Group | Organizational | Public/Rhetorical | **Mass/Media** | Cultural
Approach to Knowing	**Positivistic/Empirical** | Interpretive/Hermeneutic | Critical

Critique

Evaluation Criteria	Scope | **Logical Consistency** | Parsimony | **Utility** | Testability | **Heurism** | Test of Time

Logical Consistency

Denis McQuail (1984) believes that the theory suffers from a lack of theoretical coherence. He thinks that some of the theory's terminology needs to be further defined. He notes that the theory relies too heavily on the functional use of media, because there are times when the media can be reckless. For example, there have been instances of sloppy, inaccurate, or unethical journalism: In 1999 a Kentucky journalist was fired after falsely reporting that she had AIDS; in the late 1990s there was an erroneous CNN report about the U.S. government's knowledge of its military's use of poisonous gas in Vietnam. What if the active consumer sought out these media for information about AIDS or the U.S. involvement in Vietnam? This irresponsibility of the media is not addressed in the theory.

Utility

The theory has been criticized because some of its central tenets may be questionable. If the key concepts of the theory are shaky, then the theory is not useful—it isn't really explaining anything. The notion of the active audience, which is critical to Uses and Gratifications, has been questioned by some critics.

Some researchers (Kubey & Csikszentmihalyi, 1990) note that people report that their television watching in particular is passive and requires little concentration. Furthermore, the theory seems to highlight a reasoning media consumer, one who does not accept everything the media present. The theory does not take into consideration the fact that individuals may not have considered all available choices in media consumption. For instance, Ryan Grant has considered two choices: Stay at home or go out to the movies. What other options could he consider? Uses and Gratifications does not pay attention to the myriad unconscious decisions made by individuals.

Heurism

We can see that the heuristic nature of the theory is without question. The research has spanned several decades, and the theory has framed a number of research studies. In addition to the early pioneers Katz, Blumler, and Gurevitch and their colleagues, others have employed the theory and its thinking in their research on home computer use (Perse & Courtright, 1993; Perse & Greenberg-Dunn, 1998), the remote control (Bellamy & Walker, 1996; Ferguson, 1992), and the Internet (Morris & Ogan, 1996).

The value of Uses and Gratifications Theory today is in its ability to provide a framework for the consideration of the audience and individual media consumers in contemporary mass communication research and theory. Uses and Gratifications may not be the defining theory in the field of mass communication, but it serves the discipline well as a "perspective through which a number of ideas and theories about media choice, consumption, and even impact can be viewed" (Baran & Davis, 2003, p. 241).

Discussion Starters

1. Are there choices other than those identified for Ryan Grant to consider in his decision to do something on Friday night? How do these alternatives relate to Uses and Gratifications Theory? Use examples in your response.

2. How active a media consumer are you? Are you always thoughtful in your choice of media content? Do you bring different levels of activeness to different media—newspapers versus radio, for example?

3. UGT has been criticized for being too apologetic of the media industries and overly supportive of the status quo. Can you explain why this is so? Do you agree with these criticisms? Does such criticism have any place in scientific theory?

4. Uses and Gratifications Theory assumes that media present content and consumers consume it. How does the Internet threaten to disrupt this model? How might UGT adapt to allow for this transformation of traditional media consumers into online media users?

5. Discuss the relevance of UGT in the early twenty-first century. Incorporate examples into your response.

6. What difference would it make, according to the theory, if Ryan's movie choice was an action/adventure film and the main choices on TV were romantic comedies? How does Uses and Gratifications Theory account for media content?

7. Are there other uses and gratifications that people may get from media that the chapter doesn't discuss? Explain your answer.

Online Learning Center (www. mhhe.com/west4e)

Visit the Online Learning Center at www.mhhe.com/west4e for chapter-specific resources, such as story-into-theory and multiple-choice quizzes, as well as theory summaries and theory connection questions.

CHAPTER 24

Spiral of Silence Theory

*Based on the research of **Elisabeth Noelle-Neumann***

Carol Johansen

Each morning, Carol Johansen attends the seniors' breakfast at the local senior center. She can afford to go out to a restaurant for breakfast, but she goes to the center because she enjoys the company. She encounters a rambunctious cast of characters, including Earl, a World War I veteran who sings Broadway songs; Nancy, a former nurse who tells lively stories about former patients; and Nick, a New England lobsterman who is an avid newspaper reader. This morning's breakfast was especially interesting because the conversation quickly turned to a newspaper article on spanking children.

Nick read the article to the group, and after he was done, he offered his opinion on the topic: "I agree with this writer. I don't see anything wrong with spanking a kid. Look at this survey in the paper. Over 60 percent of the state believes it's okay to spank, but only 40 percent of the country does. Nowadays, though, you can't lay a hand on a kid. They're ready to sue you, or you'll get some state worker to come into your own house and take your kid away. It's not right."

"I agree," said Nancy. "I can tell you that my neighbor's daughter is almost 8 and a holy terror. But her mother won't touch her! I don't get it. If that was my child, I wouldn't mind putting her over my knee and giving her a good wallop! The girl's mom and dad don't want to send 'the wrong message' to her so she gets away with a lot."

Earl became more interested in the subject as Nancy spoke. Like the others, Earl had a strong opinion on the subject: "Look. How many people at this table were spanked when they were little?" All seven raised their hands. "And how many of you think that you're violent people?" None showed any response. "There. That's my point. Today, they tell you that if you spank your own kid, then that kid is going to end up violent. But look at us. We aren't violent. We don't hurt anyone. There's just too much of this political correctness out there, and too many parents simply have no rights anymore."

Carol continued glancing at one of Nick's newspapers. She, like the others, had an opinion on the subject. But her thoughts differed from those of the others. She did not believe in spanking a child at all. She had been spanked like the rest of her friends, but her dad had not known when to stop. Carol had often been physically abused. She thought about the number of parents who are not able to stop at just one slap on the behind. She also thought about what hitting accomplished. Children can be taught right and wrong, she felt, without being hit.

"Hey, Carol," Nick interrupted, "you're pretty quiet. What's your take on all this?"

Carol thought for a quick moment. Should she disagree with the rest of them? What about all the people in her community who also agree with spanking? Carol recalled seeing a news program on the topic about a week ago, and the reporter had interviewed several adult children who had been spanked and who felt that spanking was the only discipline to use on them during their childhood.

She knew that she disagreed with her breakfast colleagues, but how could she begin to explain all of her thoughts? They wouldn't understand. It's probably better simply to go with the flow, she surmised.

"Oh, I don't know. I can see how some kids need 'special attention.' But sometimes, parents get too angry."

"C'mon Carol," Nancy interrupted. "You can't have it both ways. There are a lot of . . ."

"Well, I guess I agree with it. I hope that it's not done that often, though."

As the volunteer arrived at the table to pour more coffee, the conversation quickly turned to other news. Privately, Carol thought about why she had deferred to the group's will. She didn't want to be alone in her viewpoint, nor did she want to explain the personal and sordid details of her past. As Nick began to talk about last night's city council meeting, Carol wondered whether she would ever speak up on the subject again.

Our opinions of events, people, and topics change periodically in our lives. Consider, for example, your opinions about dating when you were a 15-year-old and your opinions about dating now. Or consider the opinions you held of your parents during your adolescence and those you hold today. Your opinions on various topics—including premarital sex and raising children—may have evolved over the years. Our opinions are not static and frequently change over the years.

One important influence on our opinions is the media. Media have helped to shape who we are today. Often, this influence is subtle; at other times it is more direct. The media's influence on public opinion is what Elisabeth Noelle-Neumann studied, dating back to the 1930s and 1940s. It was in the early 1970s, however, that she conceptualized the Spiral of Silence Theory.

Although Noelle-Neumann's theory is pre-Internet age, her interpretation of the media's influence still holds true. Today, given the popularity in usage of blogs, e-mail, Listservs, and YouTube, we are bombarded with mediated messages. The messages emanating from websites, television news, and e-commentary have contributed to our cultural discourse. Indeed, these media have even affected the direction of public discourse on socially significant issues (Butsch, 2007). Finally, the theory is important to address "because it directly relates to speech freedom, which is the cornerstone of our democracy" (Liu, 2006). Therefore, the value of examining Spiral of Silence Theory remains high.

Noelle-Neumann focuses on what happens when people provide their opinions on a variety of issues that the media have defined for the public. The Spiral of Silence Theory suggests that people who believe that they hold a minority viewpoint on a public issue will remain in the background where their communication will be restrained; those who believe that they hold a majority viewpoint will be more encouraged to speak. Noelle-Neumann (1983) contends that the media will focus more on the majority views, underestimating the minority views. Those in the minority will be less assertive in communicating their opinions, thereby leading to a downward spiral of communication. Interestingly, those in the majority will overestimate their influence and may become emboldened in their communication. Subsequently, the media will report

Because of their enormous power, media have a lasting and profound effect on public opinion. Mass media work simultaneously with majority opinion to silence minority beliefs on cultural and social issues in particular. A fear of isolation prompts those with minority views to examine the beliefs of others. Individuals who fear being socially isolated are prone to conform to what they perceive to be the majority view. Every so often, however, the silent majority raises its voice in activism.

on their opinions and activities. This theory, then, adheres to the belief that we alluded to in Chapter 2. Groups are highly influential in our lives.

The minority views of Carol Johansen and the behavior of her breakfast friends underscore the gist of the Spiral of Silence Theory. Listening to her colleagues' opinions on spanking, Carol feels that she is alone in thinking that spanking is wrong. The theory suggests that Carol is influenced by media reports of over 60 percent of the state supporting spanking for discipline and also by her own recollection of a television news show that lauded the benefits of spanking by adult children who had been spanked themselves. Carol perceives her opinion to be a minority view, and consequently she speaks less. Conversely, those in our sample who agree with spanking as discipline (Nick, Nancy, and Earl) are no doubt inspired by the state survey responses; this prompts even more assertive communication on their part.

The difference between this majority and minority view at the senior center is further clarified by Noelle-Neumann (1991). She believes that those in the majority have the confidence to speak out. They may display their convictions by wearing buttons, brandishing bumper stickers, and emblazoning their opinions on the clothes they wear. Holders of minority views are usually cautious and silent, which reinforces the public's perceptions of their weakness. Nick, Nancy, and Earl are clearly confident in their opinions, whereas Carol fosters a sense of weakness by her lack of assertiveness in expressing her opinion.

The Spiral of Silence Theory uniquely intersects public opinion and media. To understand this interface better, we first unravel the notion of public opinion, a key component of the theory. We then examine three assumptions of the theory.

The Court of Public Opinion

As a researcher, Noelle-Neumann was interested in clarifying terms that may have multiple meanings. At the core of the Spiral of Silence Theory is a term that is commonly accepted but one that she felt was misconstrued: public opinion. As a founder and director of the Allensbach Institute, a polling agency in Germany, Noelle-Neumann contended that interpretations of *public opinion* have been misguided. In fact, although she identified more than fifty definitions of the term since the theory's inception, none satisfied her.

Although many years have passed since the theory's original expression, the concept of public opinion "is particularly encumbered by the thicket of confusion, misunderstandings, and communication problems" (Noelle-Neumann & Petersen, 2004, pp. 339–340). Attempting to provide some understanding of this key term in the theory, Noelle-Neumann (1984, 1993) has provided some clarity. She separates *public opinion* into two discrete terms: *public* and *opinion*.

She notes that there are three meanings of **public**. First, there is a legal association with the term. Public suggests that it is open to everyone, as in "public lands" or "public place." Second, public pertains to the concerns or issues of people, as in "the public responsibility of journalists." Finally, public represents the social-psychological side of people. That is, people not only think inwardly but also think about their relationships to others. The phrase "public eye" is relevant here. Noelle-Neumann concludes that individuals know whether they are exposed to or sheltered from public view, and they adjust themselves accordingly. She claims that the social-psychological side of public has been neglected in previous interpretations of public opinion, and yet "this is the meaning felt by people in their sensitive social skin" (1993, p. 62).

An **opinion** is an expression of an attitude. Opinions may vary in both intensity and stability. Invoking the early French and English interpretation of opinions, Noelle-Neumann notes that opinion is a level of agreement of a particular population. In the spiral of silence process, opinion is synonymous with something regarded as acceptable.

Putting all of this together, Noelle-Neumann defines **public opinion** as the "attitudes or behaviors one must express in public if one is not to isolate oneself; in areas of controversy or change, public opinions are those attitudes one *can* express without running the danger of isolating oneself" (p. 178). So, for Carol Johansen, her opinion on spanking would not be regarded as acceptable by her breakfast club. Because she fears being isolated from her particular early-morning community, she silences her opinions.

Noelle-Neumann and Petersen (2004) argue that public opinion is a dynamic process and limited by time and place. To that end, they note that "a spiral of silence only holds sway over a society for a limited period of time" (p. 350). So, there are both short- and long-term components to public opinion. For instance, in 2008, there was a difference between the public's opinion of having the first African American as a U.S. presidential candidate (short-term) and the public's opinion pertaining to race relations. In fact, Noelle-Neumann and Petersen note that in the United States, public opinion pertaining to race may pose a threat to "social cohesion" (p. 350).

Essentially, public opinion refers to the collective sentiments of a population on a particular subject. Most often, the media determine what subjects will be of interest to people, and the media often make a subject controversial. For example, the drug Viagra, used to treat impotence, was considered a medical marvel until the media discovered that many health plans covered this drug but did not cover female contraceptives. Many media outlets subsequently

public
legal, social, and social-psychological concerns of people

opinion
expression of attitude

public opinion
attitudes and behaviors expressed in public to avoid isolation

reported that this was an overtly sexist practice. Noelle-Neumann (1991) notes that public opinion may be influenced by who approves or disapproves of our views. In 2005 the U.S. Congress voted to repeal Medicare and Medicaid coverage of Viagra. Your opinion on whether you support this congressional action will likely be shaped by spokespeople on both sides of the issue as well as by friends and family members. A spiral of silence is the response to the shifting opinions of others.

Assumptions of Spiral of Silence Theory

With public opinion as our backdrop to the theory, we now explore three assumptions of the Spiral of Silence Theory. Noelle-Neumann (1991, 1993) has previously addressed these assertions:

- Society threatens deviant individuals with isolation; fear of isolation is pervasive.
- This fear of isolation causes individuals to try to assess the climate of opinion at all times.
- Public behavior is affected by public opinion assessment.

The first assumption asserts that society holds power over those who do not conform through threat of isolation. Noelle-Neumann believes that the very fabric of our society depends on people commonly recognizing and endorsing a set of values. And it is public opinion that determines whether these values have equal conviction across the populations. When people agree on a common set of values, then fear of isolation decreases. When there is a difference in values, fear of isolation sets in.

Like many theorists, Noelle-Neumann is concerned with the testability of this assumption. After all, she notes, are members of a society really threatened with isolation? How could this be? She believes that simple polling could not tap this area (for instance, How much do you fear isolation?). Questions such as these ask respondents to think too abstractly, because it's likely that few respondents have ever thought about isolation.

Noelle-Neumann employs the research values of Solomon Asch (1951), a social psychologist in the 1950s. Asch conducted the following laboratory experiment more than fifty times with eight to ten research subjects:

Which of the following lines on the right is equal to the line on the left?

_____   1. _____

                       2. _____

                       3. _____

You are probably quick to say that line 3 is equal to the line on the left. The group of research subjects, however, disagreed. After going around the room, the experimenter's assistants (who were in on the experiment) all named line 1 as the one that was equal to the line on the left. The unsuspecting subjects began to name line 1 as the correct response. In fact, Asch discovered that several times around, the unsuspecting subjects named the incorrect response. Asch believed that individuals frequently feel great pressure to agree with others, even though the others are incorrect. Borrowing from the theory, there is a very real fear of isolation.

Elizabeth Blakeslee (2005) of the *New York Times* notes that Asch's research conclusions on social conformity still exist today. She reports on the implications of following a group in many areas of society, including jury decisions and elections. She notes that "the unpleasantness of standing alone can make a majority opinion seem more appealing than sticking to one's own beliefs" (p. D3).

Responding to primary criticisms of the Asch studies—that people did not have a real fear of isolation but rather a lack of confidence in their own judgment—Noelle-Neumann engaged in a more realistic threat-of-isolation test. She believed that requiring subjects to assess a moral or aesthetic conviction was more realistic than any laboratory experiments conducted by Asch. Indeed, these moral issues should be contemporary (in the public spotlight) and issues on which the public is divided. Think about gay marriage, abortion rights, human cloning, marijuana for medical use, and other topics on which divergent points of view exist.

For Noelle-Neumann, freedom to smoke was (and continues to be) an issue "in the spotlight." During interviews with smokers, she showed them a picture with a person angrily saying, "It seems to me that smokers are terribly inconsiderate. They force others to inhale their health-endangering smoke." Respondents were asked to phrase responses to the statement. The results indicated that in the presence of nonsmokers, many smokers were less willing to support smokers' rights overtly.

The second assumption of the theory identifies people as constant assessors of the climate of public opinion. Noelle-Neumann contends that individuals receive information about public opinion from two sources: personal observation and the media. First, let's discuss how people are able to personally observe public opinion and then examine the role of the media.

quasi-statistical
sense
personal estimation
of the strength of
opposing sides on
a public issue

Noelle-Neumann (1991) states that people engage in a quasi-statistical ability to appraise public opinion. A **quasi-statistical sense** means that people are able to estimate the strength of opposing sides in a public debate. They are able to do this by listening to the views of others and incorporating that knowledge into their own viewpoints. For instance, Carol Johansen's quasi-statistical sense makes her believe that she is the only person at her breakfast table who opposes spanking. She can see that she is vastly outnumbered on the topic and therefore is able to assess the local public opinion on the subject. Noelle-Neumann calls this a quasi-statistical frequency "organ" in that she believes that people like Carol are able to numerically estimate where others fall on the topic. The theorist states that this organ is on "high alert" during periods of instability. So our quasi-statistical sense works overtime when we see that our opinions on a subject are different from those of the majority around us. This sense is, as a rule, an unconscious process.

Personal observations of public opinion can often be distorted and inaccurate. Noelle-Neumann (1993) calls the mistaken observations about how most people feel **pluralistic ignorance**. She notes that people "mix their own direct perceptions and the perceptions filtered through the eyes of the media into an indivisible whole that seems to derive from their own thoughts and experiences" (p. 169). Consider Carol's assessment of the opinions on spanking. With the vast majority of people around her supporting this type of discipline, she may believe that she is clearly in the minority. One or both sides in the debate, however, can overestimate their ability to estimate opinion. Especially with such lopsided support on a topic (as with the group at the senior center), Noelle-Neumann believes that people can become disillusioned.

People not only employ their personal observations of public opinion but also rely on the media. Yet Noelle-Neumann insists that the media's effects are frequently indirect. Because people are inherently social in nature, they talk about their observations to others. People seek out the media to confirm or disconfirm their observations and then interpret their own observations through the media. This can be illustrated through Carol's future behaviors. First, if she returns home from the senior center and reveals her beliefs on spanking to others, she may encounter several neighbors who share her opinion. Next, if she watches the evening news and learns that the majority of the country oppose spanking, this will resonate deeply with her. She will also be affected by any media reports that disproportionately publicize opposition to spanking. Finally, later discussions that Carol might have on the subject may invoke the media. She may tell others that even the media reports underscore her point of view. We will return to the powerful role of the media in the Spiral of Silence Theory a bit later in the chapter.

The final assumption of the theory is that the public's behavior is influenced by evaluations of public opinion. Noelle-Neumann (1991) proposes that public behavior takes the form of either speaking out on a subject or keeping silent. If individuals sense support for a topic, then they are likely to communicate about it; if they feel that others do not support a topic, then they maintain silence. She continues, "The strength of one camp's signals, or the weakness of the other's, is the driving force setting the spiral in motion" (p. 271). In sum, people seem to act according to how other people feel.

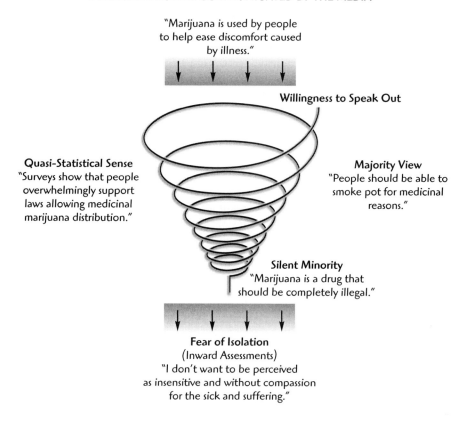

PUBLIC OPINION AS COMMUNICATED BY THE MEDIA

Figure 24.1
The Spiral of
Silence: Medicinal
Marijuana

"Marijuana is used by people
to help ease discomfort caused
by illness."

Willingness to Speak Out

Quasi-Statistical Sense
"Surveys show that people
overwhelmingly support
laws allowing medicinal
marijuana distribution."

Majority View
"People should be able to
smoke pot for medicinal
reasons."

Silent Minority
"Marijuana is a drug that
should be completely illegal."

Fear of Isolation
(Inward Assessments)
"I don't want to be perceived
as insensitive and without compassion
for the sick and suffering."

Noelle-Neumann believes that human beings have an aversion to discussing topics that do not have the support of the majority. To test this assumption, consider interviewing people on your campus about a controversial issue such as physician-assisted suicide. If straw polls in your campus newspaper show that almost 70 percent of the campus opposes this, then according to the theory, students, faculty, and staff are probably going to be less inclined to speak out in favor of the practice. A willingness to speak out may have more to do with one's convictions and an assessment of overall trends in society. That is, if there is a liberal climate on your campus, there may be more willingness to speak out; if a conservative climate exists, people may feel less inclined to offer their opposition.

These three assumptions are important to consider as we further delineate Noelle-Neumann's theory. In Figure 24.1, we illustrate several concepts and themes emerging from the theory's assumptions.

Personal opinions, a fear of being alone in those opinions, and public sentiment lay the groundwork for discussing the remainder of the theory. Each of these areas is influenced by a powerful part of U.S. society: the media. Let's now overview the powerful influence of the media in the Spiral of Silence Theory.

The Media's Influence

As we have discussed, the Spiral of Silence Theory rests on public opinion. Noelle-Neumann (1993) cautions, however, that "much of the population adjusts its attitudes to the tenor of the media" (p. 272). Nancy Eckstein and Paul Turman (2002) agree. They claim that "the media may provide the force behind the spiral of silence because it is considered a one-sided conversation, an indirect public form of communication where people feel helpless to respond" (p. 173). A willingness to speak out depends greatly on the media. Without support from others for divergent views, people will remain consonant with the views offered in the media. In fact, Noelle-Neumann (1993) believes that the media even provide words and phrases so people can confidently speak about a subject. If no repeated words or expressions are used, people fall silent. The extent to which Carol Johansen in our opening scenario will offer her views about spanking, then, will rest on what position the various media have taken on the subject. Yet, as George Gerbner (Cultivation Analysis, Chapter 22) says, television is the most influential of all media forms, although the Internet continues to be highly important.

In explaining why the media have such influence, Noelle-Neumann believes that the public is not offered a broad and balanced interpretation of news events. Consequently, the public is given a limited view of reality. This restrictive approach to covering news narrows an individual's perception.

Consider the theorist's three characteristics of the news media: ubiquity, cumulativeness, and consonance. **Ubiquity** refers to the fact that the media are pervasive sources of information. Because media are everywhere, they are relied on when people seek out information. For instance, Nick, a member of Carol Johansen's morning group, is quick to point out the recent surveys done in the state about perceptions of spanking. He has the source immediately at hand. And as the media strive for agreement from the majority of the public, they will be everywhere.

The **cumulativeness** of the media refers to the process of the media repeating themselves across programs and across time. Frequently, you will read a story in the morning newspaper, listen to the same story on the radio as you drive to work, and then watch the story on the evening news. Noelle-Neumann calls this a "reciprocal influence in building up frames of reference" (1993, p. 71). It can become problematic when the original source is left unquestioned, and yet four media (newspaper, radio, television, and the Internet) rely on that source. The theory suggests that conformity of voice influences what information gets released to the public to help them develop an opinion.

Finally, **consonance** pertains to the similarities of beliefs, attitudes, and values held by the media. Noelle-Neumann states that consonance is produced from a tendency for newspeople to confirm their own thoughts and opinions, making it look as if those opinions were emanating from the public. Each of these three qualities—ubiquity, cumulativeness, consonance—allows for majority opinions to be heard. Those wishing to avoid isolation remain silent.

It is not surprising that the media are influential in public opinion. Many surveys have demonstrated that people consider the media to have too much

ubiquity
the belief that media are everywhere

cumulativeness
the belief that media repeat themselves

consonance
the belief that all media are similar in attitudes, beliefs, and values

Research Notes

Eckstein, N. J., & Turman, P. D. (2002). "Children are to be seen and not heard:" Silencing students' religious voices in the university classroom. *Journal of Communication and Religion, 25,* 166–192.

This article is about one of the first research studies to examine the role of religion in the classroom from a communication vantage point. Eckstein and Turman explore how instructors silence students while discussing "controversial" issues, such as religion. The researchers note that silencing "often provides the task of marginalizing, excluding, centering, and privileging students in classroom discussion" (p. 175). They looked at three silencing behaviors: naming (uncovering a person's belief system), not-naming (avoiding problemitizing the fact that there are different belief systems), and smoothing over (passing on quickly to another student or topic). The results of the study show that "teachers' specific silencing behaviors of naming, not-naming, and smoothing over play a significant role in the silencing of students' religious beliefs during classroom discussion" (p. 185). Furthermore, they found that naming had the most significant effect on silencing, followed by smoothing over and not-naming. The authors conclude with a discussion of the consequences of silencing student views.

Moy, P., Domke, D., & Stamm, K. (2001). The spiral of silence and public opinion on affirmative action. *Journalism and Mass Communication Quarterly, 78,* 7–25.

The topic of affirmative action is rife with public opinion in the United States. People tend to favor or not favor affirmative action policies, and government, education, religion, and the media have all weighed in on this very controversial topic. Moy and her colleagues tested the principle "fear of isolation" in the Spiral of Silence Theory, which the authors consider the "driving force" (p. 16) behind the theory. They studied public discussions of affirmative action and analyzed data from more than 200 randomly selected adults. Looking at Initiative 200, a 1998 Washington state ballot proposal designed to remove race, ethnicity, and gender from consideration in hiring and public education, Moy and associates sampled ferry passengers in the greater Seattle area. The participants completed a questionnaire "in public" (p. 13) to ascertain the public's reaction to this topic. Results of the study indicated that people had a real fear of being isolated. However, unlike the Spiral of Silence Theory, Moy and her colleagues discovered that one's family and friends were instrumental in one's willingness to speak out. These reference groups remained influential. The media (e.g., newspapers) were somewhat influential; however, they were not as significant as Noelle-Neumann had originally proposed. The study concludes with a call for future research looking at the *process* of media effects on public opinion.

power in U.S. society. Consider also that, as we discussed in Chapter 22, information is frequently filtered through news reporters and their agencies. As a result, what is presented—or in the case of this theory, what is perceived—may not be an accurate picture of reality. For instance, most people can attest to the diversity found in the United States, and yet most media do not report with this diversity in mind. Imagine, for instance, the anxiety and frustration of many disabled individuals as they read or listen to media reports about the success of the Americans with Disabilities Act passed in the early 1990s, when the high percentage of disabled people who remain unemployed or who continue to experience discrimination in the workplace is often not reported. Or perhaps you have read or heard about the success of affirmative action policies, neglecting the fact that much of today's discrimination is often covert and subtle (Jandt, 2004). Maybe you have read about the many people who have been forced off of welfare, but you probably haven't seen many stories describing the dire circumstances of many families as a result of this decreased funding. If the media report these "success" stories often enough, Noelle-Neumann says, they are setting the news agenda—identifying what should be noticed, deciding what questions should be asked, and determining whether various social policies and programs are effective. In other words, people experience the climate of public opinion through the mass media.

As you can see, then, when people look to media for a glimpse into the perceptions and beliefs of the population, they are likely to receive anything but an impartial representation. **Dual climates of opinion** often exist—that is, a climate that the population perceives directly and the climate the media report. For instance, Carol Johansen may compare her personal perceptions of spanking with those surveyed perceptions published in the newspaper. What is remarkable is that despite the differences in opinion, many people decide to remain silent. To understand what motivates people to speak out, Noelle-Neumann developed the train test.

dual climates of opinion
difference between the population's perception of a public issue and the way the media report on the issue

The Train Test

Examining whether or not people will speak out requires a methodology that is clear, testable, representative, and replicable. To prove this, Noelle-Neumann conceptualized the train test (today the test can be applied on a plane or bus as well). The **train test** is an assessment of the extent to which people will speak out with their own opinion. According to the Spiral of Silence Theory, people on two different sides of an issue will vary in their willingness to express views in public. To study this, the researchers gave respondents sketches showing two people in conversation. The researcher asked a respondent, "Which of the two would you agree with, Person A or Person B?" This question would then be followed up with a more pivotal question; for example, one that might test opinions pertaining to food safety. Essentially, the train (or plane or bus) test asks people a question such as the following:

train test
assessment of the extent to which people will speak out

> Suppose that you have a five-hour train ride ahead of you, and a person sits next to you and starts to discuss the problems of food safety. Would you talk or not talk about the topic to the person?

This question was repeated several times with various subjects. It focused on a number of topics, ranging from nuclear power plants to abortion to racial segregation. The test revealed a number of factors that help determine whether a person will voice an opinion. They include the following:

- Supporters of a dominant opinion are more willing to voice an opinion than those in the minority opinion.
- Because of a fear of isolation, people tend to refrain from publicly stating their position if they perceive that this perception will attract laughter, mockery, or similar threats of isolation.

Theory Application in Groups (TAG)

Noelle-Neumann's theory is based on her experiences working at a polling agency in Germany. As a group, discuss the implications of developing theory with results emanating from one country. Be sure to include the consequences of the Spiral of Silence as well as other theories having their origins in or outside of the United States.

- There are various ways of speaking out—for example, hanging posters, displaying bumper stickers, and distributing flyers.
- People are more likely to voice an opinion if it agrees with their own convictions as well as fits within current trends and the spirit of the age.
- People will voice an opinion if it aligns with societal views.
- People tend to share their opinions with those who agree with them more than with those who disagree.
- People draw the strength of their convictions from a variety of sources, including family, friends, and acquaintances.
- People may engage in **last-minute swing,** or jumping on the bandwagon of the popular opinion during the final moments of conversation.

last-minute swing
jumping on the bandwagon of popular opinion after opinions have been expressed

The train test has proved to be an interesting approach to studying public opinion. The method simulates public behavior when two schools of thought exist on a subject. For those who are willing to speak out, there are opportunities to sway others. And there are times when the minority opinion speaks out loudly. We now examine this group.

The Hard Core

Every now and then, the silent minority rises up. This group, called the **hard core,** "remains at the end of a spiral of silence process in defiance of the threats of isolation" (Noelle-Neumann, 1993, p. 170). Noelle-Neumann recognizes that like most things in life, there is an exception to every rule or theory. The hard core represents a group of individuals who know that there is a price to pay for their assertiveness. These deviants try to buck the dominant way of thinking and are prepared to directly confront anyone who gets in their way (Figure 24.2).

Noelle-Neumann invokes the work of social psychologist Gary Shulman in attempting to understand the hard core better. Shulman argues that if the majority opinion becomes large enough, the majority voice becomes less powerful because no alternative opinions exist. A few years back, for instance, it was not uncommon for people to believe that those with AIDS should be quarantined (majority opinion). It didn't take long, however, for people's opinions to reject this narrow-minded view, primarily as a result of the hard core's efforts to educate

hard core
group(s) at the end of the spiral willing to speak out at any cost

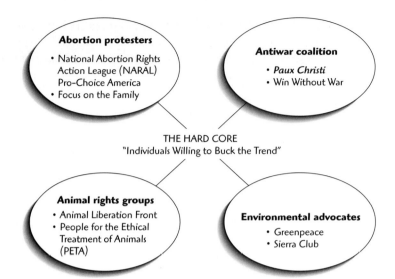

Figure 24.2
Examples of the "Hard Core" in the United States

THE HARD CORE
"Individuals Willing to Buck the Trend"

Abortion protesters
• National Abortion Rights Action League (NARAL) Pro-Choice America
• Focus on the Family

Antiwar coalition
• *Paux Christi*
• Win Without War

Animal rights groups
• Animal Liberation Front
• People for the Ethical Treatment of Animals (PETA)

Environmental advocates
• Greenpeace
• Sierra Club

the public. In fact, ironically, the media were pressed into educating the public about AIDS. It was not long before this silent hard core discovered that others had adopted their view. In this situation, the hard core was instrumental in changing public opinion.

For further evidence of the hard core, let's discuss an example pertaining to religion and religious opinion. Although we realize that not all people believe in God, God pervades our intellectual, political, and popular culture. For instance, people often say "God bless you" when others sneeze. In the political environment, each session of the U.S. Congress begins with some sort of prayer (there's even a U.S. House of Representatives chaplain), and many politicians conclude their speeches with "God bless America." "In God We Trust" appears on paper money, and the Pledge of Allegiance contains clear references to God ("one nation under God").

Despite pervasive references to God, many people in the United States do not believe in God. Some of these individuals contend that the country's Constitution requires a separation between church and state, and therefore any religious references in tax-supported venues should be eliminated. However, this opinion may not be shared by the majority because over half of the country affiliates with an organized religion (Lindner, 2008). Whether the media report on visits by the pope, present video clips of politicians leaving religious services each week, or solicit quotes for news stories from the clergy, they continue to imply that religion is an integral part of people's lives.

The minority—civil libertarians who advocate extracting religion from public-supported activities—have been vocal regarding their opinions; these hard-core dissenters have not blended into the background. Some of the effects of this hard core can be seen in that the Pledge of Allegiance is no longer required in every school district. In fact, in 2002 a federal appeals court in San Francisco ruled that the Pledge was unconstitutional in that it referenced God and violated the separation of church and state clause. Although the ruling was unsuccessfully appealed to the U.S. Supreme Court, it prompted considerable discussion on the references to God in state-sponsored efforts. The hard core might also claim victory as they see villages and cities remove religious icons (nativity sets, crucifixes, and so forth) from city parks during holidays. And with media outlets covering such legal victories, the hard core may be reconfiguring majority opinion.

Noelle-Neumann (1993) indicates that the hard core consists of people like Don Quixote, a literary figure who, because of his outdated clothing and weaponry, found himself ridiculed, defeated, and isolated. This tragic hero, according to Noelle-Neumann, had a desire to engender the respect of the world; his endless and futile combats were testimony to his undying commitment to chivalry. She concludes, "The 'hard core' [like Quixote] remains committed to the past, retaining the old values while suffering the isolation of the present" (p. 218). She adds that the hard core is the minority at the end of the spiral of silence who defy any threats of isolation.

Integration, Critique, and Closing

The Spiral of Silence Theory is one of the few theories in communication that focuses on public opinion. Indeed, the theory has been identified as an important foundation for examining the human condition (Csikszentmihalyi, 1991). The consequence of studying public opinion as Elisabeth Noelle-Neumann proposes is identified by Mihaly Csikszentmihalyi: "In an electoral democracy, but indeed even in the most tyrannical forms of government . . . the right to lead and to decide must eventually rest on the agreement of a significant segment of the population" (p. 288). The theory has been called "dynamic" (Merten, 1985), meaning that it underscores the process nature of communication that we discussed in Chapter 1. We examine two criteria for theory effectiveness: logical consistency and heurism.

Integration

Communication Tradition	Rhetorical	Semiotic	Phenomenological	**Cybernetic**	**Socio-Psychological**	Socio-Cultural	Critical
Communication Context	Intrapersonal	Interpersonal	Small Group	Organizational	Public/Rhetorical	**Mass/Media**	Cultural
Approach to Knowing	**Positivistic/Empirical**	Interpretive/Hermeneutic	Critical

Critique

| Evaluation Criteria | Scope | **Logical Consistency** | Parsimony | Utility | Testability | **Heurism** | Test of Time |

Logical Consistency

Noelle-Neumann's theory has not avoided substantial criticism. And much of that criticism pertains to the lack of logical consistency in several of the terms and concepts. Charles Salmon and F. Gerald Kline (1985) state that the Spiral of Silence fails to acknowledge a person's ego involvement in an issue. At times, people may be willing to speak because their ego is involved in the topic (for example, if a promotion at work depends on assertiveness). Carroll Glynn, Andrew Hayes, and James Shanahan (1997) raise the issue of various selectivity processes, such as cognitive dissonance, which we explored in Chapter 7. Individuals will avoid a topic that conflicts with their own views. Glynn and colleagues also note that there is little empirical support for the claim that people speak out only because they perceive support for their views. J. David Kennamer (1990) supports this criticism: "[I]t is hard to imagine either the pro-life or the pro-choice sides of the abortion issue giving up the fight because they perceive themselves to be in the minority" (p. 396).

Carroll Glynn and Jack McLeod (1985) note two additional shortcomings pertaining to the logical consistency of the theory. First, they believe that the fear of isolation may not motivate people to express their opinions. They claim that Noelle-Neumann did not empirically test her assumption that fear of isolation prompts people to speak out. Second, they argue that Noelle-Neumann does not acknowledge the influence that people's communities and reference groups have on their opinions. They believe that she focuses too much on the media. Along with that concern, the fact that the development of the Spiral of Silence relies on the media in 1985 West Germany troubles Glynn and McLeod. They doubt whether the characteristics of the media then and there (ubiquitous, cumulative, and consonant) apply to the media in the United States today. During their examination of a U.S. presidential election, Glynn and McLeod discovered little support for media bias. They do not question the relatively intimate bond among media in Germany, but they do wonder whether the theory has limited cultural application in the United States.

Noelle-Neumann has responded to several of her critics, notably in defending her emphasis on the media. She remains convinced that the media is instrumental in public opinion. She writes that "by using words and arguments taken from the media to discuss a topic, people cause the point of view to be heard in public and give it visibility, thus creating a situation in which the danger of isolation is reduced" (Noelle-Neumann, 1985, p. 80). She continues by noting that not once did the spiral of silence process contradict the media's position on a topic (Noelle-Neumann, 1993). In terms of application across cultures, Noelle-Neumann agrees that any theory of public opinion must have cross-cultural applicability. However, she posits, it is important to note that most U.S. researchers desire a rational explanation for human behavior, but not all behavior can be explained sensibly. Still, she does accept that the train test may be limited in cross-cultural adaptation. As a result, Noelle-Neumann updated the version to read:

> Assume you are on a five-hour bus trip, and the bus makes a rest stop and everyone gets out for a long break. In a group of passengers, someone

Theory Into Practice

Soshanna

The fact that the media have power over the public is really nothing new to me. I think an example of this is the war in Iraq. There is no way that the public bought into that war, but the president kept telling people that we will get rid of terrorism if we invade Iraq, and the media kept reporting it over and over again. Now, of course, we know that the invasion had nothing to do with terrorism. But the fact that the media reported the "justification" on TV, radio, and the Internet just kept those of us who hated the invasion more silent, while those so-called "patriots" had their voices heard in media broadcasts.

T*I*P

> starts talking about whether we should support [insert topic] or not. Would you like to talk to this person, to get to know his or her point of view better, or would you prefer not to? (p. 217)

Of course, you may doubt whether simply changing a train test to a bus test broadens the cross-cultural application of the theory.

Heurism

The theory has attracted writers and scholars who have discussed its merits in a variety of ways. First, some writers (Simpson, 1996) have attempted to discredit the theory because of its lack of application beyond one culture; other scholars have supported the cross-cultural application of the theory (Moy, Domke, & Stamm, 2001). This sort of scholarly dialogue enhances the heuristic appeal of the theory.

Researchers have employed the theory and many of its central concepts in their studies, including the following topics: declaring English as the official language of the United States (Lin & Salwen, 1997), religion in the classroom (Eckstein & Turman, 2002), the Persian Gulf War in the 1990s (Signorielli, Eveland, & McLeod, 1995), communication apprehension (Neuwirth, Frederick, & Mayo, 2007), college student sexual values (Chia & Lee, 2008), chat rooms (McDevitt, Kiousis, & Wahl-Jorgensen, 2003), and computer-mediated communication (Ernste, Fan, Sheets, & Elmasry, 2007). Such an array of topics and activity suggests that the theory and its prevailing concepts are worth studying.

The Spiral of Silence will continue to generate discussion among media scholars. The theory has sustained considerable criticism, and with a central emphasis on political discussion, researchers will continue to assess the theory's vitality. We live in a political world, dominated by a bold and intrusive Western media. Whether people openly express majority or minority viewpoints on an issue may not be directly proportional to the media's involvement on the issue, but it is clear that the public will come to rely on the media in the global society. The theory, therefore, may have lasting effects that have not been imagined.

Discussion Starters

1. Carol Johansen feels embarrassed about offering her opinions to a group that does not share her beliefs. Consider a similar time in your life. Did you speak out, or did you decide to remain quiet? What motivated your decision?

2. Discuss the times that you have been part of the hard-core minority. How did you behave? How did your confidence and self-esteem influence your behavior?

3. Does it make a difference to you to learn that Noelle-Neumann was once a newspaper journalist for Nazi publications? Why or why not?

4. Do you believe that the U.S. media are ubiquitous, consonant, or cumulative? Justify your answer.

5. Noelle-Neumann believes that the media help to influence minority views. Based on your observations of the media over the past several years, do you agree or disagree with this claim? What examples can you provide to defend your position?

6. Comment on the influence of the Internet on public opinion.

7. What do you suppose influences the "last-minute swings" of people?

Online Learning Center (www. mhhe.com/west4e)

Visit the Online Learning Center at www.mhhe.com/west4e for chapter-specific resources, such as story-into-theory and multiple-choice quizzes, as well as theory summaries and theory connection questions.

CHAPTER 25

Media Ecology Theory

*Based on the research of **Marshall McLuhan***

Tiera Abrams

Tiera Abrams was bored. She was studying for her midterm in statistics and needed a break. She felt as though she would freak out if she continued to look at and memorize any more calculations. As she got up to get a drink, she thought about going online to a chat room she had found while surfing the Internet. Tiera figured a 5-minute break from studying wouldn't hurt too much. She liked the chat rooms because they featured like-minded people all together in one place. As she sat and chatted on e-mail, she became particularly interested in a man from Canada. As a New Yorker, Tiera was accustomed to meeting interesting people every day. Today, though, she soon found herself in private e-mail discussions with Marcus. Marcus seemed very different from any other person she had "chatted" with over the Internet—so much so that the two exchanged e-mail addresses.

Over the course of a month, Tiera and Marcus continued to e-mail each other. They were amazed how much they had in common. They both loved country music and had dozens of country music CDs. They also were amazed to find out that they were both "tech junkies" in that they both were interested in the latest palm organizers and personal video recorders, and they couldn't imagine what life would be like without digital cable (Tiera's local cable company offered 800 channels!). They also talked about each other's family and each other's views of relationships. Neither of them was especially excited about being married, and

neither one wanted children. Tiera thought that Marcus was simply too good to be true. And Marcus seemed to be quite enamored with her. All of this, and they had never even met in person!

Eventually, they decided to talk over the phone. Tiera was quite nervous; she wasn't sure whether she and Marcus would make as good a "connection" talking to each other as they had through e-mail. The conversation went great! They talked nonstop and covered a range of topics. Of course, they couldn't talk that long because of the long distance. Yet the half-hour phone call would be the beginning of something more significant.

In fact, after the phone call, Tiera called her best friend to tell her about it. The two talked for hours. Tiera was seriously thinking of trying to hook up with her newfound friend, but she still felt a bit afraid of the entire thing. She had heard horror stories about these sorts of Internet connections and wasn't sure if she should meet Marcus in Albany, a city in upstate New York. Tiera had relatives in Albany whom she could stay with, and she thought it would be a good central location for the two to meet. She decided that during spring break she would meet Marcus and would make sure that her friends and mother knew where she was all the time.

As she drove, Tiera talked to her friends and family on her cell phone. She assured them that she would be careful and had thought about the trip a lot before she made her decision. Despite their urging her to stay at home, Tiera wanted to meet the man whom she thought would be part of her future.

The two met at a parking lot in a strip mall outside of Albany. When Tiera saw Marcus's car, she dialed her cell phone to her mother and got out of the car to meet him (even though she was confident that everything would go okay, she didn't want to take any chances). Marcus was a complete gentlemen. They took separate cars to a restaurant, had dinner, went to the bar to have a drink, and talked all the while they were together. As they stood outside the restaurant, Tiera and Marcus spoke of getting together the next day for breakfast. She said that she could be reached at her uncle's house and gave Marcus the phone number. The two embraced and went to their respective cars.

As she pulled out of the parking lot of the restaurant, Tiera was a bit surprised to hear her cell phone ring. It was Marcus. He called to thank her again and to tell her to have a great night's sleep. When she hung up the phone, Tiera's head was spinning. She still couldn't believe that all of this happened because she went online during a night of studying!

Technology is often described as the most important influence on society. Few can challenge this claim. The Western world is filled with examples of how technology influences life. For instance, no doubt many of you begin your day by turning off your alarm clock, waiting for the coffeemaker to finish, turning on morning television, and going to work or school, immediately booting up the computer once you start the workday. Maybe you rely on instant messaging or blog on a subject near and dear to you. Perhaps you use a hand-held electronic organizer for your appointments or respond to voice mail by using your cell phone. When you return home, you probably turn on the television or radio to listen to the day's events. And it's fair to say, you begin and end each weekday in pretty much the same manner, probably unaware of your reliance on communication technology.

Like a lot of people today, Tiera Abrams finds herself in the middle of what could be called tech-dating. Although she is a self-described "tech junkie," very few could have predicted—even twenty years ago—that our society would find itself where Tiera Abrams is. There was a time when seeing a person up close was a primary prerequisite to communication with that person (your authors remember it well). Yet the technological times we live in have been expanded to the extent that "up close" simply means up close to one's computer monitor!

One theorist who could understand and interpret Tiera's relational circumstance is Marshall McLuhan. In his book *Understanding Media* (1964; Gordon, 2002), McLuhan wrote about the influence of technologies such as clocks, televisions, radios, movies, telephones, and even roads and games. Although today we would not classify some of these as technologies, at the time, McLuhan was interested in the social impact of these primary mediated forms of communication. In other words, what is the relationship between technology and members of a culture? It's fair to say that McLuhan himself was part of the culture's media. He appeared regularly on television talk shows, spoke to policy-makers, had a cameo role in the Woody Allen film *Annie Hall,* and even was interviewed by *Playboy* (Jenkins, 2008).

Society has evolved as its technology has evolved. From the alphabet to the Internet, we have been affected by, and affect, electronic media. In other words, the medium *is* the message. The laws of media—enhancement, obsolescence, retrieval, and reversal—demonstrate that technology affects communication through new technology. Media Ecology Theory centers on the principles that society cannot escape the influence of technology and that technology will remain central to virtually all walks of life.

McLuhan was a Canadian scholar of literary criticism who used poetry, fiction, politics, musical theatre, and history to suggest that mediated technology shapes people's feelings, thoughts, and actions. McLuhan suggests that we have a symbiotic relationship with mediated technology; we create technology, and technology in turn re-creates who we are.

Electronic media have revolutionized society, according to McLuhan. In essence, McLuhan feels that societies are highly dependent on mediated technology and that a society's social order is based on its ability to deal with that technology. Recall that this theory was conceptualized nearly fifty years ago and, even today, McLuhan's assertion about technology rings true. Indeed, "since the public's growing consciousness of the Internet and the World Wide Web, starting in the mid-1990s, McLuhan's reputation has experienced an astounding upsurge" (Morrison, 2006, p. 170). Media, in general, act directly to mold and organize a culture. This is McLuhan's Media Ecology Theory (MET). Although some writers have referred to the theory as Technological Determinism, the growing consensus among scholars is that the term is an overstatement of McLuhan's theory (Cohen, 2000; Grosswiler, 1997; Levinson, 2001) and that it renders an audience passive and detached. In fact, audiences in McLuhan's writings are capable of being active: "Today, electronics and automation make mandatory that everybody adjust to the vast global environment as if it were his [*sic*] little home town" (McLuhan & Fiore, 1968, p. 11).

Because it centralizes the many types of media and views media as an environment unto itself, scholars aptly term McLuhan's work Media Ecology. For our purposes, we define **media ecology** as the study of how media and communication processes influence human perception, feeling, understanding, and value (Parameswaran, 2008). Given that McLuhan's writing spans a number of different academic disciplines, given that it focuses on a variety of technologies (e.g., radio, television, and so forth), and given that it pertains to the intersection of technology and human relationships and how media affect human perception and understanding (Postman, 1971), the ecological view of media proposed by McLuhan is appropriate and sensible. Paul Levinson (2000) describes the relationship of Media Ecology to communication this way: "McLuhan's work was startlingly distinct from the others [scholars] in that he

media ecology
the study of how media and communication processes affect human perception, feeling, emotion, and value

put communications at center stage. Indeed, in McLuhan's schema, there was nothing else on the stage."

McLuhan (1964) based much of his thinking on his mentor, Canadian political economist Harold Adams Innis (1951). Innis felt that major empires in history (Rome, Greece, and Egypt) were built by those in control of the written word. Innis argued that Canadian elites used a number of communication technologies to build their "empires." Those in power were given more power because of the development of technology. Innis referred to the shaping power of technology on a society as the **bias of communication.** For Innis, people use media to gain political and economic power and, therefore, change the social order of a society. Innis claimed that communication media have a built-in bias to control the flow of ideas in a society.

McLuhan extended the work of Innis. Philip Marchand (1989) observes that "not long after Innis's death, McLuhan found an opportunity to explore the new intellectual landscape opened up by his [Innis's] work" (p. 115). McLuhan, like Innis, felt that it's nearly impossible to find a society that is unaffected by electronic media. In fact, Michael Bugeja (2005) tends to agree; he notes that "the media use learners in a symbiotic marketing relationship. Content becomes biased in the process" (p. 133). Our perceptions of the media and how we interpret those perceptions are the core issues associated with MET. We now discuss these themes in the three main assumptions of the theory.

bias of communication
Harold Innis's contention that technology has a shaping power on society

Assumptions of Media Ecology Theory

We have noted that the influence of media technology on society is the main idea behind Media Ecology Theory. Let's examine this notion a bit further in the three assumptions framing the theory:

- Media infuse every act and action in society.
- Media fix our perceptions and organize our experiences.
- Media tie the world together.

Our first assumption underscores the notion that we cannot escape media in our lives: Media permeate our very existence. We cannot avoid nor evade media, particularly if we subscribe to McLuhan's broad interpretation of what constitutes media. Many Media Ecology theorists interpret media in far-reaching terms. For instance, in addition to looking at more traditional forms of media (e.g., radios, movies, and television), McLuhan also looks at the influence that numbers, games, and even money can have on society. We explore these three in more detail in order for you to understand the breadth of McLuhan's definition of media.

McLuhan (1964) views numbers as mediated. He explains: "In the theater, at a ball, at a ball game, in church, every individual enjoys all those others present. The pleasure of being among the masses is the sense of the joy in the multiplication of numbers, which has long been suspect among the literate members of

Western society" (p. 107). McLuhan felt that in numbers a "mass mind" (p. 107) was constructed by the elites in society to establish a "profile of the crowd" (p. 106). Therefore, it may be possible to create a homogenized population, capable of being influenced.

In addition to numbers, McLuhan looks at games in society as mediated. He observes that "games are popular art, collective, social reactions to the main drive or action of any culture" (p. 235). Games are ways to cope with everyday stresses and, McLuhan notes, they are models of our psychological lives. He further argues that "all games are media of interpersonal communication" (p. 237), which are extensions of our social selves. Games become mass media because they allow for people to simultaneously participate in an activity that is fun and that reflects who they are.

An additional mediated form is money. McLuhan concludes that "like any other medium, it is a staple, a natural resource" (p. 133). The theorist also calls money a "corporate image" that relies on society for its status and sustenance. Money has some sort of magical power that allows people access. Money allows people to travel the globe, serving as transmitters of knowledge, information, and culture. McLuhan notes that money is really a language that communicates to a diverse group, including farmers, engineers, plumbers, and physicians.

McLuhan, then, contends that media—interpreted in the broadest sense—are ever-present in our lives. These media transform our society, whether through the games we play, the radios we listen to, or the televisions we watch. At the same time, media depend on society for "interplay and evolution" (p. 49).

A second assumption of Media Ecology Theory relates to our previous discussion: We are directly influenced by media. Although we alluded to this influence earlier, let's be more specific about how McLuhan views the influence of media in our lives.

Media Ecology theorists believe that media fix perceptions and organize our lives. McLuhan suggests here that media are quite powerful in our views of the world. Consider, for instance, what occurs when we watch television. If television news reports that the United States is experiencing a "moral meltdown," we may be watching stories on child abductions, illegal drug use, or teenage pregnancies. In our private conversations, we may begin to talk about the lack of morals in society. In fact, we may begin to live our lives according to the types of stories we watch. We may be more suspicious of even friendly strangers, fearing they may try to kidnap our child. We may be unwilling to support laws legalizing medicinal marijuana, regardless of their merits, because we are concerned about possible increases in drug activity. We may also aggressively advocate an "abstinence-only" sex education program in schools, fearing that any other model would cause more unwanted pregnancies.

What occurs with each of these examples is what McLuhan asserts happens all the time: We become (sometimes unwittingly) manipulated by television. Our attitudes and experiences are directly influenced by what we watch on television, and our belief systems apparently can be negatively affected by television. Some writers (e.g., Bugeja, 2005) contend that McLuhan perceived television as instrumental to the erosion of family values. Marie Winn (2002) underscores the effect of television by calling it a "plug-in drug."

A third assumption of Media Ecology Theory has elicited quite a bit of popular conversation: Media connect the world. McLuhan used the phrase **global village** to describe how media tie the world into one great political, economic, social, and cultural system. Recall that although the phrase is almost a cliche these days, it was McLuhan who argued that the media can organize societies socially. Electronic media, in particular, have the ability to bridge cultures that would not have communicated prior to this connection.

The effect of this global village, according to McLuhan (1964), is the ability to receive information instantaneously (an issue we return to later in the chapter). As a result, we should be concerned with global events, rather than remaining focused on our own communities. He observes that "the globe is no more than a village" (p. 5) and that we should feel responsible for others. Others "are now involved in our lives, as we in theirs, thanks to the electric media" (p. 5).

Let's revisit our opening example of Tiera Abrams to illustrate this assumption further. As a consumer of the Internet, Tiera frequently visited "chat rooms," which allowed her to communicate with a number of different people at once. During this time, she encountered Marcus, whom she decided to meet. As a Canadian, Marcus would not normally visit the same social places as Tiera. It was electronic media that allowed this international relationship to get off the ground. If the two were to continue to see each other, they would naturally find out more about the other's family, community, and culture.

The global village of Marshall McLuhan follows the General Systems perspective we outlined in Chapter 3. You will recall that Systems theorists believe that one part of a system will affect the entire system. Media Ecology theorists believe that the action of one society will necessarily affect the entire global village. Therefore, floods in Europe, famine in Africa, and war in the Middle East affect the United States, Australia, and China. According to McLuhan, we can no longer live in isolation because of "electronic interdependence" (McLuhan & Fiore, 1996).

You have now been introduced to the primary assumptions of MET. McLuhan's theory relies heavily on a historical understanding of media. He asserts that the media of a particular time period were instrumental in organizing societies. He identifies four distinct time periods, or **epochs**, in history (Table 25.1). We address them next.

global village
the notion that humans can no longer live in isolation, but rather will always be connected by continuous and instantaneous electronic media

epoch
era or historical age

Making Media History and Making "Sense"

McLuhan (1962, 1964) and Quentin Fiore (McLuhan & Fiore, 1967, 1996) claim that the media of an era define the essence of a society. They present four eras, or epochs, in media history, each of which corresponds to the dominant mode of communication of the time. McLuhan contends that media act as extensions of the human senses in each era, and communication (technology) is the primary cause of social change (Hakanen, 2007).

Table 25.1 McLuhan's Media History

HISTORICAL EPOCH	PROMINENT TECHNOLOGY/ DOMINANT SENSE	McLUHAN'S COMMENTS
Tribal Era	Face-to-Face Contact/Hearing	"An oral or tribal society has the means of stability far beyond anything possible to a visual or civilized and fragmented world" (McLuhan & Fiore, 1968, p. 23).
Literate Era	Phonetic Alphabet/Seeing	"Western man [woman] has done little to study or to understand the effects of the phonetic alphabet in creating many of his [her] basic patterns of culture" (McLuhan, 1964, p. 82).
Print Era	Printing Press/Seeing	"Perhaps the most significant of the gifts of typography to man [woman] is that of detachment and noninvolvement—the power to act without reacting" (McLuhan, 1964, p. 173).
Electronic Era	Computer/Seeing, Hearing, Touching	"The computer is by all odds the most extraordinary of all the technological clothing ever devised . . . since it is the extension of our central nervous system" (McLuhan & Fiore, 1968, p. 35).

The Tribal Era

According to McLuhan, during the **tribal era**, hearing, smell, and taste were the dominant senses. During this time, McLuhan argues, cultures were "ear-centered" in that people heard with no real ability to censor messages. This era was characterized by the oral tradition of storytelling whereby people revealed their traditions, rituals, and values through the spoken word. In this era, the ear became the sensory "tribal chief" and for people, hearing was believing.

tribal era
age when oral tradition was embraced and hearing was the paramount sense

The Literate Era

This epoch, emphasized by the visual sense, was marked by the introduction of the alphabet. The eye became the dominant sensory organ. McLuhan and Fiore (1996) stated that the alphabet caused people to look at their environment in visual and spatial terms. McLuhan (1964) also maintained that the alphabet made knowledge more accessible and "shattered the bonds of tribal man" (p. 173). Whereas the tribal era was characterized by people speaking, the **literate era** was a time when written communication flourished. People's

literate era
age when written communication flourished and the eye became the dominant sense organ

messages became centered on linear and rational thinking. Out was storytelling; in were mathematics and other forms of analytic logic. This "scribal world" had the unintended consequence of forcing communities to become more individualistic rather than collectivistic (McLuhan & Fiore, 1967). People were able to get their information without help from their communities. This was the beginning of people communicating without the need to be face-to-face.

The Print Era

print era
age when gaining information through the printed word was customary, and seeing continued as the dominant sense

The invention of the printing press heralded the **print era** in civilization and the beginning of the industrial revolution. Although it was possible to do a great deal of printing by woodcut prior to this era, the printing press made it possible to make copies of essays, books, and announcements. This provided for even more permanency of record than in the literate age. The printing press also allowed people other than the elite to gain access to information. Furthermore, people didn't have to rely on their memories for information as they had to do in the past.

McLuhan (1964) observed that the book was "the first teaching machine" (p. 174). Consider his words today. Very few courses in college exist without a textbook. Even with technological teaching approaches such as distance learning or interactive television, the large majority of courses still require textbooks. Books remain indispensable in the teaching—learning process.

Exemplifying the print era more specifically, McLuhan writes:

> Margaret Mead has reported that when she brought several copies of the same book to a Pacific island there was great excitement. The natives had seen books, but only one copy of each, which they had assumed to be unique. Their astonishment at the identical character of several books was a natural response to what is after all the most magical and potent aspect of print and mass production. It involves a principle of extension by homogenization that is the key to understanding Western power. (p. 174)

What McLuhan notes here is that mass production produces citizens who are similar to each other. The same content is delivered over and over again by the same means. This visual-dependent era, however, produced a fragmented population because people could remain in isolation reading their mass-produced media.

The Electronic Era

Few can argue with the fact that the age we live in now is electronic. Interestingly, McLuhan (1964) and his colleague (McLuhan & Fiore, 1967) note that this epoch, characterized by the telegraph, telephone, typewriter, radio, and television, has brought us back to tribalization and the art of oral communication. Instead of books being the central repository of information, electronic media decentralized information to the extent that individuals are now one of several primary sources of information. This era has returned us to a primitivelike

Research Notes

Calavita, M. (2003). Within the context of many contexts: Family, news media engagement, and the ecology of individual political development among "Generation Xers." *Communication Review, 6,* 23–43.

The politics of fifteen young people (22–33 years old) were analyzed to determine who and what influenced their "political socialization" (p. 24). Prompted by "the apparently sorry state of this generation's political and civic attitudes and orientations" (p. 25), Calavita investigated the attitudes of a sample of young people who had completed two years of college. The researcher felt that "the news media is an environment in which individuals develop politically [and] the news media are of subtle-but-fundamentally powerful ecological importance" (p. 24) in shaping individuals. This study underscores the importance of family members—specifically parents—in contributing toward Generation Xers' political identity. According to several participants in this research, the media and family intersect to form a special "connective tissue" (p. 29) between the child and the world of politics. Calavita affirms that Generation Xers vicariously experienced their parents' news media "engagement." Two participants, for example, remembered the day President Nixon resigned because their parents were watching it on television, and at one point they watched their mother crying as the news unfolded.

The results of this research suggest that the political leanings of the participants' parents influenced Generation Xers. Furthermore, the research results underscore "the media ecology theorization of media as environments with structuring biases" (p. 24).

Strate, L. (2004). A media ecology review. *Communication Research Trends, 23,* 3–6.

Strate presents an essay that is a tribute to two leading scholars of Media Ecology, Walter Ong and Neil Postman. The two are posthumously honored by Strate, who articulates their contributions to Media Ecology Theory. First, Strate examines the influences Ong had on current questions pertaining to the media and the ecological issues surrounding media. Ong remains a crucial influence on how Media Ecology has evolved both as a cultural perspective and as a theoretical model. Strate then presents a tribute to Neil Postman, a more contemporary figure in Media Ecology (in fact, Postman conceptualized the media ecology "movement"). Postman, clearly influenced by Marshall McLuhan, looked at Media Ecology as a "field of inquiry" (p. 4) whereas in McLuhan's writings, Media Ecology is viewed in more practical terms. The essay is important as it contributes to our understanding of two central figures in Media Ecology and their relationship to Marshall McLuhan, the media pioneer associated with the theory.

---

reliance on "talking" to one another. Today, though, we define "talking" differently than the way it occurred in the tribal era. We talk through television, radio, records/tapes/CDs, photographs, answering machines, cell phones, blogs, and e-mail. The **electronic era** allows different communities in different parts of the world to remain connected, a concept we discussed earlier as the global village.

McLuhan (1964) provocatively relates a description of various technologies in the electronic age:

The telephone: speech without walls.

The phonograph: music hall without walls.

The photograph: museum without walls.

electronic era
age in which electronic media pervades our senses, allowing for people across the world to be connected

The electric light: space without walls.

The movie, radio, and TV: classroom without walls (p. 283).

The electronic era presents unique opportunities to reevaluate how media influence the people they serve. This age allows for ear and eye and voice to work together.

This historical presentation of media by McLuhan suggests that the primary media of an age prompts a certain sensory reaction in people. McLuhan and Fiore (1968) theorize that a **ratio of the senses** is required by people, which is a conversation of sorts between and among the senses. That is, a balance of the senses is required, regardless of the time in history. For instance, with the Internet, we reconcile a variety of senses, including visual stimulation of website pictures and the auditory arousal of downloaded music.

ratio of the senses
phrase referring to the way people adapt to their environment (through a balance of the senses)

The Medium Is the Message

the medium is the message
phrase referring to the power and influence of the medium—not the content—on a society

Media Ecology Theory is perhaps best known for the catchphrase **the medium is the message** (McLuhan 1964), a "humble and fascinating" phrase (Hodge, 2003, p. 342). Although followers of McLuhan continue to debate the precise meaning of this equation, it appears to represent McLuhan's scholarly values: The content of a mediated message is secondary to the medium (or communication channel). The medium has the ability to change how we think about others, ourselves, and the world around us. So, for instance, in our opening example of Tiera Abrams, what she and Marcus communicated is less important than that they communicated via a computer, the Internet, and e-mail.

McLuhan did not dismiss the importance of content altogether. Rather, as Paul Levinson (2001) points out, McLuhan argued that content gets our attention more than the medium does. McLuhan thinks that although a message affects our conscious state, it is the medium that largely affects our unconscious state. So, for example, we often unconsciously embrace television as a medium while receiving a message broadcast around the world. Consider the fact that the 2001 terrorist attacks in New York City, the train bombs in Madrid in 2004, Hurricane Katrina's devastating effects in 2005, and the 2008 earthquake in China were reported not only immediately after the events but, in some cases, during the events (interestingly, all these events occurred in the morning rush hours at each city around 9 A.M.). Many of us went to TV immediately and instinctively, captivated by the horror and the images as they occurred. We were pretty much unconscious of the medium, but rather consumed with the message. Nonetheless, we turned to television again and again for updates as the days and months progressed, rather unaware of its importance in our lives. This represents McLuhan's hypothesis that the medium shapes the message and it is, ironically enough, our unawareness of the medium that makes a message all the more important.

McLuhan and Fiore (1967) claim that in addition to the medium being the message, the medium is the "massage." By changing one letter, they creatively presented readers with another view of media. It's not clear whether the authors were making a pun on the "mass-age" or whether they were reinforcing McLuhan's earlier writings on the power of the media. McLuhan and Fiore argue that not only are we influenced by the media, but we can become seduced by it. As a population, we are entranced with new technologies. For instance, it is now customary for national media such as the *New York Times* and *USA Today* to feature special sections on technology and culture. New gadgets, gizmos, and technological inventions (and their prices) are featured for those desiring the latest. Indeed, the medium massages the masses, is part of the "mess-age" (McLuhan & Parker, 1969), and can be understood in a "mass-age" (McLuhan & Nevitt, 1972). James Morrison (2006) sums it up best by stating that "'the medium is the message' because the contents of a medium vary and may even be contradictory, but the medium's effects remain the same, no matter what the content" (p. 178).

We have presented several key assumptions and issues associated with Media Ecology Theory. We have also discussed media in very broad terms. McLuhan said that some unifying and systematic way of differentiating media was necessary. The result was an interesting analysis of hot and cool media.

Gauging the Temperature: Hot and Cool Media

To understand the "large structural changes in human outlook" (McLuhan, 1964, p. vi) of the 1960s, McLuhan set out to classify media. He explains that media can be classified as either hot or cool, language he borrowed from jazz slang. This classification system remains confounding to many scholars, and yet it is a pivotal aspect of the theory. We distinguish between the two media next and provide examples of each in Figure 25.1.

Hot media are described as media that demand very little from a listener, reader, or viewer. Hot media are high-definition communications that have

hot media
high-definition communication that demands little involvement from a viewer, listener, or reader

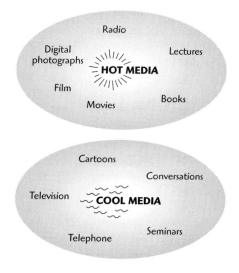

Figure 25.1
Examples of McLuhan's Hot and Cool Media

relatively complete sensory data; very little is left to the audience's imagination. Hot media, therefore, are low in audience participation. Meaning is essentially provided. An example of a hot medium is a movie, because it requires very little of us. We sit down, watch the film, react, maybe eat some popcorn, and then watch the credits. Hot media give the audience what they need—in this case, entertainment.

We should add that McLuhan believes that radio is a hot medium. He acknowledges that radio can serve as background sound, as noise-level control, or for listening pleasure. No involvement is needed with radio. However, McLuhan wrote before the proliferation of radio talk shows. Would he consider radio to be low involvement today?

cool media
low-definition communication that demands active involvement from a viewer, listener, or reader

Unlike hot media, **cool media** require a high degree of participation; they are low definition. Little is provided by the medium, so much has to be filled in by the listener, reader, or viewer. Cool media require audiences to create meaning through high sensory and imaginative involvement. Consider, for instance, cartoons. Generally, we get a few frames of illustrations and perhaps some brief phrases. Cartoons are low definition and provide very little visual information. We need to determine the meaning of the words and the pictures, and even supply missing words or ideas that are not provided in the cartoon.

Let's make one more point about cool media. Interestingly, McLuhan (1964) contended that television can be considered a cool medium. He argued that TV is a medium that requires viewers to be actively involved. In fact, he notes that television "engages you. You have to be *with* it" (p. 312). Yet, with the digital age upon us, television has taken on new meaning that perhaps even McLuhan could never have imagined. Would he still consider television a cool medium today? In a personal interview with media scholar Guido Stempel, Michael Bugeja (2005) reports that Stempel considers television to be "passive . . . [e]xcept for the remote control. In that sense . . . television is interactive" (p. 125). Bugeja and others wonder how McLuhan would place HDTV (high-definition television), which has the precise and clear audio and visual quality.

To illustrate the hot and cool media, McLuhan analyzed the 1960 presidential debates between John F. Kennedy and Richard Nixon. McLuhan discovered that for those who watched the debate on television, Kennedy had won because he exuded an objective, cool persona, perfect for the cool medium. For those who listened to the debates on the radio (a hot medium), Nixon was the winner. He was considered hot (which, in fact, his sweating showed he was!). So, the medium influences others' perceptions. Arthur Asa Berger (2007) notes that McLuhan's thinking pertaining to hot and cool media is prompting more research interest as communication theorists try to understand the passion that people have for their cell phones.

The Circle Is Complete: The Tetrad

We continue our discussion of Media Ecology Theory by examining the most recent expansion of McLuhan's thinking about the media. With his son, Eric (McLuhan & McLuhan, 1988), and to respond to those who believed that

there was no scientific grounding in his work, McLuhan developed a way to look further into the effects of technology on society. His expansion of the theory included a thorough discussion of the **laws of media.**

Although McLuhan's earlier work identified in this chapter did not fully take into account the advent of the computer, his posthumous work with his son took into consideration the influence of the Internet. Their work was an effort to bring the theory full circle: Technology affects communication through new technology, the impact of the new technology affects society, and the changes in society cause further changes in technology. McLuhan and McLuhan offer the **tetrad** as an organizing concept that allows scholars to understand the past, present, and current effects of media.

To give us a new way of looking at the role of technology in our culture, McLuhan and McLuhan offer four laws of media, phrased as questions (Table 25.2): (1) What do media *enhance?* (2) What do media make *obsolete?* (3) What do media *retrieve?* (4) What do media *reverse?* Let's examine each and identify examples of their role in culture. We pay particular attention to the role of the Internet in our discussion.

laws of media
further expansion of Media Ecology Theory with focus on the impact of technology on society

tetrad
organizing concept to understand the laws of media

Enhancement

The first law of media is **enhancement**; that is, media enhance or amplify society. The telephone enhanced the spoken word found in face-to-face conversations. Radio, of course, amplified the voice across distance. Television amplified the word and the visual across continents.

enhancement
law that states media amplify or strengthen society

Table 25.2 Laws of Media

LAWS OF MEDIA	DESCRIPTION
Enhancement	What does the medium enhance or amplify?
Obsolescence	What does the medium push aside or make obsolete?
Retrieval	What does the medium retrieve from the past?
Reversal	When pushed to its limits, what does the medium reverse or flip into?

The Internet has enhanced society in different ways. First, it has the potential to enhance a number of senses, including sight and sound. Second, the existence of the Internet has enhanced the accessibility of information. For instance, we can now obtain birth records, credit card balances, and missing person information over the Internet. Third, the Internet can enhance class division. The "haves and the have-nots" exist along this information superhighway. Finally, decentralization of authority is enhanced by the Internet. No longer do our political leaders solely possess information; that information becomes available online.

Obsolescence

McLuhan and McLuhan (1988) note that the second law of media is that media eventually render something obsolete or out of date. Television made radio obsolete, although many of us continue to turn to radio each day while we drive. Levinson (2001) notes that radio rendered motion pictures obsolete, which in turn resulted in fewer movies to watch. VCRs and DVD players may have also attempted to make movies obsolete, but we know that their efforts have been only somewhat successful.

obsolescence
law that states media eventually render something out of date

The Internet, too, has brought about **obsolescence.** For example, as we learned earlier, the global village now exists, thanks largely to the Internet. The geographical splits are pretty hard to find; even the remote villages of Africa are becoming accessible by the Internet. Second, the Internet is slowly targeting micromedia (specific audiences) rather than macromedia (large masses), thereby making traditional media outlets such as CBS, NBC, and ABC change their news reporting. Finally, face-to-face dialogues are becoming outdated with the Internet. Former "tribal" conversations are now electronically derived.

Retrieval

retrieval
law that states media restore something that was once lost

The third law is **retrieval,** meaning that media recover or restore something that was once lost. What older, previously obsolesced media is brought back? Television, for instance, restored the importance of the visual that radio did not achieve, but that was once in face-to-face conversations. Radio retrieved the town crier, the prominent voice of newsworthy events well over 200 years ago in the United States. Print retrieved the tribe's universality of knowledge. And the Internet recovers a community that was once lost to other media. For instance, chat rooms visited by people like Tiera Abrams from our opening vignette have electronically rekindled conversations that flourished before radio and television.

Reversal

reversal
law that states media will—when pushed to their limit—produce or become something else

When "pushed to the limit of its potential" (McLuhan & McLuhan, 1988, p. 99), what do media produce or become? What do media reverse into? When too many constraints exist on a medium, it will "overheat" and become ineffective. **Reversal** contains characteristics of the system from which it arose. For

instance, the public's desire to have access to entertainment in a relatively cheap medium led to the creation of radio dramas and comedy programs. The need to "see" what was heard led to the creation of these programs on television. Yet we can videotape television programs and what was once seen by millions of people at the same time is reversed into private videotaped "performances." Television, then, reversed into the early days of the print era when people could consume media privately.

The Internet—as a medium pushed to its potential—reverses society into a new and unique place. The Internet has the potential to bring tribal people together when they discuss websites or chat room conversations with one another. Looking at the number of people who "surf the net" each day, we can confidently state that the Internet can isolate people just as television can. With the ability to download music, television shows, and short films, the Internet has reversed itself into a medium with significant visual and auditory appeal. Finally, the Internet is a medium that "flips" on its user. That is, although it can serve to erode power, it can also perpetuate power differences among people. As a result, the Internet provides opportunities for both. Furthermore, the Internet has ushered in a generation of youth who "think like Pentium rather than like Plato" (Bugeja, 2005, p. 132).

Carrying the McLuhan Banner: Postman and Meyrowitz

Two influential contemporary scholars have worked to integrate McLuhan's thinking into their own scholarship. Neil Postman (1992), in *Technopoly: The Surrender of Culture to Technology*, and Joshua Meyrowitz (1985), in *No Sense of Place*, remain influential in understanding McLuhan. We close our discussion with an overview of this scholarly expansion.

Neil Postman, who died in 2003, is credited with formally introducing the term *media ecology* in 1968 (Gencarelli, 2006). Postman's biography is an interesting one and is available elsewhere (Thaler, 2006; Gencarelli, 2006). Nonetheless, it is important to give you a glimpse into Postman's credentials.

As Thomas Gencarelli (2006) observes, "Postman is first and foremost an educator" (p. 239). Indeed, most of his books pertained to public education in the United States. In some cases, he encouraged changes to the educational system by stating that it needed to be revitalized. Nowhere can that revitalization occur other than with an infusion of technology, according to Postman. The media environment, he believed, helped shape children's lives. Television, in particular, was ripe in allowing young people to be exposed to all sorts of information that was originally intended for adults. This conflation of the child and adult worlds was an ongoing concern for Postman.

Postman was clearly a man who practiced what he preached. Jim Benning (2003) relates a relevant anecdote. Shopping for a new car, Postman is quoted as saying: "Why do I need electric windows? My arm and hand work. If I were paralyzed I could use an electric window." His colleague and friend noted that "Neil would always take what he would call an ecological perspective, a balanced view."

Postman wrote over 200 articles for the public and over 20 popular and scholarly books. Postman's research is underscored by a central theme: "All technologies are human impositions into the natural order of things and, as a result, change that order" (Gencarelli, 2006, p. 244). Among the most influential of his published works is *Technopoly: The Surrender of Culture to Technology*. In the book, Postman (1992) hypothesized that technology negatively changes the fabric of society. Specifically, he believed that culture is subservient to the invisible (e.g., I.Q. scores) and visible (e.g., computers).

technopoly
a term coined by Postman that means we live in a society dominated by technology

Postman coined the term **technopoly**, which means that we live in a culture in which technology dominates our thinking and behaviors. In a technopoly, Postman argued, technological tools serve to take over the culture in which they thrive. We live in a society where being technologically driven may result in being driven mad! We trust that our technology will bring us safety and salvation, and seem to lose any sense of humility, discipline, and rationality regarding our reliance on and trust in current media. As a result, Postman laments that "tradition, social mores, myth, politics, ritual, and religion have to fight for their lives" (p. 28). Postman, like McLuhan, asked whether we want to live in a culture with such unwavering dependence on technology.

In addition to Postman, Joshua Meyrowitz's (1985) research interconnects with McLuhan's work. Meyrowitz's *No Sense of Place* ushered in a unique way of thinking related to space. First, he argues that space is more than physical (Dresner, 2006). That is, social situations such as contesting a parking ticket at city hall include more than the physical surroundings of the building and courtroom. Meyrowitz contends that the influence that communication has on the situation also needs to be considered.

As a communication scholar, Meyrowitz is interested in uncovering the effects of communication technology, namely, television, on a social situation. Consider, for instance, a private discussion between a husband and wife on marital infidelity. The discussion is likely to be free-wheeling, underscoring the intimacy that the couple shares. Now, put that discussion in front of a live

Oprah television audience. A new pattern of communication will begin, with different information flow and new rules of conduct. It is this new communication medium that Meyrowitz is interested in and one that has cultural consequences. Television is a medium that reconfigures boundaries that were once in place (Dresner, 2006).

Meyrowitz agrees with McLuhan that electronic media have social consequences. Meyrowitz expands the notion that power relations and social class can be traced to electronic media. He draws on sociology research to conclude that media have brought about a blurring of formerly distinct roles or places. He states that "many Americans may no longer seem to 'know their place' because the traditionally interlocking components of 'place' have been split apart by electronic media. Wherever one is now—at home, at work, or in the car—one may be in touch and tuned in" (p. 308).

Meyrowitz points to television. For instance, examine talk shows and you can get a sense of how the blurring of place occurs. What was once private (for instance, discussing your mother's alcoholism) is now public on *Jerry Springer*. Masculine and feminine roles now blur. Even our political leaders are now at the level of everyone else. In fact, in small states such as Maine, the governor can be contacted directly by phone, e-mail, or fax!

Both Postman and Meyrowitz remain articulate and effective stewards of Marshall McLuhan. They carry the banner which boldly proclaims that electronic media have unraveled Western society's foundation and many of its core values. To be sure, the two scholars prompt us to consider McLuhan's work in more contemporary ways. As Gary Wolf (1996) noted in *Wired* magazine: "McLuhan is relevant" (p. 124).

Integration, Critique, and Closing

You probably have already figured out that Marshall McLuhan has caused quite a reaction in both academic and public circles. His ideas are provocative, and at times, have been unilaterally dismissed by many. In fact, if you reviewed his original work, you may be challenged by frequently eccentric writing style. Some have labeled his thinking "McLuhanacy" (Gordon, 1982), while others feel his writing is equivalent to "genre bending" (Carey, 1998).

McLuhan's work and reputation, however, have been invoked with considerable regard. *Wired* magazine named him their "Patron Saint," and *Life* magazine called him the "Oracle of the Electronic Age." There exists a concentration in McLuhan Studies at the University of Toronto, a McLuhan newsletter, a *McLuhan Studies* journal, symposia on McLuhan's research, a McLuhan festival, a McLuhan reading club, and even a secondary high school in Canada named the Marshall McLuhan Catholic School. It's hard to escape his influence both in research and in societies around the world. The theory, despite its popularity, has been evaluated by scholars and writers. We will examine these critiques on the criteria of testability and heurism.

Integration

Communication Tradition	Rhetorical | Semiotic | Phenomenological | Cybernetic | Socio-Psychological | **Socio-Cultural** | **Critical**
Communication Context	Intrapersonal | Interpersonal | Small Group | Organizational | Public/Rhetorical | **Mass/Media** | Cultural
Approach to Knowing	Positivistic/Empirical | Interpretive/Hermeneutic | **Critical**

Critique

Evaluation Criteria	Scope | Logical Consistency | Parsimony | Utility | **Testability** | **Heurism** | Test of Time

Testability

Media Ecology Theory has been criticized because many of its concepts are difficult to understand, thereby making testability of the theory challenging and, indeed, nearly impossible. The question becomes apparent: How does one test something one has trouble understanding?

Criticism pertaining to the testability of the theory is represented in comments that have been offered by media scholars over the years. For instance, critics have blasted MET as "overly optimistic" about the role of technology in society (Baran & Davis, 2009). They believe that McLuhan put too much emphasis on how much technology influences society, making the very foundation of the theory rather shaky. George Gordon (1982) is more direct: "Not one bit of sustained and replicated scientific evidence, inductive or deductive, has to date justified any one of McLuhan's most famous slogans, metaphors, or dicta" (p. 42). Dwight Macdonald (1967) also attacked McLuhan's writing, noting that "he has looted all culture from cave painting to *Mad* magazine for fragments to shore up his system against ruin" (p. 203).

A great deal of criticism has been directed at McLuhan's use of words and his clarity. To some, his ideas make little sense. Some writers believe that McLuhan failed to define his words carefully and used too much exaggeration. In the *Chronicle of Higher Education,* Paul Levinson (1999) concludes that his work "was not your professor's writing—no long paragraphs of logically developed argument" (p. B10). He writes in a zigzag fashion, weaving in one point after another with no apparent topic sentence or sustained idea. Although some writers indict this process, McLuhan (1967) offers no apology: "I don't explain—I explore" (p. i).

Heurism

Media Ecology Theory and McLuhan's thinking have been met with considerable enthusiasm. Because McLuhan was a key figure in popular culture, it's important to keep in mind that his writing has prompted both academic and lay reaction. One hallmark of the heuristic value of Media Ecology Theory is the fact that there is now a Media Ecology Association (www.media-ecology.org). This organization is dedicated to promoting the theory in both practical and theoretical ways, thereby ensuring the theory's visibility. The association publishes a journal (*EME: Explorations in Media Ecology*) dedicated to the theory, a testimony to the fact that mass communication scholars continue to integrate the theory into their research.

Researchers have discussed McLuhan and his contributions in a variety of ways. Scholars have provided a comprehensive understanding of the theory and have discussed the theory's influential pioneers (Lum, 2006). Additional writers have applied several of McLuhan's premises in research (Strate & Wachtel, 2005). Furthermore, many of the theory's concepts have been incorporated into research on such diverse topics as human–computer interaction (Edsall, 2007) and YouTube as "cool" media (Trier, 2007). Media Ecology Theory, then, has high heuristic value.

Marshall McLuhan and Media Ecology Theory will continue to resonate for years to come. Perhaps one day we will revisit McLuhan's original thinking on historical epochs in media history! New media will continue to evolve in our society and so will the application of McLuhan's thinking. Was McLuhan an absurd reactionary? Or was McLuhan a cultural prophet? On his gravestone are the words "The Truth Will Set You Free." Did McLuhan think he discovered Truth? Or, even in his death, does he continue to play with our imaginations? Perhaps one of McLuhan's biographers, Philip Marchand (1989), best illustrates McLuhan's contribution to the study of media: "McLuhan's comments had at least one virtue: They seemed to suggest that the world was more interesting than any of us had previously thought it to be" (p. xiii).

Discussion Starters

1. Discuss whether Tiera Abrams's experience with an online relationship is representative of the future of relationships or if similar experiences will eventually fade away.

2. How might Media Ecology theorists like Marshall McLuhan react to the current news on television today? What would be his major criticisms and his major objections? What would he be particularly interested in?

3. Do you agree or disagree with McLuhan regarding television being a cool medium? Use examples to defend your view.

4. Suppose you were asked to have dinner with scholars Neil Postman and Joshua Meyrowitz. What types of questions would you ask them? How would the conversation proceed?

5. Interpret and comment on the following statement: "Technology is the end of our beginning." Use examples to defend your view.

6. Discuss your response to theorists who choose to be part of the popular culture, including participating on talk shows and appearing in films?

7. Apply any principle of MET to (a) YouTube, (b) Google, and (c) Facebook.

Online Learning Center    www. mhhe.com/west4e

Visit the Online Learning Center at www.mhhe.com/west4e for chapter-specific resources, such as story-into-theory and multiple-choice quizzes, as well as theory summaries and theory connection questions.

Culture and Diversity

W E ALL BELONG TO A CULTURAL COMMUNITY. SOME of us are members of a culture with a long history in the United States. Others of us belong to cultures that have recently found prominence in this country. As you learned in Chapter 1, the term *culture* has many different meanings. The theories presented in this section underscore the various interpretations and issues pertaining to culture and highlight the importance of looking at culture and human behavior.

We have selected four communication theories that fall under "Culture and Diversity": Face-Negotiation Theory, Communication Accommodation Theory, Muted Group Theory, and Standpoint Theory. We chose these theories because they represent a cross-section of what it means to be a member of a cultural community.

Each of these theories takes into consideration what happens when we communicate with people who come from different cultural backgrounds with different cultural expectations. For example, Face-Negotiation Theory points to the cultural effects of conflict. The theory answers the question "How do members from different cultures manage their interpersonal conflict?" Focusing on the role of both verbal and nonverbal communication in conversations, Communication Accommodation Theory rests on the belief that people from various cultural communities will adjust and adapt their communication to accommodate others. In Muted Group Theory, women are viewed as less powerful and less eloquent because their words have been provided by men to suit men's experiences. Finally, Standpoint Theory states that people view the world according to their positions in life. So the theory considers socioeconomic class and its application to a variety of marginalized populations, including women, the poor, gay men and lesbians, and many racial and ethnic communities.

Each theory in this section centers on the role that society plays in communication between and among cultural groups. Reading and learning about the theories will expose you to a variety of important themes: dominance, control, oppression, power, cultural identity, conflict, and politeness.

CHAPTER 26

Face-Negotiation Theory

*Based on the research of **Stella Ting-Toomey***

Professor Jie Yang and Kevin Johnston

The first ten weeks of her academic term in the United States had gone quite well. As a faculty member from China, Jie Yang felt that the communication courses she taught were well attended by students who were eager to participate. Students frequently asked her questions about what Chinese life was like, often concentrating on college life in particular. Jie was more than willing to answer their questions. She, too, had asked students about life in the United States and about what students thought of Chinese–U.S. relations. Although there were a few intercultural difficulties in translation, overall she felt that excellent relationships had been cultivated in such a short period of time. She had no reason to think that things wouldn't continue to unfold comfortably.

Her instincts, however, were incorrect. As her intercultural communication class began to prepare for their individual presentations, class members were showing signs of tension. In addition to a written final project on a research topic of their choice, Professor Yang had asked that each student provide a brief oral presentation of what they had studied. Throughout the term, she had listened to student complaints about the library staff, about how difficult it was to do research in their small college library, and about the time crunch. Still, she believed in her assignments and didn't back down despite the complaining.

One evening after class, Kevin Johnston, a graduating senior, challenged Professor Yang directly. He complained that there simply wasn't going to be enough time to complete his final presentation. He believed that Professor Yang was asking too much of him, considering that he had missed two weeks of class early in the term because of pneumonia. "It's not fair," Kevin lamented. "This is too much for me right now."

Professor Yang was sympathetic to Kevin's concerns. She agreed that he was under some pressure and reassured him that he was capable of finishing his project despite his past attendance record. "You're an excellent student, Kevin," the professor related. "And based on what I see, I know that you're very upset. But you're a hard worker and I know you want to do your best. You surely don't want me to treat you any differently than the others. Everyone is under pressure here."

Kevin wouldn't hear of it. "This is too much! I refuse to believe that you won't let a good student have some extra time. It's not like I'm not going to do it." Kevin continued by outlining his plan. If she would give him an "incomplete," then he would turn in the final paper two weeks after the class ended. "I'll try to give my presentation on what I've written," he continued, "but I'm not sure it's going to be that good."

Professor Yang was growing weary of the discussion. "Kevin, you underestimate yourself. You have a few weeks left. I trust you'll be able to finish it thoroughly."

The tone of the conversation quickly changed. "Look," Kevin interrupted, "I don't think you know the American system yet. I'm being up front and honest about the fact that I won't be able to finish the project. You keep telling me that I will. I know that you've only been in the States a short time, but you've got to give students a chance. Right now, I feel like I'm talking to a brick wall." His voice now matched the passion of his words.

Professor Yang wouldn't concede. "Kevin, in this class, we all have time constraints and outside responsibilities. I, like others, have a great deal to accomplish before the end of the term. But we can't simply abandon our responsibilities. You're a reasonable student. I'll make you a deal. How about if you turn in a detailed outline of your paper, I'll approve it; you write about two-thirds of the paper and then see if you have time to finish the rest."

Kevin followed her lead. "I can't promise you that my paper is gonna be the best. But if you'll look it over before I turn it in, that will help a lot."

"All any professor can ask is for students to do their best," Professor Yang replied, wondering if she made the right decision. "And you should know that I do expect you to do your best. I'm sure you will get everything done on time."

As Kevin walked away from his conversation, he couldn't help but think about a different approach to his conflict. He knew that he had work to do and that the boundaries had been clearly set for him by Professor Yang.

Working out conflicts like Kevin's is not easy. In the United States particularly, individuals try to manage their conflicts in a solution-oriented manner, frequently disregarding the other's cultural values or norms. Although people from a number of different cultures share Kevin's approach, some cultures would not endorse his strategies for conflict resolution.

Kevin finds himself in a situation common to many students. Yet, unlike many students, Kevin overtly confronts Professor Yang about her expectations. Although he was given the assignment in the early part of the term, he knows that the remaining time will not be sufficient to complete the task. He then tries to negotiate a different result with his professor. His dominating approach does little to rattle Professor Yang; she calmly works toward closure on this conflict.

Kevin's conflict with Professor Yang underscores the thinking behind Face-Negotiation Theory (FNT) by Stella Ting-Toomey. The theory is multifaceted, incorporating research from intercultural communication, conflict, politeness, and "facework," a topic we explore later in the chapter. Face-Negotiation Theory has cross-cultural appeal and application because Ting-Toomey has focused on a number of different cultural populations, including those in Japan, South Korea, Taiwan, China, and the United States. This is underscored by Ting-Toomey's (1988) comments: "Culture provides the larger interpretive frame in which 'face' and 'conflict style' can be meaningfully expressed and maintained" (p. 213). This theory underscores an earlier discussion of culture we undertook in Chapter 2. Issues of self and identity are also part of this theory (relevant to, for instance, intrapersonal communication); however, these areas are discussed with culture as the overarching framework.

Ting-Toomey asserts that members from different cultural backgrounds have various concerns for the "face" of others. This concern leads them to handle conflict in different ways. These comments form the backdrop to Face-Negotiation Theory.

Our opening example of Kevin Johnston and Professor Yang represents the heart of FNT. Representing two different cultural backgrounds, Kevin and his professor seem to have two different interpretations of how to manage the difficulty that Kevin is having with his final project. Kevin clearly desires to turn his work in late, whereas Professor Yang wants him to turn it in with the rest of the class. She tries to ease the conflict between the two by highlighting Kevin's qualities, and clearly she does not want to embarrass Kevin. Rather, she encourages him to work out this conflict by focusing on his ability to get things done, not the remaining time left in the term.

Professor Yang and Kevin Johnston engage in behavior that researchers have termed *face*. Because face is an extension of one's self-concept, it has become the focus of much research in a number of fields of study. In fact, because Face-Negotiation Theory rests primarily on this concept, let's first interpret the meaning behind the term and then examine the central assumptions of the theory.

About Face

Ting-Toomey bases much of her theory on face and facework. Face is clearly an important feature of life, a metaphor for self-image that pervades all aspects of social life (Domenici & Littlejohn, 2006). The concept of face has evolved in interpretation over the years. It originates with the Chinese, who, as Ho argues, have two conceptualizations of face: *lien* and *mien-tzu,* two terms describing identity and ego.

face
a metaphor for the public image people display

Erving Goffman (1967) is generally credited with situating face in contemporary Western research. He noted that **face** is the image of the self that people display in their conversations with others. Ting-Toomey and her colleagues (Oetzel, Ting-Toomey, Yokochi, Masumoto, & Takai, 2000) observe that face pertains to a favorable self-worth and/or projected other worth in interpersonal situations. People do not "see" another's face; rather, face is a metaphor for the boundaries that people have in their relationships with others. Goffman (1967) described face as something that is maintained, lost, or strengthened. At the time of his writing, Goffman did not envision that the term would be applied to close relationships. As a sociologist, he believed that face and all that it entailed was more applicable to the study of social groups. Over time, however, the study of face has been applied to a number of contexts, including close relationships and small groups.

Ting-Toomey incorporates some of the thinking from research on politeness that concludes that the desire for face is a universal concern (Brown & Levinson, 1978). Ting-Toomey (1988, 1991, 2004) expands on Goffman's thinking and argues that face is a projected image of one's self and the claim of self-respect in a relationship. She believes that face "entails the presentation of a civilized front to another individual" (Ting-Toomey, 1994a, p. 1) and that face is an identity that two people conjointly define in a relational episode. Further, face is a "socially approved self-image and other-image consideration issues" (Ting-Toomey & Chung, 2005, p. 268). Ting-Toomey and her colleague Beth Ann Cocroft (1994) succinctly identify face as a "pancultural phenomenon" (p. 310), meaning that individuals in all cultures share and manage face; face cuts across all cultures. Lori DeWitt (2006) notes that face is co-created by those who are involved in an interaction.

Regarding our opening story, Ting-Toomey and other Face-Negotiation theorists would be interested in knowing that Professor Yang is from China and Kevin Johnston is American. Their cultural variability influences the way that they relate to each other and the way face is enacted. That is, Ting-Toomey believes that although face is a universal concept, there are various representations of it in various cultures. Face needs exist in all cultures, but all cultures do not manage the needs similarly. Ting-Toomey contends that face can be interpreted in two primary ways: face concern and face need. **Face concern** may relate to either one's own face or the face of another. In other words, there is a self-concern and an other-concern. Face concern answers the question, "Do I want attention drawn toward myself or toward another?" **Face need** refers to an inclusion–autonomy dichotomy. That is, "Do I want to be associated with others (inclusion) or do I want dissociation (autonomy)?"

Face and Politeness Theory

As we noted earlier, Ting-Toomey was influenced by research on politeness. Politeness theory (Brown: & Levinson, 1978, 1987) contends that people will use a politeness strategy based on the perception of face threat. The theory suggests, according to Danette Ifert Johnson (2007), that a single message can provoke more than one face threat and can both support and threaten face needs simultaneously, and that politeness and face threats influence subsequent messages. Drawing on over a dozen different cultures around the world, politeness researchers (Brown & Levinson, 1987) discovered that two types of universal needs exist: positive face needs and negative face needs. **Positive face** is the desire to be liked and admired by significant others in our lives; **negative face** refers to the desire to be autonomous and unconstrained. Karen Tracy and Sheryl Baratz (1994) note that these "face wants" are part and parcel of relationships. They support their claim as follows:

> Recognition of existing face wants explains why a college student who wanted to borrow a classmate's notes typically would not ask for them boldly ("Lend me your notes, would you?"), but more frequently would ask in a manner that paid attention to a person's negative face wants ("Would it be at all possible for me to borrow your notes for just an hour? I'll Xerox them and get them back to you right away"). (p. 288)

Brown and Levinson's research illustrates a dilemma for individuals who try to meet both types of face needs in a conversation. Trying to satisfy one face need usually affects the other face need. For instance, our opening example shows that Professor Yang wants Kevin to work at achieving his full potential. Her positive face needs, however, are met with the challenges of putting in more time with Kevin, thereby costing her negative face needs.

face concern
interest in maintaining one's face or the face of others

face need
desire to be associated or disassociated with others

positive face
desire to be liked and admired by others

negative face
desire to be autonomous and free from others

How do people in individualistic and collectivistic cultures negotiate face in conflicts? Face-Negotiation Theory is based on face management, which describes how people from different cultures manage conflict negotiation to maintain face. Self-face and other-face concerns explain the conflict negotiation between people from various cultures.

Facework

facework
actions used to deal with face needs/wants of self and others

When communicators' positive or negative face is threatened, they tend to seek some recourse or way to restore their or their partner's face. Ting-Toomey (1994a), following Brown and Levinson, defines this as **facework,** or the "actions taken to deal with the face wants of one and/or the other" (p. 8). Stella Ting-Toomey and Leeva Chung (2005) also comment that facework is "about the verbal and nonverbal strategies that we use to maintain, defend, or upgrade our own social self-image and attack or defend (or 'save') the social image of others" (p. 268). In other words, facework pertains to how people make whatever they're doing consistent with their face. Ting-Toomey equates facework with a "communication dance that tiptoes" between respect for one's face and the face of another. So Professor Yang's comments to Kevin about his ability to complete the project and presentation illustrate how the professor simultaneously saves her face (not reneging on the assignment) and also Kevin's face (providing him praise).

tact facework
extent to which a person respects another's autonomy

Te-Stop Lim and John Bowers (1991) extend the discussion by identifying three types of facework: tact, solidarity, and approbation. First, **tact facework** refers to the extent that one respects another's autonomy. This allows a person freedom to act as he or she pleases while minimizing any impositions that may restrict this freedom. For instance, Professor Yang engages in tact facework with Kevin while he relates his problems with the course assignments. She could, of course, respond to him by stating that he should just keep quiet and work, but instead she uses tact facework strategies—she asks him for suggestions while avoiding directives.

solidarity facework
accepting another as a member of an in-group

The second type of facework, **solidarity facework,** pertains to a person accepting the other as a member of an in-group. Solidarity enhances the connection between two speakers. That is, differences are minimized and commonalities are highlighted through informal language and shared experiences. For instance, Professor Yang notes that, like Kevin, she has responsibilities, and people cannot simply go back on their duties because of a time crunch. Her conversational style reflects an approachable professor, not one who uses language reflecting a status difference.

approbation facework
focusing less on the negative aspects and more on the positive aspects of another

The final type of facework is **approbation facework,** which involves minimizing blame and maximizing praise of another. Approbation facework exists when an individual focuses less on the negative aspects of another and more on the positive aspects. It is clear that despite her real feelings about Kevin's experiences, Professor Yang employs approbation facework by noting that he is a hard worker and an excellent student. She also explains that he has the ability to get everything accomplished. In other words, she recognizes Kevin's positive attributes while avoiding blame.

Our introductory comments on face and facework form an important backdrop to the understanding of Face-Negotiation Theory. The theory proposed by Ting-Toomey also rests on a number of other issues needing attention and clarification. We begin to unravel the theory in more detail by presenting three key assumptions of FNT.

Assumptions of Face-Negotiation Theory

A number of assumptions of Face-Negotiation Theory take into consideration the key components of the theory: face, conflict, and culture. With that in mind, the following guide the thinking of Ting-Toomey's theory:

- Self-identity is important in interpersonal interactions, with individuals negotiating their identities differently across cultures.
- The management of conflict is mediated by face and culture.
- Certain acts threaten one's projected self-image (face).

The first assumption highlights **self-identity**, or the personal features or character attributes of an individual. In their discussion of face, William Cupach and Sandra Metts (1994) observe that when people meet, they present an image of who they are in the interaction. This image is "an identity that he or she wants to assume and wants others to accept" (p. 3). Self-identity includes a person's collective experiences, thoughts, ideas, memories, and plans (West & Turner, 2009). People's self-identities do not remain stagnant but rather are negotiated in their interactions with others. People have a concern with both their own identity or face (self-face) and the identity or face of another (other-face).

self-identity
personal attributes of another

Just as culture and ethnicity influence self-identity, the manner in which individuals project their self-identities varies across cultures. Mary Jane Collier (1998) relates that cultural identity is enacted and "contested in particular historical, political, economic, and social contexts" (p. 132). Delores Tanno and Alberto Gonzalez (1998) note that there are "sites of identity," which they define as "the physical, intellectual, social, and political locations where identity develops its dimensions" (p. 4). Self-identity, therefore, is influenced by time and experience. Consider, for example, the self-identity of a politician as she begins her new term in office. She most likely will be overwhelmed and perhaps frustrated by her new position and the responsibilities that go along with it. Yet, over time and with experience, that frustration will be replaced with confidence and a new perspective on her identity as a representative of others.

Theory Into Practice

Irene

I can tell you that coming from China, the discussion about face(work) rings true to me. In Beijing, we are very concerned not to make others feel bad. We also try to stay clear of conflict because we believe that arguing is not the best way to get to a resolution. I remember in one of my classes in America my professor said something that was very incorrect. But, I didn't say anything because I knew it would cause more problems in our conversation.

Inherent in this first assumption is the belief that individuals in all cultures hold a number of different self-images and that they negotiate these images continuously. Ting-Toomey (1993) states that a person's sense of self is both conscious and unconscious. That is, in scores of different cultures, people carry images that they habitually or strategically present to others. Ting-Toomey believes that how we perceive our sense of self and how we wish others to perceive us are paramount to our communication experiences.

The second assumption of Face-Negotiation Theory relates to conflict, which is a central component of the theory. Conflict in this theory, however, works in tandem with face and culture. For Ting-Toomey (1994b), conflict can damage the social face of individuals and can serve to reduce the relational closeness between two people. As she relates, conflict is a "forum" for face loss and face humiliation. Conflict threatens both partners' face, and when there is an incompatible negotiation over how to resolve the conflict (such as insulting the other, imposing one's will, and so forth), the conflict can exacerbate the situation. Ting-Toomey states that the way humans are socialized into their culture influences how they will manage conflict. That is, some cultures, like the United States, value the open airing of differences between two people; other cultures believe conflict should be handled discreetly. We return to these cultural orientations a bit later in the chapter.

This confluence of conflict, face, and culture can be exemplified in our story of Professor Yang and Kevin Johnston. It is apparent that Kevin's conflict with Professor Yang centers on his desire to receive an "incomplete" and her determination to have him complete the project. Because Professor Yang does not acquiesce to his wishes, Kevin tries to maintain his face by agreeing to his professor's compromise. In other words, he expresses a need to preserve his face with his professor. And, as we mentioned earlier, Professor Yang saves Kevin's face by lauding his abilities. This face-saving seems to prevent an escalation of conflict between the student and his professor. Finally, we note that

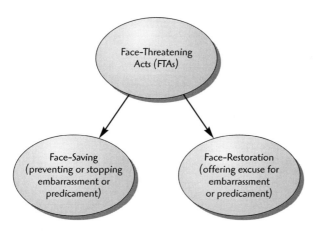

Figure 26.1
Face-Maintenance Framework
Source: Adapted from Ting-Toomey & Cole, 1990.

Professor Yang is from China, a culture shown by research to be more concerned with creating positive face than the United States (Samovar, Porter, & McDaniel, 2007).

A third assumption of Face-Negotiation Theory pertains to the effects that various acts have on one's face. Incorporating politeness research, Ting-Toomey (1988) asserts that face-threatening acts (FTAs) threaten either the positive or the negative face of the interactants. FTAs can be either direct or indirect and occur when people's desired identity is challenged (Tracy, 1990). Direct FTAs are more threatening to the face of others, whereas indirect FTAs are less so.

Ting-Toomey and Mark Cole (1990) note that two actions make up the face-threatening process: face-saving and face restoration. **Face-saving** involves efforts to prevent events that either elicit vulnerability or impair one's image. Face-saving often prevents embarrassment. For instance, one of your author's best friend's primary language is French. Although he does speak fluent English, he periodically uses French phrases in his conversations with others. Because others are usually not prepared for this, your author introduces him as someone whose primary language is French. In this example, your author is using a face-saving technique.

face-saving
efforts to avoid embarrassment or vulnerability

Face restoration occurs after the loss of face has happened. Ting-Toomey and Cole (1990) observe that people attempt to restore face in response to the events. For instance, people's excuses are face-restoration techniques when embarrassing events occur (Cupach & Metts, 1994). Excuses ("I thought it was her job") and justifications ("I'm not a morning person") are commonplace in face restoration. These face-maintenance strategies and their relationship to each other are represented in Figure 26.1.

face restoration
strategy used to preserve autonomy and avoid loss of face

So far, we have detailed face and facework as well as three primary assumptions of Face-Negotiation Theory. We now turn our attention to a discussion of additional dimensions of the theory. First, we explore individualism and collectivism, and then we examine how conflict functions in the theory.

Table 26.1 Rankings of Individualism and Collectivism Around the World*

RANK	COUNTRY	RANK	COUNTRY
1	United States	28	Turkey
2	Australia	29	Uruguay
3	Great Britain	30	Greece
4/5	Canada/Netherlands	31	Philippines
4/5	Netherlands	32	Mexico
6	New Zealand	33/35	Yugoslavia
7	Italy	33/35	Portugal
8	Belgium	33/35	East Africa
9	Denmark	36	Malaysia
10/11	Sweden	37	Hong Kong
10/11	France	38	Chile
12	Ireland	39/41	Singapore
13	Norway	39/41	Thailand
14	Switzerland	39/41	West Africa
15	Germany	42	Salvador
16	South Africa	43	South Korea
17	Finland	44	Taiwan
18	Austria	45	Peru
19	Israel	46	Costa Rica
20	Spain	47/48	Pakistan
21	India	47/48	Indonesia
22/23	Japan	49	Colombia
22/23	Argentina	50	Venezuela
24	Iran	51	Panama
25	Jamaica	52	Ecuador
26/27	Brazil	53	Guatemala
26/27	Arab countries		

*The lower the number, the more individualistic the country is rated; the higher the number, the more collectivistic the country is rated.

Source: Hofstede, 2001.

Individualistic and Collectivistic Cultures

Culture is not a static variable. It is interpreted along many dimensions. To this end, Ting-Toomey examines culture and how it interrelates with face and conflict by employing thinking derived from both Harry Triandis (1972, 1988) and Geert Hofstede (1980, 2001). Both were instrumental in identifying the cultural variability used to explain cultural differences in behavior. Culture can be organized around two ends of a continuum: individualism and collectivism. At one end is a culture that places a premium on the value of individual identity; at the other end is a culture that values group identity. Individualistic cultures are "independent self" cultures, and collectivistic cultures are "interdependent self" cultures. Cultures across the world vary in individualism and collectivism (Table 26.1). These two dimensions play a prominent role in the way that facework and conflict are managed.

Ting-Toomey and her colleagues Ge Gao, Paula Trubisky, Shizhong Yang, Hak Soo Kim, Sung-Ling Lin, and Tsukasa Nishida (1991) clarify that individualism and collectivism apply not only to national cultures, but also to co-cultures within national cultures. That is, for example, different racial and ethnic groups within the United States may vary in their individualism and collectivism. For example, Ting-Toomey and her colleagues observe that whereas many European Americans in the United States identify with individualistic values and beliefs, when first-generation immigrant groups from Mexico or Japan arrive, they tend to retain their collectivistic orientation. Let's explore the concepts of individualism and collectivism a bit further.

Individualism and Collectivism

In Chapter 6, we briefly discussed these terms. You may recall that when people emphasize the individual over the group, they are articulating an individualistic perspective. **Individualism** refers to the tendency of people to highlight individual identity over group identity, individual rights over group rights, and individual needs over group needs (Ting-Toomey, 1994b). Individualism is the "I" identity (I want, I need, and so forth). Larry Samovar, Richard Porter, and Edwin McDaniel (2007) believe that individualism was likely the first value that developed in the early formation of the United States. They believe that "Individualism emphasizes individual initiative ('Pull yourself up by your own boot straps'), independence ('Do your own thing'), individual expression ('The squeaky wheel gets the grease'), and even privacy ('A man's [woman's] home is his [her] castle')" (Samovar & Porter, 1995, p. 85). Individualistic values highlight freedom, honesty, comfort, and personal equality, among others (Ting-Toomey & Chung, 2005).

individualism
a cultural value that places emphasis on the individual over the group

As you see, individualism involves self-motivation, autonomy, and independent thinking. Individualism suggests direct communication with another. Think about Kevin Johnston's comments expressing his desire to complete his project on his own time. He is projecting individualism to Professor Yang.

According to intercultural communication scholars, individualism is esteemed in the United States (Jandt, 2006). In addition to the United States, a number of other cultures are viewed as individualistic. Australia, Great Britain, Canada, the Netherlands, and New Zealand are examples of individualistic cultures. Italy, Belgium, and Denmark are also considered individualistic. These cultures stress individual achievement and value independence.

Whereas individualism focuses on one's personal identity, collectivism looks outside the self. Ting-Toomey (1994b) comments that **collectivism** is the emphasis of group goals over individual goals, group obligations over individual rights, and in-group needs over individual wants. Collectivism is the "we" identity (we can do this, we are a team, and so forth). People in a collectivistic culture value working together and viewing themselves as part of a larger group. Collectivistic societies, consequently, value inclusion. Collectivistic values emphasize harmony, respecting parents' wishes, and fulfillment of another's needs, among others.

collectivism
a cultural value that places emphasis on the group over the individual

Examples of collectivistic cultures include Indonesia, Colombia, Venezuela, Panama, Mexico, Equador, and Guatemala. In these countries, we should point out, the general population is poor; in fact, some of the most severe poverty in the world is found in these countries. Therefore, it's fair to say that people in some of these cultures are guided less by rules and function as a group more out of physical and economic necessity.

Face Management and Culture

So, how do individualism and collectivism relate to Ting-Toomey's theory? Ting-Toomey and Chung (2005) argue that "members [of cultures] who subscribe to individualistic values tend to be more self-face-oriented and members who subscribe to group-oriented-values tend to be more other- or mutual-face oriented in conflict" (p. 274). If you are a citizen of an individualistic society, you are more likely to be concerned with controlling your own autonomy and boundaries for behavior. You would also want choices to satisfy self-face needs. Dissatisfied with the assignment and its deadline, Kevin Johnston is seeking autonomy and wants another choice from his professor. Ting-Toomey believes that in individualistic cultures, **face management** is overt in that it involves protecting one's face, even if it comes to bargaining. Kevin Johnston engages in face negotiation that promotes confrontation, and as Ting-Toomey notes, members of individualistic cultures like Kevin will tend to use more autonomy-preserving face strategies in managing their conflict than will members of collectivistic societies.

Collectivistic cultures "are concerned with the adaptability of self-presentation image" (Ting-Toomey, 1988, p. 224). Adaptability, then, allows for interdependent bonds with others (positive face). What this means is that members of collectivistic communities consider their relationship to others when discussing matters and feel that a conversation requires ongoing maintenance by both communicators. For instance, Professor Yang makes efforts to demonstrate her connection to Kevin by empathizing with his conflict. She also demonstrates a collectivistic orientation by asking whether it would be fair to grant Kevin an extension and not offer the same alternative to other students. Professor Yang, then, as a member of a collectivistic culture, seeks both self-face and other-face needs.

Ting-Toomey believes that conflict is often present when members from two different cultures—individualistic and collectivistic—come together and that individuals will use a number of different conflict styles. Face-Negotiation Theory takes into consideration the influence culture has on the way conflict is managed.

Managing Conflict Across Cultures

The individualistic–collectivistic cultural dimension influences the selection of conflict styles. These styles refer to patterned responses, or typical ways of handling conflict across a variety of communication encounters (Ting-Toomey et al., 1991; Ting-Toomey & Chung, 2005). The styles include avoiding (AV), obliging (OB), compromising (CO), dominating (DO), and integrating (IN). In **avoiding**, people will try to stay away from disagreements and dodge unpleasant

face management
the protection of one's face

avoiding
staying away from disagreements

Research Notes

Kim, M., Lee, H., Kim, I. D., & Hunter, J. E. (2004). A test of a cultural model of conflict styles. *Journal of Asian Pacific Communication, 14,* 197–222.

Conflict, according to the researchers, "occurs in specific cultural settings" (p. 197). To this end, the research team examined and tested a model of conflict styles across various ethnic groups in Hawaii. Kim and associates argue that it is important to examine the link between individualistic and collectivistic cultural values and preferred conflict styles. An "ethnocultural" model of conflict styles was conceptualized to help explain "why individuals with different cultural orientations would prefer one set of conflict styles over another" (p. 199). Over 200 undergraduate students studying in Hawaii were selected because of the diversity of the student body (e.g., Japanese, White, Chinese, Filipino, Part Hawaiian, Mixed–no Hawaiian, Korean, and Samoan). Questionnaires with three conflict scenarios were provided to participants as well as a Conflict Inventory examining the five styles of conflict management (dominating, obliging, integrating, avoiding, and compromising) and a Face-Maintenance Inventory that looked at how individuals preserve or threaten the face of another. The results of the research showed that an individual's culture made a difference on preference for conflict style. Three clusters, or dimensions, of conflict styles emerged in the analysis: compromising/integrating, obliging/avoiding, and dominating. Furthermore, the researchers found that some of the previous research that showed preferred conflict styles and particular face-maintenance strategies should be reconsidered. In sum, the findings of this study

indicate that previous research on culture and conflict management may need reexamination due to "logical flaws" (p. 214) present in the research.

Oetzel, J. G., & Ting-Toomey, S. (2003). Face concerns in interpersonal conflict: A cross-cultural empirical test of the face negotiation theory. *Communication Research, 30,* 599–624.

Oetzel and Ting-Toomey present a study that tests the fundamental principle of Face-Negotiation Theory: "Face is an explanatory mechanism for culture's influence on conflict behavior" (p. 599). The researchers were interested in styles of conflict management (dominating, obliging, integrating, avoiding, and compromising) and face concerns. Over 750 participants from four countries (the United States, Japan, Germany, and China) were given questionnaires that asked them to recall a conflict with a person of the same sex and same ethnic/cultural group. The questionnaire was written in various languages to ensure "conceptual equivalence" (p. 608). The results of the research indicated that (1) a person's cultural individualism–collectivism influenced conflict style and that (2) self-face concern was associated with the dominating style of conflict and other-face concern was associated with avoiding and integrating conflict styles. Furthermore, Oetzel and Ting-Toomey found that members from collectivistic cultures were more avoiding and less integrating than members from individualistic cultures. Finally, members from collectivistic cultures have higher other- and self-face concerns than members from individualistic cultures. The authors provide further validation for Face-Negotiation Theory with specific modifications and implications explained in the research.

---

exchanges with others ("I'm busy" or "I don't want to talk about that"). The **obliging** style includes a passive accommodation that tries to satisfy the needs of others or goes along with the suggestions of others ("Whatever you want to do is okay with me"). In **compromising**, individuals try to find a middle road to resolve impasses and use give-and-take so that a compromise can be reached ("I'll give up the first week of my vacation; you give up one week of yours").

obliging
satisfying the needs of others

compromising
using give-and-take to achieve a middle-road resolution

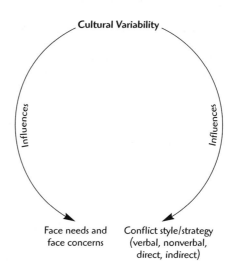

Figure 26.2
Cultural Variability, Face, and Conflict

Cultural Variability

Influences   Influences

Face needs and   Conflict style/strategy
face concerns   (verbal, nonverbal,
                         direct, indirect)

dominating
using influence or authority to make decisions

integrating
collaborating with others to find solutions

The **dominating** style includes those behaviors that involve using influence, authority, or expertise to get ideas across or to make decisions ("I'm in the best position to talk about this issue"). Finally, the **integrating** style is used by people to find a solution to a problem ("I think we need to work this out together"). As opposed to compromising, integrating requires a high degree of concern for yourself and for others. In compromising, a moderate degree exists.

Ting-Toomey believes that the decision to use one or more of these styles will depend on the cultural variability of communicators. Yet conflict management necessarily takes into consideration the concern for self-face and other-face. We illustrate this relationship in Figure 26.2. From our opening story, Kevin Johnston, using a dominating style of conflict management, apparently has little concern for the face of his professor (self-face). Professor Yang, however, is more compromising in the way that she handles the conflict with her student (other-face).

Let's continue to clarify Ting-Toomey's discussion of conflict management by identifying the relationship of conflict style to facework. Ting-Toomey notes

Theory Application in Groups (TAG)

Because conflict and culture are primary themes of Face-Negotiation Theory, explain how mediators of conflict should be trained. Center your discussions on the importance of understanding conflict from a variety of cultural viewpoints and give examples.

several relationships among conflict styles and face concern/face need. First, both AV and OB styles of conflict management reflect a passive approach to handling conflicts. A CO style represents a mutual-face need by finding middle-ground solutions to a conflict. Finally, a DO style reflects a high self-face need and a need for control of the conflict, whereas the IN conflict style indicates a high self-face/other-face need for conflict resolution.

With respect to comparisons across five cultures (Japan, China, South Korea, Taiwan, and the United States), Ting-Toomey and her research colleagues (1991) made a number of discoveries:

- Members of U.S. culture use significantly more dominating styles of conflict management (than Japanese and Koreans).
- The Taiwanese report using significantly more integrating styles of conflict management.
- The Chinese and Taiwanese use significantly more obliging conflict styles (than the United States).
- The Chinese use higher degrees of avoidance as a conflict style than other cultural groups.
- The Chinese use a higher degree of compromising than other cultures.

Their research also showed that collectivistic cultures (China, Korea, and Taiwan) had a higher degree of other-face concern.

It is clear from the research on face and conflict that cultural variability influences the way conflict is managed. Let's reflect on our opening discussion of Kevin Johnston and Professor Yang. According to Face-Negotiation Theory, because Professor Yang is a member of the Chinese culture—defined as a collectivistic society—she is likely to compromise with Kevin in their conflict. As you saw in our opening, she does try to compromise by asking him to write up a detailed outline and then write about two-thirds of the paper (not the entire paper). She also has a high degree of other-face concern. Kevin, on the other hand, is very dominating in his conflict style and possesses a great deal of self-face concern.

Integration, Critique, and Closing

Face-Negotiation Theory assumes that people of various cultures are concerned with the presentation of their face. It is a theory that artfully infuses conflict into its framework, explaining why members of two different cultures, for instance, manage conflict differently. Ting-Toomey asserts that different cultural values exist in dealing with conflict, and these conflictual episodes, in turn, are influenced by the face concerns and face needs of communicators. FNT has a rich history, and we discuss two criteria for the theory's effectiveness: heurism and logical consistency.

Integration

Communication Tradition	Rhetorical | Semiotic | Phenomenological | Cybernetic | **Socio-Psychological** | Socio-Cultural | Critical
Communication Context	Intrapersonal | Interpersonal | Small Group | Organizational | Public/Rhetorical | Mass/Media | **Cultural**
Approach to Knowing	**Positivistic/Empirical** | Interpretive/Hermeneutic | Critical

Critique

Evaluation Criteria	Scope | **Logical Consistency** | Parsimony | Utility | Testability | **Heurism** | Test of Time

Logical Consistency

Interestingly, Face-Negotiation Theory has received some clarification from Ting-Toomey herself, prompting refinement of the theory. Recall that the theory rests on the differing experiences and perceptions of individualistic and collectivist cultures. Ting-Toomey uses this foundation to lay out the essence of her theory. At times, however, this cultural dimension may not fully explain cultural differences. In her own research, Ting-Toomey and colleagues (1991) discovered some discrepancies. She found that Japanese respondents showed more concern for self-face than U.S. respondents. In addition, although Ting-Toomey proposes that individualistic cultures are not usually compromising in their conflict styles, the highly individualistic U.S. respondents used a significantly high degree of compromising when faced with a conflict. In this study, then, the "I" identity of the U.S. respondents was displaced.

Ting-Toomey and Cocroft (1994) respond to these differences in expectations by noting that looking at facework from the individualistic and collectivistic orientation "is a necessary starting point for facework behavior research" (p. 314). The researchers also state that many of the facework category systems in research reflect individualism–collectivism thinking, and therefore, Face-Negotiation Theory must necessarily begin from this vantage point.

Additional issues surrounding the logical consistency of Face-Negotiation Theory remain. As we have mentioned, Ting-Toomey (1988) has positioned the theory within the politeness perspective of Brown and Levinson (1987). She incorporates a number of the components of their thinking, including positive face and negative face. Yet Tracy and Baratz (1994) believe that such labeling in Brown and Levinson's framework "may be too general to capture the face-concern most central to an interactant" (p. 290). That is, other issues pertaining to face concern exist that are not identified by the researchers. Ting-Toomey's application and integration of politeness research, then, may warrant further reflection and consideration. Ting-Toomey and Cocroft (1994) agree with the fact that Brown and Levinson have presented an original template from which to draw, but report data that demonstrates several problems with their research.

Heurism

Ting-Toomey's Face-Negotiation Theory has sparked interest among intercultural communication researchers, making it highly heuristic. Several of the key concepts and features of the theory have been studied. For instance, conflict management examined within the framework of "face" has been investigated with Malaysians (Rose, Suppiah, Uli, & Othman, 2008) and across various other cultures, including Japan, Germany, Mexico, and the United States (Oetzel, Ting-Toomey, Chew-Sanchez, Harris, Wilcox, & Stumpf, 2003). The theory has been woven into research looking at family problems in Japan (Child, Pearson, & Nagao, 2006). In addition, on a more practical note, the theory has been incorporated into research on intercultural training and development pertaining to conflict (Ting-Toomey, 2007).

Face-Negotiation Theory will continue to intrigue communication researchers. Particularly at a time when culture pervades all aspects of life and the global village is becoming smaller, the theory will have lasting appeal. When people from two different cultures have a conflict, understanding how they maintain and negotiate face will have implications beyond the encounter. Ting-Toomey has given us an opportunity to think about how we can mediate the potential difficulties in communication among cultures, and she elegantly presents important information on a world dependent on communication.

Discussion Starters

1. If he had to do it over again, what communication strategies would you recommend for Kevin Johnston in his conflict with Professor Yang? How might he save his own face and the face of his professor?

2. Have you been to one of the countries categorized here as collectivistic? If so, what communication differences did you notice between that culture and U.S. culture?

3. Do you believe that Face-Negotiation Theory relies on people being reasonable agents who are capable of handling conflict? Can conflict become unreasonable? Explain with examples.

4. Interpret the following statement by Ting-Toomey through description and example: "Collectivists need to work on their ethnocentric biases as much as the individualists need to work out their sense of egocentric superiority." Do you agree or disagree with her view?

5. What evidence do you have that face maintenance is a critical part of U.S. society? Use examples in your response.

6. Discuss the role of power in facework. How can it both help and hinder face-saving in your interactions with others?

7. Apply any concept or feature of FNT to a job interview.

Online Learning Center www. mhhe.com/west4e

Visit the Online Learning Center at www.mhhe.com/west4e for chapter-specific resources, such as story-into-theory and multiple-choice quizzes, as well as theory summaries and theory connection questions.

CHAPTER 27

Communication Accommodation Theory

*Based on the research of **Howard Giles***

Luke Tomsha and Roberto Hernandez

As an upcoming spring graduate, 22-year-old Luke Tomsha was already preparing for the onslaught of interviews he would face graduating with a 3.86 grade point average. Luke knew that his grades were excellent, and as a double major (Spanish and communication), he felt that his chances of landing a good job were pretty good.

Luke's day to shine was upon him. He got an interview with a large accounting firm looking to hire someone in their human resources department. The position required proficiency in two languages. He flew to Denver for his first face-to-face interview with Roberto Hernandez, the HR director. The interview would be one that both men would remember for quite some time.

"Buenos dias, Luke," Roberto said.

"Good morn . . . I mean, buenos dias to you, Mr. Hernandez," Luke replied. Already, the initial tension eased. Luke immediately felt comfortable with his future boss.

Roberto continued, "Please, have a seat. I hope your flight last night was fine. I know that this time of the year can get a little bumpy, especially over the Rockies."

"Oh, it was great. I like to fly. This time, I got a chance to watch a movie that I hadn't seen yet. Personally, I love movies while I fly. It distracts me from the other noise and loud talking," Luke responded.

Their conversation continued. Luke was certainly a bit on edge but noticed that his accelerated speech rate slowed to match that of his interviewer. Yet Luke still felt awkward because he did not know exactly when Mr. Hernandez would change the subject from flying to the job.

Roberto began to talk further about his two sons, both of whom love to fly. "Like you, I love to fly," Roberto related. "My wife, though, is a different story. I wish she had the same attitude as you."

Luke replied, "Hey, maybe it's simply *machismo,* but I'm never afraid to fly."

Roberto was struck by Luke's use of the term *machismo.* Was he adjusting his speech to Spanish simply because Roberto was Mexican? As an interviewer, he knew that job candidates get nervous, and maybe this was simply a nervous habit of his. Of course, it didn't escape Roberto's notice that Luke was speaking Spanish to a Mexican American man who happened to have a strong accent. Yet he didn't want to make anything out of it. "I trust you've come here with a lot of questions, Luke. Let me begin by answering one that we haven't really addressed over the phone—your salary."

"Está bien—that's okay. I just need to know more about the job and what it involves. We can get to the salary a bit later if you'd like," Luke answered.

"Ah . . . no," said Roberto. "I can tell you that based on your application, you are an excellent candidate, and we are willing to pay you top dollar. We're all happy to see your interest."

"Thanks," Luke remarked. "I have to say that I wasn't ready to immediately discuss salary, but, hey, I appreciate it. Muchas gracias," he said with a slight smile.

Roberto was now agitated by Luke's frequent insertion of Spanish words into the conversation. He could handle the initial greeting; after all, he had initiated it. But Luke's continuing in this manner only made Roberto more uneasy. He didn't know whether to ask Luke to leave or simply to say how confused he was over Luke's persistent behavior. Of course, he could choose to remain silent and simply send Luke a rejection letter. Roberto decided to confront the young college student instead.

"Luke, I'm a bit taken aback by your odd inclusion of Spanish. I realize that you are interviewing with a Chicano, and I know I began with a friendly welcome in Spanish. But, frankly, it's a bit much, don't you think? Maybe I'm reaching here, but it's . . ." Roberto stared at the young job candidate.

"Mr. Hernandez," Luke explained, "I'm sorry if I've offended you. I realize that I break into Spanish, and to be honest with you, yeah, I guess it was a bit inappropriate. I was using Spanish to show you some respect, to ah . . . to show that I can weave Spanish into our conversation. . . . I really am sorry if I was out of place."

Luke was extremely nervous. He wasn't sure what Mr. Hernandez would say next. He was mad at himself for sounding like an idiot and assumed that he had lost the job. Maybe he had tried too hard to adapt to his interviewer. Maybe an interview was the worst place for him to demonstrate his fluency in Spanish. Maybe he had misread the situation.

"Listen, Luke," Roberto advised. "I've been around this firm for almost fifteen years. I've seen people come and go. I want you to be one of those who come and stay. I hope you don't get too upset by this. I know that I should've started out with a traditional Denver greeting and . . ."

". . . and I think," Luke interrupted, "that I should keep my mouth shut and not pretend I'm some expert in a foreign language! Really, I'm sorry about this."

Roberto smiled. "Now, let's get on with the rest of this interview."

When two people speak, they frequently mimic each other's speech and behavior. Often, we will talk to another who uses the same language we do, gestures similarly, and even speaks at a similar rate. We, in turn, may respond in kind to the other communicator. Imagine, for instance, situations where you have spoken to someone who has not gone to college. Chances are that you avoided using jargon that is unique to high school or college life—for example, talking about midterms or finals ("bombed the exam"), studying ("hit the books"), classes ("I need another elective"), and so forth.

Although we all have these types of experiences at the interpersonal level, sometimes there are group- or culture-based differences, such as perceived differences in age group, in accent or ethnicity, or in the pace and rate of speech. Whether in an interpersonal relationship, in a small group, or across cultures, people adjust their communication to others. This adaptation is at the core of Communication Accommodation Theory (CAT), developed by Howard Giles. Formerly known as Speech Accommodation Theory (but later conceptualized more broadly to include nonverbal behaviors and speaking patterns), Communication Accommodation Theory rests on the premise that when speakers interact, they adjust their speech, their vocal patterns, and their gestures to accommodate others. Giles and his colleagues believe that speakers have various reasons for being accommodative to others. Some people wish to evoke a listener's approval, others want to achieve communication efficiency, and still others want to maintain a positive social identity (Giles, Mulac, Bradac, & Johnson, 1987). As you can see in our opening story, however, we do not always achieve what we aim for. As we found while discussing Face-Negotiation Theory, adaptation and self-identity are important markers in our communication with others.

Communication Accommodation Theory had its beginnings in 1973, when Giles first introduced the notion of an "accent mobility" model, which is based on various accents heard in interview situations (similar to the situation with Luke and Roberto). Much of the subsequent theory and research has remained sensitive to the various communication accommodations undertaken in conversations among diverse cultural groups, including the elderly, people of color, immigrants, and the visually impaired (for example, Gallois, Callan, & Johnstone, 1984; Gallois, Franklyn-Stokes, Giles, & Coupland, 1988; Klemz, 1977; Moon & Nelson, 2008; Nussbaum, Pitts, Huber, Krieger, & Ohs, 2005). We discuss this theory with this cultural variability in mind.

To get a sense of the central characteristic of CAT, we first delineate what is meant by the word *accommodation*. For our purposes, **accommodation** is defined as the ability to adjust, modify, or regulate one's behavior in response to another. Accommodation is usually done unconsciously. We tend to have internal cognitive scripts that we draw on when we find ourselves in conversations with others. In a conversation with a 15-year-old girl, you might find yourself using teen vocabulary; with an 85-year-old, you might slow your speech and use more facial animation. This is all done without much thought and can occur overtly or covertly.

accommodation
adjusting, modifying, or regulating behavior in response to others

Like several other theories in this book, Communication Accommodation Theory relates to other research first conducted in another field, in this case, social psychology. To this end, it's important to address the theoretical vehicle that launched Giles's thinking: Social Identity Theory.

Communication Accommodation Theory • Theory at a Glance

This theory considers the underlying motivations and consequences of what happens when two speakers shift their communication styles. During communication encounters, people will try to accommodate or adjust their style of speaking to others. This is primarily done in two ways: divergence and convergence. Groups with strong cultural pride often use divergence to highlight group identity. Convergence occurs when there is a strong need for social approval, frequently from powerless individuals.

Social Psychology and Social Identity

Much of the research and theory in the field of social psychology pertain directly to how people search for meaning in the behaviors of others and how this meaning influences future interactions with others. Stephen Worchel (1998) summarizes the field this way: "Typically, social psychology searches for effects [of behaviors] and the causes of these effects" (p. 53). One of the central concepts discussed in the research of social psychology is identity. According to Jessica Abrams, Joan O'Connor, and Howard Giles (2003), "accommodation is fundamental to identity construction" (p. 221). Recognizing the importance of the self and its relationship to group identity, Henri Tajfel and John Turner (1986) developed **Social Identity Theory.** This theory suggests that a person's self-concept is comprised of a personal identity (e.g., body characteristics, psychological behaviors) as well as a social identity (e.g., affiliation with a group) (Giles, Willemyns, Gallois, Anderson, 2007). Researchers and theorists in Social Identity suggest that people are "motivated to join the most attractive groups and/or give an advantage to the groups to which one belongs (in-group)" (Worchel, Rothgerber, Day, Hart, & Butemeyer, 1998, p. 390). When people are given an opportunity, Worchel and colleagues contend, they will provide more resources to their own groups, rather than to out-groups. And when in-groups are identified, an individual decides the extent to which the group is central to his or her identity. Social identity, then, is primarily based on the comparisons that people make between **in-groups** (groups to which a person feels he or she belongs) and **out-groups** (groups to which a person feels he or she does not belong).

Tajfel and Turner (1986) note that people strive to acquire or maintain positive social identity, and when social identity is perceived as unsatisfactory, they will either join a group they feel more at home in or make the existing group a more positive experience. Summing up the Social Identity perspective, Tajfel and Turner observe that "the basic hypothesis, then, is that pressures to evaluate one's own group positively through in-group/out-group comparisons lead social groups to attempt to differentiate themselves from each other" (p. 16). Tajfel and Turner note that communication exists on a continuum from "interindividual" to "intergroup." So, according to the theory, the more that Luke perceives Roberto to be either a "Chicano" or a "boss" rather than simply "Mr. Hernandez," the more Luke will rely on stereotypes or group-level impressions to understand Roberto's behavior.

Giles drew from some of the thinking related to Social Identity Theory. He felt that we accommodate not only to *specific* others, but also to those we perceive as members of other groups. Thus, intergroup variables and goals influence the communication process. Giles, like many social psychologists, believes that people are influenced by a number of behaviors. Specifically, he argues that an individual's speech style (accent, pitch, rate, interruption patterns) can affect the impressions that others have of the individual. Giles and Smith (1979) also comment that the nature of the setting, the conversation topic, and the type of person with whom one communicates will all intersect to determine the speech manner one adopts in a given situation. If an individual is viewed

Social Identity Theory
a theory that proposes a person's identity is shaped by both personal and social characteristics

in-groups
groups in which a person feels he or she belongs

out-groups
groups in which a person feels he or she does not belong

favorably, communicator A will shift his or her speech style to become more like that of communicator B; that is, communicator A has *accommodated* communicator B. Giles and Smith maintain that people adjust their speech style to accommodate how they believe others in the conversation will best receive it. In our opening, you can see how Luke shifts his speech to accommodate what he believes (incorrectly) Mr. Hernandez will appreciate.

Communication Accommodation Theory is based on many of the same principles and concepts as Social Identity Theory. Giles was influenced by the belief that when members of different groups come together, they compare themselves. If their comparisons are favorable, a positive social identity will result. Jake Harwood (2006) thoughtfully sums up the importance of social identity and group membership: "Even our closest interpersonal relationships are imbued with group identifications that both join us to those within our groups and separate us from those not in our groups" (p. 89).

With this theoretical footing in place, we now turn our attention to the assumptions guiding the development of Communication Accommodation Theory. As we discuss these, you will be able to sense the influence of social psychology, and Social Identity Theory in particular.

Assumptions of Communication Accommodation Theory

Giles and other Accommodation Theory proponents would be interested in the accommodation taking place between Luke Tomsha and Roberto Hernandez. Their conversation exemplifies a number of issues that underlie the basic assumptions of the theory. Recalling that accommodation is influenced by a number of personal, situational, and cultural circumstances, we identify several assumptions below:

- Speech and behavioral similarities and dissimilarities exist in all conversations.
- The manner in which we perceive the speech and behaviors of another will determine how we evaluate a conversation.
- Language and behaviors impart information about social status and group belonging.
- Accommodation varies in its degree of appropriateness, and norms guide the accommodation process.

Many principles of CAT rest on the first assumption that there are similarities and dissimilarities between communicators in a conversation. Past experiences, you may recall, form a person's field of experience, a concept we discussed in Chapter 1. Whether in speech or behaviors, people bring their various fields of experiences into a conversation (West & Turner, 2009). These varied experiences and backgrounds will determine the extent to which one person will accommodate another. The more similar our attitudes and beliefs are to those of others, the more we will be attracted to and accommodate those others.

Let's look at a few examples to illustrate this assumption. Consider our opening scenario with Luke and Roberto. They are clearly from different professional backgrounds with different levels of work experience. Presumably, they are products of different family backgrounds with different beliefs and values. The two are clearly dissimilar in some ways, yet they are similar in others—for example, they both like to fly, and they both have an interest in working at the accounting firm.

To illustrate this assumption further, consider the following dialogue between a grandparent and a teenage granddaughter:

GRANDMOTHER: I don't know why you're wearing all black. You'll have people talking.

GRANDDAUGHTER: So? People talked about your generation wearing weird stuff too. It's the style now.

GRANDMOTHER: But we only wore black for funerals.

GRANDDAUGHTER: Yeah, and that's because back then, that's the most excitement you had! You people never had any fun.

GRANDMOTHER: You would be surprised how much fun we had. It was different from what you think now. We did a lot when I was younger.

In this conversation, the granddaughter draws conclusions about the grandparent using group-based expectations: Older people can't understand teenagers. This expectation influences the teenager's communication with her grandmother.

The second assumption rests on both perception and evaluation. Communication Accommodation is a theory concerned with how people both perceive and evaluate what takes place in a conversation. **Perception** is the process of attending to and interpreting a message, whereas **evaluation** is the process of judging a conversation. People first perceive what takes place in a conversation (for instance, the other person's speaking abilities) before they decide how to behave in a conversation. Consider, for example, Luke's response to Roberto. The interviewer's informality at the beginning of the interview is perceived by Luke as a good way to break the ice and eliminate some of his tension. Luke's subsequent behavior reflects a relaxed style (too relaxed). Luke is like most people in an interview: He gets a sense of the interview atmosphere (perception) and then reacts accordingly (evaluation).

Motivation is a key part of the perception and evaluation process in Communication Accommodation Theory. That is, we may perceive another person's speech and behaviors, but we may not always evaluate them. This often happens, for instance, when we greet another person, engage in small talk, and simply walk on. We normally don't take the time to evaluate such a conversational encounter.

Yet there are times when perceiving the words and behaviors of another leads to our evaluation of the other person. We may greet someone, for instance, and engage in small talk, but then be surprised when we hear that the other person recently got divorced. According to Giles and colleagues (1987), it is then that we decide our evaluative and communicative responses. We may

perception
process of attending to and interpreting a message

evaluation
process of judging a conversation

express our happiness, our sorrow, or our support. We do this by engaging in an accommodating communication style.

The third assumption of Communication Accommodation Theory pertains to the effects that language has on others. Specifically, language has the ability to communicate status and group belonging between communicators in a conversation. Consider what occurs when two people who speak different languages try to communicate with each other. Giles and John Wiemann (1987) discuss this situation:

> In bilingual, or even bidialectal, situations, where ethnic majority and minority peoples coexist, second language learning is dramatically unidirectional: that is, it is very common for the dominant group to acquire the linguistic habits of the subordinate collectivity. . . . Indeed, it is no accident that cross-culturally what is "standard," "correct," and "cultivated" language behavior is that of the aristocracy, the upper or ruling classes and their institutions. (p. 361)

The language used in a conversation, then, will likely reflect the individual with the higher social status. In addition, group belonging comes into play because inferred in this quotation is a desire to be part of the "dominant" group.

To understand this assumption better, let's return to our opening. In the interview situation with Mr. Hernandez, Luke's language and behaviors are guided by the interviewer. This is what normally occurs in interviews: The individual with the higher social status sets the tone through his or her language and behaviors. Although Roberto is a member of a co-culture that has been historically oppressed, he nonetheless has the power to establish the interview's direction. Those wishing to identify with or to become part of another's group—for example, Luke wishing to be offered a job by Mr. Hernandez—will usually accommodate.

The fourth and final assumption focuses on norms and issues of social appropriateness. We note that accommodation can vary in social appropriateness and that accommodation is rooted in norm usage. It's important to understand that accommodation may not always be worthwhile and beneficial. Certainly, there are times when accommodating another is important, yet there are also times when accommodation is inappropriate. For instance, Melanie Booth-Butterfield and Felicia Jordan (1989) found that people from marginalized cultures are usually expected to adapt (accommodate) to others.

Norms have been shown to play some role in Giles's theory (Gallois & Callan, 1991). **Norms** are expectations of behaviors that individuals feel should or should not occur in a conversation. The varied backgrounds of communicators like Luke and Roberto, for instance, or those of a grandparent and grandchild will influence what they expect in their conversations. The relationship between norms and accommodation is made clear by Cynthia Gallois and Victor Callan (1991): "Norms put constraints of varying degree . . . on the accommodative moves that are perceived as desirable in an interaction" (p. 253). Therefore, the general norm that a younger person is obedient to an older person suggests that Luke will be more accommodative in his communication to Mr. Hernandez. Of course, the interview context itself entails special expectations for behavior.

norms
expectations of behavior in conversations

Theory Into Practice

Cassie

I'm so into conversations that when I read about CAT, I immediately understood what it was all about. When we talked about how language communicates status, I thought about my doctor. I'm originally from Barcelona so I don't have the best English. One time, I went in to see my doctor to have her examine me (I had tingling up and down my left leg). After some testing, she told me that I needed this test and that test and I never understood a single thing she was saying. I tried to ask her questions, but I gave up eventually. She had more status than I did because she knew what she was talking about and I didn't. (I should say that she is no longer my doctor and that I'm okay.)

These four assumptions form the foundation for the remainder of our discussion of the theory. We now examine the ways that people adapt in conversations.

Ways to Adapt

Communication Accommodation Theory suggests that in conversations people have options. They may create a conversational community that entails using the same or similar language or nonverbal system, they may distinguish themselves from others, or they may try too hard to adapt. These choices are labeled convergence, divergence, and overaccommodation. We examine each next and illustrate them in Figure 27.1.

Convergence: Merging Thoughts Ahead

convergence
strategy used to adapt to another's behavior

The first process associated with CAT is termed *convergence*. Giles, Nikolas Coupland, and Justine Coupland (1991) define **convergence** as "a strategy whereby individuals adapt to each other's communicative behaviors" (p. 7). People may adapt to speech rate, pause, smiling, eye gaze, and other verbal and nonverbal behaviors. Convergence is a selective process; we do not always choose to enact a convergent strategy with people. When people do converge, they rely on their perceptions of the other person's speech or behaviors. What this means is that Luke Tomsha's decision to use Spanish in his interview with Roberto Hernandez is partially based on his knowledge that Mr. Hernandez began the interview with a greeting in Spanish; Luke attempts to converge with the opening tone set by his interviewer.

In addition to the perception of the other's communication, convergence is also based on attraction (Giles, 2008). Usually, when communicators are attracted to others, they will converge in their conversations. Attraction is a broad term that encompasses a number of other characteristics, such as liking, charisma, and credibility. Giles and Smith (1979) believe that a number of factors affect our attraction for others—for example, the possibility of future interactions

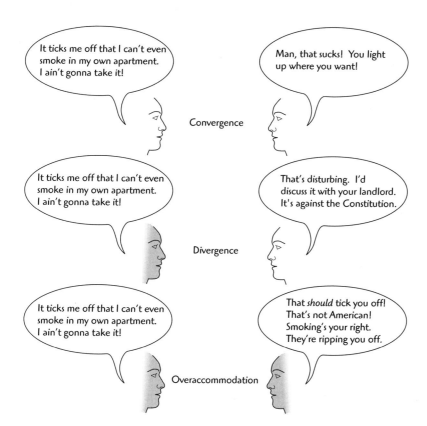

Figure 27.1
Ways to Adapt or Accommodate in Conversation

with the listener, the speaker's ability to communicate, and the status differential between communicators. Having similar beliefs, having a similar personality, or behaving in similar ways causes people to be attracted to each other and is likely to prompt convergence. Remember, however, that uncovering similarities occurs over time. People may not instantly know whether they are attracted to each other and whether this will lead to identifying their similarities. And the relational history between communicators may be a critical issue in convergence. For instance, Richard Street's (1991) research indicates that physicians differ in their convergence patterns with first-time patients and with repeat patients. He cautions, however, that differences in convergence may be explained by looking at the traditional roles of doctor and patient as well as the time lag between visits.

At first view, convergence may appear to be a positive accommodating strategy, and it usually is. Our discussion so far implies that the other person is viewed as similar to the individual or that at least one is attracted to the other in a conversation. Yet, as we explained previously, convergence may be based on stereotypical perceptions. As Giles and colleagues (1987) conclude, "Convergence is often cognitively mediated by our stereotypes of how socially categorized others will speak" (p. 18). What this means is that people will converge toward stereotypes rather than toward real speech and behaviors.

Theory Application in Groups (TAG)

An essential feature of Communication Accommodation Theory is the notion of convergence. In small groups, discuss the possible range of reactions to and evaluations of the issue of convergence in intercultural encounters. Be sure to discuss the ways people converge and how others might react to that convergence.

indirect stereotyping
imposing outdated and rigid assumptions of a cultural group upon that group

There are obvious implications of stereotypical convergence. For example, gay fathers and lesbian mothers report that too many people—including educators—rely on outdated stereotypes of gay men and lesbians when they communicate with them (West & Turner, 1995). Examining the cultural experiences of African Americans, Mark Orbe (1998) notes that African Americans are often identified in stereotypical ways. He points out that **indirect stereotyping** exists; that is, stereotyping when European Americans talk to their African American friends about what they believe to be African American "subjects" (sports, music, and so forth). Some African Americans report that if they speak nonstandard dialect, they are especially prone to stereotypical reactions. Marsha Houston (2004) agrees. She notes that when describing themselves, White women in particular identify their speech as appropriate and standard and describe African American female speech as nonstandard, incorrect, or deviant.

Other cultural groups have also been the target of stereotyping. Edwin Vaughan (1998), for example, contends that blind people are repeatedly addressed as if they are deaf. Shobha Pais (1997) maintains that Asian Indian women in the United States are often perceived as strange because of their sari (fabric draped over the shoulder and head) or *salwar kameez* (pantsuit). And Charmaine Shutiva (2004) bemoans the fact that the Native American culture is erroneously viewed as stoic and unemotional, when in reality, it involves a great deal of humor and joy. These examples demonstrate that a number of cultural groups continue to be stereotyped. Stereotyped perceptions may influence the extent to which an individual will converge.

Before we leave our discussion of convergence, let us briefly discuss the evaluation of convergence. Specifically, what occurs when people attempt to converge in their conversations? How do people respond? We have already illustrated a number of examples that demonstrate both positive and negative consequences of convergence. But how do we know how our convergence will be met?

First, we need to consider that an evaluation of convergence usually depends on whether the convergence is thoughtful. When convergence is perceived as good, it can enhance the dialogue; when it is perceived as bad, it can break down the communication process. If a communicator speaks or behaves in a style similar to a listener's, the convergence will probably be favorably perceived. But converging to ridicule, tease, or patronize will most likely be perceived negatively. There is a fine line between whether or not convergence will be perceived in the intended way. Consider, for instance, what happens when a nurse speaks to a patient in a nursing home about eating lunch (Ryan, Maclean, & Orange, 1994):

NURSE: It's time for lunch, Mrs. James.

RESIDENT: But I'm not hungry. And I don't particularly like this kind of soup.

NURSE: Everyone has to eat now, Mary. We have to get on with our day's work. Besides that, we can't suit everyone's tastes all of the time. We don't make the soup just for you, you know.

RESIDENT: I'd really rather just rest in my room and have a cup of tea later.

NURSE: Look, dearie, if you don't eat now, you won't get anything later. Let's stop being so fussy, all right?

RESIDENT: Fine.

In this conversation, you can see how convergence by the nurse might be construed as condescending by Mrs. James. In fact, Ryan and colleagues found that this style of communicating was rated as less respectful, less nurturing, and more frustrating for the resident. There are other standards of evaluating convergence, including the norms of the situation (Did the speaker converge in an offensive way?), the ability to pull it off effectively (How does a 50-year-old use the "cool" talk of a high school student?), and the value of a language to a community (Should European Americans employ Black English vernacular in their interactions with African Americans?).

Divergence: Vive la Différence

Accommodation is an optional process in which two communicators decide to accommodate, one does, or neither does. Giles (1980) believes speakers sometimes accentuate the verbal and nonverbal differences between themselves and others. He terms this **divergence** or nonaccommodation. Divergence differs greatly from convergence in that it is a dissociation process. Instead of showing how two speakers are alike in speech rate, gestures, or posture, divergence is when there are no attempts to demonstrate similarities between speakers. In other words, two people speak to each other with no concern about accommodating each other. No effort is made to "reduce social distance or to make communication smoother" (Giles et al., 2007, p. 144). Divergence has not received as much research attention as convergence, and so our knowledge about the process is limited to a few claims about its function in Communication Accommodation Theory.

First, divergence should not be misconstrued as an effort to disagree or to not respond to another communicator. Divergence is not the same as inattentiveness. When people diverge, they have simply chosen to dissociate themselves from the communicator and the conversation. The reasons for divergence vary. And, according to Giles (2008), not all divergences are negatively perceived.

divergence
strategy used to accentuate the verbal and nonverbal differences between communicators

Divergence is a way for members of various cultural communities to maintain social identity. Giles and his colleagues (1987) observe that there are occasions when people—namely, racial and ethnic groups—"deliberately use their language or speech style as a symbolic tactic for maintaining their identity, cultural pride, and distinctiveness" (p. 28). Individuals may not wish to converge in order to preserve their cultural heritage. Imagine, for example, that you are traveling in France; everywhere you go the French people you encounter encourage you to speak French. You are surprised at that until you realize that you, as a visitor, should not expect the French to converge to your language.

We've already learned that some cultural groups are immediately stereotyped and that people communicate with this categorization in mind. It's no wonder, then, that some cultural groups remain committed to divergence in their conversations with others. To illustrate this point, consider the conclusions of Richard Bourhis and Giles (1977). In this classic study, the research team studied Welsh people who were very proud of their ethnic identity but who did not know the Welsh language. As they learned the language, the researchers asked several questions in a standard English format. During the question-and-answer period, the researchers asked the group why they wanted to learn Welsh since it is "a dying language with a dismal future." The Welsh sample rebutted with not only a strong Welsh dialect but also Welsh words and phrases. Remarkably, the group could link together difficult Welsh words! The group, then, began to diverge from the English that was spoken to them, ostensibly out of ethnic pride.

A second reason people diverge pertains to power and role differences in conversations. Divergence frequently occurs in conversations when there is a power difference between the communicators and when there are distinct role differences in the conversation (physician–patient, parent–child, interviewer–interviewee, and so forth) (Street, 1991; Street & Giles, 1982). Street (1991), for instance, comments that "interactants having greater status may speak for longer periods, initiate most of the conversational topics, speak more slowly, and maintain a more relaxed body posture than does the less powerful" (p. 135). Divergence, then, occurs when one person wishes to render another one less powerful. Consider, for instance, the interview situation of Luke and Roberto. Because Roberto is in the more powerful position as the person conducting the interview and the one who will ultimately decide whether Luke will be offered the position, he exercises considerable influence on the content and structure of the interview. As an interviewer who holds more status than Luke, Roberto could engage in language and stories that are unique to the company (and unknown by Luke), ask questions about Luke's qualifications (which Luke cannot ask of Roberto), talk for a greater proportion of the interview time, and effectively use silence as an interview strategy. In other words, CAT maintains that because Roberto and Luke hold different roles in the conversation, one is able to freely diverge from the conversation of the other.

Finally, although not as often as for the reasons cited previously, divergence is likely to occur because the other in the conversation is viewed to be a "member of undesirable groups, considered to hold noxious attitudes, or display a deplorable appearance" (Street & Giles, 1982, p. 195). To this end, Giles and his colleagues (1987) contend that divergence is used to contrast self-images in a conversation. To understand this point, consider the number of so-called undesirable groups in society today. Reynolds (2008), for instance, notes that homeless people are historically part of what society labels as unappealing or vulgar. Employing the accommodation principle of divergence, then, a homeless man asking for money outside a movie theater may find himself in a conversation with a communicator (we'll call this person Pat) who wishes to diverge to demonstrate differences between the two. Pat's divergence may take the form of an increased rate of speech or a more clipped manner. Pat may also use vocabulary and pronunciation that clearly mark him as a member of the upper-middle class. In each case, the divergence is carried out by the individual who wishes to imply a status difference between the two.

Giles and colleagues (1987) conclude that such divergence enacted by Pat may have the goal of bringing another's behavior (and appearance) "to an acceptable level" (p. 32) and that Pat's divergence is a type of self-disclosure that illustrates that certain kinds of speech and behavior are not shared between two people. As is often the case, the homeless person's situation is viewed as his problem. Divergence is simply a way of further communicating this value. As our third assumption points out, language and behaviors frequently communicate status.

Overaccommodation: Miscommunicating With a Purpose

Jane Zuengler (1991) observes that **overaccommodation** is a term attributed to people who, although acting from good intentions, are perceived, instead, as patronizing or demeaning. Overaccommodation has the effect of making the target feel worse. Consider, for example, the overaccommodation taking place in Luke Tomsha's interview. Luke's efforts in speaking Spanish are undermined by Roberto's perception that Luke is patronizing him. In this case, and as some researchers (Coupland, Coupland, Giles, & Henwood, 1988) argue, the overaccommodation yields poor communication. Luke is not trying to patronize Roberto Hernandez. Although the speaker apparently has the intention of showing respect, the listener perceives it as distracting and disrespectful.

Overaccommodation can exist in three forms: sensory overaccommodation, dependency overaccommodation, and intergroup overaccommodation (Zuengler, 1991). Let's define these and present an example of each.

Sensory overaccommodation occurs when a speaker overly adapts to another who is perceived as limited in some way. Limitation, in this sense, refers to either a linguistic or a physical limitation. That is, a speaker may believe that he or she is sensitive to another's language disability or physical disability, but overdoes the accommodation. For example, in her study on patients with Alzheimer's disease, Heidi Hamilton (1991) felt that she had underestimated the level of competence of an Alzheimer's patient and found herself overaccommodating. Because Hamilton believed that Alzheimer's patients typically respond better to questions about the here and now rather than about past times or places, she kept this in mind as she framed her conversations with patients.

overaccommodation
attempt to overdo efforts in regulating, modifying, or responding to others

sensory overaccommodation
overly adapting to others who are perceived as limited in their abilities (physical, linguistic, or other)

Research Notes

Bunz, U., & Campbell, S. W. (2004). Politeness accommodation in electronic mail. *Communication Research Reports, 21,* 11–25.

In this article, Bunz and Campbell apply accommodation principles to e-mail messages. The researchers were interested in whether people accommodated to verbal politeness strategies while using e-mail with others. Giles's notion of convergence in Communication Accommodation Theory was of particular interest. More than 120 students were recruited from public speaking courses to participate in this study. The average age was around 19 years old. The researchers engaged in a somewhat covert undertaking by notifying participants that a visiting professor (fictitious Dr. Chris Aitken) at the university was looking for people to complete a survey for a study. Bunz and Campbell told students that the professor would contact them via e-mail with more information if they expressed interest. Once the e-mail addresses were collected, each student received an e-mail message from the visiting professor. The e-mail asked why the student was participating, with "politeness indicators" such as "please," "thank you," "I would appreciate," and "I'm grateful" used in the study (p. 16). The results of the research showed that many of the politeness cues were accommodated by students. When Dr. Aitken used politeness within the text of the message, participants accommodated by also including politeness markers in their e-mail responses. Bunz and Campbell conclude by identifying additional lines of research looking at levels of formality, friendliness, and personalness, which they are currently undertaking.

Williams, A., & Garrett, P. (2002). Communication evaluations across the lifespan: From adolescent storm and stress to elder aches and pains. *Journal of Language and Social Psychology, 21,* 101–126.

The researchers looked at almost 500 community adults ages 20 to 59, to assess their experiences with family members ages 13 to 16, 65 to 85, and their own age. Examining what they term "intergenerational communication research" (p. 102), the authors set out to look at the extent to which various populations had contact with each other and the perceptions that various age groups had of each other. All participants completed a questionnaire asking about their contact exposure.

Williams and Garrett found that respondents between 20 and 29 years of age reported more contact with their peer group and less contact with elder and younger groups. Those in the 50 to 59 age group reported more frequent contact with elder populations, but also with their peer group. The perception of young teenage populations was the most negatively perceived, with views such as "noncommunicative," "less accommodative," and "more self-promotional" characterizing this group. Furthermore, there was less respect toward this young population than for the elder or peer groups. The results are interpreted within a Communication Accommodation framework, and the researchers call for replication of their research for further validation.

It turned out, however, that she underestimated the mental capabilities of her interviewees. Hamilton believed that she spent much more interview time on the environment surrounding the Alzheimer's patient than was necessary. This resulted in making patients seem more incompetent than they actually were.

The second type of overaccommodation is **dependency overaccommodation**, which occurs when a speaker places the listener in a lower-status

dependency overaccommodation
occurs when speakers place listeners in a lower-status role

role, and the listener is made to appear dependent on the speaker. In dependency overaccommodation, the listener also believes that the speaker controls the conversation to demonstrate higher status. This can be seen by examining the treatment of a number of immigrant populations in the United States.

Many cultural groups are marginalized in the United States, and dependency overaccommodation, it appears, may be one reason for this ostracizing. For instance, during assimilation into their new communities, many refugees are made to feel subordinate when conversing with others. Although government workers may believe that during their conversations with refugees they are doing what is right (helping refugees understand various procedures and rules associated with documentation), refugees may feel quite dependent on the speaker (immigration official). Given that many newly arrived strangers do not know the English language, do not have a basic understanding of cultural values or norms, and do not have a clear sense of their job skills (Martin & Nakayama, 2008) their perceptions of dependency are warranted.

In addition to sensory and dependency overaccommodation, there is a third type of overaccommodation called **intergroup overaccommodation**. This involves speakers lumping listeners into a particular group, failing to treat each person as an individual. At the heart of this overaccommodation is stereotyping, and there can be far-reaching consequences. Although maintaining racial and ethnic identity is critical, individual identity is equally important.

intergroup overaccommodation occurs when speakers place listeners in cultural groups without acknowledging individual uniqueness

Consider when a speaker uses language that assigns a listener to a particular cultural group. The speaker may feel comfortable suggesting, for instance, that Mexican Americans have never been given a chance to succeed in the United States because they have been busy raising their families. To a Mexican American, this generalization may be perceived negatively. Communicating with this perception in mind may cause some Mexican Americans to accommodate negatively.

Overaccommodation usually results in listeners perceiving that they are less than equal. There are serious implications to overaccommodation, including losing motivation for further language acquisition, avoiding conversations, and forming negative attitudes toward speakers and society (Zuengler, 1991). If one goal of communication is achieving intended meaning, overaccommodation is a significant roadblock to that goal.

Integration, Critique, and Closing

Communication Accommodation Theory focuses on the role of conversations in our lives and the influence that communication and culture has on those conversations. The theory articulates a number of important points regarding the role communication patterns and styles play for communicators and for the message. To understand the theory's value to the communication discipline, we evaluate the theory using the following three criteria: scope, testability, and heurism.

Integration

Critique

Scope

The boundaries of the theory are rather expansive. You may recall that the theory originally examined speech; it was later expanded to include the nonverbal arena. Giles (2008) underscores the broad scope of Communication Accommodation Theory by stating that over the years, it "began to take propositional forms that became increasingly more complex and, arguably, more demanding on readers" (p. 166). Its scope, however, does not necessarily undermine the theory's integrity. The cross-disciplinary interest in the theory suggests that efforts to delimit it may not be the best course of action. The changing nature of culture in Western society suggests that a theory of this nature may need to be extensive in order to understand multiple populations.

Testability

The strengths of the theory may be quite significant because the theory has elicited little scholarly criticism. Still, a few concerns pertaining to the testability

Theory Into Practice

Michael

I work in a nursing home that specializes in Alzheimer's disease. We have more than a hundred residents with the disease, all of whom are at various stages of the disease. I have heard the "baby talk" from staff to residents before, and I've heard it a lot. We're trained and told not to talk this way and to treat every resident with dignity—that includes talking like an adult. But I've seen my co-workers talk down to the residents, and the residents, in turn, talk that way. It's pathetic. If anything, I wish the staff would accommodate with speech that is less demeaning and more considerate.

of the concepts have been identified. In short, some scholars contend that a few of the central features of the theory warrant further examination. Judee Burgoon, Leesa Dillman, and Lesa Stern (1993), for example, question the convergence–divergence frame advanced by Giles. They believe that conversations are too complex to be reduced simply to these processes. They also challenge the notion that people's accommodation can be explained by just these two practices. For instance, what occurs if people both converge *and* diverge in conversations? Are there consequences for the speaker? The listener? What influence, if any, does race or ethnicity play in this simultaneous process? One might also question whether the theory relies too heavily on a rational way of communicating. That is, although the theory acknowledges conflict between communicators, it also rests on a reasonable standard of conflict. Perhaps you have been in conflicts that are downright nasty and with people who have no sense of reason. It appears that the theory ignores this possible dark side of communication. Still, Giles (Gallois, Ogay, & Giles, 2005) is clear in noting that a great deal of work is still to be done before the process of accommodation can be fully understood.

Heurism

Without doubt, Giles and his colleagues have conceptualized a theory rich in heuristic value. The theory has been incorporated in a number of different studies. For instance, accommodation has been studied with law enforcement (Giles et al., 2007), with physicians (Hajek, Villagran, & Wittenberg-Lyles, 2007), with the elderly (Harwood, 2002), on the job (McCroskey & Richmond, 2000), in advertising (Moon & Nelson, 2008), in conjunction with e-mail (Bunz & Campbell, 2004), and even with messages left on telephone answering machines (Buzzanell, Burrell, Stafford, & Berkowitz, 1996). There is no doubt that the theory is heuristic and has lasting scholarly value in the communication field.

In his earlier writings on the theory, Giles challenged researchers to apply Communication Accommodation Theory across the life span and in different cultural settings. For the most part, his suggestions have been heeded. His research has broadened our understanding of why conversations are so complex. Through convergence, Giles sheds light on why people adapt to others in their interactions. Through divergence, we can understand why people choose to ignore adapting strategies. He has pioneered a theory that has helped us better understand the culture around us and the influences of accommodation on the diverse relationships within society.

Discussion Starters

1. What divergent strategies can you develop to rewrite our opening example of Luke Tomsha and Roberto Hernandez? Incorporate real dialogue in your response.

2. Explain how convergence might function in the following relationships: teacher–student, therapist–client, and supervisor–subordinate. In your response, choose a conversational topic that might be unique to the relationship and integrate convergence accordingly.

3. We have noted that overaccommodation results in miscommunication. Some research in Communication Accommodation Theory has also examined underaccommodation, or the process of not adapting sufficiently to another communicator. What do you believe are some examples of underaccommodation?

4. Giles contends that self-perception can influence the accommodation process. How does a person's self-perception affect accommodation? Provide examples to illustrate your thoughts.

5. CAT has been framed in the intercultural communication context. Based on your understanding of the theory, under what additional context(s) can the theory be understood?

6. How does accommodation lead to social identity? Explain using examples from your life.

7. Discuss a situation in which accommodation might backfire on an individual.

Online Learning Center (www. mhhe.com/west4e)

Visit the Online Learning Center at www.mhhe.com/west4e for chapter-specific resources, such as story-into-theory and multiple-choice quizzes, as well as theory summaries and theory connection questions.

CHAPTER 28

Muted Group Theory

*Based on the research of **Cheris Kramarae***

Patricia Fitzpatrick

Patricia Fitzpatrick sat in the back row in her Political Science 100 lecture; she closed her eyes, letting the professor's words wash over her. She was wondering what in the world had possessed her to go back to college at the age of 40. It had seemed like a good idea when she first thought about finishing the B.A. she had begun over twenty years ago, but now she thought she must have been out of her mind to try this. She felt like she was not understanding a word her professors said, and she was having an extremely difficult time keeping current with her assignments. Most of the other students were much younger than she, and seemed to have a lot more disposable income. She really hadn't spoken to many of them beyond a quick hello. All in all, this college idea was turning into a big hassle.

It wasn't supposed to be this way. Initially, she had thought it would improve her self-esteem if she could finish her degree. She was also hoping it might get her out of the dead-end job she had with Hudson's Department Store. She worked nights as a shipping clerk for the store, sending out orders for their mail-order business. She had been working for Hudson's for the past seven years, and it did not seem as if there was much possibility for advancement there. It was a pretty boring job with low pay, and Patricia was hopeful that a degree might give her more opportunities. As a single mom with three kids, she really needed a better job.

But Patricia was starting to despair about her prospects. One of the most disturbing things so far had been how tongue-tied she felt in class. She had so much trouble articulating what she wanted to say about the material, that she ended up not saying anything in most of her classes. Patricia worried that this would count against her, especially in her smaller classes, where the professors really seemed to encourage class participation. She had expected that she would have a lot to say as she learned new things, but she was finding it difficult to express her opinions. So, instead of increasing her self-esteem, college was making her feel worse about herself.

Actually, this wasn't the first time that Patricia had felt inarticulate. She admitted to herself that she had had a hard time speaking up long before she returned to college. At work, she was the only woman on her shift, and the men didn't seem to pay attention to her when she spoke. Once she had tried to compare something at work to an experience she had had teaching her son to read, and the other workers had looked at her like she was nuts. Then they all had started laughing and calling her "Mom." Another time she had been the chair of a committee at her daughter's school. The committee was supposed to research ways the school could raise money for more computer equipment. Patricia had to get up in front of representatives from the parents' group, teachers, and administrators and report on the committee's findings. Although the report had been okay, Patricia thought she had paused too much while she spoke. Even though she had spent a great deal of time preparing for the speech, she had still found herself groping for words occasionally.

She had hoped that college would help her become more articulate. It would be wonderful to be able to speak up and say what was on her mind. Patricia wasn't ready to give up, but things certainly weren't going as planned.

Some researchers analyzing Patricia's situation might be tempted to examine her individual traits, noting that she might have problems with shyness or a fear of communicating. However, the theory that we discuss in this chapter offers a different approach to explaining Patricia's problems. Muted Group Theory (MGT) asserts that, as a female, as a single mom, and as a person of low income, Patricia is a member of several groups whose experiences are not well served by her language system—a language system that was devised primarily by well-to-do men to represent their own experiences. In other words, MGT focuses on the power to name experiences (Wood, 2008). Thus, Patricia and others are muted because their native language often does not provide a good fit with their life experiences. Muted Group Theory explains that women trying to use man-made language to describe their experiences is somewhat like native English speakers learning to converse in Spanish. To do so, they have to go through an internal translation process, scanning the foreign vocabulary for the best word to express their thoughts. This process makes them hesitant and often inarticulate as they are unable to use the language fluently for their purposes. In the process, muted groups metaphorically lose their voice (Wood, 2008).

As Cheris Kramarae (1981) observes,

> The language of a particular culture does not serve all its speakers equally, for not all speakers contribute in an equal fashion to its formulation. Women (and members of other subordinate groups) are not as free or as able as men are to say what they wish, when and where they wish, because the words and the norms for their use have been formulated by the dominant group, men. (p. 1)

Yet it isn't the case that all women are silenced and all men have voice. MGT allows us to understand any group that is silenced by the inadequacies of their language. Furthermore, muting may take place as a result of the unpopularity of the views that a person is trying to express. Muted Group theorists criticize dominant groups and argue that hegemonic ideas often silence other ideas. Anita Taylor and M. J. Hardman (2000) comment that some feminist groups can become dominant within the feminist movement and then mute the voices of other women who question their ideology. Taylor and Hardman advance the example of Matilde Joslyn Gage, a nineteenth-century feminist who argued views that made her unpopular with the other feminists of the day such as Elizabeth Cady Stanton. As a result of advancing ideas that were considered too radical, "she became a *persona non grata* among the women of the movement" (pp. 2–3) who had more power; consequently, Gage's voice was muted and lost to future generations.

Language serves its creators (and those who belong to the same groups as its creators) better than those in other groups who have to learn to use the language as best they can. This is the case because the variety of experiences of the creators are named clearly in language, whereas the experiences of other groups are not. Due to their problems adapting to a language they did not create, people from other groups appear less articulate than those from groups like the creators. Sometimes these muted groups create their own language to compensate for their problems with the dominant group's language.

As you can probably guess from our discussion thus far, MGT is a critical theory as we defined it in Chapter 3. That is, MGT points out problems with the status quo and suggests ways to remediate these problems. Later in this chapter, we describe some of the action steps advocated by Muted Group proponents.

Origins of Muted Group Theory

Muted Group Theory originated with the work of Edwin and Shirley Ardener, social anthropologists who were concerned with social structure and hierarchy. In 1975, Edwin Ardener noted that groups making up the top end of the social hierarchy determine the communication system for the culture. Lower-power groups in the society, such as women, the poor, and people of color, have to learn to work within the communication system that the dominant group has established. Turning this generalization to the specific case of women in a culture, Edwin Ardener observed that social anthropologists study women's experiences by talking almost exclusively to men. Thus, not only do women have to contend with the difficulties of a language that does not completely give voice to their thoughts, but their experiences are represented through a male perspective (Ardener, 2005).

In 1975, Edwin Ardener commented on why ethnographers (who at the time were mainly men) tended to speak and listen to men in the cultures they studied. Ardener noted, "Those trained in ethnography evidently have a bias towards the kinds of model that men are ready to provide (or to concur in) rather than towards any that women might provide. If the men appear 'articulate' compared with the women, it is a case of like speaking like" (p. 2). Further, Shirley Ardener (1978) observed that women's mutedness is the counterpart to men's deafness. Thus, she explains that women (or members of any subordinate group) do speak, but their words fall on deaf ears, and when this happens over time, they tend to stop trying to articulate their thoughts, and

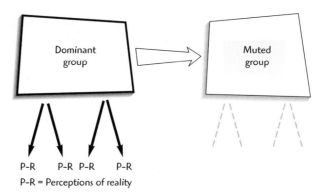

Figure 28.1
**Muted Group
Theory**
Source: Adapted from
Ardener, 1975.

P-R = Perceptions of reality

they may even stop thinking them. In Ardener's words, "Words which continually fall upon deaf ears may, of course, in the end become unspoken, or even unthought" (p. 20).

The Ardeners might argue that Patricia Fitzpatrick is twice muted: once by the failure of her language to act as an accurate tool for her use and once by anyone who labels her as inarticulate rather than poorly served by language. For Edwin Ardener, muted groups are rendered inarticulate by the dominant group's language system, which grows directly out of their worldview and experience. For the muted group, what they say first has to shift out of their own worldview and be compared to the experiences of the dominant group. Thus, articulations for the muted group are indirect and broken (Figure 28.1).

This line of thinking is especially true for the English language because it was developed and formalized by male clerics and academics. Because women were not instrumental in formalizing the English language, and were dominated in the culture that created it, Kramarae theorized that women would be a muted group. As Anita Taylor and M. J. Hardman (2000) observe,

> English does not name concepts important to women but to men (e.g.,
> one can have a "seminal" idea; but was one ever described as "ovular"?).
> English also devalues concepts important to women but not to men
> (again, the "seminal" idea is an example; if one nurtured or incubated
> an idea it would have quite a different feeling, as would ovulating it).
> English uses male referents and terms (e.g., the "generic" he and the
> conclusion that number is more important than gender for the third-
> person indefinite pronoun). (p. 8)

For these reasons, among others, MGT concludes that women are silenced by their language.

Two examples should clarify this line of thinking. One example comes from the work of Hilary Callan (1978), who suggests that many female nurses have difficulties with assuming authority. Callan argues that this difficulty is not because they are unable to take orders or to give them but rather because they experience a tension between elements of their self-definition. Nurses have been defined by others as either battle-axes who have renounced femininity or superfeminine angels of mercy. These two extremes pose problems for nurses themselves, who struggle to reconcile the complexities of their situations and self-perceptions with the two labels. Furthermore, as Callan concludes,

> The nurses' problem—and mine as ethnographer—is that the capacities and handicaps they may have [as] biological females are manifested and mapped on to a terrain of experience which includes (among many other things) the existence of traditional male authority patterns (which may or may not be an authentic model for women) as well as the relevant parts of the profession's own encapsulated history. (p. 212)

Thus, language constrains these nurses as they struggle to define themselves and their own profession. Language fails to serve their needs.

A second example comes from the work of Helen Sterk (1999), who has spent several years gathering birth stories from mothers in an effort to understand the experience of birth from the mothers' point of view. A central issue that Sterk identifies is that although birth seems to be the quintessential female experience, for many women, birth is medically managed in such a way that they feel somewhat removed from it. If a woman gives birth in a hospital, the language of the process is mainly the doctor's. The progress of the birth experience is noted in the observing doctor's language as to how many centimeters a woman's cervix has dilated, for example. As Sterk explains, this language is completely insufficient for women, and they are frequently reduced to repeating, "I simply cannot explain how I felt."

Makeup of Muted Groups

Much of the theorizing and application of Muted Group Theory has focused on women as a muted group. Yet, as researchers such as Mark Orbe (1998) and Michael Hechter (2004) note, the theory can be validly applied to any nondominant group. Orbe suggests that in the United States and several other cultures, the society privileges specific characteristics and perspectives: European American, male, heterosexual, able-bodied, youthful, middle and upper class, and Christian. People with these perspectives form the **dominant group,** or the group that holds the power in the culture. Other groups that coexist with the dominant group are generally subordinate to it in that they do not have access to as much power as do members of the dominant group. Thus, African Americans, gays and lesbians, the elderly, the lower class, disabled people, non-Christians, and Asian Americans (Martin & Nakayama, 2006) all can be members of muted groups, in the same way that women are.

dominant group
the group that holds the power in a given culture

In fact, some researchers have suggested that men might be part of a muted group as well. Radhika Chopra (2001) examines the issue of muting for nurturing fathers. Chopra argues that the discourse of mothering represented by Nancy Chodorow's (1978) book, *The Reproduction of Mothering,* reduced the father to a "depersonalized cipher" whose presence is "posited as an absence, in contrast with the hands-on vital involvement of the mother" (p. 447). Chopra notes that this discourse not only silences the father but also fails to account for fathering in other societies or periods of history where the distant, silent father did not exist.

Chopra points to fathers in the early American colonial period who were very involved in teaching their children both reading and writing skills as well as moral and religious teachings. Further, Chopra notes that ethnographies of societies like the Trobriand islanders (Weiner, 1976) allow a glimpse at fathers who maintained lifelong relationships with their children that are "characterized by love, protection, and nurture" (p. 448).

Although some Muted Group theorists might disagree that fathers are ever in a low-power position, Chopra concludes that giving voice to "father-care" is a critical process that will remove the category of caregiving from female ownership and in so doing transform the concept of gender identity completely. Yet, because most of the research in the area of Muted Group Theory has focused on men as the dominant group and women as the muted group, we shall pay most attention to that relationship in this chapter.

In training our focus on men and women, we need to clarify two terms: *sex* and *gender*. Generally, researchers use **sex** to mean biological categories, male and female, determined by the presence of XX chromosomes for females and XY chromosomes for males. Philip Smith (1985) observes that most people believe that sex is "an inherent and/or God-given attribute of individuality, an inalienable, incontrovertible fact of human existence" (p. 20). In contrast, **gender** is defined as the learned behaviors that constitute femininity and masculinity in a given culture. Thus, gender is changeable and reflects whatever the culture accepts at a given time for these roles. Currently, it is within the definition of masculinity to have pierced ears, and it is within the definition of femininity to have tattoos. At an earlier time, these attributes would not have been deemed appropriate. However, it is also the case that the terms *sex* and *gender* are often blurred because women are socialized to be feminine and men are encouraged to be masculine. Therefore, we will use the terms interchangeably in this chapter.

sex
biological category divided into male and female

gender
social category consisting of the learned behaviors that constitute masculinity and femininity for a given culture

Assumptions of Muted Group Theory

After the Ardeners' groundwork in developing the concepts of Muted Group Theory, Cheris Kramarae (1981) built on the theory to focus it more specifically on communication. Additionally, as Kramarae comments, her aims are somewhat more limited than those of the Ardeners, who were concerned with applying Muted Group Theory across many cultures. Kramarae's interest is in the "questions the theory raises and [the] explanations it . . . provide[s] for the communication patterns among and between women and men in Great Britain and the United States" (1981, p. 4). Toward this end, Kramarae first isolates three assumptions she believes are central to MGT.

- Women perceive the world differently than men because of women's and men's different experiences and activities rooted in the division of labor.

- Because of their political dominance, men's system of perception is dominant, impeding the free expression of women's alternative models of the world.

"Talk to me, Alice. I speak woman."

- In order to participate in society, women must transform their own models in terms of the received male system of expression. (p. 3)

We will review each of these assumptions in turn.

Gender-Based Differences in Perception

This first assumption begins with the premise that the world is a different place for women and men and that their experiences differ. Furthermore, the assumption posits an explanation for these differences. The explanation lies in the division of labor that allocates work on the basis of sex, such that women are responsible for tasks in the home and men are responsible for work outside the home. The division of labor began in Western countries in the eighteenth and nineteenth centuries as a result of social transformations, in large part related to the industrial revolution (Coontz, 1988). The industrial revolution took work out of the home and made it a paid activity. Prior to that, work had been intertwined with home life because all members of the family contributed to the family's survival, usually on subsistence farms. No one was literally paid for their specific labor; the money the family realized came from selling their produce or livestock, the result of collective work by the entire family.

The separation of the workplace from the home led to a recognition of the two as separate spheres; the conceptualization of public and private came about, and the family was classed as private life (Tronto, 1993). The result of this division was to cast women's role in the home, or private life, and men's role in the workplace, or public life. This had the effect of clearly delineating women's tasks in the home and sharply dividing what women's responsibilities were in contrast to men's. Stephanie Coontz (1988) notes that this trend occurred in all classes and ethnic groups in the United States except African Americans.

You can see the logic of blaming the division of labor for men's and women's differing worldviews. When people's occupations differ greatly, they tend to see the world in different ways. If your day is spent caring for children and the home, your experiences will vary a great deal from those of someone whose day is spent selling merchandise to others. Further, Sandra Bem (1993) argues that this initial division also created what she labels a **gender polarization** lens that caused people to see women and men as very different from each other. In 1909, Clara E. Hasse, a student at Milwaukee Downer Women's College, wrote a senior essay revealing how she looked through the lens of gender polarization. She wrote about the topic of single-sex schooling, saying, "It were far better not to class girls with boys while receiving their education, the most important reason being that they are so entirely different and therefore should be taught diversely" (p. 10). To the extent that we in the United States have subscribed to the notion that women and men are radically different from each other, we might expect that they have been treated differently. Different treatment should certainly result in different experiences.

As we have written elsewhere with Judy Pearson (Pearson, West, & Turner, 1995), "From birth it is clear that male and female babies are treated differently. . . . Male [infants] are more likely than female infants to be described as 'strong,' 'solid,' or 'independent.' Female infants, on the other hand, are often described as 'loving,' 'cute,' and 'sweet'" (p. 49). In Chapter 5, when we discussed Symbolic Interaction Theory, we commented on the power of other people's predictions on self-concept formation. We can see how males and females are treated differently and expected to do different activities. Even when women work outside the home, they are often still expected to take primary responsibility for the home and care for children or elderly parents as the need arises (Wood, 1994). Arlie Hochschild (1989) talks about the phenomenon of the **second shift**, where working mothers put in eight hours at their paid job and then come home to do a second shift there.

One study (Turner, 1992) asked respondents to describe situations that they believe are uniquely experienced by their own sex and for which, currently, no word exists and then to give those experiences a name. This was patterned after an activity Judy Pearson (1985) calls creating "genlets" or "sexlets." The results were not completely supportive of Muted Group Theory because men generated essentially the same number of "genlets" as women, indicating that language fails men as well as women.

However, the types of words created did differ between men and women. Men coined words concerned with drinking and competition, whereas women created words focusing on relationships and personal issues such as appearance. Women also noted experiences where they felt fearful or uncertain, and this concern was not included in the men's words. For instance, women coined the word *herdastudaphobia,* which meant feeling fear when passing a group of strange men on the street, and they created the word *piglabelphobia,* to designate a woman's tendency to limit what she eats in front of a date for fear of being labeled a pig. Women also coined the term *Brinkley-mirror,* to refer to the insecurity women feel at being compared to glamour models. Men created words such as *scarfaholic,* an eating contest among men; *gearheaditis,* an obsession with fixing up your car to have it be the best on the road; and *Schwarzenegger-syndrome,* working out overtime to build muscles bigger than the other guys'. Interestingly, when men focused on issues of eating and body building, their concern was competitive. When women addressed these same issues, their concern was for their own insecurities and their desire to please others. Thus, the assumption that men and women have different experiences was supported by these results. All of these instances support the first assumption of MGT: that women perceive the world differently from men because of women's and men's different experiences and activities rooted in the division of labor.

Male Dominance

The second assumption of Muted Group Theory goes beyond simply noting that women and men have different experiences. This assumption states that men are the dominant group, and their experiences are given preference over women's. Specifically, men are in charge of naming and labeling social life, and women's experiences are often unnamed as a result. Women then have difficulties talking about their experiences. For example, Kramarae (1981) tells the following story about a woman who attended a workshop on the topic of women as a muted group and spoke about a common problem she experienced with her husband:

> She and her husband, both working full-time outside the home, usually arrive home at about the same time. She would like him to share the dinner-making responsibilities but the job always falls upon her. Occasionally, he says, "I would be glad to make dinner. But you do it so much better than I." She was pleased to receive this compliment but as she found herself in the kitchen each time she realized that he was using a verbal strategy for which she had no word and thus had more difficulty identifying and bringing to his awareness. She told the people at the seminar, "I had to tell you the whole story to explain to you how he was using flattery to keep me in my female place." She said she needed a word to define the strategy, or a word to define the person who uses the strategy, a word which would be commonly understood by both women and men. (p. 7)

In this example, the woman had difficulty naming her experience although she knew something was occurring that she wished to talk about. In a similar fashion, Patricia Fitzpatrick from our opening vignette is experiencing problems speaking out in class, talking to the other students, speaking to her co-workers, and generally articulating her ideas. She is uncomfortable about her difficulties, and she is blaming herself because things are not working out as she planned.

Muted Group Theory takes a different perspective, however, noting that these problems are not the result of women's inadequacies but rather are caused by the unresponsiveness of the language women have to express themselves. MGT argues that any speaker would be inarticulate if there were no words to describe her or his thoughts.

Muted Group Theory asserts that men's political dominance allows their perceptions to be dominant. This forces alternative perceptions—those that women hold as a result of their different experiences—into a subordinate position. Women's communication is constrained because of this subordinate position. Dale Spender (1984) suggests that when people talk about sex and use the word *foreplay,* men's perspective is privileged. Most women would say that one of the things they like best about intimate contact is cuddling. Calling it "foreplay" relegates the activity to something of lesser importance than the "main event" of sexual intercourse. Spender argues that when women talk about sexual activity using language like "foreplay," they are not able to give full expression to their experience, and many times they do not even realize that language is separating them from their own sense of the experience.

Cindy Reuther and Gail Fairhurst (2000) discuss the "glass ceiling" for women in organizational hierarchies and comment on how (White) men's experiences dominate the world of work. They observe that patriarchal values tend to reproduce themselves in organizations to men's advantage. They note:

> The practices leading to the replication of white males in senior levels are based in ideology. In often subtle and unconscious ways (e.g., in language, dress, and work rituals), white women and men and women of color are pressured to commit to patriarchal and white interests and value systems. The upshot is that replication promotes conformity rather than a pluralistic system in which individuals can interact and work according to personal principles. (p. 242)

Overall, then, MGT assumes that men's, especially White men's, experiences are dominant and women and people of color need to subordinate their own experiences to the extent that they can in order to partake in social and organizational success.

Women's Translation Processes

The final assumption of Muted Group Theory speaks to the process of translation that women must go through in order to participate in social life. Women's task is to conceptualize a thought and then scan the vocabulary, which is really better suited to men's thinking, for the best words for encoding that thought. You can see how this renders women less fluent speakers than men. Tillie Olsen (1978), the author of *Silences,* says that although men are supposed to tell it straight, women have to "tell it slant" (p. 23).

The pauses that worry Patricia Fitzpatrick in our opening scenario are attributable, according to MGT, to this cumbersome process of translation that women have to engage in when speaking. Some researchers (Hayden, 1994) suggest that women's groups engage in a great deal of overlaps and simultaneous speaking because they are helping one another cope with a language system that is not well suited to their tasks. Thus, when women speak with one another, they collaborate on storytelling—not so much because women are collaborative by nature but rather because they need to help one another find the right words to encode their thoughts.

Some of the problems inherent in the translation process are highlighted by examining instances when women's words for experiences do become part of the general vocabulary. Before the 1970s, the term *sexual harassment* did not exist. Women who experienced what we now call sexual harassment had nothing to use for labeling their experiences. As Gloria Steinem has said, before the term was accepted into the vocabulary, women simply accepted harassment as part of life. For instance, Angie had a job in a library years ago, and her boss was a male who liked to comment on her figure and compare it to his wife's. At the time, Angie could only say that she had a bad job with a horrible boss. This lack of terminology makes the experience individual and minimizes the inappropriateness of the behavior in the workplace. Labeling it sexual harassment places it in a category, suggests some coping strategies, and points to its seriousness. Furthermore, giving the experience a term, *sexual harassment,* allows us to see that it exists broadly and is supported at many levels of society. Social change is possible when we recognize the phenomenon with a label. Similarly, the terms *date rape, marital rape,* and *stalking* all name crimes that without the labels might simply be seen as individual problems and not be recognized as serious offenses. Without these words, women faced silence when they wanted to talk about their experiences, and they were at a loss for instituting social change.

Marsha Houston and Cheris Kramarae (1991) point out that silencing can be accomplished *by* women as well, as can be seen by examining some talk between African American and European American women. Their observation is that silencing occurs not only through preventing talk but also by shaping and controlling the talk of others. When White women criticize African American women's talk as "confrontational," "the message to black women in white women's pejorative use of this term is, 'Talk like me, or I won't listen'" (p. 389). If subordinate group members hear this message and try to conform to it, their talk is slowed and disempowered. When Patricia Fitzpatrick, from our opening story, thinks about how her contributions sound and attempts to speak like the other students, she is hampered in her fluency.

The Process of Silencing

The central assertion of Muted Group Theory is that members of marginalized groups are silenced and rendered inarticulate as speakers. This silencing does not rely on explicit enforcement or coercion. As Robin Sheriff (2000) observes, silencing of muted groups is a socially shared phenomenon. "Unlike the activity of speech, which does not require more than a single actor, silence demands collaboration and the tacit communal understandings that such collaboration presupposes. Although it is contractual in nature, a critical feature of this type of silence is that it is both a consequence and an index of an unequal distribution of power" (p. 114). Thus, silence is accomplished through a social understanding of who holds the power and who does not (Gendrin, 2000). In this section we will briefly review a few of the methods used to accomplish this power distribution and resulting silencing. This is not an exhaustive list of methods of silencing. Perhaps you can think of other ways you have experienced or observed. Some researchers (Wall & Gannonleary, 1999) argue that understanding these processes is the most important contribution that MGT can make to communication research.

Ridicule

Houston and Kramarae (1991) point out that women's speech is trivialized. "Men label women's talk chattering, gossiping, nagging, whining, bitching (Cut the cackle!)" (p. 390). Men often say that women talk about meaningless things and claim that they cannot understand how women spend so much time on the phone talking to their girlfriends. Women themselves often refer to their own talk as gabbing or gossiping. Women are also told that they have no sense of humor, and this is an opportunity for ridicule. Also, women's concerns are often trivialized by men as not being important enough to listen to, yet women are expected to be supportive listeners for men. Even in the medical context, women report that their doctors may ridicule or trivialize their concerns (Brann & Mattson, 2004).

Ritual

Some people have pointed out that many social rituals have the effect of silencing women or advocating that women are subordinate to men. One such ritual is the wedding ceremony. There are a number of aspects in the traditional ceremony that silence the bride. First, the groom stands at the front while the bride is "delivered" to him on the arm of her father. The father then "gives her away" to the groom. Furthermore, the groom stands at the right hand of the minister (or whoever officiates), and this is traditionally a place of higher status than the bride's position, to the left. The groom says the vows first. The bride wears a veil and a white gown to indicate that she has been "preserved" for the groom. The groom is told at the end that he may kiss the bride. The couple is pronounced "man" and "wife," and traditionally, the bride changes her name to the groom's. In many services, the couple is introduced immediately after the vows as Mr. and Mrs. John Smith. In her (1981) book, Kramarae talks about the process she went through concerning her name changes. When she married, her husband's name was Kramer and her name upon marriage became Cheris Rae Kramer. At the time of her marriage, it was not legal for a wife to keep her own name. Later the laws changed, and Kramarae combined her husband's last name with her middle name and created her own name. This change was accomplished with a great deal of discussion and controversy, and many people questioned her judgment. Kramarae points out that no one questioned her

Research Notes

Brann, M., & Mattson, M. (2004). Reframing communication during gynecological exams: A feminist virtue ethic of care perspective. In P. M. Buzzanell, H. Sterk, & L. H. Turner (Eds.), *Gender in applied communication contexts* (pp. 147–168). Thousand Oaks, CA: Sage.

This study builds on the concept of voice that is critical to Muted Group Theory. The authors write the chapter to "give voice to women's concerns about gynecological exams" (p. 147). Brann and Mattson argue that the biomedical model obscures issues of gender and effectively silences women by making them marginal to issues of their own health.

To assist in reframing this model to be more responsive to women patients, the authors' study examined women's concerns about gynecological exams. Seventy-nine women completed a paper-and-pencil survey consisting of thirteen mainly open-ended questions, and returned it to the authors through the mail. The sample was relatively diverse with an age range from 18 to 71.

The authors coded the responses by themes and found that women reported several concerns, including discomfort, discovering pathology, and the communication climate that exists during the exam. Brann and Mattson used these data to advocate reframing the gynecological exam to respond to a feminist ethic of care. In revealing the voices of their respondents and suggesting changes based on their concerns, Brann and Mattson responded to the central concerns framed by Muted Group Theory.

Gendrin, D. M. (2000). Homeless women's inner voices: Friends or foes? In M. J. Hardman & A. Taylor (Eds.), *Hearing many voices* (pp. 203–219). Cresskill, NJ: Hampton Press.

Gendrin illustrates Muted Group Theory's concern with giving voice to marginalized groups. Gendrin examines intrapersonal communication (or the inner voices) of homeless women, observing that her study is "based on the notion that individuals experience some internal disequilibrium when they feel out of place with the larger social environment" (p. 206). Thus, the author asserts that homeless women are a group out of the mainstream and, as such, good candidates to be muted.

Over the course of one year, Gendrin contacted seventy-five residents at a women's shelter to participate in her study. The women were mainly single and had one or two children. They had been homeless between one month and eight years. The women responded to a questionnaire that was orally administered in an interview format. There were four different instruments in the questionnaire, including a survey of internal conversations, a measure of life satisfaction, a loneliness scale, and a relationship satisfaction scale. Of the seventy-five participants, thirty-five provided actual scripts of their internal dialogues.

Gendrin concludes that "homeless women's inner voices reflect longing for a happier past or a better future, talk of the pain of broken relationships, addiction, and abuse" (p. 214). Furthermore, she notes that these inner voices link the homeless women to their past and provide some continuity for them despite all the changes in their lives. The author argues that inner dialogues seem to help homeless women and provide them with some support.

husband throughout the entire process, and his name remained unchanged. Although many couples work to individualize the ceremony and have changed some of these aspects, the traditional ritual implies subordination of the bride.

Control

Researchers have noted that men control many decisions, such as what goes into history books, leaving women's history untapped (Smith, 1979). In addition,

Theory Into Practice
Ethan

When I started reading about Muted Group Theory, it really seemed wrong to me. I mean there are a lot of times I am not sure exactly how to put my thoughts into words and I'm a white, heterosexual guy, so I don't qualify for any of the muted groups that the book talks about. But when I read about that sexual harassment didn't have a name for a long time, it did make me think that maybe the theory had a point. I guess it would be pretty hard to talk about something if there were literally no word to describe it. And I can see how you'd think it was something that just happened to you and not some big thing that was going on with a lot of people if there were no words for it.

the media are controlled by men; women's talk and contributions get less coverage in mainstream media. Furthermore, many communication practices place men as central and women as eclipsed. For instance, men talk more than women in mixed-sex interactions despite conventional wisdom to the contrary. In an analysis of sixty-three previous studies examining U.S. men's and women's talk in a variety of contexts, men's talk time exceeded women's in sixty-one of the cases (James & Drackich, 1993).

A communication behavior that keeps men in control is interruptions. When men interrupt women, the women often switch to talk about whatever topic the men raise. When women interrupt men, this is usually not the case. Men frequently go back to what they originally were talking about (DeFrancisco, 1991). In addition, Victoria DeFrancisco has concluded that men often fail to attend to their partners' talk; they refuse to consider what the women are speaking about and shift the conversation to a topic of their preference (DeFrancisco, 1991).

Harassment

Elizabeth Kissling (1991) writes about street harassment, noting that women do not have free access to public streets. Men control public spaces in that women walking there may receive verbal threats (sometimes couched as compliments). Sexual harassment in the workplace is another method of telling women that they do not belong out of the domestic sphere. Mary Strine (1992) shows how some talk in universities naturalizes harassment, making it seem like an acceptable practice. When women who have experienced sexual harassment are labeled as hysterical, overly sensitive, or troublemakers, their concerns are dismissed and defined as unimportant (Buzzanell, 2004; Clair, 1993; Clason, 2008; Dougherty, 2001).

Strategies of Resistance

As we mentioned at the beginning of this chapter, Muted Group Theory is a critical theory; as such, it goes beyond explaining a phenomenon—such as women's muting—to advocating change in the status quo. Houston and

Kramarae (1991) offer several strategies for this purpose. One strategy of resistance consists of naming the strategies of silencing as we have suggested. Through this process, the silencing is made accessible and a topic for discussion. A second approach advocated by Houston and Kramarae is to reclaim, elevate, and celebrate "trivial" discourse. Houston and Kramarae mention that women are beginning to celebrate and study oral histories, diaries and journals, and the so-called alternative means of expression like sewing, weaving, and other handwork that is often done by women. Through examining these forums for expression, women are recognizing the "effectiveness, impact, and eloquence of women's communicative experiences as well as men's" (Foss & Foss, 1991, p. 21).

Women also are creating a new and more representative language to capture their experiences. Although changing the language is an ambitious task, language is malleable, and as new concepts enter our culture, new words are created to describe them. Think of all the words we now have to talk about computers and computer-mediated communication (itself a new term!). Suzette Elgin (1988) invented a whole language, which she calls Laadan, focusing on women's experiences. Kramarae and Paula Treichler (1985) compiled a feminist dictionary to give woman-centered definitions to words of importance in women's experiences.

Through naming strategies of silencing, reclaiming, elevating, and celebrating women's discourse, and creating new language for uniquely gendered experiences, muting can be resisted. In short, there are many approaches to changing the situation that MGT delineates and explains.

Integration, Critique, and Closing

Muted Group Theory has many adherents, but as you would expect with such a politically charged theory, it also has detractors. As you think about MGT, let's consider the criteria of utility and test of time as we evaluate the theory.

Integration

Communication Tradition	Rhetorical	**Semiotic**	Phenomenological	Cybernetic	Socio-Psychological	Socio-Cultural	**Critical**
Communication Context	Intrapersonal	Interpersonal	Small Group	Organizational	Public/Rhetorical	Mass/Media	**Cultural**
Approach to Knowing	Positivistic/Empirical	Interpretive/Hermeneutic	**Critical**

Critique

| Evaluation Criteria | Scope | Logical Consistency | Parsimony | **Utility** | Testability | Heurism | **Test of Time** |

T*I*P

Theory Into Practice

Victor

When I first read Muted Group Theory, I didn't like it. I felt like I was being blamed for something I didn't do. It's not my fault that some women don't speak up. But the more I thought about the arguments of the theory, the more it did make some sense to me. As a Black man in a predominately White university, I think I keep silent sometimes because I am not sure if what I have to say will fit with what the rest of the students are thinking. I know my perspective is a lot different, and I am not always willing to share that. The theory ought to talk about the ways that being a single member of a group in with a bunch of people from the dominant group doesn't only mute you. Sometimes it makes you talk in an uncomfortable way. Like in class when they all turn to me for the "Black opinion" about something or another. I really hate that.

Utility

First, like Standpoint Theory, Muted Group Theory has been criticized for not being useful because it engages in essentialism, or the belief that all men are essentially the same and all women are essentially the same and the two differ from each other. These critics note that there is great difference within groups; sometimes the difference within a group (such as women) can be greater than the difference between groups (women and men). Some theorists approach this from the perspective of other influences on communication besides gender, such as status, age, ethnicity, or upbringing. Others disavow the notion of influences altogether, claiming that both individuals and groups are constantly changing through communication. Therefore, any attempt to state unequivocally what women or men are like falsely "freezes" those groups in time, as if they have a natural, unchangeable essence.

Supporters of MGT agree that there are many groups that are muted and many standpoints. However, being female is to be part of a central group in our culture, and thus, even though women are not all alike and there is no essential womanness that all women possess, women in the United States are often treated alike. This treatment forms a common set of experiences that allows MGT to make generalizations about men and women.

Furthermore, some critics fault the usefulness of MGT because they note that women do speak out in public forums, and they point to women like Hillary Rodham Clinton and Condoleeza Rice as examples of women who are not muted at all. Muted Group theorists would agree that some women have gained a public forum, but they would also point out that they may have done so by becoming extremely adept at translation. Women who bring a uniquely female perspective to the table have not fared as well, according to these theorists. They argue that until we are able to hear from a wide diversity of voices rather than forcing all who wish to speak out to conform to a narrow range of options defined by the dominant group, we will still need the critical commentary of Muted Group Theory.

Test of Time

Some critics of MGT argue that the theory has not been sufficiently integrated into empirical research. Related to this notion is the fact that the theory was derived thirty years ago, and the theory's assumptions have not been updated. Should the theory's assumptions be discarded because the theory has not undergone refinement over the years? Proponents of the theory would respond to this charge of sustainability in two ways: First, more testing needs to be done, and second, a critical theory like MGT is not as conducive to hypothesis testing as some other theories are (for instance, Uncertainty Reduction Theory). The theory has been integrated into communication scholarship, but the extent to which it has withstood the test of time remains in question.

Certainly Muted Group Theory is provocative and causes us to think about biases in language. It also shines a light on what we accept and what we reject from speakers. MGT also explains some problems women experience in speaking out in many settings. It is up to us to decide if these issues form a systematic bias against subordinate groups and in favor of the dominant group, as Muted Group Theory asserts.

Discussion Starters

1. Do you think Muted Group Theory provides a good explanation for the difficulties in her classes and elsewhere faced by Patricia Fitzpatrick from our opening story? Why or why not? What other explanations might you offer to understand her situation?

2. Have you had the experience of fumbling for words to describe something that you were feeling or something that happened to you? Do you think Muted Group Theory explains that experience for you? Why or why not?

3. Can you coin terms for experiences that women have and men do not? What about the reverse? Do you agree with MGT that the English language fits the male experience of the world better than the female experience? Explain your answer.

4. We mentioned that one criticism of MGT is that it overstates the problem that women have with language. Do you agree or disagree with this criticism?

5. Have any of the reforms that are suggested by MGT taken hold in our language? Give examples of changes in the language that have made it more responsive to women's experiences.

6. What other social groups might be muted in the United States? Does MGT provide a good explanation for groups, other than women, who are silenced? Why or why not?

7. If MGT is a critical theory, what actions has it stimulated? How has it advocated for change?

Online Learning Center (www. mhhe.com/west4e)

Visit the Online Learning Center at www.mhhe.com/west4e for chapter-specific resources, such as story-into-theory and multiple-choice quizzes, as well as theory summaries and theory connection questions.

CHAPTER 29

Standpoint Theory

Based on the research of **Nancy C. M. Hartsock**

Angela Coburn and Latria Harris

Angela Coburn banged her books together and left class with a frown. She was really steaming. Usually she enjoyed her linguistics class and she liked Professor Townsend. But today she was upset and offended. Professor Townsend had explained the concepts of denotation and connotation by discussing a case that she had read about in the newspaper. The case concerned a European American aide to the mayor of Washington, D.C., who had lost his job for using the word *niggardly* in a meeting with two others, one European American and one African American. The aide had been explaining that he had very little money in the budget and so had to spend it sparingly. When Angela had read the report of this event, she had gasped out loud. As an African American, the sound of that word was extremely offensive to her. No matter that the aide said it meant "miserly"; she knew a racial slur when she heard one. She was older than most of the students at Mead University, and she remembered the civil rights struggles of the 1960s. Further, she knew that there was a lot of racism in the United States, even today. So Angela couldn't believe it when she heard Professor Townsend begin to tell the story of the aide in Washington to illustrate the lesson. There were racist students at Mead—even in class with her—and Angela felt that using that example sent the wrong message.

She was still fuming later that evening when she met Latria Harris at the coffee shop for their study group. Latria was also in Professor Townsend's linguistics class, and she and Angela studied together every Wednesday. Angela enjoyed their meetings; they helped her keep on top of the assignments for a challenging class, and it was nice to socialize with another African American woman at the university. Angela and Latria got along well despite the difference in their ages and circumstances. Angela was a 48-year-old mother of three grown children; her husband had left her many years ago, and she had raised the kids alone. She'd always struggled financially and had been on welfare for a few years; now things were looking up. She had begun her studies toward a B.A. six years ago, and she was hoping to finish this year. Latria was a 20-year-old single woman who had come to college straight from a college-prep high school, and her parents were quite wealthy.

As soon as Angela sat down, she burst out with her displeasure at Professor Townsend and the linguistics class. She spoke about how upset she was for some time until she noticed a blank look on Latria's face. "Don't you agree with me, Latria?" Angela asked.

"Well," Latria responded, "I saw how upset it made you, but I can't say that I felt the same. My family doesn't use that word, but it doesn't really bother me to hear it. I know a lot of people who use it. Also, I understood Townsend's point. The words sound alike but are defined completely differently. I guess Townsend was trying to say that people's connotations about the meaning of the one word may poison their responses to the other word."

Angela looked at Latria in silence for a while. Finally, she spoke: "Latria, I understand the point too. I just think a different example should have been used to illustrate it. Those words sound too much alike for me. And that's all some of the racists around here need to hear—a professor speaking a word like that. They will start to think it's okay to say such a thing. And it is not okay. No way. People have died because of that word."

Latria looked at Angela in some disbelief. "I know you're upset, but I think you are carrying this too far. I want to stand by you in this, but I just can't see it as such a big deal."

Angela and Latria fell silent, each pursuing her own thoughts. Finally, Angela said, "Girl, I guess we aren't going to agree about this. Maybe we should just get to studying this week's assignments." Angela smiled as she spoke and looked warmly at her friend, so Latria opened her book with relief. The last thing she wanted to do was to offend or disrespect Angela. Latria gave Angela a lot of credit for everything she had gone through and for how hard she worked at all her classes. Really, Angela was an inspiration to Latria. She grinned back at Angela as they began their work.

Standpoint Theory provides an entry point for understanding some of the dynamics that Angela and Latria experience as they talk about their linguistics course. Standpoint Theory provides a framework for understanding systems of power. This framework is built on knowledge generated from the everyday lives of people—acknowledging that individuals are active consumers of their own reality and that individuals' own perspectives are the most important sources of information about their experiences (Riger, 1992; Wood, 2007). Standpoint Theory gives authority to people's own voices.

The theory claims that people's experiences, knowledge, and communication behaviors are shaped in large part by the social groups to which they belong. Thus, insofar as Angela and Latria share membership in social groups, they may share a standpoint. The fact that they are both African American women makes their standpoints similar, but standpoints are always multiple, and their economic differences cause their standpoints to diverge. In addition, Standpoint Theory argues that there is no objective standard for measuring standpoints. Essentially, all statements, assertions, and theories must be understood as simply representing a subjective social location (Davis, 2008). Thus, Latria's position is valid in regard to her standpoint, whereas Angela's position is true to hers.

Everyday people, not the elite, provide the framework for Standpoint Theory because of the belief that they possess knowledge different from that of those in power. This knowledge forges standpoints in opposition to those in power. Standpoints come from resisting those in power and refusing to accept the way society defines their group (Wood, 2004). Standpoint Theory advocates criticizing the status quo because it is a power structure of dominance and oppression. Furthermore, in this critique are possibilities for "envisioning more just social practices" (Hartsock, 1997, p. 373). Thus, Standpoint Theory points to the problems in the social order and suggests new ways of organizing social life so that it will be more equitable and just. In this regard, the theory belongs to the class of theories we call critical theories (see Chapter 2).

Historical Foundations of Standpoint Theory

Although communication researchers have only recently begun to apply Standpoint Theory to studies of communication behavior (see, for example, Wood, 2008), it is a theoretical framework with a long history. In fact, although we are profiling the theory as conceptualized by Nancy Hartsock, she is only one of many researchers who have contributed to developing this theory.

Standpoint Theory's rich history begins in 1807, when the German philosopher Georg Wilhelm Friedrich Hegel discussed how the master–slave relationship engendered different standpoints in its participants. Hegel wrote that although slaves and masters live in a common society, their knowledge of that society is vastly different. These differences stem from the very different positions they occupy within the society. Hegel argued that there can be no single vision concerning social life. Each social group perceives a partial view of society. Karl Marx also claimed that the position of the worker (vis-à-vis class) shapes the worker's access to knowledge.

Nancy Hartsock drew on Hegel's ideas and Marxist theory to begin to adapt Standpoint Theory for use in examining relations between women and men. From her work with these ideas, Hartsock published "The Feminist Standpoint: Developing the Ground for a Specifically Feminist Historical Materialism." Hartsock was concerned with the debates regarding feminism and Marxism that occurred in the 1970s and early 1980s, focusing on the absence of women's issues in Marxist theory. Hartsock's interest was to "make women present" in Marx's theory and, in so doing, to forge a feminist-Marxist theory (Hartsock, 1997).

Hartsock is interested in expanding Marx's account to include all human activity rather than simply focusing on what was primarily male activity within capitalism. She focuses on Marx's claim that "a correct vision of class society is available from only one of the two major class positions in capitalist society" (Hartsock, 1983, p. 106). On the basis of this proposal, Hartsock observes, Marx developed a powerful critique of class structure. Hartsock suggests that it is Marx's critique of class relationships rather than his critique of capitalism that is most helpful to feminists.

Hartsock applies Hegel's concepts about masters and slaves and Marx's notions of class and capitalism to issues of sex (the biological categories of male and female) and gender (the behavioral categories of masculinity and femininity). This is a common adaptation of the theory, and consequently people sometimes refer to Standpoint Theory as Feminist Standpoint Theory, as Nancy Hartsock labeled it in 1983. In some ways this complicates matters because there is no consensus on the exact meaning of "feminist." Many authors have noted that there are different kinds of feminism (Cirksena & Cuklanz, 1992). For our purposes, we need to acknowledge this diversity, yet stipulate that the defining characteristic that unites all types of **feminism** is a focus on women's particular social position and a desire to end any suppression based on sex or gender.

This brings us to an interesting difference between this theory and many others in this book. In many ways, Standpoint Theory expresses and embodies

feminism
focusing on women's social position and desiring to end oppression based on gender

People are situated in specific social locations; they occupy different places in the social hierarchy based on their membership in social groups (poor, wealthy, men, women, European American, African American, Latino, uneducated, well educated, and so forth). Because of these social locations, individuals view the social situation from particular vantage points. Those vantage points formed in opposition to those in power, resisting the social definition given to them by those in power, become standpoints. No standpoint allows a person to view the entire social situation completely—all standpoints are partial—but people on the lower rungs of the social hierarchy do see more than their own position.

a critique of other mainstream theories and approaches to research. The critique lodged by Standpoint theorists begins with the observation that most research in the past has flowed from one common perspective: that of the White, middle-class male. Some feminist researchers argue that traditional approaches to research inquiry are male defined and block women's unique perspectives. Thus, the critique continues, this White, middle-class male perspective has served to silence any other perspective as a valued contributor to scientific knowledge (Chafetz, 1997).

This critique acknowledges that Feminist Standpoint Theory must begin by highlighting the relationship between power and knowledge. In doing so, "feminist standpoint theory tries to hold together two tensions: the search for better knowledge and the commitment to the idea that knowledge is always intertwined with issues of power and politics. As a consequence, the foundational tenet of feminist standpoint theory is that knowledge always arises in social locations and is structured by power relations" (O'Brien Hallstein, 2000, p. 3). In other words, Standpoint Theory begins with an imperfect epistemology, one devised by men in power, and seeks to develop a better epistemology, while recognizing that knowledge is not separable from politics.

It is important to keep in mind that although the feminist version of Standpoint Theory is the one that is commonly conceptualized, Standpoint Theory can be used to analyze a variety of standpoints, such as, for example, those that Angela and Latria bring to their conversation, based on race, class, and economic status. In this chapter, we explain the theory as Nancy Hartsock details it, applying its principles to women's particular standpoint. Yet it is wise to remember that a variety of standpoints, such as those provided by status, race, and so on, can be explained by the theory, which also lends itself well to application in other co-cultural groups: "Standpoint focuses on perspectives of women, but could also take the perspectives of African American women, poor white women/men, nonwhite women and men and individuals belonging to minority ethnic and religious groups outside modern Western society"

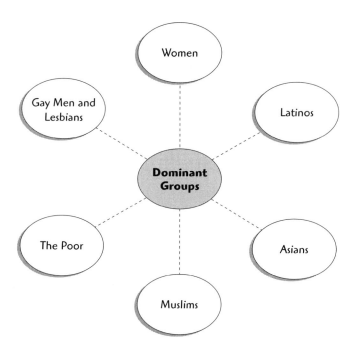

Figure 29.1
Relationship of Multiple Groups in U.S. Society
Source: Adapted from Wood (2004).

(Wallace & Wolf, 1995, p. 270). Other theorists, such as Etsuko Kinofuchi and Mark Orbe (2008), use Standpoint Theory to examine race and culture.

The social hierarchy is not fixed. There are continual struggles in society to determine which group is dominant and who has the right to speak for them and for others (Figure 29.1). The debate over undocumented immigrants being allowed to work in the U.S. reflects this struggle. Who has the right to "speak" on behalf of this population?

Assumptions of Standpoint Theory

Feminist Standpoint Theory rests first on a few general beliefs that Janet Saltzman Chafetz (1997) says characterize any feminist theory: (1) Sex or gender is a central focus for the theory; (2) sex or gender relations are viewed as problematic, and the theory seeks to understand how sex or gender is related to inequities and contradictions; (3) sex or gender relations are viewed as changeable; and (4) feminist theory can be used to challenge the status quo when the status quo debases or devalues women.

In addition, Standpoint Theory, as Hartsock conceptualizes it, rests on five specific assumptions about the nature of social life:

- Material life (or class position) structures and limits understandings of social relations.

- When material life is structured in two opposing ways for two different groups, the understanding of each will be an inversion of the other. When

Theory Into Practice

Connie

The idea that a rich person's idea of poverty is limited makes sense. I know when I started at the university, I made friends with a lot of girls who came from much wealthier families than I do. It was pretty hard to make them understand that I really had to work part-time and I couldn't afford to go out for pizza every other night. They kind of looked at me funny and I knew they thought I was just making excuses for not hanging out with them. I definitely felt like they did not understand where I was coming from at all. But I did see what their lives were like—or at least I thought I did.

there is a dominant and a subordinate group, the understanding of the dominant group will be both partial and harmful.

- The vision of the ruling group structures the material relations in which all groups are forced to participate.
- The vision available to an oppressed group represents struggle and an achievement.
- The potential understanding of the oppressed (the standpoint) makes visible the inhumanity of the existing relations among groups and moves us toward a better and more just world.

We will discuss each of these assumptions briefly. They are framed in the modified Marxist perspective that Hartsock favors.

The first assumption sets forth the notion that individuals' location in the class structure shapes and limits their understandings of social relations. Our chapter-opening story of Angela and Latria illustrates the power of one's location in society for shaping understanding. Because of Angela's standpoint, based on her difficult circumstances raising her children alone and struggling to finish her degree, and on her age, her response to the class discussion differs sharply from Latria's, whose class background and age have somewhat shielded her from the bitterness that influences Angela's viewpoint. In a simple example, a rich person's understanding of poverty is severely limited.

Second, Feminist Standpoint Theory assumes that all standpoints are partial, but those of the ruling class can actually harm those of the subordinate group. This point leads naturally to the third assumption, which asserts that the ruling group structures life in such a way as to remove some choices from the subordinate group. Hartsock comments that in the United States people have very little choice about participating in a market economy, which is the preferred mode for the ruling class. As Hartsock (1997) comments, the vision of the rulers structures social life and forces all parties to participate in this structure. "Truth is, to a large extent, what the dominant groups can make true; history is always written by the winners" (p. 96). Furthermore, the ruling class promotes propaganda that describes the market as beneficial and virtuous.

The fourth assumption asserts that the subordinate group has to struggle for their vision of social life. This leads to the final assumption, which claims that this struggle results in a clearer, more accurate vision for the subordinate group than that possessed by the ruling class. With this clear vision, the subordinate group can see the inherent inhumanity in the social order and can thus attempt to change the world for the better. This set of assumptions leads to the conclusion that although all standpoints are partial, the standpoint of an oppressed group is formed through careful attention to the dominant group. This isn't true in reverse. Thus, members of oppressed groups have a more complete standpoint than do members of dominant groups.

Added to these assumptions that characterize Hartsock's Marxist view of Standpoint Theory, most conceptions also embody a set of beliefs about knowledge and knowledge gathering.

- All knowledge is a product of social activity, and thus no knowledge can be truly objective.

- Cultural conditions "typically surrounding women's lives produce experiences and understandings that routinely differ from those produced by the conditions framing men's lives" (Wood, 1992, p. 14). These different understandings often produce distinct communication patterns.

- It is a worthwhile endeavor to understand the distinctive features of women's experience.

- We can only know women's experience by attending to women's interpretations of this experience.

The standpoint approach suggests both what is worth studying (ontology) and how to go about studying it (epistemology). First, the assertion is made that knowledge is not an objective concept but rather is shaped subjectively by knowers. This suggests an approach to knowing that is much different from that suggested by a belief in objective truth.

The second belief points to the different social locations that men and women inhabit in the United States even when they work and live in what seem to be similar situations. In a study examining sexual harassment in the workplace, Debbie Dougherty (2001) begins with a notion derived from ST that while sexual harassment may be dysfunctional for women, it may serve some functions for men. She used discussion groups and interviews with the employees of a large health-care organization and discovered that what women saw as dysfunctional and distressful behaviors, men interpreted as a form of coping behavior for work-related stressors, a mode of therapy, and a means for demonstrating camaraderie. Dougherty concludes that her findings indicate how different social locations have shaped men's and women's reactions to sexual harassment. Dougherty also discusses how managers can use this information to develop workshops that address how functions can be satisfied for men without providing distress for women in the organization.

The third belief deals with ontology, or what is worth knowing. This assumption places marginalized people (women) at the starting place for theorizing and research. This makes Standpoint Theory feminist and somewhat revolutionary by replacing the dominant standpoint with standpoints outside the cultural mainstream. Sandra Harding (1991) comments on this by saying, "What 'grounds' feminist standpoint theory is not women's experiences but the view from women's lives . . . we start our thought from the perspective of lives at the margins" (p. 269).

Finally, Standpoint Theory operates from the belief that the only way to achieve Harding's sentiment is by having women talk about their experiences and interpret them. The research participant is an active partner in the endeavor. It is a continuing goal for Feminist Standpoint theorists to develop new methodologies that give voice to those who have been silenced previously (Ford & Crabtree, 2002).

Through these assumptions and beliefs we get a picture of Standpoint Theory as an evolving framework, grounded in Marxism, but rejecting some of the central tenets of that perspective in favor of a feminist approach. Standpoint Theory seeks to understand the influence that a particular location exerts on people's views of the world and on their communication. In this quest, researchers in Standpoint Theory wish to begin with the marginalized and focus on their stories and interpretations. As Standpoint theorists work with research participants, they recognize the limited view of their own vision and they acknowledge the subjective nature of truth(s).

Key Concepts of Standpoint Theory

The theory rests on several key concepts: standpoint, situated knowledges, and sexual division of labor. We will discuss each concept in the next section.

Standpoint

standpoint
an achieved position based on a social location that lends an interpretative aspect to a person's life

The central concept of the theory, **standpoint,** is a location, shared by a group experiencing outsider status, within the social structure, that lends a particular kind of sense making to a person's lived experience. Furthermore, from Hartsock's perspective, "A standpoint is not simply an interested position (interpreted as bias) but is interested in the sense of being engaged" (1998, p. 107). The concept of engagement is amplified by researchers who distinguish between a standpoint and a perspective (Hirschmann, 1997; O'Brien Hallstein, 2000). As O'Brien Hallstein observes, it is easy to confuse the two, but there is a critical difference. A perspective is shaped by experiences that are structured by a person's place in the social hierarchy. A perspective may lead to the achievement of a standpoint but only through effort. As O'Brien Hallstein argues, standpoints are only achieved after thought, interaction, and struggle. Standpoints must be actively sought; they are not possessed by all people who have experienced oppression. Standpoints are achieved through experiences of

Research Notes

Dougherty, D. S. (2001). Sexual harassment as [dys]functional process: A feminist standpoint analysis. *Journal of Applied Communication Research, 29,* 372–402.

This study was undertaken to answer two research questions: (1) How do women and men discursively construct sexual harassment in organizations? and (2) How do men and women discursively reinforce and resist constructions of sexual harassment in organizations? To answer these questions, Dougherty conducted focus groups with employees in a large health-care organization.

Eleven women and twelve men with an average age of 38 years participated in three types of focus groups: all men, all women, and mixed sex. These focus groups were videotaped as they discussed sexual harassment in the workplace. After the group discussions, Dougherty held one-on-one interviews with the participants. They viewed the videotapes, and Dougherty asked each participant to elaborate on the discussion and contribute ideas and opinions that he or she may not have voiced in the group context.

These methods yielded 1,011 single-spaced pages of transcript data, which Dougherty subjected to thematic analysis. Among her conclusions were the notions that men and women operate from different standpoints and thus have developed different discursive practices and meanings for these practices around the topic of sexual harassment. Whereas men saw sexual harassment as sometimes functioning to develop workplace camaraderie, demonstrate caring, and provide stress reduction, women saw none of these functions. In fact, women found sexual harassment dysfunctional. Based on these differences, women and men actually talk about sexual harassment quite differently.

Ford, L. A., & Crabtree, R. D. (2002). Telling, re-telling and talking about telling: Disclosure and/as surviving incest. *Women's Studies in Communication, 25,* 53–87.

This study is autoethnographic: One of the authors (Crabtree) provides the story of her own incest experience to her friend (Ford), the other author. The authors note that "in this text we reflexively examine ourselves as subjects and objects, and through the dialogic form become both authors of our experience and audience to each other" (p. 54). They use Feminist Standpoint Theory to frame the study, giving its historical background and discussing the commonality–difference tension implicit in the theory.

Much of the article is written as a dialogue between the two researchers, recounting Crabtree's story and Ford's reactions. The article breaks another boundary by including some of the comments of the academic reviewer that the editor has chosen to review the piece for publication. The authors splice literature reviews throughout the dialogue where they add information to the personal narrative. Crabtree focuses on the telling and retelling her experiences; that is, she explains when and how and whom she chose to tell and what the results of the telling were.

The authors conclude by stating that they hope their dialogue "will become part of the larger disciplinary dialogue on power, ideology, research methods, feminist standpoint theory, disclosure, incest survivorship and other areas where ideas, values, and meaning are contested" (p. 84).

---

oppression added to active engagement, reflection, and recognition of the political implications of these experiences.

Furthermore, standpoints are not free of their social and political contexts. As Sandra Harding (1991) notes, "standpoints are socially mediated" (p. 276). Because standpoints are defined by specific social locations, they are by necessity **partial,** or incomplete. The location allows only a portion of social life to

partial
a recognition that no one has a complete view of the social hierarchy

Theory Application in Groups (TAG)

In small groups, discuss the difference between a standpoint and a perspective. Prepare a statement for the rest of the class that represents the group's consensus on that question.

be viewed by any particular group. In addition, the political aspect of standpoints stresses that individuals go through a developmental process in acquiring them. As Welton (1997) states, developing a standpoint requires "active, political resistance to work against the material embodiment of the perspective and experience of the dominant group. It is the act of having to push against the experience-made-reality of the hegemonic group, that makes it a political standpoint and potentially liberating" (p. 11). Moreover, as O'Brien Hallstein (1999, 2000) argues, standpoints are political because they are achieved in collaboration and dialogue with others rather than in isolation.

A specific type of standpoint is described by Patricia Hill Collins (1986, 1989, 1991) when she describes herself as an African American woman academic. This social position places her as an **outsider within,** or a person who normally would be marginalized but has somehow gained access to the inside. In the case of outsiders moving into a social location that historically excluded them, Collins suggests that a particular clarity of vision occurs. Ruth Frankenberg (1993) concurs, saying that "the oppressed can see with the greatest clarity, not only their own position but . . . indeed the shape of social systems as a whole" (p. 8) (see also work by Patton, 2004, for elaboration of the outsider within). This clarity of vision suggests, as Standpoint Theory argues, that the lower positions on the hierarchy possess the greatest accuracy in their standpoints, where **accuracy** refers to the ability to transcend the limits of partial vision and see beyond one's own specific social location.

outsider within
a person in a normally marginalized social position who has gained access to a more privileged location

accuracy
the ability to see more than what's available to one's own specific social location

situated knowledges
what anyone knows is grounded in context and circumstance

Situated Knowledges

Donna Haraway (1988) contributes the term **situated knowledges,** meaning that any person's knowledge is grounded in context and circumstances. Haraway's concept suggests that knowledges are multiple and are situated in experience. For example, what one person learns from her position as a caregiver for her ailing parents is different from the knowledge that another person develops from her position as an electrical engineer. The notion of situated knowledges reminds us that what we know and do is not innate but rather is the result of learning from our experiences. So if the engineer cared for elderly family members, she also would learn the caregiving knowledge. A similar point is made in discussions of Black feminist standpoints (Reynolds, 2002). Different local communities may define the standpoint somewhat differently depending on their experiences.

Sexual Division of Labor

Hartsock's Marxist-inspired Feminist Standpoint Theory rests on the notion that men and women engage in different occupations based on their sex, which results in a **sexual division of labor.** Not only does this division simply assign people to different tasks based on sex, but it also exploits women by demanding work without providing wages while making "women responsible for the unwaged maintenance and reproduction of the current and future labor force" (Chafetz, 1997, p. 104). Furthermore, the inequities that women suffer in the workplace when involved in labor for wages are linked to their responsibility for unwaged domestic work. In addition, as Nancy Hirschmann (1997) points out, a feminist standpoint "enables women to identify the activities they perform in the home as 'work' and 'labor,' productive of 'value,' rather than simply the necessary and essential byproducts of 'nature' or the function of biology which women 'passively' experience" (p. 81). Thus, Standpoint Theory highlights the exploitation and distortion that result when labor is divided by sex.

sexual division of labor
allocation of work on the basis of sex

Relationship to Communication

Standpoint Theory has become popular with communication researchers because it advances a reciprocal relationship with communication behavior and standpoints. Communication is responsible for shaping our standpoints to the extent that we learn our place in society through interaction with others. Thus, we can imagine that when Angela's mother told her stories about her African American heritage and about her ancestors who were slaves, Angela learned much about her standpoint. Every time a teacher told Angela that she probably could not go to college and receive a B.A. degree, communication shaped her standpoint. By the same token, Latria's standpoint was also shaped by communication, although the content may have been very different. Latria probably did not hear stories of slavery and may have been encouraged to go to college by her teachers. Thus, communication from others shaped different standpoints for the two women.

Similarly, one of the assumptions of the theory is that those who share a standpoint will also share certain communication styles and practices. Thus, for example, we expect that women who take care of children communicate in a maternal fashion, whereas men who are not responsible for such caregiving do not (Ruddick, 1989). Marsha Houston (1992) has cited the example of communication behaviors among African American women—like loud talking and interrupting—which are shaped by their standpoints and misunderstood by those outside the group. Houston points out that some European American researchers interpret these communication behaviors differently (and usually more negatively) than do members of the group themselves.

In addition, Roseann Mandziuk (2003) points out how communication, in the form of commemorative campaigns, may try to establish standpoints in public consciousness. Mandziuk analyzes three recent campaigns that sought to commemorate Sojourner Truth and observes how they competed for the right to establish her persona in public memory. As Mandziuk notes, each of the three campaigns set forth differing standpoints for Truth, and "the questions of location, character, and ownership variously occupied the center of the debates" (p. 287).

Standpoint Theory, therefore, illustrates the centrality of communication in both shaping and transmitting standpoints. The theory points to the use of communication as a tool for changing the status quo and producing change. By giving voice to those whose standpoints are infrequently heard (Buzzanell, 2004), the methods associated with the theory focus on communication practices. As Julia Wood (1992a) notes, "Whether women's own voices are granted legitimacy seems especially pertinent to communication scholars' assessments of the value of alternative theoretical positions" (p. 13). The concepts of voice, speaking out, and speaking for others are important to Standpoint Theory and Standpoint epistemology, and they are all concepts rooted in communication.

Integration, Critique, and Closing

Standpoint Theory, or Feminist Standpoint Theory, has generated a great deal of research, interest, and spirited controversy. As you examine the value of this theory, keep in mind one of the most critical of all evaluation criteria: Utility.

Integration

Communication Tradition	Rhetorical	Semiotic	Phenomenological	Cybernetic	Socio-Psychological	Socio-Cultural	**Critical**
Communication Context	Intrapersonal	Interpersonal	Small Group	Organizational	Public/Rhetorical	Mass/Media	**Cultural**
Approach to Knowing	Positivistic/Empirical	Interpretive/Hermeneutic	**Critical**

Critique

Evaluation Criteria	Scope	Logical Consistency	Parsimony	**Utility**	Testability	Heurism	Test of Time

Utility

essentialism
the belief that all women are essentially the same, all men are essentially the same, and the two differ from each other

The complaint most commonly leveled against Standpoint Theory revolves around essentialism, and a great deal has been written on this topic. As we discussed in Chapter 27 with reference to Muted Group Theory, **essentialism** refers to the practice of generalizing about all women (or any group) as though they were essentially the same. Essentialism obscures the diversity that exists among women. Our opening story of Angela and Latria illustrates the mistake we make if we engage in essentialism. Although they are both African American women attending the same university, the differences between them cause them to interpret the classroom discussion differently. Because Standpoint Theory focuses on the location of social groups, many researchers have argued that it is essentialist. For example, Catherine O'Leary (1997) argues that although Standpoint Theory has been helpful in reclaiming women's experiences as suitable research topics, it contains a problematic emphasis on the universality of this experience at the expense of differences among women's experiences.

Implicit (and often explicit) in this critique are the ways that many White women researchers have excluded the standpoints and voices of women of color, women who are disabled, lesbians, poor women, and women from developing nations (Collins, 1990). Yet this criticism may be unfair to Hartsock's conceptualization of the theory. Hartsock (1981) has stated that although there are many differences among women, she is pointing to specific aspects of women's experience that are shared by many: unpaid household labor and provision of caregiving and nurturance. Hirschmann (1997) argues that Feminist Standpoint Theory really does accommodate difference by allowing for a multiplicity of feminist standpoints. Hirschmann suggests that standpoints can be developed from Hartsock's framework that will bring a useful approach to the tension between shared identity and difference. Wood (1992a) concurs with this rebuttal, and she suggests that Standpoint Theory is different from essentialist views of women in one important way.

The theory does not suggest that men and women are fundamentally different (or have different essences); rather, ST begins with the assumption that social and cultural conditions that typically surround women's lives produce different experiences and understandings from the social and cultural conditions typically surrounding men's lives. Wood concludes, "There is nothing in the logic of standpoint epistemology that precludes analysis of the intersections among conditions that structure race, class, and gender relations in any given culture" (p. 14). Thus, Angela and Latria's conversation could be understood as a constellation of standpoints—some of which shape their experiences in a similar fashion and some of which cause them to diverge significantly.

More current studies conducted using a Standpoint framework have made the tension between difference and commonality central to their approach (Andrews, 2002). For example, Katrina Bell, Mark Orbe, Darlene Drummond, and Sakile Camara (2000) used Black Feminist Standpoint Theory to examine African American women's communication practices. Bell and her colleagues purposely collected information from very diverse women in an effort to capture different lived experiences. This resulted in a sample of women who shared a racial identity but differed in terms of many of their other social locations including age, religion, sexual identity, and so forth.

The researchers found that despite their diversity, the participants in their study did share a multiple consciousness of oppression as a result of racism, sexism, classism, and heterosexism. Yet the participants also voiced ways in which the issue of diversity existed among African American women. Throughout their data, the participants described other aspects of their identity that became salient in their interactions with others and in many instances impeded their

Theory Into Practice

Jennie

I thought Feminist Standpoint Theory was interesting, but I noticed that none of the examples referred to my specific social location. I am a Cherokee Indian, and I am very proud of my heritage. But it's certainly true that we Native Peoples are on the very bottom rungs of the social hierarchy. If anyone should have an accurate picture of the whole social structure by being on the bottom looking up, it'd be us. I guess there's always another "out" group to study. I also was thinking about the tensions between commonality and difference mentioned in the chapter. I know I get annoyed when White students assume that all Indians are the same and think that I know everything about the Crow or the Blackfeet, even though I am Cherokee and we have very different cultures.

sense of connection with African American women. As such, the researchers saw multiple consciousness as a "dynamic process of constant negotiation" (p. 50). Thus, the researchers conclude that Black Feminist Standpoint Theory allows for the assumption of commonality of oppression while acknowledging various expressions of this common experience.

In a study of academic women, Debbie Dougherty and Kathleen Krone (2000) also sought to apply Standpoint Theory to a group of diverse women to capitalize on the creative tensions between similarity and difference. They interviewed four women in the same department in an academic institution and from the interviews they created a narrative that, although fictional, attempted to capture the standpoints voiced in the interviews. Then they had the participants comment on the narrative and identify areas for change and develop action plans. In this process, the researchers found both commonality and difference among the standpoints of the participants.

The women agreed that their standpoints were shaped by a sense of isolation, a strong desire for community, and the feeling of invisibility. Yet they differed in their consciousness of their own oppression. However, rather than ignoring these differences or using them to divide themselves from one another, the women used differences to strengthen their relationship. The researchers note that the critique focused on essentialism may miss the point. Dougherty and Krone observe that "differences and similarities create and recreate each other, becoming so intertwined that they are difficult to separate" (p. 26).

A second area of criticism related to utility concerns the notion of dualisms, or dualistic thinking. Feminists (Cirksena & Cuklanz, 1992) note that much of Western thought is organized around a set of oppositions, or **dualisms.** Reason and emotion, public and private, and nature and culture are just a few of the pairs of opposites that are common organizing principles in Western thinking. Feminists have been concerned with these dualisms for two related reasons: First, dualisms usually imply a hierarchical relationship

dualisms
organizing things around pairs of opposites

between the terms, elevating one and devaluing the other. When we suggest that decisions should be made rationally, not emotionally, for example, we are showing that reason holds a higher value in our culture than does emotion. Related to this issue is the concern that these dualisms often become gendered in our culture. In this process, men are associated with one extreme and women with the other. In the case of reason and emotion, women are identified with emotion. Because our culture values emotion less than reason, women suffer from this association. Feminist critics are usually concerned with the fact that dualisms force false dichotomies onto women and men, failing to see that life is less either/or than both/and, as Relational Dialectics Theory (Chapter 12) holds.

O'Leary (1997) argues that Standpoint Theory does not present us with a sufficiently complex understanding of experience, and as a result, it still rests on a dualism between subjective experience and objective truth. O'Leary suggests that Hartsock's framework cannot accommodate the complexities of multiple knowledges. Yet Hartsock specifically allows for this very thing within her original theory, arguing for clusters of standpoints. Overall, as Hartsock (1997) notes, the controversies engendered by Standpoint Theory indicate a "fertile terrain" for debate and open the possibilities for expanding and refining the theory so that it is more responsive to diversity and clearer about the distinctions between subjectivity and objectivity.

In sum, Standpoint Theory presents us with another way of viewing the relative positions, experiences, and communication of various social groups. It has a clear political, critical bent, and it locates the place of power in social life. It has generated much controversy as people find it either offensive or compatible with their own views of social life. The theory may be compatible with other theories, enabling us to combine them to get more useful explanations for human communication behaviors.

Scholars need to continue refining Standpoint Theory, applying it to other co-cultural groups and resolving some of the issues of essentialism and dualism that critics have uncovered. Standpoint Theory holds much promise for illuminating differences in the communication behaviors of different social groups.

Discussion Starters

1. Do you accept the argument of Standpoint Theory that all standpoints are partial? Explain your answer. How does the case of Angela and Latria, from the beginning of the chapter, illustrate this claim?

2. Give an example of situated knowledges in a specific context.

3. The chapter identifies Standpoint Theory as a feminist theory. Discuss how a theory can be identified with a political ideology? Explain your answer.

4. If all truths are understood as coming from some subjective standpoint, how is it possible for people to communicate? If there is no

objective truth, how do we reach agreement among people with different standpoints?

5. What are the limits of difference that ground a standpoint? Might we eventually end up with standpoints that are so particular that only relatively few people share them? How would this help us to understand communication between and among people?

6. How well do you think more recent scholarship has done in incorporating the tension between sharing a common standpoint and recognizing differences? Give some examples.

7. Take a position on the essentialist argument relative to Standpoint Theory, and defend your position.

Online Learning Center   (www. mhhe.com/west4e)

Visit the Online Learning Center at www.mhhe.com/west4e for chapter-specific resources, such as story-into-theory and multiple-choice quizzes, as well as theory summaries and theory connection questions.

On the Horizon . . .

Chapter 30
Moving in New
Directions 519

WE CONCLUDE OUR BOOK WITH AN EXAMINA-
tion of how communication theory functions in our professional and personal lives. We hope that as you read this
material, you continue to realize that communication the-
ory is not esoteric nor unfamiliar. We hope that taking this course and reading this text
help you understand the links between being an everyday theorist and a professional
scholar.

We know that you may not be enrolled as a communication major nor do you
have plans to pursue this academic area of study. Nonetheless, the following information will be of some value to you as a consumer of theory and research. You have just
completed a challenging and important journey, and this final point along the way
asks you to think about the "theoretical horizon" in communication.

As we wrote this book, we imagined relating communication theory in an inviting
and practical way. We continue this goal in this final chapter by presenting some future
uses and applications of communication theory. We illustrate the usefulness of having
a background in communication in a number of different career paths. While reflecting on this material, keep in mind that we live in a world that requires theoretical
thinking. You now have the basic tools to work toward understanding communicating
with your self, in your relationships, and with others in the society in which you live.

Moving in New Directions

Laura Niles and Mike Salinsky

Laura Niles and Mike Salinsky hurried across campus to the Brew Bayou. They ordered lattes, sat down at their favorite table, and smiled at each other. They had been going for coffee together every Tuesday and Thursday after their Intro to Communication class, and this morning they had just finished the final exam.

"This is the mother of all coffee breaks today," Mike laughed. "I am so psyched to be finished with our first year! There were some days when I thought we'd never make it."

Laura laughed quietly, thinking of all she and Mike had been through since they started their first year at Milton College. It was hard to believe how much had happened in less than a year. Last summer, she and Mike hadn't even known each other and now they were so close. He was her best friend at school, and she really valued their friendship.

She looked over at Mike and asked, "How do you think you did on the Comm final?"

Mike put down his coffee and seemed to think seriously about the question. Then he smiled broadly and said, "I really think I did well . . . no, I *know* that I did well. But I'll be honest. A lot had to do with studying with you. You helped me focus on the important concepts and organize the material. It made a big difference. That question on the relationship of the self and communication was really a breeze after we covered Symbolic Interactionism, Uncertainty Reduction Theory,

and Standpoint Theory last week. I think I nailed that answer, thanks, of course, to our study session. How did you do?"

"I felt the same way," Laura said. "Studying with you always helps me, and this time we really focused on the right stuff. Because we went over that material on Expectancy Violations Theory, I think I really gave a good answer on that question about nonverbal communication."

Laura and Mike smiled at each other. "It feels great, doesn't it?" Mike asked.

"I agree," Laura nodded as she spoke. "Plus, I really think I learned a lot this term. Just look at us. I think I understand a lot more about us because of this theory class."

Mike put down his coffee and leaned over to Laura, saying, "Yeah, it sounds a little dumb, but when we talked about men and women's friendships, it did help me understand us . . . just a bit better. I have really never had a close female friend before you. And you already know that our friendship means a lot to me."

"I feel the same way. There were so many things we talked about in that class that applied to my life," Laura observed. "Remember that section on dialectics? That told me a lot about what I'm going through with my mother—that stuff on separation and closeness pretty much describes us to a T."

Laura and Mike grinned at each other, feeling pretty satisfied with themselves. "Now," Mike said, "the only problem will be getting some type of a job where we can use this stuff. My dad is still asking me what jobs I can get after graduation with a communication major."

"Yeah," Laura agreed. "We should go to the internship meeting at the beginning of next semester; I bet we can find some good job possibilities there."

"Great idea. Let's plan to do that. Meanwhile, we better finish this caffeine and get studying for our exam!"

As the two finished drinking their coffees and pulled their books together to leave, they both thought about how much fun this term had been. Who would have thought that theory would apply to them and to their lives?

Mike and Laura have taken a course like the one you are now finishing. Their comments reveal that they found the material involving and relevant. We hope you, too, have observed that communication is important. As a college student, it is estimated that you spend 75 percent of your day communicating, and this is expected to continue throughout your life (Morreale & Vogl, 1998). Communication skills are increasingly important in today's information age. New information technology continues to revolutionize the process of communication and affects how we engage in that process. You don't have to be a communication professional to know how important communication is to people's lives. An economics professor notes, "We are living in a communications revolution comparable to the invention of printing. . . . In an age of increasing talk, it's wiser talk we need most" (McCloskey, 1993, p. 12). Laura and Mike concluded that wiser talk is informed by theories about communication. We hope you agree.

We also hope that after reading this book you feel, like Mike and Laura, that you have gained an understanding of your own communication behaviors and how they affect important relationships in your life, as well as how the media influence us all. It is true that communication theory pervades our daily activities, and its application to everyday life and our careers cannot be overstated.

Still, like Mike and Laura, you might be wondering how a knowledge of communication theory and a major in communication might help you in securing a job. Although we, and other liberal arts experts, recognize that attaining a job is not the only goal of your college experience, we also know that it is necessary to consider future employment prospects to help you pay the bills! If you are a communication major, you may already be aware of the employment opportunities awaiting you. If you are not a communication major, you should know that a communication degree provides an excellent background for a wide variety of jobs.

The theories covered in this text offer rich possibilities for application in both work and leisure activities. We should try to engage in "practicing theory." Sandra Petronio (1999) agrees, observing that we need to seize the opportunity to translate scholarly ideas into practical applications.

To conclude our text on communication theory, we wish to do the following: (1) Identify some prominent areas that are on the theoretical horizon; (2) suggest career paths for those with a communication degree; and (3) propose

Calvin and Hobbes

by Bill Watterson

tips for seeking that career using your degree. In short, we want to study for your final exam with you—both the actual final you may take in this class and the lifelong final you take when you apply what you learned in a meaningful way outside the classroom. We expect that the issues you have learned in this class will continue to apply to your daily lives long after you take the final exam at the end of the term.

It's clear that as a society, and as this text implies, the United States recognizes the value of communication. Communication skills relate directly to getting a job (DuBrin, 2007) and in 2008 the National Association of Colleges and Employers (www.naceweb.org) reported that communication skills rank in the top three skills employers look for in new hires in nearly all professions. Finally, learning about communication helps us to improve our lives physically, emotionally, and psychologically (e.g., Helpguide.org, 2008). With over 12 million hits from a Google search of "value of communication in life," people within (and outside of) the United States continue to place a premium on the importance of communication.

Thinking About the Future

Throughout this book, we have introduced you to theoretical thinking and the application of this thinking to research questions investigating the communication process. We have profiled many specific theories about communication and illustrated how they affect our understanding of communication processes. And although it is our contention that these theories help you to achieve "wiser talk," no one theory we have discussed reveals everything there is to know about communication in all its complexities. As we pointed out in Chapter 3, theory is like a lens that focuses your attention on some areas of communication. Yet, in so doing, it also blinds you to other areas that are outside the parameters of the lens. Furthermore, this lens of theory points to what we value as researchers and as a society—for example, open and disclosive communication, developing relationships, disseminating information, and individual

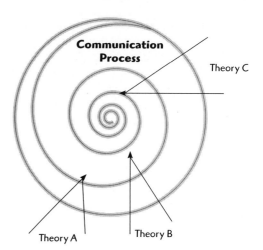

Figure 30.1
How Theory Acts as a Lens

effects on communication behaviors. In concentrating on these values, we often ignore other communication practices that are not valued by us, even though they may occur frequently in our interactions—for example, deception, short-term relationships, computer-mediated communication, and destructive communication (Figure 30.1).

Focusing is inevitable, and in many ways it is a useful process. Without focusing, we cannot understand the nuances of a particular phenomenon. Putting some aspects of the communication process under the microscope, so to speak, allows for a fine-grained picture of those aspects. If we try to see everything at once, our vision is too cluttered, and we cannot concentrate sufficiently on the details.

It is also the case, however, that blocking out some things so that we can concentrate on others may lead to bias and inaccurate or oversimplified thinking. We may be overlooking extremely important parts of the process that would change our perspective completely if we only moved or widened our lens slightly. Recall the old story of the blind men examining an elephant. Each man only examines one small part of the elephant and thus gets a distorted impression of what an elephant is like. The man who feels the tail, for instance, says an elephant is like a rope, whereas the man who feels the tusk thinks an elephant is like a sword. It is our argument that several trends in modern life compel us to examine communication in somewhat different ways than theorists have done in the past.

It is clear how important and relevant communication is in our lives. Thus, it is critical that we continue to think in meaningful ways about the communication process. We must continue to widen and change our lenses to understand what we focus on and what we leave out. When researchers study areas that we once took for granted, new insights are gained. For instance, researchers have already begun to study the effects of new technology on the teaching–learning process (Leeman, 2007). One result of this sort of research is the ability for colleges and universities to determine whether teaching online courses is in the best interests of the school, teacher, and student. This information is an important beginning in unraveling the complexities of electronic teaching. Thus, when we observe that technology is changing interpersonal relationships (such as those found on Facebook profiles), we necessarily expand that discussion to include looking at the role of technology in the classroom.

We believe that four themes suggest important trends for the future of our culture and will affect our future and help us refocus: technology, work and family life, aging and health, and culture and identity. As we reviewed the theories in this book, we discovered areas where cultural change and development have left gaps. There are issues that our theories do not explain. We suggest that these changes call for new theoretical thinking. When issues of equality between women and men became critical in our culture, feminists promoted theoretical thinking like Standpoint Theory and Muted Group Theory to help us explain these issues. In the same way, now that we have entered the twenty-first century, we need to move in new directions theoretically. Although the theories we have reviewed in this book explain a great deal about communication, some developments in our social life cry out for new thinking to aid our understanding. The four themes we have listed provide a starting place for this new thinking. We will review each of the themes briefly, suggesting how they may have an impact on our daily lives and on our theoretical thinking.

Technology

The theme of technology is inescapable for anyone living today. Every day we are bombarded with messages from various technological innovations ranging from our telephones (cell or standard) to our computers, televisions, and fax machines. The use of technology is not limited to the young, who are growing up in a world pervaded by technological innovations. For instance, Daniel Kadlec (2007) notes that among adults over 50, 54 percent use the Internet, retired people spend an average of nine hours online, and that this level of activity peaks around the age of 70. He refers to this population as "senior netizens" (p. 94).

The boundaries between interpersonal communication and computers are not clear-cut. The two often overlap, as the subfield computer-mediated communication (CMC) demonstrates. The fact that interpersonal communication and mass communication cannot always be viewed as separate contexts has implications for our theorizing. For example, when we think about a theory like Relational Dialectics Theory (Chapter 12), we are directed to think about people in face-to-face relationships. The salience of closeness and distance as a pervasive tension seems most applicable when you think of dating partners, spouses, or parents and children. That dialectic may not be as relevant in a relationship that is conducted online. The mediated nature of the relationship may necessitate a new theory to describe it (Tong, Van Der Heide, Langwell, and Walther, 2008).

When we consider a theory like Social Penetration Theory (Chapter 10), we are reminded of one of the biases that Martin Lea and Russell Spears (1995) point out: the idea that relationships move from one point to another. As Lea and Spears note, the metaphor of movement is pervasive in our theories about relationship development. The very name Social Penetration connotes the move from a surface level to deeper and deeper levels of intimacy. Yet, as the writers suggest, this metaphor may preclude our study of CMC, which occurs outside the realm of movement as described by Social Penetration Theory. We need other theories to help us understand what happens in online relationships.

Some researchers note that we are no longer a nation of readers. Instead, people get most of their information from interactive media or from television. This has had serious implications for newspapers as well as for interpersonal communication patterns. Furthermore, news outlets have the capacity to create electronic newspapers specifically tailored to individual needs and interests. Marketers are already capable of targeting specific individuals and of sending ads that deal with products they are likely to buy. If you use Amazon.com, for example, the company probably knows more about your reading habits than you do yourself.

With all these individualized, targeted media abounding, what will hold us together as a community? Years ago, the television set served as a focal point for families to gather around and come together. When a television episode of *All in the Family, The Cosby Show, Seinfeld,* or *60 Minutes* was aired, the episode was talked about the next morning at breakfast, at the office, or at the gym.

Today, however, different technologies have caused our society to redefine what it means to be a community. Many of our theories of mass communication presume that the same messages are reaching the masses. In the technological world of tomorrow, that may not be the case. Technological changes and innovations change our communication behaviors and may even change the process of communication. New theoretical developments in CMC have been enlightening. For instance, Joseph Walther and his colleagues (e.g., Westerman, Van Der Heide, Klein, and Walther, 2008) have been instrumental in advancing our knowledge of how CMC influences interpersonal relationships. This line of research continues and will be informative as our culture continues to grapple with the role of technology in our personal and professional lives.

On the other hand, we may not be as different in our use of new technologies as some have predicted. Carole Blair (2006) comments that the particular type of technology may change but that the process of using it to communicate may not be all that different. She notes that even the narrative traditions of oral societies may constitute a technology, using that term broadly. Blair's argument is that "communication depends upon material supports or technologies. That is, we make use of various 'technologies'—understood broadly—to communicate with others: e.g., language, ritual behavior, visual symbols, electronic or virtual media, and so forth" (p. 55). Regardless of whether new technologies constitute a communication revolution or simply an evolution, we will need to examine our theories to see how well they explain questions of communication technologies.

Work and Family Life

A second trend in our society involves increased pressures to balance work and home, or family life. Many companies are seeking ways to assist employees with the difficult task of juggling a lot of different stressors. Consequently, even in a poor economic climate, companies are instituting perks for their employees, such as in-house services like laundries and child-care centers. These steps help employees manage the ever-increasing demands of home and work (Medved, 2007). As Christena E. Nippert-Eng (1996) points out, the way we divide life and erect boundaries is socially constructed. Boundaries are arbitrary, cultural distinctions. One of the important boundaries constructed in Western culture has been that between home and work. Yet, in today's culture, we see more interplay between these two categories. Consider, for instance, how many people are working from their homes or how many families now homeschool their children (Edley, 2004; Kirby, Golden, Medved, Jorgensen, & Buzzanell, 2003).

Although in many ways the blurring of these boundaries may be helpful, it is confusing as well. In times of confusion, we can turn to theory for guidance. As we noted in this book, communication theories on organizational life are often quite separate from those that explain relational life. Yet, as people spend more and more time on the job, many important relationships contain elements of both work life and social life. As Theodore Zorn (1995) observes, we know very little about the dynamics of friendship at work. This is especially the case, Zorn notes, when the personal relationship involves people at different hierarchical work levels. When a boss is an employee's friend or is romantically linked with a subordinate, what theories explain the development of their relationship? Although romantic ties between a supervisor and a subordinate have been broadly discussed, these relationships can vary tremendously from one organization to another and from one individual relationship to another. Again, we need theories to begin to explain our experiences in these situations.

People's experience of work has changed over time (Soterin, Buzzanell, & Turner, 2007). It is now rare for people to stay with one organization for their entire work life. Thus, the number of workplace relationships has increased tremendously, and we need to pay attention to this phenomenon to help us understand our interactions. As people move to different workplaces, they experience different organizational climates and cultures. Some companies may consider themselves a "family" and thus foster interpersonal ties among their employees. Other companies may have a more formal approach and may discourage personal relationships among employees. Theoretical thinking can be helpful in sorting out these differences.

Communication is a process that both maintains and integrates the boundary between work and family. For example, when we speak differently at work and at home, we use talk to maintain a distance between the two realms. Think about the vocabulary you use with your family and with your co-workers. Often we may be more formal at work, or we may use work-related jargon on the job. Yet this is not always the case. Nippert-Eng (1996) writes about a son who took a summer job working for his father. The son, Kim, saw and heard a different side of his father while at work: ". . . his father's style of talk was not only chock full of expletives at work but . . . these were often hurled in red-faced, yelling fits at his subordinates" (p. 77). The all-male, blue collar industrial environment promoted a side of his dad that Kim had never fathomed. Theories are needed to explain the processes of separating and integrating work and family.

In addition, Nippert-Eng comments that "cross-realm talk," or talk that functions to integrate the two areas of life, is important. As we spend more and more time working, we deprive our families of a communication resource if we do not engage in cross-realm talk. The same is true, to a lesser extent perhaps, in the workplace. Nippert-Eng points out that our personal lives and problems do not disappear when we go to work. Co-workers who are also personal friends can provide needed support. Communication scholars, including Erika Kirby and Kathleen Krone (2002), Annis Golden (2000), and Caryn Medved (2007) have begun examining the work–family relationship and the communication surrounding this delicate balance in life. We can expect to read about further theoretical developments in this area over the next few years.

Aging and Health

As medical advances help our population live longer, we are confronting more issues of aging. According to the U.S. Census Bureau (www.census.gov), the population of those 65 and older will grow from 34 million to 82 million in 2050, a 135 percent increase. In 2030, the number of seniors over the age of 65 will constitute nearly 20 percent of the entire population of the United States. This brings to the forefront issues of coping with age and diseases of the elderly. General health-care concerns and life-threatening diseases have created new communication challenges.

Many theories in communication tend to center on youthful relationships: dating, early marriage, and parenting of young and adolescent children. The discipline does not have many theories that address marriages that have lasted for fifty years, parents communicating with adult children, or older family members who require at-home care. What occurs, for instance, when an elderly parent is taken into an adult child's home? What effects are there on the family? On the senior? What support systems will help offset communication difficulties?

Communication professionals have applied existing theoretical thinking to problems of aging and health care. For example, some research has examined physician–patient communication, specifically medical interviews, through the prism of the Narrative Paradigm (Chapter 20). In these studies (Sharf, 1990; Sharf & Poirier, 1988), researchers reported that doctors and patients did not find that each other's stories fulfilled the criteria for a good story. The authors conclude that a narrative-based training program for health-care professionals would improve the quality and the experience of medical interviews for both patients and physicians. To further demonstrate the need to understand health-related issues in our society, consider the words of Barron Lerner, a physician who worked with Catherine, a colleague/patient with a highly aggressive form of cancer. Lerner (2002) thoughtfully relates a story that showed Catherine's health deteriorating:

> Catherine soon announced that she was tired. We hugged and I said goodbye. She died the the next day. I will always remember my last encounter with Catherine as one of the greatest privileges I have had as a doctor, and as a friend. Displaying unbelievable dignity and grace, Catherine taught us how patients cope with severe illness. And she taught us how we should care for patients. We should be frank, attentive, and patient. Most important, we should not emotionally distance ourselves from the sick. (p. D4)

This example illustrates the importance of applying theoretical thinking to practical problems. Ethical questions abound when we have the medical technology to prolong life, clone life, and create life. In fact, Matthew Kreuter, David Farrell, Laura Olevitch, and Laura Brennan (2000) explore the confluence of health, humans, and technology. They found that human communication experts now have a number of nonprint technologies (e.g., interactive computer kiosks, video games, Internet sites) at their disposal to get health-oriented messages across to various populations (seniors, infants, caretakers, and so forth).

Aging and health issues will preoccupy communication researchers for some time to come. Scholars such as Dawn Braithwaite and Teresa Thompson (2000) have already begun an ambitious undertaking to understand one area related to health communication better: disability. They have called for more theoretical thinking in the area of communication and disability, from perceptions of people with disabilities in the media to how disability issues are dealt with in the classroom. Their work has inspired other scholars to work toward developing a conceptual framework related to a pressing health-related topic in the twenty-first century.

Culture and Identity

As our society becomes increasingly diverse in terms of race and ethnicity, issues of culture and identity become important. Researchers have called for inclusion of diversity in definitions of family (Turner & West, 2006), in dating relationships (Houston & Schwartz, 1995), and in politics (Sullivan & Turner, 1996). Yet so much more attention is needed on the issues of cultural and racial diversity. How do we need to change our current institutional structures to embrace a more diverse society? How do we address issues of language and cultural values as the workforce becomes increasingly diverse? New theories such as Co-Cultural Communication Theory (Orbe, 1998) are being tested and are beginning to be embraced by scholars to understand culture, identity, and community.

Furthermore, as Tsukasa Nishida (1996) points out, "In order to understand the communication behaviors of any culture, it is important to examine them in light of communication theories that have developed within the culture itself" (pp. 102–103). Nishida's point rests on the problems of cultural ethnocentrism that arise when the proponents of a theory do not have the same values as the culture to which they are applying the theory. Thus, cultural sensitivity and awareness are critically important considerations for future theorizing about communication in various cultures.

Stella Ting-Toomey and Leeva Chung (1996) point out that identity is a meaningful issue for future theorizing in communication. They note that given the large number of marriages across cultures in the United States, several questions become salient. They ask, "How do members from two contrastive groups negotiate their identity differences? How do the offspring of intergroup marriages conceptualize their cultural identities? How do these identities affect their interpersonal relationship development patterns?" (p. 255). They observe that gender and ethnic identity issues need more conceptual frameworks. They ask, "How do we know when gender and/or ethnicity will be salient when a person constructs his or her identity?" What are the conditions that prompt someone to identify himself as a 45-year-old European American male college professor rather than an adventurous, fun-loving, risk-taking man, for example? Theoretical thinking will help us find answers to these important questions about culture and identity.

Thinking About Career Opportunities

We can also apply our theoretical knowledge to career options. It's important to clarify that our emphasis on applying theoretical thinking to the world of work does not indicate that we believe that education is the same as vocational training. Far from it. A college education is much more than training for one specific job, as we hope you agree. Instead, understanding the process of communication and the ability to think critically about the process enables you to live a fuller life as well as to be better at whatever you eventually decide to do for your career. We certainly believe, however, that many careers await people who have the skills and critical tools that you are acquiring. For an example of various careers related to communication, in particular, see Table 30.1.

We have identified several important areas that you should consider in your career opportunities. Remember, however, that this list should not be viewed as a substitute for your own efforts; planning and strategizing a career in communication should begin as you enter college. You can learn the "rules of the job game" throughout your academic career. Although these suggestions are aimed at those who are communication majors, they are also applicable for nearly every other major on a college or university campus.

Remain Ethical

Without doubt, your ethics will always be challenged at work. In fact, beginning in 2002, a large number of corporate scandals challenged the bedrock of ethical principles in the United States. As we mentioned in Chapter 1, stay focused on what is right and wrong while at work. Be honest with yourself.

Table 30.1 Careers Related to Communication

FIELDS	CAREERS	RELATED COURSES
Advertising	Copy writer, media planner, advertising specialist, media sales representative	Persuasion, advertising and society, mass media, media production, small group communication, communication theory, ethics, listening
Communication Education	High school speech teacher, debate coach, college or university professor, language arts coordinator, communication curriculum specialist	Oral interpretation, public speaking, interpersonal communication, research methods in communication, cross-cultural communication, communication theory, ethics, listening
Electronic and New Media	Broadcasting station manager, director of broadcasting, film editor, news director, technical director, actor, news anchor, announcer, researcher	Public speaking, interpersonal communication, mass communication, media research, media theory, media criticism, studio and field production, media ethics, visual communication, listening, organizational communication
Journalism	Reporter, editor, copy writer, script writer, news service researcher, technical writer	Public speaking, media theory, media research, print journalism, media ethics, visual communication, listening
Public Relations	Publicity manager, press agent, corporate public affairs specialist, fund raiser, media analyst, researcher	Business and professional communication, public speaking, interpersonal communication, media theory, media research, ethics, listening
Business	Sales representative, manager, negotiator, customer service representative, communication trainer, human resources manager	Public speaking, business and professional communication, interpersonal communication, organizational communication, managerial communication, small group communication, interviewing, ethics, listening
Health Care	Health educator, medical grants writer, hospital director of communication, hospice manager, health-care counselor, medical training supervisor	Health communication, interpersonal communication, ethics, public relations, conflict and communication, family communication, communication theory, research methods, listening
International Relations	Corporate representative, translator, student tour coordinator, diplomat, foreign relations officer, foreign correspondent	Intercultural communication, international communication, nonverbal communication, communication theory, research methods, ethics, conflict and communication, political communication, persuasion, listening
Law	Public defender, corporate attorney, public interest attorney, legal secretary, paralegal, legal reporter, law professor, arbitrator	Public speaking, interpersonal communication, media law, legal communication, argumentation and debate, persuasion, listening, small group communication, conflict and communication, ethics, communication theory
Social and Human Services	Public administrator, social worker, recreational supervisor, human rights officer, counselor, religious leader	Public speaking, interpersonal communication, family communication, listening, small group communication, ethics, communication theory, conflict and communication

Table 30.2 Principles of Ethical Communication

- We advocate truthfulness, accuracy, honesty, and reason as essential to the integrity of communication.
- We endorse freedom of expression, diversity of perspective, and tolerance of dissent to achieve the informed and responsible decision making fundamental to a civil society.
- We strive to understand and respect other communicators before evaluating and responding to their messages.
- We promote access to communication resources and opportunities as necessary to fulfill human potential and contribute to the well-being of families, communities, and society.
- We promote communication climates of caring and mutual understanding that respect the unique needs and characteristics of individual communicators.
- We condemn communication that degrades individuals and humanity through distortion, intimidation, coercion, and violence and through the expression of intolerance and hatred.
- We are committed to the courageous expression of personal convictions in pursuit of fairness and justice.
- We advocate sharing information, opinions, and feelings when facing significant choices while also respecting privacy and confidentiality.
- We accept responsibility for the short- and long-term consequences of our own communication and expect the same of others.

Source: National Communication Association (www.natcom.org).

Work toward producing the best product, whether working by yourself, with a supervisor, or with a team of colleagues. Perhaps ethics is best summed up with the following question: Are you doing your very best? We have provided a doctrine of ethical beliefs articulated by the National Communication Association (Table 30.2). Examine these and construct your own ethical principles. Remember, ethical questions surround us each day. Being ethical is the most important characteristic of being human.

Be Flexible

As you enter the workforce, you will need to be flexible about working either independently or with a team. You will also be required to work in various office environments, which means that you will have to adjust to the people and the context. Being flexible does not mean being uncommitted. Flexibility suggests that to be successful at work, you should be willing to take on new jobs, work with difficult people, hone new skills, and respond to circumstances that may seem ridiculous. The workplace, like the college classroom, can be quite unpredictable, and being flexible in response to this unpredictability will give you an edge over others.

Embrace Diversity

We have already mentioned that the United States is more culturally diverse than ever. This fact should not only be acknowledged but dealt with directly. As consumers in and of the global village that McLuhan (Chapter 25) talked about, we have no choice but to work toward understanding people who are different from us. We must welcome the diversity that is currently part of the fabric of the United States and of the world. Simply admitting that the world is diverse is insufficient. We must work toward understanding that diversity. We might do this by reading, volunteering in agencies that assist diverse populations, or cultivating respect for the language, customs, and traditions of various racial, ethnic, and religious groups. We might also review the history of the United States to understand those groups who have been disparaged, marginalized, oppressed, and overlooked. As you can see, embracing diversity involves more than realizing that the world is filled with different kinds of people.

Cultivate New Technologies

Like diversity, new technologies will remain part of the U.S. landscape forever. Years ago, merely being able to type sixty words per minute was sufficient for job security. Now, of course, the technological vista is vastly different. Most jobs require some sort of technological know-how. Computer-aided design and computer-assisted systems tie all work environments together. Cell phones, beepers, interactive television, podcasting, and social networking sites such as MySpace, Friendster, and Facebook are also important to technological understanding. Whether you find yourself gathering, creating, sorting, storing, or distributing information, technology will be present. Being able to work with new technologies, even some you are presently unfamiliar with, will be the hallmark of a lasting employee.

Yet, as we mention technological competency, we are aware of the variations in computer usage and technological availability. For instance, not all people in the United States have Internet access nor do they use the Internet consistently. In fact, CNET news (2008) reports that "the digital divide is apparently alive and well" (p. 1). A survey reported by CNET indicates that about 20 million homes, or 18 percent, are without access to the Internet. More specific numbers reported by the Internet and American Life Project of the Pew Research Center show a disparity among various age groups. For instance, the Pew Foundation (2008) notes the following percentages of Internet use:

18–29:	91%
30–49:	86%
50–64:	74%
65+:	38%

In addition, some variability exists with educational attainment:

Less than high school:	38%
High school:	66%
Some college:	87%
College + :	95%

Finally, further evidence of the digital divide is apparent by examining Pew's survey of household income:

Less than $30,000:	56%
$30,000–49,000:	79%
$50,000–74,000:	92%
$75,000+:	95%

As you can see, there are some important differences among people. There may be a host of issues and variables that influence these variations. Nonetheless, we need to caution ourselves against thinking that everyone in the country uses the Internet the same way.

Maintain Creativity

There is a saying in the corporate world that, too often, people can't "think out of the box." At the core of this saying is the inability to think creatively. Too often, we are unable or refuse to color outside the lines. Alexander Hiam in *The Futurist* (1998) reports that "visual thinking" can be a valuable way of looking at a problem. He continues:

> Draw a diagram or picture of the problem you're working on, or think up visual analogies by asking yourself to name 10 things that the problem looks like. Then seek ways of generating fresh perspectives by analyzing these images: Ask yourself why the problem looks like that thing. (p. 33)

Try using visual thinking in your college life as well. You will be surprised to discover what Hiam concludes: "It pays to discuss not just *what* you think but *how* you think" (p. 33).

Don't Forget Basic Skills

There is no doubt that although society continues to evolve, the need to sharpen basic skills in reading, writing, listening, and speaking will never go out of style. Too often as career opportunities unfold, we tend to neglect one or several of these basic life skills. Yet what career is absolved from knowing how to locate, understand, and interpret information? Can you name a career that does not rely in some way on memos, letters, manuals, reports, or graphs? Is there a career that doesn't require workers to receive and to send verbal and nonverbal messages? And, important to this course you are now concluding, there are virtually no careers that do not ask people to organize their ideas and to communicate them orally. Reading, writing, listening, and speaking are central to all careers, and you should continue building these skills both inside and outside the college classroom.

Keep a Sense of Humor

We don't have to discuss this recommendation in too much detail. We're sure you understand what it means to have a sense of humor. As you have experienced in college, at home, or in your workplace, things can and do go wrong. Sometimes it may seem that splashing hot coffee on your face would be less painful than continuing your day! Well, before you start brewing (and stewing), make a genuine effort to see the funny side of life. We're not suggesting that you laugh at everything that goes wrong (although there might be some value to that suggestion!). Rather, we encourage you to not take your job or your work too seriously.

Conclusion

We hope you agree with us that thinking theoretically is a practical as well as a conceptual enterprise. Certainly, we have many theoretical resources now to help us understand our communication processes in relationships at home, at work, and via mass media. In addition, the four trends in our social life discussed in this chapter will undoubtedly affect our communication behaviors and the process of communication in unexpected ways. Understanding the process of communication contributes to solving today's problems and those we will encounter in the future. As our technological expertise grows, our involvement in work merges with issues of family life, and our society ages and becomes more diverse, we will need to examine and understand the communication dynamics inherent in all these changes. The more knowledge you acquire about how communication affects and is affected by social trends, the more valuable you will be to employers.

Learning about what the future holds for you can be both exciting and daunting. As you sort through the opportunities, keep an open mind. As a student of communication, your broad knowledge and skills will be attractive to employers in a variety of areas. This communication theory course is one step toward a rewarding career path. Knowing current theory, recognizing what challenges lie ahead for future theory, and applying that theory are additional steps to help you move in new directions.

Glossary

The following is a list of terms presented in this text. As you review the list, keep in mind that there may be more than one way to define a particular term. This is a result of theorists interpreting a concept differently based on the context of their theory. When this occurs, we have listed the term twice and included the chapter number to which each definition refers (in parentheses).

abstract symbol symbol representing an idea or thought

accommodation adjusting, modifying, or regulating behavior in response to others

accuracy the ability to see more than what's available to one's own specific social location

act communication behaviors indicating a person's ambiguity in receiving a message (17)

act one prong of the pentad; that which is done by a person (19)

actions activities based on intentional choice responses

activeness refers to how much freedom the audience really has in the face of mass media

active strategies reducing uncertainties by means other than direct contact

activity refers to what the media consumer does

adjustment organizational responses to equivocality

affective exchange stage stage of social penetration that is spontaneous and quite comfortable for relational partners

affiliative constraints refers to when members withhold their input rather than face rejection from the group

agency behaviors or activities used in social environments (15)

agency one prong of the pentad; the means used to perform the act (19)

agent a person engaging in behaviors or activities in social environments (15)

agent one prong of the pentad; the person performing the act (19)

alienation perception that one has little control over his or her future

allocative resources material assistance used to help groups accomplish their goals

applied research research to solve a problem or create a policy

approbation facework focusing less on the negative aspects and more on the positive aspects of another

arousal increased interest or attention when deviations from expectations occur

arrangement a canon of rhetoric that pertains to a speaker's ability to organize a speech

attitude a later addition to the pentad; the manner in which the agent positions himself or herself relative to others

audience analysis an assessment and evaluation of listeners

authoritative resources interpersonal assistance used to help groups accomplish their goals

autonomy and connection an important relational tension that shows our conflicting desires to be close and to be separate

avoiding staying away from disagreements

axiology a branch of knowledge focused on what is worth knowing

axioms truisms drawn from past research and common sense

behavioral sequences a series of actions designed to achieve a goal

behavioral uncertainty degree of uncertainty related to behaviors

behavior control the power to change another's behavior

belief in the inherent morality of the group assumption that the group members are thoughtful and good; therefore the decisions they make will be good

bias of communication Harold Innis's contention that technology has a shaping power on society

body part of an organizational strategy in a speech that includes arguments, examples, and important details to make a point

boundaries a property of systems theory stating that systems construct structures specifying their outer limits

boundary coordination one of the processes in the privacy rule management system; describes how we manage private information that is co-owned

boundary linkage the connections forming boundary alliances between people

boundary ownership rights and privileges accruing to co-owners of private information

boundary permeability how much information is able to pass through a boundary

boundary turbulence conflicts about boundary expectations and regulation

breadth number of topics discussed in a relationship

breadth time amount of time spent by relational partners discussing various topics

buyer's remorse postdecision dissonance related to a purchase

calibration a property of systems theory stating that systems periodically check the scale of allowable behaviors and reset the system

causal argument an assertion of cause and effect, including the direction of the causality

cause an antecedent condition that determines an effect

channel pathway to communication

characterological coherence a type of coherence referring to the believability of the characters in the story

charmed loop rules of meaning are consistent throughout the loop

civic spaces a metaphor suggesting that speakers have "locations" where the opportunity to persuade others exists

closed-mindedness a group's willingness to ignore differences in people and warnings about poor group decisions

co-cultures groups of individuals who are part of the same larger culture, but who can be classified around various identities (e.g., race, sex, age, etc.).

code converting raw data to a category system

coercive power perception that another person has the ability to enact punishment

cognitions ways of knowing, beliefs, judgments, and thoughts

cognitive arousal mental awareness of deviations from expectations

cognitive dissonance feeling of discomfort resulting from inconsistent attitudes, thoughts, and behaviors

cognitive uncertainty degree of uncertainty related to cognitions

coherence a principle of narrative rationality judging the internal consistency of a story

cohesiveness the degree of togetherness between and among communicators (2)

cohesiveness a cultural value that places emphasis on the group over the individual (14)

collective boundary a boundary around private information that includes more than one person

collective rationalization situation in which group members ignore warnings about their decisions

collectivism prioritizing group needs or values over the needs or values of an individual (we-identity)

communication a social process in which individuals employ symbols to establish and interpret meaning in their environment

communication apprehension a general sense of fear of speaking before an audience

communicator reward valence the sum of the positive and negative characteristics of a person and the potential for him or her to carry out rewards or punishments

comparison level (CL) a standard for what a person thinks he or she should get in a relationship

comparison level for alternatives (CLalt) how people evaluate a relationship based on what their alternatives to the relationship are

compromising using give-and-take to achieve a middle-road resolution

concepts labels for the most important elements in a theory

conclusion part of an organizational strategy in a speech that is aimed at summarizing a speaker's main points and arousing emotions in an audience

concrete symbol symbol representing an object

concurrence seeking efforts to search out group consensus

conscientious objectors group members who refuse to participate because it would violate personal conscience

consonance the belief that all media are similar in attitudes, beliefs, and values

consonant relationship two elements in equilibrium with each other

constitutive rules organize behavior and help us to understand how meaning should be interpreted

consubstantiation when appeals are made to increase overlap between people

content the conversion of raw data into meaning

contexts environments in which communication takes place

contextual dialectics tensions resulting from the place of the relationship within the culture

contradiction the central feature of the dialectic approach; refers to oppositions

control direction over the important concepts in a theory

convergence strategy used to adapt to another's behavior

cool media low-definition communication that demands active involvement from a viewer, listener, or reader

coordination trying to make sense of message sequencing

costs elements of relational life with negative value

counter-hegemony when, at times, people use hegemonic behaviors to challenge the domination in their lives

covering law approach a guideline for creating theory suggesting that theories conform to a general law that is universal and invariant

critical approach an approach stressing the researcher's responsibility to change the inequities in the status quo

cultivation differential the percentage of difference in response between light and heavy television viewers

cultural communication communication between and among individuals whose cultural backgrounds vary

cultural patterns images of the world and a person's relationship to it

culture a community of meaning and a shared body of knowledge

culture wars cultural struggles over meaning, identity, and influence

cumulativeness the belief that media repeat themselves

cycles series of communication behaviors that serve to reduce equivocality

cyclic alternation a coping response to dialectical tensions; refers to changes over time

data the raw materials collected by the researcher to answer the questions posed in the research or to test a hypothesis

decoding receiving and comparing messages

deductive logic moving from the general (the theory) to the specific (the observations)

deliberative rhetoric a type of rhetoric that determines an audience's course of action

delivery a canon of rhetoric that refers to the nonverbal presentation of a speaker's ideas

dependency overaccommodation occurs when speakers place listeners in a lower-status role

depenetrate slow deterioration of relationship

depth degree of intimacy guiding topic discussion

dialectic approach an approach framing contradiction as both/and

direct exchange an exchange where two people reciprocate costs and rewards

discursive consciousness a person's ability to articulate personal goals or behaviors

disinhibition searching a passive strategy involving watching a person's natural or uninhibited behavior in an informal environment

dispositional matrix the beliefs you have about relationships

disqualifying a substrategy of integration; refers to exempting certain issues from the general pattern

dissonance ratio a factor in determining magnitude of dissonance; the amount of consonant cognitions relative to the dissonant ones

dissonant relationship two elements in disequilibrium with each other

divergence strategy used to accentuate the verbal and nonverbal differences between communicators

diversion a category of gratifications coming from media use; involves escaping from routines and problems

division when two people fail to have overlap in their substances

dominant group the group that holds the power in a given culture

dominant-hegemonic position operating within a code that allows one person to have control over another

dominating using influence or authority to make decisions

double interact loops cycles of an organization (e.g., interviews, meetings) to reduce equivocality

dramatistic ratios the proportions of one element of the pentad relative to another element

dual climates of opinion difference between the population's perception of a public issue and the way the media report on the issue

dualisms organizing things around pairs of opposites

dualistic approach an approach framing contradiction as two separate entities

duality of structure rules and resources used to guide organizational decisions about behaviors or actions

duration organizational rule stating that decisions regarding equivocality should be made in the least amount of time

dyadic uniqueness distinctive relationship qualities

effect a condition that inevitably follows a causative condition

effective matrix the transformations you are able to make to your given matrix, by learning a new skill, for example

effort organizational rule stating that decisions regarding equivocality should be made with the least amount of work

electronic era age in which electronic media pervades our senses, allowing for people across the world to be connected

enactment interpretation of the information received by the organization

enculturation performances organizational behaviors that assist employees in discovering what it means to be a member of an organization

enhancement law that states media amplify or strengthen society

enmeshment extent to which partners identify themselves as part of a system

entry phase the beginning stage of an interaction between strangers

environment situation or context in which communication occurs

epideictic rhetoric a type of rhetoric that pertains to praising or blaming

episodes communication routines that have recognized beginnings, middles, and endings

epistemology a branch of knowledge focused on how we know things

epoch era or historical age

equifinality a property of systems theory stating that systems can achieve the same goals through different means

equivocality the extent to which organizational messages are uncertain, ambiguous, and/or unpredictable

essentialism the belief that all women are essentially the same, all men are essentially the same, and the two differ from each other

ethics perceived rightness or wrongness of an action or behavior

ethos the perceived character, intelligence, and goodwill of a speaker

evaluation process of judging a conversation

exit phase the stage in a relationship when people decide whether to continue or leave

expectancies thoughts and behaviors anticipated in conversations

expert power perception that another person has the ability to exert influence because of special knowledge or expertise

explanation the ability to interpret the meaning of behavioral choices

exploratory affective exchange stage stage of social penetration that results in the emergence of our personality to others

face a metaphor for the public image people display

face concern interest in maintaining one's face or the face of others

face management the protection of one's face

face need desire to be associated or disassociated with others

face restoration strategy used to preserve autonomy and avoid loss of face

face-saving efforts to avoid embarrassment or vulnerability

facework actions used to deal with face needs/wants of self and others

false consciousness Gramsci's belief that people are unaware of the domination in their lives

fate control the ability to affect a partner's outcomes

feedback communication given to the source by the receiver to indicate understanding (meaning) (1)

feedback a subprocess of calibration; information allowing for change in the system (3)

feminism focusing on women's social position and desiring to end oppression based on gender

fidelity a principle of narrative rationality judging the credibility of a story

field journal personal log to record feelings about communicating with people in a different culture from one's own

field of experience overlap of sender's and receiver's culture, experiences, and heredity in communication

first order effects a method for cultivation to occur; refers to learning facts from the media

forensic rhetoric a type of rhetoric that pertains to speakers prompting feelings of guilt or innocence from an audience

fraction of selection Schramm's idea of how media choices are made; the expectation of reward divided by the effort required

Frankfurt School theorists a group of scholars who believed that the media were more concerned with making money than with presenting news

fresh act something new developed from action or behavior

gender social category consisting of the learned behaviors that constitute masculinity and femininity for a given culture

gender polarization viewing men and women as polar opposites

generalized exchange an exchange where reciprocation involves the social network and isn't confined to two individuals

generalized other the attitude of the whole community

given matrix the constraints on your choices due to the environment and/or your own skill levels

global village the notion that humans can no longer live in isolation, but rather will always be connected by continuous and instantaneous electronic media

glosses outdated words in a speech

good reasons a set of values for accepting a story as true and worthy of acceptance; provides a method for assessing fidelity

grand theories theories that attempt to explain all of a phenomenon such as communication

grounded theory theory induced from data and analysis

group insulation a group's ability to remain unaffected by outside influences

groupthink a way of group deliberation that minimizes conflict and emphasizes the need for unanimity

guilt tension, embarrassment, shame, disgust, or other unpleasant feeling

habitual rules nonnegotiable rules that are usually created by an authority figure

hard core group(s) at the end of the spiral willing to speak out at any cost

Hawthorne experiments a set of investigations that ushered in a human relations approach to organizations

hegemony the domination of one group over another, usually weaker, group

heurism a criterion for evaluating theories; refers to the amount of research and new thinking stimulated by the theory

hierarchy an organizing principle whereby things or people are ranked one above the other (2)

hierarchy a property of systems theory stating that systems consist of multiple levels (3)

high-context cultures cultures, like Japan, where the meaning of a message is in the context or internalized in listeners

homeostatic a term for a stable system that isn't changing

homogeneity group similarity

hot media high-definition communication that demands little involvement from a viewer, listener, or reader

hypotheses testable predictions of relationships between concepts that follow the general predictions made by a theory

I the spontaneous, impulsive, creative self

ice age analogy a position stating that television doesn't have to have a single major impact, but influences viewers through steady limited effects

identification when two people have overlap in their substances

ideology framework used to make sense of our existence

illusion of invulnerability belief that the group is special enough to overcome obstacles

illusion of unanimity belief that silence equals agreement

imperviousness to influence refers to audience members' constructing their own meaning from media content

importance a factor in determining magnitude of dissonance; refers to how significant the issue is

indirect stereotyping imposing outdated and rigid assumptions of a cultural group upon that group

Individual Differences Perspective a specific approach to the idea of limited effects; concentrates on the limits posed by personal characteristics

individualism a cultural value that places emphasis on the individual over the group

inductive logic moving from the specific (the observations) to the general (the theory)

information environment the availability of all stimuli in an organization

in-groups groups in which a person feels he or she belongs

integrating collaborating with others to find solutions

integration a coping response to dialectical tensions; refers to synthesizing the opposition; composed of three substrategies

intentionality occurs when people's prior motives determine use of media

interactional dialectics tensions resulting from and constructed by communication

interactional expectations an individual's ability to carry out the interaction

interactional model of communication view of communication as the sharing of meaning with feedback that links source and receiver

interactive strategies reducing uncertainties by engaging in conversation

interdependence a property of systems theory stating that the elements of a system affect one another

intergroup overaccommodation occurs when speakers place listeners in cultural groups without acknowledging individual uniqueness

internal and external stress pressure exerted on the group by issues and events both inside and outside of the group

interpersonal communication face to face communication between people

interpersonal meaning the result when two people agree on each other's interpretations of an interaction

interpretive approach an approach viewing truth as subjective and stressing the participation of the researcher in the research process

intimacy the feeling state of knowing someone deeply in all ways because that person is significant in one's life

intimate distance very close spatial zone spanning 0–18 inches

intrapersonal communication communication with oneself

introduction part of an organizational strategy in a speech that includes gaining the audience's attention, connecting with the audience, and providing an overview of the speaker's purpose

invention a canon of rhetoric that pertains to the construction or development of an argument related to a particular speech

irrelevant relationship two elements that have no meaningful relation to each other

lack of decision-making procedures failure to provide norms for solving group issues

lack of impartial leadership refers to groups led by individuals who put their personal agenda first

language a shared system of verbal and nonverbal symbols

last-minute swing jumping on the bandwagon of popular opinion after opinions have been expressed

laws of media further expansion of Media Ecology Theory with focus on the impact of technology on society

legitimate power perception that another person has the ability to exert influence because of title or position

life scripts clusters of past or present episodes that create a system of manageable meanings with others

limited effects the perspective replacing Mass Society Theory; holds that media effects are limited by aspects of the audience's personal and social lives

linear model of communication one-way view of communication that assumes a message is sent by a source to a receiver through a channel

literate era age when written communication flourished and the eye became the dominant sense organ

logical consistency a criterion for evaluating theories; refers to the internal logic in the theoretical statements

logos logical proof; the use of arguments and evidence in a speech

looking-glass self our ability to see ourselves as another sees us

loop the reflexiveness of levels in the hierarchy of meaning

low-context cultures cultures, like the United States, where most of the meaning is in the code or message

macrotheory a theory with extensive boundaries

magnitude of dissonance the quantitative amount of discomfort felt

mainstreaming the tendency for heavy viewers to perceive a similar culturally dominant reality to that pictured on the media although this differs from actual reality

mass communication communication to a large audience via various channels (e.g., radio, Internet, television, etc.)

mass media channels or delivery modes for mass messages

Mass Society Theory the idea that average people are the victims of the powerful forces of mass media

material coherence a type of coherence referring to the congruence between one story and other related stories

Me the reflective, socially aware self

meaning what people extract from a message

media ecology the study of how media and communication processes affect human perception, feeling, emotion, and value

memory a canon of rhetoric that refers to a speaker's effort in storing information for a speech

message words, sounds, actions, or gestures in an interaction

metaphor a figure of speech that helps to make the unclear more understandable

microtheory a theory with limited boundaries

mid-range theory a theory that attempts to explain a specified aspect of a phenomenon such as communication

mind the ability to use symbols with common social meanings

minimal justification offering the least amount of incentive necessary to obtain compliance

models simplified representations of the communication process

monologic approach an approach framing contradiction as either/or

morphogenic a term for when a system recalibrates (or changes)

mortification one method of purging guilt, by blaming ourselves

motion refers to the processual nature of relationships

movements activities based on stimulus-response

narration an account to which listeners assign meaning

narrative rationality a standard for judging which stories to believe and which to disregard

narrow theory a theory that attempts to explain a very limited aspect of a phenomenon such as communication

negative face desire to be autonomous and free from others

negotiated position accepting dominant ideologies, but allowing for cultural exceptions

neo-Marxist limited embracement of Marxism

networks communication patterns through which information flows

neutralizing a substrategy of integration; refers to compromising between the oppositions

new media computer-related technology

noise distortion in channel not intended by the source

nominal concepts concepts that are not directly observable

norms expectations of behavior in conversations

novelty and predictability an important relational tension that shows our conflicting desires to have stability and change

obliging satisfying the needs of others

observations focused examination within a context of interest; may be guided by hypotheses or research questions

obsolescence law that states media eventually render something out of date

ontology a branch of knowledge focused on the nature of reality

openness the acknowledgment that within all human systems the boundaries are permeable

openness and protection an important relational tension that shows our conflicting desires to tell our secrets and to keep them hidden

operationalize making an abstract idea measurable and observable

opinion expression of attitude

oppositional position substituting alternative messages presented by the media

order or hierarchy a ranking that exists in society primarily because of our ability to use language

organizational communication communication within and among large, extended environments

organizational culture the essence of organizational life

organizational rituals routines that pertain to the organization overall

orientation stage stage of social penetration that includes revealing small parts of ourselves

outcome whether people continue in a relationship or terminate it

out-groups groups in which a person feels he or she does not belong

out-group stereotypes stereotyped perceptions of group enemies or competitors

outsider within a person in a normally marginalized social position who has gained access to a more privileged location

overaccommodation attempt to overdo efforts in regulating, modifying, or responding to others

overestimation of the group erroneous belief that the group is more than it is

Palo Alto team a group of scholars who believed that a person "cannot not communicate"

paradigm shift a significant change in the way most people see the world and its meanings

parametric rules rules that are set by an authority figure but are subject to some negotiation

parasocial interaction the relationship we feel we have with people we know only through the media

parsimony a criterion for evaluating theories; refers to the simplicity of the explanation provided by the theory

partial a recognition that no one has a complete view of the social hierarchy

particular others individuals who are significant to us

passion performances organizational stories that employees share with one another

passive strategies reducing uncertainties by unobtrusive observation

pathos emotional proof; emotions drawn from audience members

pentad Burke's method for applying Dramatism

perception process of attending to and interpreting a message

performance metaphor suggesting that organizational life is like a theatrical presentation

personal boundary a boundary around private information that includes just one person

personal distance spatial zone of 18 inches to 4 feet, reserved for family and friends

personal identity a category of gratifications coming from media use; involves ways to reinforce individual values

personal idioms private, intimate expressions stated in a relationship

personal meaning the meaning achieved when a person brings his or her unique experiences to an interaction

personal phase the stage in a relationship when people begin to communicate more spontaneously and personally

personal relationships a category of gratifications coming from media use; involves substituting media for companionship

personal rituals routines done at the workplace each day

personal space individual's variable use of space and distance

personnel organizational rule stating the most knowledgeable workers should resolve equivocality

phenomenology a personal interpretation of everyday life and activities

physical arousal bodily changes as a result of deviations from expectations

physical (external) noise bodily influences on reception of message

physiological noise biological influences on reception of message

pluralistic ignorance mistaken observation of how most people feel

political performances organizational behaviors that demonstrate power or control

positive face desire to be liked and admired by others

positivistic/empirical approach an approach assuming the existence of objective reality and value neutral research

power the degree of dependence a person has on another for outcomes (11)

power imposition of personal will on others (15)

practical consciousness a person's inability to articulate personal goals or behaviors

praxis refers to the choice-making capacity of humans

prediction the ability to forecast one's own and others' behavioral choices

pre-interactional expectations the knowledge or skills a communicator brings to an interaction

pressures on dissenters direct influence on group members who provide thoughts contrary to the group's

pressure toward uniformity occurs when group members go along to get along

primary territories signal a person's exclusive domain over an area or object

print era age when gaining information through the printed word was customary, and seeing continued as the dominant sense

privacy rule attributes one of the features of privacy rule characteristics; describes how people acquire rules and the properties of rules

privacy rule characteristics one of the processes in the privacy rule management system; describes the nature of privacy rules

private boundaries the demarcation between private information and public information

private disclosures the process of communicating private information to another

private information information about things that matter deeply to a person

problem-solving groups sets of individuals whose main task is to make decisions and provide policy recommendations

process ongoing, dynamic, and unending occurrence

productive exchange an exchange where both partners incur costs and benefits simultaneously

proxemics study of a person's use of space

psychological noise cognitive influences on reception of message

public legal, social, and social-psychological concerns of people

public and private dialectic a contextual dialectic resulting from a private relationship and public life

public communication the dissemination of information occurs from one person to many others (audience)

public distance spatial zone of 12 feet and beyond, reserved for very formal discussions such as between professor and students in class

public image outer layer of a person; what is available to others

public opinion attitudes and behaviors expressed in public in order to avoid isolation

public territories signal open spaces for everyone, including beaches and parks

punctuate how individuals interpret or emphasize an episode

pure research research to generate knowledge

purpose one prong of the pentad; the goal the agent had for the act

Pygmalion effect living up to or down to another's expectations of us

quasi-statistical sense personal estimation of the strength of opposing sides on a public issue

ratio of the senses phrase referring to the way people adapt to their environment (through a balance of the series)

rational world paradigm a system of logic employed by many researchers and professionals

rationale a factor in determining magnitude of dissonance; refers to the reasoning employed to explain the inconsistency

reactivity searching a passive strategy involving watching a person doing something

real and ideal dialectic a contextual dialectic resulting from the difference between idealized relationships and lived relationships

real concepts concepts that are directly observable

receiver recipient of a message

reciprocity communication that mirrors the previous communication behavior (9)

reciprocity the return of openness from one person to another (10)

redemption a rejection of the unclean and a return to a new order after guilt has been temporarily purged

referent power perception that another person has the ability to achieve compliance because of established personal relationships

reflexivity a person's ability to monitor his or her actions or behaviors

reframing a substrategy of integration; refers to transforming the oppositions

regulative rules guidelines for people's behavior

relational uncertainty a lack of certainty about the future and status of a relationship

relationship agreement and understanding between two people

relationships the ways in which the concepts of a theory relate to one another

reliability the stability and predictability of an observation

requisite variety engaging in communication that is as complex as the messages received

resonance occurs when a viewer's lived reality coincides with the reality pictured in the media

resources stories, symbols, and images that people use to make sense of their world (6)

resources attributes or material goods that can be used to exert power in an organization (15)

response reaction to equivocality

retention collective memory allowing people to accomplish goals

retrieval law that states media restore something that was once lost

reversal law that states media will—when pushed to their limit—produce or become something else

reward power perception that another person has the ability to provide positive outcomes

reward/cost ratio balance between positive and negative relationship experiences

rewards elements of relational life with positive value

rhetoric a speaker's available means of persuasion

ritual performances regular and recurring presentations in the workplace

ritual perspective a position depicting the media as representers of shared beliefs

roles positions of group members and their relationship to the group

role taking the ability to put oneself in another's place

rule development one of the features of privacy rule characteristics; describes how rules come to be decided

rule properties the characteristics of a rule that reveal how stable or changeable it is

rules general routines that the organization or group follows in accomplishing goals (15)

rules guidelines in organizations as they review responses to equivocal information (17)

rules approach a guideline for creating theory that builds human choice into explanations

scapegoating one method of purging guilt, by blaming others

scene one prong of the pentad; the context surrounding the act

scientific method the traditional method for doing research involving controlled observations and analysis to test the principles of a theory

scope a criterion for evaluating theories; refers to the breadth of communication behaviors covered in the theory

secondary territories signal a person's affiliation with an area or object

second order effects a method for cultivation to occur; refers to learning values and assumptions from the media

second shift the phenomenon of working women putting in eight hours on the job and another day's work at home

segmentation a coping response to dialectical tensions; refers to changes due to context

selection a coping response to dialectical tensions; refers to prioritizing oppositions (12)

selection choosing the best method for obtaining information (17)

selective attention a method for reducing dissonance by paying attention to information that is consonant with current beliefs and actions

selective exposure a method for reducing dissonance by seeking information that is consonant with current beliefs and actions

selective interpretation a method for reducing dissonance by interpreting ambiguous information so that it becomes consistent with current beliefs and action

selective retention a method for reducing dissonance by remembering information that is consonant with current beliefs and actions

selectivity audience members' use of media reflects their existing interests

self imagining how we look to another person

self-appointed mindguards individuals who protect the group from adverse information

self-censorship group members minimize personal doubts and counterarguments

self-concept a relatively stable set of perceptions people hold about themselves

self-disclosure personal messages about the self disclosed to another (9)

self-disclosure purposeful process of revealing information about oneself (10)

self-esteem the degree of positive orientation people have about themselves

self-fulfilling prophecy a prediction about yourself causing you to behave in such a way that it comes true

self-identity personal attributes of another

semantic noise linguistic influences on reception of message

semiotics the study of signs

sensemaking creating awareness and understanding in situations that are complex or uncertain

sensory over-accommodation overly adapting to others who are perceived as limited in their abilities (physical, linguistic, or other)

sex biological category divided into male and female

sexual division of labor allocation of work on the basis of sex

significant symbols symbols whose meaning is generally agreed upon by many people

situated knowledges what anyone knows is grounded in context and circumstance

situational contexts environments that are limited by such factors as the number of people present, the feedback, the space between communicators, among others

small group communication communication among at least three individuals

social the notion that people and interactions are part of the communication process

Social Categories Model a specific approach to the idea of limited effects; concentrates on the limits posed by group membership

social constructionism belief that people co-construct their social reality in conversations

social distance spatial zone of 4-12 feet, reserved for more formal relationships such as those with co-workers

Social Identity Theory a theory that proposes a person's identity is shaped by both personal and social characteristics

social integration reciprocity of communication behaviors in interaction

social penetration process of bonding that moves a relationship from superficial to more intimate

social performances organizational behaviors intended to demonstrate cooperation and politeness with others

social reality a person's beliefs about how meaning and action fit within an interpersonal interaction

social rituals routines that involve relationships with others in the workplace

society the web of social relationships humans create and respond to

solidarity facework accepting another as a member of an in-group

Sophists teachers of public speaking (rhetoric) in ancient Greece

source originator of a message

speech act action we perform by speaking (e.g., questioning, complimenting, or threatening)

stable exchange stage stage of social penetration that results in complete openness and spontaneity for relational partners

standpoint an achieved position based on a social location that lends an interpretative aspect to a person's life

strange loop rules of meaning change within the loop

stranger-on-the-train revealing personal information to strangers in public places

structural coherence a type of coherence referring to the flow of the story

structuration the production, reproduction, and transformation of social environments through rules and resources in relationships

structure the rules and resources used to sustain a group or organization

style a canon of rhetoric that includes the use of language to express ideas in a speech

substance the general nature of something

subsystems smaller systems that are embedded in larger ones

success organizational rule stating that a successful plan of the past will be used to reduce current equivocality

suprasystems larger systems that hold smaller ones within them

surveillance a category of gratifications coming from media use; involves collecting needed information

syllogism a set of propositions that are related to one another and draw a conclusion from the major and minor premises

symbol arbitrary label given to a phenomenon

synergy the intersection of multiple perspectives in a small group

system a group or organization and the behaviors that the group engages in to pursue its goals

systems approach a guideline for creating theory that acknowledges human choice and the constraints of the systems involved

tact facework extent to which a person respects another's autonomy

tactical rules unstated rules used to achieve a personal or interpersonal goal

task-oriented groups sets of individuals whose main goal is to work toward completing jobs assigned to them

task rituals routines associated with a particular job in the workplace

technopoly a term coined by Postman that means we live in a society dominated by technology

territoriality person's ownership of an area or object

test of time a criterion for evaluating theories; refers to the theory's durability over time

testability a criterion for evaluating theories; refers to our ability to test the accuracy of a theory's claims

tetrad organizing concept to understand the laws of media

theatre of struggle competition of various cultural ideologies

the medium is the message phrase referring to the power and influence of the medium—not the content—on a society

the negative rejecting one's place in the social order; exhibiting resistance

theorems theoretical statements derived from axioms, positing a relationship between two concepts

theory an abstract system of concepts and their relationships that help us to understand a phenomenon

theory of sociocultural evolution Darwin's belief that only the fittest can survive challenging surroundings

thick boundaries closed boundaries allowing little or no information to pass through

thick description explanation of the layers of meaning in a culture

thin boundaries open boundaries allowing all information to pass through

thought an inner conversation

threat threshold tolerance for distance violations

topics an aid to invention that refers to the arguments a speaker uses

totality acknowledges the interdependence of people in a relationship

train test assessment of the extent to which people will speak out

trajectory pathway to closeness

transactional model of communication view of communication as the simultaneous sending and receiving of messages

transgression a violation of relational rules, practices, and expectations

transmissional perspective a position depicting the media as senders of messages across space

tribal era age when oral tradition was embraced and hearing was the paramount sense

ubiquity the belief that media are everywhere

uncertainty avoidance an attempt to avoid ambiguous situations

unwanted repetitive patterns (URPs) recurring, undesirable conflicts in a relationship

utility a criterion for evaluating theories; refers to the theory's usefulness or practical value (4)

utility using the media to accomplish specific tasks (23)

validity the truth value of an observation

values standards and principles in a culture

victimage the way we attempt to purge the guilt we feel as part of being human

violation valence perceived negative or positive assessment of an unexpected behavior

violence index a yearly content analysis of prime-time network programming to assess the amount of violence represented

whistle-blowing process in which individuals report unethical or illegal behaviors or practices to others

wholeness a fundamental property of systems theory stating that systems are more than the sum of their individual parts

References

Aakhus, M. (2007). Communication as design. *Communication Monographs, 74,* 112–117.

Abrams, J., O'Connor, J., & Giles, H. (2003). Identity and intergroup communication. In W. B. Gudykunst (Ed.), *Cross-cultural and intercultural communication* (pp. 209–224). Thousand Oaks, CA: Sage.

Adams, K., & Galanes, G. J. (2009). *Communicating in groups.* Boston: McGraw-Hill.

Afifi, T. D. (2003). "Feeling caught" in stepfamilies: Managing boundary turbulence through appropriate communication privacy rules. *Journal of Social and Personal Relationships, 20,* 729–755.

Agustin, C., & Singh, J. (2005). Curvilinear effects of consumer loyalty determinants in relational exchanges. *Journal of Marketing Research, 42,* 96–108.

Alboher, M. (2008, May 29). Hot ticket in B-school: Bringing life values to corporate ethics. *The New York Times,* C5.

Alkhazraji, K. M. (1997). The acculturation of immigrants to U.S. organizations: The case of Muslim employees. *Management Communication Quarterly, 11,* 217–265.

Allen, B. J. (2007). Theorizing communication and race. *Communication Monographs, 74,* 259–264.

Allen, R. L., & Hatchett, S. (1986). The media and social reality effects: Self and system orientation of Blacks. *Communication Research, 13,* 97–123.

Allman, J. (1998). Bearing the burden or baring the soul: Physicians' self-disclosure and boundary management regarding medical mistakes. *Health Communication, 10,* 175–197.

Altman, I. (1975). *The environment and social behavior.* Monterey, CA: Brooks/Cole.

Altman, I., & Taylor, D. A. (1973). *Social penetration: The development of interpersonal relationships.* New York: Holt, Rinehart & Winston.

Altman, I., Vinsel, A., & Brown, B. (1981). Dialectic conceptions in social psychology: An application to social penetration and privacy regulation. In L. Berkowitz (Ed.), *Advances in experimental social psychology* (pp. 130–145). New York: Academic Press.

Alwood, E. (1997, October 14). The power of persuasion: The media's role in addressing homosexual issues in the future. *The Advocate,* 54.

Andersen, K. E. (2003). *Recovering the civic culture: The imperative of ethical communication.* Boston: Pearson/Allyn & Bacon.

Anderson, R., & Ross, V. (2002). *Questions of communication: A practical introduction to theory* (2nd ed.). New York: St. Martin's Press.

Anderson, T. L., & Emmers-Sommer, T. M. (2006). Predictors of relationship satisfaction in online romantic relationships. *Communication Studies, 57,* 153–172.

Andrews, M. (2002). Feminist research with nonfeminist and anti-feminist women: Meeting the challenge. *Feminism & Psychology, 12,* 55–77.

Angus, I., Jhally, S., Lewis, J., & Schwichtenberg, C. (1989). On pluralistic apology. *Critical Studies in Mass Communication, 6,* 441–449.

Apker, J., Propp, K. M., & Ford, W. S. Z. (2005). Negotiating status and identity tensions in healthcare team interactions: An exploration of nurse role dialectics. *Journal of Applied Communication Research, 33,* 93–115.

Appel, E. C. (2003). Rush to judgment: Burlesque, tragedy, and hierarchical alchemy in the rhetoric of America's foremost political talkshow host. *Southern Communication Journal, 68,* 217–230.

Ardener, E. (1975). The "problem" revisited. In S. Ardener (Ed.), *Perceiving women* (pp. 19–27). London: Malaby Press.

Ardener, S. (1978). Introduction: The nature of women in society. In S. Ardener (Ed.), *Defining females* (pp. 9–48). New York: Wiley.

Ardener, S. (2005). Muted group theory excerpts. *Women and Language, 28,* 50–72.

Arneson, P. (2007). A conversation about communication ethics with Kenneth A. Andersen. In P. Arneson (Ed.), *Exploring communication ethics* (pp. 131–142). New York: Peter Lang Publishing.

Arnett, R. C., Harden-Fritz, J., & Bell, L. M. (2008). *Communication ethics literacy: Dialogue and difference.* Thousand Oaks, CA: Sage.

Arnhart, L. (1981). *Aristotle on political reasoning: A commentary on rhetoric.* DeKalb: Northern Illinois University Press.

Aron, A., & Aron, E. N. (1989). *The heart of social psychology: A backstage view of a passionate science* (2nd ed.). Lexington, MA: Lexington Books.

Aronson, E. (1969). The theory of cognitive dissonance: A current perspective. In L. Berkowitz (Ed.), *Advances in experimental social psychology* (pp. 1–34). New York: Academic Press.

Asch, S. E. (1951). Effects of group pressure upon the modification and distortion of judgments. In J. Guetzkow (Ed.), *Groups, leadership, and men: Research in human relations* (pp. 177–190). New York: Russell & Russell.

Austin, J. L. (1975). *How to do things with words.* Cambridge, MA: Harvard University Press.

Ayres, D. M., Ayres, J., & Hopf, T. S. (1995). Reducing communication apprehension among at-risk children. *Communication Reports, 8,* 178–184.

Bandura, A. (1977). *Social learning theory.* Englewood Cliffs, NJ: Prentice-Hall.

Banks, S. P., & Riley, P. (1993). Structuration theory as an ontology for communication research. In S. A. Deetz (Ed.), *Communication yearbook 16* (pp. 167–196). Newbury Park, CA: Sage.

Bantz, C. R. (1989). Organizing and the social psychology of organizing. *Communication Studies, 40,* 231–240.

Baran, S. J., & Davis, D. K. (2009). *Mass communication theory: Foundations, ferment, and future* (5th ed.). Belmont, CA: Wadsworth.

Barge, J. K. (2004). Articulating CMM as a practical theory. *Human Systems, 15,* 193–204.

Barge, J. K., & Pearce, W. B. (2004). A reconnaissance of CMM research. *Human Systems, 13,* 13–32.

Barker, R. T., Rimler, G. W., Moreno, E., & Kaplan, T. E. (2004). Family business members' narrative perceptions: Values, succession, and commitment. *Journal of Technical Writing and Communication, 34,* 291–320.

Barnes, S. B. (2003). *Online connections: Internet interpersonal relationships.* Cresskill, NJ: Hampton.

Barnlund, D. C. (1970). A transactional model of communication. In K. K. Sereno & C. D. Mortensen (Eds.), *Foundations of communication theory* (pp. 83–102). New York: Harper.

Bartoo, H., & Sias, P. M. (2004). When enough is too much: Communication apprehension and employee information experiences. *Communication Quarterly, 52,* 15–26.

Baxter, L. A. (1984). Trajectories of relationship disengagement. *Journal of Social and Personal Relationships, 1,* 29–48.

Baxter, L. A. (1988). A dialectical perspective on communication strategies in relationship development. In S. Duck (Ed.), *Handbook of personal relationships* (pp. 257–273). New York: Wiley.

Baxter, L. A. (1990). Dialectical contradictions in relationship development. *Journal of Social and Personal Relationships, 7,* 69–88.

Baxter, L. A. (2006). Relational dialectics theory: Multivocal dialogues of family communication. In D. O. Braithwaite & L. A. Baxter (Eds.), *Engaging theories in family communication: Multiple perspectives* (pp. 130–145). Thousand Oaks, CA: Sage.

Baxter, L. A., & Babbie, E. R. (2004). *The basics of communication research.* Belmont, CA: Wadsworth.

Baxter, L. A., & Braithwaite, D. O. (2008). Relational dialectics theory. In L. A. Baxter & D. O. Braithwaite (Eds.), *Engaging theories in interpersonal communication: Multiple perspectives* (pp. 349–361). Thousand Oaks, CA: Sage.

Baxter, L. A., Braithwaite, D. O., Bryant, L., & Wagner, A. (2004). Stepchildren's perceptions of the contradictions in communication with stepparents. *Journal of Social and Personal Relationships, 21,* 447–467.

Baxter, L. A., Braithwaite, D. O., Golish, T. D., & Olson, L. N. (2002). Contradictions of interaction for wives of elderly husbands with adult dementia. *Journal of Applied Communication Research, 30,* 1–26.

Baxter, L. A., & Montgomery, B. M. (1996). *Relating: Dialogues and dialectics.* New York: Guilford Press.

Baxter, L. A., & Sahlstein, E. M. (2000). Some possible directions for future research. In S. Petronio (Ed.), *Balancing the secrets of private disclosures* (pp. 289–300). Mahwah, NJ: Erlbaum.

Baxter, L. A., & Wilmot, W. W. (1985). Interaction characteristics of disengaging, stable, and growing relationships. In R. Gilmour & S. Duck (Eds.), *The emerging field of personal relationships.* Hillsdale, NJ: Erlbaum.

Beavin-Bevelas, J. (1990). *Equivocal communication.* Newbury Park, CA: Sage.

Belasen, A. T. (2007). *The theory and practice of corporate communication: A competing values perspective.* Thousand Oaks, CA: Sage.

Bell, K. E., Orbe, M. P., Drummond, D. K., & Camara, S. K. (2000). Accepting the challenge of centralizing without essentializing: Black feminist thought and African American women's communicative experiences. *Women's Studies in Communication, 23,* 41–62.

Bellamy, R. V., & Walker, J. R. (1996). *Television and the remote control: Grazing on a vast wasteland.* New York: Guilford Press.

Bean, C. J., & Eisenberg, E. (2006). Employee sensemaking in the transition to nomadic work. *Journal of Organizational Change Management, 19,* 210–222.

Bem, D. J. (1967). Self-perception: An alternative interpretation of cognitive dissonance phenomena. *Psychological Review, 74,* 183–200.

Bem, S. (1993). *The lenses of gender: Transforming the debate on sexual inequality.* New Haven, CT: Yale University Press.

Benning, J. (2003). Remembering Neil Postman. Retrieved July 24, 2008 from the World Wide Web: www.alternet.org

Berger, A. A. (2007). *Media & society: A critical perspective.* Lanham, MD: Rowman & Littlefield.

Berger, C. R. (1977). The covering law perspective as a theoretical basis for the study of human communication. *Communication Quarterly, 25,* 7–18.

Berger, C. R. (1979). Beyond initial interaction: Uncertainty, understanding, and the development of interpersonal relationships. In H. Giles & R. St. Clair (Eds.), *Language and social psychology* (pp. 122–144). Oxford: Blackwell.

Berger, C. R. (1982). *Social cognition and the development of interpersonal relationships: The quest for social knowledge.* Paper presented at the First International Conference on Personal Relationships, Madison, WI.

Berger, C. R. (1986). Uncertain outcome values in predicted relationships: Uncertainty reduction theory then and now. *Human Communication Research, 13,* 34–38.

Berger, C. R. (1987). Communicating under uncertainty. In M. E. Roloff & G. R. Miller (Eds.), *Interpersonal processes: New directions in communication research* (pp. 39–62). Newbury Park, CA: Sage.

Berger, C. R. (1995). Inscrutable goals, uncertain plans, and the production of communicative action. In C. R. Berger & M. Burgoon (Eds.), *Communication and social processes* (pp. 1–28). East Lansing: Michigan State University Press.

Berger, C. R. (2005). Slippery slopes to apprehension: Rationality and graphical depictions of increasingly threatening trends. *Communication Research, 32,* 3–28.

Berger, C. R., & Bradac, J. J. (1982). *Language and social knowledge: Uncertainty in interpersonal relations.* London: Arnold.

Berger, C. R., & Calabrese, R. J. (1975). Some explorations in initial interaction and beyond: Toward a developmental theory of interpersonal communication. *Human Communication Research, 1,* 99–112.

Berger, C. R., & Gudykunst, W. B. (1991). Uncertainty and communication. In. B. Dervin & M. J. Voight (Eds.), *Progress in communication sciences* (Vol. 10, pp. 21–66). Norwood, NJ: Ablex.

Berger, C. R., & Kellerman, K. (1994). Acquiring social information. In J. A. Daly & J. Weimann (Eds.), *Strategic interpersonal communication* (pp. 1–31). Hillsdale, NJ: Erlbaum.

Berger, C. R., & Roloff, M. E. (1980). Social cognition self-awareness and interpersonal communication. In B. Dervin & M. Voigt (Eds.), *Progress in communication sciences* (Vol. 2, pp. 158–172). Norwood, NJ: Ablex.

Berscheid, E., & Walster, E. H. (1978). *Interpersonal attraction.* Reading, MA: Addison-Wesley.

Bienenstock, E. J., & Bianchi, A. J. (2004). Activating performance expectations and status differences through gift exchange: Experimental results. *Social Psychology Quarterly, 67,* 310–318.

Bishop, J. W., Scott, K. D., Goldsby, M. G., & Cropanzano, R. (2005). A construct validity study of commitment and perceived support variables: A multifoci approach across different team environments. *Group Organizational Management, 30,* 153–180.

Blair, C. (2006). Collective memory. In G. J. Shepherd, J. St. John, & T. Striphas (Eds.), *Communication as . . . Perspectives on theory* (pp. 51–59). Thousand Oaks, CA: Sage.

Blakeslee, S. (2005, June 28). What other people say may change what you see. *The New York Times,* p. 11.

Blalock, H. M. (1969). *Theory construction: From verbal to mathematical formulations.* Englewood Cliffs, NJ: Prentice Hall.

Blanquicett, C., Amsbary, J. H., Mills, C., and Powell, L. (2007). Examining the perceptions on doctor–patient communication. *Human Communication, 10,* 421–436.

Blau, P. M. (1964). *Exchange and power in social life.* New York: Wiley.

Blumer, H. (1969). *Symbolic interactionism: Perspective and method.* Englewood Cliffs, NJ: Prentice Hall.

Blumler, J. G. (1979). The role of theory in uses and gratifications studies. *Communication Research, 6,* 9–36.

Blumler, J. G. (1985). The social character of media gratifications. In K. E. Rosengren, L. A. Wenner, & P. Palmgreen (Eds.), *Media gratifications research: Current perspectives* (pp. 41–60). Beverly Hills, CA: Sage.

Blumler, J. G., & McQuail, D. (1969). *Television in politics: Its uses and influence.* Chicago: University of Chicago Press.

Bochner, A. (1985). Perspectives on inquiry: Representation, conversation, and reflection. In M. L. Knapp & G. R. Miller (Eds.), *Handbook of interpersonal communication* (pp. 27–58). Beverly Hills, CA: Sage.

Book, P. L. (1996). How does the family narrative influence the individual's ability to communicate about death? *Omega, 33,* 323–341.

Booth-Butterfield, M., Booth-Butterfield, S., & Koester, J. (1988). The function of uncertainty reduction in alleviating primary tension in small groups. *Communication Research Reports, 5,* 146–153.

Booth-Butterfield, M., & Jordan, F. (1989). Communication adaptation among racially homogeneous and heterogeneous groups. *Southern Communication Journal, 54,* 253–272.

Bormann, E. G. (1996). Symbolic convergence theory and communication in group decision making. In R. Y. Hirokawa & M. S. Poole (Eds.), *Communication and group decision making* (pp. 81–113). Thousand Oaks, CA: Sage.

Bostrom, R. N. (2003). Theories, data, and communication research. *Communication Monographs, 70,* 275–294.

Bostrom, R. N. (2004). Empiricism, paradigms, and data. *Communication Monographs, 71,* 343–351.

Boulding, K. (1990). *Three faces of power.* Newbury Park, CA: Sage.

Bourhis, R. Y., & Giles, H. (1977). The language of intergroup distinctiveness. In H. Giles (Ed.), *Language, ethnicity and intergroup relations* (pp. 119–135). London: Academic Press.

boyd, d. m., & Ellison, N. B. (2007). Social network sites: Definition, history, and scholarship. *Journal of Computer-Mediated Communication, 13,* 11. http://jcmc.indiana.edu/vol13/issue1/boyd.ellison .html

Boyle, M. P., Schmierbach, M., Armstrong, C. L., McLeod, D. M., Shah, D. V., & Pan, Z. (2004). Information seeking and emotional reactions to the September 11 terrorist attacks. *Journalism & Mass Communication Quarterly, 81,* 155–167.

Boysen, G. A. (2008). Revenge and student evaluations of teaching. *Teaching of Psychology, 35,* 218–222.

Braithwaite, D. O., & Baxter, L. A. (1995). "I do" again: The relational dialectics of renewing marriage vows. *Journal of Social and Personal Relationships, 12,* 177–198.

Braithwaite, D. O., & Baxter, L. A. (2008). Introduction: Meta-theory and theory in interpersonal communication research. In L. A. Baxter & D. O. Braithwaite (Eds.), *Engaging theories in interpersonal communication: Multiple perspectives* (pp. 1–18). Thousand Oaks, CA: Sage.

Braithwaite, D. O., & Thompson, T. L. (2000). Communication and disability research: A productive past and bright future. In D. O. Braithwaite & T. L. Thompson (Eds.), *Handbook of communication and disabilities* (pp. 507–516). Mahwah, NJ: Erlbaum.

Braithwaite, D. O., Toller, P. W., Daas, K. L., Durham, W. T., & Jones, A. C. (2008). Centered but not caught in the middle: Stepchildren's perceptions of dialectical contradictions in the communication of co-parents. *Journal of Applied Communication Research, 36,* 33–55.

Brann, M., & Mattson, M. (2004). Reframing communication during gynecological exams: A feminist virtue ethic of care perspective. In P. M. Buzzanell, H. Sterk, & L. H. Turner (Eds.), *Gender in applied communication contexts* (pp. 147–168). Thousand Oaks, CA: Sage.

Brasfield, R. (2007). Rereading *Sex and the City:* Exposing the hegemonic feminist narrative. *Journal of Popular Film and Television, 34,* 130–139.

Brashers, D. E. (2001). Communication and uncertainty management. *Journal of Communication, 3,* 477–497.

Brenders, D. A. (1987). Fallacies in the coordinated management of meaning: A philosophy of language critique of the hierarchical organization of coherent conversation and related theory. *Quarterly Journal of Speech, 73,* 329–348.

Brilhart, J. K., Galanes, G. J., & Adams, K. (2001). *Effective group discussion* (10th ed.). New York: McGraw-Hill.

Brooks, D. E., & Ward, C. J. (2007). "Crash" course: Assessing students' engagement with pedagogies of diversity. *Journalism & Mass Communication Educator, 62,* 244–262.

Brown, P., & Levinson, S. (1978). Universals in language usage: Politeness phenomenon. In E. Goody (Ed.), *Questions and politeness* (pp. 56–89). Cambridge: University Press.

Brown, P., & Levinson, S. C. (1987). *Politeness: Some universals in language use.* Cambridge, UK: Cambridge University Press.

Brown, R. (1965). *Social psychology.* New York: Free Press.

Brownstein, A. L., Read, S. J., & Simon, D. (2004). Bias at the racetrack: Effects of individual expertise and task importance on predecision reevaluation of alternatives. *Personality and Social Psychology Bulletin, 30,* 891–909.

Brummett, B. (1993). Introduction. In B. Brummett (Ed.), *Landmark essays on Kenneth Burke* (pp. xi–xix). Davis, CA: Hermagoras Press.

Bruning, S. D., Castle, J. D., & Schrepfer, E. (2004). Building relationships between organizations and publics: Examining the linkage between organization–public relationships, evaluations of satisfaction, and behavioral intent. *Communication Studies, 55,* 435–446.

Bruss, M. B., Morris, J. R., Dannison, L. L., Orbe, M. P. Quitugua, J. A., & Palacios, R. T. (2005). Food, culture, and family: Exploring the coordinated management of meaning regarding childhood obesity. *Health Communication, 18,* 155–175.

Bryant, J., & Miron, D. (2004). Theory and research in mass communication. *Journal of Communication, 54,* 662–704.

Bryant, L. E. (2003). Stepchildren's perceptions of the contradictions in communication with stepfamilies formed post bereavement. Unpublished doctoral dissertation, University of Nebraska, Lincoln.

Budd, M., Entman, R. M., & Steinman, C. (1990). The affirmative character of U.S. cultural studies. *Critical Studies in Mass Communication, 7,* 169–184.

Budd, M., & Steinman, C. (1992). Cultural studies and the politics of encoding research. In S. A. Deetz (Ed.), *Communication yearbook 15* (pp. 251–262). Newbury Park, CA: Sage.

Buffington, D., & Fraley, T. (2008). Skill in black and white: Negotiating media images of race in a sporting context. *Journal of Communication Inquiry, 32,* 292–310.

Bugeja, M. (2005). *Interpersonal divide: The search for community in a technological age.* Oxford: University Press.

Bunz, U., & Campbell, S. W. (2004). Politeness accommodation in electronic mail. *Communication Research Reports, 21,* 11–25.

Bureau of Justice Statistics. (2004). Violent victimization rates by age, 1973–2003. Retrieved September 13, 2005, from the World Wide Web: www.ojp.usdoj.gov/bjs/glance/tables/vagetab.htm

Burgess, E. W. (1926). The family as a unity of interacting personalities. *The Family, 7,* 3–9.

Burgess, E. W., & Locke, H. J. (1953). *The family: From institution to companionship* (2nd ed.). New York: American Book Co.

Burgoon, J. K. (1978). A communication model of personal space violations: Explication and an initial test. *Human Communication Research, 4,* 129–142.

Burgoon, J. K. (1994). Nonverbal signals. In M. L. Knapp & G. R. Miller (Eds.), *Handbook of interpersonal communication* (pp. 229–285). Newbury Park, CA: Sage.

Burgoon, J. K., Coker, D. A., & Coker, R. A. (1986). Communicative effects of gaze behavior: A test of two contrasting explanations. *Human Communication Research, 12,* 495–524.

Burgoon, J. K., Dillman, L., & Stern, L. A. (1993). Adaption in dyadic interaction: Defining and operationalizing patterns of reciprocity and compensation. *Communication Theory, 3,* 295–316.

Burgoon, J. K., & Hale, J. L. (1988). Nonverbal expectancy violations: Model elaboration and application to immediacy behaviors. *Communication Monographs, 55,* 58–79.

Burgoon, J. K., & Jones, S. B. (1976). Toward a theory of personal space expectations and their violations. *Human Communication Research, 2,* 131–146.

Burgoon, J. K., & Walther, J. B. (1990). Nonverbal expectancies and the evaluative consequences of violations. *Human Communication Research, 17,* 232–265.

Burke, K. (1945). *A grammar of motives.* New York: Prentice Hall.

Burke, K. (1950). *A rhetoric of motives.* New York: Prentice Hall.

Burke, K. (1965). *Permanence and change.* Indianapolis: Bobbs-Merrill.

Burke, K. (1966). *Language as symbolic action: Essays on life, literature, and method.* Berkeley: University of California Press.

Burke, K. (1968). Dramatism. In D. L. Sills (Ed.), *The international encyclopedia of the social sciences,* 7 (pp. 445–452). New York: Macmillan/Free Press.

Burke, K. (2007). On persuasion, identification, and dialectical symbols. *Philosophy and Rhetoric, 39,* 333–339.

Burrell, G., & Morgan, G. (1979). *Sociological paradigms and organisational analysis.* London: Heinemann.

Butsch, R. (2007). *Media and public spheres.* New York: Palgrave Macmillan.

Buttle, F. A. (1994). The coordinated management of meaning: A case exemplar of a new consumer research technology. *European Journal of Marketing, 8,* 76–100.

Buzzanell, P. M., Burrell, N. A., Stafford, R. S., & Berkowitz, S. (1996). When I call you up and you're not there: Application of communication accommodation theory to telephone answering machine messages. *Western Journal of Communication, 60,* 310–336.

Buzzanell, P. M. (2004). Revisiting sexual harassment in academe: Using feminist ethical and sensemaking approaches to analyze macrodiscourses and micropractices of sexual harassment. In P. M. Buzzanell, H. Sterk, & L. H. Turner (Eds.), *Gender in applied communication contexts* (pp. 25–46). Thousand Oaks, CA: Sage.

Buzzanell, P. M., & Turner, L. H. (2003). Emotion work revealed by job loss discourse: Backgrounding-foregrounding of feelings, construction of normalcy, and (re)instituting of traditional masculinities. *Journal of Applied Communication Research, 31,* 27–57.

Callan, H. (1978). Harems and overlords: Biosocial models and the female. In S. Ardener (Ed.), *Defining females* (pp. 200–219). New York: Wiley.

Campbell, D. T. (1965). Variation and selective retention in socio-cultural evolution. In H. R. Barringer, G. I. Blanksten, & R. W. Mack (Eds.), *Social change in developing areas* (pp. 19–49). Cambridge, MA: Schenkman.

Carey, J. W. (1975). A cultural approach to communication. *Communication, 2,* 1–22.

Carey, J. W. (1989). *Communication as culture.* Boston: Unwin Hyman.

Carey, J. W. (1998). Marshall McLuhan: Genealogy and legacy. *Canadian Journal of Communication, 23,* 13–21.

Carlson, J. M. (1983). Crime show viewing by pre-adults: The impact on attitudes toward civil liberties. *Communication Research, 10,* 529–552.

Carveth, R., & Alexander, A. (1985). Soap opera viewing motivations and the cultivation hypothesis.

Journal of Broadcasting & Electronic Media, 29, 259–273.

Cast, A. D. (2003). Power and the ability to define the situation. *Social Psychology Quarterly, 66,* 185–201.

Caughlin, J. P., & Afifi, T. D. (2004). When is topic avoidance unsatisfying? Examining moderators of the association between avoidance and dissatisfaction. *Human Communication Research, 30,* 479–513.

Caughlin, J. P., & Petronio, S. (2004). Privacy in families. In A. Vangelisti (Ed.), *Handbook of family communication* (pp. 379–412). Mahwah, NJ: Erlbaum.

Cavanaugh, J. C., & Parks, D. C. (1993). Vitality for life: Psychological research for productive aging. *APS Observer* (Vol. 2; special issue, report 2, pp. 1–2). American Psychological Society.

Chafetz, J. S. (1997). Feminist theory and sociology: Underutilized contributions for mainstream theory. *Annual Review of Sociology, 23,* 97–120.

Chen, Y. W. (2006). The Twain have met! Investigating crucial indicators for intercultural friendship levels between international students from four East Asian countries and U.S. Americans. Paper presented at the annual meeting of the International Communication Association, Singapore.

Chesebro, J. W. (1993). Preface. In J. W. Chesebro (Ed.), *Extensions of the Burkeian system* (pp. vii–xxi). Tuscaloosa: University of Alabama Press.

Chia, S. C., & Lee, W. (2008). Pluralistic ignorance about sex: The direct and the indirect effects of media consumption on college students' misperception of sex-related peer norms. *International Journal of Public Opinion Research, 20,* 53–73.

Child, J. T., Pearson, J. C., & Nagao, M. (2006). Elusive·family problems reported by Japanese college students: An examination of theme variation and methodology. *Journal of Intercultural Communication Research, 35,* 45–59.

Cho, Y. (2008). We know where we're going, but we don't know where we are: An interview with Lawrence Grossberg. *Journal of Communication Inquiry, 32,* 102–122.

Chodorow, N. (1978). *The reproduction of mothering.* Berkeley: University of California Press.

Chopra, R. (2001). Retrieving the father: Gender studies, "father love" and the discourse of mothering. *Women's Studies International Forum, 24,* 445–455.

Cirksena, K., & Cuklanz, L. (1992). Male is to female as _____ is to: A guided tour of five feminist frameworks for communication studies. In L. Rakow (Ed.), *Women making meaning: New feminist directions in communication* (pp. 18–44). New York: Routledge.

Clair, R. P. (1993). The use of framing devices to sequester organizational narratives: Hegemony and harassment. *Communication Monographs, 60,* 113–136.

Clark, G. (2004). *Rhetorical landscapes in America: Variations on a theme from Kenneth Burke.* Columbia: University of South Carolina Press.

Clason, M. (2008). Constructions of masculinity and femininity and their impact on sexual harassment in the workplace. Unpublished dissertation, Marquette University, Milwaukee, WI.

Cline, R. J. W., & McKenzie, N. J. (2000), Dilemmas of disclosure in the age of HIV/AIDS: Balancing privacy and protection in the health care context. In S. Petronio (Ed.), *Balancing the secrets of private disclosures* (pp. 71–82). Mahwah, NJ: Erlbaum.

Cline, R. W. (1990). Detecting groupthink: Methods for observing the illusion of unanimity. *Communication Quarterly, 38,* 112–126.

CNET News. (2008). Survey: One-fifth of Americans have never used email. Retrieved December 2, 2008 from the World Wide Web: www.news.cnet.com/8301-10784_3-9946706-7.html

Cohen, E. (2007). Expectancy violations in relationships with friends and media figures. Paper presented at the annual meeting of the International Communication Association, San Francisco, CA.

Cohen, H. (2000). Revisiting McLuhan. *Media International Australia: Culture and Policy, 5,* 3–9.

Collier, M. J. (1998). Researching cultural identity: Reconciling interpretive and postcolonial perspectives. In D. V. Tanno & A. Gonzalez (Eds.), *Communication and identity across cultures* (pp. 122–147). Thousand Oaks, CA: Sage.

Collins, P. H. (1986). Learning from the outsider within: The sociological significance of black feminist thought. *Social Problems, 33,* 14–32.

Collins, P. H. (1989). A comparison of two works on Black family life. *Signs, 14,* 875–884.

Collins, P. H. (1990). *Black feminist thought: Knowledge, consciousness, and the politics of social empowerment*. Boston: Unwin Hyman.

Collins, P. H. (1991). *Black feminist thought: Knowledge, consciousness, and the politics of empowerment*. New York: Routledge.

Condit, C. M. (1992). Post-Burke: Transcending the substance of dramatism. *Quarterly Journal of Speech, 78,* 349–355.

Conquergood, D. (1992). Life in Big Red: Struggles and accommodations in a Chicago polyethnic tenement. In L. Lamphere (Ed.), *Structuring diversity: Ethnographic perspectives on the new immigration* (pp. 95–144). Chicago: University of Chicago Press.

Conquergood, D. (1994). Homeboys and hoods: Gang communication and cultural space. In L. R. Frey (Ed.), *Group communication in context: Studies of natural groups* (pp. 23–55). Hillsdale, NJ: Erlbaum.

Conrad, C., & Macom, E. A. (1995). Revisiting Kenneth Burke: Dramatism/logology and the problem of agency. *Southern Communication Journal, 61,* 11–28.

Cook, K. S., & Rice, E. (2003). Social exchange theory. In J. Delamater (Ed.), *Handbook of social psychology* (pp. 53–76). New York: Kluwer Academic/Plenum.

Cooley, C. H. (1972). *Human nature and social order*. Glencoe, IL: Free Press.

Coontz, S. (1988). *The social origins of private life*. New York: Verso.

Cooper, J., & Fazio, R. H. (1984). A new look at dissonance theory. In L. Berkowitz (Ed.), *Advances in experimental social psychology* (pp. 229–266). Orlando, FL: Academic Press.

Cooper, J., & Stone, J. (2000). Cognitive dissonance and the social group. In D. J. Terry & M. A. Hogg (Eds.), *Attitudes, behavior, and social context: The role of norms and group membership* (pp. 227–244). Mahwah, NJ: Erlbaum.

Cooper, J. M. (1986). *Reason and human good in Aristotle*. Indianapolis, IN: Hackett Publishing.

Cooper, J. M. (1996). An Aristotelian theory of the emotions. In A. O. Rorty (Ed.), *Essays on Aristotle's* Rhetoric (pp. 238–257). Berkeley: University of California Press.

Cooper, L. (1932). *The rhetoric of Aristotle*. New York: Appleton-Century-Crofts.

Coplin, W. (2004). *10 things employers want you to learn in college*. Berkeley, CA: Ten Speed Press.

Cottrell, N. B., Wack, D. L., Sekerak, G. J., & Rittle, H. (1968). Social facilitation of dominant responses by the presence of an audience and the mere presence of others. *Journal of Personality and Social Psychology, 9,* 245–250.

Coupland, N., Coupland, J., Giles, H., & Henwood, K. (1988). Accommodating the elderly: Invoking and extending a theory. *Language in Society, 17,* 1–41.

Courtright, J. (1978). A laboratory investigation of groupthink. *Communication Monographs, 45,* 229–246.

Cox, S. A., & Kramer, M. W. (1995). Communication during employee dismissals: Social exchange principles and group influences on employee exit. *Management Communication Quarterly, 9,* 156–190.

Craig, R. T. (1999). Communication theory as a field. *Communication Theory, 9,* 119–161.

Craig, R. T. (2007). Communication theory as a field. In R. T. Craig & H. L. Muller (Eds.), *Theorizing communication: Readings across traditions* (pp. 63–98). Thousand Oaks, CA: Sage.

Craig, R. T., & Muller, H. L. (2007). *Theorizing communication: Readings across traditions*. Thousand Oaks, CA: Sage.

Cronen, V. E. (1995a). Coordinated management of meaning: The consequentiality of communication and the recapturing of experience. In S. J. Sigman (Ed.), *The consequentiality of communication* (pp. 17–66). Hillsdale, NJ: Erlbaum.

Cronen, V. E. (1995b). Practical theory and the tasks ahead for social approaches to communication. In W. Leeds-Hurwitz (Ed.), *Social approaches to communication* (pp. 217–242). New York: Guilford Press.

Cronen, V. E., & Pearce, W. B. (1981). Logical force in interpersonal communication: A new concept of the "necessity" in social behaviors. *Communication, 6,* 5–67.

Cronen, V. E., Chen, V., & Pearce, W. B. (1988). The coordinated management of meaning in intercultural communication: A critical theory in the pragmatic tradition. In Y. Y. Kim & W. Gudykunst (Eds.), *Theories in intercultural communication* (pp. 66–98). Newbury Park: Sage.

Cronen, V. E., Pearce, W. B., & Harris, L. M. (1982). The coordinated management of meaning: A theory of communication. In F. E. X. Dance (Ed.), *Human communication theory* (pp. 67–89). New York: Harper & Row.

Cronen, V. E., Pearce, W. B., & Snaveley, L. M. (1979). A theory of rule-structure and types of episodes, and a study of perceived enmeshment in undesired repetitive patterns (URPs). In D. Nimmo (Ed.), *Communication yearbook 3* (pp. 225–239). New Brunswick, NJ: Transaction Books.

Csikszentmihalyi, M. (1991). Reflections on the "Spiral of Silence." In J. A. Anderson (Ed.), *Communication yearbook 14* (pp. 294–298). Newbury Park, CA: Sage.

Cubrick, K. N., & Chory, R. M. (2007). Exposure to television makeover programs and perceptions of self. *Communication Research Reports, 24,* 283–291.

Cultural Environment Movement. (1996). Viewers' declaration of independence. *Cultural environment monitor, 1,* 1.

Cupach, W. R., & Metts, S. (1994). *Facework.* Thousand Oaks, CA: Sage.

Cushman, D. P., & Cahn, D. D. (1985). *Communication in interpersonal relationships.* Albany, NY: SUNY Press.

Cushman, D. P., & Pearce, W. B. (1977). Generality and necessity in three types of human communication theory: Special attention to rules theory. In B. Ruben (Ed.), *Communication yearbook 1* (pp. 173–182). New Brunswick, NJ: Transaction Books.

Cushman, D., & Whiting, G. C. (1972). An approach to communication theory: Toward consensus on rules. *The Journal of Communication, 22,* 217–238.

Dainton, M., & Aylor, B. (2001). A relational uncertainty analysis of jealousy, trust, and maintenance in long-distance versus geographically close relationships. *Communication Quarterly, 49,* 172–188.

Dance, F. E. X. (1967). Toward a theory of human communication. In F. E. X. Dance (Ed.), *Human communication theory* (pp. 288–309). New York: Holt.

Daniels, T. D., Spiker, B. D., & Papa, M. J. (2008). *Perspectives on organizational communication.* Boston: McGraw-Hill.

Darwin, C. (1948). *The origin of species.* New York: Random House.

Davis, K. (2008). Intersectionality as buzzword: A sociology of science perspective on what makes a feminist theory successful. *Feminist Theory, 9,* 67–85.

DeFrancisco, V. (1991). The sounds of silence: How men silence women in marital relationships. *Discourse and Society, 2,* 355–370.

Delaney, T. (2008). *Simpsonology.* Amherst, NY: Prometheus Books.

Derlega, V. J., Metts, S., Petronio, S., & Margulis, S. T. (1993). *Self-disclosure.* Newbury Park, CA: Sage.

de Sousa Santos, B. (2006). Globalizations. *Theory, Culture, & Society, 23,* 393–399.

DeWitt, L. (2006). Face-Negotiation theory. *North Dakota Speech and Theatre Journal, 19,* 38–42.

Dickson, F. C., & Walker, K. L. (2001). The expression of emotion in later-life married men. *Communication Quarterly, 49,* 66–71.

Dillon, R. K., & Galanes, G. J. (2002). Public dialogue: Communication theory as public affairs praxis. *Journal of Public Affairs, 6,* 79–91.

Dimmick, J., Chen, Y., & Li, Z. (2004). Competition between the Internet and traditional news media: The gratification-opportunities niche dimension. *The Journal of Media Economics, 17,* 19–33.

Dimmick, J., Sikand, J., & Patterson, S. J. (1994). The gratifications of the household telephone: Sociability, instrumentality, and reassurance. *Communication Reports, 21,* 643–663.

Dindia, K. (1994). The intrapersonal-interpersonal dialectical process of self-disclosure. In S. Duck (Ed.), *Dynamics of relationships* (pp. 27–56). Thousand Oaks, CA: Sage.

Dindia, K. (2003). Definitions and perspectives on relational maintenance communication. In D. J. Canary & M. Dainton (Eds.), *Maintaining relationships through communication: Relational, contextual, and cultural variations* (pp. 1–30). Mahwah, NJ: Erlbaum.

Dobkin, B. A., & Pace, R. C. (2006). *Communication in a changing world.* New York: McGraw-Hill.

Doherty, W. J., Boss, P. G., LaRossa, R., Schumm, W. R., & Steinmetz, S. K. (1993). Family theory and methods. In P. G. Boss, W. J. Doherty, R. LaRossa, W. R. Schumm, & S. K. Steinmetz (Eds.), *Sourcebook of family theories and methods: A contextual approach* (pp. 313–341). New York: Plenum.

Domagalski, T. A., & Steelman, L. A. (2007). The impact of gender and organizational status on anger expression. *Management Communication Quarterly, 20,* 297–315.

Domenici, K., & Littlejohn, S. W. (2006). *Facework: Bridging theory and practice.* Thousand Oaks, CA: Sage.

Donnelly, J. H., & Ivancevich, J. M. (1970). Post-purchase reinforcement and back-out behavior. *Journal of Marketing Research, 7,* 399–400.

Dougherty, D. S. (2001). Sexual harassment as [dys]functional process: A feminist standpoint analysis. *Journal of Applied Communication Research, 29,* 372–391.

Dougherty, D. S., & Krone, K. J. (2000). Overcoming the dichotomy: Cultivating standpoints in organizations through research. *Women's Studies in Communication, 23,* 16–40.

Dow, B. J. (1990). Hegemony, feminist criticism and *The Mary Tyler Moore Show. Critical Studies in Mass Communication, 7,* 261–274.

Dray, W. (1957). *Laws and explanation in history.* London: Oxford University Press.

Dresner, E. (2006). Middle region phenomena and globalization. *The International Communication Gazette, 68,* 363–378.

DuBrin, A. J. (2007). *Human relations: Interpersonal job-oriented skills.* New York: Prentice-Hall.

Duck, S. (1994). *Meaningful relationships.* Thousand Oaks, CA: Sage.

duGay, P., Hall, S., Janes, L., Mackay, H., & Negus, K. (1997). *Doing cultural studies: The story of the Sony Walkman.* London: Sage/The Open University.

Duggan, A. P., & Parrott, R. L. (2001). Physicians' nonverbal rapport-building behaviors and patients' talk about the subjective component of illness. *Human Communication Research, 27,* 299–311.

Durham, W. T. (2008). The rules-based process of revealing/concealing the family planning decisions of voluntarily child-free couples: A communication privacy management perspective. *Communication Studies, 59,* 132–147.

Eckstein, N. J., & Turman, P. D. (2002). "Children are to be seen and not heard": Silencing students' religious voices in the university classroom. *Journal of Communication and Religion, 25,* 166–192.

Edley, P. P. (2004). Entrepreneurial mothers' balance of work and family: Discursive constructions of time, mothering, and identity. In P. M. Buzzanell, H. Sterk, & L. H. Turner (Eds.), *Gender in applied communication contexts* (pp. 255–273). Thousand Oaks, CA: Sage.

Edsall, R. (2007). Cultural factors in digital cartographic design: Implications for communication to diverse users. *Cartography and Geographic Information Science, 34,* 121–129.

Eisenberg, E. M., & Goodall, H. L. (2004). *Organizational communication: Balancing creativity and constraint.* Boston: Bedford/St. Martin's.

Eisenberg, E. M., Goodall, H. M., & Tretheway, A. (2006). *Organizational communication: Balancing creativity and constraint.* New York: Bedford Books.

Eisenberg, E. M. (2007). *Strategic ambiguities: Essays on communication, organization, and identity.* Thousand Oaks, CA: Sage.

Elgin, S. (1988). *A first dictionary and grammar of Laadan* (2nd ed.). Madison, WI: Society for the Furtherance and Study of Fantasy and Science Fiction.

Elkin, R. A., & Leippe, M. R. (1986). Physiological arousal, dissonance, and attitude change: Evidence for a dissonance-arousal link and a don't remind me effect. *Journal of Abnormal and Social Psychology, 51,* 55–65.

Elkins, J. R. (2001) Narrative theory and literary criticism. Retrieved September 11, 2002 from the World Wide Web: www.wvu.edu/lawfac/jelkins/lawyerslit/theories.htm

Ellison, N., Heino, R., & Gibbs, J. (2006). Managing impressions online: Self-presentation processes in the online dating environment. *Journal of Computer-Mediated Communication, 11,* article 2. (http://jcmc.indiana.edu/vol11/issue2/ellison.html)

Emmers, T. M., & Canary, D. J. (1996). The effect of uncertainty reduction strategies on young couples' relational repair and intimacy. *Communication Quarterly, 44,* 166–182.

Emmers-Sommer, T. M. (2003). When partners falter: Repair after a transgression. In D. J. Canary & M. A. Dainton (Eds.), *Maintaining relationships through communication: Relational, contextual, and cultural variations* (pp. 185–208). Mahwah, NJ: Erlbaum.

Engen, D. E. (2002). The communicative imagination and its cultivation. *Communication Quarterly, 50,* 41–57.

England, P. (1989). A feminist critique of rational-choice theories: Implications for Sociology. *The American Sociologist, 20,* 14–28.

Engleberg, I. N., & Wynn, D. (2007). *Working in groups: Communication principles and strategies.* Boston: Allyn & Bacon.

Englehardt, E. E. (2001). *Ethical issues in interpersonal communication.* Fort Worth, TX: Harcourt.

Erbert, L. A. (2000). Conflict and dialectics: Perceptions of dialectical contradiction in marital conflict. *Journal of Social and Personal Relationships, 17,* 638–659.

Ernste, T., Fan, D., Sheets, P., & Elmasry, M. (2007). Conservative, liberal, or moderate? The public opinion and computer-mediated communication. Paper presented at the annual meeting of the International Communication Association, San Francisco, CA.

Eyal, K., & Finnerty, K. (2007). The portrayal of consequences of sexual intercourse on prime-time programming. *Communication Research Reports, 24,* 225–233.

Faber, R. J. (2000). The urge to buy: A uses and gratifications perspective on compulsive buying. In S. Ratneshwar, D. G. Mick, & C. Huffman (Eds.), *The why of consumption* (pp. 177–196). London: Routledge.

Ferguson, D. A. (1992). Channel repertoire in the presence of remote control devices, VCRs and cable television. *Journal of Broadcasting & Electronic Media, 36,* 83–91.

Fernback, J. (2007). Beyond the diluted community concept: A symbolic interactionist perspective on online social relations. *New Media & Society, 9,* 49–69.

Festinger, L. (1957). *A theory of cognitive dissonance.* Stanford, CA: Stanford University Press.

Festinger, L., & Carlsmith, J. M. (1959). Cognitive consequences of forced compliance. *Journal of Abnormal and Social Psychology, 58,* 203–210.

Festinger, L., Riecken, H. W., & Schacter, S. (1956). *When prophecy fails.* Minneapolis: University of Minnesota Press.

Ficara, L. C., & Mongeau, P. A. (2000, November). *Relational uncertainity in long-distance college student dating relationships.* Paper presented at the annual meeting of the National Communication Association, Seattle, WA.

Fiese, B. H. (2003). Coherent accounts of coping with a chronic illness: Convergences and divergences in family measurement using a narrative analysis. *Family Process, 42,* 439–451.

Finklehor, D., & Ormrod, R. (2000, June). Kidnapping of juveniles: Patterns from NIBRS. *Juvenile Justice Bulletin.* Washington, DC: U.S. Department of Justice, Office of Justice Programs: Office of Juvenile Justice and Delinquency Prevention.

Fisher, W. R. (1984). Narration as a human communication paradigm: The case of public moral argument. *Communication Monographs, 51,* 1–22.

Fisher, W. R. (1985). The narrative paradigm: An elaboration. *Communication Monographs, 52,* 347–367.

Fisher, W. R. (1987). *Human communication as narration: Toward a philosophy of reason, value, and action.* Columbia: University of South Carolina Press.

Fiske, S. T., & Taylor, S. E. (1984). *Social cognition.* Reading, MA: Addison-Wesley.

Flanagin, A. J. (2007). Commercial markets as communication markets: Uncertainty reduction through mediated information exchange in online auctions. *New Media & Society, 9,* 401–423.

Flint, D. J. (2006). Innovation, symbolic interaction and customer valuing: Thoughts stemming from a service-dominant logic of marketing. *Marketing Theory, 6,* 349–362.

Foa, U., & Foa, E. (1974). *Societal structures of the mind.* Springfield, IL: Thomas.

Ford, L. A., & Crabtree, R. D. (2002). Telling, retelling and talking about telling: Disclosure and/as surviving incest. *Women's Studies in Communication, 25,* 53–87.

Forte, J. A. (2004). Symbolic interactionism and social work: A forgotten legacy, part 2. *Families in Society, 85,* 521–530.

Forte, J. A., Barrett, A. V., & Campbell, M. H. (1996). Patterns of social connectedness and shared grief work: A symbolic interactionist perspective. *Social Work With Groups, 19,* 29–51.

Foss, K., & Foss, S. (1991). *Women speak: The eloquence of women's lives.* Prospect Heights, IL: Waveland Press.

Foss, S. (1994). A rhetorical scheme for the evaluation of visual imagery. *Communication Studies, 45,* 213–224.

Foss, S., Foss, K., & Trapp, R. (1991). *Contemporary perspectives on rhetoric.* Prospect Heights, IL: Waveland Press.

Fox, C. (2002). Beyond the "tyranny of the real": Revisiting Burke's pentad as research method for professional communication. *Technical Communication Quarterly, 11,* 365–388.

Frankenberg, R. (1993). *White women, race matters: The social construction of Whiteness.* Minneapolis: University of Minnesota Press.

French, J. R. & Raven, B. (1959). *The bases of social power.* Ann Arbor: University of Michigan Press.

Frewin, K., & Tuffin, K. (1998). Police status, conformity and internal pressure: A discursive analysis of police culture. *Discourse & Society, 9,* 173–185.

Frey, L. R., Botan, C. H., & Kreps, G. L. (2000). *Investigating communication: An introduction to research methods* (2nd ed.). Boston: Allyn & Bacon.

Frymier, A. B. (2005). Students' classroom communication effectiveness. *Communication Quarterly, 53,* 197–212.

Frymier, A. B., & Houser, M. A. (2002). The teacher-student relationship as an interpersonal relationship. *Communication Education, 49,* 207–219.

Fujishin, R. (2007). *Creating effective groups: The art of small group communication.* Lanham, MD: Rowman & Littlefield.

Gabriel, Y. (2008). Spectacles of resistance and resistance of spectacles. *Management Communication Quarterly, 21,* 310–326.

Gallois, C., & Callan, V. J. (1991). Interethnic accommodation: The role of norms. In H. Giles, J. Coupland, & N. Coupland (Eds.), *Contexts of accommodation: Developments in applied sociolinguistics* (pp. 245–269). Cambridge: Cambridge University Press.

Gallois, C., Callan, V. J., & Johnstone, M. (1984). Personality judgments of Australian aborigine and White speakers: Ethnicity, sex, and context. *Journal of Language and Social Psychology, 3,* 39–57.

Gallois, C., Franklyn-Stokes, A., Giles, H., & Coupland, N. (1988). Communication accommodation theory and intercultural encounters: Intergroup and interpersonal considerations. In Y. Y. Kim & W. B. Gudykunst (Eds.), *Theories in intercultural communication* (pp. 157–185). Newbury Park, CA: Sage.

Gallois, C., Ogay, T., & Giles, H. (2005). Communication accommodation theory. In W. Gudykunst (Ed.), *Theorizing about intercultural communication* (pp. 121–148). Thousand Oaks, CA: Sage.

Galvin, K. (2004). The family of the future: What do we face. In A. Vangelisti (Ed.), *Handbook of family communication* (pp. 675–698). Mahwah, NJ: Erlbaum.

Garnett, J. L., & Kouzmin, A. (2007). Communicating throughout Katrina: Competing and complementary conceptual lenses on crisis communication. *Public Administration Review, 67,* 171–187.

Gastil, J., Leighter, J., Deess, E. P., & Black, L. (2008). From small group member to citizen: Measuring the impact of jury deliberation on citizen identity and civic norms. *Human Communication Research, 34,* 137–169.

Gecas, V., & Burke, P. J. (1995). Self and identity. In K. S. Cook, G. A. Fine, & J. S. House (Eds.), *Sociological perspectives on social psychology* (pp. 41–67). Boston: Allyn & Bacon.

Geertz, C. (1973). *The interpretation of cultures.* New York: Basic Books.

Geertz, C. (1983). *Local knowledge.* New York: Basic Books.

Gencarelli, T. F. (2006). Neil Postman and the rise of media ecology. In C. M. K. Lum (Ed.), *Perspectives on culture, technology, and communication: The media ecology tradition* (pp. 201–25). Cresskill, NJ: Hampton.

Gendrin, D. M. (2000). Homeless women's inner voices: Friends or foes? In M. J. Hardman & A. Taylor (Eds.), *Hearing many voices* (pp. 203–219). Cresskill, NJ: Hampton Press.

Gerbner, G. (1998). Cultivation analysis: An overview. *Mass Communication and Society, 3/4,* 175–194.

Gerbner, G. (1999). What do we know? In J. Shanahan & M. Morgan (Eds.), *Television and its viewers: Cultivation theory and research* (pp. ix–xiii). Cambridge: Cambridge University Press.

Gerbner, G., & Gross, L. (1972). Living with television: The violence profile. *Journal of Communication, 26,* 173–199.

Gerbner, G., Gross, L., Jackson-Beeck, M., Jeffries-Fox, S., & Signorielli, N. (1978). Cultural indicators: Violence profile No. 9. *Journal of Communication, 28*, 176–206.

Gerbner, G., Gross, L., Jackson-Beeck, M., Jeffries-Fox, S., & Signorielli, N. (1978). Cultural indicators: Violence profile No. 9. *Journal of Communication, 28*, 176–206.

Gerbner, G., Gross, L., Morgan, M., & Signorielli, N. (1982). Charting the mainstream: Television's contributions to political orientations. *Journal of Communication, 32*, 100–127.

Gerbner, G., Gross, L., Morgan, M., & Signorielli, N. (1986). Living with television: The dynamics of the cultivation process. In J. Bryant & D. Zillman (Eds.), *Perspectives on media effects* (pp. 17–40). Hillsdale, NJ: Earlbaum.

Gibbs, J. L., Ellison, N. B., & Heino, R. D. (2006). Self-presentation in online personals: The role of anticipated future interaction, self-disclosure and perceived success in Internet dating. *Communication Research, 33*, 152–177.

Giddens, A. (1979). *Central problems in social theory: Action, structure, and contradiction in social analysis.* Berkeley: University of California Press.

Giddens, A. (1984). *The constitution of society: Outline of the theory of structuration.* Berkeley: University of California Press.

Giddens, A. (1993). *New rules of sociological method: A positive critique of interpretive sociologies* (2nd ed.). Cambridge, UK: Polity Press.

Gilder, G. F. (1994). *Life after television.* New York: Norton.

Giles, H. (2008). Communication accommodation theory. In L. A. Baxter & D. O. Braithwaite (Eds.), *Engaging theories in interpersonal communication* (pp. 161–174). Los Angeles: Sage.

Giles, H., Coupland, N., & Coupland, J. (1991). Accommodation theory: Communication, context, and consequence. In II. Giles, J. Coupland, & N. Coupland (Eds.), *Contexts of accommodation: Developments in applied sociolinguistics* (pp. 1–68). Cambridge: Cambridge University Press.

Giles, H., Mulac, A., Bradac, J. J., & Johnson, P. (1987). Speech accommodation theory: The first decade and beyond. In M. L. Mclaughlin (Ed.), *Communication yearbook 10* (pp. 13–48). Newbury Park, CA: Sage.

Giles, H., & Smith, P. M. (1979). Accommodation theory: Optimal levels of convergence. In H. Giles, & R. N. St. Clair (Eds.), *Language and social psychology* (pp. 231–244). Oxford: Blackwell.

Giles, H., & Wiemann, J. (1987). Language, social comparison, and power. In S. Chaffee & C. R. Berger (Eds.), *Handbook of communication science* (pp. 350–384). Newbury Park, CA: Sage.

Giles, H., Willemyns, M., Gallois, C., & Anderson, M. C. (2007). Accommodating a new frontier: The context of law enforcement. In K. Fiedler (Ed.), *Social accommodation* (pp. 129–162). New York: Psychology Press.

Ginnett, R. (2005). What can leaders to do avoid groupthink? *Leadership in Action, 25*, 13.

Glascock, J., & Ruggerio, T. E. (2004). Representations of class and gender of primetime Spanish-language television in the United States. *Communication Quarterly, 52*, 390–402.

Glynn, C. J., Hayes, A. F., & Shanahan, J. (1997). Perceived support for one's opinions and willingness to speak out: A meta-analysis of survey studies on the spiral of silence. *Public Opinion Quarterly, 61*, 452–463.

Glynn, C. J., & McLeod, J. M. (1985). Implications of the spiral of silence for communication and public opinion research. In K. R. Sanders, L. L. Kaid, & D. Nimmo (Eds.), *Political communication yearbook 1984* (pp. 43–65). Carbondale: Southern Illinois University Press.

Goffman, E. (1967). *Interaction rituals: Essays on face-to-face interaction.* Garden City, NY: Doubleday.

Goffman, E. (1974). *Frame analysis: An essay on the organization of experience.* New York: Harper & Row.

Golden, A. (2000). What we talk about when we talk about work and family: A discourse analysis of parental accounts. *Electronic Journal of Communication/La Revue Electronique de Communication, 10.*

Golden, J. L., Berquist, G. F., Coleman, W. E., Sproule, J. M., & Golden, R. (2007). *The rhetoric of Western thought: From the Mediterranean world to the global setting.* Dubuque, IA: Kendall-Hunt.

Golish, T. D., & Powell, K. A. (2003). "Ambiguous loss": Managing the dialectics of grief associated with premature birth. *Journal of Social and Personal Relationships, 20*, 309–334.

Gong, G. (2004). When Mississippi Chinese talk. In A. Gonzalez, M. Houston, & V. Chen (Eds.), *Our voices: Essays in culture, ethnicity, and communication* (pp. 104–113). Los Angeles: Roxbury.

Gonzalez, A., & Gonzalez, J. (2002). The color problem in sillyville: Negotiating white identity in one popular "kid-vid." *Communication Quarterly, 50,* 410–422.

Gonzalez, A., Houston, M., & Chen, V. (2004). Introduction. In A. Gonzalez, M. Houston, & V. Chen (Eds.), *Our voices: Essays in culture, ethnicity, and communication* (pp. 1–13). Los Angeles: Roxbury.

Goodboy, A. L., & Myers, S. A. (2008). The effect of teacher confirmation on student communication and learning outcomes. *Communication Education, 57,* 153–178.

Gordon, G. (1982, January). An end to McLuhanacy. *Educational Technology, 44,* 39–45.

Gordon, W. T. (Ed.) (2002). *Marshall McLuhan: Understanding Media.* Berkeley, CA: Gingko Press.

Gouran, D. S. (1998). The signs of cognitive, affiliative, and egocentric constraints in patterns of interaction in decision-making and problem-solving groups and their potential effects on outcomes. In J. Trent (Ed.), *Communication: Views from the helm for the 21st century* (pp. 98–102). Needham Heights, MA: Allyn & Bacon.

Gouran, D. S., & Hirokawa, R. Y. (1996). Functional theory and communication in decision-making and problem-solving groups. In R. Y. Hirokawa & M. S. Poole (Eds.), *Communication and group decision making* (pp. 55–80). Thousand Oaks, CA: Sage.

Gouran, D. S., Hirokawa, R. Y., & Martz, A. E. (1986). A critical analysis of factors related to decisional processes involved in the *Challenger* disaster. *Central States Speech Journal, 37,* 119–135.

Gray, H. (1989). Television, Black Americans, and the American dream. *Critical Studies in Mass Communication, 6,* 376–386.

Greene, K., & Kremar, M. (2005). Predicting exposure to and liking of media violence: A uses and gratifications approach. *Communication Studies, 56,* 71–93.

Greene, K., Derlega, V. J., Yep, G. A., & Petronio, S. (2003). *Privacy and disclosure of HIV in interpersonal relationships.* Mahwah, NJ: Erlbaum.

Griffin, C. L. (2009). *Invitation to public speaking.* Belmont, CA: Wadsworth.

Gross, M., Guerrero, L. K., & Alberts, J. K. (2004). Perceptions of conflict strategies and communication competence in task-oriented dyads. *Journal of Applied Communication Research, 32,* 249–271.

Grossberg, L. (1986). Is there rock after punk? *Critical Studies in Mass Communication, 3,* 50–74.

Grossberg, L. (1997). *Bringing it all back home: Essays on cultural studies.* Durham, NC: Duke University Press.

Grosswiler, P. (1997). *The method is the message: Rethinking McLuhan through critical theory.* Montreal: Black Rose Books.

Gudykunst, W. B. (1995). Anxiety/uncertainty management (AUM) theory. In R. Wiseman (Ed.), *Intercultural communication theory* (pp. 8–58). Thousand Oaks, CA: Sage.

Gudykunst, W. B., Chua, E., & Gray, A. (1987). Cultural dissimilarity and uncertainty reduction processes. In M. McLaughlin (Ed.), *Communication yearbook, 10* (pp. 456–469). Newbury Park, CA: Sage.

Gudykunst, W. B., & Hammer, M. R. (1987). The influences of ethnicity, gender, and dyadic composition on uncertainty reduction in initial interactions. *Journal of Black Studies, 18,* 191–214.

Gudykunst, W. B., & Matsumoto, Y. (1996). Cross-cultural variability of communication in personal relationships. In W. B. Gudykunst, S. Ting-Toomey, & T. Nishida (Eds.), *Communication in personal relationships across cultures* (pp. 19–56). Thousand Oaks, CA: Sage.

Gudykunst, W. B., & Nishida, T. (1984). Individual and cultural influence on uncertainty reduction. *Communication Monographs, 51,* 23–36.

Gudykunst, W. B., & Nishida, T. (1986a). Attributional confidence in low- and high-context cultures. *Human Communication Research, 12,* 525–549.

Gudykunst, W. B., & Nishida, T. (1986b). Social penetration in close relationships in Japan and the United States. In R. Bostrom (Ed.), *Communication yearbook 7* (pp. 592–610). Beverly Hills, CA: Sage.

Gudykunst, W. B., Yang, S. M., & Nishida, T. (1985). A cross-cultural test of uncertainty reduction theory: Comparison of acquaintances, friends, and dating relationships in Japan, Korea, and the United States. *Human Communication Research, 11,* 407–454.

Guerrero, L. K., & Bachman, G. F. (2008). Communication following relational transgressions in dating relationships: An investment-model explanation. *Southern Communication Journal, 73*, 4–23.

Hajek, C., Villagran, M., & Wittenberg-Lyles, E. (2007). The relationships among perceived physician accommodation, perceived outgroup typicality, and patient inclinations toward compliance. *Communication Research Reports, 24*, 293–302.

Hakanen, E. A. (2007). *Branding the teleself: Media effects discourse and the changing self.* Lanham, MD: Rowman & Littlefield.

Hall, E. T. (1966). *The hidden dimension.* Garden City, NY: Anchor/Doubleday.

Hall, E. T. (1977). *Beyond culture.* Garden City, NY: Anchor/Doubleday.

Hall, E. T. (1990). *Beyond culture.* New York, NY: Anchor Books.

Hall, E. T. (1992). *An anthropology of everyday life.* New York: Doubleday/Anchor Books.

Hall, E. T., & Hall, M. R. (1990). *Understanding cultural differences.* Yarmouth, ME: Intercultural Press.

Hall, S. (1980a). Encoding/decoding. In S. Hall, D. Hobson, A. Lowe, & P. Willis (Eds.), *Culture, media, language* (pp. 128–138). London: Hutchinson.

Hall, S. (1980b). Cultural studies and the centre: Some problematic and problems. In S. Hall, D. Hobson, A. Lowe, & P. Willis (Eds.), *Culture, media, language* (pp. 15–47). London: Hutchinson.

Hall, S. (1981). The whites of their eyes: Racist ideologies and the media. In G. Bridges & R. Brunt (Eds.), *Silver linings: Some strategies for the eighties* (pp. 28–52). London: Lawrence and Wishart.

Hall, S. (1989). Ideology and communication theory. In B. Dervin, L. Grossberg, B. J. O'Keefe, & E. Wartella (Eds.), *Rethinking communication: Paradigm issues* (pp. 40–51). Newbury Park, CA: Sage.

Hall, S. (1992). Cultural studies and its theoretical legacies. In L. Grossberg, C. Nelson, & P. Treichler (Eds.), *Cultural studies* (pp. 277–294). New York: Routledge.

Hall, S. (1997). The problem of ideology: Marxism without guarantees. In S. Hall (Ed.), *Representation: Cultural representations and signifying practices* (pp. 30–46). London: Sage/The Open University.

Halpert, J., & Burg, J. H. (1997). Mixed messages: Coworker responses to the pregnant employee. *Journal of Business and Psychology, 12*, 241–253.

Hammersley, M. (1992). *What's wrong with ethnography? Methodological explorations.* London: Routledge.

Haraway, D. (1988). Situated knowledges: The science question in feminism and the privilege of partial perspective. *Signs, 14*, 575–599.

Harding, S. (1987). Introduction: Is there a feminist method? In Sandra Harding (Ed.), *Feminism and methodology* (pp. 1–14). Bloomington: University of Indiana Press.

Harding, S. (1991). *Whose science, whose knowledge? Thinking from women's lives.* Ithaca, NY: Cornell University Press.

Hargie, O., Tourish, D., & Wilson, N. (2002). Communication audits and the effects of increased information: A follow-up study. *The Journal of Business Communication, 39*, 414–436.

Haridakis, P. M., & Rubin, A. M. (2005). Third-person effects in the aftermath of terrorism. *Mass Communication & Society, 8*, 39–59.

Harmon-Jones, E. (2000). An update on cognitive dissonance theory, with a focus on the self. In A. Tesser, R. B. Felson, & J. M. Suls (Eds.), *Psychological perspectives on self and identity* (pp. 119–144). Washington, DC: American Psychological Association.

Harris, M., & Cullen, R. (2008). Renovation as innovation: Transforming a campus symbol and a campus culture. *Perspectives: Policy and Practice in Higher Education, 12*, 4–51.

Harris, T. E., & Sherblom, J. C. (2008). *Small group and team communication.* Boston: Allyn & Bacon.

Hart, R. P. (1997). *Modern rhetorical criticism.* Boston: Allyn & Bacon.

Hartley, J. (2003). *A short history of cultural studies.* London: Sage.

Hartsock, N. (1981). Political change: Two perspectives in power. In C. Bunch (Ed.), *Building feminist theory: Essays from Quest, a feminist quarterly* (pp. 55–70). New York: Longman.

Hartsock, N. (1983). The feminist standpoint: Developing the ground for a specifically feminist historical materialism. In S. Harding & M. B. Hintikka (Eds.), *Discovering reality* (pp. 283–310). Boston: Ridel.

Hartsock, N. C. M. (1997). Standpoint theories for the next century. *Women and Politics, 18,* 93–101.

Harwood, J. (2000). Communicative predictors of solidarity in the grandparent-grandchild relationship. *Journal of Social and Personal Relationships, 17,* 743–766.

Harwood, J. (2006). Communication as social identity. In G. Shepherd, J. St. John, & T. Striphas (Eds.) *Communication as . . . : Perspectives on theory* (pp. 84–90). Thousand Oaks, CA: Sage.

Hatch, M. J. (2006). Organizational theory: Modern, symbolic, and postmodern perspective. Oxford: Oxford University Press.

Hayden, S. (1994). Interruptions and the construction of reality. In L. H. Turner & H. M. Sterk (Eds.), *Differences that make a difference: Examining the assumptions in gender research* (pp. 99–106). Westport, CT: Bergin & Garvey.

Hechter, M. (2004). From class to culture. *The American Journal of Sociology, 110,* 400–445.

Heider, F. (1958). *The psychology of interpersonal relations.* New York: Wiley.

Heidlebaugh, N. J. (2008). Invention and public dialogue: Lessons from rhetorical theories. *Communication Theory, 18,* 27–50.

Helpguide.org. (2008). Relationship help: Building great relationships using emotional intelligence. Retrieved December 2, 2008 from the World Wide Web: www.helpguide.org/mental/improve_relationships.htm

Hempel, C. (1952). *Fundamentals of concept formation in empirical science.* Chicago: University of Chicago Press.

Herek, G. M., Janis, I. L., & Huth, P. (1987). Decision making during international crises: Is quality of process related to outcome? *Journal of Conflict Resolution, 31,* 203–226.

Herrmann, A. (2007). Narrative and ethnography as existential phenomenological approaches to organizational sensemaking. Paper presented at the annual meeting of the International Communication Association, San Francisco, CA.

Herzog, H. (1944). Motivations and gratifications of daily serial listeners. In P. F. Lazarsfeld & F. N. Stanton (Eds.), *Radio Research, 1942–1943.* New York: Duell, Sloan and Pearce.

Hetsroni, A. (2001). What do you really need to know to be a millionaire? Content analysis of quiz shows in America and in Israel. *Communication Research Reports, 18,* 418–428.

Hiam, A. (1998, October). Obstacles to creativity—and how you can remove them. *The Futurist,* 30.

Hickson, M., Stacks, D. W., & Moore, N. J. (2007). *Nonverbal communication: Studies and applications.* New York: Oxford.

Hirokawa, R. Y., Erbert, L., & Hurst, A. (1996). Communication and group decision-making effectiveness. In R. Y. Hirokawa & M. S. Poole (Eds.), *Communication and group decision making* (pp. 269–300). Thousand Oaks, CA: Sage.

Hirokawa, R. Y., Gouran, D. S., & Martz, A. E. (1988). Understanding the sources of faulty group decision making: A lesson from the *Challenger* disaster. *Small Group Behavior, 19,* 411–433.

Hirschmann, N. J. (1997). Feminist standpoint as postmodern strategy. *Women and Politics, 18,* 73–92.

Hochschild, A. R., with Anne Machung. (1989). *The second shift: Working parents and the revolution at home.* New York: Viking Penguin.

Hodge, B. (2003). How the medium is the message in the unconscious of 'America online.' *Visual Communication, 2,* 341–353.

Hofstede, G. (1980). *Culture's consequences: International differences in work-related values.* Beverly Hills, CA: Sage.

Hofstede, G. (1991). *Cultures and organizations: Software of the mind.* London: McGraw-Hill.

Hofstede, G. (2001). *Culture's consequences: Comparing values, behaviors, institutions, and organizations across nations.* Thousand Oaks, CA: Sage.

Hollingshead, A. B., Wittenbaum, G. M., Paulus, P. B., Hirokawa, R. Y., Ancona, D. G., Peterson, R. S., Jehn, K. A., & Yoon, K. (2005). A look at groups from the functional perspective. In M. S. Poole & A. B. Hollingshead (Eds.), *Theories of small groups: Interdisciplinary perspectives* (pp. 21–62). Thousand Oaks, CA: Sage.

Hoppe-Nagao, A., & Ting-Toomey, S. (2002). Relational dialectics and management strategies in marital couples. *Southern Communication Journal, 67,* 142–159.

Hopper, R., Knapp, M. L., & Scott, L. (1981). Couples' personal idioms: Exploring intimate talk. *Journal of Communication, 31,* 23–33.

Houston, M. (1992). The politics of difference: Race, class, and women's communication. In L. F. Rakow (Ed.), *Women making meaning: New feminist directions in communication* (pp. 45–59). New York: Routledge.

Houston, M. (2004). When Black women talk with White women: Why the dialogues are difficult. In A. Gonzalez, M. Houston, & V. Chen (Eds.), *Our voices: Essays in culture, ethnicity, and communication* (pp. 119–125). Los Angeles: Roxbury.

Houston, M., & Kramarae, C. (1991). Speaking from silence: Methods of silencing and of resistance. *Discourse and Society, 2,* 387–399.

Houston, M., & Schwartz, P. (1995). The relationships of lesbians and of gay men. In J. T. Wood & S. Duck (Eds.), *Under-studied relationships: Off the beaten track* (pp. 89–121). Thousand Oaks, CA: Sage.

Hsu, C. (2004). Sources of differences in communication apprehension between Chinese in Taiwan and Americans. Paper presented at the annual meeting of the International Communication Association, New Orleans, LA.

Hughes, P. C., & Dickson, F. C. (2006). Relational dynamics in interfaith marriages. In L. H. Turner & R. West (Eds.), *The family communication sourcebook* (pp. 373–388). Thousand, Oaks, CA: Sage

Huitema, D., van de Kerkhof, M., Pesch, U. (2007). The nature of the beast: Are citizens' juries deliberative or pluralistic? *Policy Sciences, 40,* 287–311.

Hunt, S. B. (2003). An essay on publishing standards for rhetorical criticism. *Communication Studies, 54,* 378–384.

Hyde, M. (2004). Introduction: Rhetorically we dwell. In M. Hyde (Ed.), *The ethos of rhetoric* (pp. xii–xxvii). Columbia: University of South Carolina Press.

Ichiyama, M. A. (1993). The reflected appraisal process in small-group interaction. *Social Psychology Quarterly, 56,* 87–99.

Ijams, K., & Miller, L. D. (2000). Perceptions of dream disclosure: An exploratory study. *Communication Studies, 51,* 135–149.

Inglis, F. (1993). *Cultural studies.* Cambridge, MA: Basil Blackwell.

Innes, M. (2002). Organizational communication and the symbolic construction of police murder investigations. *British Journal of Sociology, 53,* 67–68.

Innis, H. (1951). *The bias of communication.* Toronto: University of Toronto Press.

James, D., & Drackich, J. (1993). Understanding gender differences in amount of talk. In D. Tannen (Ed.), *Gender and conversational interaction* (pp. 281–312). Oxford: University Press.

Jameson, J. K. (2004). Negotiating automony and connection through politeness: A dialectical approach to organizational conflict management. *Western Journal of Communication, 68,* 257–277.

Jandt, F. E. (2004). *An introduction to intercultural communication* (4th ed.). Thousand Oaks, CA: Sage.

Jandt, F. E. (2006). *An introduction to intercultural communication* (5th ed.). Thousand Oaks, CA: Sage.

Janis, I. L. (1972). *Victims of groupthink: A psychological study of foreign-policy decisions and fiascoes.* Boston: Houghton Mifflin.

Janis, I. L. (1982). *Groupthink: Psychological studies of policy decisions and fiascoes.* Boston: Houghton Mifflin.

Janis, I. L. (1989). *Crucial decisions: Leadership in policymaking and crisis management.* New York: Free Press.

Janis, I. L., & Gilmore, J. B. (1965). The influence of incentive conditions on the success of role-playing in modifying attitudes. *Journal of Personality and Social Psychology, 1,* 17–27.

Jaworski, A., & Coupland, J. (2005). Othering in gossip: "You go out you have a laugh and you can pull yeah okay but like . . ." *Language in Society, 34,* 667–694.

Jeffres, L. W., Atkin, D. J., & Neuendorf, K. A. (2001). Expanding the range of dependent measures in mainstreaming and cultivation analysis. *Communication Research Reports, 18,* 408–417.

Jenkins, H. (2008, April 4). Is the medium still the message? *The Chronicle of Higher Education, 54,* 30.

Jia, W. (2001). *The remaking of the Chinese character and identity in the 21st century.* Westport, CT: Ablex.

Johanneson, R. L., Valde, K. S., & Whedbee, K. E. (2008). *Ethics in human communication.* Prospect Heights, IL: Waveland.

Johnson, A. J., Wittenberg, E., Haigh, M., Wigley, S., Becker, J., Brown, K., & Craig, E. (2004). The process of relationship development and deterioration: Turning points in friendships that have terminated. *Communication Quarterly, 52,* 54–68.

Johnson, D. I. (2007). Politeness theory and conversational refusals: Associations between various types of face threat and perceived competence. *Western Journal of Communication, 71*, 196–215.

Jourard, S. M. (1971). *The transparent self* (rev. ed.). New York: Van Nostrand.

Jucks, R., & Bromme, R. (2007). Choice of words in doctor-patient communication: An analysis of health-related Internet sites. *Health Communication, 21*, 267–277.

Kadlec, D. (2007, February 12). Senior netizens. *Time*, 94.

Katz, E., Blumler, J. G., & Gurevitch, M. (1974). Utilization of mass communication by the individual. In J. G. Blumler & E. Katz (Eds.), *The uses of mass communication: Current perspectives on gratifications research* (pp. 19–32). Beverly Hills, CA: Sage.

Katz, E., Gurevitch, M., & Haas, H. (1973). On the use of the mass media for important things. *American Sociological Review, 38*, 164–181.

Kaufman, J. M., & Johnson, C. (2004). Stigmatized individuals and the process of identity. *The Sociological Quarterly, 45*, 807–833.

Kaye, B. K., & Johnson, T. J. (2004). A web for all reasons: Uses and gratifications of Internet components for political information. *Telematics and Informatics, 21*, 197–223.

Kellermann, K., & Reynolds, R. (1990). When ignorance is bliss: The role of motivation to reduce uncertainty in uncertainty reduction theory. *Human Communication Research, 17*, 5–35.

Kellner, D., & Hammer, R. (2004). Critical reflections on Mel Gibson's *The Passion of the Christ. Logos, 3*, 3–4.

Kelly, C., & Zak, M. (1999). Narrativity and professional communication: Folktales and community meaning. *Journal of Business and Technical Communication, 13*, 297–317.

Kennamer, J. D. (1990). Self-serving bias in perceiving the opinions of others. *Communication Research, 17*, 393–404.

Kennedy, G. A. (1991). *Aristotle on Rhetoric: A theory of civil discourse.* New York: Oxford University Press.

Kenneth Burke's Literary Trust. (2006). On persuasion, identification, and dialectical symmetry. *Philosophy & Rhetoric, 39*, 333–339.

Kephart, W. M. (1950). A quantitative analysis of intragroup relations. *American Journal of Sociology, 60*, 544–549.

Keyton, J. (2005). *Communication and organizational culture.* Thousand Oaks, CA: Sage.

Keyton, J., Ferguson, P., & Rhodes, S. C. (2001). Cultural indicators of sexual harassment. *Southern Communication Journal, 67*, 33–50.

Kimberling, C. R. (1982). *Kenneth Burke's dramatism and popular arts.* Bowling Green: Bowling Green University Press.

Kinefuchi, E., & Orbe, M., P. (2008). Situating oneself in a racialized world: Understanding student reactions to *Crash* through standpoint theory and context-positionality frames. *Journal of International and Intercultural Communication, 1*, 70–90.

Kirby, E. L., Golden, A., Medved, C., Jorgensen, J., & Buzzanell, P. M. (2003). An organizational communication challenge to the discourse of work and family research: From problematics to empowerment. In P. Kalbfleisch (Ed.), *Communication yearbook 27* (pp. 1–44). Mahwah, NJ: Lawrence Erlbaum.

Kirby, E. L., & Krone, K. J. (2002). The policy exists but you can't really use it: Communication and the structuration of work-family policies. *Journal of Applied Communication, 30*, 50–77.

Kirkwood, W. (1992). Narrative and the rhetoric of possibility. *Communication Monographs, 59*, 30–47.

Kissling, E. (1991). Street harassment: The language of sexual terrorism. *Discourse and Society, 2*, 121–135.

Knapp, M. L. (1978). *Nonverbal communication in human interaction.* New York: Holt, Rinehart & Winston.

Knapp, M. L., & Hall, J. A. (2010). *Nonverbal communication in human interaction.* Wadsworth/Cengage: Boston.

Knapp, M. L., & Vangelisti, A. L. (2000). *Interpersonal communication and human relationships* (4th ed.). Boston: Allyn & Bacon.

Knapp, M. L., & Vangelisti, A. L. (2009). *Interpersonal communication and human relationships* (6th ed.). Boston: Allyn & Bacon.

Knobloch, L. K. (2008). Uncertainty reduction theory. In L.A. Baxter & D.O. Braithwaite (Eds.), *Engaging theories in interpersonal communication:*

Multiple perspectives (pp. 133–144). Thousand Oaks, CA: Sage.

Knobloch, L. K., Miller, L. E., Bond, B. J., & Monnone, S. E. (2007). Relational uncertainty and message processing in marriage. *Communication Monographs, 74,* 154–180.

Knobloch, L. K., & Solomon, D. H. (2003). Responses to changes in relational uncertainty within dating relationships: Emotions and communication strategies. *Communication Studies, 54,* 282–305.

Knox, R. E., & Inkster, J. A. (1968). Postdecision dissonance at posttime. *Journal of Personality and Social Psychology, 8,* 310–323.

Koenig Kellas, J. (2008). Narrative theories. In L. A. Baxter & D.O. Braithwaite (Eds.), *Engaging theories in interpersonal communication: Multiple perspectives* (pp. 241–254). Thousand Oaks, CA: Sage.

Kramarae, C. (1981). *Women and men speaking: Frameworks for analysis.* Rowley, MA: Newbury House.

Kramarae, C., & Treichler, P. (1985). *A feminist dictionary.* Boston: Pandora.

Kramer, M. W. (2004). Toward a communication theory of group dialectics: An ethnographic study of a community theater group. *Communication Monographs, 71,* 311–332.

Kramer, M. W. (2005). Communication and social exchange processes in community theater groups. *Journal of Applied Communication Research, 33,* 159–182.

Kramer, M. W., & Berman, J. E. (2001). Making sense of a university's culture: An examination of undergraduate students' stories. *Southern Communication Journal, 66,* 297–311.

Kreuter, M., Farrell, D., Olevitch, L., & Brennan, L. (2000). *Tailoring health messages: Customizing communication with computer technology.* Mahwah, NJ: Erlbaum.

Kubey, R., & Csikszentmihalyi, M. (1990). *Television and the quality of life: How viewing shapes everyday experience.* Hillsdale, NJ: Erlbaum.

Kubic, K. N., & Chory, R. M. (2007). Exposure to television makeover programs and perceptions of self. *Communication Research Reports, 24,* 283–292.

Kurtz, H. (1998, August 13). Homicide rate down, except on the evening news. *San Francisco Chronicle,* p. A8.

Lamoureux, E. L. (1994). Rhetorical dilemmas in Catholic discourse: The case of bishop John J. Meyers. *Communication Studies, 45,* 281–293.

Langellier, K. M., & Peterson, E. E. (2004). *Storytelling in daily life.* Philadelphia: Temple University Press.

La Poire, B. A., & Burgoon, J. K. (1992). A reply from the heart: Who are Sparks and Greene and why are they saying all these horrible things? *Human Communication Research, 18,* 472–482.

LaPoire, B. A., & Burgoon, J. K. (1996). Usefulness of differentiating arousal responses within communication theories: Orienting response or defensive arousal within nonverbal theories of expectancy violation. *Communication Monographs, 63,* 208–230.

LaRose, R., & Eastin, M. S. (2004). A social cognitive theory of Internet uses and gratifications: Toward a new model of media attendance. *Journal of Broadcasting & Electronic Media, 48,* 358–377.

LaRossa, R., & Reitzes, D. C. (1993). Symbolic interactionism and family studies. In P. G. Boss, W. J. Doherty, R. LaRossa, W. R. Schumm, & S. K. Steinmetz (Eds.), *Sourcebook of family theories and methods: A contextual approach* (pp. 135–163). Thousand Oaks, CA: Sage.

Lash, S. (2007). Power after hegemony: Cultural studies in mutation. *Theory, Culture, & Society, 24,* 55–78.

Lavelle, J. J., Rupp, D. E., & Brockner, J. (2007). Taking a multifoci approach to the study of justice, social exchange, and citizenship behavior: The target similarity model. *Journal of Management, 33,* 841–866.

Lea, M., & Spears, R. (1995). Love at first byte? Building personal relationships over computer networks. In J. T. Wood & S. Duck (Eds.), *Understudied relationships: Off the beaten track* (pp. 197–233). Thousand Oaks, CA: Sage.

Leathers, D., & Eaves, M. H. (2008). *Successful nonverbal communication: Principles and applications.* Boston: Allyn & Bacon.

Leeds-Hurwitz, W. (1990). Notes on the history of intercultural communication: The foreign service institute and the mandate for intercultural training. *Quarterly Journal of Speech, 76,* 262–281.

Leeman, N. (2007, Fall). The web resides at the hub of learning. *Nieman Reports, 61,* 70–71.

Leo, J. (2001, July 23). Is there an echo? *Newsweek,* 17.

Lerner, B. H. (2002, July 23). In the death of a doctor, a lesson. *The New York Times,* p. D4.

Lester, J. (2008). Performing gender in the workplace: Gender socialization, power, and identity among women faculty members. *Community College Review, 35,* 277–305.

Leung, L., & Wei, R. (2000). More than just talk on the move: Uses and gratifications of the cellular phone. *Journalism & Mass Communication Quarterly, 77,* 308–320.

Levine, T. R., Anders, L. N., Banas, J., Baum, K. L., Endo, K., Hu, A. D. S., & Wong, C. H. (2000). Norms, expectations, and deception: A norm violation model of veracity judgments. *Communication Monographs, 67,* 123–137.

Levinson, P. (1999, October 15). McLuhan for the millenium. *Chronicle of Higher Education, 48,* B10.

Levinson, P. (2000). McLuhan and media ecology. In *Proceedings of the Media Ecology Association,* vol. 1. Retrieved August 15, 2005 from the World Wide Web: www.media-ecology.org/publications/proceedings/v1/McLuhan

Levinson, P. (2001). *Digital Mcluhan: A guide to the information millennium.* London: Routledge.

Levy, M., & Windahl, S. (1985). The concept of audience activity. In P. L. Palmgreen, L. A. Wenner, & K. E. Rosengren (Eds.), *Media gratifications research: Current perspectives* (pp. 109–122). Beverly Hills, CA: Sage.

Lewis, J., & Morgan, M. (2001). He may not be a liberal but he plays one on TV: Imagining the ideology of President Clinton. *The Communication Review, 4,* 327–346.

Li, H. (2006). Backchannel responses as misleading feedback in intercultural discourse. *Journal of Intercultural Communication Research, 35,* 99–116.

Lim, T., & Bowers, J. W. (1991). Facework, solidarity, approbation, and tact. *Human Communication Research, 176,* 415–450.

Lin, C. A., & Salwen, M. B. (1997). Predicting the spiral of silence on a controversial issue. *Howard Journal of Communications, 8,* 129–141.

Lindner, E. W. (2008). *Yearbook of American & Canadian churches.* Nashville, TN: Abingdon Press.

Lingle, J. H., & Ostrom, T. M. (1981). Principles of memory and cognition in attitude formation. In R. E. Petty, T. M. Ostrom, & T. C. Brock (Eds.), *Cognitive responses in persuasive communications* (pp. 399–420). New York: McGraw-Hill.

Littlejohn, S., & Foss, K. (2008). *Theories of human communication* (9th ed.). Wadsworth/Cengage: Boston.

Liu, J. (2006). A cross-national and double-sided test of 'sprial of silence' theory: Culture, governmental form & personality. Paper presented at the annual meeting of the International Communication Association, San Francisco.

Long, E. (1989). Feminism and cultural studies. *Critical Studies in Mass Communication, 6,* 427–435.

Longley, J., & Pruitt, D. G. (1980). Groupthink: A critique of Janis' theory. *Review of Personality and Social Psychology, 1,* 74–93.

Lord, C. (1994). The intention of Aristotle's *Rhetoric.* In E. Schiappa (Ed.), *Landmark essays on classical Greek rhetoric* (pp. 157–168). Davis, CA: Hermagoras Press.

Lucas, K., & Sherry, J. L. (2004). Sex differences in video game play: A communication-based explanation. *Communication Research, 31,* 499–523.

Lucaites, J. L., & Condit, C. M. (1985). Reconstructing narrative theory: A functional perspective. *Journal of Communication, 35,* 9–108.

Lull, J. (1982). How families select television programs: A mass-observational study. *Journal of Broadcasting, 26,* 801–811.

Lum, C. M. K. (2006). Notes toward an intellectual history of media ecology. In C. M. K. Lum (Ed.), *Perspectives on culture, technology, and communication: The media ecology tradition* (pp. 1–60). Cresskill, NJ: Hampton.

Lyman, S. M. (1990). *Civilization: Contents, discontents, malcontents, and other essays in social theory.* Fayetteville, AK: University of Arkansas.

Macdonald, D. (1967). He has looted all culture.... In G. Stearn (Ed.), *McLuhan: Hot & cool* (pp. 56–77). New York: Dial.

MacIntrye, A. (1981). *After virtue: A study in moral theory.* Notre Dame, IN: University of Notre Dame Press.

Mamali, C., & Paun, G. (1982). Group size and the genesis of subgroups: Objective restrictions. *Revue Roumaine Des Sciences Sociales—Serie de Psychologie, 26,* 139–148.

Mandziuk, R. M. (2003). Commemorating Sojourner Truth: Negotiating the politics of race and gender in the spaces of public memory. *Western Journal of Communication, 67,* 271–291.

Marchand, M. (1989). *Marshall McLuhan: The medium and the messenger.* New York: Ticknor & Fields.

Markey, P. M., & Markey, C. N. (2007). Romantic ideals, romantic obtainment, and relationship experiences: The complementarity of interpersonal traits among romantic partners. *Journal of Social and Personal Relationships, 24,* 517–533.

Mars, M. M., & Giner, M. B. (2007). Connecting organizational environments with the instructional technology practices of community college faculty. *Community College Review, 34,* 324–343.

Marsh, C. (2006). Aristotelian ethos and the new morality: Implications for media literacy and media ethics. *Journal of Mass Media Ethics, 21,* 338–352.

Martin, J., & Nakayama, T. (2006). *Intercultural communication in contexts.* New York: McGraw-Hill.

Martin, J. N., & Nakayama, T. K. (2008). *Experiencing intercultural communication: An introduction.* New York: McGraw-Hill.

Marx, K. (1963). *The communist manifesto of Karl Marx and Friedrich Engels.* New York: Russell & Russell.

Maslow, A. H. (1970). *Motivation and personality* (2nd ed.). New York: Harper & Row.

Matheson, C. (2001). The Simpsons *and philosophy: The d'oh! of Homer.* Ottawa, IL: Open Court.

Marx, K., & Engels, F. (1848). *The Communist manifesto.* New York: Penguin Books.

Matthews, M. W. (2003). I think, you think, we all think groupthink. Retrieved October 28, 2008 from the World Wide Web: http://www.extremelysmart.com/yankee/03h-groupthink.php

Matz, D. C., & Wood, W. (2005). Cognitive dissonance in groups: The consequences of disagreement. *Journal of Personality and Social Psychology, 88,* 1–22.

McCabe, C. (2008). An interview with Stuart Hall, December 2007. *Critical Quarterly, 50,* 12–54.

McClish, G. (2007). A man of feeling, a man of colour: James Forten and the rise of African American deliberative rhetoric. *Rhetorica, 25,* 297–328.

McCloskey, D. (1993). The neglected economics of talk. *Planning for Higher Education, 22,* 11–16.

McCroskey, J. C., & Richmond, V. P. (2000). Applying reciprocity and accommodation theories to supervisor/subordinate communication. *Journal of Applied Communication Research, 28,* 278–289.

McDevitt, M., Kiousis, S., & Wahl-Jorgensen, K. (2003). Spiral of moderation: Opinion expression in computer-mediated discussion. *International Journal of Public Opinion Research, 15,* 454–71.

McGregor, G. (1995). Gender advertisements then and now: Goffman, symbolic interactionism, and the problem of history. In N. K. Denzin (Ed.), *Studies in symbolic interaction* (pp. 3–42). Greenwich, CT: JAI Press.

McKinney, D. H., & Donaghy, W. C. (1993). Dyad gender structure, uncertainty reduction, and self-disclosure during initial interaction. In P. Kalbfleish (Ed.), *Interpersonal communication: Evolving interpersonal relationships* (pp. 33–50). Hillsdale, NJ: Erlbaum.

McLuhan, M. (1962). *The Gutenberg galaxy.* New York: Mentor.

McLuhan, M. (1964). *Understanding media.* New York: Mentor.

McLuhan, M., & Fiore, Q. (1967). *The medium is the massage: An inventory of effects.* New York: Bantam Books.

McLuhan, M., & Fiore, Q. (1968). *War and peace in the global village.* New York: Bantam Books.

McLuhan, M., & Fiore, Q. (1996). *The medium is the massage: An inventory of effects.* San Francisco: HardWired.

McLuhan, M., & McLuhan, E. (1988). *Laws of media: The new science.* Toronto: University of Toronto Press.

McLuhan, M., & Nevitt, B. (1972). *Take today: The executive as dropout.* New York: Harper & Row.

McLuhan, M., & Parker, H. (1969). *Counterblast.* New York: Harcourt, Brace & World.

McPherson, M. B., & Liang, Y. (2007). Students' reactions to teachers' management of compulsive communicators. *Communication Education, 56,* 18–33.

McQuail, D. (1984). With the benefits of hindsight: Reflections on uses and gratifications research. *Critical Studies in Mass Communication, 1,* 177–193.

McQuail, D., Blumler, J. G., & Brown, J. (1972). The television audience: A revised perspective. In D. McQuail (Ed.), *Sociology of mass communication* (pp. 135–165). Harmondsworth, England: Penguin Books.

Mead, G. H. (1934). *Mind, self and society: From the standpoint of a social behaviorist.* Chicago: University of Chicago Press.

Medved, C. E. (2007). Investigating family labor in communication studies: Threading across historical and contemporary discourses. *Journal of Family Communication, 7,* 225–243.

Meisenbach, R. J., Remke, R. V., Buzzanell, P. M., & Liu, M. (2008). "They allowed": Pentadic mapping of women's maternity leave discourse as organizational rhetoric. *Communication Monographs, 75,* 1–24.

Melia, T. (1989). Scientism and dramatism: Some quasi-mathematical motifs in the work of Kenneth Burke. In H. W. Simmons & T. Melia (Eds.), *The legacy of Kenneth Burke* (pp. 156–173). Madison: University of Wisconsin Press.

Merritt, B. D. (1991). Bill Cosby: TV auteur? *Journal of Popular Culture, 24,* 89–102.

Merten, K. (1985). An essay: Public opinion—our social skin. *Journalism Quarterly, 62,* 649–653.

Metts, S., & Lamb, E. (2006). Methodological approaches to the study of family communication. In L. H. Turner & R.West (Eds.), *The family communication sourcebook* (pp. 83–108). Thousand, Oaks, CA: Sage.

Metzger, M. J. (2004). Privacy, trust, and disclosure: Exploring barriers to electronic commerce. *Journal of Computer-Mediated Communication, 9,* 204–223.

Meyer, M. D. E. (2003). "It's me. I'm it": Defining adolescent sexual identity through relational dialectics in *Dawson's Creek. Communication Quarterly, 51,* 262–280.

Meyrowitz, J. (1985). *No sense of place.* New York: Oxford University Press.

Miike, Y. (2007). An Asiacentric reflection on Eurocentric bias in communication theory. *Communication Monographs, 74,* 272–278.

Milkie, M. A. (1999). Social comparisons, reflected appraisals, and mass media: The impact of pervasive beauty images on Black and White girls' self-concepts. *Social Psychology Quarterly, 62,* 190–210.

Miller, G. R. (1981). Tis the season to be jolly: A yuletide 1980 assessment of communication research. *Human Communication Research, 7,* 371–377.

Miller, G. R., & Steinberg, M. (1975). *Between people: A new analysis of interpersonal communication.* Chicago: Science Research Associates.

Miller, K. (2005). *Communication theories: Perspectives, processes, and contexts.* New York: McGraw-Hill.

Millhous, L. M. (2004). Projected measures of motivation and media choice. *Communication Research Reports, 21,* 154–163.

Minnebo, J., & Eggermont, S. (2007). Watching the young use illicit drugs: Direct experience, exposure to television and the stereotyping of adolescents' substance use. *Young, 15,* 129–144.

Minnebo, J., & Van Acker, A. (2004). Does television influence adolescents' perceptions of and attitudes toward people with mental illness? *Journal of Community Psychology, 32,* 257–275.

Modaff, D. P., DeWine, S., & Butler, J. (2008). *Organizational communication: Foundations, challenges, and misunderstandings.* Boston: Pearson.

Molitor, F. T. (1994). The effects of television exposure on the cultivation of AIDS-related fears: A test of a new model for predicting resonance. *Dissertation Abstracts International, 54*(7-A), 2372.

Molm, L. D. (2001). Theories of social exchange and exchange networks. In G. Ritzer & B. Smart (Eds.), *Handbook of social theory* (pp. 260–272). London: Sage.

Monge, P. R. (1973). Theory construction in the study of communication: The system paradigm. *Journal of Communication, 23,* 5–16.

Monge, P. R., & Contractor, N. (2003). *Theories of communication networks.* Oxford: University Press.

Mongeau, P. A., & Henningsen, M. L. (2008). Stage theories of relationship development. In L. A. Baxter & D. O. Braithwaite (Eds.), *Engaging theories in interpersonal communication* (pp. 363–376). Thousand Oaks, CA: Sage.

Mongeau, P. A., Jacobsen, J., & Donnerstein, C. (2007). Defining dates and first date goals: Generalizing from undergraduates to single adults. *Communication Research, 34*, 526–527.

Montgomery, B. M. (1992). Communication as the interface between couples and culture. In J. A. Andersen (Ed.), *Communication yearbook 15* (pp. 475–507). Newbury Park, CA: Sage.

Montgomery, E. (2004). Tortured families: A coordinated management of meaning analysis. *Family Process, 43*, 349–372.

Moon, D. (2008). Concepts of "culture": Implications for intercultural communication research. In M. K. Asante, Y. Miike, & J. Yin (Eds.), *The global intercultural communication reader* (pp. 11–26). New York: Routledge.

Moon, S., & Nelson, M. R. (2008). Exploring the influence of media exposure and cultural values on Korean immigrants' advertising evaluations. *International Journal of Advertising, 27*, 299–330.

Moran, R. (1996). Artifice and persuasion: The work of metaphor in the *Rhetoric*. In A. O. Rorty (Ed.), *Essays on Aristotle's* Rhetoric (pp. 385–398). Berkeley: University of California Press.

Morgan, J. N. (2004). Organizational cultures and communication. *Communication Teacher, 18*, 128–131.

Morgan, M. (1986). Television and the erosion of regional diversity. *Journal of Broadcasting & Electronic Media, 30*, 123–129.

Morreale, S. P., & Vogl, M. W. (Eds.). (1998). *Pathways to careers in communication*. Annandale, VA: NCA.

Morris, M., & Ogan, C. (1996). The Internet as mass medium. *Journal of Communication, 46*, 39–50.

Morrison, E. W. (2002). Information seeking within organizations. *Human Communication Research, 28*, 229–242.

Morrison, J. C. (2006). Marshall McLuhan: The modern Janus. In C. M. K. Lum (Ed.), *Perspectives on culture, technology, and communiction: The media ecology tradition* (pp. 163–200). Cresskill, NJ: Hampton.

Moskowitz, D., & Roloff, M. (2007). On HIV disclosure: A literature review. Paper presented at the annual meeting of the International Communication Association, San Francisco.

Moskowitz, D. A., & Roloff, M. E. (2007). The ultimate high: Sexual addiction and the bug chasing phenomenon. *Sexual Addiction and Compulsivity, 14*, 21–40.

Motley, M. T. (1990). On whether one can(not) not communicate: An examination via traditional communication postulates. *Western Journal of Speech Communication, 54*, 1–20.

Mottet, T. P., Beebe, S. A., Raffeld, P. C., & Medlock, A. L. (2004). The effects of student verbal and nonverbal responsiveness on teacher self-efficacy and job satisfaction. *Communication Education, 53*, 150–163.

Moy, P., Domke, D., & Stamm, K. (2001). The spiral of silence and public opinion on affirmative action. *Journalism and Mass Communication Quarterly, 78*, 7–25.

Mulrine, A. (2008, June 2). To battle groupthink, the Army trains a skeptics corps. *U.S. News & World Report, 30*, 32.

Mumby, D. K., & May, S. (2005). Introduction: Thinking about engagement. In S. May & D. K. Mumby (Eds.), *Engaging organizational theory & research* (pp. 1–14). Thousand Oaks, CA: Sage.

Murdock, G. (1989). Cultural studies: Missing links. *Critical Studies in Mass Communication, 6*, 436–440.

Murray, J. (2003). An other-Burkean frame: Rhetorical criticism and the call of the other. *Communication Studies, 54*, 169–187.

Muthusamy, S. K., & White, M. A. (2005). Learning and knowledge transfer in strategic alliances: A social exchange view. *Organization Studies, 26*, 415–441.

Myers, M. (2007). The use of pathos in charity letters: Some notes toward a theory and analysis. *Journal of Technical Writing and Communication, 37*, 3–16.

Myers, S. A., & Anderson, C. M. (2008). *The fundamentals of small group communication*. Thousand Oaks, CA: Sage.

Nakayama, T. K., & Krizek, R. L. (1995). Whiteness: A strategic rhetoric. *Quarterly Journal of Speech, 81*, 291–309.

National Association of Colleges and Employers. (2007). *The Job Outlook 2008*. Bethlehem, PA: National Association of Colleges and Employers.

National Association of Colleges and Employers. (2008). Perfect job candidate pairs communication skills with strong work ethic. Retrieved December 2, 2008 from the World Wide Web: http://www.naceweb.org/press

Neel, J. (1994). *Aristotle's voice: Rhetoric, theory & writing in America*. Carbondale: Southern Illinois University Press.

Nelson, C. (1989). Writing as the accomplice of language: Kenneth Burke and poststructuralism. In H. W. Simons & T. Melia (Eds.), *The legacy of Kenneth Burke* (pp. 156–173). Madison: University of Wisconsin Press.

Neuliep, J. W., & Grohskopf, E. L. (2000). Uncertainty reduction and communication satisfaction during initial interaction: An initial test and replication of a new axiom. *Communication Reports, 13*, 67–77.

Neuwirth, K., Frederick, E., & Mayo, C. (2007). The spiral of silence and fear of isolation, *Journal of Communication, 57*, 450–468.

Newcomb, H. (1978). Assessing the violence profile studies of Gerbner and Gross: A humanistic critique and suggestion. *Communication Research, 5*, 264–283.

Nichols, M. H. (1952). Kenneth Burke and the new rhetoric. *The Quarterly Journal of Speech, 38*, 133–134.

Nippert-Eng, C. E., (1996). *Home and work*. Chicago: University of Chicago Press.

Nishida, T. (1996). Communication in personal relationships in Japan. In W. B. Gudykunst, S. Ting-Toomey, & T. Nishida (Eds.), *Communication in personal relationships across cultures* (pp. 102–121). Thousand Oaks, CA: Sage.

Nkomo, S. M., & Cox, T. (1996). Diverse identities in organizations. In S. R. Clegg, C. Hardy, & W. R. Nord (Eds.), *Handbook of organizational studies* (pp. 338–356). London: Sage.

Noelle-Neumann, E. (1983). The effect of media on media effects research. *Journal of Communcation, 33*, 157–165.

Noelle-Neumann, E. (1984). *The spiral of silence: Public opinion—our social skin*. Chicago: University of Chicago Press.

Noelle-Neumann, E. (1985). The spiral of silence—A response. In K. R. Sanders, L. L. Kaid, & D. D. Nimmo, (Eds.), *Political communication yearbook, 1984* (pp. 43–65). Carbondale: Southern Illinois University.

Noelle-Neumann, E. (1991). The theory of public opinion: The concept of the spiral of silence. In J. A. Anderson (Ed.), *Communication yearbook 14* (pp. 256–287). Newbury Park, CA: Sage.

Noelle-Neumann, E. (1993). *The spiral of silence: Public opinion—our social skin* (2nd ed.). Chicago: University of Chicago Press.

Noelle-Neumann, E., & Petersen, T. (2004). The spiral of silence and the social nature of man. In L. L. Kaid (Ed.), *Handbook of political communication* (pp. 339–356). Mahwah, NJ: Lawrence Erlbaum.

Nomai, A. J., & Dionisopoulos, G. N. (2002). Framing the Cubas narrative: The American Dream and the capitalist reality. *Communication Studies, 53*, 97–111.

Nussbaum, J. F., Pitts, M. J., Huber, F. N., Krieger, J. L. R., & Ohs, J. E. (2005). Ageism and ageist language across the life span: Intimate relationships and non-intimate interactions. *Journal of Social Issues, 61*, 287–305.

O'Brien Hallstein, D. L. (1999). A postmodern caring: Feminist standpoint theories, revisioned caring and communication ethics. *Western Journal of Communication, 63*, 32–56.

O'Brien Hallstein, D. L. (2000). Where standpoint stands now: An introduction and commentary. *Women's Studies in Communication, 23*, 1–15.

O'Leary, C. M. (1997). Counteridentification or counterhegemony? Transforming feminist standpoint theory. *Women and Politics, 18*, 45–72.

O'Neill, B. S., & Arendt, L. A. (2008). Psychological climate and work attitudes: The importance of telling the right story. *Journal of Leadership & Organizational Studies, 14*, 353–370.

Oetzel, J., Ting-Toomey, S., Chew-Sanchez, M. I., Harris, R., Wilcox, R., & Stumpf, S. (2003). Face and facework in conflicts with parents and siblings: A cross-cultural comparison of Germans, Japanese, Mexicans, and U.S. Americans. *Journal of Family Communication, 3*, 67–93.

Oetzel, J. G., Ting-Toomey, S., Yokochi, Y., Masumoto, T., & Takai, J. (2000). A typology of facework behaviors in conflicts with best friends and relative strangers. *Communication Quarterly, 48*, 397–419.

Olsen, T. (1978). *Silences*. New York: Delacorte Press.

Orbe, M. P. (1998). *Constructing co-cultural theory: An explication of culture, power, and communication*. Thousand Oaks, CA: Sage.

Ota, H., Giles, H., & Somera, L. (2007). Beliefs about intra- and intergenerational communication in Japan, the Phillipines, and the United States: Implication for older adults' subjective well-being. *Communication Studies, 58*, 173–188.

Ott, B. (2003). "I'm Bart Simpson, who the hell are you?" A study in postmodern identity (re)construction. *Journal of Popular Culture, 37*, 56–82.

Pacanowsky, M. E. (1983). A small town cop. In L. L. Putnam & M. E. Pacanowsky (Eds.), *Communication and organizations: An interpretive approach* (pp. 261–282). Beverly Hills, CA: Sage.

Pacanowsky, M. E. (1989). Creating and narrating organizational realities. In B. Dervin, L. Grossberg, B. J. O'Keefe, & E. Wartella (Eds.), *Rethinking communication* (pp. 250–257). Newbury Park, CA: Sage.

Pacanowsky, M. E., & O'Donnell-Trujillo, N. (1982). Communicaton and organizational cultures. *Western Journal of Speech Communication, 46*, 115–130.

Pacanowsky, M. E., & O'Donnell-Trujillo, N. (1983). Organizational communication as cultural peformance. *Communication Monographs, 50*, 127–147.

Pacanowsky, M. E., & O'Donnell-Trujillo, N. (1990). Communication and organizational cultures. In S. R. Corman, S. P. Banks, C. R. Bantz, & M. E. Mayer (Eds.), *Foundations of organizational communication: A reader* (pp. 142–153). New York: Longman.

Pais, S. (1997). Asian Indian families in America. In M. K. DeGenova (Ed.), *Families in cultural context* (pp. 173–190). Mountain View, CA: Mayfield.

Papa, M. J., Daniels, T. D., & Spiker, B. K. (2008). *Organizational communication: Perspectives and trends*. Thousand Oaks, CA: Sage.

Parameswaran, K. (2008). Interactive television programmes: A study in *media ecology. Language in India, 8*, 2.

Palmgreen, P., Wenner, L. A., & Rosengren, K. E. (Eds.). (1985). *Media gratifications research: Current perspectives*. Beverly Hills, CA: Sage.

Papacharissi, Z., & Rubin, A. M. (2000). Predictors of Internet use. *Journal of Broadcasting & Electronic Media, 44*, 175–196.

Parks, M. R. (1982). Ideology in interpersonal communication: Off the couch and into the world. In M. Burgoon (Ed.), *Communication yearbook 5* (pp. 79–108). New Brunswick, NJ: Transaction Books.

Parks, M. E. (1982). Ideology in interpersonal communication: Off the couch and into the world. In M. Burgoon (Ed.), *Communication Yearbook 5* (pp. 79–107). New Brunswick, MJ: Transaction Books.

Parks, M., & Adelman, M. (1983). Communication networks and the development of romantic relationships: An expansion of uncertainty reduction theory. *Human Communication Research, 10*, 55–80.

Patterson, B. R. (2007). Relationship development revisited: A preliminary look at communication in friendship over the lifespan. *Communication Research Reports, 24*, 29–37.

Patton, T. O. (2004). Reflections of a Black woman professor: Racism and sexism in academia. *Howard Journal of Communications, 15*, 185–200.

Pavitt, C., & Johnson, K. (2002). Scheidel and Crowell revisited: A descriptive study of group proposal sequencing. *Communication Monographs, 69*, 19–32.

Pearce, W. B. (1976). The coordinated management of meaning: A rules-based theory of interpersonal communication. In G. R. Miller (Ed.), *Explorations in interpersonal communication* (pp. 17–35). Beverly Hills, CA: Sage.

Pearce, W. B. (1989). *Communication and the human condition*. Carbondale: Southern Illinois University Press.

Pearce, W. B. (1994). *Interpersonal communication: Making social worlds*. New York: HarperCollins.

Pearce, W. B. (1995). A sailing guide for social constructionists. In W. Leeds-Hurwitz (Ed.), *Social approaches to communication* (pp. 88–112). New York: Guilford Press.

Pearce, W. B. (2004). *Using CMM: The coordinated management of meaning*. Woodside, CA: Pearce and Associates.

Pearce, W. B. (2006). The coordinated management of meaning (CMM). In W. B. Gudykunst (Ed.), *Theorizing about intercultural communication* (pp. 35–54). Thousand Oaks, CA: Sage.

Pearce, W. B. (2007). *Making social worlds: A communication perspective*. Malden, MA: Blackwell.

Pearce, W. B., & Conklin, F. (1979). A model of hierarchical meanings in coherent conversation and a study of indirect responses. *Communication Monographs, 46,* 75–87.

Pearce, W. B., & Cronen, V. E. (1980). *Communication, action, and meaning: The creation of social realities*. New York: Praeger.

Pearce, W. B., Cronen, V. E., & Conklin, F. (1979). On what to look at when analyzing communication: A hierarchical model of actors' meanings. *Communication, 4,* 195–220.

Pearce, W. B., & Littlejohn, S. W. (1997). *Moral conflict: When social worlds collide*. Thousand Oaks, CA: Sage.

Pearce, W. B., & Pearce, K. A. (2000). Extending the theory of the coordinated management of meaning (CMM) through a community dialogue process. *Communication Theory, 10,* 405–423.

Pearson, J. C. (1985, October). *Innovation in teaching gender and communication: Excluding and including women and men*. Paper presented at the annual conference of the Organization for the Study of Communication, Language, and Gender, Lincoln, NE.

Pearson, J. C., & VanHorn, S. B. (2004). Communication and gender identity: A retrospective analysis. *Communication Quarterly, 52,* 284–299.

Pearson, J. C., West, R., & Turner, L. H. (1995). *Gender and communication* (3rd ed.). Madison, WI: Brown & Benchmark.

Peplau, L. A., & Beals, K. P. (2004). The family lives of lesbians and gay men. In A. Vangelisti (Ed.), *Handbook of family communication* (pp. 233–248). Mahwah, NJ: Lawrence Erlbaum.

Perloff, R. M. (1993). *The dynamics of persuasion*. Hillsdale, NJ: Erlbaum.

Perse, E. M., & Courtright, J. A. (1993). Normative images of communication media: Mass and interpersonal channels in the new media environment. *Human Communication Research, 19,* 485–503.

Perse, E. M., & Greenberg-Dunn, D. (1998). The utility of home computers and media use: Implications of multimedia and connectivity. *Journal of Broadcasting & Electronic Media, 42,* 435.

Peterson, I. (2002, August 14). Questions about germ scientist after Princeton anthrax finding. *The New York Times*, p. A21.

Petronio, S. (1991). Communication boundary management: A theoretical model of managing disclosure of private information between married couples. *Communication Theory, 1,* 311–335.

Petronio, S. (2000). The boundaries of privacy: Praxis of everyday life. In S. Petronio (Ed.), *Balancing the secrets of private disclosures* (pp. 37–49). Mahwah, NJ: Erlbaum.

Petronio, S. (2002). *Boundaries of privacy: Dialectics of disclosure*. Albany, NY: SUNY Press.

Petronio, S. (2004). Road to developing communication privacy management theory: Narrative in progress, please stand by. *Journal of Family Communication, 4,* 193–207.

Petronio, S., & Caughlin, J. P. (2006). Communication privacy management theory: Understanding families. In D. O. Braithwaite & L. A. Baxter (Eds.), *Engaging theories in family communication: Multiple perspectives* (pp. 35–49). Thousand Oaks, CA: Sage.

Petronio, S., & Durham, W. T. (2008). Communication privacy management theory. In L. A. Baxter & D. O. Braithwaite (Eds.), *Engaging theories in interpersonal communication: Multiple perspectives* (pp. 309–322). Thousand Oaks, CA: Sage.

Petronio, S., Ellemers, N., Giles, H., & Gallois, C. (1998). (Mis)communicating across boundaries: Interpersonal and intergroup considerations. *Communication Research, 25,* 571–595.

Petronio, S., & Kovach, S. (1997). Managing privacy boundaries: Health providers' perceptions of resident care in Scottish nursing homes. *Journal of Applied Communication Research, 25,* 115–131.

Petronio, S., & Martin, J. N. (1986). Ramifications of revealing private information: A gender gap. *Journal of Clinical Psychology, 42,* 499–506.

Petronio, S., Martin, J. N., & Littlefield, R. (1984). Prerequisite conditions for self-disclosing: A gender issue. *Communication Monographs, 51,* 268–273.

Petronio, S., Reeder, H. M., Hecht, M. L., & Ros-Mendoza, T. M. (1996). Disclosure of sexual abuse by children and adolescents. *Journal of Applied Communication Research, 24,* 181–199.

Petronio, S., Sargent, J., Andea, L., Reganis, P., & Cichocki, D. (2004). Family and friends as healthcare advocates: Dilemmas of confidentiality and privacy. *Journal of Social and Personal Relationships, 21,* 33–52.

Pew Internet & American Life Project. (2008). Demographics of Internet users. Retrieved December 2, 2008 from the World Wide Web: www.pewinternet.org/trends/user_demo_10%2020%2008.htm

Philipsen, G. (1995). The coordinated management of meaning theory of Pearce, Cronen, and associates. In D. Cushman & B. Kovacic (Eds.), *Watershed traditions in human communication theory* (pp. 13–43). Albany, NY: SUNY Press.

Phillips, D. C. (1992). *The social scientists' bestiary.* Oxford, England: Pergamon Press.

Planalp, S. (1987). Interplay between relational knowledge and events. In R. Burnett, P. McGhee, & D. Clarke (Eds.), *Accounting for relationships: Social representations of interpersonal links* (pp. 173–191). London: Methuen.

Planalp, S., & Honeycutt, J. M. (1985). Events that increase uncertainty reduction in personal relationships. *Human Communication Research, 11,* 593–604.

Planalp, S., & Rivers, M. (1988). *Changes in knowledge of relationships.* Paper presented at the annual meeting of the International Communication Association, New Orleans, LA.

Planalp, S., Rutherford, D. K., & Honeycutt, J. M. (1988). Events that increase uncertainty in personal relationships II: Replication and extension. *Human Communication Research, 14,* 516–547.

Poole, M. S. (1983). Review of *Communication, action and meaning: The creation of social realities. Quarterly Journal of Speech, 69,* 223–224.

Poole, M. S. (1990). Do we have any theories of group communication? *Communication Studies, 41,* 237–247.

Poole, M. S. (1998). The small group should be the fundamental unit of communication research. In J. Trent (Ed.), *Communication: Views from the helm for the 21st century* (pp. 94–97). Needham Heights, MA: Allyn & Bacon.

Poole, M. S. (2007). Generalization in process theories of communication. *Communication Methods and Measures, 1,* 1–10.

Poole, M. S., & DeSanctis, G. (1990). Understanding the use of group decision support systems: The theory of adaptive structuration. In J. Fulk & C. Steinfield (Eds.), *Organizations and communication technology* (pp. 175–195). Thousand Oaks, CA: Sage.

Poole, M. S., & McPhee, R. D. (2005). Structuration theory. In S. May & D. K. Mumby (Eds.), *Engaging organizational theory & research* (pp. 171–195). Norwood, NJ: Ablex.

Poole, M. S., Seibold, D. R., & McPhee, R. D. (1986). A structurational approach to theory-building in group decision-making research. In R. Y. Hirokawa & M. S. Poole (Eds.), *Communication and group decision-making* (pp. 237–264). Beverly Hills, CA: Sage.

Poole, M. S., Seibold, D. R., & McPhee, R. D. (1996). The structuration of group decisions. In R. Hirokawa & M. S. Poole (Eds.), *Communication and group decision making* (pp. 114–146). Thousand Oaks, CA: Sage.

Postman, N. (1971). *Teaching as a subversive activity.* New York: Delta.

Postman, N. (1992). *Technopoly: The surrender of culture to technology.* New York: Knopf.

Potter, W. J. (1991). The relationships between first and second order measures of cultivation. *Human Communication Research, 18,* 92–113.

Potter, W. J. (1993). Cultivation theory and research: A conceptual critique. *Human Communication Research, 19,* 564–601.

Preston, E. H. (1990). Pornography and the construction of gender. In N. Signorielli & M. Morgan (Eds.), *Cultivation analysis: New directions in media effects research* (pp. 107–122). Newbury Park, CA: Sage.

Punyanunt-Carter, N. (2007). Using attachment theory to study communication motives in father-daughter relationships. *Communication Research Reports, 24,* 311–318.

Radway, J. (1984). *Reading the romance: Women, patriarchy, and popular literature.* Chapel Hill: University of North Carolina Press.

Radway, J. (1986). Identifying ideological seams: Mass culture, analytical methods, and political practice. *Communication, 9,* 93–123.

Ramirez, A., & Wang, Z. (2008). When online meets offline: An expectancy violations theory perspective on modality switching. *Journal of Communication, 58,* 20–39.

Raschick, M., & Ingersoll-Dayton, B. (2004). The costs and rewards of caregiving among aging spouses and adult children. *Family Relations, 53,* 317–325.

Raven, B. H. (1993). The bases of power: Origins and recent developments. *Journal of Social Issues, 49,* 227–251.

Rawlins, W. K. (1992). *Friendship matters: Communication, dialectics, and the life course.* New York: Aldine De Gruyter.

Rayburn, J. D., & Palmgreen, P. C. (1984). Merging uses and gratifications and expectancy-value theory. *Communication Research, 11,* 537–562.

Real, M. R. (1996). *Exploring media culture.* Thousand Oaks, CA: Sage.

Reimer, B., & Rosengren, K. E. (1990). Cultivated viewers and readers: A life-style perspective. In N. Signorielli & M. Morgan (Eds.), *Cultivation analysis: New directions in media effects research* (pp. 181–206). Newbury Park, CA: Sage.

Reuther, C., & Fairhurst, G. T. (2000). Chaos theory and the glass ceiling. In P. Buzzanell (Ed.), *Rethinking organization and managerial communication from feminist perspectives* (pp. 236–253). Thousand Oaks, CA: Sage.

Reynolds, J. (2008). *The face of homelessness.* Hemet, CA: Theatron Media.

Reynolds, P. D. (2007). *A primer in theory construction: An A&B Classics Edition.* Boston: Allyn & Bacon.

Reynolds, T. (2002). Rethinking a Black feminist standpoint. *Ethnic and Racial Studies, 25,* 591–606.

Rhys, W. R., & Bywater, I. (1954). *Rhetoric.* New York: Modern Library.

Richards, I. A. (1936). *The philosophy of rhetoric.* New York: Oxford University Press.

Richmond, V. P., McCroskey, J. C., & Hickson, M. L. (2008). *Nonverbal behavior in interpersonal relations.* Boston: Allyn & Bacon.

Richmond, V. P., Smith, R. S., Heisel, A. D., & McCroskey, J. C. (2001). Nonverbal immediacy in the physician-patient relationship. *Communication Research Reports, 18,* 211–216.

Riger, S. (1992). Epistemological debates, feminist voices: Science, social values, and the study of women. *American Psychologist, 47,* 730–740.

Roberts, K. C. (2004). Texturing the narrative paradigm: Folklore and communication. *Communication Quarterly, 52,* 129–142.

Roberts, W. R. (1984). Rhetoric. In J. Barnes (Ed.), *The complete works of Aristotle* (pp. 2152–2269). Princeton, NJ: Princeton University Press.

Roethlisberger, F. L., & Dickson, W. (1939). *Management and the worker.* New York: Wiley.

Roffers, M. (2002). Personal communication, Milwaukee, WI.

Rogers, L. E., & Escudero, V. (2004). Theoretical foundations. In L. E. Rogers & V. Escudero (Eds.), *Relational communication: An interactional perspective to the study of process and form.* Mahwah, NJ: Lawrence Erlbaum.

Roloff, M. E. (1981). *Interpersonal communication: The social exchange approach.* Beverly Hills, CA: Sage.

Rorty, A. O. (1996). Structuring rhetoric. In A. O. Rorty (Ed.), *Aristotle's* Rhetoric (pp. 1–33). Berkeley: University of California Press.

Rose, R., Suppiah, W., Uli, J., & Othman, J. (2007). A face concern approach to conflict management—A Malaysian perspective. *Journal of Social Sciences, 2,* 121–126.

Rose, R. A. (2006). A proposal for integrating structuration theory with coordinated management of meaning theory. *Communication Studies, 57,* 173–196.

Rosenfeld, L. B., & Bowen, G. L. (1991). Marital disclosure and marital satisfaction: Direct-effect versus interaction-effect models. *Western Journal of Speech Communication, 55,* 69–81.

Rosenthal, R., & Jacobson, L. (1968). *Pygmalion in the classroom: Teacher expectation and pupils' intellectual development.* New York: Holt, Rinehart & Winston.

Rowland, R. C. (1987). Narrative: Mode of discourse or paradigm? *Communication Monographs, 54,* 264–275.

Rowland, R. C. (1989). On limiting the narrative paradigm: Three case studies. *Communication Monographs, 56,* 39–53.

Rubin, A. M. (1981). An examination of television viewing motives. *Communication Research, 8,* 141–165.

Rubin, A. M. (1994). Uses, gratification and media effects research. In J. Bryant & D. Zillman (Eds.), *Media effects: Advances in theory and research* (pp. 281–301). Hillsdale, NJ: Erlbaum.

Rubin, L. (1998, March). *Friends and kin.* Speech presented at the conference on Successful Relating in Couples, in Families, between Friends, and at Work, Tucson, AZ.

Rubin, A. M., & Step, M. M. (2000). Impact of motivation, attraction, and parasocial interaction on talk radio listening. *Journal of Broadcasting & Electronic Media, 44,* 635–654.

Rudd, J. E. (Ed.) (2007). *Communicating in global business negotiations: A geocentric approach.* Thousand Oaks, CA: Sage.

Ruddick, S. (1989). *Maternal thinking: Towards a politics of peace.* Boston: Beacon Press.

Russ, T. L., Simonds, C. J., & Hunt, S. K. (2002). Coming out in the classroom . . . An occupational hazard: The influence of sexual orientation on teacher credibility and perceived student learning. *Communication Education, 51,* 311–324.

Rutenberg, J., & Zeleny, J. (2008, May 15). The politics of the lapel, when it comes to Obama. *The New York Times,* A27.

Ryan, E. E. (1984). *Aristotle's theory of rhetorical argumentation.* Montreal: Les Editions Ballarmin.

Ryan, K. M. (2007). He's a rebel: A discourse analysis of Nike's Bode Miller Olympic advertising campaign. Paper presented at the annual meeting of the International Communication Association, San Francisco, CA.

Rydell, R. J., Hugenberg, K., & McConnell, A. R. (2006). Resistance can be good or bad: How theories of resistance and dissonance affect attitude certainty. *Personality and Social Psychology Bulletin, 32,* 740–750.

Rydell, R. J., McConnell, A. R., & Mackie, D. M. (2008). Consequences of discrepant explicit and implicit attitudes: Cognitive dissonance and increased information processing. *Journal of Experimental Social Psychology, 44,* 1526–1532.

Sabatelli, R. M., & Shehan, C. L. (1993). Exchange and resource theories. In P. G. Boss, W. J. Doherty, R. LaRossa, W. R. Schumm, & S. K. Steinmetz (Eds.), *Sourcebook of family theories and methods: A contextual approach* (pp. 385–411). New York: Plenum.

Sabatine, F. J. (1989). Rediscovering creativity: Unlearning old habits. *Mid-American Journal of Business, 4,* 11–13.

Sahlstein, E. M. (2004). Relating at a distance: Negotiating being together and being apart in long-distance relationships. *Journal of Social and Personal Relationships, 21,* 689–710.

Salem, P. (2007). Making sense of knowledge management. *RCA Vestnik (Russian Communication Association), 1,* 47–68.

Salmon, C. T., & Kline, F. G. (1985). The spiral of silence ten years later: An examination and evaluation. In K. Sanders, L. L. Kaid, & D. Nimmo (Eds.), *Political communication yearbook 1984* (pp. 3–29). Carbondale: Southern Illinois University Press.

Salmon, G., & Faris, J. (2006). Multi-agency collaboration, multiple levels of meaning: Social constructionism and the CMM model as tools to further our understanding. *Journal of Family Therapy, 28,* 272–292.

Samovar, L. A., & Porter, R. E. (1995). *Communication between cultures* (3rd ed.). Belmont, CA: Wadsworth.

Samovar, L. A., Porter, R. E., & McDaniel, E. (2007). *Communication between cultures* (7th ed.). Belmont, CA: Wadsworth.

Sapir, E. (1921). *Language: An introduction to the study of speech.* New York: Harcourt, Brace & World.

Satir, V. (1988). *The new peoplemaking.* Mountain View, CA: Science and Behavior Books.

Schell, J. (1982). *The fate of the earth.* New York: Avon Books.

Schoeman, F. D. (Ed.). (1984). *Philosophical dimensions of privacy: An anthology.* London: Cambridge University Press.

Schramm, W. L. (1954). *The process and effects of mass communication.* Urbana: University of Illinois Press.

Schrodt, P. (2002). The relationship between organizational identification and organizational culture: Employee perceptions of culture and identification in a retail sales organization. *Communication Studies, 53,* 189–202.

Schrodt, P., Witt, P. L., Myers, S. A., Turman, P. D., Barton, M. H., & Jernberg, K. A. (2008). Learner empowerment and teacher evaluations as functions of teacher power use in the college classroom. *Communication Education, 57,* 180–200.

Schultz, B. G. (1996). *Communicating in the small group* (2nd ed.). New York: HarperCollins.

Schwartz, J. (2005, April 4). Some at NASA say its culture is changing, but others say problems still run deep. *The New York Times*, pp. 1–3.

Schwartz, J., & Wald, M. L. (2003, March 9). 'Groupthink' is 30 years old, and still going strong. *The New York Times*, pp. 4–5.

Schwichtenberg, C. (1987). Articulating the people's politics: Manhood and right-wing populism in the A-Team. *Communication, 9,* 389–398.

Seinfeld, J. (1993). *SeinLanguage*. New York: Bantam Books.

Selby, G. (2000). The limits of accommodation: Frederick Douglas and the Garrisonian abolitionists. *Southern Communication Journal, 66,* 52–66.

Shanahan, J., & Jones, V. (1999). Cultivation and social control. In D. Demers & K. Viswanath (Eds.), *Mass media, social control and social change* (pp. 35–61). Ames, IA: Iowa State Press.

Shanahan, J., & Morgan, M. (1999). *Television and its viewers: Cultivation theory and research*. Cambridge: Cambridge University Press.

Shannon, C., & Weaver, W. (1949). *The mathematical theory of communication*. Urbana: University of Illinois Press.

Sharf, B. F. (1990). Physician-patient communication as interpersonal rhetoric: A narrative approach. *Health Communication, 2,* 217–231.

Sharf, B. F., & Poirier, S. (1988). Exploring (un)common ground: Communication and literature in a health care setting. *Communication Education, 37,* 224–236.

Sharkey, W. F., Park, H. S., & Kim, R. K. (2004). Intentional self-embarrassment. *Communication Studies, 55,* 379–399.

Shaw, M. E. (1981). *Group dynamics: The psychology of small group behavior*. New York: McGraw-Hill.

Sheriff, R. E. (2000). Exposing silence as cultural censorship: A Brazilian case. *American Anthropologist, 102,* 114–132.

Sherry, J., Lucas, K., Rechtsteiner, S., Brooks, C., & Wilson, B. (2001, May). *Video game uses and gratifications as predictors of use and game preference*. Paper presented at the annual meeting of the International Communication Association, Washington, DC.

Shimanoff, S. (1980). *Communication rules: Theory and research*. Beverly Hills, CA: Sage.

Shinnar, R. S., Young, C. A., & Meana, M. (2004). The motivations for and outcomes of employee referrals. *Journal of Business Psychology, 19,* 271–283.

Showalter, E. (1997, December). The professor wore Prada. *Vogue, 80, 86,* 92.

Shutiva, C. (2004). Native American culture and communication through humor. In A. Gonzalez, M. Houston, & V. Chen (Eds.), *Our voices: Essays in culture, ethnicity, and communication* (pp. 134–139). Los Angeles: Roxbury.

Siebold, D. R., & Myers, K. K. (2006). Structuring. In G. Shepherd, J. St. John, & T. Striphas (Eds.), *Communication as . . . Perspectives on theory* (pp. 143–152). Thousand Oaks, CA: Sage.

Signorielli, N. (1990). Television's mean and dangerous worlds: A continuation of the cultural indicators perspective. In N. Signorielli & M. Morgan (Eds.), *Cultivation analysis: New directions in media effects research* (pp. 85–106). Newbury Park, CA: Sage.

Signorielli, N., Eveland, W. P., & McLeod, D. M. (1995). Actual and perceived U.S. public opinion: The spiral of silence during the Persian Gulf war. *International Journal of Public Opinion Research, 7,* 91–109.

Simmons, V. N., Webb, M. S., & Brandon, T. H. (2004). College-student smoking: An initial test of an experiential dissonance-enhancing intervention. *Addictive Behaviors, 29,* 1129–1141.

Simpson, C. (1996). Elisabeth Noelle-Neumann's "spiral of silence" and the historical context of communication theory. *Journal of Communication, 46,* 149–173.

Smith, D. (1979). A peculiar eclipsing: Women's exclusion from man's culture. *Women's Studies International, 1,* 281–295.

Smith, K. L., & Belgrave, L. L. (1994). Experiencing hurricane Andrew: Environment and everyday life. In Norman K. Denzin (Ed.), *Studies in symbolic interaction* (pp. 251–273). Greenwich, CT: JAI Press.

Smith, P. M. (1985). *Language, the sexes, and society*. Oxford, England: Basil Blackwell.

Smudde, P. M. (2004). Implications on the practice and study of Kenneth Burke's idea of a "public relations counsel with a heart." *Communication Quarterly, 52,* 420–432.

Snyder, M. (1979). Self-monitoring processes. In L. Berkowitz (Ed.), *Advances in experimental social psychology* (Vol. 12, pp. 86–131). New York: Academic Press.

Soar, M. (2000). Encoding advertisements: Ideology and meaning in advertising production. *Mass Communication & Society, 3,* 415–437.

Sokolon, M. (2005). Emotions in political rhetoric: Why does Aristotle think we get angry first and emulate last? Paper presented at the annual meeting of the Southwest Political Science Association, New Orleans, LA.

Soterin, P., Buzzanell, P. M., & Turner, L. H. (2007). Colonizing family: A feminist critique of family management texts. *Journal of Family Communication, 7,* 245–263.

Sparks, G. G., & Greene, J. O. (1992). On the validity of nonverbal indicators as measures of physiological arousal: A response to Burgoon, Kelley, Newton, and Keeley-Dyreson. *Human Communication Research, 18,* 445–471.

Sparks, G. G., & Ogles, R. M. (1990). The difference between fear of victimization and probability of being victimized: Implication for cultivation. *Journal of Broadcasting & Electronic Media, 34,* 351–358.

Speer, R. B., & Trees, A. R. (2007). The push and pull of stepfamily life: The contribution of stepchildren's autonomy and connection-seeking behaviors to role development in stepfamilies. *Communication Studies, 58,* 377–394.

Spender, D. (1984). *Man made language.* London: Routledge & Kegan Paul.

Sproule, J. M. (1980). *Argument.* New York: McGraw-Hill.

Stacks, D. W., Hill, S. R., & Hickson, M. (1991). *Introduction to communication theory.* Fort Worth, TX: Holt, Rinehart & Winston.

Stafford, L. (2005). *Maintaining long-distance and cross-residential relationships.* Mahwah, NJ: Erlbaum.

Stafford, L. (2008). Social exchange theories. In L. A. Baxter & D. O. Braithwaite (Eds.), *Engaging theories in interpersonal communication: Multiple perspectives* (pp. 377–389). Thousand Oaks, CA: Sage.

Steele, C. M. (1988). The psychology of self-affirmation: Sustaining the integrity of the self. In L. Berkowitz (Ed.), *Advances in experimental social psychology* (Vol. 21, pp. 261–302). San Diego. Academic Press.

Steele, C. M., Spencer, S. J., & Lynch, M. (1993). Self-image, resilience, and dissonance: The role of affirmational resources. *Journal of Personality and Social Psychology, 64,* 885–896.

Steiner, L. (1988, August). *Oppositional decoding as an act of resistance.* Paper presented at the annual conference of the Association for Education in Journalism and Mass Communication, Norman, OK.

Sterk, H. (1999). Personal communication, Milwaukee, WI.

Stern, L. A., & Taylor, K. (2007). Social networking on Facebook. *Journal of the Communication, Speech, & Theatre Association of North Dakota, 20,* 9–20.

Stockstill, C. J., & Roach, D. (2007). Communication apprehension in high school athletes. *Texas Speech Communication Journal, 32,* 53–64.

Strate, L., & Wachtel, E. (2005). *The legacy of McLuhan.* Cresskill, NJ: Hampton Press.

Straus, S. G. (1997). Technology, group processes, and group outcomes: Testing the connections in performance in computer-mediated and face-to-face groups. *Human-Computer Interaction, 12,* 227–266.

Strine, M. S. (1992). Understanding how things work: Sexual harassment and academic culture. *Journal of Applied Communication Research, 20,* 391–400.

Stroud, S. R. (2001). Technology and mythic narrative: *The Matrix* as technological hero-quest. *Western Journal of Communication, 65,* 416–441.

Sullivan, P. A., & Turner, L. H. (1993). *The Zoe Baird spectacle: Silences, sins, and status.* Paper presented at the annual meeting of the Speech Communication Association, Miami, FL.

Sullivan, P. A., & Turner, L. H. (1996). *From the margins to the center: Contemporary women and political communication.* Westport, CT: Praeger.

Sun, C. F., & Scharrer, E. (2004). Staying true to Disney: College students' resistance to criticism of *The Little Mermaid. The Communication Review, 7,* 35–55.

Sundarajan, N., & Spano, S. (2004). CMM and the co-construction of domestic violence. *Human Systems, 15,* 45–58.

Sunnafrank, M. (1986). Predicted outcome value during initial interactions: A reformulation of uncertainty reduction theory. *Human Communication Research, 13,* 191–210.

Surber, J. P. (1998). *Culture and critique: An introduction to the critical discourses of cultural studies.* Boulder, CO: Westview Press.

Suter, E. A. (2008). Discursive negotiation of family identity: A study of U.S. families with adopted children from China. *Journal of Family Communication, 8,* 126–147.

't Hart, P. (1990). *Groupthink in government: A study of small groups and policy failure.* Amsterdam: Swets and Zeitlinger.

't Hart, P. (1998). Preventing groupthink revisited: Evaluating and reforming groups in government. *Organizational Behavior and Human Decision Processes, 73,* 306–313.

Tajfel, H., & Turner, J. C. (1986). The social identity theory of intergroup behavior. In S. Worchel & W. Austin (Eds.), *The psychology of intergroup relations* (pp. 7–24). Chicago, IL: Nelson Hall.

Tan, A. S. (1982). Television use and social stereotypes. *Journalism Quarterly, 59,* 119–122.

Tanno, D. V., & Gonzalez, A. (1998). Sites of identity in communication and culture. In D. V. Tanno & A. Gonzalez (Eds.), *Communication and identity across cultures* (pp. 3–7). Thousand Oaks, CA: Sage.

Taylor, A., & Hardman, M. J. (2000). Introduction: The meaning of voice. In A. Taylor & M. J. Hardman (Eds.), *Hearing many voices* (pp. 1–27). Cresskill, NJ: Hampton Press.

Taylor, D. A., & Altman, I. (1987). Communication in interpersonal relationships: Social penetration processes. In M. E. Roloff & G. R. Miller (Eds.), *Interpersonal processes: New directions in communication research* (pp. 257–277). Newbury Park, CA: Sage.

Taylor, J. R., & Van Every (2000). *The emergent organization: Communication as its site and surface.* Mahwah, NJ: Erlbaum.

Thaler, P. (2006). The legacy of Neil Postman, and the coming of age of media ecology. *Review of Communication, 6,* 369–373.

Theiss, J. A., & Solomon, D. H. (2006). A relational turbulence model of communication about irritations in romantic relationships. *Communication Research, 33,* 391–418.

Theye, K. (2008). Shoot, I'm sorry: An examination of narrative functions and effectiveness within Dick Cheney's hunting accident apologia. *Southern Communication Journal, 73,* 160–177.

Thibaut, J., & Kelley, H. (1959). *The social psychology of groups.* New York: Wiley.

Thoburn, N. (2007). Patterns of production: Cultural studies after hegemony. *Theory, Culture, & Society, 24,* 79–94.

Tidwell, L. C., & Walther, J. B. (2002). Computer-mediated communication effects on disclosure, impressions, and interpersonal evaluations: Getting to know one another a bit at a time. *Human Communication Research, 28,* 317–348.

Timmer, S. G., Sedlar, G., & Urquiza, A. J. (2004). Challenging children in kin versus nonkin foster care: Perceived costs and benefits to caregivers. *Child Maltreatment, 9,* 251–262.

Ting-Toomey, S. (1988). Intercultural conflict styles: A face negotiation theory. In Y. Y. Kim & W. B. Gudykunst (Eds.), *Theories in intercultural communication* (pp. 213–238). Newbury Park, CA: Sage.

Ting-Toomey, S. (1991). Intimacy expression in three cultures: France, Japan, and the United States. *International Journal of Intercultural Relations, 15,* 29–46.

Ting-Toomey, S. (1993). Communicative resourcefulness: An identity negotiation perspective. In R. Wiseman & J. Koester (Eds.). *Intercultural communication competence* (pp. 72–111). Newbury Park, CA: Sage.

Ting-Toomey, S. (1994a). Face and facework: An Introduction. In S. Ting-Toomey (Ed.), *The Challenge of facework* (pp. 1–14). Albany, NY: SUNY Press.

Ting-Toomey, S. (1994b). Managing intercultural conflicts effectively. In L. A. Samovar & R. E. Porter (Eds.), *Intercultural communication: A reader* (pp. 360–372). Belmont, CA: Wadsworth.

Ting-Toomey, S. (2004). Translating conflict face-negotiation theory into practice. In D. Landis, J. Bennett, & M. Bennett (Eds.), *Handbook of intercultural training* (pp. 215–240). Thousand Oaks, CA: Sage.

Ting-Toomey, S. (2007). Intercultural conflict training: Theory-practice approaches and research challenges. *Journal of Intercultural Communication Research, 36,* 255–271.

Ting-Toomey, S., & Chung, L. (1996). Cross-cultural interpersonal communication: Theoretical trends and research directions. In W. B. Gudykunst, S. Ting-Toomey, & T. Nishida (Eds.), *Communication in personal relationships across cultures* (pp. 237–261). Thousand Oaks, CA: Sage.

Ting-Toomey, S., & Chung, L. C. (2005). *Understanding intercultural communication*. Los Angeles: Roxbury.

Ting-Toomey, S., & Cocroft, B. A. (1994). Face and facework: Theoretical and research interests. In S. Ting-Toomey (Ed.), *The challenge of facework* (pp. 307–340). Albany, NY: SUNY.

Ting-Toomey, S., & Cole, M. (1990). Intergroup diplomatic communication: A face-negotiation perspective. In F. Korzenny & S. Ting-Toomey (Eds.), *Communication for peace: Diplomacy and negotiation* (pp. 77–95). Newbury Park, CA: Sage.

Ting-Toomey, S., Gao, G., Trubisky, P., Yang, Z., Kim, H. S., Lin, S., & Nishida, T. (1991). Culture, face maintenance, and styles of handling interpersonal conflict: A study in five cultures. *The International Journal of Conflict Management, 2,* 275–296.

Toller, P. W. (2005). Negotiation of dialectical contradictions by parents who have experienced the death of a child. *Journal of Applied Communication Research, 33,* 46–66.

Toner, R. (2008, May 24). '88 campaign offers a lesson in using symbols as bludgeons. *The New York Times,* A1, A21.

Tong, S. T., Van Der Heide, B., Langwell, L., & Walther, J. B. (2008). Too much of a good thing? The relationship between number of friends and interpersonal impressions on Facebook. *Journal of Computer-Mediated Communication, 13,* 531–549.

Toulmin, S. (1958). *The uses of argument*. London: Cambridge University Press.

Tracy, K. (1990). The many faces of facework. In H. Giles & W. P. Robinson (Eds.), *Handbook of language and social psychology* (pp. 209–226). New York: Wiley.

Tracy, K., & Baratz, S. (1994). The case for case studies of facework. In S. Ting-Toomey (Ed.), *The challenge of facework* (pp. 287–306). Albany, NY: SUNY.

Trenholm, S. (1991). *Human communication theory*. Englewood Cliffs, NJ: Prentice-Hall.

Triandis, H. C. (1972). *The analysis of subjective cultures*. New York: Wiley.

Triandis, H. C. (1988). Collectivism vs. individualism: A reconceptualization of a basic concept in cross-cultural psychology. In G. Verma & C. Bagley (Eds.), *Cross-cultural studies of personality, attitudes and psychology* (pp. 60–95). London: Macmillan.

Trier, J. (2007). "Cool" engagements with YouTube. *Journal of Adolescent & Adult Literacy, 50,* 598–604.

Tronto, J. C. (1993). *Moral boundaries: A political argument for an ethic of care*. New York: Routledge.

Trujillo, N. (1983). Performing Mintzberg's roles: The nature of managerial communication. In L. Putnam & M. E. Pacanowsky (Eds.), *Communication and organizations: An interpretive approach* (pp. 73–98). Beverly Hills, CA: Sage.

Trussell, N., & Lavrakas, P. J. (2004). The influence of incremental increases in token cash incentives on mail survey response: Is there an optimal amount? *Public Opinion Quarterly, 68,* 349–367.

Turkle, S. (2005). *The second self: Computers and the human spirit*. Cambridge, MA: MIT Press.

Turnage, A. K. (2007). Email flaming behaviors and organizational conflict. *Journal of Computer-Mediated Communication, 13.*

Turner, J. H. (1978). *The structure of sociological theory*. Homewood, IL: Dorsey Press.

Turner, J. H. (1986). *The structure of sociological theory* (4th ed.). Chicago: Dorsey Press.

Turner, L. H. (1990). The relationship between communication and marital uncertainty: Is her marriage different from his marriage? *Women's Studies in Communication, 13,* 57–83.

Turner, L. H. (1992). An analysis of words coined by women and men: Reflections on the muted group theory and Gilligan's model. *Women and Language, 25,* 21–26.

Turner, L. H., & West, R. (2006). *Perspectives on family communication* (3rd ed.). New York: McGraw-Hill.

Turow, J. (2003). *Media today: An introduction to mass communication* (2nd ed.). Boston: Houghton Mifflin.

UCLA Center for African American Studies (2002). Prime time in black and white: Making sense of the

2002 Fall season. *The CAAS Research Report, 1*, 1–12.

Ulmer, R., Sellnow, T. L., & Seeger, M. W. (2007). *Effective crisis communication*. Thousand Oaks, CA: Sage.

Van Assche, T. (2007). Wedded to groupthink: Consistency of concurrence seeking following threat and opportunity groupthink decisions. Paper presented at the annual meeting of the International Studies Association, Chicago, IL.

van der Westhuizen, P. C., Oosthuizen, I., Wolhuter, C. C. (2008). The relationship between an effective organizational culture and student discipline in a boarding school. *Education and Urban Society, 40*, 205–225.

Van Epps, G. (2008). *Relooking unit cohesion: A sensemaking approach*. Ft. Leavenworth, KS: U.S. Army Command.

VanLear, C. A. (1991). Testing a cyclical model of communicative openness in relational development: Two longitudinal studies. *Communication Monographs, 58*, 337–361.

VanLear, C. A. (1996). Communication process approaches and models: Patterns, cycles, and dynamic coordination. In J. H. Watt & C. A. VanLear (Eds.), *Dynamic patterns in communication processes* (pp. 35–70). Thousand Oaks, CA: Sage.

Vaughan, C. E. (1998). *Social and cultural perspectives on blindness: Barriers to community integration*. Springfield, IL: Thomas.

Venn, C. (2007). Cultural theory and its futures. *Theory, Culture, & Society, 24*, 49–54.

Waldeck, J. H., Seibold, D. R., & Flanigan, A. J. (2004). Organizational assimiliation and communication technology use. *Communication Monographs, 71*, 161–183.

Waldron, V. R., & Lavitt, M. R. (2000). Welfare-to-work: Communication competencies and client outcomes in a job training program. *Southern Communication Journal, 66*, 1–15.

Walker, L. (1984). *The battered woman syndrome*. New York: Springer.

Wall, C. J., & Gannonleary, P. (1999). A sentence made by men: Muted group theory revisited. *European Journal of Women's Studies, 6*, 21–35.

Wallace, W. L. (1971). *The logic of science in sociology*. Chicago: Aline Atherton.

Wallace, W. L. (1983). *Principles of scientific sociology*. New York: Aldine.

Wallace, R. A., & Wolf, A. (1995). *Contemporary sociological theory: Continuing the classical tradition*. Englewood Cliffs, NJ: Prentice Hall.

Walther, J. B. (2009). Social information processing theory. In L.A. Baxter & D.O. Braithwaite (Eds.), *Engaging theories in interpersonal communication* (pp. 391–404). Los Angeles: Sage.

Walther, J. B., & Burgoon, J. K. (1992). Relational communication in computer-mediated communication. *Human Communication Research, 19*, 50–88.

Wang, Q., Fink, E. L., & Cai, D. A. (2008). Loneliness, gender, and parasocial interaction: A uses and gratifications approach. *Communication Quarterly, 56*, 87–109.

Watzlawick, P., Beavin, J. H., & Jackson, D. D. (1967). *Pragmatics of human communication*. New York: Norton.

Weedon, C. (2004). *Identity and culture: Narratives of difference and belonging*. New York: Open University.

Weick, K. (1969). *The social psychology of organizing*. Reading, MA: Addison-Wesley.

Weick, K. (1979). *The social psychology of organizing* (2nd ed.). Reading, MA: Addison-Wesley.

Weick, K. (1995). *Sensemaking in organizations*. Thousand Oaks, CA: Sage.

Weick, K. E., & Sutcliffe, K. M. (2007). *Managing the unexpected: Resilient performance in an age of uncertainty*. San Fancisco: Jossey-Bass.

Weiner, A. B. (1976). *Women of value, men of renown: New perspectives in Trobriand exchange*. Austin: University of Texas Press.

Welton, K. (1997). Nancy Hartsock's standpoint theory: From content to "concrete multiplicity." *Women and Politics, 18*, 7–24.

West. R., & Turner, L.H. (2009). *Understanding interpersonal communication: Making choices in changing times*. Boston: Wadsworth/Cengage.

Westerman, D., Van Der Heide, B., Klein, K., & Walther, J. B. (2008). How do people really seek out information about others? Information seeking across Internet and traditional communication sources. Paper presented at the annual meeting of the International Communication Association, San Francisco, CA.

Whitchurch, G. G., & Constantine, L. L. (1993). Systems theory. In P. G. Boss, W. J. Doherty, R. LaRossa, W. R. Schumm & S. K. Steinmetz (Eds.), *Sourcebook of family theories and methods: A contextual approach* (pp. 325–352). New York: Plenum.

White, A. M. (2006). "You've got a friend": African American men's cross-sex feminist friendships and their influence on perceptions of masculinity and women. *Journal of Social and Personal Relationships, 23*, 523–542.

White, G. B. (2006). Analogical power and Aristotle's model of persuasion. *Analogical Reasoning, 6*, 67–68.

White, J. M., & Klein, D. M. (2002). *Family theories* (2nd ed.). Thousand Oaks, CA: Sage.

White, J. M., & Klein, D. M. (2008). *Family theories.* Thousand Oaks, CA: Sage.

Whorf, B. L. (1956). Languages and logic. In J. B. Carroll (Ed.), *Language, thought, and reality: Selected writings of Benjamin Lee Whorf* (pp. 233–245). Cambridge, MA: MIT Press.

Wicklund, R. A., & Brehm, J. W. (1976). *Perspectives on cognitive dissonance.* Hillsdale, NJ: Erlbaum.

Willis-Rivera, J. L., & Meeker, M. (2002). De Que Colores: A critical examination of multicultural children's books. *Communication Education, 51*, 269–279.

Wilson, B. J., Martins, N., & Marske, A. L. (2005). Children's and parents' fright reactions to kidnapping stories in the news. *Communication Monographs, 72*, 46–70.

Wilmot, W. (1987). *Dyadic communication.* New York: Random House.

Windahl, S. (1981). Uses and gratifications at the crossroads. In G. C. Wilhoit & H. DeBock (Eds.), *Mass communication review yearbook* (pp. 113–132). Beverly Hills, CA: Sage.

Winn, M. (2002). *The plug-in drug: Television, computers, and family life.* New York: Penguin.

Wolf, G. (1996). Channeling McLuhan. Retrieved March 3, 2003, from the World Wide Web: www.wired.com.

Wolf, M. A., Meyer, T. P., & White, C. (1982). A rules-based study of television's role in the construction of social reality. *Journal of Broadcasting, 26*, 813–829.

Wood, J. (2007). *Gendered lives: Communication, gender, and culture* (7th ed.). Belmont, CA: Wadsworth.

Wood, J. C. (2004, July). Lecture delivered at the Hope Summer Institute, Decorah, Iowa.

Wood, J. T. (1992). Gender and moral voice: Moving from woman's nature to standpoint epistemology. *Women's Studies in Communication, 15*, 1–24.

Wood, J. T. (1994). *Who cares? Women, care, and culture.* Carbondale: Southern Illinois University Press.

Wood, J. T. (2008). Critical feminist theories. In L. A. Baxter & D.O. Braithwaite (Eds.), *Engaging theories in interpersonal communication: Multiple perspectives* (pp. 323–334). Thousand Oaks, CA: Sage.

Wood, J. T., Dendy, L. L., Dordek, E., Germany, M., & Varallo, S. M. (1994). Dialectic of difference: A thematic analysis of intimates' meanings for differences. In K. Carter & M. Prisnell (Eds.), *Interpretive approaches to interpersonal communication* (pp. 115–136). New York: SUNY Press.

Woodward, G. C. (1997). *Perspectives on American political media.* Needham Heights, MA: Allyn & Bacon.

Worchel, S. (1998). A developmental view of the search for group identity. S. Worchel, J. Morales, D. Paez, & J. Dechamps (Eds.), *Social identity: International perspectives* (pp. 53–74). London: Sage.

Worchel, S., Rothgerber, H., Day, E. A., Hart, D., & Butemeyer, J. (1998). Social identity and individual productivity within groups. *British Journal of Social Psychology, 37*, 389–413.

Wright, K. (2000). Perceptions of on-line support providers: An examination of perceived homophily, source credibility, communication and social support within on-line support groups. *Communication Quarterly, 48*, 44–59.

Yerby, J. (1995). Family systems theory reconsidered: Integrating social construction theory and dialectical process. *Communication Theory, 5*, 339–365.

Yetiv, S. A. (2003). Groupthink and the Gulf crisis. *British Journal of Political Science, 33*, 419–442.

Young, S. L. (1998). Where silenced voices speak out: The hidden power of informal communication networks. *Women and Language, 21*, 21–30.

Zagacki, K. S. (2007). Constitutive rhetoric reconsidered: Constitutive paradoxes in G.W. Bush's Iraq war speeches. *Western Journal of Communication, 71,* 272–283.

Zajonc, R. B. (1965). Social facilitation. *Science, 149,* 269–274.

Zanna, M. P., & Cooper, J. (1976). Dissonance and the attribution process. In J. H. Harvey, W. J. Ickes, & R. F. Kidd (Eds.), *New directions in attribution research* (pp. 199–218). Hillsdale, NJ: Erlbaum.

Zillman, D., & Wakshlag, J. (1985). Fear of victimization and the appeal of crime drama. In D. Zillman & J. Bryant (Eds.), *Selective exposure to communication* (pp. 141–151). Hillsdale, NJ: Erlbaum.

Zimbardo, P. G., Ebbesen, E. B., & Maslach, C. (1977). *Influencing attitudes and changing behavior.* New York: Random House.

Zorn, T. E. (1995). Bosses and buddies: Constructing and performing simultaneously hierarchical and close friendship relationships. In J. T. Wood & S. Duck (Eds.), *Under-studied relationships: Off the beaten track* (pp. 122–147). Thousand Oaks, CA: Sage.

Zuengler, J. (1991). Accommodation in native-nonnative interactions: Going beyond the "what" to the "why" in second-language research. In H. Giles, J. Coupland, & N. Coupland (Eds.), *Contexts of accommodation: Developments in applied sociolinguistics* (pp. 223–244). Cambridge: Cambridge University Press.

Name Index

Ting-Toomey, S., 208, 448, 449, 450, 451, 452, 453, 454, 455, 456, 457, 458, 459, 460, 461, 462, 463, 528
Toller, P. W., 212
Tomsha, L., 469
Toner, R., 7
Tong, S. T., 523
Toulmin, S., 349
Tourish, D., 151, 163
Tracy, K., 451, 455, 462
Trapp, R., 338
Treichler, P., 497
Trenholm, S., 4
Tretheway, A, 287
Triandis, H., 456
Trier, J., 445
Tronto, J. C., 489
Trubisky, P., 456
Trussell, N., 193
Tuffin, K., 288
Turkle, S., 40
Turman, P. D., 418, 419, 425
Turnage, A. K., 40
Turner, J., 333
Turner, J. C., 468
Turner, J. H., 46, 125, 199
Turner, L. H., 69, 122, 124, 159, 168, 182, 453, 469, 474, 490, 495, 525, 527
Turow, J., 400

Uli, J., 463
Ulmer, R., 306
Urquiza, A. J., 194, 199

Valde, K. S., 16
Van Acker, A., 389
Van Assche, T., 255
van de Kerkhov, M., 255
Van Der Heide, B., 523, 524
Van Epps, G., 306
Van Every, E. J., 298, 306
Vangelisti, A., 174, 182
VanHorn, S. B., 77, 81
VanLear, C. A., 6, 182
Vaughan, E., 474

Villagran, M., 481
Vinsel, A., 182
Vogl, M. W., 520
Voloudakis, M., 141
von Bertalanffy, L., 60, 294

Wachtel, E., 445
Wack, D. L., 243
Wagner, A., 212
Wahl-Jorgensen, K., 425
Wakshlag, J., 389
Wald, M. L., 242, 256
Waldeck, J. H., 38
Waldron, V. R., 38
Walker, J. R., 408
Wall, C. J., 494
Wallace, R. A., 504–505
Wallace, W. L., 62
Walster, E. H., 119
Walther, J. B., 136, 163, 164, 523, 524
Wang, Q., 393
Ward, C. J., 36
Watzlawick, P., 6, 9, 58
Weaver, W., 11, 12, 30, 148
Webb, M., 121
Weedon, C., 363, 368
Wei, R., 405
Weick, K., 290, 292, 293, 294, 296, 297, 298, 299, 300, 301, 302, 303, 304, 305, 306
Weick, K. E., 304
Weiner, A. B., 488
Welton, K., 510
Wenner, L., 401
West, R. L., 168, 182, 453, 469, 474, 490, 527
Westerman, D., 524
van der Westhuizen, P. C., 288
Whedbee, K. E., 16
Whitchurch, G. G., 58
White, Am. M., 124, 326
White, C., 57
White, J. M., 50, 189
White, M. A., 199
Whiting, G. C., 96, 97, 106
Whorf, B., 331

Wicklund, R., 121, 126
Wiemann, J., 471
Wigley, S., 172
Wilcox, R., 463
Willemyns, M., 468
Williams, A., 478
Williams, T., 370
Willis-Rivera, J. L., 42
Wilmot, W. W., 14, 159
Wilson, B. J., 380, 382, 389, 405
Wilson, N., 151, 163
Windahl, S., 400, 401
Winfrey, O., 38
Winn, M., 432
Wittenbaum, G. M., 251
Wittenberg, E., 172
Wittenberg-Lyles, E., 481
Wittgenstein, L., 94
Wolf, A., 504–505
Wolf, M. A., 57
Wolhuter, C. C., 288
Wood, J. C., 502, 503, 512, 513
Wood, J. T., 214, 490, 507
Wood, W., 118, 123, 484
Woods, T., 40
Woodward, G., 366
Worchel, S., 468
Wright, K., 40
Wynn, D., 242

Yang, S. M., 161, 456
Yep, G. A., 232
Yerby, J., 50, 65
Yetiv, S. A., 241, 251
Yokochi, Y., 450
Yoon, K., 251
Young, C. A., 124
Young, S. L., 61

Zagacki, K. S., 39
Zajonc, R., 243
Zak, M., 350
Zanna, M. P., 116
Zeleny, J., 7
Zillman, D., 389
Zimbardo, P. G., 117
Zorn, T., 211, 525
Zuengler, J., 477, 479

Subject Index

personal phase of, 151
subtexts of, 35
uncertainty reduction and, 152
communication, intrapersonal,
32–34
repetitiveness of, 33
communication, mass, 40–41
changes in, 40
Communication Privacy
Management (CPM), 220
assumptions of, 222–223
basic suppositions of, 223–228
consistency of, 233–234
criticism of, 233–235
evolution of, 221–222
heurism of, 234–235
integration of, 233
utility of, 234
communicator reward valence,
139–140
The Communist Manifesto
(Marx), 31
Communists, 249
comparison level (CL), 191–192
comparison level for alternatives
(CLalt), 191–192
computer-mediated
communication
(CMC), 523
concepts, 48. *See also*
self-concept
nominal, 49
operationalizing, 61
real, 49
specificity of, 70
concurrence seeking, 247
conflicts, 6, 454
avoiding, 458–461
compromising, 458–461
across cultures, 458–461
dominating, 458–461
integrating, 458–461
obliging, 458–461
in social situations, 403
conscientious objectors, 254
consciousness
discursive, 265
false, 367
practical, 265
consensus seeking, 240
consistency, 69, 116
in attitudes, 116
in behaviors, 116
in beliefs, 116
of Communication Privacy
Management, 233–234

of Cultivation Analysis,
388–389
of Cultural Studies, 373
of Face-Negotiation
Theory, 462
increasing, 118
of Narrative Paradigm, 355
in narratives, 350, 351–352
of Organization Information
Theory, 305–306
of Organizational Cultural
Theory, 287–288
restoring, 116
of Rhetorical Theory, 325
of Spiral of Silence Theory,
424–425
in theory, 113
of Uses and Gratification
Theory, 407–408
contexts, 32, 68
collating, 42
situational, 32
contradiction, 205
control, 51, 225–226
behavior, 193
fate, 193
of men, 495–496
as silencing, 495–496
convergence, 61, 472–475
attraction and, 472
evaluation of, 474–475
intention of, 475
maintaining social identity, 476
relational history and, 473
stereotypes and, 473
conversation. *See also* speech
flow of, 94
inner, 86
Coordinated Management of
Meaning (CMM), 75, 93
assumptions of, 94–97
core of, 97–101
criticism of, 109–111
evolution of, 109
heurism of, 110–111
integration of, 109
parsimony of, 109–110
refinement of, 109
scope of, 109
stages of, 110
utility of, 110
coordination
challenge of, 104, 106, 108
degree of, 104–105
influence on, 105–106
moral order and, 105

no, 104
partial, 105
perfect, 104
Corporate Ethics Statements, 18
The Cosby Show, 369–370
as "Black America," 370
as educational tool, 370
cosubstantiation, 333
Couch, Carl, 79
Counter Heg, 369
counter-hegemony. *See also*
hegemony
audience and, 373
in *The Simpsons*, 370–371
courtrooms, 322
CPM. *See* Communication
Privacy Management
creativity, 532
credibility, 472
crime. *See also specific crimes*
contextualizing, 19
critical thinking, 22
critical tradition, 31
criticism
of Aristotle, 325
of Cognitive Dissonance
Theory, 124–127
of Communication
Accommodation Theory,
479–481
of Communication Privacy
Management, 233–235
Coordinated Management of
Meaning, 109–111
of Cultivation Analysis,
388–391
of Cultural Studies, 373–375
of Dramatism, 338–341
of Expectancy Violations
Theory, 141–143
of Face-Negotiation Theory,
461–463
of Groupthink, 254–256
of interactional model, 13
of Muted Group Theory,
497–499
of Narrative Paradigm,
355–357
of Organization Information
Theory, 305–306
of Organizational Cultural
Theory, 287–288
of Relational Dialectics Theory,
216–217
of Rhetorical Theory,
324–326

education
  AIDS, 422
  attainment of, percentage
    of, 531
  communication, 529
  The Cosby Show as tool
    for, 370
  enrollment patterns, 19
  ethics, 17
  goal of, 520
  online, 522–523
efficiency, 467
either/or prepositions, 331
electronic interdependence, 432
elevator, 131
emotions, 90
employee commitment, 194
enmeshment, 100
environment, 8
  advocates of, 422
environment, information.
    See information environment
episodes, 99–100
  clusters of, 100–101
  culture and, 100
  perspective on, 99
  punctuating, 99
epistemology, 52, 53, 507
equifinality, 60
equivocality, 297
  principles of, 301–302
  reducing, 299
equivocality, reducing
  behavior cycles, 302
  enactment stage in, 303
  retention stage in, 304
  rules, 302
  selection stage in, 303–304
essentialism
  of Muted Group Theory, 498
  of Standpoint Theory, 512–513
ethics, 15–22. *See also* Corporate
    Ethics Statements
  aging, 527
  business, 17–18
  career, 528, 530
  culture and, 16
  education, 17
  entertainment, 17
  health, 527
  industry, 17–18
  medicine, 17
  as moral decision making, 16
  National Communication
    Association doctrine
    on, 530

politics, 17
religion, 17, 18
shifting standards of, 16
strategies, 21
studying, 16
technology, 17
violating, 16
ethnocentrism, 527–528
ethos, 314, 325
eulogies, 323
evaluation, 470
  of convergence, 474–475
  of relationships, 191–192
  theory, 71
"everyday" issues, 220
  groupthink in, 252
EVT. *See* Expectancy Violations
    Theory
exchange
  direct, 196
  generalized, 196
  productive, 196–197
  structures, 196–197
expectancy violation, 130
Expectancy Violations Theory
    (EVT), 75, 130
  assumptions of, 134–137
  clarity of, 142
  criticism of, 141–143
  integration of, 141
  scope of, 142
  testability of, 142–143
  utility of, 142
expectations, 134
  attractiveness and, 136–137
  for behavior, 269
  culture and, 136
  deviation from, 139–140
  group-based, 470
  influences on, 135
  interactional, 135
  observations and, 136
  past experience and, 136
  predictions and, 136
  pre-interactional, 135
expected activity outcomes, 406
experience
  field of, 13
  inviting, 42
  past, 14
  personal, making
    sense of, 23
  theory and, relationship
    between, 50
explanation, 148
eye contact, 140

face
  Chinese conceptualization
    of, 450
  concern, 451
  desire for, 450
  as extension of self-concept,
    450
  humiliation, 454
  loss, 454
  maintenance, 455
  management, 458
  need, 451
  negative, 451
  politeness theory and, 451
  positive, 451
  restoration, 455
  saving, 454, 455
  self, 462
  wants, 451
Face-Negotiation Theory, 449
  assumptions of, 453–455
  consistency of, 462
  criticism of, 461–463
  heurism of, 463
  integration of, 462
  refinement of, 462
Facebook, 523
face-threatening acts (FTAs), 455
facework, 452–453
  approbation, 452
  solidarity, 452
  tact, 452
family. *See also* stepfamilies
  business, 348
  diversity in, 527
  eroded by television, 432
  future of, 525–526
  income, 532
  policies, 272
  as private life, 489
fate control, 193
The Fate of the Earth
    (Schell), 354
feedback, 12, 59–60, 294, 301
  providing, 295
  requesting, 295
feminism, 339
  dictionary, 497
  dominant groups in, 484
  uniting, 503
"The Feminist Standpoint:
    Developing the Ground
    for a Specifically Feminist
    Historical Materialism"
    (Hartsock), 503
feminist-Marxist theory, 503

field journal, 283
focus, 522
foreign policy, 241, 251
foreplay, 492
forewarnings, 241
foster care, 194
Frankfurt School theorists,
    363–364
free
  speech, 20
  will, 53
fresh act, 262
FTAs. *See* face-threatening acts
future, 521–528
  culture, 527–528
  family, 525–526
  health, 526–527
  identity, 527–528
  technology, 523–524
  trends, 523
  workplace, 525–526
The Futurist (Haim), 532

Gage, Matilde Joslyn, 484
Game Theory, 189, 193
  win-lose notion in, 190
games, 431. *See also* video games
gangs, 282
Geertz, Clifford, 275
gender. *See also* men; women
  bias in ethnography, 485
  as changeable, 488, 505
  criteria for rules, 229–230
  dualism and, 515
  identity, 488
  perception and, 489–491
  polarization, 490
  problematic relations
    regarding, 505
  sex and, blurring of, 488
  in Spanish television, 380
  video games and, 402
General Systems Theory (GST),
    58, 294–295
generalizations, 63
genlets, 490
gentlemen's club, 250
global village, 432, 440
God, 422
Golden Mean, 18
Google, 521
Government Accountability
    Project, 20
Gramsci, Antonio, 367
Gregory, Alex, 84
grief, 90

Groening, Matt, 207
group(s). *See also* in-groups;
    out-groups
  based expectations, 470
  freezing, 498
  intergroup variables, 468
  language and, 471
  marginalized, 479
  relationship of U.S., 505
  solidarity, 197
  undesirable, 477
groups, dominant, 487
  within feminist movement, 484
  men as, 491–492
groups, muted, 487–488
  men in, 487–488
  women as, 486–487
groups, small, 35–36, 240
  activities of, 242
  affiliative constraints of, 243
  close-mindedness in, 249
  collective rationalization
    in, 249
  complexity of, 243
  conformity, 245
  constraining behavior of, 263
  dominant voices in, 246
  influence in, 244
  inherent morality of, belief
    in, 249
  insulation, 246
  invulnerability illusion of,
    248–249
  majority of support in, 254
  out-group stereotypes in, 249
  overestimation of, 248–249
  pressure on dissenters in,
    250–251
  problem-solving, 242, 243
  recommendations for, 252
  self-appointed mindguards
    in, 250
  self-censorship in, 250
  stress, 247
  structural factors in, 246–247
  task-oriented, 242
  unanimity in, illusion of, 250
  uniformity pressures in,
    250–251
Groupthink
  antecedent conditions of,
    245–247, 248
  appeal of, 256
  assumptions of, 242–244
  criticism of, 254–256
  development of, 241

in everyday lives, 252
heurism of, 255–256
influence of, 256
integration of, 254
oversimplifying, 252
preventing, 252–254
promoting, 246
recognizing, 245
scope of, 255
symptoms of, 247–251
test of time, 256
testability of, 255
GST. *See* General Systems Theory
guilt, 333–335
  purging, 334, 340
Guinier, Lani, 122
gynecological exams, 495

habituation, 320
Haim, Alexander, 532
Hall, Stuart, 361
Hartsock, Nancy, 503
Hasse, Clara E., 490
Hawthorne experiments, 38
health
  ethics, 527
  future of, 526–527
health care
  advocates, 228–229
  career in, 529
Hegel, Georg Wilhelm
    Friedrich, 503
hegemony, 367–369. *See also*
    counter-hegemony consent
    and, 367
Hempel, Carl, 50
heurism, 70
  of Cognitive Dissonance
    Theory, 127
  of Communication Accommo-
    dation Theory, 481
  of Communication Privacy
    Management, 234–235
  of Coordinated Management
    of Meaning, 110–111
  of Cultivation Analysis, 389
  of Cultural Studies, 374
  of Dramatism, 340–341
  of Face-Negotiation
    Theory, 463
  of Groupthink, 255–256
  of Media Ecology Theory,
    444–445
  of Narrative Paradigm, 357
  of Organization Information
    Theory, 306

of Organizational Cultural
Theory, 288
of Rhetorical Theory, 326
of Social Exchange
Theory, 199
of Social Penetration Theory,
182–183
of Spiral of Silence Theory, 425
of Uncertainty Reduction
Theory, 155–156, 164
of Uses and Gratification
Theory, 408
hierarchy, 37, 59, 334
of needs, 394
of organized meaning, 97
social, 366
history books, 495
HIV. *See* human
immunodeficiency virus
homeless, 477
women, 495
homeostatic, 60
homicide rate, 382
homogeneity, 244
Hovland, Carl, 30–31
Hudson, Rock, 361
human immunodeficiency virus
(HIV), 232
human services, 529
humor, 181
career and, 532–533
Hurricane Katrina, 403
hypothesis, 56

I, 88
ice age analogy, 382
identification, 332–333
ideology, 365
impression management, 125
incest, 509
income, 532
individual
freedom, 83
society and, 83
society and, interdependency
between, 77
Individual Differences
Perspective, 393
individualism, 101
inductive logic, 60
industrial revolution, 489
industrial safety, 4
influence, exerting, 268
information environment,
297–299
ambiguity in, 296

multiple sources in, 298
organizations dependence
on, 296
in-groups, 468. *See also* group(s)
The Insider, 15–16
integration
of Cognitive Dissonance
Theory, 124
of Communication
Accommodation
Theory, 480
of Communication Privacy
Management, 233
of conflicts, 458–461
of Coordinated Management
of Meaning, 109
of Cultivation Analysis, 388
of Cultural Studies, 373
dialectics, of relational, 214
of Dramatism, 338
of Expectancy Violations
Theory, 141
of Face-Negotiation
Theory, 462
of Groupthink, 254
of Media Ecology Theory, 444
of Muted Group Theory, 497
of Narrative Paradigm,
354–355
of Organization Information
Theory, 305
of Organizational Cultural
Theory, 287
of Relational Dialectics
Theory, 216
of Rhetorical Theory, 324
social, 268–269
of Social Exchange Theory, 197
of Social Penetration
Theory, 181
of Spiral of Silence Theory, 423
of Standpoint Theory, 512
of Structuration Theory, 270
of Symbolic Interaction
Theory, 89
of Uncertainty Reduction
Theory, 163
of Uses and Gratification
Theory, 407
intentionality debate, 8–10
interaction
goal of, 79
meaning created in, 80–82
self-concepts and, 82–83
interactional model, 12–14
criticism of, 13

interdependence, 58
electronic, 432
Interdependence, Theory
of, 187
international relations,
career in, 529
Internet, 20. *See also* media, new
age and, 523
dot com bust, 293
education on, 522–523
enhancement, 439–440
growth of, 406
motivations for, 406
political information on, 402
relationships, 523
use of, percentage of, 531
Internet and American Life
Project of the Pew Research
Center, 531
interruptions, 496
intimacy, 225
isolation
fear of, 414, 415, 420
standpoints shaped by, 514

Janis, Irving, 240
jargon, 466
"Jeanne Clery Act," 19
Jefferson, Thomas, 251
Jerry Springer, 399
job satisfaction, 281
Johnson, Lyndon, 378
journalism, 529
justification, minimal, 119–120

Kaplan, Eric, 107
Kennedy, John F., 438
Kennedy, Ted, 340
kidnapping, 380, 382
knowing
approaches to, 50–52
critical approach to, 51–52
interpretive approach to, 51
positivistic approach to, 51
knowledge
moral, 279
power and, relationship
between, 504
situated, 510
Kopechne, Mary Jo, 340
Kuhn, Manford, 78

Laadan, 497
labels, 7, 133
labor, division of, 489–490, 511
Lacy, Clifton R., 377

memory
  attitude organizing, 119
  in rhetoric, 319–320
men. *See also* gender
  at birth, 490
  control of, 495–496
  defining research inquiry, 504
  dominance of, 491–492
  interruptions and, 496
  in muted groups, 487–488
  role in workplace, 489
mental calculus, 223
message, 11
Meyrowitz, Joshua,
    442–443
MGT. *See* Muted Group
    Theory
microtheory, 222
mind, 86
Mind, Self, and Society
    (Mead, G.), 77, 85
models, 11. *See also specific
    models*
money, 431
Montgomery, Barbara, 202
moral habits, 322
moral knowledge, 279
moral order, 105
moral theory, 347
morphogenic, 60
mortification, 334
motion, 205
movements, 57
multiple mode problem, 126
Muted Group Theory
    (MGT), 484
  assumptions of, 488–493
  assumptions of, dated, 499
  criticism, 497–499
  discarding, 499
  essentialism of, 498
  integration, 497
  origins of, 485–487
  test of time, 499
  utility of, 498–499
My Fair Lady, 87–88

"naïve psychologists," 45
narrative
  choosing among, 348–349
  coherence, 351–353
  competing, 349
  consistent, 350, 351–352
  fidelity, 352
  interdisciplinary approach
    to, 348

logic, 346
  public, 348
  rational world
    paradigm v., 347
  rationality, 351
  traditional logic v., 349
  truth in, 350
  universality of, 347
Narrative Paradigm, 344
  assumptions of, 346–350
  conservative bias of,
    355–356
  consistency of, 355
  context in, 350
  criticism of, 355–357
  heurism of, 357
  integration of, 354–355
  key concepts in, 350–354
  scope of, 355
  testability of, 357
  utility of, 355–356
National Association of Colleges
    and Employers, 311
National Commission on the
    causes and Prevention of
    Violence, 378
National Communication
    Association, 337
  doctrine of ethical
    beliefs, 530
National Safety Society, 4
needs and motivation
    theory, 394
negative, 334
Negro Leagues, 272
neo-Marxist, 364
networks, 36
New Yorker Collection,
    10, 84, 107, 276,
    349, 489
newspapers, 395
  electronic, 524
Nichols, Marie Hochmuth,
    338–339
nicknames, 208
Nixon, Richard, 438
No Sense of Place (Meyrowitz),
    442–443
noise, 30
  external, 12
  psychological, 12
  semantic, 12
nonverbal communication,
    15, 130
norms, 471
numbers, 430–431

nurses, 286
  authority issues with,
    486–487
  "care coordinator role" of, 298
  stereotypes, 486–487

Obama, Barack, 7
observations, 61
offensive displays, 133
one dollar/twenty dollars study,
    119–120
onion analogy, 172–174
ontology, 52, 507
openness, 59
  culture and, 168–169
  protection and, 208–209
  value of, 169
opinion
  change in, 411
  confidence in, 412
  dual climates of, 420
  ego and, 426
  as expression of attitude, 413
  hard core, 421–423
  last-minute swings of, 421
  media influence on, 411
  minority, 411
  on religion, 422
  societal views and, 421
opinion, public, 412–414
  behavior and, 414, 416–417
  media and, 415–416
  personal observation and,
    415–416
  on race, 413
order, 334
Organization Information
    Theory, 292
  ambiguity in, 298
  assumptions of, 296–297
  consistency of, 304–306
  criticism of, 305–306
  focus of, 293
  heurism of, 306
  integration of, 305
  key concepts in, 297–301
  theoretical latticework
    of, 304
  utility of, 306
Organizational Cultural
    Theory, 275
  assumptions of, 278–282
  consistency of, 288
  criticism of, 287–288
  integration of, 287
  utility of, 288

organizational culture. *See* culture, organizational

organizational rituals, 285

organizations. *See also* culture, organizational
  books on, 275
  dependence on information, 296
  evolution of, 292
  guidelines for, 299
  information adequacy in, 281
  interrelationships in, 294
  job satisfaction in, 281
  living system metaphor for, 291
  people in, importance of, 278–279
  as static units, 306
  symbols in, 279
  technology into, introduction of new, 291
  time/space in, 269–270
  women and glass ceiling in, 492

otherness, 30

others
  generalized, 88–89
  particular, 88

out-groups, 468. *See also* group(s)

overaccommodation, 477–479. *See also* accommodation
  dependency, 478–479
  intergroup, 479
  miscommunication from, 477
  sensory, 477–478

ownership, 225–226
  boundary, 231

Palo Alto team, 9

paradigm, 344, 396
  limited effects, 406
  narrative v. rational world, 347
  national, 344–345
  rational world, 345, 346, 349
  shift, 345
  soundness, 349–350

parametric rules, 57

parasocial interaction, 396

parsimony, 70
  of Coordinated Management of Meaning, 109–110
  of Dramatism, 338–339
  of Relational Dialectics Theory, 216
  of Structuration Theory, 271

pathos, 314

patriotism, 7

PDC. *See* Public Dialogue Consortium

pentad, 335–337
  act, 335
  agency, 336
  agent, 336
  attitude, 337
  purpose, 336
  scene, 335

perception, 470. *See also* self-perception
  dissonance and, 118–119
  gender and, 489–491

performance, 284–285
  enculturation, 286–287
  passion, 285
  political, 286
  social, 286

Persian Gulf crisis, 251

personal
  dialog theory, 202
  idioms, 179
  shoppers, 525

personal space, 130
  affiliation and, 131

perspective
  on episodes, 99
  standpoint and, 508
  taking, 86

persuasion, 38–39, 221, 332. *See also* public speaking; rhetoric; speech
  Cognitive Dissonance Theory and, 120–124
  media and, 372

phenomenological tradition, 29–30

phenomenology, 29–30

PIRG. *See* Public Interest Research Group

Plato, 312, 323

Pledge of Allegiance, 7, 422–423

pluralistic ignorance, 416

politeness, 450
  in electronic mail, 478
  face and, 451
  theory, 451

political
  figures, 210
  performance, 286
  socialization, 435

politics, 20
  diversity in, 527

positive reinforcement, 267

Postman, Neil, 441–442

POV. *See* predicted outcome value

power, 193
  coercive, 267
  difference, 476
  expert, 268
  imbalances, 52
  knowledge and, relationship between, 504
  legitimate, 268
  meaning and, 366
  referent, 267
  reward, 267
  struggle for, 366
  as two-way street, 263
  type as resource, 267
  understanding systems of, 502

practical discipline, 63

pragmatists, 78

praxis, 206

predicted outcome value (POV), 163

predictions, 147
  behavior, 152
  expectations and, 136
  on mass media, 401
  relationship, 170
  social penetration, 170

presidential debates, 1960, 438

primary territories, 133

printing press, 434

Prisoner's Dilemma, 189–190

privacy. *See also* boundaries
  management dialectics, 227–228

privacy rule
  attributes, 231
  characteristics, 229–231
  management system, 226–227, 229–233

private information, 223–225

probabilistic laws, 56

probing, 208–209

PROD. *See* Proportional Representation of Diversity index

proletariat, 363

Proportional Representation of Diversity index (PROD), 387

proxemics, 131

public, 413. *See also* opinion, public
  distance, 132–133
  image, 172
  narrative, 348
  territories, 133

Public Dialogue Consortium
(PDC), 102
Public Interest Research Group
(PIRG), 20
public relations, career in, 529
public speaking, 38–39, 221. *See
also* persuasion; rhetoric;
speech
as audience centered, 313
death and, 311
"how to" for, 311
studying, 311
Pygmalion effect, 87–88

quasi-statistical sense, 416
Quixote, Don, 423

racetrack, 121
radio, 395
rationale, 117–118
rationality, 188–189
narrative, 351
tests for, 351
rationalizing, 189
in groups, 249
RDT. *See* Relational Dialectics
Theory
reactivity searching, 158
receiver, 11
reciprocity, 56, 154, 172–173
indirect, 196
trust and, 174
Redeemer, 335
redemption, 333–335
reflected appraisals, 87
reflexivity, 264–266
rejection, fear of, 243
*Relating: Dialogues and
Dialectics* (Baxter &
Montgomery), 202
relational development, 204
Relational Dialectics Theory
(RDT), 202
assumptions of, 204–205
criticism of, 216–217
goal of, 216
integration of, 216
parsimony of, 216
utility of, 216
relationships, 49
abusive, 192
age and, 526–527
consonant, 114
contradictory desires in, 204
dating, 151, 159
depenetration of, 170

developed, 158–161
disengagement of, 182
dissolution of, 170
dissonant, 114
doctor-patient, 4, 526–527
dramatic metaphor in, 329
ebb-and-flow patterns in, 216
evaluation of, 191–192
of groups in U.S., 505
intimate, 169
irrelevant, 114
maintenance, 172
master-slave, 503
meaning and, 100
misrepresentation in, 199
need for personal, 398
negative, 186–187
nonintimate, 169
number of, 35
online, 523
outcome of, 187
platonic, 141
positive, 186
predictions, 170
speaker-audience, 313
teacher-student, 136
tearing up, 172–174
trajectory of, 168
transgressions of, 171
uncertainty in, 151, 159
workplace, 525
worth of, 186
youthful, 526
relationships, long distance
romantic (LDRs), 213
reliability, 64
religion. *See also specific religions*
in classroom, 419
opinions on, 422
research
applied, 63
breadth/depth of, 23
intergenerational, 478
limitations of, 65
male defined, 504
naturalistic, 282–283
process of, 60–65
pure, 62–63
values in, 53
resonance, 383–384
resources, 105
allocative, 266
authoritative, 266–267
power type as, 267
rules and, distinction
between, 266

respect, professional, 136
rhetoric, 39, 313. *See also*
persuasion; public speaking;
speech
arrangement in, 317–319
artistic unity in, 317
body in, 318
canons of, 316–321
conclusion in, 318
deliberative, 321, 323
delivery in, 321
epideictic, 321, 323
forensic, 321–322
glosses in, 319
introduction in, 318
invention in, 316–317
memory in, 319–320
metaphor in, 319
simplicity in, 317
style in, 319
types of, 321–324
voice manipulation in, 321
word appropriateness in, 319
word choice in, 319
word imagery in, 319
Rhetoric (Aristotle), 309, 311
organization of, 325
A Rhetoric of Motives
(Burke), 332
Rhetorical Theory
assumptions of, 313–315
consistency of, 325
criticism of, 324–326
heurism of, 326
integration of, 324
test of time, 326
rhetorical tradition, 28–29
rituals
cultural, 148
organizational, 285
personal, 284
perspective on media, 378
as silencing, 494–495
social, 285
task, 284–285
role, 36
taking, 86–87
Roloff, Michael, 187
Rostow, Walt, 250
rules, 93. *See also* privacy rule
altering existing, 262
blueprint of, 259
constitutive, 106–107
contextual criteria for,
229–230
creating new, 262

social networking, 4, 20–21, 156
social order
    problems in, 502
    technology and, 429
social outcomes, 406
social penetration, 168
    predictions, 170
Social Penetration Theory
    (SPT), 168
    affective exchange stage of,
        179–180
    assumptions of, 169–171
    criticism of, 181–183
    exploratory affective exchange
        stage of, 178
    heurism of, 182–183
    integration of, 181
    orientation stage of, 177–178
    reward/cost ratio in, 175–176
    scope of, 181–182
    stable exchange stage of,
        180–181
    stages of, 176–181
social performance, 286
social privilege, 487
social process, influence of, 84
social psychology, 468–469
The Social Psychology of
    Organizing (Wieck), 293
social reality, 96
    of contradictions, 205
    dominant, 386
social rituals, 285
social services, 529
social situations
    awareness of problems created
        by, 403
    conflicts in, 403
    interactions creating, 96
    tensions in, 403
social status, 471
social structure, 84
socialization, political, 435
society, 88–89
    competing, 369
    diversity in, 527
    individual and, 83
    individual and, interdependency
        between, 77
    internalizing, 86
    media maintaining, 378
sociocultural evolution, theory
    of, 295–296
socio-cultural tradition, 31
socio-psychological, 30–31
Sophists, 312

source, 11
speech. See also conversation;
        persuasion; public speaking;
        rhetoric
    act, 99
    behavior similarities/
        dissimilarities in, 469
    cross-realm, 526
    free, 20
    style, 468–469
    women and collaborative, 492
    women and trivialized, 494
Speech Accommodation Theory.
        See Communication
        Accommodation Theory
Spiral of Silence Theory, 386, 411
    assumptions of, 414–417
    consistency of, 424–425
    criticism of, 423–425
    heurism of, 424
    integration of, 423
SPT. See Social Penetration
        Theory
ST. See Standpoint Theory
stability measure, 192
Standpoint Theory (ST), 502
    assumptions of, 505–508
    assumptions of, second
        set, 507
    criticism of, 512–515
    essentialism of, 512–513
    framework for, 502
    history of, 503–505
    integration, 512
    key concepts of, 508–511
standpoints, 508–510
    community and, 514
    constellation of, 513
    developing, 510
    invisibility feeling and, 514
    isolation and, 514
    outsider within, 510
    partial, 509
    perspective and, 508
    political aspect of, 510
    social context of, 509
Stanton, Elizabeth Cady, 484
Starr, Kenneth, 334
state, separation between church
        and, 422
status quo, 51
    challenging, 54
    criticizing, 502
    women devalued by, 505
Stempel, Guido, 438
stepfamilies, 228

stereotypes
    convergence and, 473
    indirect, 474
    nurse, 486–487
    targets of, 474
Stevens, Mick, 276, 349, 489
stranger-on-the-train
        phenomenon, 171
street harassment, 496
structuration, 260–261
Structuration Theory, 259
    assumptions of, 262–264
    criticism of, 270–272
    difficulty in reading, 271
    elements of, 264–269
    integration of, 270
    parsimony of, 271
    scope of, 271
structure, 260
    duality of, 266–268
    need for, 259
subculture, 41
substance, 332–333
    ambiguity of, 333
subsystems, 59
subtle realism, 51
suicide, doctor-assisted, 19, 417
suprasystems, 59
"survival of the fittest," 295
syllogisms, 315–316
symbol, 7, 77
    abstract, 7
    behavioral, 279
    concrete, 7
    effectiveness of, 280
    motivation through, 330
    in organizations, 279
    physical, 279
    significant, 86
    systems, 329
    verbal, 279, 280
Symbolic Interaction Theory (SI),
        75, 77
    assumptions of, 79–85
    Chicago School of, 78
    criticism of, 89–91
    glance at, 79
    history of, 78–79
    integration, 89
    Iowa School of, 78
    key concepts of, 85–89
    scope of, 89
    testability of, 90–91
    themes of, 79–85, 85
    utility of, 90
synergy, 36

system(s)
   class, 363
   disruptions in, 294
   of power, 502
   symbol, 329

Taoism, 18
Technological Determinism.
   See Media Ecology Theory
technological lens, 34
technology
   availability of, 531
   competence and, 531
   cultivating new, 531–532
   culture and, 428
   in electronic age, 435–436
   influence of, 428
   introduced into
      organizations, 291
   social order and, 429
   trends, 523–524
technopoly, 442
*Technopoly: The Surrender of
   Culture to Technology*
   (Postman), 442
television, 57, 377. *See also*
   media, mass; *specific shows*
   bending in, 386
   blending in, 386
   blurring in, 386, 443
   boundaries and, 443
   as central cultural arm, 381
   class in Spanish, 380
   computer hybrid with, 404
   cultural function of, 381
   family values eroded by, 432
   gender in Spanish, 380
   influence of, 381
   manipulation through, 431
   motivation for, 395
   uniqueness of, 379–380
tenure, 133
terministic screens, 331
territoriality, 133–134
   prevention and, 133
   reaction and, 133
testability, 70
   of Cognitive Dissonance
      Theory, 127
   of Communication
      Accommodation Theory,
      480–481
   of Expectancy Violations
      Theory, 142
   of Groupthink, 255
   of Media Ecology Theory, 444

of Narrative Paradigm, 357
of Social Exchange
   Theory, 199
of Symbolic Interaction
   Theory, 90–91
tetrad, 439
theater, 93
   reconsideration of, 94
   of struggle, 369
theorems, 155
theory, 45, 67. *See also*
   macrotheory; microtheory
   building, 55–60
   complex spatial network
      and, 50
   components of, 48–49
   consistency, 113
   covering law approach to,
      55–56
   criticism of, 48
   defining, 46–49
   evaluating, 71
   generality level of, 47–48
   goals, 49
   grand, 47
   grounded, 61
   guidelines, 55, 56
   as lens, 50, 522
   limitations of, 65
   midrange, 47–48
   narrow, 48
   practicing, 520
   rules approach to, 55, 57–58
   stage, 169
   systems approach, 55, 58–60
   testing, 54
   values in, 53
thought, 86
threat threshold, 138
time alternation, 208–209
time, test of, 70–71
   and Cultivation Analysis,
      389–391
   and Groupthink, 256
   and Muted Group Theory, 499
   and Rhetorical Theory, 326
Toner, Robin, 7
topic, 317
   selection, 208
torture, 102
totality, 205
tourism, 340–341
toxic shock syndrome, 361
traditions, 27–32, 67
   critical, 31
   cybernetic, 30

phenomenological, 29–30
rhetorical, 28–29
semiotic, 29
socio-cultural, 31
socio-psychological, 30–31
train test, 420–421
   limits to, 424–425
trained incapacities, 331
transactional model, 14–15
trickster, 340
Truth, Sojourner, 511–512
turning points, 172
twenty-statements self-attitudes
   questionnaire, 78
"two heads are better than
   one," 244

uncertainty, 259
   acceptance, 158
   aversiveness of, 150
   avoidance, 162
   behavioral, 148
   cognitive, 148
   within dating, 151, 159
   interpersonal settings and, 150
   in marriage, 159
   relational, 160
uncertainty reduction
   interpersonal communication
      and, 152
   proactive, 149
   retroactive, 149
   satisfaction and, 155
Uncertainty Reduction Theory
   (URT), 69, 147
   active strategies of, 157
   antecedent conditions of, 157
   assumptions of, 150–153
   axioms of, 153–155
   criticism of, 163–165
   expansion of, 69, 155–163
   goal of, 147
   heurism of, 155–156, 164–165
   integration of, 163
   interactive strategies of,
      157–158
   passive strategies of, 157
   reformulation of, 163
   scope of, 69
   utility of, 163–164
   validity of, 164
understanding, 3
Understanding Media
   (McLuhan), 428
unwanted repetitive patterns
   (URP), 108, 171

URP. *See* unwanted repetitive patterns
URT. *See* Uncertainty Reduction Theory
Uses and Gratification Theory, 393
  acceptance of, 396
  assumptions of, 397–400
  consistency of, 407–408
  criticism of, 407–408
  heurism of, 408
  integration of, 407
  new media and, 404–406
  stages in, 394–397
  terminology of, 407
  utility of, 408
utility, 70
  of Cognitive Dissonance Theory, 125–127
  of Communication Privacy Management, 234
  of Coordinated Management of Meaning, 110
  of Cultivation Analysis, 389
  of Cultural Studies, 373–374
  of Dramatism, 339–340
  of Expectancy Violations Theory, 142
  of media, 400
  of Muted Group Theory, 498–499
  of Narrative Paradigm, 355–356
  of Organization Information Theory, 306
  of Organizational Cultural Theory, 288

  of Relational Dialectics Theory, 216
  of Social Exchange Theory, 198–199
  of Standpoint Theory, 512–515
  of Symbolic Interaction Theory, 90
  of Uncertainty Reduction Theory, 163–164
  of Uses and Gratification Theory, 408

validity, 64
values, 279
  affirmed through media, 404
  collectivistic, 457
  debate over, 54
  eroded by television, 432
  individualistic, 457
  openness, 169
  reinforced through media, 404
  in research, 53
  study of, 323
  in theory, 53
variables, 30
Viagra, 413–414
victimage, 334, 340
Victims of Groupthink (Janis), 240
video games
  gender and, 402
  motivations for, 405
  social interactions and, 405–406
Vietnam War, 248–251
  bombings in, 249

Viewers' Declaration of Independence, 387
violation valence, 138–139
  examples of, 139
Violence Index, 378
  criticism of, 379

Weaver, Warren, 11
wedding
  ceremony, 494–495
  rings, 80
Western Electric Hawthorne Plant, 38
whistle-blowing, 21, 252–253
"Who am I?", 82
wholeness, 58
Wieck, Karl, 293
wishful thinking, 395
withdrawal, 208–209
women
  at birth, 490
  collaborative speech of, 492
  dictionary, 497
  fluency of, 492
  glass ceiling for, 492
  homeless, 495
  interruptions and, 496
  invented language for, 497
  as muted group, 486–487
  in public forums, 498
  role in home, 489
  second shift of, 490
  status quo devalues, 505
  translation process of, 492–493
  trivialized speech of, 494